Praise for *Mussolini's Italy*

"Shrewd, lucid, exhaustively documented and totally unsentimental . . . among its greatest virtues is [Bosworth's] eye for what made Italian Fascism Italian. . . . A cautionary tale that all of us, Italian and non-Italian, would do well to remember."
—*The New York Times Book Review*

"A powerful work of scholarship, beautifully written, which should be read by anyone interested in twentieth-century Europe, or indeed the antecedents of modern-day Italy."   —*The Economist*

"[Bosworth is] one of the most outstanding historians of modern Italy . . . absorbing . . . fascinating . . . Bosworth's deep knowledge of Italy . . . is continually illuminating." —*The Washington Post Book World*

"With this insightful, comprehensive study, Bosworth secures his place as one of the two leading historians in the English-speaking world . . . of twentieth-century Italy. Bosworth begins with an admission that he has embarked on an 'impossible project': 'to unveil the lives of Italians' from all walks of life 'under a generation of dictatorship.' Impossible, indeed, but what a grand attempt at a synthesis of social and political history he produces."
—*Publishers Weekly* (starred and boxed review)

"A breathtakingly ambitious history that defies its author's own warning: 'Aspiring to write the total history of a totalitarian society is a delusion.' . . . Superb—and timely."
—*Kirkus Reviews* (starred review)

"A lively portrait in Mussolini's Italy of the lives of ordinary Italians under Fascism. . . . In mesmeric detail, Bosworth puts Mussolini squarely behind the worst atrocities of post-Risorgimento Italy."
—Ian Thomson, *The Spectator*

"[A] superbly evocative account . . . Profound in its scholarship and humane in its judgments."
—Christopher Clark, *Sunday Telegraph* (UK)

"Everybody with an interest in the everyday life of Italians under Mussolini's dictatorship will have to read Richard Bosworth's *Mussolini's Italy*. . . . Such a book was long overdue. . . . One cannot recommend this book too highly."
—Tobias Abse, *Literary Review* (UK)

"[A] penetrating new book . . . Bosworth's fine book, studded with crisply drawn vignettes of Mussolini's main collaborators and with fascinating details of how ordinary Italians coped with Fascist rule in the provinces, pulls no punches."
—Tony Barber, *Financial Times Magazine* (UK)

"This book ranges very widely, synthesizing in often colorful prose the author's compendious knowledge of Italian social and political history. . . . Bosworth deftly documents Fascism's uneven and complex political and ideological history, charting Mussolini's torturous road to power, the gathering political appeal of his leadership, and the final implosion of the system. This scholarly and passionate book will doubtless be required reading for students of modern Italy, but it deserves still a wider audience than that." —*Bookforum*

PENGUIN BOOKS

MUSSOLINI'S ITALY

R. J. B. Bosworth's prizewinning *Mussolini* was greeted on publication in 2002 as the definitive life of Il Duce. Bosworth is professor of history at the University of Western Australia and has been a Visiting Fellow at a number of institutions, including the Italian Academy at Columbia University, Clare Hall (Cambridge), Balliol College (Oxford), All Souls College (Oxford), and the University of Trento.

R. J. B. BOSWORTH

Mussolini's Italy

Life under the Fascist Dictatorship
1915–1945

PENGUIN BOOKS

PENGUIN BOOKS

Published by the Penguin Group
Penguin Group (USA) Inc., 375 Hudson Street, New York, New York 10014, U.S.A.
Penguin Group (Canada), 90 Eglinton Avenue East, Suite 700, Toronto,
Ontario, Canada M4P 2Y3 (a division of Pearson Penguin Canada Inc.)
Penguin Books Ltd, 80 Strand, London WC2R 0RL, England
Penguin Ireland, 25 St Stephen's Green, Dublin 2, Ireland (a division of Penguin Books Ltd)
Penguin Group (Australia), 250 Camberwell Road, Camberwell,
Victoria 3124, Australia (a division of Pearson Australia Group Pty Ltd)
Penguin Books India Pvt Ltd, 11 Community Centre, Panchsheel Park, New Delhi – 110 017, India
Penguin Group (NZ), cnr Airborne and Rosedale Roads, Albany,
Auckland 1310, New Zealand (a division of Pearson New Zealand Ltd)
Penguin Books (South Africa) (Pty) Ltd, 24 Sturdee Avenue, Rosebank, Johannesburg 2196, South Africa

Penguin Books Ltd, Registered Offices:
80 Strand, London WC2R 0RL, England

First published in Great Britain by Allen Lane, Penguin Books Ltd 2005
First published in the United States of America by The Penguin Press,
a member of Penguin Group (USA) Inc. 2006
Published in Penguin Books (UK) 2006
Published in Penguin Books (USA) 2007

1 3 5 7 9 10 8 6 4 2

THE LIBRARY OF CONGRESS HAS CATALOGED THE HARDCOVER EDITION AS FOLLOWS:
Mussolini's Italy : life under the fascist dictatorship, 1915–1945 / R.J.B. Bosworth
p. cm.
Includes index.
ISBN 1-59420-078-5 (hc.)
ISBN 978-0-14-303856-6 (pbk.)
1. Italy—History—1914–1945. 2. Fascism—Italy. 3. Mussolini, Benito, 1883–1945. I. Title.
DG571.B715 2006
945.091—dc22   2005052127

Printed in the United States of America

For Nicholas, Oliver and Ella

Therefore doth heaven divide
The state of man in divers functions,
Setting endeavour in continual motion;
To which is fixed, as an aim or butt,
Obedience: for so work the honey-bees,
Creatures that by a rule in nature teach
The act of order to a peopled kingdom.
They have a king, and officers of sorts;
Where some, like magistrates, correct at home,
Others, like merchants, venture trade abroad,
Others, like soldiers, armed in their stings,
Make boot upon the summer's velvet buds;
Which pillage they with merry march bring home
To the tent-royal of their emperor:
Who, busied in his majesty, surveys
The singing masons building roofs of gold,
The civil citizens kneading up the honey,
The poor mechanic porters crowding in
Their heavy burdens at his narrow gate,
The sad-ey'd justice, with his surly hum,
Delivering o'er to executors pale
The lazy yawning drone. I this infer,
That many things, having full reference
To one consent, may work contrariously;
As many arrows, loosed several ways,
Fly to one mark; as many ways meet in one town;
As many streams meet in one salt sea;
As many lines close in the dial's centre;
So may a thousand actions, once afoot,
End in one purpose, and be all well borne
Without defeat. (*Henry V*, I. 2.183–213)

A highly politic and decidedly war-mongering Shakespearean Archbishop of
Canterbury sketching a corporate state. For Fascist bees, see chapter 8.

Contents

List of illustrations		xiii
List of abbreviations		xvi
Note on further reading		xix
Maps		xx
Preface		xxiii

	Introduction	1
1	One Italy or another before 1914	9
2	Liberal and dynastic war	37
3	Popular and national war	66
4	1919	93
5	Becoming a Fascist	121
6	Learning to rule in the provinces	150
7	Learning to rule from Rome	184
8	Building a totalitarian dictatorship	215
9	Forging Fascist society	249
10	Placing Italy in Europe	277
11	Going to the people	307
12	Dictating full-time	339
13	Becoming imperialists	367
14	Embracing Nazi Germany	396
15	Lurching into war	431
16	The wages of Fascist war	463

17 Losing all the wars   498
18 The Fascist heritage   531

Conclusion   561
Notes   573
Index   663

List of illustrations

1. Piero Bolzon, officer, gentleman and Fascist. (Reading University Library)
2. An early squad. (Reading University Library)
3. Pius XI inaugurating Holy Year, 1925. (*L'Illustrazione Italiana*)
4. The complexity of salutes in Fascist Italy, Rome, 1926. (Reading University Library)
5. Mussolini smiling and striding (with Achille Starace), Rome, 1927. (*L'Illustrazione Italiana*)
6. Mussolini and Edda becoming respectable in the Borghese gardens, Rome, 1927. (*L'Illustrazione Italiana*)
7. Victor Emmanuel and Mussolini in civvies at the harvest. (*L'Illustrazione Italiana*)
8. Mussolini meets peasants in the Pontine marshes. (*L'Illustrazione Italiana*)
9. The athletic Renato Ricci and his boy scouts, Rome, 1930. (*Rivista dell'ONB di Bolzano*, from Biblioteca Comunale, Trento)
10. Boy scouts from Bolzano at Rome zoo, 1930. (*Rivista dell'ONB di Bolzano*, from Biblioteca Comunale, Trento)
11. The Sala del Mappamondo with a very small *Duce* at a desk in the corner. (Touring Club Italiano/Alinari Archives Management, Milano)
12. Dante and Battisti joined as ghosts, Trento, 1935. (Biblioteca Comunale, Trento)
13. Fascist scout piping, 1935. (Biblioteca Comunale, Trento)
14. Fascist boys on holiday, 1935. (Biblioteca Comunale, Trento)

15. Teenage Mussolinis as toughs. (Biblioteca Comunale, Trento)
16. Roberto Farinacci. (Biblioteca Comunale, Trento)
17. 'Liberated Tigreans' and the Fascist white man's burden, 1935. (*Il Legionario*, from Biblioteca Comunale, Trento)
18. Little migrant Fascists in Melbourne, Australia, 1936. (*Il Legionario*, from Biblioteca Comunale, Trento)
19. A seventy-six-year-old lady named Camilla donates her wedding ring after fifty-six years of marriage, 1936. (*Il Legionario*, from Biblioteca Comunale, Trento)
20. Cesare De Vecchi di Val Cismon as Minister of Education, 1936. (*Il Legionario*, from Biblioteca Comunale, Trento)
21. Giuseppe Bottai being scholarly. (*Il Legionario*, from Biblioteca Comunale, Trento)
22. Fiat in Ethiopia, 1936. (*Il Legionario*, from Biblioteca Comunale, Trento)
23. Vittorio Mussolini's wedding – the Mussolinis in high society, 1937. (*L'Illustrazione Italiana*)
24. Queen Elena, being statuesque, 1937. (*Il Legionario*, from Biblioteca Comunale, Trento)
25. Achille Starace, the King and small children, Rome 1937. (*Il Legionario*, from Biblioteca Comunale, Trento)
26. Princess Maria José and baby prince Victor Emmanuel, 1937. (*Il Legionario*, from Biblioteca Comunale, Trento)
27. Mussolini, Italo Balbo and small migrant Fascists in Libya, 1937. (*Il Legionario*, from Biblioteca Comunale, Trento)
28. A Caesarian trio for 'the New Roman Empire', 1937. (*Il Legionario*, from Biblioteca Comunale, Trento)
29. Camelized troops outside the Victor Emmanuel monument, 1937. (AKG)
30. Church and State in the rain, 1938. (*Il Legionario*, from Biblioteca Comunale, Trento)
31. Galeazzo Ciano as Fascist pin-up, 1938. (AKG)
32. Fascist and Savoyard ceremony, 1939. (AKG)
33. The Axis licked. (*L'Illustrazione Italiana*)
34. Italians pleased to become POWs, Calabria, September 1943. (by permission of the Trustees of the Imperial War Museum, London)

35. Schoolteacher partisan, Val d'Aosta, 1944. (by permission of the Trustees of the Imperial War Museum, London)

List of abbreviations

ACS	Archivio Centrale dello Stato (Rome)
AN	Alleanza Nazionale (National Alliance – post-fascists)
ANC	Associazione Nazionale dei Combattenti (National Returned Soldiers' League)
ANI	Associazione Nazionalista Italiana (Italian Nationalist Association)
AOI	Africa Orientale Italiana (Italian East Africa)
BMOO	Benito Mussolini, *Opera omnia* (edited by E. and D. Susmel), 44 vols (Florence, 1951–62; 1978–80)
BN	Brigate Nere (Black Brigades)
CGdL	Confederazione Generale del Lavoro (General Confederation of Labour)
CIGA	Compagnia Italiana Grandi Alberghi (Italian Major Hoteliers' League)
CIL	Confederazione Italiana del Lavoro (Italian Labour Confederation – Catholics)
CISNAL	Confederazione Italiana Sindacati Nazionali Liberi (Italian Free National Trade Union – neo-fascists)
CP	Confinati politici: fascicoli personali (personal files of those sent to *confino*)
DC	Democrazia Cristiana (Christian Democracy)
DDI	I documenti diplomatici italiani, third to eighth series
DGPS	Direzione Generale di Pubblica Sicurezza (Directorate of Public Security)
EIAR	Ente Italiano Audizioni Radiotelefoniche (Italian Radio Company)

EUR	Esposizione Universale Italiana (Italian Universal Exhibition)
FIOM	Federazione Italiana degli operai metallurgici (Italian Metalworkers' Union)
GUF	Gioventù Universitaria Fascista (Fascist University Youth)
INPS	Istituto Nazionale di Previdenza Sociale (National Insurance Institute)
IRI	Istituto per la Ricostruzione Industriale (Institute for the Reconstruction of Industry)
MI	Ministero dell'Interno (Ministry of the Interior)
MRF	Mostra della Rivoluzione Fascista (Exhibition of the Fascist Revolution)
MSI	Movimento Sociale Italiano (Italian Social Movement – neo-fascists)
MVSN	Milizia Volontaria per la Sicurezza Nazionale (Voluntary Militia for National Security)
NATO	North Atlantic Treaty Organization
ONB	Opera Nazionale Balilla (Fascist boy scouts)
OND	Opera Nazionale Dopolavoro (National After-work Group)
ONMI	Opera Nazionale per la Protezione della Maternità e dell'Infanzia (National agency for mothers and children)
OVRA	Fascist Secret Police (the initials have no direct meaning)
PCd'I	Partito Comunista d'Italia (Italian Communist Party in 1920s)
PCI	Partito Comunista Italiano (Italian Communist Party after Fascism)
PNF	Partito Nazionale Fascista (National Fascist Party)
PNM	Partito Nazionale Monarchico (National Monarchist Party)
PPI	Partito Popolare Italiano (Italian Popular Party – Catholics)
PSI	Partito Socialista Italiano (Italian Socialist Party)
RSI	Repubblica Sociale Italiana (Italian Social or 'Salò' Republic)

SCP	Segreteria del Capo di Polizia (Senise-Chierici 1940–43) (Secretariat of the Chief of Police)
SPDCO	Segreteria particolare del Duce: Carteggio ordinario (general papers of the *Duce*'s personal office)
SPDCR	Segreteria particolare del Duce: Carteggio riservato (special papers of the *Duce*'s personal office)
SPEP	Situazione politica ed economica delle provincie (Review of the political and economic situation in the provinces)
TCI	Touring Club Italiano (Italian Touring Club)
UIL	Unione Italiana del Lavoro (Italian Labour Union – syndicalists)
UQ	Uomo Qualunque (Common Man Party)

Note on further reading

The research material used in writing this book can be traced in the notes. For published sources up to 2000, see the extensive bibliography in my biography of Mussolini (London: Edward Arnold, 2002, pp. 520–63). Though now becoming dated, the fullest bibliography on the Fascist era is R. De Felice, *Bibliografia orientativa del fascismo* (Rome, 1991). My thanks to Sage, publishers of the *European History Quarterly*, and to Cambridge University Press, publishers of *Contemporary European History*, for permission to reprint material first published in these journals.

Map 1 **Italy in the 1930s**

SOUTH
TYROL

Bolzano

Trento Tolmezzo
Udine

Como Trieste
Milan Venice Fiume
Cremona Verona
Turin Mantua
Alessandria Ferrara
Parma
Genoa Bologna
La Spezia Forlì Riccione
Oneglia Sarzana Empoli
Livorno Pisa Florence
Siena Perugia

Adriatic

I T A L Y

Sea

Lagosta

Bastia

Corsica
(Fr.)

Tremiti Is.

Rome *The Gargano*

Foggia
Benevento Bari
Island of Naples
Ponza Brindisi
Taranto Lecce
Sassari Gallipoli

Sardinia

Tyrrhenian   Sea

Cagliari

Lipari Is.
Messina
M e d i t e r r a n e a n   S e a Palermo Reggio di Calabria

Sicily
Catania
Augusta
Gela

Pantelleria

Malta

Isole
Pelagie

Acquisitions 1919/20

Northern boundary
of Italy 1914

0   200 km
0   100 mi

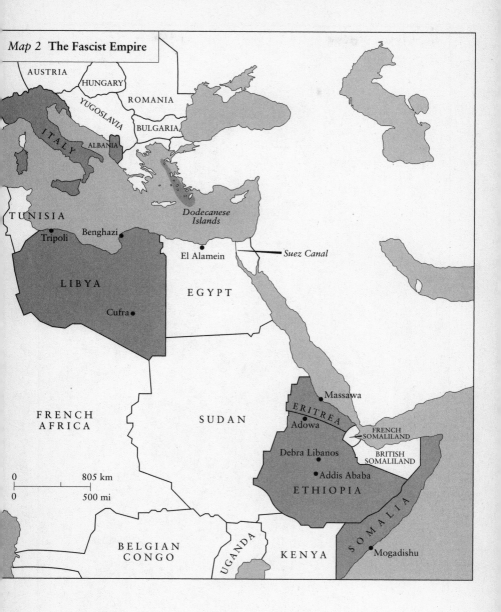

Map 2 **The Fascist Empire**

AUSTRIA
HUNGARY
ROMANIA
YUGOSLAVIA
BULGARIA
ITALY
ALBANIA

TUNISIA

Tripoli
Benghazi

Dodecanese
Islands

Suez Canal

El Alamein

LIBYA

EGYPT

Cufra

FRENCH
AFRICA

SUDAN

Massawa

ERITREA

Adowa

FRENCH
SOMALILAND

0   805 km
0   500 mi

Debra Libanos

BRITISH
SOMALILAND

Addis Ababa

ETHIOPIA

BELGIAN
CONGO

UGANDA

KENYA

SOMALIA

Mogadishu

Map 3 Italy in 1943–5

Area under Nazi administration after 1943

0   200 km

0   100 mi

Dongo

Salò

Milan

Turin

Venice

Trieste

SALO

Verona

REPUBLIC

Genoa

Bologna

Ravenna

GOTHIC   LINE

Adriatic

Florence

Livorno

Perugia

I · T · A · L · Y

Corsica
(Fr.)

Sea

Termoli

Rome

Monte
Cassino

GUSTAV LINE

Anzio

Bari

Naples

Salerno

Taranto

Sardinia

Tyrrhenian Sea

Mediterranean Sea

Palermo

Messina

Sicily

Catania

Syracuse

Tunis

Malta

Preface

> The recovery of the voices lost within the totalizing narratives
> of modernization and nationalization is one of the most chal-
> lenging tasks facing historians today, but before we can even
> begin to identify and listen to these voices, we must first under-
> stand the mechanisms by which they have been (and continue
> to be) silenced.

> B. Porter, *When nationalism began to hate: imagining politics*
> *in nineteenth-century Poland*, p. 137.

I began to research and write this book very soon after I had completed my biography of Mussolini. I was stimulated to a degree by
what seemed to me a sensible comment from a reviewer in the
Spectator. Jonathan Sumption said, very kindly, that my book was
'the best biography [of Mussolini] in English to date'. Then came the
rub. Sumption continued: 'Yet the main reflection which it provokes
is the inadequacy of biography as a vehicle for explaining' terrible
events. Really to comprehend inter-war Italy, he ran on, 'one would
have to dig into the life of the small towns and cities and the thousands of local institutions and associations of provincial Italy to
understand why so many Italians' accepted the 'Italian dictatorship'.
'Inter-war Italy was a fragmented country with a large apolitical peasantry and a developed system of local clientage and power-broking, in
which mutual favours counted for a great deal more than ideology. At
this level, Fascism was often no more than a convenient label, appro-
priated by local interests which had existed before Mussolini was ever

heard of and endured long after his death. Against this inherently unstable background, the *Duce* survived because he was cunning enough to be many things to many men. Perhaps this is just politics. Perhaps it is a fraud. But if so it may well be that those Italians who cared were willing participants in the deception.'

Scanning these words, I could only agree while rather regretting that my effort to produce a biography where a Great Bad Man had been deliberately placed in context and where the limits of his free will had been closely described had not won over my reviewer. But, with the extraordinary good fortune that has been my fate as a writer of history over the last decade, Simon Winder of Penguin, nudged by the excellent Clare Alexander, was soon in touch, suggesting that I produce a history of the life of Italians under the Fascist dictatorship which lasted a generation. That is what I have done in this new study, a book that I wryly call to myself 'Mussolini without Mussolini'. It is true that readers will be able to locate the regime's leader in its pages, especially in chapter 12. But he certainly has not been given a prominent part in the story, all the more because I trust that anyone interested in him can turn to my biography or to the growing list of other accounts of the *Duce*'s rule.

My task, rather, has been to unveil the lives of Italians under a generation of dictatorship, be they men, women or children, party officials and party intellectuals or anti-Fascists, landowners and industrialists or workers and peasants, all coming from the many and varied regions of Italy or, on occasion, emigrants passed beyond the national border. It is, of course, an impossible project. Aspiring to write the total history of a totalitarian society is a delusion. Yet any reader who consults the book's pages will find that a vast array of people turn up in my tale and that it spans from Sardinia to Sicily, from Turin to Reggio Calabria, from Trieste to Bari and beyond. There are many stories in the pages that follow and my hope must be that readers will find them emblematic and will draw a general picture from their impressionist detail.

In this preface I do not want to start composing another parallel book. Rather it is time to express gratitude. *Mussolini's Italy* was written over a fifteen-month period in 2003–5 and in three beautiful and stimulating places. I remain a staff member of the University of

Western Australia, whose antipodean architecture, with its campanile and colonnades and worthy slogans etched into walls, has an air that De Chirico, if not Mussolini, might recognize. It is a generous place for a historian, especially one who is given such free rein to research and write. My thanks to the Vice Chancellor, Alan Robson, for his acceptance that the humanities cannot and should not be circumscribed too severely by the intellectual and ethical narrowness spreading in contemporary Australia. Among my work colleagues, Rob Stuart has been a helpfully critical reader, Giuseppe Finaldi a delightfully zestful substitute when I laid aside my teaching programme, Philippa Maddern, a head of school of infinite dedication to and love for the discipline of history. Such doctoral or proto-doctoral students as Marianne Hicks, David Ritter, Sarah Finn, Michael Ondaatje and, especially, Frances Flanagan, who doubled as an error-corrector, have kept my enthusiasm glowing, as of course have what are becoming my memories of two generations of marvellous Australian undergraduates, determined not to be dumbed down. Similarly sustaining my commitment to the history trade were Reto Hofmann, Ben Mercer, Samantha Quinn and Yavor Siderov, once of UWA and now of the world. I should not forget that UWA is Australia's foremost centre for Italian studies, where Finaldi, Loretta Baldassar, Nick Harney, Susanna Iuliano and others constitute a new cohort to replace that splendid historian of the Renaissance, Lorenzo Polizzotto, and me as we approach academic, if not writing, retirement. Born and bred in Sydney and a teacher at the university there for two decades, I am also heavily in debt to many people in that place, notably Gianfranco Cresciani, 'my first student' and therefore my early teacher, and, as for all my books, the two Whites, Graham and Shane, civilized and rigorous Americanists, who hammer away at an Italianist's inelegance and confusion. When I am trying to be a cosmopolitan historian and stay a loyal, if lonely, Australian fan of the Pakistan cricket team (with support from Wasim), it may be that I am being happily structured by my origins in Sydney, traditionally the most outward-looking of Australian cities.

The second site for the writing of my study of life under the dictatorship was Trento and its fine university, which welcomed me as a visiting professor in the first half of 2004. I am enormously indebted to Gustavo Corni and Mark Gilbert for the invitation to go there and for the lightness of my teaching load once I had arrived. Similarly the libraries of the city were perfect places in which to research. I should never have known of the (alleged) link between *italianità* and local bees if I had not worked in Trento. In the usual seductive Italian fashion, the city itself is a jewel. Each morning from a flat in the *foresteria* at Sardagna I could look down on cathedral, castle, river and walls or up to the framing Alps (and imagine sad, lingering echoes of battle from the terrible First World War fought along the summits I could see).

For quite a time my computer may have lived at Trento but the research for this book has been done, in 2002–4 and over many years before that, in a host of Italian libraries and, above all, in the efficient Archivio centrale dello stato, redolently housed in the model Fascist suburb of EUR in Rome. Too many friends have helped me in my Italian years to be listed here but I must mention Patrizia Dogliani (herself the author of a penetrating study of Fascist society), Dante Bolognesi, Fabio and Ariella Malusà, Giovanni and Susanna Minelli, Gino and Patty Rizzo, Mario and Giovanna Ronchetti-Rosselli and Paul Corner for their hospitality towards and intellectual engagement with a wandering Australian.

If there are any moments in my text where my prose glitters, it is the result of my being hunched over my computer in a third place, All Souls College, Oxford. I came to that sanctuary in September 2004 with a not-quite-finished first draft and found myself immersed in a restless sea of scholarship. My old friend Jim Adams, my new friends, the modern historians of the place, Noel Malcolm, Hew Strachan, Ian Maclean and Robin Briggs, such fellow visitors as Richard Yeo and Walter Stephens and a host of All Soulsians may have on occasion terrified me with their span and understanding but they were unfailingly generous and welcoming and courteously ready to listen to Fascist tales. They sent me back to my computer to polish and polish again, helped now by the commentaries on my MS that I was receiving from such other English friends as Roger Absalom, Carol Jefferson-Davies and Christopher Duggan, and by responses to my various papers at this or that British centre, as well as from the ever-perceptive Simon Winder and the similarly rigorous and encouraging Scott Moyers of Penguin's New York office. When I talked Fascism with Nick Stargardt and Lyndal Roper, Jonathan Morris and Carl Levy, Martin Blinkhorn and Bob Moore, Martin Conway and Chris Clark, I was reminded that it was to a degree possible to be a British Italianist even while being Australian.

Allen Lane/Penguin were endlessly responsive to my authorial worries. My special thanks to Jane Robertson for her perceptive sub-edit, to Alison Hennessey for tracking down issues relating to the photographs, and to Richard Duguid and Elisabeth Merriman for their careful editorial work.

I have visited Italy at least once per year since 1967 and, even when not there, I have constantly benefited from reading Italian research and scholarship. Appropriately, Italians, since Fascism, have argued passionately about the meaning of their dictatorship. My debt to their labours can be tracked in my notes, while my stance on their disputes can be found in another of my books, *The Italian dictatorship* (London, 1998). Among the historians of the last decades, special acknowledgement must be given to Renzo De Felice (1929–96), the author of a massively detailed and more than 6,000-page biography of Mussolini, which doubles as a political history of the dictatorship. I have quite a number of political and methodological disputes with De Felice's work but it would be churlish to deny that his archival labours have left behind a mine of material that no later historian in the field can ignore.

A further complication in what might be my 'real' ethnic identity may result from my participation in Italian debates. Can I claim thereby to be in some part 'Italian'? Perhaps. But nationality is not the beginning or end of identity. My time at Oxford was sweetened by the smaller and yet embracing world of family matters. My fellowship at All Souls coincided with one held at Wolfson College by my criminologist daughter, Mary. For a decade she had been based in the USA but was now living in the same block of flats as Michal and I. Mary, Anthony and baby Ella kept reminding me that an Australian, as well, is a familist and glad to be one. So, too, did Edmund, who, despite the business of his banking life, continues to read and apparently enjoy his father's prose. And, of course, it goes without saying to anyone who knows me, in every event, whether geographical or intellectual, I was accompanied by Mike, best of wives, friends and intellectual partners.

While my life composing this book in 2003–5 has been a continuous delight, the greater world has not seemed so benign. I am not convinced that Fascism is somehow back. Paul Ginsborg's nightmare at the end of his recent study of Berlusconi of '*piccoli Forzisti*' (Berlusconian scouts) going to bed in 2013 'clutching in their small palms the medals of Silvio Berlusconi, as the "piccoli Balilla" did with that of Il Duce in 1935'[1] is too feverish for my tastes. Yet the world which lives under the hegemony of economic rationalism and which seems every day more in the care of neoconservatives is a frighteningly irrational and brutal place. The ghosts of Fascists past may indeed break open the champagne when they hear of the current approval of pre-emptive strikes and the cheerful acceptance that vast collateral damage may accompany them. Spin on the one hand and fundamentalism on the other are similarly retrograde ideas or practices, of powerful influence on Italians between the wars, then and thereafter properly damned, but now seemingly resuscitated. Renzo De Felice made himself unpopular to me, among others, by his insistence during the 1970s and 1980s that the then Italian Republic was morally not necessarily better than Fascism. But perhaps his comment needs restating. Can we be sure today that we are the moral superiors of Fascist Italians?

For any Anglo-Saxon writing about modern Italy, there is a further issue. In English-language treatment of that past, the presence of a superciliousness sprung from a racist belief that Anglo-Saxons are always and inevitably purer and more efficient than Italians can easily enough be traced in the scholarship. On both counts, there are reasons to avoid cheap moralizing about Fascist sins. As the new millennium advances, I may in this book still want to argue that the Italian dictatorship was a murderous regime, no proper model for any believer in the good of humankind. But I must also accept that the democracies of our times (not to mention the dictatorships) have not yet brought us to happiness and, sadly, may presently be transporting us away from that desired state. The battle is not over. Historic Fascism is probably dead and buried but, in our future, anti-Fascism, loosely defined as a sustained search for liberty, equality, fraternity and sorority, must go on. In that hope, I dedicate this book to Ella, Oliver and Nicholas of the newest generation.

Introduction

Adolf Hitler continues to stand as a sort of banal shorthand for our terrible past, even in a new millennium. Every understanding of the Second World War and of the 'locust years' that preceded that appalling conflict is refracted through our comprehension of the 'mad' *Führer*. It is the ghost of Adolf Hitler who, history tells us, carried the world to total war and, with blind and (pseudo-)scientific fanaticism, to the massacre of the Jews in the 'final solution'. After we have learned the lessons of such history, it is the ghost of Adolf Hitler who pushes us to our understanding of the world. It is the ghost of Adolf Hitler who persuades us that our opponents comprise The Other – the imponderable, incomprehensible, fundamentalist, 'mad'. It is the ghost of Adolf Hitler who ensures that we think of all dictators and all societies that have the misfortune to be ruled by them as the replica of his murderous and inexorable regime.

But letting Hitler be our history teacher and implicit model is not a good idea. At the onset of the Balkan wars of the 1990s, the still Yugoslav journalist Slavenka Drakulic warned against the resurfacing of terrible simplifiers. 'Once the concept of "otherness" takes root,' she wrote sadly, 'the unimaginable becomes possible.'[1] It is a comment that should be kept in mind when turning to examine what I some years ago called the 'Italian dictatorship'. From 1922 to 1943 and then, in a terrible coda in central and northern Italy, from September 1943 to April 1945, the Italian people fell under the domination of a vicious and retrograde tyranny. It banned rival parties, arbitrarily imprisoned or drove into exile their leaders and, before and after 1922, killed from 2,000 to 3,000 of its political opponents. It destroyed the free press, liquidated non-Fascist trade unions, infringed the rule of law, sponsored a secret police, tempted Italians to spy on, and inform against, each other and reaffirmed crudely patriarchal practices. It talked about building a corporate state that the world would marvel at and thereby unite bosses and workers and bring welfare and justice to all. In practice, however, the dictatorship's economic performance was patchy at best. Its erratic pursuit of free trade at first and autarchy or protection thereafter did nothing to lessen Italy's relative financial and technological weakness or to improve the Italian population's lower standard of living compared with the richer and greater powers to its north and west.

Any glimpse of economic advance was blighted by the fact that Fascist Italy indulged in almost constant warfare, during the 1920s 'restoring order' in its empire, in 1935 invading Ethiopia, after 1936 impelling 'volunteers' to fight on the insurgent side in the Spanish Civil War, and in 1939 occupying Albania, its erstwhile puppet. After allying with Nazi Germany in the original Axis of Evil, this dictatorship wilfully entered all the Second World Wars, from June 1940 against Britain and France, from June 1941 against the USSR and from December that year against the USA, despite the millions of Italo-Americans who had moved across the Atlantic. In October 1940 Fascist Italy launched its own dismally incompetent attack on Greece and, after being rescued by the Germans in March–April 1941, was a brutal, if erratic, administrator of the Nazi-fascist new order in the Balkans and the rest of occupied Europe. Italy's foreign policy adventures had been prefigured at the beginning of the Fascist movement, when the doctrine of pre-emption and the ready acceptance of collateral damage on innocent bystanders were integral elements of 'squadrism' and its motorized and armed raids on fascism's political opponents. Always in theory and sometimes in practice, Fascists savagely eliminated their enemies without by your leaves and without pondering the complexities of life. If, in 1920–21, it was right to sally forth against socialist or Catholic foes at home, so, eventually, when opportunity came, it was just and necessary to launch aggressive foreign wars.

By then, Fascism had also become openly racist, whatever contradictions that policy line entailed in the light of Italians' lowly slot on most racial hierarchies. After initial forays into public racism in its

African empire, in 1938 the dictatorship brought in wide-ranging anti-Semitic legislation. The Italian persecution of the Jews was not the same as the German, but from 1943 the Salò Republic (RSI or Repubblica Sociale Italiana) officially proclaimed Jews enemies of the nation and its bureaucrats and politicians actively helped the Germans transport some 7,000 Italian Jews to their doom in the east. Earlier, Fascist Italy had sought belatedly to bear the imperial white man's burden and did so with severe damage to its subject peoples' lives and spirits. In Libya and Ethiopia, Italian armed forces murdered with a will: Italy may have been a latecomer to European imperialism but it was no gentler than the rest. By bombing sacred sites at Cufra and Debra Libanos, Italians sought ruthlessly to cancel any rival native history that might contest its own. Before and after 1940 Fascist rhetoric was unrestrained in extolling the virtues of war and killing, each being inscribed as the essence of Fascist manhood. And, on more than one occasion, wicked words were followed with evil deeds.

It was for Fascism that the malign term 'totalitarianism' was invented and, if they did not coin it, Fascists adopted it as the special badge of the regime. In theory at least, the dictatorship became a place where everyone had to ask not what their state would do for them but what they would and must do for the overweening state. Fascism was new and 'revolutionary', so the formula ran, because it had found a way to rally the masses in their deepest souls behind an authoritarian form of government. Mussolini himself regularly explained that the key to his regime lay in its harnessing of youth, trade unionism and leisure through the instrumentalities of a single and ubiquitous party. There was much talk about a 'liturgy' becoming engrained in every Italian mind where, by implication, it must oust the ancient belief system of the Catholic Church or the modern ones of the liberal nation, consumer capitalism and socialist humanism, in favour of a new and Fascist 'civic religion'. Here, in contemporary parlance, was what might be labelled Fascist fundamentalism. Regime propagandists spread an extreme and in retrospect ludicrous personality cult in which Mussolini was elevated into an all-seeing and all-knowing god, a Man who, Italians were assured, radiated a divine light and possessed an omniscient intuition. As the basic regime slogan went: 'Mussolini is always right' (*Mussolini ha sempre ragione*). At its most fanatical this cult required that Italians abandon contact with the world outside their leader, bow down and worship Him (like the Deity, he was habitually addressed in the capitalized form), purging from their minds everything that was not Fascist (or Mussolinian).

The Axis alliance with Nazi Germany had its ups and downs. Yet it was always in some sense 'natural'. Despite their national distinctiveness, Nazism and Italian Fascism and the array of lesser fascist movements did retain some commonality, being more like each other as societies than was their totalitarian rival, Stalinist communism, or their half-embarrassed progenitor and later frequent butt, conservative liberalism.[2] At a minimum, Mussolini and his dictatorship acted as a model for Adolf Hitler when, during the 1920s, the *Führer* was still a peripheral and unsuccessful figure on the crowded and quarrelsome German right and the German dictator never altogether abandoned his gratitude for this spiritual patronage. The Fascist regime was a willing if often gullible sponsor of a slew of other rightists, who dreamed of the murderous overthrow of democratic systems and of the launching of new wars to enforce the national grandeur they regarded as ideal. Among them were Ante Pavelić and the Croatian Ustasha, perhaps the most odious of all inter-war fascist-like movements, and those brutal and dissident Spanish officers who, after 1936, excised what they saw as the pustule of social democracy in their country, with a death toll that ran into hundreds of thousands.

Here, then, was a regime that, at a minimal count, with its repressive policies at home and its aggressive wars in its empire and in Europe, must bear responsibility for the premature death of a million people. It holds a prominent place in the black book of human misdeeds in the twentieth century.

At the same time, this dictatorship (like so many others) was deeply corrupt. Mussolini's henchmen had their snouts in any trough around. All ruling elites are rapacious but some are more rapacious than others. Under Fascism, patron–client ties flourished and the special personal reference or *raccomandazione* was a necessary part of life. Roberto Farinacci, the roughest and toughest *ras* (local boss), the 'real' Fascist, pronounced as his solution to the problem of getting through life not some ideological credo but the more familiar nostrum: 'I never forget my friends'.[3]

Like landmines in the present Third World, political tests lay not far below the surface under this intrusive regime. Fascist welfare trickled down only to those deemed deserving in their Fascism. As Paul Corner has acutely noted: in this system, 'the rules were in many ways unwritten rules and could only be guessed at – something that gave the authorities a great deal of discretionary power'.[4] Yet, for all the political meddling and persecution, this permanent unpredictability meant that there was always a possibility that rules could be circumvented or bent to the advantage of the ruthless and the smart. For some prison; for others amnesty. For some endless petty persecution; for others rich reward arrived from the skies (or the *Duce*'s office). For some daily apprehension; for others status and power. Hope and hopelessness grew together. This trickiness at the root of Fascism, the variability in its behaviour, the perpetual overt gap between its theory and its practice, meant that, while it was conquering or seeming to conquer, the dictatorship remained a nervous regime, unsure where it would end, unclear about the succession to Mussolini, unconvinced that it had swept away all opposition, talking big because it was always most likely that it was little. When, in the middle of the 1930s, Fascism, by most measures, had won the consent, however passive, of its subjects, still Mussolini neurotically insisted on daily conversations with his cynical, apolitical, pitiless and able Chief of Police, Arturo Bocchini. The leader quizzed his official obsessively about the state of public opinion, asking if traces of anti-Fascism had surfaced. Despite its proclamation of empyrean grandeur and its assertion that it had invented '*the* ideology of the twentieth century', this was a regime that never comfortably settled into office and hid its unease with pratings about 'permanent revolution', permanently about to start.

Lies abounded. Fascism proclaimed that its fundamental aim was national and social unity; that was what the *fasces*, rods bound around a retributive axe, symbolized. Yet Italy between the wars remained a place marked by an intricate regional hierarchy, a country where some parts (the great cities, the numerous historic towns, the 'north') were deemed civilized and others (backwoods *paesi* or villages, the countryside, the 'south') 'barbarous'. Most Italians clung to this knowledge, deeply inscribed in mental maps of their own, ones that had been by no means reliably nationalized and homogenized but instead reflected individual, family, class, gender and *paese* experience. Peasants knew they were peasants, *poveri cristi*, who had much in common with each other and were separated by a yawning chasm from landowners, town-dwellers and the bourgeoisie. Women, even the richest and best-educated ones, could scarcely aspire to equality with men. Emigration connected Italians along migrant chains to France or Belgium, New York or Buenos Aires, more securely than they were wedded to those extensive parts of Italy where they had never been and which were often literally beyond their ken, let alone to the exotic national empire in Benghazi, Tirana or Mogadishu. Paradoxically for a society heralding national homogeneity, the punishment system for the tiniest display of political dissidence was grounded in the reality of difference and not the myth of uniformity. Those men and women dispatched to *confino* (forced residence elsewhere) were meant to suffer and bend their heads because they had to live among foreigners and in a foreign clime, sitting out their years among the 'barbarous', even though all the while they were in Italy.

If geography was a shifting subject for many Italians, so was history. Membership in the party could be adroitly backdated, personal records rewritten with aplomb. Here was a regime that was undergirded by 'spin', long before that word had been given its current ubiquity. The Fascist dictatorship is often best understood as a 'propaganda state', one where nothing was what it was said to be and where everything that mattered lay in the words. Along with spin – perhaps its natural partner – went a profound cynicism, a way of viewing a citizen's surrounds and the world which deeply characterized the dictator, the leader or *Duce*, and which rarely left the minds of most Italians. Under this dictatorship, there may have been chatter about the philosophical acuity of Michels, Mazzini (and Mussolini), but Machiavelli (in vulgarized version) offered the handiest guide for comprehending the human condition.

A paradox lies at the heart of this book as it seeks to recount what the Fascists said they were doing, what they were actually doing and how the Italian people, in their class, gender, age, regional, religious, urban, rural and other diversities, coped with this dictatorship's version of totalitarianism. No serious historian should want to forget or forgive the crimes and wickedness of a misrule that lasted a generation. Yet the story of Fascism, of the Fascists and of Italian men and women in their era is not a simple one. This was neither a regime nor a society which was completely 'Other'. Lacking the power and the purpose to wipe clean the minds of its subjects and forge genuine 'new men' and 'new women', the dictatorship left a thousand histories still blooming in Italy and the Italies. In instance after instance, Italians, with power or without, from the top of society to the bottom, behaved in ways that may have been tinctured by Fascism but were at the same time deeply coloured by other factors, especially those which eddied powerfully through Italian society, moving with rhythms and effects diverse from that of the dictatorship.

In telling this tale, I shall introduce readers to Fascist bosses, some of them war criminals who never went before an international court, the overwhelming majority killers at one or other moment of their lives. One of my tasks in this book is to trace the careers of such unlovely underlings of the *Duce* as Roberto Farinacci, Dino Grandi, Italo Balbo, Giuseppe Bottai, Giuseppe Volpi, Giuseppe Giuriati, Achille Starace and the rest to illustrate how they twisted and turned in their understanding and deployment of Fascism. At the same time, attention will often switch from 'great men' to the little Fascists of the regions, towns and suburbs and will give place as well to those Italians who sought to get on with their lives, doing their best to ignore the dictatorship and, wittingly or unwittingly, deny it control over their minds. I shall therefore trace a varied set of journeys through a totalitarianism that somehow never became fully normalized and that always remained open to some form of manipulation or at least to the expectation of it.

The richly textured histories of these people will be full of loyalties and perceptions that were not merely Fascist. Time and again, Italians proved able to give lip-service to totalitarianism while retaining a sense of self. I shall talk of an everyday constituted by Catholicism, the family, gender understandings, the special flavour of different regions, towns and villages and by those who found an identity or identities outside the nation. Comprehending the fluctuating story of 'lite' Fascist totalitarianism, sceptical Fascist fundamentalism, a Fascist liturgy that failed to make itself catholic and universal, Fascist wars that were frequently more toughly fought with words than with weapons, can act as a counter to the pervasive power of Hitler's ghost. Reviewing the uneven experience of a people pent-up for two decades under the sway of a dictatorship of this Fascist sort may help us to the happy realization that, even in the worst of times, human fallibility, human hope and human struggle somehow obscure, delay and derail those determined to apply a simple and single answer, a seamless solution, to any question that matters. It might also allow us to examine in a more perceptive manner other dictatorships, great or petty and be they commanding countries, business concerns or just groups of individuals. Under the rule of Benito Mussolini, the history of Italian men and women – of intellectuals and businesspersons, landowners and peasants, priests and kings, the dictator, his henchmen and those committed to some form of anti-Fascism – was not cut off from the history of us all.

I

One Italy or another before 1914

The balcony stands there still today, jutting from the upper floor of the Palazzo Venezia, the building tourist guides describe as the first great Renaissance palace built in mid-fifteenth-century Rome. From this place, successively on 2 October 1935 and 9 May 1936, Benito Mussolini, *Duce* of Fascism, announced the invasion of Ethiopia and hailed a military triumph which, the dictator boasted, had brought empire back to the 'fatal hills of Rome'. Here also, on 7 May 1938, Mussolini and Adolf Hitler together acknowledged the plaudits of the populace at the propaganda peak of the *Führer*'s most successful visit to Italy. From that balcony on 10 June 1940, the Italian leader joined his Axis ally, Nazi Germany, in the war against the 'plutocratic' and 'decadent' liberal democratic states, Britain and France. Entry into the conflict, he roared, marked 'the logical development of our revolution'.[1] 'Balcony Empire', a pair of American journalists christened the regime in sardonic response.[2] Certainly the most familiar image in the history and memory of Fascism is of the dictator speechifying at one venue or another, his jutting fleshy chin, rolling eyes, florid gestures and vehement phrases caught by the newsreels of the time. The *Duce*'s oratorical technique now seems quaint, a period piece which prompts neither terror nor faith but rather a condescending smile. *Italiani*, we are assured in such bestsellers as *Captain Corelli's Mandolin* or such prize-winning films as *Life is beautiful*, or just by commonsense, are *brava gente*; Italians are nice people, bumbling of course, no doubt corrupt, but charming always. They incarnate their particular variety of cuisine, fashion, style and elegant love-making; they could not practise murder or mayhem. Of all the nations in the world, it seems, Italians are the last to be typecast as willing executioners.

My favourite bumper sticker reminds me that 'paranoids have ene-mies, too', and stereotypes do generally contain a grain of truth. In this book, I shall have cause to relate Italian charm, Italian corruption and Italian blunderings. Yet, any glimpses of *bravi italiani* and even *bravi fascisti* should not be read with excessive complacency. The Fascist dictatorship does not deserve to be given its historical place bathed in that pink glow of nostalgia, which is better left to the sort of adver-tisements and soft-porn movies which, over the last decades, have filled Italian television screens, perhaps occupied Italian minds and certainly have assisted the financial and political career of Silvio Berlusconi. Between the wars, Fascist Italy paved the first and fundamental path towards the destruction of Marxism, socialism, communism and lib-eral democracy, mapping a short way to repress any followers of those ideologies who hoped to be the humanist heirs of the French Revolution and Enlightenment. Here was the ideology that did not altogether die in 1945 and whose more recent epigones include the Ba'athists of Syria and Iraq and so Saddam Hussein (and Iyad Allawi).

If, outside its western fringe, Europe, by the end of 1938, had proved that the mixture of parliamentarism, capitalism and self-determination, heralded in 1919 by President Woodrow Wilson, led only to autocracy or worse, then Italy had pioneered the path to this wreck of individual and social freedom. From its first moment, Fascist Italy was a state that did not hide or apologize for its social Darwinism and war-mongering, its use of social and military terror and its fondness for pre-emptive assault. Despite Italy's signature to conventions banning its use, poison gas, the most obvious weapon of mass destruction of the time, was dropped by Mussolini and the Royal and National Italian Army on Libyans and Ethiopians and its wider deployment thereafter was seriously contemplated. As early as 1920, Mussolini spoke in favour of 'ethnic cleansing' in the Balkans and, during the Second World War, Aldo Vidussoni, a Fascist party secretary, envisaged the liquidation of all Slovenes. Expressing its own special version of racism, the Italian dictatorship played a significant part in escorting the world to 'Auschwitz'. In almost every sense the regime headed by Mussolini constituted the first and truest fascism and was a deadly enemy of what is best or most humane about humankind. It was not merely a joke.

Nor was it the product of 'one man alone', as Winston Churchill phrased it for immediate political purposes during the war. When Mussolini barked and bellowed on his balcony, the camera noticed the excited and jostling throng, an audience composed of the people of Italy, or of Rome, or of Fascism, spread out across the square below – Piazza Venezia. They were what the regime dubbed an 'oceanic crowd', the indispensable extras, those who shouted *'DUCE, DUCE, DUCE!'* in an apparent ecstasy of faith and commitment, men and women who had learned, according to the Fascist creed, that their fate as the subjects of the regime was to 'believe, obey and fight'. The task of this book is to enter their minds and review their habits and behaviour. How did they, the Italians, those who came to the square and those who did not, live their generation of Fascism, dictatorship, violence, repression, racism and war? How did they imagine and fashion their lives under totalitarianism, Italian-style?

As I begin to answer these questions, I shall make my words pan across the surrounds of what the Fascist press liked to call the sacramental meeting of *Duce* and people, and then on through the different regions of Italy and beyond to wherever Italians might be found. My intention here is to paint a backdrop for the scenes to follow. In this and later chapters, I shall populate my story with a range of characters, some of them Mussolini's henchmen, the leaders of the regime, but others men and women of street, city and countryside, whose stories can be reconstructed through the archives or other available sources. This book, in other words, will recount both the story of Fascist dictatorship and that of 'everyday Mussolinism'; it will portray how ordinary Italians lived their lives in times that Fascism swore to make extraordinary.

Palazzo Venezia and its Piazza lay in the heart of Rome, since 1871 the capital of Italy and a city – publicists took pains to remember – called 'eternal', the predestined citadel and inspiration of the empires of the 'First', 'Second' and 'Third' Italies, of Rome, Renaissance and Risorgimento. Looking down on the square from the south was the Capitol, sublimely sacred site of the classical imperium. To the east stood the Coliseum, by 1940 visible from the balcony down the Via dell'Impero, or Empire Street, itself the jewel of Fascist urban planning and renewal. To the west the Corso Vittorio Emanuele led to the

Vatican, while the other Corso ran from the Piazza Venezia towards the Milvian bridge, where, to his immediate military and political benefit, the Emperor Constantine had seen the vision of the Cross, and on to the Via Flaminia and those other Roman roads which fanned out across Italy and beyond.

The environment of the dictator's balcony was thus resonant, suffused with histories in need of narration and understanding. Yet in 1940 the biggest building, the most imposing, the most glaring in its refulgent whiteness, the edifice with the most stentorian architectural message, has not yet been mentioned, although it still imposes itself on any visitor to Rome. Along the southern edge of the Piazza Venezia and guarding the entry of the Via dell'Impero stood the Victor Emmanuel monument or *Vittoriano*, the *monumentissimo*, typewriter or wedding cake, as its critics more scoffingly styled it. Given its massive size (its surface alone occupied 17,000 square metres), its jingoism, its bravado, it must, even on that early summer day of 10 June 1940, have dwarfed the loquacious dictator and the restless crowd. Perhaps leader and people were no more than homunculi; perhaps Italian history limited their free will and shadowed their choices; but, if the signals of the 'Third Italy' are to be decoded, a picture of the Victor Emmanuel monument may be a good place to start.

The building is not a Fascist one. Rather it honours King Victor Emmanuel II, who, with arithmetical irony, was the first king of Italy (1861–78). Planned since 1880, opened on 4 June 1911 – the usually sober Prime Minister, Giovanni Giolitti, had saluted a 'national anthem in marble'[3] – but not fully finished until much later, the *Vittoriano* was designed to be the most sacred and the most visible symbol of that Italy which, it was said, had been 're-united' in the Risorgimento. To the disgust of the Vatican and its sympathizers throughout the world,[4] the monument's statuary displayed a medley of liberal gods – Thought, Action, Sacrifice, Law, Force, Peace, Unity, Liberty – not all of whom were treasured by Fascism. The meaning of the monument could be adapted, however. After the First World War, the stepped and pillared building was surmounted by Winged Victories charging towards the west, thus promising to deal either with the Vatican or with France, Britain and those other powers which, Fascist theory argued, immured Italy in the Mediterranean.

Special focus of the worship of the nation was the 'Altar of the Fatherland', finally completed in 1925 with a representation of the goddess of Rome, reborn, as Fascist phrasing had it, through that 'national love which fights and wins' and through 'hard work which builds and sows'. It had been here, on 4 November 1921, third anniversary of the victory of Vittorio Veneto, that Italy's 'unknown soldier' of the Great War was patriotically interred. After 1922 Mussolini, too, would regularly use the site, especially while, through the second decade of the regime, one Fascist war succeeded another.

The monument also broadcast a spatial message. Its construction entailed the demolition of a number of medieval and Renaissance buildings, a cloister, a library and a hospice, some classical mosaics, and the Palazzetto Venezia, a wing of the greater Palazzo, in total amounting to 'hectares of urban fabric'.[5] A contemporary commentator has briefly stated that, in regard to the city's texture, 'the *Vittoriano* is a catastrophe'.[6] Liberal and Fascist town-planners thought the sacrifice worthwhile, however, because the levelling of the monument's surrounds set the new building hard up against the classical Capitol. By 1935 the *Vittoriano* stood at the centre of axes proceeding to the Coliseum, to the various republican and imperial fora, and to the Theatre of Marcellus and the Temple of Janus, where classical Romans had disclosed whether the present was a time of peace or of war. The Victor Emmanuel monument constituted the visible proof that the ghosts of Italies past and especially those of the all-conquering Roman empire were welcome in the new nation. The monument made concrete in the most literal of senses the alleged fact that the Third Italy was organically connected with the First and Second Italies. It proclaimed that the nation was eternal and that its inhabitants were primordially and exclusively Italian. The very heaviness of the building (somewhat ironically countered by its dazzling whiteness) promised an infrangible national unity. As an Italian historian has explained, the monument and the remade Piazza Venezia, 'adjacent as they were to the classical Forum, constituted, or were meant to constitute, the "Italic Forum" of modern Rome'.[7]

Fascism was much given to enthusing about unity; its own symbol, the *fasces* – lictors' rods tied with rope and made more ominous by an axe, sharpened for the punishment of dissenters, traitors and enemies

– pledged the dictatorship to bind Italians inseparably together. But, in some senses, Liberal Italy had got there first in the Victor Emmanuel monument. After 1860 the Liberal leadership had been soon troubled by the thought that Italy had been made but Italians still needed to be. Both *Vittoriano* and *fasces* made it evident that, from 1860 to 1945 (and beyond), the first task confronting the politicians who had taken up residence in the Third Rome was to complete (or commence) the nationalization of the masses. In the sacramental liturgy of the modern Italian nation, the steps of the *Vittoriano* and the paving stones of the Piazza Venezia were meant to mark the holy place where the subjects of the peninsula, a territory so recently dismissed as a 'mere geographical expression' – many of whose people seemed to their leaders wayward and imponderable, if not actively murderous – could join in a communion, experience a mystic patriotic transubstantiation, be born anew or now be inscribed as Italians and know that their identities were above all national.

So went hope or theory. In 1882, the very year when Giuseppe Sacconi's project for the Victor Emmanuel monument was sketched, the French writer Ernest Renan remarked with optimistic democracy that a nation entailed a 'daily plebiscite'. At once, however, he added pessimistically that 'forgetting and, I would say, historical error are an essential factor in the creation of a nation';[8] such an entity was unimaginable without the bolstering of lies from the past. In no place, certainly in no capital city, were ambiguity and falsehood more evident than in Rome.

After all, much can be revealed about the history of states and societies by examining their main cities. Britain and France were modernized, centralized and ruled by imperial London and imperial Paris; Russia, facing east and west, was perennially torn by the duel between Moscow and St Petersburg; Spain was split between the artificiality and tyranny of Madrid and the Mediterranean localism or cosmopolitanism of Barcelona; in Germany, Berlin offered efficiency and industrialization or, by contrast, militarism and authoritarianism – though maybe Vienna or Bonn or Weimar or Frankfurt was the 'real' capital.

Italy, like Germany, was one of the new nations of the nineteenth century and Rome faced many competitors among the nation's urban centres: Milan, site of the national stock market, commerce and much journalism; Florence, most celebrated for its cultural and artistic heritage; Naples, capital of the south, of connections with the new world and, still in 1914, the metropolis with the greatest population; Turin, solid city of heavy industry and cradle of the Royal Savoy dynasty, to name but a few. What could Rome offer to counter these rivals? Its history spoke of Empire but, ever since the Cross triumphed over the ruins of the Capitol, Rome had become the heart of the world-girding empire of the Church. This universal Catholic imperium was not easy to reconcile with the little nation of Italy. The political mixture of the Risorgimento had been etched with anti-clericalism: Italian modernity seemed irrational without it. As late as 1889 Prime Minister and sometime liberal terrorist, now turned nationalist, Francesco Crispi, took pleasure in erecting a statue to Giordano Bruno, martyr to the obscurantism and brutality of the Counter-Reformation. In reply, a bishop with special religious charge over Rome could still hope that God would yet 'hunt from His breast the criminal [Liberal] wolves', who were devouring the 'holy city'.[9] In 1911 the Jesuit journal, *Civiltà Cattolica*, greeted the programme of the national fiftieth anniversary celebrations with the dampening homily that 'a year of mourning' was the best approach to the history so far of United Italy. Rather than relying on a trumpery nation-state, Italians, the Jesuits counselled, should direct their minds towards St Peter's, which offered 'the security of remaining completely firm in the face of the assaults of Hell'.[10] The cold war between Catholic Church and Italian state was not formally overcome until the signature of the Lateran Pacts between Mussolini and Pope Pius XI in February 1929. That treaty, however much a good business deal for each contracting party, did not snuff out the conflict of charisma and meaning between God's anointed and Fascism's totalitarian chief, with poor little King Victor Emmanuel III (1900–1946) clinging to a distant third place as the inspiration for or manipulator of Roman and Italian spiritual life.

Rome had other problems, too. The late nineteenth and early twentieth centuries were the age of gold and iron, of railways, battleships and modernized banking. The sinews of industry stiffened the ability of a Great Nation to rage in the European and non-European worlds. But Rome drew its income from bureaucracy, building speculation and the pleasing leisure and wantonness of tourism. No factory chimneys belched the promise of power over the eternal city's restaurants and ruins. Its oldest bank (and one of the few not to fail in the financial crisis of the 1890s) honoured the Holy Ghost (Banco di Santo Spirito) and flourished in the Catholic interest. Those who mingled in Rome's central streets were frequently foreigners trying their best to ignore the present while they sought uplift or entertainment from the past. Arnold Toynbee, English classicist and philosophical historian in the making, learned from his Mediterranean tour in 1911–12 that the Ancients could not have been like the Moderns. The latter were rightly denominated 'dagos'. A present-day Italian or Greek (he saw no reason to distinguish between the two) was 'a parasite . . . his nature is unsuccessful imitation.'[11] In September 1910 the radical young socialist journalist Benito Mussolini hinted at local doubts about the allure of history to foreign visitors when he lambasted the national capital: 'Rome, the parasitic city of cheap low-grade hotel-keepers, shoe-shine boys, prostitutes, priests and bureaucrats'. Rome, he complained with earnest ideological devotion, was a 'city without a proletariat worthy of the name [and] . . . not the centre of national policy. Rather it was the place from which contagion spread over national political life.'[12] Rome, it sometimes seemed, was the least Italian and least modern of places. Often, for all the propaganda stoking its myth, it was the city least loved by those Italians who did not live there.

While he was pondering the meaning of the nation, Ernest Renan noted that science, and especially the new science of racism, was particularly ill equipped to explain Italy. All societies, he argued, were multiple. But 'Italy is the country that most embarrasses ethnography: Gallic, Etruscan, Pelasgic, Greek, not to mention the many other elements, have interbred here, forming an indecipherable blend.'[13] The insistence that Italy is a country of division, contradiction and nuance is another of those maxims familiar to any who contemplate the national story. No doubt the alleged failure of nationalization can in its turn be exaggerated to distort the historical record. For quite a few Italians it was possible to craft a nationalism embracing regional diversity. Yet anyone who attempts to survey pre-First World War Italy cannot avoid seeing variation and difference.

If modernity and progress are what matter, then Italy's emblematic city in 1914 was Turin, the capital of Piedmont, far to the north-west and less than a hundred kilometres from the French border, a territory with many centuries of its own history, one that was scarcely identical with that of Rome or Florence or Naples. For all its idiosyncrasy, Piedmont had donated its rulers to the new Italian nation. However, although Victor Emmanuel II and Umberto I had found their resting place in Rome's restored Pantheon, once offered to the Emperor Augustus by Marcus Agrippa, their predecessors, the kings of Piedmont-Sardinia, lay buried at the Basilica of Superga which stands on a hill above Turin. Count Camillo Benso di Cavour, the political impresario of the Risorgimento, with his ambiguous boast *'je suis italien avant tout'*, sprang from an eminent Piedmontese noble family. Also Piedmontese were Giolitti, the dominant politician of the years from 1900 to 1914, Luigi Cadorna, the general who led Italian forces into the First World War (he was known to speak a heavily Piedmontese dialect),[14] and Pietro Badoglio, the key military figure of the Fascist years and, in 1943, Mussolini's immediate successor. A Piedmontese ethos never ceased to be a basic component of the thought and practice of the Italian officer corps and can be traced in other segments of the administrative apparatus of the Italian state.

But, with the onset of the twentieth century, Turin was acquiring a new face. It was evolving into the city of the Agnellis and Fiat and of modern Italian heavy industry. Simultaneously it became the fulcrum of the Italian left. Before 1914 its growing socialist movement welcomed Antonio Gramsci and Palmiro Togliatti, two immigrants from Sardinia, who, for forty years, were destined to lead the Italian Communist Party. These young men were drawn to study at Turin University, the most ideologically lively in the nation. As early as 1897, when as a region Piedmont still held only third place in the nation in industrial employment, Turin had already sent two socialists as its deputies to the parliament in Rome. By 1913 three fifths of the seats in the urban government were occupied by socialists. Turin was the dynamo of Italian Marxist theorizing and trade union practice, and the place where, in response, industrial employers had begun organizing on their own behalf. In Turin, 'planning' and 'progress' were positive terms and the nationally important local paper *La*

Stampa could cheerfully portray a local administration working as 'a business agency serving the city's future'. Municipal expenditure doubled from 1899 to 1909.[15] Fiat's own output increased by 120 per cent between 1906 and 1911 and, during that time, the company opened branches in Austria, the United States and Argentina, and manufactured its first airplane.

Head of Fiat and founder of an industrial dynasty was Giovanni Agnelli, born in 1866 into the Piedmontese gentry. Agnelli, like so many of his class, was destined for the army and in 1889 became a lieutenant in the socially prestigious cavalry. He also dabbled in politics and agriculture and, along with members of his aristocratic Turin club, had a youthful yen for fast cars. Determined to harness the new technology, Agnelli took permanent leave from his regiment and in 1899, with a noble colleague, founded Fiat. For a while it was only one company among many, almost all of which soon failed, several in the economic downturn of 1907. But Agnelli was a hard-headed businessman and open to the new world. In 1903 he visited the USA to examine factory practice and he remained a student of American business methods and a pioneer advocate of Taylorism and the scientific organization of labour. In July 1905 King Victor Emmanuel III made an official visit to the Fiat factory (it was patriotically situated in Via Dante). By 1911 Fiat employed 6,500 workers and the invasion of Libya brought the chance for state contracts, smoothed by Agnelli's personal or regionally enhanced ties with Prime Minister Giolitti. On occasion, Agnelli did evince a dislike of interfering 'priestlings, professors and state officials', the foes of 'the nation's productive elements', but, at least until the war, his self-estimation retained some humility. He did not yet perceive politics as an arena where business people naturally led the way. In 1914–15 Agnelli was not at the forefront in advocating Italian commitment to the First World War, rendered cautious by the knowledge that his firm had contracts with the British and German navies and the Russian army.[16] However, once entry was determined, he set about exploiting the beckoning financial opportunity.

Antonio Gramsci, destined to be the Italian Marxist of greatest intellectual span and profundity and so the guide of that working class forming itself in Fiat and other factories, was born in 1891 at Ales, up country from the humble Sardinian port of Oristano. His birthplace was a world away from modernity. In peasant Sardinia, the inhabitants refused subjugation to the mathematical discipline of the Christian calendar, preferring to record the years with the name of those major events that stirred and afflicted their *paese*.[17] In studying peasant Italy, assumptions about everyday experience should not stale an ability to see the infinite variety of pre-modern imagining. Although he himself always retained an intellectual interest in and empathy towards it, Gramsci's family did not belong to this traditional world. Rather, Gramsci sprang from the southern bureaucracy. His grandfather was a colonel in the *carabinieri*; his father a public official, who, in 1897, fell into disgrace amid accusations of peculation and spent the years 1900–1904 in jail. Helped by an elder brother and more generally impelled by the desire to reverse his kin's downward social mobility, by 1911 Gramsci had moved to Turin, winning a scholarship in the same exams sat by Togliatti. Soon the two were busily reading socialist philosophy, practising socialist journalism and establishing themselves as critical, revolutionary, intellectuals. In Turin, it has been estimated that by 1914 four fifths of the socialist party membership of 1,000 were workers, but students were also attracted to the new movement and its protean but alluring talk of revolution. Gramsci was no dully vulgar Marxist; rather he was enquiring and independent enough to be much taken with Taylorism and, during the autumn of 1914, flirted with those schismatic comrades soon to be led by Mussolini, who were breaking from the mainstream socialist cause in quest of a different sort of revolution in Italy's military campaign. In the end, however, Gramsci did not yield to nationalist temptation, and in 1915 he joined the staff of the local socialist weekly, *Il Grido del Popolo*, and campaigned against the war.[18]

Agnelli, on the one hand, and Gramsci, on the other, each incarnated those new social forces that were spreading the second industrial revolution, with its advantages and discontents, across Europe. Neither man fitted easily into an Italy defined by the Rome of tourism, religion and national myth. Each instead reflected Turin. Even under Fascist dictatorship, the city retained much of its particularity. Its citizens never fully sacrificed their localism or their cosmopolitanism to the demands of totalitarian nationalization. Rather, Piedmontese continued to say to themselves in dialect: 'I'm off to Italy' (*ndé 'n Italia*) whenever they had to cross the regional border, and cherished the knowledge that 'Italians' were rogues and swindlers or, more charitably, that they were just soft and self-indulgent southerners, perpetually prey to their childish passions. Each Piedmontese, by contrast, was deemed a person who was 'not impulsive, does not give himself over to enthusiasms, does not get carried away, never gets excited; he sees things as they are'.[19]

If Turin was the most modern face of northern Italy, away to the east Venice emitted more mixed messages. This ancient and imperial republican city was still the major port on the Adriatic but was struggling to adapt to modernity and to a presence in an Italian nation. Of its population of 160,000, 30,000 lived below the poverty line. Commentators regularly underlined the damp and insanitary character of local housing, and the vulnerability of Venetians to tuberculosis and malaria, not to mention the fact that the city had the second or third highest suicide rate in the country, those who killed themselves doing so either for love or out of desperation at their social conditions. In May 1911 even a Liberal paper condemned the appalling environment at the Murano glass factories where, in habitual flouting of Italy's weak labour legislation, children of ten endured shifts beside the ovens and young girls were forced to work through the night. Another of the city's diseases was cholera; the epidemic of 1911 was first denied and then concealed by the Giolitti government, which feared the news might discountenance the tourist trade during the patriotic celebration of the nation's fiftieth anniversary. Cholera, suicide and romance were transmuted by German writer Thomas Mann into his novella *Death in Venice*, and the idea that Venice, despite its natural, architectural and artistic beauty, was really a tomb remained a common and powerful one.[20]

There were socialists in Venice, just as there were in Turin. The city had a socialist deputy, Elia Musatti, and it also boasted a *Fascio giovanile 'Carlo Marx'* (the Karl Marx Socialist Youth Group). Most members were local workers but Venice, because it always drew an international clientele – before 1914, the Lido was one of the best-regarded bathing establishments in Europe – was a magnet for intellectuals, people who believed that their ideas, like diamonds, could carve the path to a better future. One was Margherita Sarfatti, later notorious as 'Benito Mussolini's Jewish mistress'.[21] On 8 April 1880 Sarfatti had been born into a wealthy Venetian family, the Grassinis, whose palazzo lay in the city's ghetto. She and her friends rejoiced in the post-Risorgimento freeing of their culture from traditional religious repression (though it had been worse in the papal territories than in the Venetian Republic or its Austrian-ruled successor from 1815 to 1866). After the 1860s most Jews felt a debt to the nation and, for a time, were more likely to applaud Italian nationalism than Zionism.

Being a woman might be a more vexing matter. The scientific criminologist Cesare Lombroso, also of Jewish descent and Liberal Italy's most internationally renowned scholar, had pronounced that 'a woman, being weaker and more passionate than a man, has more need of the support and restraint of the family to keep her in the right way, from which she is more easily turned than a man, on account of the slippery path of prostitution that is always open to her'.[22] In both rural and urban Italy, women could rarely detect anything that was modern in their lives. The Risorgimento had scarcely proved a 'national revolution' for them. Their illiteracy level had fallen from an 81 per cent high in 1860, but by 1911 it was still reckoned at 42 per cent. A paltry 250 Italian women attended Italian universities in 1900. Many women still perished in childbirth (or in crude abortions designed to prevent it) and female life expectancy did not match that of males until the 1920s.[23]

None the less, however erratically and inconsistently, some change in the gender order was in the air. Giolittian Italy saw the growth of clubs and newspapers canvassing the female cause and, in 1908, Rome hosted the first National Congress of Italian Women. The journal *Scena Illustrata* made a stuttering start on the ladder to modernity when, in 1901, it held a 'Cinderella contest', inviting its readers to send in their foot measurements, presumably for princely appraisal. Women, or men, had to wait until 1911 and the anniversary celebrations for Italy's first beauty contest. One who reproved such developments was Pope Benedict XV (1914–22). He anathematized those fashion changes that were reducing the heaviness of female apparel: 'Christian mothers, I cry for you. I cry tears of blood for your daughters, great and small . . . Their shameless immodesty . . . wounds me to the heart . . . I curse the infamous fashion for nudity that profanes their virginal candour . . . Even in families who think of themselves as respectable and Christian, they cheerfully shed stockings and the indispensable parts of their underwear . . . On roads and paths, at school and at home, girls of 7 to 14, young ladies of 16 to 23, on bicycles or on foot, adopt attitudes which are repugnant to the most elementary Christian and social decency.'[24]

Benedict XV would not have been impressed by Margherita Grassini, even though, as a girl, she and her father had been received by Pope Leo XIII (1878–1903) and she had grown up closer to Catholic than Jewish religion. In 1898 Margherita married local lawyer Cesare Sarfatti, at the time a Republican, although, before long, the two were proclaiming their commitment to socialism. They soon had two sons (the elder of whom was destined to die in the war and have his memory posthumously Fascistized).[25] In 1902 the Sarfattis moved to Milan, where each cut a dash in socialist politics, and Margherita became a celebrated journalist and cultural critic. By 1914 she boasted 'the most brilliant salon in Milan'[26] and had taken as a lover Mussolini, who had arrived in Milan in 1912 from the Romagna as the aspiring editor of the socialist paper *Avanti!*

Among Sarfatti's contacts were the flamboyant and self-publicizing writers Gabriele D'Annunzio and Filippo Tommaso Marinetti. Each made plain his dislike for the other, just as each, with unpatriotic anxiety, sought to be lionized in Paris, still the real cultural capital of Europe, in the hope of escaping the intellectual tedium and mediocrity of parochial little Italy. Each none the less found a place for Venice in the web of romance, masculinity, power and fakery that they wove around themselves. Marinetti, the Futurist, launched the scandalous idea that Venice, weighed down by its cultural treasures and tourist appeal, was emasculating a national thrust towards real modernity. The best way to deal with the wretched place, he suggested lightly, was to deploy artillery to hurtle its crumbling buildings into its canals. D'Annunzio, who favoured a more ornate, or even rococo, personality than that being marketed by his younger colleague, did not seek to puncture the romance of the city. He did, however, try to write Venice into the nation, when, in 1908, he premiered his play *La Nave* there and shouted its patriotic theme that Italy must engage in sea-borne expansion. Some years earlier, Stelio, a character in D'Annunzio's novel *Il Fuoco* (The Flame), who was given to haranguing the masses from a balcony, had pronounced: 'throughout the whole world, I know of no other place than here on these sluggish waters, except perhaps Rome, where an alert, ambitious man can activate the power of his intellect and direct all his energies towards the supreme ideal . . . In Venice', he added portentously, 'one cannot feel except through music or think through images. They come from everywhere in such profusion, endlessly, they are more real and alive than the people who jostle us in a narrow street.'[27]

For all the self-conscious and avant-garde posturing of Sarfatti and those other intellectuals for whom Venice mattered, the most significant individual in the city and one who became an emblematic figure in twentieth-century Italian history was Giuseppe Volpi.[28] This lawyer son of an engineer with claims to patrician ancestry was born in 1877. By the start of the new century he had renounced his profession, establishing himself as one of Italy's wealthiest, most adventurous and best-connected business leaders. His Società Adriatica di Elettricità, curiously abbreviated as 'SADE', dominated energy supply in the Veneto and surrounding regions. But Volpi had simultaneously begun his penetration of the Balkans. Victor Emmanuel III's wife, Elena, was a Montenegrin princess, and sentiment, interest and the evocation of the imperial histories of Rome and Venice suggested that Italy must not be behindhand in its commerce in that region or anywhere in the eastern Mediterranean. By 1912 Volpi had installed himself as the trusted agent of Giolitti, smoothing the path of more orthodox diplomats towards the Treaty of Lausanne, by which the Ottoman Empire accepted the loss of Libya to Italian arms. Volpi was also closely connected with the Banca Commerciale Italiana which was directed by Giuseppe Toeplitz and near to Giolitti. So common was it to view Volpi as a friend of German banking that the Nationalist Ezio Maria Gray, enemy of Giolittian neutralism in 1914–15, tried to damn Volpi as 'an undesirable alien'.[29]

Gray and Volpi each eventually played major roles in the Fascist dictatorship. But already in 1917 Volpi turned Venice towards its future when he persuaded the government and the banks to approve the creation of Porto Marghera as a major industrial site on the mainland side of the lagoon. Thereafter Volpi liked to think of himself as the unofficial ruler of Venice. Certainly he was its most influential citizen and embodied a special version of modernity present in Venice, not one that exactly replicated the situation in Rome or Turin.

Some thousand kilometres south of Venice, and well away from most modern preoccupations, lay the Sicilian port of Messina. If scrutiny of northern cities unveils certain themes, analysis of a southern centre uncovers others. Like so many settlements in Sicily, Messina was an ancient city, having acquired its name in 493 BC, when a homesick Greek tyrant longed for his home region of Messenia in the Peloponnese. Before the First World War, however, Messina acquired a more sinister significance. Struck by an earthquake on the morning of 28 December 1908, Messina fell to the ground. Up to 100,000 people died in the city and surrounding *comuni*, whether in Sicily or, across the strait, in Calabria – some flattened by the quake, others overwhelmed by the tsunami or tidal wave which swept in from the sea. Whatever the exact toll, it overshadows the 5,000 or so Italians killed fighting for national unification in 1859–61 and the similar number who perished at Adua, the battle humiliatingly lost to the Ethiopians in 1896. Much about peasant life, especially in the south, is embodied in the statistic that from 1894 to 1908 Calabria averaged 5,000 dead each year, victims of one natural disaster or another.[30]

Before the earthquake, Messina had been Italy's fourth largest trading port, with imports and exports being valued at 71 million lire in 1908. Modernization of a kind was in the air. Bilateral agricultural agreements which, in recent years, Italy had signed with Germany, Austria and Switzerland, nourished a commerce in cordials and citrus. Was not Messina the place which had inspired J. W. Goethe to write Mignon's song: 'Do you know the land where the lemon tree blooms'? Emigration was another growing business; the United States employed both a Consul and a Vice-Consul in the city. Tourism was increasing but little developed. Oscar Browning, MA, once of King's College, Cambridge, warned against too sedulously romantic thoughts of fraternization with local peasants. They were, he wrote, 'very wretched and degraded . . . The common living room is shared by pigs and poultry and even occasionally by an ass and a mule.'[31] Nevertheless, Messina was the railway junction where trains from the mainland reassembled after crossing straits once deemed perilous because of the presence of Scylla and Charybdis. Further south, the Prussian baron Wilhelm von Glöden, stylish photographer of naked local boys (he was well enough regarded to mount a public exhibition of his work in Rome during the 1911 anniversary celebrations), was updating Taormina as Sicily's prime tourist site. Rich northern European gays were drawn to places where they could savour 'purely Greek profiles' among the young male inhabitants.[32] Von Glöden had taken up residence in Taormina in 1876 and was not to be dislodged by Fascism, despite its homophobia. People of his social eminence were laws unto themselves and so, as one historian has remembered, von Glöden was appreciated as a person who brought guests to that part of Sicily: 'Customers [of his artistic photography] and friends who cared to lay on a car and a picnic lunch were rewarded, it is said, by the short loan of one of the numerous young [male] models while the Baron took an afternoon siesta.'[33]

The earthquake exacted a terrible toll on Messina and its surrounding region. One extended family of sixty was reported to have counted only two survivors. Another man lost his wife and eight children.[34] In Reggio Calabria, the barracks collapsed, killing all but three of the 850 soldiers stationed there.[35] Perhaps the loss of these agents of contemporary authority could be endured by the local inhabitants. One observer noted that, at Reggio, peasants from the villages in the interior arrived in the city marshalled by their priests, just as they might have done in the Middle Ages. It was now a little dangerous to search for food or medicine, however, since looters were shot without questions being asked and unknown 'foreigners' from out of town could easily have their identities and actions misinterpreted.[36] With a more severely geopolitical reference, one contemporary journalist judged the earthquake disaster as the equivalent of a military defeat like that suffered by France at Sédan in 1870,[37] and the precariousness of Italy's position as the least of the great powers was made evident when well-informed rumour bruited that Austrian Chief of General Staff Conrad von Hötzendorff had advised his emperor to launch a preventive war against Italy and so reverse the losses of the Risorgimento.[38]

The most celebrated Italian to endure the earthquake was Gaetano Salvemini, thirty-five-year-old professor of history at Messina

University and recent author of an impressive study of the French Revolution. Salvemini was also a prominent and intellectually lively member of the socialist movement. At first it was assumed that he had been entombed with the rest and a series of eulogistic obituaries mourned his death. The twenty-five-year-old Mussolini, always anxious to assert his own claims to intellectuality, sent a telegram conventionally regretting the loss of 'one of the finest figures in the world of Italian socialism'.[39] But while his wife, five small children and sister-in-law perished, Salvemini survived. He had wandered the streets of the ruined city for some days before being recognized by chance by King Victor Emmanuel III, arrived at Messina on a royal visit of succour. Given a squad of soldiers to help him dig, Salvemini then sought his family. But, after two days of labour, fresh falls from the structure and the terrible smell caused the rescuers to abandon their effort. 'I made a mistake in not killing myself on the first day,' Salvemini was left to remark in agony.[40]

Salvemini would become a Cato-like critic of both Giolitti and Mussolini – after 1925 he became an exile or *fuoruscito*, professor of Italian history at Harvard University for a time and the best-known anti-Fascist publicist in the English-speaking world.[41] In his rectitude, Salvemini owed quite a bit to his calamity in the earthquake. As his biographer has noted: 'from 1909 onwards, although he worked with his usual energy for the same [democratic] ideal, his life was pervaded by a veil of sadness and pessimism.'[42] Nor was Salvemini the only anti-Fascist intellectual to be marked by the Italian peninsula's vulnerability to natural disaster. Liberal philosopher, historian and upper-class anti-Fascist Benedetto Croce lost his parents and sister in an earthquake on Ischia in July 1883, Croce himself being buried under their collapsed hotel for a night, unable to respond to the fading cries of his father for help.[43]

Novelist, sometime communist, later anti-communist (and alleged Fascist informer) Ignazio Silone survived an earthquake in the Marsica, an area of great estates to the east of Rome, in January 1915 (just as Italian politicians were trying to work out how and when to join the First World War). This disaster, Silone recalled, 'in thirty seconds killed thirty thousand people'. He detected a timeless meaning in the event: 'What surprised me most was to see with what matter-of-factness the people accepted this tremendous catastrophe. In an area like ours, in which so many injustices went unpunished, the frequency of earthquakes seemed so plausible a fact that it required no explanation.' Equally predictable, he explained, was the nature of the reconstruction, or lack of reconstruction, which followed. State welfare merely became the opportunity for 'intrigue, fraud, embezzlement, favouritism, scheming and thievery of every sort', in which the local rich were the only certain beneficiaries.[44]

Similar charges had accompanied attempts by the Liberal government to repair the damage to Messina. When the Fascist regime took over, it claimed that the Liberals had only built 125 new edifices per annum, a replacement rate which implied that rehousing would not be complete for eighty years.[45] But Fascism, too, lagged behind in the refurbishment of the city. In 1937 Mussolini himself complained to his Minister of Public Works that the initial wooden huts survived and seemed to have become 'eternal and inviolable'.[46] In 1958, well after Fascism's fall, it was alleged that 10,000 Messinesi still subsisted in 'temporary' accommodation.[47]

The vagaries, corruption and weakness of the Italian state here evidenced must preoccupy any historian of Liberal, Fascist and Republican Italy. But in 1908 at least one public official did his duty and deserves to have his story told. Antonio Barreca was an itinerant postman on the Siracusa–Messina run. According to his memoirs, self-published in 1931, by which time he could call himself *Cavaliere* Barreca, the postman had lodged by chance on the night of 27–28 December with a widow and her granddaughter. Surviving the first impact, Barreca realized the women were trapped. Braving the inky darkness and the hellish sounds all around, he broke into the women's room and, despite their lack of appropriate clothing, persuaded them to crawl out and live.

Barreca was not gallant merely to females in distress. For a time at least he did possess an appropriate sense of the duty of a state official. Donning his postman's uniform and cloak, he began to battle his way through fire, misery and death to that bastion of government authority and connection to Rome and the wider world – the railway station. It took him two hours to get there. But the station had also been overwhelmed by disaster. The *capostazione* could only cry that he had lost his family and tens of workers in the disaster. The telegraph was down, the post office a shell and the railway line leading south blocked. Barreca, whose own family was in Siracusa and presumably safe, refused to be downcast and trudged along the buckled track until he could find a working transmitter. After twenty kilometres and three hours of walking, he reached the station of Scaletta Zanclea. There the railway's telegraph line was broken but the post office building, despite being scarred by large and ominous cracks, was for the moment intact. Local officials refused to enter it. But Barreca surmounted this last danger and tapped out a terrible message, obediently directing it to his superior, the Director of the Provincial Postal System at Siracusa: 'Miraculously escaped alive, I do not know what has happened to my fellow workers. Messina destroyed.'[48]

Alas for Antonio Barreca. At Siracusa his seniors had difficulty believing that their subordinate could be so light-headed as to claim that a whole city had been destroyed and the local prefect sternly drafted an order for Barreca's arrest. Nor was Rome swift to respond. Carlo Schanzer, the Minister of Posts and Telegraphs, carried the news with tardiness and incredulity to Giolitti, who had not yet visited Sicily, although he was serving as Prime Minister for the third time, expostulating: 'But this fellow must be a madman! How can anyone say that Messina has been destroyed?'[49] Only when information came from other sources, and officers from a Russian fleet exercising in the Mediterranean landed at the ruined port, did action ensue.

Nor was Barreca's post-earthquake experience to be altogether happy. He was summoned to Rome in April 1909, briefly hailed as the epitome of a state official, accorded the ineffable pleasure of a personal meeting with Schanzer and, responsibly and formally, given a public examination so that he could be promoted to a higher and better paid grade. However, he quickly decided that the experience had left him with a nervous condition that obliged him to cease work and subsist on his postman's pension. Unable, however, to live the honourable and leisured life to which he aspired, he became locked in endless litigation with a government reluctant to raise his pension. He was cheered by thanks from the landlady's granddaughter, who had moved to Milan where, he wrote, she 'had the good fortune to be sought in marriage by a lawyer'. The couple came to Sicily for their honeymoon and took pains to locate Barreca and proffer advice and encouragement, personal and legal. But, at least until 1931, no more charity could be wrung from the stern bureaucrats in Rome and Barreca was left to write his memoirs. In the preface he acknowledged with hopeful Fascist piety the inestimable benefits brought to Italy and his home island by the *Duce* but omitted to mention that he was still waiting for his own reward.

Barreca was not unique in his behaviour and world-view. The aspiration to become a client, with an accommodating, generous, powerful and enduring patron, penetrated deeply into many Italian souls. As one historian of Liberal Italy has acutely remarked: 'clientelism was one of the factors which cemented the [prevailing] system of state, professions and market'.[50]

With a certain rigour, the Liberal government was swift to preach 'realism' in dealing with Messina. On 3 January 1909 Giolitti declared martial law in the stricken city, despite the fact that, according to the constitution, a state of siege was only possible in the face of enemy troops. The local commander, General Francesco Mazza, shot looters out of hand. The King's cousin, the Duke of Aosta, headed a relief committee, and on 11 January 1909, only a fortnight after the earthquake, abruptly rejected the idea that welfare payments should be channelled to 'peasants and poor workers'. The aim of the state, he made clear in phrases which echo through Liberal ideology, must be that 'fit men honourably earn their living and not become unused to work . . . It is immoral to subsidize a wave of vagabonds and render men lazy.' In the eyes of officialdom, the poor had not lost much in the tragedy since they did not have much to lose. Such government assistance as there could be – and ministers and economists were fighting off a run against the lira on international markets[51] – should, the relief committee agreed, be confined to the middling classes and especially to those small proprietors who had 'lost everything'.[52]

The government's indifference to the suffering poor was echoed by the tone of newspaper reports. The bourgeois Rome paper *La Tribuna*, which often acted as a mouthpiece for Giolitti, published the news that *paesani* from hill villages, devastated by the earthquake but very unlikely to be succoured by officialdom, were wreaking a traditional rural revenge on an urban centre. They were roaming the debris of Messina and joining those prisoners who had survived the collapse of the town jail in sacking the place. Emboldened by the chaos, these wild men coveted gold and other jewellery and were said to have shoved such ornaments into the bags they carried, sometimes with finger or ear attached. It was even alleged that they had slashed their loot from living bodies, callously slicing off the hands of those who were trying to scrabble free from the wreckage.[53] The Reformist Socialist Meuccio Ruini, whose ideology ought to have made him optimistic about humankind, could read one lesson from the earthquake: 'Man is a wolf. The only perfect organization to emerge from the carnage has been the organization of murder and theft. What a beast of prey man really is!'[54] His more radical party comrade, Oddino Morgari, knew that a Divine Being did not exist but suggested that the earthquake made it necessary to invent God in order to curse Him.[55]

Some historians talk glibly about Liberal Italy being a 'democracy'. But it was very far from being a society that had achieved liberty, equality or sorority. French journalist Jean Carrère stated that, when he was touring Sicily and Calabria in 1909, the peasant population of those regions where 'the ground trembled', were 'subi, résigné et vaincu' (overwhelmed, reduced to lethargy, beaten). When recounting the sentiments expressed by the ruling class about the earthquake, it is not difficult to see why or to understand how such southerners remained impervious to cheap nationalist rhetoric about a homogeneous and united people.

The American Consul and Vice-Consul and their wives died in Messina.[56] But their deaths did not curtail the grand currents that, during the years leading to 1914, were expelling so many Italians from their country. In 1913, the year when departures peaked, 407,475 Italians entered North America, 148,850 the countries of South America and 307,627 left for Europe, France and Germany, with each country receiving more than 80,000. Of the regions, the north-west lost 175,224, the north-east 123,853, central Italy 208,641 and the south 364,780. Sicily alone bid farewell to 146,061 of its inhabitants.[57]

These Italians outside Italy most frequently migrated along 'chains', which ran from their village to some settlement in a host country. Each *paese* of migration had a *Weltpolitik*, in both practice and imagination, one that was not easy to reconcile with national policy. In 1904 a report in the official *Bollettino dell'Emigrazione* noted that, in the USA, it was 'very rare for a farm worker from southern Italy to disembark without having a relation, a fellow villager or some sort of friend whom he can contact . . . All southern Italians, whether they plan to be here on a temporary basis or permanently, are grouped by region, by *paese*, by village or by family.' They expected to be hired to work as groups, shopped in their own special places and even hired lawyers of their own. Their catchphrase was 'who does not possess *paesani* will not be happy in any aspect of life'.[58]

Governmental attitude to these departures fluctuated, with the most common position being expressed by economist and sometime prime minister Luigi Luzzatti, who in 1901 told parliament that 'it was useless discussing whether Italian emigration is a good or an ill. It is simply a necessity.'[59] As the expatriation grew, however, so did a concern, prompted by stories of exploitation of the emigrants and by the increasing authority achieved by racial theoretics and Social Darwinism and the resulting fear that Italy was voluntarily wasting valuable bloodstocks. Moderate liberal and editor Olindo Malagodi concluded that emigration was the most obvious token of 'national inferiority'.[60] New generation intellectuals, generally hostile to the Giolittian order and, from 1910, grouped in the Associazione Nazionalista Italiana (Italian Nationalist Association), sought remedy in power politics. Their leading philosopher, Enrico Corradini, argued that emigration gave proof of Italy's national failure, a sad contrast with the rising strength of Japan, for example, a country that concentrated its population and mustered them to stand alert against their foes. Like Japan, Corradini urged, a renewed, more authoritative and authoritarian Italy must accept that war was 'the supreme act', for which the nation should urgently and ruthlessly prepare.[61]

Also interested in the migration issue was the Catholic Church. Giovanni Battista Scalabrini, the bishop of Piacenza, whose patriotic brother had been a key agent of anti-clerical Prime Minister Crispi, established the order of Scalabrinians to watch over the personal and religious fate of the emigrants. Scalabrinian 'missionaries' sought to reconcile *religione e patria*, Catholicism and Italy, preaching that a rapprochement between Church and State could allow the nation to resume its past glories. Italy, in this gospel, was the emigrants' common mother and the bonds with their home must never be fractured.[62]

Romolo Murri was another priest troubled by the migration and national questions, although, unlike Scalabrini, his path led to a loss of his vocation, the gain of a Swedish wife and the embrace of Fascism. In 1913 Murri toured Latin America, publishing his impressions in the establishment journal *Nuova Antologia*. Italians were obvious and numerous in this new world and a handful were making their fortune, he noted. However, corruption and excess were all too evident, clientelism was pervasive and the poor and unsuccessful were oppressed and derided. The Italian language (or presumably the dialects which the emigrants actually spoke) soon surrendered to the dominant Spanish, he remarked sadly, and 'the woman, more plastic and adaptable than man, more in need of social contact, more fearful of fights and disputes' was, he believed, 'the first to abandon any national sense, taking on local practices, absorbing the new language' and assimilating in the interests of her children.[63] Yet, for some, he contended, a countering process was possible. The better migrants learned from their treatment and experiences that they were indeed Italian. They ignored past class or ideological cleavages, marking in themselves 'for the first time our country and its imprint'. As one migrant told him: 'I came to look for "America". Instead, in America, I discovered and learned to know Italy.'[64]

This ironical course through which the initial localism and cosmopolitanism of the emigrants transmogrified into nationalism and Fascism is another theme worth remembering in the history of Mussolini's dictatorship. Migration was, after all, often not envisaged by an emigrant as a permanent step. Rather, emigrants frequently conceived of themselves as 'sojourners' who, in an act comparable with accepting conscription into the army, hoped to make their fortune and, after years of hard service, bring it and them 'home' to the *paese*. Even in 1913, 111,298 Italians came back from North America, 64,726 from South America, while repatriations from Europe were naturally more numerous.[65] On many occasions the returnees were labelled *Americani* by those who had stayed at home and they may well have expressed their local identity in a fashion amended by their time away. A minority followed more narrowly the model of nationalism that Murri had outlined. Amerigo Dumini, for example, the Fascist thug who organized the slaying of moderate socialist politician Giacomo Matteotti in 1924, was born at St Louis, Missouri, in 1896. He was the child of (temporary) emigrants (his father was a Tuscan painter), whose choice of his first name hinted at their surviving patriotism. Dumini was sent home to be educated and there won by the siren call of the national effort in the First World War. In 1919, according to his own account, he was turned into a Fascist after suffering public abuse from a socialist mob who assaulted him outside Florence's Duomo, merely because he was wearing uniform.[66]

A rather more sophisticated returned migrant was Edmondo Rossoni, eventually the leading advocate of Fascist trade unionism. Rossoni had been born in 1884, one year after Mussolini, at Tresigallo, in the province of Ferrara, some eighty kilometres north of the *Duce*'s birthplace, Predappio. Like many another ambitious youth of the Po valley, Rossoni was active in socialist politics, but in 1907 he renounced the party in despair at its moderation. This swerve in his ideology prompted him to leave Italy, first for Nice and then Brazil, and eventually in 1910 the USA. In his new country, Rossoni remained a revolutionary, however. Dismayed by the pronounced Anglo-Saxon American belief in the racial inferiority of Italians, he was soon demanding 'the creation of a strictly Italian working-class union'. Enough of an internationalist to condemn the attack on Libya as 'monstrous',[67] Rossoni, by August 1914, supported Italian intervention in the First World War, although he still advocated 'revolution' as the prime war aim. During the hostilities Rossoni was employed until 1916 as a publicist of the nation among emigrants in the USA, before returning to Italy to speak for the patriotic Fascio d'azione interventista (Interventionist League). In 1918–19, as secretary-general of the syndicalist Unione Italiana del Lavoro, that group which had long stood separate from the mainstream socialist party and demanded national rather than class unions, he at first mistrusted what he feared was the reactionary bent of Mussolini's *fasci di combattimento*. However, in 1921, he merged his movement into what was becoming the Fascist party, having determined to be an Italian, to rejoice in the 'national imprint' and to privilege 'national revolution' over the socialist variety.

Emigrants were not the only Italians to live outside the borders of the Kingdom of Italy. After 1915 patriotic propaganda called the world conflict Italy's 'last war of the Risorgimento', intended finally to bring all Italians in Europe home to their nation.[68] Indeed, in the Trentino, north of Verona, in the city of Trieste and its hinterland, and in Istria, Italians bore Habsburg rule. The memoirs of Diego De Castro, a self-consciously middle-class resident in the Adriatic fishing port of Pirano, provide a textured image of local identity, in which class, gender and ethnicity wove yet other patterns of Italianness. 'The first measure' of a person, De Castro contended, was the 'level of his or her *italianità*'. However, he continued, society was split in each of Istria's towns into three distinct classes. 'First-class people', among whom he placed himself, had their own *caffè* and, he maintained, no one from an inferior class presumed to enter such a place. 'First-class people' also spoke their own language. If he strayed to Capodistria (seventeen kilometres to the north-east), Parenza, Umago or other nearby towns, he found local 'first-class people' talking an 'Italian' which he could at once recognize and which was more familiar than the tongue of the lower classes of his own town. Nor was language the only social marker since dress codes, too, were very diverse for each group. All behaviour was conditioned by class. A 'first-class man' (as distinct from a woman) only entered the portals of the local church for weddings, baptisms and funerals, since priests were esteemed automatic friends of Austria. Some features of life remained primitive. There was no running water available at Pirano and someone from the humble classes collected his laundry each day and dumped it into the sea for washing. In old age, De Castro still thought of himself as having been an 'irredentist' (that is, one who believed that his lands should be 'redeemed' by the Italian nation) but admitted that he had not foreseen the ruin of the Austrian Empire in the First World War.[69]

During the Fascist regime, the most publicly revered figure in these irredentist regions was the 'martyr' Cesare Battisti, born in 1875 to a well-off family at Trento. This Italian-speaking city of the Counter-Reformation had been an independent prince-bishopric until 1803, when it fell under Habsburg control. Battisti studied law at Florence University but returned to his home town to become active in politics and journalism. In 1848 and 1866 local elites aspired to be united with Italy, resenting both the economic travail of the city and what they regarded as increasing pressure to become German. Whether peasants outside the town shared this nationalism is doubtful (a little further north, they spoke dialects of German, while certain Alpine valleys were surviving redoubts of Ladin or Romansch). Battisti at first conceived of himself as a socialist, urging the cessation of ethnic quarrelling. None the less his enthusiasm for being Italian kept breaking through, as it did, for example, when in 1896 a monument to Dante, who had been reconstructed as a symbol of the Italian language, culture, history and future, was inaugurated at Trento. From 1900 Battisti edited a daily called *Il Popolo* (The People) to inform the Trentino region about his ideas, and a nationalist populism began to fray his commitment to orthodox socialism, while the fact that the Austrian authorities doggedly sequestered the paper on repeated occasions kept Battisti in the news. He remained an attractive and ambiguous enough figure to be sought out by Mussolini when the latter moved to Trento as orthodox socialist party secretary in January 1909. After July 1914 Battisti fled across the border and campaigned vigorously for Italian intervention. When Italy did enter the war in May 1915 Battisti volunteered for service. Captured by the Austrians, in July 1916 he was hanged as a traitor in the Trento castle ditch. The callousness of an Austrian lieutenant, who had himself photographed beside the swinging corpse, confirmed Battisti's place on an honour-roll of national heroes[70] and stiffened the resolution of officers to avenge the 'pain and horror' of his end.[71] Despite certain ambiguities in their story, the irredentist regions would provide crucial support for Fascism as it gathered strength, and the special attitudes and traditions of this frontier continued to mark the Fascist movement and sponsor its more drastic actions.

This excursion around the Italian peninsula and beyond has indicated that, just before the outbreak of the First World War, Italians found many diverse and even contradictory ways to be themselves. An acknowledgement of regional, class and gender difference is only a first step towards understanding the complexity and variety of Italian life. The currents of very many histories continued to fret and to fashion the paths by which Italians were adjusting to modernity. If Fascism really was fully to nationalize, homogenize and unite Italians, then much work lay ahead.

Blackening the horizon in 1914 was the First World War. After it was decided, in May 1915, that Italy must join the conflict, the war proved a bloody, costly and wrenching event and the eventual national 'victory' was partial and uncertain. As if to prove the point, on that day in November 1921 when Liberal Italy, with some desperation given its buffeting from the social, economic and political crisis of the rise of Fascism, buried its Unknown Soldier under the Altar of the Fatherland attached to the Victor Emmanuel monument in central Rome, the socialist paper *Avanti!* held its own line. 'The Unknown Soldier is one of yours, proletarians!' the paper urged editorially. 'Honour him in silence and curse the war!'[72] Socialists and officialdom, it was plain, had contrasting memories of the great conflict and, a historian should add, Italy's war had not been identical with that still celebrated in English-speaking recollections of the Western Front. No doubt, much about Italy was drastically amended by four years of battle, but its trauma, however profound, did not eliminate texture and diversity in the transmission of Italian pasts to a future. One matter is certain, however. Although quite a few strands in Fascism's nature can be traced before 1914, first and foremost the national dictatorship was to be the product of Italy's war.

2

Liberal and dynastic war

In 1914, by almost every index, Italy was the least of the great powers. Nor, despite huffing and puffing about imperial conquest and racial prowess, would that ranking be much altered during the Fascist years. When the First World War began, Italy's population tallied some 35 million, up from 25 million in 1860, but behind France's at 39 million and not gaining on the rapidly augmenting inhabitants of Britain, Germany, Austria-Hungary and Russia. Available hospital beds had increased by 58 per cent[1] and, although with great regional and class variation, the health of the nation was improving. Life expectancy for Italians grew from thirty at the time of the Risorgimento to forty-seven in 1900, but in this regard too Italy lagged behind the Western powers and only narrowly exceeded Spain. Contrary to some legend, Italy's birth rate was not especially high, at 21.7 per thousand in 1913, falling below that of France or Sweden.[2] Social gains were often precariously won. Among the casualties of Italy's war were infants; the numbers who died in the first year of life returned to almost 200 per thousand births as a result of the medical and food deprivation imposed by the conflict.[3] In 1914 Italy's most numerous city, at just over 700,000, was still, as it had been for centuries, Naples, despite the glaring absence of modern industry in a place still half regretful at the loss of its past as capital of the kingdom of the Two Sicilies. Next came Rome and Milan, each at more than 600,000, then Turin, Palermo and Genoa.

Worth noting, by contrast, was the fact that Italy long possessed the greatest number of urban centres boasting a population above 20,000, each likely to be conscious of its special history and virtue. Recent research has criticized too gross a division of Italy into a developed north and a 'backward' south. Historians have underlined that each region possessed its own 'south' and emphasized that landowners could contrive a path to capitalist development for their world or, more simply, to enhanced profit for themselves. Despite such changes, the urban fabric of the country was arranged in Italians' minds with studied hierarchy and continuity. The most fundamental difference elevated those who lived within a *città*'s walls (where some form of *civiltà*, civilization and citizenship bloomed) above the *contadini*, peasants of one kind or another, who did not. At the same time, each urban settlement claimed a precise rung on a ladder of significance and desirability. Some jostling was possible, especially between one town and its nearest neighbour of a similar size. But, when Mussolini advanced from Predappio to Forlì to Bologna to Milan and, more equivocally, to Rome, while in his secret soul he longed for Paris, he was following an imagined upward path any educated Italian might understand and applaud. Nationalist and Fascist bluster about a united nation could never shake the basic knowledge of Italians that some places in their peninsula outranked others.

Italy's relatively small population and relatively tardy urban growth reflected the fact that the peninsula lacked many of the minerals that steeled Britain, Germany and even France for industrialization and war. Although, with the coming of the twentieth century, hydroelectricity filled some gaps in Italy's deficient energy supplies, throughout the period from 1860 to 1945 the nation remained dependent on coal imports. Its domestic production in 1914 was a risible 0.9 million tons, sadly inferior to Britain's 292 million, Germany's 277 million, Austria-Hungary's 47 million, France's 40 million and Russia's 36.2 million tons.[4] In 1916 the young officer Carlo Emilio Gadda, destined to write for Fascism and then, after 1945, to become its most scabrous critic, linked Italy's mineral dearth to its other God-given woes: 'The lack of iron and coal', he remonstrated in his war diary, 'and the frequency of earthquakes are the . . . major explanations why the Italian nation is "less adapted to the current environment" (in the Darwinian sense of the word) of our era.'[5] Certainly, whether under Liberal or Fascist rule, Italy's international behaviour and restricted economic development were frequently conditioned by the need for energy imports. Just before the Second World

War, it became clear that there were parts of Italy where natural gas lay untapped, but its effective exploitation had to await the Republic after 1946. Italy occupied Libya in 1911–12 but failed to uncover or exploit the territory's massive oil resources. Italian economists and geologists, learned in the classics, preferred instead to fantasize about 'restoring' Libya to the position it had once held in imperial Roman grain production. Until the fall of Fascism, the colony's greatest mineral export was salt.

In 1913 Italy's per capita gross national product stood at an index of 43 to the 100 of the USA (France was 56, Germany 54 and Britain 83) and, although an appreciable growth rate had been achieved during the Giolittian decade, Italy was still yielding ground to Germany, the USA and Japan, and was not catching France.[6] Italy's banking system had all but collapsed in the first half of the 1890s, amid allegations of endemic corruption and incompetence; national finances had only been bailed out through the acceptance of foreign expertise and implicit foreign control, notably from Germany, which, to 1915, in the view of the more nationalist or paranoid of commentators, exercised a stranglehold over the Italian exchequer and ruthlessly practised dumping on to the Italian market.[7] In reality, Germany was scarcely alone in its treatment of Italy. Other countries, notably Britain, France and Belgium, maintained their own quasi-imperial encampments in sectors of the national economy. The Vatican, rich fount of capital, dominated the Banco di Roma, the financial group most directly involved in proselytizing Liberal Italy's imperial adventure in Libya – the future Pope Pius XII (1939–58) sprang from a family prominent in that bank's management. The national budget regularly teetered into deficit, the currency was vulnerable to crises, real or imagined, and surplus was achieved only through the monies that reached Italy either from emigrant remittances or through tourism. This latter was to prove the most lasting and lucrative money-spinner, though with somewhat unpredictable effects. Much tourist spending was informal, went unrecorded and untaxed and, by definition, lay outside the formal reckoning of the budget; the massive tourist presence was yet another factor which subtly limited the rigour of Fascist totalitarianism and which perennially checked plans to impose a strong state in full control of Italian lives.

The bumpy national drive towards industrialization and modernity was hugely regionally imbalanced. In 1911 80.3 per cent of the workforce of the Abruzzi-Molise was employed in agriculture against 39.2 per cent in Liguria. At that time, 35.6 per cent of Lombards worked in industry, while only 14.3 per cent of Calabrians found similar employment, somehow defined. In Lazio 4.2 per cent of the labour force held bureaucratic jobs, in Sardinia 2.6 per cent but in Lombardy only 1.5 per cent. Illiteracy in Piedmont had fallen to 11 per cent. It reached 25.2 per cent in the Veneto and 32.7 per cent in the Emilia-Romagna (each regions where Mussolini for a time worked as a schoolteacher), 58 per cent in Sicily and 69.6 per cent in Calabria.[8] Three hundred and thirty of every 1,000 Italian recruits in 1914 were illiterate, as against 220 in the Austro-Hungarian armies, 68 in the French forces and one in the German.[9] Female rates of illiteracy were always much higher than male. Italy remained a country where a little learning was treasured and rewarded; schoolteachers in 1910 earned four times the average pay of industrial workers[10] and the status of intellectual work, especially among intellectuals, was valued still more highly. The Mussolini who was still not a *Duce* was anxious to be called *professore*, granted his qualifications to teach primary school French.

The availability of figures about many aspects of Italian society is a product of that statistical revolution which has been described as underpinning the 'making of Italy'.[11] But the fondness of Italian experts for tabulating information in regional lists hid differences within the regions, which frequently were as great as those from one area to the next. In some senses, the plethora of statistics simultaneously 'unmade' Italy or at least divided it, by cherishing the capital cities of each region or province and slighting their hinterlands and countryside. Moreover, the peasants of the peninsula and especially of the south preserved a traditional reluctance to expose to government inspectors the exact details of their lives. Very frequently, peasants viewed any official as someone who was either the malign agent of a foreign army of occupation, or the spy of their bailiffs and landowners, or both.

Outside the Po valley and a few other plains, the Italian countryside is notoriously convoluted. The Apennine and Alpine mountain chains steeply sunder one settlement from the next. Well into the twentieth century, travelling in much of the peninsula was dangerous and unpredictable. In the countryside of Sardinia, hotels were unknown because people there had not yet imagined that a person could stay away amid the perils of a night without family contact.[12] In many an upland, roads waited to be paved over ancient muddy paths, still most easily trod by the feet of man and donkey. Even in the 1950s, an anthropologist reported, villages in the Salento, an area of low hills in the hinterland of Lecce, were still only connected by cart-tracks. There, peasants regarded the surfaced 'national roads' or high-ways, which led to Bari, Naples or Rome, as foreign and alien, not for them.[13]

Inadequate roads symbolized the partial and erratic penetration of the state into Italian lives. As the twentieth century began, the cele-brated bandit Giuseppe Musolino held Aspromonte, the rugged hills of southern Calabria, in thrall. Modernized enough to give interviews to eager journalists even while the police were hunting him, Musolino ignited much moralizing from urban Italians and visiting foreigners about the 'traditional backwardness' and 'bloodthirstiness' of his region.[14] It was, after all, true that the Mafia in Sicily, the 'ndrangheta in Calabria and, in a different manner, the Camorrà in Naples owed quite a bit to the impenetrability of the local terrain. Each criminal group constituted a sort of anarcho-feudalist set of cells or families, better integrated into its regional society than were the agents of the national government. Geography also ensured that much of the national railway was thriftily built down the Adriatic and Mediterranean coasts, sometimes literally along the sandhills behind the beach. This placement left crucial parts of the Italian transport system nakedly exposed to a superior navy, while bombing from the sea rather than from the air was regarded as the greater strategic threat.

Diseases resulting from poverty and poor diet also haunted quite a few sections of the peninsula. Simple starvation took a regular toll. Even in sophisticated Milan in 1913, female workers were reported to spend from 50 per cent to 90 per cent of their wages on food and such sustenance as they managed was still deficient. When officials meas-ured their weight, they discovered that these women fell well below the national average. Despite the agricultural fertility of at least some parts of the national territory, Italy imported grain. A bumper harvest in 1913[15] gave extra confidence the following year to those politicians who wanted Italy to join the war at once. A reduction in the import bill, however temporary, permitted greater military expenditure.

One good year, however, could scarcely overcome ancient deficiencies. Pellagra still smote the poor of the Po valley, although its effect was beginning to lessen before 1914 as rapidly unionizing peasants began to demand meals composed of something more than polenta.[16] In 1909 a parliamentary commission, investigating why rural people might be emigrating from Calabria, found that meat there was a food 'treated with religious reverence or collective madness in a transgression which happened but once per year'. In many *paesi*, even vegetables were not a matter of everyday consumption. The peasants of one *comune* allegedly sustained themselves over a whole winter exclusively on figs. Bread remained the staff of life but its character differed drastically from one class and region to the next. In the Calabrian saying, a 'white bread woman' was identical with a *signora*, while the head of a peasant family was instead accustomed to bake the family bread supply once per month. 'Hard bread keeps the family together', the optimistic saying went. Only with the processes of social change unleashed by overseas emigration did (dried) fish, coffee and tea penetrate inland settlements and bring variety to local tables.[17] A statistician recorded that coffee use went up in Italy by 90 per cent from 1900 to 1913. Sugar consumption doubled in the same period.[18] The effect on peasant lives was uneven, however. As late as the Second World War, the inhabitants of a *paese* near the Ferramonti di Tarsia concentration camp in Calabria willingly surrendered their sugar ration for use by the confined *signori* in the camp, because the villagers had not yet imagined that honey could be replaced as a sweetener.[19]

Malaria was another scourge of the flat areas of the peninsula. The mosquito ruled the Pontine marshes, just outside the imperial gates of Rome. It did so as well in the Maremma in the hinterland of Grosseto in Tuscany, where, when the twentieth century began, bandits still roamed unchecked.[20] Some reduction in the malign effect of malaria occurred from the 1890s, when government schemes were initiated to provide cheap quinine to the populace. But the budget for such matters could not survive the First World War and, in 1917–19, the death and debility rates soared.[21] Ignorance about medical matters remained profound. When cholera struck the Puglian port of Barletta in 1910, local socialists, jaunty paladins of science and modernity, blamed the disease on the arrival there of gypsies and, in some ethnographic confusion, persuaded the national paper *Avanti!* to warn against 'those Russians with rough and unkempt beards whose ignorance and filth fit them for classification in the lower spheres of the animal kingdom'.[22] Although such humanist socialists as the reformist leader Filippo Turati believed fervently in worker education and sought a future where the Italian masses could outstrip the educational attainments of the British or Germanic worlds, modern knowledge remained alien to many peasant communities. In Messina, a local told a visiting journalist after the earthquake that there the humble classes automatically addressed all members of the bourgeoisie as *professore*, a word which expressed an unbridgeable gulf in intellect and imagination as much as it did in respect or a desire to learn.[23]

Amid the pre-1914 atmosphere of continued international crises and the threat or promise of war, Italy's economic and social limitations entailed military weakness too. In that world where Social Darwinian assumptions that nations were locked into a struggle for the fittest dominated every elite's common sense, Italy's pretensions even to be the least of the great powers often looked hollow. In 1913, Italy managed to provide military training to only 24.7 per cent of its available male class against Germany's 74 per cent and France's 87 per cent. One problem was the lack of fit potential recruits, the other the feebleness of the writ of Liberal administration across wide tracts of national territory.[24] In every European chancellery and on every European parade ground, it was assumed that Italians could not fight. The humiliating naval defeats by Austria at Lissa in 1866 and the unavenged imperial loss to Emperor Menelik's Ethiopians at Adua thirty years later confirmed that prejudice. Germany's 'maker', Otto von Bismarck, had provided the most widely circulated summary of the new Italy's limited military prowess. The Italians, he said mockingly, were a people with a 'very large appetite and very poor teeth'. In the affairs of the world, he added peremptorily, 'as to Italy, she does not count'.[25]

Bismarck made these comments about a power that from 1882 was, and until 1914 remained, a member of the Triple Alliance with Germany and Austria-Hungary and so apparently stood in the opposite camp to the rival Triple Entente of France, Britain and Russia. But in diplomacy, too, Italy was the most ambiguous of the powers. Its leaders convinced few foreigners to alter their appraisal of Italian strength and reliability when they resuscitated the familiar Latin phrase about 'friends and allies' to justify their many connections with Britain and France, while explaining how Italy stayed tied to Austria-Hungary, always its most likely enemy in any general conflict. True to this frayed record, Italy, alone of the great powers but in parallel with all the little Balkan states, except Serbia, did not join the war at its beginning in August 1914. When, nine months later, Italy's leaders found reason to fight, they took their country into battle against the nation's old allies.

Like most European states, Italy was a monarchy. Since the assassination of his father, Umberto I, in 1900 (the killer was an anarchist returned from an emigrant's life in New Jersey), Italy's king was Victor Emmanuel III. He remained head of state through the Fascist years, abdicating belatedly in May 1946, just before the referendum through which Italians opted for a republic. In the *belle époque*, Victor Emmanuel, tiny, uxorious, with scholarly interests in numismatics and a leisure-time devotion to photography (and hunting), did not register greatly in the social, sporting and political pages compared with such busy self-publicists as Kaiser Wilhelm II of Germany, Edward VII of Britain or 'Foxy' Ferdinand of Bulgaria. A man of few public words, Victor Emmanuel preferred platitude to fame. Visiting Messina after the earthquake he was recorded by the press as having muttered 'It is terrible, terrible' and back in the Quirinale, the royal palace in Rome, he advised his government with consummate cliché that now was a time when 'everyone will do his duty'.[26] Marketed somewhat unconvincingly to the nation during the First World War as the *re soldato* (soldier king), Victor Emmanuel restricted his diary entries to facts and appointments and, at no time in his life, brought joy to journalists seeking copy. Both stern and timid, Victor Emmanuel III for the most part dedicated himself to being a constitutional sovereign, whose seeming propriety was undermined by his conservative bent in times of trouble.

Italy's liberalism found its most telling expression in the national bicameral parliament. Crucial politically was the Chamber of Deputies.[27] To some degree the lower house was checked and balanced by the Senate, a citadel of ex-generals, cultural luminaries and politicians whose careers had taken a turn for the worse. Even Fascism did not bother to reform it far. The national parliament was not a place where one ideologically defined party replaced another after elections fought over clear and rival political programmes, however. For the first decades after the Risorgimento, almost all members of the political elite defined themselves as liberals of one kind or another. They were defenders of the Risorgimento settlement and, simultaneously, men (women in Italy did not get the vote until after the fall of Fascism) who had emerged from and were integrated into a local power base and patronage system. Each parliamentarian, by definition, assumed the advantages and duties of being a patron. In Giolitti's governments from 1903 to 1913, a sociologist has estimated (although his categories hide a frequent overlapping), 4 per cent of office-holders were landowners, 29 per cent lawyers, 4 per cent other professions, 16 per cent 'technical' intellectuals, 10 per cent humanist intellectuals, 16 per cent military personnel, 16 per cent bureaucrats. Only 1 per cent was best identified as devoted to industry and commerce and 4 per cent were otherwise defined. There were no workers or peasants. Among ordinary deputies, lawyers and journalists predominated and numbers in these occupations varied little even among the socialists. In 1913 80 per cent of deputies defined as being from the *Estrema* (Far Left) were university graduates.[28] Perhaps the most pervasive organization for those in or near the political world was Freemasonry, membership of which long remained all but mandatory for the military and for the civic professions. Liberal Italians held an array of religious attitudes but the first and most menacing institutional enemy against which leaders of the new state long rallied was the Catholic Church.

The twentieth century ruptured the tranquillity of this liberal world of gentlemen and *notabili*. The coming crisis was foreshadowed in Milan in 1898, when rioters, both Catholic and socialist, were ruthlessly repressed by the army. For two years thereafter, the Prime Minister was a Piedmontese general, Luigi Pelloux, who aimed to shore up law and order. His key backer, Italy's most significant conservative liberal, Sidney Sonnino, intellectually more sophisticated than his soldier leader, talked of the need to 'return to the constitution', stipulating a more authoritarian form of government, a greater censorship of the press, a more rigorous suppression of social discontent and a more active and knowing nationalization of the masses. During the next decade it became increasingly apparent that the most direct challenge to the existing order came from the socialist movement, with its flaunted dedication to international revolution. A number of revolutionary groups united in 1892 to form the Italian Socialist party and, by 1900, the PSI had elected thirty-three deputies to the Chamber. The party remained damaged by schism, however, and the speed of its electoral advance did not approach that of the German Social Democratic Party. None the less, in 1913, the PSI did boast fifty-two deputies, while the Chamber contained a further twenty-seven members who called themselves syndicalists or reformists but, in their minds at least, were still pledged to a socialist future of some kind, even though the mainstream party's formal mass base remained fragile. In 1914 it counted 1,300 members in Milan, 530 in Rome, 110 in Naples and 25 in Palermo.[29]

As elsewhere in Europe, organized party life did not limit itself to the parliamentary forum. The national trade union, the moderate and even reformist Confederazione Generale del Lavoro (CGdL), was founded in 1906 and, five years later, had attracted to its ranks 384,000 workers. But unity was brittle here, too. In 1912, a syndicalist union, the UIL, broke from the CGdL and claimed more than 100,000 supporters, many of them drawn from the older group.

Marx had mocked the 'idiocy of rural life' but Italian Marxism was unusual in its penetration of the peasant world, at least in the Po valley and especially among day labourers or *braccianti*. Federterra (the National Federation of Land Workers) gave social hope and political impulse to the poorest families in the northern countryside, which juddered with the changes unleashed by a rapidly capitalizing agriculture. In the south, by contrast, pre-capitalist landowners were not queasy about grasping their customary power; historian Frank Snowden has traced the ruthless employment by the wealthy of armed squads, designed to deal with any sign of mutiny among the day labourers of Puglia. 'Force', Snowden concluded, 'was no accidental feature' of life there; rather 'an integral part of labour discipline'. Among the Apulian peasantry, 'squadrism was not an invention of the fascists'.[30]

Strikes, lockouts and social violence were on the rise in Liberal Italy, although the active commitment of Italian socialism to full-blown revolution may be doubted. The patriotism aroused by the Libyan war in 1911–12 exposed some revolutionaries to seduction by the nation. When, in the midst of the imperial conflict in March 1912, an anarchist tried to kill Victor Emmanuel III, three leading reformist socialists, Leonida Bissolati of Cremona, Ivanoe Bonomi of Mantua and Angiolo Cabrini, born in Codogno but active in Rome, felt obliged to accompany other parliamentarians in delegation to the Quirinal Palace. There they respectfully voiced the nation's alleged relief at the King's escape. At the next socialist party congress, held in July 1912 at Reggio Emilia, the PSI again split, the most vehement attacks on the three moderates coming from the young 'maximalist' or radical, Benito Mussolini, who soon took over the editorship of the party's paper *Avanti!* from Claudio Treves, another reformist, and, later, for good measure, fought a duel against him.[31]

The other mass force growing in late Liberal Italy was political Catholicism, although its adepts did not coalesce in the Partito Popolare Italiano or Popular Party until 1919. The PPI's first leader was the Sicilian priest Luigi Sturzo. Similarly, it was not until March 1918 that the Catholics joined in a national trade union, the Confederazione Italiana del Lavoro (CIL), designed to save some workers from what was widely feared in the Church hierarchy to be godless socialism. However, as early as 1889, a Catholic Social Studies Association (Unione cattolica per gli studi sociali) had come into existence, 'favouring the maintenance and the development of faith and commitment in the countryside, especially opposing the insidious attack of [protestant] sects and other propaganda encouraging disbelief and socialism'. By 1914 quite a few 'white' or Catholic unions were flourishing in such clerical and agricultural areas as the Veneto and Marche. Although even moderate CGdL secretary Rinaldo Rigola condemned these bodies as constituting 'nothing more than a bunch of systematic black-legs',[32] some Catholic unionists were as zealous in demanding improvements in pay and conditions as were the socialists. Before and after the war, Catholicism could not be placed with full certainty on the left–right political axis, even though in most instances the sympathies of Catholic leaders were conservative and anti-socialist. Catholic banks, large and small, were, for example, hostile to the reforms undertaken by Giolitti in 1911–12 which imposed greater state control over the national insurance business. In 1913 Catholics from the social and financial elite signed the so-called 'Gentiloni Pact' that, for the first time since the Risorgimento, implicitly ended the papal veto, or *non expedit*, on the active participation by the pious in elections. In the subsequent poll it was thought that 228 deputies owed their success to the Catholic interest and they tended to align themselves on the more conservative and patriotic wing of Italian liberalism. Already in October 1911 the Bishop of Cremona, Geremia Bonomelli, hailed the attack on Libya as a 'crusade' in which national tricolour and Christian cross were together raised in triumph against the Muslim foe.

A few weeks later another commentator, the free trade economist Maffeo Pantaleoni, was more extreme in his language. In Libya, he wrote, 'the present bastardized population, the result of the cross-breeding of whatever is filthiest in the human races, should be driven out and destroyed, and replaced with good, Italian, blood'.[33] Pantaleoni was not the first Italian to vent the phrases of colonialist racism and genocide.[34] However, during the prelude to the First World War, such views were given a greater profile through the establishment of the Nationalist Association and the sale of its paper, *L'Idea Nazionale*, the first issue of which came out on 1 March 1911, the fifteenth anniversary of the unavenged Adua defeat.

The Nationalists won six seats in the Chamber of Deputies as a result of the 1913 elections, although they were braided more deeply into elite culture than this trifling figure suggests. In 1914 many a Liberal father was possessed of a Nationalist son. Entrants to the Ministry of Foreign Affairs in those years, for example, drawn to a man from the best and brightest of their world, were very likely to welcome Nationalist urging of a more forward policy in Africa, the Balkans, the eastern Mediterranean and the rest of Europe and simultaneously to second the demand for greater domestic discipline to marshal the nation to meet what might well be the coming and at least half-desired challenge of war.[35]

The most important Nationalist politician was the journalist Luigi Federzoni, whose electoral victory in Rome in 1913 signalled a more general switch to patriotic policies among the Italian elite. Born into the Bologna bourgeoisie in 1878, he began his career on the local paper, *Il Resto del Carlino*. In 1905 he transferred to the national capital and there he stayed. He worked first for *Il Giornale d'Italia* (a relatively conservative paper near Sonnino), before becoming a founder of *L'Idea Nazionale*. Writing under the archly busy pseudonym Giulio de Frenzi, he made his name by passionately attacking what he regarded as craven Italian efforts to ingratiate themselves with German tourists holidaying beside Lago di Garda. In and around the town he ironically labelled 'Desenzano am See', everyone spoke German on occasions that mattered, he complained. 'Italian', he charged, was reduced to being 'a kind of dialect with which one can hope to be understood in the lowest grade dives on the Verona side of the lake'.[36] Federzoni naturally espoused the cause of imperial advance on Libya, hoping that the Italian seizure of the Ottoman-ruled Dodecanese islands in 1912 would not be temporary, as the government (mendaciously) promised, but would instead signal the first step towards an Italian domination of 'all the islands, Anatolia and the whole eastern Mediterranean, and perhaps more besides'.[37] Federzoni was similarly forward in advocating the *italianità* of Dalmatia. The Croat language, he wrote in 1910, did not exist; it was a fake and fabrication in the same way that Esperanto was. The humiliating naval defeat at Lissa in 1866, Federzoni urged, must be overturned and Italy must 'resume' its destined place as the only civilizing force in the region, replacing the obsolescent Habsburg empire.[38]

A noxious message was being inscribed, one of border nationalism. It was destined to mark Italians' relationship with their neighbours, especially those to the north-east, for two generations and more. Taking Federzoni's phrasing a step further, another nationalist wrote later that Slovenes were 'constitutional idiots, lacking in brain power, thick-headed and presumptuous yokels'.[39] As a third journalist put it, all Balkan peoples were barbarous thieves.[40] Such quick and chill stereotypes led Fascist Italians towards what is now called ethnic cleansing as the way of dealing with Slovenes. Luigi Federzoni and the Nationalists paved the way for such attitudes and policies. Federzoni himself was long to be a Fascist Minister, member of the ruling Grand Council and one of the most influential, typical and malign Italians of his generation.

While Nationalists clamoured for Italy to acquire more strenuous government, the Liberal Italian state was expanding. The number of bureaucrats in its pay rose from 98,000 in 1882 to 260,000 in 1911.[41] At the summit of the system stood the prefects, whose position as the agents of centralized government, largely on the Napoleonic model, had been confirmed by an early post-Risorgimento parliament in 1865, leading the radical Salvemini sardonically to christen Liberal Italy a 'prefectocracy'.[42] Prefects managed law and order in a broad sense. One memoirist, stationed for a time at Saluzzo in Piedmont, remembered Giolitti arriving during an election campaign with 'precise and absolute' orders about which candidates were to be elected and which not. Seconding the prefect in each city was the local *Questore* or police chief. Giolitti was notorious in some circles[43] for commanding his prefects and their police to 'hold the ring' in social disputes, certainly between workers and industrialists and, less reliably, between peasants and landowners. At the same time, however, the Giolittian state was inventing repressive policing practices that would be honed under Fascism. Not for nothing would Mussolini's long-term police chief, Arturo Bocchini, commence his career in the pre-war bureaucracy. Under the Liberals, such dubiously liberal actions as the compilation and retention of lists of political dissidents, secret telephone tapping, preventive forced residence (*domicilio coatto*) and *confino*, that is, the extended relegation of a person to a *paese* in the south or to a remote island off the Italian coast, began.

The worst example of the ruthless treatment of prisoners in Liberal Italy occurred, predictably, through colonial policy. In October 1911 Giolitti ordered the cramming on to the desolate Tremiti islands of hundreds of Libyan families who had objected to the arrival of Italian occupiers in their homeland. Virtually nothing had been done to prepare for the presence of the internees, no shelter was available and food supplies arrived erratically and inadequately. By June 1912 almost a third were dead, with the toll being worst among children and old people. The fate of the Libyans was not helped by the fact that the islanders, ignored by national governments until then, were themselves regular victims of epidemics of cholera and typhus, depending on the season.[44]

As so often in Italy a disjunction yawned between the theories of liberalism and the practice of law and criminal justice. Tuscany had led the world in the abolition of capital punishment in 1853 and the Chamber of Deputies passed similar legislation for the nation in 1865, although full implementation was long held up in the Senate. The death penalty was not restored until 1926, despite the pressure brought to bear by the widely publicized criminological researches of Cesare Lombroso and others, estimating that murder was six times more common in Liberal Italy than in France and nine times more frequent than in Britain.[45] Most of these slayings were poor-on-poor killings – they should qualify too sentimental a view of the native 'niceness' of the 'Italian people' – but quite a number of Italians suffered from the brutal and authoritarian governing habits of the elites, their bailiffs and other agents, who, across tracts of Italy, were not squeamish in using violence and murder if they perceived a threat to their social power.

This, then, was the Liberal Italy whose political chiefs, from July 1914 to May 1915, puzzled whether and when to take the nation into the war, on which side, for what reward and at what cost. In those months, the personality who, in Fascist retrospect, was to be apotheosized as the deciding figure, was Benito Mussolini. Who, then, was this *Duce* in the making? Born in July 1883, Mussolini came from the popular, but not the poorest, classes of the Romagna. His father was a blacksmith and local socialist activist, who, in his time, turned almost respectable as deputy mayor of his home *paese*, Predappio, and before his death in 1910, innkeeper of the patriotically named hostelry, Il Bersagliere, of Forlì. Mussolini's mother (she died in 1906, still in her forties) was the local schoolteacher, a believing Catholic, possessed of a sense of service to her community. Mussolini himself qualified to teach primary and then secondary school French, although, he later frankly acknowledged, without fully mastering the language. For a while he cadged employment in a succession of humble schools at one locality or another across northern Italy, but his joy lay in politics and journalism. He was good at both and, as has been noted, in December 1912 was nominated editor of the socialist paper *Avanti!* He had not yet celebrated his thirtieth birthday.

In order to take up this job, he moved to Milan, which became his political redoubt. In 1914 he was living there with his comrade-wife, Rachele. Mussolini scarcely confined himself to one woman and gadded restlessly across a range of political activities, always parading his temerity and savagery and, on occasion, doing something to conceal his naked ambition by casting it in ideological phrases. In 1913–14 he edited his own fortnightly journal, with the hopeful title, *Utopia*. Margherita Sarfatti was among his certain contributors and his probable financiers.[46] Unlike Hitler, Mussolini did not need to be made by the First World War. In 1914, even though his rivals and enemies within the socialist movement were rallying against him and he may well have been riding for a fall, Mussolini had made a name for himself as a young man of talent and ruthlessness. He had, for example, proved well able to sack staff on *Avanti!* who did not come up to his standards. In less than two years, he had quadrupled the paper's circulation.

Although, from time to time, patriotic heresy could taint the young *Duce*'s social pronouncements, for the most part he tried to be champion of the workers of the world. During the Libyan war, he served six months in jail under a set of eight charges including 'fomenting violence, resisting police orders, infringing the freedom of recruits and businessmen, and damaging railway, telegraph and telephone lines'.[47] He was also noisy in berating the Nationalists, whom he wrote off as lickspittles of monarchy, army and war.[48] In June 1914 the newshound Mussolini was to the fore in playing up the social disturbances known as 'Red Week', at the peak of which revolutionaries, stirred up by the socialist conference at Ancona in April, attempted full-scale insurrection. As a historian of Liberal Italy portrayed it evocatively: 'Local dictators proclaimed republics, the red flag was hoisted above town halls, taxes were abolished and prices reduced by decree, churches were attacked . . . landlords' villas sacked, troops disarmed and even a general captured.'[49] In Bologna, forces hostile to the 'revolutionaries' already displayed their mettle, with members of the

Associazione Nazionalista Italiana augmenting the previous deployment of 'civilian patrols' to curb working-class actions and now presenting themselves in arms to help the police reimpose order.[50] In this
conflict, Mussolini for the moment stood on the other side of the barricades; on 10 June, destined to be a redolent date in Fascist history,
he urged: 'We must take up again our anti-militarist propaganda to
ensure that bayonets are only raised when we [socialists] want them
to be . . . Our propaganda must break into the barracks, where
currently the sons of the people are taught how to kill their own
brothers.'[51]

As Archduke Franz Ferdinand made his way to Sarajevo, Mussolini
remained an extreme socialist, committed to pulling down the Liberal
order in the interests of a world-spanning revolution. The outbreak of
the war did not at first alter that situation. However, by September
1914, the attachment of the editor of *Avanti!* to the official line of
neutralism was crumbling. In October, Mussolini broke from the
party, proclaiming that, although still a believing socialist, he was certain that the cause of social overturn could be better hurried by war
than by Italy remaining at peace. Mussolini thus joined the ranks of
the interventionists, a motley crew in terms of political background,
although the great majority nourished a deep belief in their intellectuality and self-importance. By 15 November Mussolini had a paper of
his own – *Il Popolo d'Italia* – to edit, being sustained by first government and later Italian business and French and British secret service
funds. *Il Popolo d'Italia*'s line emphasized the irrelevance of past
ideological stances now that all men confronted the onrush of war
and urged that the young and audacious must seize 'history' by the
throat and wrench it in the direction which most advantaged the
active segment of society. Mussolini, the bonny wrangler, also spilled
much ink on polemical attacks against those socialists who stubbornly
cleaved to the view that neutrality was the best choice for Italy. They
were, he proclaimed, *canaille*, cannibals, hysterics. Although he
occasionally remembered that he had grown up a socialist, Mussolini,
with his cutting phrases and slashing debating style, was digging an
abyss between himself and his erstwhile party.

Despite his high words, Mussolini was still only a bit player among
the interventionists. *Professor* Mussolini, as he liked to be called,

could scarcely mix it socially with D'Annunzio, Marinetti, Corradini, Federzoni and a gaggle of patriotic writers. It was true that the future *Duce* was a client of the Minister of Colonies, Martini, but the relationship was a distant one and Mussolini was too far down the social ladder to have the gall to ask to meet the politician most influential in funding him. None the less, the experience of interventionism was to be crucial in forging Mussolini and other young and aspiring men into Fascists. In February 1915, the editor of *Il Popolo d'Italia* was presaging the future when he already defined himself and his small band of followers as 'we, interventionists and fascists'.[52]

At Cremona, one of the clients of Bissolati, the reformist socialist (and Freemason) whose expulsion from the socialist party in 1912 propelled him on a course through which, in 1915, he became a middle-aged volunteer at the front and, in 1916–18, a government minister,[53] was the young railway worker Roberto Farinacci. Even after the war, Farinacci (born 1892) was still respectfully given to saluting Bissolati as his *duce*.[54] Early on, Farinacci had acquired a reputation for energy as well as for vitriolic anti-clericalism directed against church worthies and the local Catholic labour organizer, Guido Miglioli. When the interventionists needed a publicist in Cremona, Farinacci was their man. The first number of his paper, the well-named *La Squilla* (The Clarion Call), came out on 18 November 1914. Very similar to Mussolini's tack in *Il Popolo d'Italia*, Farinacci fused the preaching of intervention with revolutionism and the excoriation of those socialists who opposed the abandonment of neutrality. In Cremona, local disputes spread beyond the verbal. On 10 April 1915 a pro-war rally at the Eden Theatre ended in a general assault on opponents of the war, with Farinacci editorializing the brawl into a military victory and boasting that his critics had now 'learned their lesson'.[55] Some vicissitudes lay ahead but Farinacci's path to being the violent and corrupt Fascist boss of his city and the second most emblematic figure in the coming dictatorship was now open.

Still younger was Dino Grandi, born 1895, and in 1914 a Bologna law student.[56] This son of a moderately prosperous landowner father and a schoolteacher mother, who did her best to fuse national and Catholic piety, thought of himself as a Mazzinian enemy of Giolitti and 'really existing liberalism'. Anxious to make his mark as that familiar Italian combination, a journalist, writer (and politician), Grandi was sent by his home-town paper, *Il Resto del Carlino*, to report on Mussolini's break from the socialist party. By early 1915 Grandi was himself the editor of a newssheet called *L'Azione* (Action), advocating the Corradinian line that the war was 'a national version of class struggle', but proclaiming itself 'national-liberal' and so dissociating himself and his friends from the more conservative social postures of the Nationalists. After 1915 Grandi rose to be a Captain among the crack Alpini (Alpine troops) and, by the end of 1920, he was a Fascist. The Ministries of Foreign Affairs and Justice awaited him, as did a period as ambassador in London and the task, in July 1943, of plotting his *Duce*'s downfall.

The youngest of the three Fascist chiefs being tempered through the interventionist campaign was Italo Balbo of Ferrara, yet another provincial capital of the Po valley and its discontents. Balbo was born in 1896, the son of two schoolteachers. His family sprang from Piedmont and relatives had held more glamorous occupations than school-teaching, while serving the kings of Savoy or Napoleon in the officer corps. Camillo Balbo, the father of the later Fascist *gerarca* (boss), was politically active, head at Ferrara of a Circolo Monarchico 'Umberto I' and the public enemy of priests and socialists. He patriotically christened his first child Maria Trieste, the first name being added at the baptismal font at the beseeching of his wife. Young Italo Balbo was another to invoke the ghosts of Risorgimento heroes – Mazzini and Giuseppe Garibaldi – in order to add lustre to his precocious efforts to combine patriotism and criticism of the existing order. Sent to complete high school at Milan in 1911, Balbo varied his teenage politics across irredentism, syndicalism, republicanism and a love of sport and technology, these last merging in his fascination with air races. He hoped to be an 'open cockpit man'. In 1913 Balbo expanded his field of political activity by seconding the unsuccessful campaign of Calabrian (and later fellow Fascist) Michele Bianchi for the Chamber of Deputies.

With the outbreak of war, Balbo swiftly stood forward as a crusader for intervention, meeting Mussolini soon after his secession from the PSI, though he remained a client of Bianchi. In October 1914 Bianchi, who was seven years older than Balbo, formed a Fascio

Rivoluzionario d'Azione to preach war entry. Balbo joined their demonstrations in Milan. But more typical of his character and behaviour at the time was his command of the Ferrara branch. There, his biographer reveals, 'he led a group of high school and technical school students who confronted the police with the ultimatum, "Either you declare war or we'll run you out of office".' He and some friends, viewing themselves in their callow way as reborn *garibaldini*, headed for the French border, hoping to join the fight on the Western Front but, lacking parental permission, they were turned back by officialdom. None the less, on 18 May 1915, at the zenith of debate about war entry, they did persuade the *Gazzetta Ferrarese* to publish the 'interventionist manifesto' of Bianchi's Fascio.[57]

Farinacci, Grandi and Balbo, each about ten years junior to Mussolini and with some diversity in political and class background, were typical zealots in the interventionist cause. They were young, northern, literate, activist and anti-socialist males who sought a political stance that was not just reactionary. They were real or aspirant members of some fraction of the middle class. Each would have been appalled to be mistaken for a simple worker or peasant and for each the thought of residence outside his city's walls among the uncivilized was nightmarish indeed.

The reaction of more sober Italians to the crisis of the war can be traced accurately enough through prefectural reports, commissioned by an anxious government, fearful that anti-national and perhaps prowar demonstrations could shove the country down a slippery slope to revolution. On 31 March 1915, Prime Minister Antonio Salandra, a southern lawyer from the most conservative wing of the liberals, ordered his prefects to 'end any restraint' in dealing with 'tumults'.[58] Anything but a politician for a mass age, Salandra, confronted with the problem that his neutralist opponent Giolitti still controlled a majority in parliament, resigned on 13 May and was then displeased to find demonstrations in favour of his ousted government and intervention sweeping every urban centre in the country. In those days, even in the south, many of the 'best people' flocked on to the streets shouting for national war. They composed the crowds of the so-called 'Radiant May'.

They were also in a minority. Most workers and virtually all peasants hated the idea of conflict and at least the latter often knew little about the nation except as a malign conscripting and taxing force. Even in relatively modern Piedmont, where quite a few peasants owned their land and the male world experienced some forms of modernization, women retained the vaguest comprehension of the wider world. When their men were drafted and taken away, the women accepted that once more they were to fight against 'Austria', but they did not understand where that country was, comprehending merely that their men must spend many days in a train or on foot to get there.[59] Peasants had neither reason nor opportunity to master the finer points of international diplomacy or ideological debate.

Other more respectable Italians also questioned the value of war entry, either generally or in the specific circumstances of 1914–15. Giolitti, leading politician of the previous decade and somewhat accidentally out of government since March 1914, argued that, since 'quite a lot' (parecchio) could be won from the Germans by negotiation, there was no need for precipitate action. Pope Benedict XV, facing an impossible world in which children of the Church had arrayed themselves on both sides of the battlelines, in despair or anger eventually damned the war as 'a pointless slaughter'. Victor Emmanuel III was scarcely a natural warrior – in disgust one patriotic young lieutenant depicted him as 'that gibbering idiot of a king'.[60] The army leadership had been trained to think that caution might be for the best. In the empire, Libya was anything but pacified (60,000 troops were required just to keep the flag flying over its coastal fortresses). Ethiopia had recently acquired the young, restless and irresponsible Lij Yasu as emperor, with effects that were difficult to prophesy, except that, in May 1914, a need was seen to dispatch more than 20,000 troops to the East African colony of Eritrea as military insurance. Most industrialists were also generally not at the forefront of pro-war demonstrations, for the moment savouring the likelihood that profit could be wrung from both sets of combatants.[61]

One typical business chief reluctant to conclude that war was Italy's only option was Luigi Vittorio Bertarelli (1859–1926), Milan-based manufacturer of sacred furnishings and, more tellingly, administrator and chief propagandist of the Touring Club Italiano. With its membership reaching almost half a million by the 1920s, this body,

founded in 1894, was a symbol of the modernization and nationalization of the Italian bourgeoisie. Pledged 'to make Italy known to
Italians', the TCI took patriotism very seriously. In 1911 it announced
that it was 'an eminently nationalist institution' and was soon to the
fore in mapping Libya and organizing elite tourist visits there. At the
same time, Bertarelli, for one, believed staunchly in a peaceful competition between the (advanced) nations, being delighted that the TCI
could boast fraternal relations with similar associations in France,
Britain, Germany and Austria. The war he regarded as a nuisance, a
potentially calamitous crack in the happy spread of technology and an
irksome infringement of the good order and mathematical precision
which he associated with clear road signs, accurate maps, well-trained
hotel staff and clean restaurants. In a sort of New Year's message for
1915, Bertarelli wrote to club members of his confidence that a great
future awaited the nation. For the present, however, he explained, 'the
work of the Touring is essentially pacific, and is [at its] most important . . . in fruitful international collaboration'. None the less, he
added in case he should be accused of *lèse-majesté* against the *patria*,
the TCI was, by definition, 'a powerful expression of national unity
and of solid social concord'.[62]

Once Italy did enter the war, the TCI played a major part in the
national effort. After all, its maps were superior to anything possessed
by the army on its own account. However, the doubts harboured by
Bertarelli, from his comfortable niche in the Milan bourgeoisie,
should be kept in mind as the story of Fascism unfolds. Even in the
Second World War, quite a few Italians retained an understanding of
the world and its purpose which was nearer to that of Bertarelli than
the militant one expressed so vociferously by the dictatorship, its chief
and his friends.

In the minds of Salandra and his foreign minister and leading political ally, Sonnino, none of these diverse currents of public opinion
mattered much. Ironically, given Churchill's eventual aphorism that
Mussolini alone had taken Italy into the Second World War, in March
1915 Salandra told Sonnino that 'we two alone' must make the decisions and plot whether and when Italy should enter the world conflict.[63] Shortly after, on 26 April, they concluded the Treaty of London
with entente negotiators, pledging their nation to rapid action in

return for territorial gains. They included the Trentino and Trieste, Istria, much of Dalmatia, the islands of the upper Adriatic and Valona in Albania. Since Christmas Day 1914 Italian forces, anxious to assert a national role in Albania, had been garrisoning the island of Saseno off the port of Valona, though hampered by their discovery that the place lacked supplies of fresh water. Britain, France and Russia also offered tantalizingly vague compensation for Italy in Asia Minor and Africa, leaving the details to be finalized at a post-war settlement.

The news of the agreement precipitated 'Radiant May' and something very like a constitutional crisis. In a springtime of *bellezza*, often to be invoked as presaging the birth of Fascism, the demonstrators carried the day in the *piazze* of urban Italy, helped by the open backing of entente agents. The wife of the British ambassador showered patriots with rose petals when they chanted for war outside the Embassy in Rome;[64] the American ambassador deemed the event 'the most inspiring' since the fall of the classical empire.[65] The doubters in parliament were too reticent to oppose them. Giolitti, Piedmontese in his world-view, feared that the dynasty was compromised. He concluded that premature and poorly prepared battle must be endured in order to avoid the threat of drastic political change at home. His weakness scarcely matched the irresponsibility of the government where Ferdinando Martini, Minister of Colonies and the most civilized and gentlemanly of the Cabinet, talked carelessly of a choice between 'external or civil war'.[66]

So Italy joined the First World War. The moderate liberal press trumpeted its joy. *Il Corriere della Sera* pronounced that national 'salvation' lay at the front; 'Italy has drawn its sword and spoken in a Roman manner from the Campidoglio', it editorialized, as if to prove that, even in Milan, the shadow of the Victor Emmanuel monument shrouded men's minds.[67] The war, the paper maintained, represented the 'pinnacle of the Risorgimento'.[68] In Venice, *Il Gazzettino* hailed the pro-war crowds as composing 'a national insurrection against traitors to the *patria*'. This paper, too, deemed the moment 'great and Roman', a time of destiny.[69] With these and other examples providing an armoury, Fascism was to have no trouble locating a national vocabulary of *romanità*, when it was time for its own legions to join in battle.

Such pro-war sentiments among the educated classes have rarely been subjected to criticism. Rosario Romeo, the best conservative Italian historian of his generation after 1945, was sure that the First World War was 'the greatest triumph of our history'.[70] It is a comment of astonishing insouciance. No doubt the war accelerated Italy's trajectory along one path to modernity. The cost was high, however, in men, materials and in more spiritual realms, where the killing fields of the war trained Fascists to be Fascists.

It did not take long in 1915 for some of the short-term calculations of Salandra and Sonnino to be shown to be wrong, as Italian troops were committed to a front which ran for 300 kilometres from the Stelvio pass near the Swiss border to the Adriatic coast, just short of Trieste. The entente's prospects had deteriorated between April and May, with the Russian spring advance against Austria-Hungary being blunted and turned back. Italy joined not so much a winning as a potentially losing side. Furthermore, in contrast to 1913, after a wet summer the recent harvest fell below average and grain stocks were low. In December 1914 the local prefect had warned that 'the province of Lecce is totally deficient in cereals, beans and other basic foodstuffs'.[71] Nor had the army covered its many deficiencies in the respite from August 1914 to May 1915. It was short of munitions, its rifles were old in design and laboriously and tardily manufactured by Italian industry. Despite massive expenditure over the last years, the army had accepted little modern military practice and was top-heavy with gentlemen officers. In July 1915 Salandra, clinging manfully to his 'short-war illusion', well after it had been rejected elsewhere, disdained the advice that stores of winter equipment should be urgently got in. Along the avenues of Milan city centre, victory flags had been hung to laud Italy's decisive war entry. By the end of August they were quietly removed, by then faded, tattered and with the colours of the *tricolore* having run together.

The divisive and impassioned nature of 'Radiant May' meant that Italy, alone of the great powers, moved to battle without being mustered into a *union sacrée*. When reformist socialists Turati and Treves, themselves vulnerable to suggestions that the *patria* was in danger, raised possible collaboration with the government, wondering whether their presence could assist in 'rallying the masses to the national cause', Salandra would have none of them.[72] Instead, he took Italy to the front split both politically and socially. In the parliament, neutralist liberals, who still saw themselves as the clients of Giolitti, outnumbered those who had opted for war. In the country at large, the noisy but quarrelsome interventionists may have occupied the intellectual high ground but the majority of the Italian population and the two mass parties in the making, the Catholics and the socialists, were, despite some backsliding, hostile to the conflict and to the way it was soon evident that it would be waged. In July 1915, one officer noted with pleasure the esprit of his men as they advanced into the mountains of the Trentino. Their singing of the 'Garibaldi hymn', 'Fratelli d'Italia', however, left the villagers they met 'rather indifferent'. The soldiers waved flags and clapped and shouted for the *patria*. While they did so, however, he added sadly: 'The mass of the population stayed silent.'[73]

It would be rash to assume that all soldiers were natural crusaders for the nation. Their understanding of political affairs was often superficial; Emilio De Bono, a general and later Fascist chief, reported that his men thought that the word '*Statuto*' (Constitution) was the special title for the first Sunday in June, when the Risorgimento was celebrated. His fellow officers, he claimed, were unlikely to remedy such ignorance. They ostentatiously preferred not to name the Prime Minister, or to mention other politicians, and deprecated reading of any kind.[74] Among the general staff in the early months of the war, a dislike and distrust of such fervent patriots and social conservatives as Federzoni was automatic and the first Nationalist offers to propagandize the troops were rejected as fatuous and damaging.[75]

In so far as any governmental effort to nationalize the masses was concerned, Salandra cleaved to tradition. In his mind and that of Army Chief of Staff Luigi Cadorna, war was a matter for the experts, that is, for the Officer Corps and the monarch or his agents. As the Prime Minister put it on 22 May: 'a war government cannot be a free government'.[76] When the cannon roared the limits of liberalism were narrow. What Salandra was expressing was the view that this was to be a dynastic war, no different from those unleashed by Cavour during the Risorgimento. (Sonnino was hoping quietly that he could match his great predecessor's skill at the diplomatic table, while the dim soldiers inflicted as little harm as possible in battle.) Interference from other politicians, intellectuals or ideologues was not to be contemplated. No hint of 'revolution' (however defined) should subvert the marshalling of the nation's strength. Salandra thought his task was to ignore change at home (he did not trouble to hide the fact that his own three sons were so-called *imboscati*,[77] men who had been found a cushy billet far from the front). This Prime Minister wanted to give no further encouragement to the enthusiasms of 'Radiant May'. War was, and must be, as it ever had been.

Thus doubtfully armed, from the spring of 1915 to the autumn of 1917 the nation's armies doggedly fought eleven battles against Austria for control of the Isonzo river, north-west of Trieste. It took three weeks after war entry was announced on 24 May for troops to be mobilized. The fact that Cadorna then had thirty-five divisions on the front against his enemies' fifteen (fourteen Austrian and one German) seemed to promise easy victory.[78] Instead the war almost at once bogged down. On the Isonzo, Italy suffered 900,000 casualties over the next two and a half years for an advance limited to thirty kilometres.[79] Soldiers were sent off to seize some Alpine precipice on the front above Trento and Rovereto, to dispute a trench on the Carso or just to die, to the war-cry '*Avanti Savoia*' (Forward Savoy), the slogan which the Piedmontese monarchy had utilized before the Risorgimento. The troops conceived of themselves as mercenaries and 'king's men' or just unlucky devils, better identified as hired warriors of the ruling dynasty or passive victims of fate than thrusting citizens of a nation in arms.

Along with the pre-1789 style management of the army went the most traditionalist diplomacy, which, until 1919, remained in the austere or purblind hands of the Foreign Minister, Sonnino. In May 1915 Italy entered the war against Austria alone, an act which at once separated the Italian cause from that of the greater powers of the entente, for whom Germany was both the real and the propaganda enemy. Only in September 1916 did Italy belatedly add Germany to its enemies (despite Salandra's objections, the nation had joined the conflict against Turkey in August 1915 and that against Bulgaria two months later). The Isonzo battles were therefore treated by everyone but the Italians as a 'sideshow'; the Austrians, after all, were most engaged in stemming the 'Russian steamroller' on their Eastern front. Of all the combatant states, Liberal Italy was least prepared for the 'new diplomacy'.

Government was also troubled. Cadorna made no attempt to hide his contempt for politicians, even ones as deferential and conservative as Salandra. He was especially unhappy at having to consult the Minister of War, in 1915–16 Vittorio Zupelli, himself a general but, in Cadorna's mind, a disgracefully 'political' one, about his management of the war. In April 1916 Cadorna's insistence meant Zupelli had to resign, and in June he was followed by Salandra. The result was the creation of a boasted 'Ministry of concord, war and victory', under the antiquated Paolo Boselli, seventy-eight years old and a Ligurian nonentity whose chief claim to fame was that he had been President of the patriotic Dante Alighieri Society. To a degree Boselli enhanced the national propaganda effort at the front, at home and abroad. However, such work remained 'fragmentary and disorganized'.[80] The Boselli cabinet did widen a touch socially and politically, through the invitation to Catholic Filippo Meda to become Minister of Finance and the consigning of posts to the reformists Bissolati and Bonomi. What Boselli's government really entailed, however, was, for the foreseeable future, the predominance of Cadorna in the running of the war and, therefore, more battles for the Isonzo at a snowballing cost. Under the 'test of war', by the end of 1916 Liberal Italy seemed to have demonstrated that the officer corps which it had inherited from Piedmont was its last bastion.

It was a stockade under siege. To the astonishment of Italian diplomats, in March 1917 Russia, the most direct enemy of Italy's main foe, Austria, collapsed into revolution. At first the news of regime change there seemed welcome but, on 27 March, Federzoni expressed alarm at the growing 'extremism' sweeping Petrograd and worried at the prospect that Russia would be forced out of the war.[81] The entry of the USA added further complications to international dealings, since the Sonninian policy of *sacro egoismo* (sacred egoism) squared badly with the 'new diplomacy' being preached with such fervour by President Woodrow Wilson. But Italy's real problems lay on the home and military fronts, where strikes, mutinies and general discontent multiplied, while victory still did not come and the holocaust of peasant soldiers continued. Suddenly, on 24 October 1917, the forces of Austria-Hungary, leavened by German troops withdrawn from the Russian front, launched an offensive, announcing their advance with a massive gas attack. It would be called the Battle of Caporetto, after a village known in Slovene as Kobarid on the upper Isonzo. Before the fighting was over, the Italians lost 40,000 dead or wounded, 280,000 POWs, 350,000 deserters or stragglers, a huge volume of arms and equipment and a slice 150 kilometres long of prime land in the Veneto.[82] With the help of eleven British and French divisions, rushed to their aid (but greeted with suspicion by the military leadership, some ordinary soliders[83] and the common people), the Italian armies eventually resisted and held on the Piave river, only about thirty kilometres from Venice and the opening to the entire Po valley. The rally occurred on 9 November, two days after the Bolsheviks had seized the Winter Palace and one day after they had announced that their new administration was offering peace, land and bread to its population. At that moment, Italy seemed very likely to follow Russia out of the war and into domestic revolution.

For the expert on the 'southern question', Giustino Fortunato (1848–1932), who embodied much of the liberalism of the Risorgimento, a sign of the times was made manifest on 2 August 1917. That day he was assaulted by his own peasants, men and women who, he complained, had been loyal servitors of his family for two centuries. 'Who would ever have thought', he lamented to Salandra, 'that so savagely terrible a state of mind' could exist among the poor? Among such people, a dreadful rumour had taken root that 'the "masters", the "bourgeois", the "scribblers"', had covertly approached the government to prolong the war at the peasantry's cost. Such conspiracy theories and the ubiquitous popular rejection of the war were not the result of malign socialist propagandizing, Fortunato had to admit. Rather, peasants returning from the front brought the bad news and themselves urged a breaking with the bosses. 'The last, vain, illusion of my life is fallen,' Fortunato remarked mournfully. It was too much. 'I had the right to a little more love and a little more respect.'[84]

Despite Fortunato's prophecy that the end of the world was nigh, in the event there was no full-scale collapse. Farinacci later wrote that the defeat at Caporetto and the resistance that it aroused signalled a break between the old Italy and his new one, the Italy of 'Fascist revolution'.[85] Although not the most reliable of historians, Farinacci had a point. In late 1917 the methods, however authoritarian, of a liberal and dynastic campaign to which the Italian state had so far clung were evidently insufficient as a means of dealing with the world crisis and, at least if Fortunato's experience meant anything, maybe Risorgimento-style liberalism was equally inadequate in keeping the home front united and purposeful. Now, instead, must be the time of national, even people's war, that variety of combat which would let slip the dogs of Fascism and sweep many of the sons of erstwhile liberals towards a toleration of, and even applause for, dictatorship.

3

Popular and national war

On 6 November 1917, with Italian forces reeling back behind the Piave river, Francesco Nitti, a worthy southern politician who generally evinced a sober accountant's approach to politics and life, grew unwontedly emotional at the seemingly disastrous fate that awaited the Italian nation at war. He wrote to the new Prime Minister, Vittorio Emanuele Orlando, who had taken office only a week earlier, with a pledge of uttermost loyalty: 'Sacrifice all of us,' he urged with a biblical ring to his words, 'and we will follow you.'[1] But Nitti's relative moderation in invoking the New Testament was too academic and meek for the times at hand and presaged his ill-starred post-war career; when in his turn he became Prime Minister he would be berated by Mussolini, D'Annunzio and others as the cowardly and treacherous *Cagoia* (Turd-face).

At the front, or among those propagandists whose task it was to revive Italian arms, the rhetoric of the moment was studded with a greater brutality and shrillness, attitudes destined to transmute into Fascism. *Il Soldato* (The Soldier), a weekly meant to be read by ordinary soldiers but written by intellectuals, some of them junior officers, had a special ring to its first issue after the Caporetto defeat. Darkness might cover the Italian earth but, its editorial advised, 'no people' had ever obtained 'greatness without having passed the test of suffering'. Now, it proclaimed, was the time for new men, a new government, a new military command; Caporetto constituted a point in national life from which there could be no turning back. The new Italy must throb with 'youth' and the 'modern'.

Fascist-to-be Paolo Orano, who was making his name as a patriotic propagandist on the journal, added that Italians must resist a barbarian invasion, now as in the past composed of wicked 'Teutons, Alemanni, Goths, Huns . . . and Vandals'. Faced with a bestial enemy ready to rape and mutilate, Italians, he charged, must dedicate themselves to 'killing, killing, killing'. They must accept that their 'men, fathers, husbands, brothers, lovers, sons die' to achieve a holy 'massacre of the barbarian, a butchering of the aggressor, a shambles of the race of prey'. The whole nation must transmogrify into an army where only one idea and one action were possible. Orano did not use the word 'Fascist'; it had not yet been invented. But what he imagined was something beyond total war, a totally total war, a totalitarian war, waged by a steely society whose purpose was victory on the field of battle and none other.[2] To a man and a woman, Italians must believe in the nation as their lay God. War must bring in its train political and cultural revolution.

To what extent, then, did Liberal Italy manage to wage a 'total' war in the period that ran from the defeat at Caporetto to the surrender of its opponents in November 1918? What was the impact of the new policies during that time on the actions and thought processes of Italian soldiers, workers, peasants, men and women, old and young, emigrants and those who stayed or had returned home? Were all the people now embraced by the nation, as Mussolini for one demanded they should be, declaring that, in the age of iron needed to fight the war, a new kind of warrior democracy of workers, peasants and soldiers could be born (and rallied to victory by himself)?[3] Who were those who fought or saw themselves as fighting for the *patria* and who were blind to its charm?

In 1919 a nationalist general concluded bitterly that, when confronted by the 'test of war', Italy had demonstrated that 'no one governed it'.[4] The crucible of combat had not forged chieftains of the fortitude and calibre of Hindenburg and Ludendorff, Lloyd George and Clemenceau. Yet the story of the Italian war effort was not one of mere chaos. Although, in 1915, the Liberal regime, in its organization of economy and society, did lag behind the greater powers, modern elements had intruded into its war administration. As early as May 1915 the business league, Confindustria, coordinated by its active secretary Gino Olivetti, a Piedmontese entrepreneur of Jewish descent, underlined the centrality of economics in war. Now, Olivetti argued, planning was everything. War could only be waged effectively by cementing the closest ties between government and business. Skilled workers, for example, should be exempt from service at the front since they were needed in the factory. Industry was dependent on cheap credit and efficient and reliable transport and these services the state must provide, although the bureaucracy must be careful not to stifle the dynamism of private enterprise. If the battle were to be won, Olivetti asserted, the factory must become the furnace, the dynamo, of national life. All else must bow to the production of munitions and the other necessities of war. To Olivetti, the model of a war economy was that which Rathenau and others were engineering in Germany. Britain, by contrast, was too liberal and too faint-hearted in imposing the labour discipline that was the iron corollary of contemporary war. Strikes must be banned but employer greed should also be curtailed and full powers assumed by the central authorities. Now was the time for all men to come to the service of the nation, whether they wanted to or not.

To some extent, it did seem that the government was listening to this Spartan counsel. In June 1915 Salandra published a decree that gave the military the right to intervene in industry to ensure the most efficient equipping of the armed forces. Lest that seem an attack on workers, in August, with Olivetti's direct approval, it was announced that a supervisory agency was being created to handle industrial disputes fairly. Under this body, both 'civilian and military workers' were guaranteed 'equal treatment', without the nation suffering the 'least interruption of work'.[5] General Alfredo Dallolio, Under-Secretary of War, another man of energy and administrative skill, tried hard to make the system function. Born in 1853 and trained as a soldier, Dallolio favoured an even more controlled and punitive labour discipline than did Olivetti, hating the idea that wartime circumstances might allow employees opportunity to seek improvements in pay and conditions. He upbraided businessmen who, fearing a labour shortage, concluded feebly that they must pamper their skilled workers.[6] From June 1917 Dallolio, who had been nominated to the Senate in February, was promoted to be the new Minister of Munitions, a position he held until May 1918, at which point he resigned, annoyed by the Minister of Finance Nitti's fussy interference in his portfolio. By the end of the war, 1,976 business concerns had been made subject to the Ministry of Munitions, along with 902,000 workers, 70 per cent of whom directly produced arms. Italy's geographical variety was displayed in the fact that 1,116 of the firms involved were located in the industrial triangle of Turin, Milan and Genoa, while only 377 functioned south of Rome or in the islands.

Under the prompting of Dallolio, production expanded, especially during the last two years of the war (as it would dismally fail to do during the Second World War). From 5.9 per cent in 1914 and 18.3 per cent in 1915, war expenditure in relation to GDP rose to 33.1 per cent in 1917–18 and, contrary to what might have been expected when the conflict began, Italian industry proved able to meet most of the national demand for armaments.[7] In this situation, the heavy industrial firm of Ansaldo saw its capital augment from 30 million lire in 1916 to 500 million in 1918, with its workforce leaping in the same period from 6,000 to 111,000. Fiat's workforce expanded from 4,300 in 1914 to more than 40,000 at the end of the war;[8] Alfa Romeo's from 200 to 4,130.[9] By 1918 Fiat, helped by the seventy-hour week it had imposed on its workforce in March 1916, had become the largest producer of vehicles in Europe, manufacturing 70,862 (including Italy's first tanks) between 1915 and 1918, as against its pre-war production of 3,300 per annum.[10] Its annual profits touched 70 per cent of investment.[11] Fiat also built aeroplane engines, machine guns and ammunition; 382 aeroplanes were manufactured in Italy in 1915, 6,523 in 1918.[12] The army had 146 heavy artillery pieces available to it in May 1915 and 2,346 in October 1917.[13] Change of another kind was evidenced in the statistic which revealed that the unskilled female factory workforce expanded from 80,000 to 140,000 from 1916 to 1917.[14]

In 1919 the distinguished economist Riccardo Bachi affirmed that war had converted the state into being 'the driving motor of the national economy'[15] and it was true that the sum of government outlays between 1915 and 1918 was double the total spent by all Italian administrations from 1860 to the onset of the war.[16] Waging the great campaign cost Italy $12,892 million, as against Germany's $32,388, Britain's $45,307, Russia's $11,778 (to 1917) and the USA's surprising $35,731 million.[17] Only 5.7 per cent of the Italian sum was raised through income tax, a figure that was higher than France's derisory 3.7 per cent, but well below Germany's 13.9 per cent and Britain's 18.2 per cent. Even in war, the government was unable or unwilling to force the wealthier sections of society to pay their share.

Taken in isolation, the economy performed in wartime in a fashion that was certainly no worse and perhaps better than might have been predicted from Italy's relative rank in the industrially developed world. As shall be seen, for all the bluster about modernization and *autarchia* (autarchy), the Fascist economy in the Second World War trailed its allies and enemies more distantly than did its Liberal predecessor in the 1914–18 war. However, between 1915 and 1918, the greater failure lay in the more informal arena of culture and society, where what might be termed the index of national spirit lagged behind that in Germany, Britain or France.

Class difference, evident everywhere, was dramatically present in Italy, both on the military and the home front. Soldiers, whose pay (after obligatory subtractions) in 1915 amounted to 0.50 lire per day, about 6 per cent of a skilled metalworker's wage, were – especially in the infantry, which took 95 per cent of all casualties – mostly peasants. In 1919, 63 per cent of war orphans (218,000 boys and girls) were reckoned to be peasant children. Although over 300,000 emigrants returned home to the draft, 5.7 million did not, the fabulous wealth of 'America' being demonstrated by the pay scales in the US army, where privates earned seventeen times as much as they did in the Italian forces. Other conditions were even better. As one emigrant, who opted to serve the USA but remained suspicious of displaying his family fortune to the world at large, confided: 'Dearest darling wife, I can tell you that I am insured for 50,000 lire. If I die you will be rich. Just don't rush off and tell the godparents as you are unfortunately so given to doing.'

When serving in the Italian army, by contrast, soldiers were often treated with contemptuous brutality by senior officers, who were themselves well paid, especially in the higher echelons. By September 1915, 700 ordinary troops in one Alpine zone had simply frozen to death.[18] Murmurings of dissent were greeted with condign punishment. Between 1915 and 1918, 870,000 of the 5.2 million Italians who joined the armed forces were denounced for infractions of discipline, about half for avoiding the draft. Of serving soldiers, 210,000 were found guilty of one crime or another and more than 4,500 were sentenced to death (at least 750 were executed, as against 500 in France and 304 in Britain).[19] In September 1919, 600,000 were amnestied in regard to their various misdemeanours,[20] in a policy which combined mercy and state weakness in a fashion that would not be wholly abandoned under the dictatorship. One typical felony for soldiers at the front was self-harm and, as early as September 1915, the capital penalty – still illegal in civilian society – was inflicted on a soldier guilty of shooting away the top of his index finger.[21] Another man was jailed for fifteen years for recording in his diary a chronicle of the anti-war strikes and demonstrations that had occurred in some parts of the country just after war entry.[22] Chief of General Staff Cadorna used a metaphor with a terrible future in the twentieth century when, on hearing of Caporetto, he concluded savagely that his army was riddled with 'vermin'.[23] Details of bad behaviour were carefully filed in the state archive and later, under Fascism, were the first matter police appraised when they were judging the appropriate punishment for a critic of the regime.

The army leadership tried to be alert to any whiff of mutiny, dispatching to military jail, for example, a corporal from Salerno, who had spent time as an emigrant in Germany and who used his knowledge of the enemy language to set up a tiny Yuletide truce, with an exchange of cigarettes and a waving of placards with 'Happy Christmas' scrawled on them, at his section of the front in 1916. A Florentine soldier, trained as a mechanic, was condemned to three years in jail when censorship disclosed that he had written home calling the patriotic 'martyr' Battisti an 'imbecile'. How hypocritical, he had mused, for Italians to bewail the Austrian decision to hang Battisti, when 'the gentlemen who run our war tribunals do the same to any poor soldier who . . . says that he does not want to join a push forward in which he will die'. A third man received six months for reporting that his comrades were being tied up and left outside overnight in freezing conditions for minor acts of indiscipline. 'Ordinary soldiers', he concluded, were 'treated worse than beasts'.[24] No wonder, then, that for many conscripts and their families at home, the name of the nation amounted to a curse. Infantry stationed at the front were reported to think of themselves as *fessi* (poor fools), those in command nearby as *fissi* (people with a steady job), men stationed behind the front as *italiani* and the inhabitants of the rest of the country as *italianissimi* (ultra-Italians), with the implication that the more 'Italian' people were the more likely they were to be shirkers, lacking any comprehension of the daily tragedy of the poor bloody foot-sloggers.[25]

Despite the harshness of conditions for serving men, even sensitive officers worried that they were not tough enough on those in their charge. The availability at officers' mess of champagne and grappa, cakes, meats and other quality foodstuffs was taken for granted. Carlo Emilio Gadda saw nothing amiss in the fact that officers' celebrations 'on the gastronomic side were no different from such festivals in peacetime'.[26] Before Caporetto, junior officers did little to challenge the practice of the generals who seldom rotated men from the frontline; service could continue without relief for months. In return, ordinary ranks endured their officers, whom in their family mail they sarcastically labelled *signori* and *studenti* (gentlemen and students)[27] as, at home, they had put up with their landowners with a sullen combination of stoicism and hostility. Men were reported especially to dislike volunteers who had not waited for the draft, disdaining them as 'mad or leprous or as cuckolds', and prompting Attilio Frescura, author of the first and most evocative account of the front, to muse: 'They cannot understand a commitment to ideology in the name of which a man will leave his goods, family and ordinary life.' Frescura contended that his troops could not 'hate' the enemy in the way that patriotic rhetoric, especially in the newspapers, demanded, because 'you cannot hate what you do not understand'.[28]

An acute summary of the mood of the troops came from patriotic writer Adolfo Omodeo, who observed that 'the peasants of the prosperous, "fat", Romagna are astonished to see the thin reddish soil of the Carso [west of Trieste] and ask their officers whether it has really been worth unleashing the wrath of God to conquer such piddling land'. Common soldiers, a patriotic priest reported, had no thought of the nation. What mattered to them were 'themselves, their families and their homes'.[29] Their responsibilities in that regard were, after all, burdensome. Frescura tallied 952 children for the 230 ordinary soldiers serving under him. Half fascinated, half appalled by the peasant world they brought before his young middle-class eyes, he noticed that, at forty, his men typically counted five, seven or ten children. By then, they were already old, 'aged by the land on which they sweated and which by now was swallowing them'.[30]

Given that family loyalty so often outweighed any sense of identity with the nation, it is no surprise to find that, among the Allies, Italy lay third behind Russia and Portugal in the proportion of its men who became POWs by the end of combat, with the tally of 530,000 not being many fewer than the total dead (578,000). The French gave up 446,300 POWs to 1,398,000 killed; the British 170,389 to 723,000.[31] Among Italian POWs, the percentage of officers was low, about 3 per cent. The Italian dead amounted to 10.3 per cent of those mobilized (France 16.8, Germany 15.4, Australia 14.5 and Serbia an appalling 37.1 per cent). Overall, 7.4 per cent of the cohort of males aged between fifteen and forty-nine failed to return from the Italian war (France 13.3, Germany 12.5, Serbia 22.7 per cent).

More than 100,000 of the POWs did not make it back to Italy. Their mortality rate in the Austrian camps reached 20 per cent (and was over 5 per cent in the German camps), with quite a few perishing from starvation. The death toll was not alleviated by a General Staff and government that, until the last months of 1918, stubbornly refused to send regular provisions to such places as Mauthausen (which was preparing for a still more sinister history in the next war). The moralist – in his own eyes – Sonnino was to the fore in rejecting attempts to ameliorate the POWs' fate. When those who had survived did repatriate, they were greeted with official suspicion, fear being expressed either that they had traitorously surrendered during the war or that they had imbibed 'subversion' from their contacts in the Germanic world. One bright suggestion was that they might for the foreseeable future be penned in a camp in Libya and there be rigorously cross-examined about the exact nature of their war experience.[32]

The elite's nervousness about the masses had a long history in Italy, where Francesco Crispi had left behind the dictum: 'Our plebs are barbarians.' In an ideal future, he added, they must respectfully accept the benefits that trickled down to them from the bourgeoisie and 'be glad to be given a place at the banquet of life'.[33] A pessimism about

the reliability of the poorer classes surfaced even in the most enlight-
ened minds when Gaetano Salvemini, for example, took the lead in
advising the military authorities not to allow wounded soldiers to seek
momentary sanctuary with their families lest the convalescents
depress public morale by talk about discomfort and death at the
front.[34] The national government was slow and hesitant in taking on
the task of what was coming to be called propaganda and so of selling Italy's special First World War. Perhaps that failure is still reflected
in English-language literature about the conflict, obsessed with the
mud and fog of the Western Front, possessing some image of more
mobile encounters on the plains of Eastern Europe, but ignorant of
Italy's Alpine terrain.

Before 1914 the Italian Foreign Ministry had flirted with the idea
of finding bureaucratic means to render 'public opinion' the secular
arm of national policy and even wondered whether Nationalist
'exaggeration' could not be a virtue, since its excess might etch a
path down which sensible and realistic diplomats could tread.[35] But,
with the outbreak of war, the organization of the media was tardy
compared with that in other combatant states. Sonnino, with his
habitual inflexibility, feared that any harnessing of the press was dis-
honest and clung to the purpose of the war as *sacro egoismo* and only
that. In his mind, the expansion of national or dynastic territory was
a self-evident good, needing no other ideological gloss to dazzle
foreign or domestic opinion. The military also started with the view
that journalists should be excluded from anywhere near the front.
Only in 1916 was Cadorna persuaded that a suitably controlled press
could improve morale.[36] Serving officers often continued to scorn
patriotic journalists as the worst kind of shirkers; Frescura, for
example, blamed the Caporetto defeat on 'lying newshounds' and
invented the verb *barzineggiare* (to Barzini-ify), with contemptuous
reference to Luigi Barzini (senior), one of the nation's most celebrated
pressmen.[37]

None the less, some journalists did make their mark, winning the
favour of the military or government. One was Virginio Gayda, who
was destined to be the noisiest of Fascist propagandists during the
Second World War. Employed by the Turin paper *La Stampa*, Gayda
had made a name for himself by first-hand observation of the Russian

Revolutions of 1917, where he also helped process those Austrian POWs whose first loyalty might be to Italy. A little earlier, Vittore Scialoja, head of the evocatively named Unione degli insegnanti italiani per la guerra nazionale (Union of Italian teachers for the national war), had taken over from the patriotic and respectable Dante Alighieri Society the task of organizing a national propaganda service at ministerial level. The pamphlets put out by the Brescia branch of his organization advised their readers, in slightly double-edged phrasing, that the war did not belong to the *signori* alone. After victory, it was predicted, 'war industries will be transformed in a trice to those of peace'; jobs would be there for all. 'Agricultural machinery will pour from the factories which now make guns, and will render the land more productive and food cheaper. Moreover, the ordinary soldiers, in great majority peasants, as a result of the wisdom of their new rulers, will obtain many new and better rental agreements, as well as insurance against sickness and death, and fertile terrain to develop for themselves.'[38] Peace, Scialoja promised, would open to all Italians the gates of the promised land.

During the emergency of Caporetto, an Under-Secretaryship for Propaganda abroad and for the Press was created, with direct responsibility to new Prime Minister Orlando. By March 1918 it had been awarded a budget of nine million lire. The Nationalist Romeo Gallenga Stuart, a writer, irredentist and anglophile, held the office until its suppression in December 1918 – Orlando's enthusiasm for the post rapidly faded as he swung round to Sonnino's view that the art of diplomacy was not assisted by loud words in the newspapers. Despite the disappointments of his career as a propagandist in the First World War, Gallenga Stuart in 1922 became a leading Fascist in his home city of Perugia and found gilded retirement in the Senate from 1929 to his death in 1938.[39]

If Liberal politicians remained suspicious of extravagant propaganda outside Italy, they were not much quicker in explaining and justifying the war to their own people and soldiery. The process of nationalizing the Italian masses limped haltingly forward. Seams of localism lay deep within the army. Many officers categorized each other on hearing a colleague's regional dialect; one self-consciously Lombard general sardonically christened the only member of his staff who addressed him in correct Italian '*el pürista*'. Officers and ordinary men literally spoke different languages, both because dialect was the norm for everyday discourse among most Italians and because the cultures of Italians varied so vastly by class and region. Language difference was all the more obvious in those parts of Italy crossed by the battlefront during the successive phases of the war. In 1916 Frescura recorded the sullen reaction of a *paese* in the hinterland of Gorizia to its 'liberation' by national troops. The young men of the place had been conscripted into the Habsburg armies and, somewhere off stage, were engaged in killing or being killed. When the first Italian forces reached the village, the old men, fearing the irruption of 'foreigners', had tried to resist with pitchforks. Firing commenced, 150 villagers died and Italian troops sacked the *paese*. Months later the *paesani* took refuge in their dialect to convey their view that Italians were *bruti scrovi* (dirty pigs). When the officer tried to chat with a local girl, he was asked plaintively: 'Should we want peace or not? Believe me. We don't know which side we are on.'[40]

Another social division, given greater depth at the front, was gender. Joanna Bourke may go too far when she claims that 'for men, combat was the male equivalent of childbirth: it was "the initiation into the power of life and death"'.[41] Yet service in the army had always been the means through which society 'made a man of a lad' and so reinforced gender division. From the fragmentary evidence available it seems that most enlisted men preferred a masculine interpretation of the gender order. The soldiers' continuing primary commitment to their families was charming – POWs were reported to switch into dialect when they wished to discuss amatory matters in family mail[42] – and violent. Peasants away from home feared that their wives might betray their 'honour' and wartime tales of a man on furlough killing his woman out of jealousy were common.[43] Other family values also surfaced. Leo Spitzer, an analyst of POW correspondence, has remarked on the ritualized prose of southern soldiers, who were still given to saluting their parents by beseeching their renewed blessing and offering to kiss their hand or their right foot in homage. Ceremonious phrases could take up half or two thirds of a letter. A modicum of modernity, almost a spontaneous people's Futurism, could creep in, however. Spitzer noted the way soldiers sent their loved ones a 'train', 'an automobile', 'an aeroplane' or a 'shrap-nel' of kisses (*baci*), or perhaps just a *bacccccccio*.[44]

Among officers, the more patriotic, who were pioneering attitudes to demography to be formalized under Fascism, counselled those of their fellows who were briefly able to return to their homes to be sure to breed boy children while they were there; the 'class of 1916' was certain to be needed by the nation in 1936. The exhaustion of the fight did not mean the end of lust. The sight of some Red Cross girls prompted Frescura to muse: 'Someone compared women to a pome-granate. I think it was D'Annunzio, who perhaps loves the fragrant and blood-red fruit which, when bitten, happily mixes the sweetness of its juices with the bitterness of its pith. I, however, who am a gour-mand, if I want to compare women with something botanical, . . . pre-fer the artichoke, which you must strip little by little so that the best of it is left to last and is the most fragrant and anticipated.' As the war continued Frescura's comments grew more misogynist. His experience as a censor of his men's mail persuaded him that any mention of 'love' was self-interested. Females stayed loyal for six months, he reckoned. After that, they grew bored. Their 'liberation' into wartime employ-ment on trams or in offices boded ill, he feared. In his imagining, the women of Italy joined ranting journalists and 'the adulterous and adulterating' businessmen responsible for deficient army supplies in opening the path to Caporetto.[45] Another officer remembered won-dering whether or not he should fall for the woman who did his wash-ing and ironing in some *paese* just behind the front, deciding not to because, he remarked acidly, 'women are the same in every country. From the sea, salt; from women, trouble.'[46]

Such careless sexism is evidence that, in Italy, as in other combat-ant societies, distinctions deepened during the war between those who served at the front and those who stayed at home. In July 1918 Carlo Emilio Gadda, by then a POW, recalled his 'livid and limitless, end-less and eternal' fury against the 'murderous dogs' who, during the Caporetto defeat, 'handed over such a lot of the *patria* to the enemy'. 'Dogs, cowards, you have torn at my flesh and insulted me. Even if you die of TB or hunger that is not enough.'[47] The term *imboscato* (shirker) had many usages in condemning those who were not directly involved in the fighting. Frescura recorded the jokey but tart way the word was bandied about by those who returned alive from a raid to greet their fellows who had stayed behind in a trench, even though, he admitted, its more ordinary meaning was fixed on those who dallied in 'Rome, where no cannon, no ships and no planes reach'.[48]

Joanna Bourke has emphasized challengingly that 'the characteristic act of men at war is not dying, it is killing'. In her analysis, the First World War provides examples of both officers and men exulting in killing; she cites a 'shy and sensitive' soldier who 'recounted that the first time he stuck a German with his bayonet was gorgeously satisfying'. It is typical of English-speaking literature that her example is taken from the Western Front; Italy does not appear in her index. But she does raise questions that need to be asked about Italy's war. To what extent did Italian soldiers bond as a result of their war experience? Was war converting them into willing executioners? As Bourke remarks, 'comradeship' has become a cliché of all 'military, cultural history' and its celebration is a ubiquitous part still of all patriotic discourse.[49]

Hailing the brotherhood of combat speedily became part of the literature of Italy's war.[50] When, after Caporetto, a more pronounced effort was made to propagandize the troops, it was natural that they and the *patria* should be compared with a family. Members of the crack Alpini were, for example, assured that they comprised a 'spiritual unit', a kith and kin, whose 'bloodstocks' were perpetually renewed by the calling up of 'sons, brothers, grandsons'. Each soldier, it was alleged, loved his unit 'with absolute devotion'.[51] The commitment grew when Italians were ranged against their neighbours. Leonida Bissolati reported the zeal with which men hunted down and exterminated 'fanaticized Slavs' who had taken to the hills at the Italians' approach.[52] In forging this 'mateship' (as Australians call it), a rhetoric could easily be adapted from the Church. The 'old boots' of the Alpini, as they were persuaded to call themselves, were said to revere a jocular 'ten commandments',[53] which charted a fraternity never to be broken or forgotten. In its own propaganda Fascism similarly offered 'decalogues' for believers to subscribe to, testimony either to totalitarian control or to an automatic recourse to the language and mindset of 'eternal' Catholicism.

The comradeship of Italian troops is all the more significant, since, after 1918, Fascism was soon proclaiming that it stood for the spirit of the trenches, asserting that it incarnated the modernized war effort of 1917–18, translated into politics. What was Fascism but the expression of a mateship that was simultaneously egalitarian and hierarchical and posited on the idea that all actions led to life or death? After October 1922 the myth was spread that Mussolini accepted the charge from King Victor Emmanuel III to become Prime Minister by promising that he embodied the 'Italy of Vittorio Veneto', that victory which, on 4 November 1918, crowned the Italian fight-back from Caporetto.[54] Mussolini's war diary was then and thereafter one of the regime's most treasured texts, with its staccato phrases bringing to the Fascist 'revolution' the legitimacy of direct contact with the front.[55] The *Duce* became the *Duce* in many ways because he was successfully marketed as Italy's 'ordinary soldier'. Revelling in the First World War formed a crucial part of Fascist ceremonial and almost all leading Fascists followed their leader in claiming that their souls had been reforged at the front. Augusto Turati was, for example, accredited to the Italian public in his new role as Fascist party secretary after 1926 when Mussolini hailed him as 'first of all a soldier. He came to Fascism almost straight from the trenches.'[56]

Turati, like Dino Grandi, had been a captain in the war, Italo Balbo and Giuseppe Bottai were lieutenants and volunteers, Achille Starace, long-serving party secretary of the 1930s, was also a captain, having been twice promoted for heroism in the field and ending the war as adjutant to a general. Of Mussolini's other henchmen, Cesare De Vecchi, born at Casale Monferrato in 1884 and eventually obtaining degrees in law, letters and philosophy, was a lieutenant in the Artillery, later elevated to be a captain in the Arditi. Emilio De Bono was a general. Although Mussolini and Farinacci obtained only non-commissioned rank (and therefore expressed a different variety of Fascism), the typical Fascist chest bristled with medals. In quite a few senses, the doctrine of Fascism would amount to a vocabulary giving verbal justification to the rise to political power and social authority of a cohort of junior officers. Did the war, then, lead directly to Fascism?

The answer is yes and no. Interventionism in 1914–15, volunteering in 1915, service at the front, the modernization of an officer's identity fostered by the nature of combat there, participation in the more urgently patriotic propaganda campaigns after Caporetto, all meshed easily with Fascism. Joanna Bourke has warned, however, that behaviour in war does not always replicate itself in peacetime, contending that, contrary to some legend, the majority of returned soldiers manage to wall off the horror or glory of their war experiences into their pasts. Her advice is worth remembering when examining the motivation of Fascism, as distinct from its justification. After 1919 Fascists sought, with increasing success, to make themselves the true and only heirs of Italy's war. But other currents ran from that war, some to remain visible under the dictatorship and others which, despite repression, more latently swayed Italian lives.

Two special features of Italy's war deserve note. One was the search – and, to 1918, the unavailing search – for charisma. The pursuit of 'leadership' is a common feature of the fighting life but usually the 'hero' is a person who can be presented as holding military command in some direct way.[57] Perhaps because the Italian nation was so partially made and its institutions so uncertainly framed, perhaps because King Victor Emmanuel III was not physically imposing, despite the desperate attempts to market him (one propagandist took pains to claim that the monarch thriftily carried a packed lunch of hard-boiled eggs to sustain himself on tours of the front),[58] perhaps because the countering charisma of the Catholic Church, embodied in Pope Benedict XV, or through its manifold saints and expansive 'history', was still so uneasily integrated into national identity, quite a few Italians can be found engaged in wartime quest for a *duce*. The poet and airman Gabriele D'Annunzio was the gaudiest candidate for the post of national warrior-saint. Frescura in June 1916 was riveted by his presence. 'When he speaks, Gabriele D'Annunzio turns into an abstraction,' he believed. 'He is not one among the crowd. Even though he dominates it, he is outside and higher up. He is not speaking to us but to someone above us, his audience. He is speaking to the race.' A visit from D'Annunzio rendered the usually sceptical Frescura 'beside himself' in a semi-mystical fashion. Deploying phrases that were endlessly repeated about Mussolini under the dictatorship, Frescura was groping for a new 'political (and national) religion'. D'Annunzio's gospel or rather what Frescura read into it transported the young officer into communion with his 'race'. The magic of words metamorphosed the unlikely figure of the womanizing and diminutive poet – who had spent most of the last decade trying erratically to pay his bills and to make a splash in Paris and whose very rhetoric was dated and ornate, scarcely spare enough for the world of the tank and the machine gun – into a hero, potentially *the* hero.

The delayed presentation until 1917–18 of the war as a popular and involving event, a crisis in which the whole nation must fuse to defeat the enemy, may have left quite a few Italians less drained by the emotional demands of patriotism than were the populations of some other combatant countries. Frescura argued that 'Caporetto was useful to Italy. I would even say that it was necessary for us. The calamity stirred a magnificent reaction. The high command was placed into the hands of a general who knew how to learn from the mistakes of the past . . . Soldiers learned that the Austrians lied when they invited us to be their brothers . . . The country understood that you could only win peace through victory and stopped harming the spirit of those at the front, while all accepted a tougher discipline. After the defeat the army undertook a vigorous moral revival; [now were organized] a regular rotation of service at the front, places for soldiers to meet and relax, newspapers, rewards, furloughs and speeches', and, with them, came a new determination to endure and to overcome.[59] Italians, Frescura was saying, were being made, as Italy moved forward to win its third and final war for the Risorgimento and national (re-)birth.

Perhaps. It is undoubtedly true that many officers – they had increased in total from 35,700 in 1914 to 176,000 in December 1918[60] – and some of their men now identified with the nation. Their sense of communion was all the greater because many of the new officers sprang from the lower middle classes of southern Italy,[61] a social group that was also becoming predominant in the bureaucracy. Starace, the eventual proponent of the populist Fascism of the 1930s, reflected something of their character and world-view – in August 1914 he had already brought attention to himself by physically attacking a group who were hymning permanent neutrality at the elegant Caffè Biffi in Milan.[62] Eventually, Starace set aside his war experience to make his sense of self wholly dependent on his ideology and *Duce*. Others of the so-called 'emerging middle classes' had a looser and more adaptable view of their place in the nation, where their patriotism, especially if they came from the south, regularly entailed a continuing loyalty to their locality and family and an eager pursuit of patron–client ties. Their conversion to Fascism often retained the same unstated but powerful qualifications that conditioned their cleaving to the nation.

However, for almost all Italians, talk of national devotion needs to be met with the query – which nation? The new enthusiasm for war after 1917 sometimes enhanced the gulf between one Italian and another. From the beginning of the campaign, despite the fact that the loyalty of established officers often seemed more to their caste than to their *patria*, those in authority were quick to deploy the language of nationalization against any judged 'bad soldiers'. Such men heard from their officers that they were 'unworthy of the army' and 'did not merit being called Italian'.[63] As the war continued and was more deeply inscribed as an ideology, so alleged 'enemies within' developed a greater profile.

Most prominent and menacing were the socialists. Already in early 1917 the aspirant journalist and politician Italo Balbo, then on an officer training course, demanded that the socialists of his home town of Ferrara should be given 'a good whipping – with the pen, and, if necessary, in some more convincing way'. They were, he wrote, de facto 'Austrians', traitors indistinguishable from the enemy.[64] The prime task of the local patriotic *fascio* must be to deal with them. Senior military judges similarly had little doubt that the socialists were evil and alien. Men could be punished merely for fraternizing with them when on leave. In February 1918 one Tuscan infantryman was sentenced to fifteen years in prison for 'inducing betrayal', after he urged his fellows to lay down their arms. His villainy was made evident by the fact that 'he is an affiliate of the Socialist party. All know the evil, poisonous work it pursues among the masses and especially among the soldiery.' Socialists, the judges maintained, were the 'agents of defeatism and *caporettismo*' (the spirit of Caporetto). With their 'tenacious and systematic opposition to the war', they were 'doing the Germans' work for them'.[65]

The Italian socialist movement was indeed having a vexed war, with the political choices required doing little either to amend the party's longstanding fondness for schism or to overcome the exclusion, sometimes the self-exclusion, of socialists from full participation in national life. Those comrades who had not followed Mussolini into the heresy of interventionism greeted the outbreak of war with some nervousness. On 23 May 1915 a manifesto hid the patriotic doubts and reservations of many of the party's leaders by proclaiming grandly that war entry was 'against the real national interest and against the suffrage and the hopes of the proletarian mass'. Only the socialists, the statement continued, had dared to counter the 'morbid' atmosphere of 'irritation, exasperation and overweening power', which partisans of the war had spread with their cynical amalgam of 'deceit and violence'. Battle, the socialists predicted fearfully, would become the excuse for 'an unbridled suppression of every liberty'. Armed conflict was destined to sow seeds of social and political hatred. The party and its members must yield neither to its temptations nor to its threats.

While attempts continued to hold the wings of the movement together, the party line was resolved in the words of Secretary Costantino Lazzari as 'neither support nor sabotage'. The negative nature of the formula made it unsatisfactory to many, however. The journalist Alberto Malatesta, reacting to the charge that the party had turned into a bunch of 'Austria-lovers', felt impelled to write in *Avanti!* in September 1915 that 'no Italian can desire the defeat of Italy. No one can hope that the ties which, with so many sacrifices, have been woven between the various members of our collectivity, should be sundered.' Every Italian must tremble at the oblation demanded of the soldiery. But these regrets and sensitivities, he concluded, did not make the war just or sensible. Three years later, a deputy was still trying to explain matters to the country, his party and himself: 'as a socialist, I do not want to play the game of the ruling class of my country. Therefore I do not actively support the war. But similarly I do not want to work for the ruling class of another country. Therefore I do not sabotage the national war effort.'[66]

In truth the Italian socialist movement possessed many of those features that, in the other combatant states, led party chiefs in August 1914 to accept a *union sacrée* where the theoretical allure of internationalism was overborne by service to the nation in peril. Italy's delayed war entry and the cynicism of the political and diplomatic

manipulations that occasioned it, however, meant that Italian socialists stayed loyal to Marxist theory and so stood apart from the nation.
Despite doubts and criticisms from the 'reformist' section of the party
headed by Filippo Turati, mainstream rank and file, as well as purists
and extremists, applauded the meetings at Zimmerwald and Kienthal,
where Lenin and others endeavoured to reactivate a Socialist
International and inspire 'revolution' and the redirection of national
into civil war in which Europe's proletarians could overthrow
Europe's bourgeoisie.

For all its internationalist dreams, Italian socialism never lost its
local character, being rooted in a different social base from that of
many European labour movements, given the power and size of
Federterra, the peasant union. In the area around Piacenza, for example, it was reported before 1914, 'in our part of the world, socialist
has become synonymous with an organized peasant'.[67] Throughout
the Po valley, where, in some towns and villages, the socialist vote had
surpassed 40 or even 50 per cent[68] before 1914 and where communal
administration was grasped by willing socialist hands, the war exacerbated an existing conflict between countryside and urban centre.
Bologna or Ferrara may have boasted many party members, but
others in these cities were having their own politics tempered by the
war and in the process were blending nationalism and anti-socialism
into a violent form of a new politics, armed against the peasants who
resided outside the urban walls. In the countryside, too, there was
deepening potential for dispute between that majority of peasant
unionists who followed the party line and those returning peasant soldiers who, especially after Caporetto, had been taught with new passion that the nation rested at the heart of their being. Here the spread
of the 'religion of the nation' carried a potential for something
approaching a religious war, since peasant socialism was itself imbri-
cated with an 'ardent lay religiosity'; peasant children might be baptized into a socialist faith, christened 'Liberty' or 'Rebel' and marked
by the sacraments of the party. From the wall of a peasant home or
meeting place, the images of Christ, Garibaldi and Marx blessed syncretic hopes in revolution,[69] ones in which localism and cosmopolitanism outweighed nationalism. Even Turati had been heard to say
that 'the local *Comune* is the truest *patria*'.[70]

Workers and peasants on occasion evinced similar attitudes. In Sesto Fiorentino, dominated by the Ginori ceramic factory, where socialism was flourishing before 1900, those conscripted into the army were reported to sing a sad ditty about the absurdity of dying for someone from the (imponderable and 'foreign') Trentino as they marched off to war.[71] In a *paese* in the province of Caserta, local women took the lead in a demonstration of 2,000, protesting when the local priest, with austere patriotism, tried to ban the annual *festa* of San Vito. The enraged crowd dragged the saint's statue from the church and bore it triumphantly through the town, crying for peace and stoning the *carabinieri*, guilty guardians of the nation-state.[72] However, it was in the rapidly industrializing city of Turin that, in August 1917, there appeared the most dramatic display of popular hostility to government. Italy's fiscal management had not been faring well in war. The reluctance to tax had meant galloping debt and inflation. In 1917 wholesale prices rose to nearly three times their level in 1914 (in 1918 four times, in 1920 six times), though real wages held up much better in Italy's First World War than they did in the Second.[73] There were evident deficiencies, however. Meat consumption, always low among the poorer sectors of society, declined by a third between the start and the end of the war.[74] Throughout the conflict the government had been tardy and partial in its effort to acquire and distribute basic food supplies. Although there were quite a few local initiatives (some organized by socialist administrations), no national rationing scheme was ever developed. On 22 August bread was rumoured to be unavailable in Turin at a time of extra political excitement fostered by an official visit from a delegation of pro-war, anti-Bolshevik socialists belonging to the Petrograd Soviet (and contested by local members of the PSI).[75]

The result was spontaneous riot in which city women played a prominent part, helping to sack bakeries, for example. On the next day, the army arrived, fortified with tanks and machine guns. Fifty people died in the resultant mêlée; more than 800 were arrested, many of them socialists, even though the party leaders had not fomented the event and the national trade union organization under Rinaldo Rigola, a reformist with a pronounced dislike of the irresponsibly revolutionist lawyers and intellectuals he feared dominated party rhetoric,[76] refused to back the action with a general strike. The troops themselves were reported to have shown no desire to fraternize with what they regarded as worker *imboscati*, living the soft life in their factories. Dallolio characteristically took the occasion to urge repression and an improvement in food supply and other conditions in Turin.[77] Quiet was soon enough restored to the city but the Turin riots indicated a lurking social crisis exacerbated by war and by the lack of space for political manoeuvre open to the socialist leadership.

Caporetto made things worse. Replaying the reaction of their comrades in other countries in 1914, quite a number of leading Italian socialists, including Rigola and Filippo Turati, now felt impelled to defend the national cause.[78] Speaking for his union, Rigola declared: 'We can philosophize as much as we want about the idiocy of the war. We can reject each and every dealing with those who wanted it. But, when the enemy tramples our native soil, we have only one duty, and that is to resist.' Lazzari, however, felt impelled to deny these sentiments, demanding instead that the party members 'follow the line already agreed and that is to work ceaselessly for peace and for socialism'.

The enhanced nationalism of the government in the aftermath of the defeat made it hard for the authorities to tolerate socialist opposition and, in February 1918, Lazzari and his deputy, Nicola Bombacci, were found guilty of culpable disloyalty and sentenced to two years in prison. The attempts by Turati and his reformist colleague Claudio Treves to affirm that the party had not deviated from its initial line of neither support nor sabotage were not tailored to convince the judges or the rank and file.[79] The atmosphere of the last year of Italy's war deepened the fissure between the moderate and adventurous wings of Italian socialism. On the one hand, great opportunity, even 'revolution', beckoned. By 1918 the Italian socialist movement was enriched by a massive influx of trade union and party members, while the peasantry, whether unionist or militarized, was agog with the promise, suddenly made in January 1918, that land would be distributed to them after the war. On the other hand, what really was the party line, about the nation, its war and 'revolution'? The initial pronouncement in November 1918 by officials that 'a more tenacious and uncompromising work' should continue, now that 'the bloody parenthesis' of the war was at last over, left unsolved many basic questions about the place of socialism in the Italian future. Brutal answers from the party's foes were not long in coming.

If, in 1914, socialism seemed the mass ideology with the most promising future, organized Catholicism, what was often called social Catholicism, was its most evident friend or foe if Italy was to move towards some developed form of democracy. In 1910 more than 100,000 Italians had signed up to Catholic or 'white' unions, as compared with the 350,000 who then belonged to the socialist Confederazione Generale del Lavoro. Political Catholicism, however, was at least as rent by the war as were the socialists. Benedict XV's first encyclical about events used conventionally reactionary phrasing to blame the conflict on egoism, materialism, 'a disrespect for authority' and 'the insubordination of the masses'. The prolongation of the war and Italian entry into it, however, required a more refined line. The Pope could scarcely endorse a conflict in which Catholics died and killed on both sides and, on 1 August 1917, during what came to be seen as the prologue to the Turin riot, the Caporetto defeat and the Bolshevik Revolution in Russia, Benedict denounced the war and pressed for a 'just and lasting' compromise peace. Throughout the appalling strife, he resisted tempting whispers from the Germans of a place for the Vatican at any peace-making held under the aegis of the central powers – the Italian government, which was appalled by the idea, had insisted on excluding such a presence in clause 15 of the Treaty of London. Later in the conflict Benedict flirted with the apparent idealism of American President Woodrow Wilson. However, the Vatican had not really been won over to the gospel of the new diplomacy. In May 1920 Benedict expressed a possible approval of the principles of the League of Nations but emphasized that the Church itself was the 'perfect model of universalism'.[80]

Other humbler Catholics wholeheartedly rejected the terrible conflict. Their most active champion was Guido Miglioli, one of the first and most activist of Catholic peasant unionists, a deputy who yielded nothing to the socialists in his fervent damning of Italy's war. Operating in the hinterland of Cremona, Miglioli was the special target of the paper edited by the rising local patriotic politician Roberto Farinacci, whose thuggish anti-clericalism grew incandescent at the sight of a pious pacifist. In December 1917 Miglioli was beaten up by interventionists while walking in Rome and, just after Christmas, he was first howled down and then stoned by Farinacci and his friends at a meeting in Cremona. Farinacci, sketching the procedure for what became squadrism, boasted: 'We could not let this provocation go unanswered, and we shouted at him: "German, swindler, traitor, sodomite, the Germans are at the Piave because of you." . . . We did too little to him . . . [He] deserved more; he deserved to be forever put out of circulation.'[81]

Affrays in the provinces there may have been but, during the previous decade, many influential Catholics had been integrating ever more closely into the Liberal state, a process displayed in the Gentiloni pact of 1913. When the Italian government entered the war, Catholic patriots rallied to the nation. Their political leader was Filippo Meda, from 1916 to 1919 Minister of Finance in the Boselli and Orlando administrations. His was an appropriate post given the massive presence of Catholic money in the Italian banking system, be it in large enterprises like the Banco di Roma or in the myriad of smaller Catholic regional banks and credit unions. Meda knew where he stood politically, socially and ideologically; in his view, pacifist Catholics sinned by 'abandoning the defenceless working masses to socialist influence'.[82] He justified his backing of Italian intervention with the argument that peace must always be accompanied by justice. That prerogative, he urged, Austria had denied Italy by its continued occupation of Italian lands and its rejection of Italian aspirations to a place in the sun in the Mediterranean.[83]

Out in society there were also quite a few signs of a patriotic salving of the political-religious wounds opened in the Risorgimento. Even before 1914 the twin worlds of emigration and imperial ambition had seen an alliance between Church and State expand. The emigrant missionary organization, the Scalabrinians, asserted their dedication to *religione e patria* (religion and nation) and Italian priests – Franciscans in the vanguard[84] – unfurled the red, white and green tricolour above their bases from Palestine to China. With the onset of war, labelled by ex-priest, now Nationalist, Romolo Murri 'the supreme religious act',[85] it was natural for these links to harden. With anti-clerical rigour, in 1865 Liberal Italy had banned the presence of chaplains in its military forces and, even during the Libyan war, they were not much encouraged. However, in April 1915 Cadorna was already suggesting that a chaplain should accompany each regiment and, in June, the Vatican created the office of Vescovo del Campo or Bishop to the Front and appointed Angelo Bartolomasi to the post at a pay equivalent to that of a major-general. Eventually more than 24,000 priests served in the national armed forces, 1,243 being decorated for courage.[86] For some, the God of their fathers swiftly merged with the God of the nation. Father Reginaldo Giuliani, a chaplain to the Arditi (and eventual Fascist), thought his men handsome and upstanding in their uniforms, 'like knights of old'. When they advanced they did not flaunt holy relics but 'a great majority', he contended, 'clung to real religion in their hearts and souls'. Giuliani readily cursed the enemy, whom he briefly character-ized as 'barbarians', 'a furious wave which [after Caporetto] sought . . . [to seize Italian lands], impelled by ancient hatreds, brutal greed and savage arrogance'.[87]

Giuliani may have been extreme in his sentiments but quite a num-ber of priests found their nationalization accelerating after 1915. A case study of Umbria has disclosed that the younger clergy in that region were likely to identify themselves with Italy and its war and to do so with greater alacrity given that the elderly teachers at their sem-inaries were so given to anathematizing patriotism. In Perugia, the local Catholic paper had affirmed after Caporetto: 'We are Italians and the cities and land and families which we must defend from the threatened enemy devastation are also Italian.' In 1918 the paper's editor blessed a victory in which 'the Italian borders assigned by Divine Providence but long opposed have now been gained'.[88]

Yet the identification between Church and nation-state was never complete and a sense of reserve lingered under Fascism. During the war the best example of the Church's claim to an eternal presence among the peoples of Italy and therefore to a seniority compared with any form of modern state came in those territories occupied by the Austrians in 1917–18. There, 800,000 Italians endured the precipitate flight of their Liberal administrators. 'In overwhelming majority,' however, a historian of these events has noted, 'priests remained at their posts, while mayors did not.' With future parallels to the Fascist war in 1943–5, priests stood up for their parishioners, proving to be their refuge in time of trouble. They were needed against the Austrian authorities, cruelly suspicious of any whiff of surviving Italian patriotism (perhaps 5,000 civilians died during the battle and 22,000 were estimated to have starved to death before Italian rule resumed). They were similarly petitioned for help against returning Italian landowners in 1919, furious about what had been done in their absence and hostile to peasant dreams, sometimes achieved in 1917–18, of seizing the land.[89]

If Catholicism had not been reduced merely to a servant of the nation, the final area of debate and doubt as peace approached lay at the heights of government. For so-called 'Liberals', the dispute in 1914–15 about how and when to enter the war had not ended. Before May 1915, Giovanni Giolitti, the most successful Liberal politician of the previous generation (he was born in 1842), had not ruled out gain to be won from the central powers by negotiation rather than armed force. In 1918, he and his large, if diminishing, band of clients still evinced an implicit opposition to the particularities of Italy's war. In any arrangement of a post-war political order, Giolitti would claim a place and do so with an interpretation of the recent past that was not the same as that of the government.

Equally perplexing was the definition of national war aims. Indeed, matters in that regard became more wrenching during the last stages of combat than they had been at the beginning. It was true that a wide-ranging but not manic set of ambitions had been inscribed in the Treaty of London through which Italy had entered the conflict. However, the Bolsheviks, after seizing power and while Trotsky still thought innocently that the purpose of Marxist foreign policy was to 'publish a few revolutionary manifestos and then close shop', had published copies of the 'secret treaties' held at Petrograd and severely embarrassed all Allied governments, including the Italian, by doing so. President Woodrow Wilson, who had brought the USA into the war earlier in 1917, was further complicating matters by insisting, except when dealing with Mexico, Japan, Nicaragua and American blacks and socialists, that a new international 'idealism' underscore any settlement. If the peace-making was destined to turn into a fight between the new politics of 'Wilson versus Lenin', then a traditional-

ist Italy, alight with national 'egoism', could expect little considera-
tion, all the more since Caporetto had only confirmed the general foreign disrespect for Italian fighting qualities and disregard for the
Italian contribution to victory.[90]

For Italy, being the least of the great powers remained a vexing fate.
Bureaucrats in the colonial ministry had entertained themselves during
the war with extravagant expansionist 'plans' for the nation to take
over not just all of East Africa but the Portuguese colonies and a great
deal of Turkey into the bargain.[91] More pressing was the 'problem' of
the Adriatic, in other words the drawing of a strategically and ethnically just border there between Italy and what many Italians deemed
the (barbarous) Slav world. Sonnino stuck to a contradictory policy in
which Italy firmly defended its interests but treated the locals as a
buyer did peasants: 'it is at the market and at the last moment that I'll
settle on a price', he pronounced.[92] Such Machiavellian realism
accorded ill with the new phraseology of the Allied campaign, pledged
to make the world safe for (liberal capitalist) democracy. No doubt
President Wilson's ideas cried out for interpretation on the ground.
The first problem of Wilsonian principles, as much of Central and
Eastern Europe was to demonstrate so sadly after 1919, was how self-
determination should work politically, given that the nationality of the
peoples of the region was even more complex and flawed than was that
of the Italian masses. It was not merely Liberal cynicism and ambition
which made the charting of Italy's north-eastern border, the one most
affected by Wilsonian ideals, such a fraught and doubtful matter. Nor
was it much surprise that, there, symptoms appeared of what has been
called the 'Habsburg disease', a fevered politics which should more
fairly be ascribed to the inadequacies of the Wilsonian prescription for
an easy marriage between liberty and nationality in that Europe where
familiar frontiers had been trampled down by the war.

Back in 1909 Federzoni had pronounced that 'the new generation
of Italians, those who are possessed with a consciousness of the
nation's historic mission, can only be nationalist and imperialist'.[93]
During the July crisis, Alfredo Rocco, destined to be a Fascist Minister
of Justice and a key framer of Fascist 'corporatism', had added that
Nationalists loved the proletariat but disdained socialism, doing so
stirred by 'a racial hatred, a hatred of those who belong to society's

builders against those who are society's destroyers'.[94] The words of each man pointed to that future where, by 1918, at home and abroad, Italy, in its version of the First World War, had won the most partial of victories, both militarily and in the more crucial arena of the affirmation of its institutions and national values. In the midst of the 1914–15 debate about intervention, *L'Idea Nazionale* wrote off parliament as 'a third-rate club, frequented by a varied collection of broken-down wind-bags, of letter writers who like official stationery, of old misanthropes who like to read a free newspaper, of rabid gamblers who could not live without their daily game'.[95] Neither the views nor the tone were destined to lose their shrillness. The post-war period was soon to see the rise of a medley of bourgeois, intellectuals and returned soldiers, who were ready to gamble the lives and well-being of their fellow citizens to convert what they took to calling a 'maimed victory' (*vittoria mutilata*)[96] into a 'real' (and Fascist) one. Men who had once automatically viewed themselves as liberals now took to infringing the rule of law (or cynically adapting it to their own gain and to the disadvantage of their enemies) and to seeing the 'armed society' of the totalized First World War as the ideal political and economic model for peacetime, too. They would act pre-emptively against their foes. In their rise, the first casualty was to be the gentler, kinder, more studied and restrained world of the Liberal *belle époque*.

4

1919

Until his fall in 1928–9, Mario Giampaoli was for quite a while the boss (or *ras* as such people were called under the regime) of Milan. A radical Fascist, he exulted at the way the revolution had made militant the citizens of his city. He naturally expected that the Milanese should render him and his *Duce* homage – just before he lost office, a tame biographer saluted him as 'the unchallengeable judge of every local political matter'. Although a committed enemy of communism, the *ras* of Milan reckoned that Fascism was rooted in the people, declaring his motto to be: 'With the people and for the people'. Giampaoli, born in Padua in 1894, had begun work as a postman, a vocation marred by a conviction for theft in 1913. The crisis of the war, however, presented opportunity and Giampaoli made a name for himself as a syndicalist, interventionist and volunteer. By the end of the conflict a political career was beckoning. Like many Italian politicians, whether Liberal or Fascist, Giampaoli shored up his authority by editing and owning a paper, a weekly which police reports alleged to have delivered him sufficient funds for the 'high life', despite his modest claim that its task was 'to educate [its readers] in the most profound sense'.[1] In the police view, rather than acting as an austere missionary of the Fascist word, Giampaoli enjoyed numerous irregular sexual relationships and indulged a predilection for heavy gambling. He funded these activities either through the direct employment of stand-over tactics or by more subtly blackmailing his victims through the small print and ambiguous statements of articles in his journal. In 1929, to police approval, Mussolini closed the paper down. It was entitled *Il 1919*.[2] Its nomination of a year, that of the birth of the so-called Fasci di combattimento at a meeting, attended by Giampaoli among others, in a building facing Piazza San Sepolcro, not far from the magnificent Milan cathedral, had, until the atmosphere soured, been enough to express a programme and an attitude. Giampaoli and his sort of Fascists were the legionaries of, and true believers in, a 'revolution' presided over by Benito Mussolini. They had unfurled their banners and taken their stand in 1919; then, they liked to proclaim, they could have done none other.

The first year of peace had been a time of crisis in Italy, as it was throughout Europe. The collapse of the central powers' armies came swiftly; events outpaced human preparation for them and the end of war had scarcely ushered in a soft and piping time of universal amity. Violence continued. In Russia, the Bolshevik Revolution had lurched into vicious civil war where sackings and massacre were everyday occurrences and where carnage among the peoples of all the Russias was aided and abetted by intervening foreign forces. In Germany, the New Year saw an attempted rising by the Spartacists, the most revolutionary faction of the socialist movement. It was put down with great savagery and its leaders, Rosa Luxemburg and Karl Liebknecht, were summarily executed. Other revolutions broke out in Hungary and Bavaria and, after moments of mayhem, met the same fate. All over Eastern Europe, where, in 1917–18, it had seemed that Germany had won the First World War, borders were unsettled, societies upturned, political legitimacy in dispute, culture in flux. Everywhere the vocabulary of war still held sway. Engraven into men's and women's minds, it naturalized slaughter for much of the post-war era. The guns at the front had fallen silent but the world remained embattled. As a recent historian has put it, Europeans in 1919 seemed to have decided that peace meant no more than 'war pursued by other means'.[3] A contemporary Fascist agreed. For Piero Bolzon, a new war immediately replaced the old one in each European city, while every political doctrine, he remarked, was 'now become a gospel of violence'.[4] Even liberalism might have to adapt to the new age.

For Italy, least of the great powers, poorest of the great economies, most fragile of the great societies and most uneasily nationalized of the great cultures, the conversion from war to peace entailed a sea of troubles. If not to the same degree as France, battles, especially those after Caporetto, were conducted on national soil and had devastated

Italian lands, physically and morally. Both its years in the Triple Alliance before 1914 and geopolitics had created many ties between the Italian economy and those of the central powers which had been wrecked by war and revived slowly, given the travails of Germanic Europe. Moreover, the Liberal elite had fought their war to victory but without identifying a 'leader' and without fully charting a set of diplomatic, political, social and economic aims. 'What comes next?' was not in 1919 a question to which Orlando or Sonnino or Nitti or Giolitti or King Victor Emmanuel III or Pope Benedict XV or the army Chief of Staff, Armando Diaz, or Agnelli and others in the business world had a speedy response. By contrast, a slew of writers and intellectuals, great and small – D'Annunzio, the Futurist Marinetti, such Nationalists as Federzoni, Rocco and the more senior philosopher, Enrico Corradini, the self-styled overlord of the crack troops, the Arditi, Ferruccio Vecchi, the heads of the various socialist factions and, for the present more limited in their appeal if not necessarily in their ambitions, Mussolini, Farinacci, Balbo, Grandi, Giampaoli and many others growing accustomed to call themselves 'Fascists' – all were anxious to express their ideas and to make or enhance their names. So many of the certainties of the old world order had been swept away by the war. Did kings rule? Should parliaments debate? Should God or his Pope be relied on for spiritual sustenance? Should the state or business best govern the economy? Should culture cleave to tradition or marry itself to modernism and the machine? Should peasants own the land? Should women be emancipated? Should emigration resume? Should Italians be united in a nationality or, perhaps, a race and, if they were, where might its borders lie? For each question, many, often contradictory, passionately contradictory, answers existed.

To be sure, within a few short years, a Fascist 'revolution' proved that Mussolini and his friends were those armed with the most effective immediate replies. Proclaiming a totalitarian 'last word', the Fascists sought to silence all debates and to impose on Italians the 'unity' and obedience of the parade ground (even if the appearance or intent of the regime should not be assumed to be identical with its reality). During the months that followed November 1918, however, this future was not yet clear, even though talk of 'revolution' was all around. When reopening the parliamentary Chamber for its first session after the war, Orlando, for one, had proclaimed, grandly but opaquely, that the war had amounted to 'the greatest political and social revolution which history had recorded'.[5]

Technically speaking, Italy had been victorious in the First World War. In the last days of October 1918, a fortnight or so before the trenches emptied on the Western Front (a primacy Italian patriots then and thereafter loved to recall), Italian armies, moving forward from the Piave and on Monte Grappa (but not yet reaching the line they had held in October 1917), found that Austrian resistance had melted away as revolution or collapse dissolved the Habsburg empire. The town of Vittorio Veneto fell on 30 October. A few days later, Italian forces 'liberated' Trento and Trieste, the key targets for those who had viewed combat as completing the Risorgimento by bringing 'unredeemed' Italians home to the nation. At 3 p. m. on 4 November, to be called 'Vittorio Veneto Day' and so marking a holy victory won in the region with that name under forces led euphoniously by King Vittorio Emanuele, fighting on the Italian front of the Great War ceased.

But what could Italy expect from the peace-making and from the mixture of utopian thoughts about peace and more aggressive ones about predation which so characterized the moment? The sound of artillery might no longer echo through the Veneto but Italian troops were not yet still. One hundred thousand of them remained on guard in Albania,[6] ostensibly a pledge of that small nation's independence but implicitly asserting that any territory washed by the Adriatic was of national interest. Italian forces also intruded into Dalmatia and insisted on garrisoning the port of Rijeka (or Fiume as the Italians called it), accepting with bad grace the presence there of French troops and the soldiers of what was becoming Yugoslavia. These last had often served in the Habsburg armies and, in Italian eyes, seemed, through some iniquitous sleight of hand, to have been translated from defeated old enemies into threatening new ones. Already on 30 October Orlando had pronounced that 'Fiume is more Italian than Rome'[7] (even though the town had not been listed among the terms of the Treaty of London). Italian soldiery also served in Turkey – Italian–Greek relations, damaged since 1911–12 by Liberal occupation of the ethnically Greek Dodecanese islands, remained tense – as well as in the Italian empire where, for example, in Libya, the First World War had left national rule weak and contested. Carlo Sforza, to be Giolitti's sensible and realistic Foreign Minister and, later, an anti-Fascist exile, was deluded enough about hopes of gain in Asia Minor to state that the area presented 'the *only* real chance to make a great Italy tomorrow'.[8]

Soldiering was one thing; diplomacy another. The year 1919 began with a state visit to Italy by Woodrow Wilson, who at that moment seemed girded with a charisma that could stun Italians and calm their fears about the future. Was the American president the saviour of humankind? Rich and poor, left and right, momentarily believed he might be. In *Il Popolo d'Italia*, Mussolini, still casting around for a line of his own through which to advance into the post-war period, enthused: 'Wilson's empire has no borders because He [sic] does not govern territories. Rather He interprets the needs, the hopes, the faith of the human spirit, which has no spatial or temporal limits.'[9]

It was true that Mussolini qualified his apotheosis of the American leader with the plea that Wilson recognize Italy's 'just rights'.[10] And, a few months later, his admiration, like that of most Italians, had withered as quickly as it had bloomed. Now Wilson was condemned as a muddled professor or worse. His '"American" way of viewing things' was deemed 'hostile both to the European and the Latin spirit'.[11] Later Fascist party secretary and, at this time, Nationalist, irredentist and highly decorated volunteer, officer and president of the Comitato per le rivendicazioni nazionali (Committee for just national claims), Giovanni Giuriati argued that Wilsonian principles had been cunningly invented to block Italian imperial advance. Wilson's flaunted ideals reeked of hypocrisy. The wealthy old states had cynically adopted its verbiage as soon as they realized that what Giuriati called Italy's 'national organism' had surmounted the test of war.[12]

Giuriati was being paranoid, as nationalists are wont to be. Yet Italy was to endure a humiliating Paris peace-making (a situation not much overcome in recent historiography where the policies and attitudes of its people and leaders receive as little mention as does Italy's overall war effort). Wilson's 'new covenant' pledged an 'open' diplomacy and so the purging of the sins of the old world in a new order that would marry liberalism, capitalism and 'self-determination' (or beneficent nationalism). This prospect squared uneasily with the habitual fate and behaviour patterns of the most precarious of the great powers, the one which could only afford to practise what has been called *imperialismo straccione*, the search for imperial rags and patches discarded or disdained by the senior powers. Structures ensured that the Liberal leadership was riding for a fall. Roberto Farinacci was soon lambasting the government for its failure at the peace-making, which he linked with its overall inadequacy in war-making. In his opinion, in 1919 'the ruling class, which governed the country for the last fifty years, gave us an example of life without grandeur. It abandoned us to the enemy in a war which it did not know how to foresee or hinder or run. Uncomprehending both of the martyrdom of our people and of the danger to the *patria*, it humili-ated and betrayed our soldiers, cursed the war, and . . . finally wasted and utterly destroyed our victory.'[13]

In Paris, it had been a bitter spring for Italy's negotiators, led by Orlando and Sonnino. By early April 1919 the regularizing of Italian frontiers emerged as the major issue confronting the peace delegates, with Wilson reluctantly accepting that the border between the Italian and Germanic worlds should be set at the watershed of the Brenner pass, even though that boundary meant that tens of thousands of German-speaking peasants would be subjugated to Italian rule. The resultant oppression of Germans should not be forgotten when reviewing the diplomacy of the 1930s nor should the profound hos-tility of almost all German nationalists, except Hitler, for their oppres-sors. However willing to force concessions on the German world, Wilson could not tolerate the Italian mapping of its territorial meet-ing with Yugoslavia. He was particularly unimpressed with the noisy campaign for Fiume, where a crisis of administration continued unabated (in summer, the lynching of nine French soldiers by an enraged Italian mob prompted Clemenceau to mutter to his Allied col-leagues twice on succeeding days that Italy was no more than 'a nation of assassins, a nation of assassins').[14] On the evening of 23 April, confronted by stalemate, Wilson appealed to what he called international 'public opinion' against the Italian negotiators, the first occasion on which the traditional secrecy of diplomatic dealing had been so patently infringed.

The next day, Orlando, expressing or feigning high dudgeon, left for Rome and Sonnino followed his Prime Minister forty-eight hours later. The two must have expected that their gesture would be greeted with contrition and they would be summoned back in triumph with their terms and conditions met. Instead, the reverse happened. In the absence of the Italians, the labours of the peace-makers were expedited. In early May, African mandates were happily distributed without contacting Rome. The great majority of political opinion in Italy was outraged at the national slight. Even Salvemini complained of harsh treatment and Mussolini used the occasion to employ to his own account the language coined by Corradini and the Nationalists when he urged in his paper that 'our future policy must be directed towards establishing a modicum of justice between us proletarians and the fatter and more bourgeois nations of the world'.[15] Beset by 'Anglican hypocrisy', Mussolini added belligerently, 'we should reply: "Hooray for an Italian Malta! Hooray for Eire! Egypt for the Egyptians!"'[16]

Briefly, while he seemed a victim of foreign bullying, Orlando saw his political star rise. However, under his aegis Italian policy had reached the deadest of ends and, after 5 May, the mortified Prime Minister and Sonnino had to crawl back to Paris. There was a price to be exacted in Italy for this latest reversal. On 19 June, a few days before the signature of the Versailles Treaty (28 June), Orlando's government fell. Nationalists filled rivers of copy with laments about the 'French peace' and its wicked mistreatment of an Italy that had been perfidiously robbed of its victory. Mussolini was little different, although, rarely averse to the main chance, he did take the occasion to hail Dante Ferraris, a patriotic Piedmontese entrepreneur of Jewish descent who had become president of Confindustria (the confederation of industrialists) and was a generous financier of patriotic causes, as the business chief who had done most to protect Italy from social and economic 'chaos and convulsion'. Ferraris may have been pleased to learn that the aspirant *Duce* admired him as 'a man of action, with an open, honest and constructive mind', rather like Mussolini, it might be thought.[17] On 3 July Mussolini added the self-estimate that, in its three months of existence, 'Fascism' had proved itself 'the most lively, brave, active and revolutionary . . . force around in Italy', although, he also took care to stress, it was a movement without too many 'political prejudices'.[18] International crisis and international failure were grist to his mill.

Francesco Nitti, the new Prime Minister, was experienced above all in financial administration and was consumed by a love of accurate statistics and a hope in the fundamental moderation of humankind – he was an early convert to the view that the Germans, whom he thought 'the most cultivated people on earth', had been traduced and persecuted at Versailles. Although he never ceased to maintain that national ambitions in the Treaty of London were justified, Nitti aimed to shift the focus of government from foreign issues to domestic affairs.

How, after all, was the economy going six months after the end of the war? In the summer of 1919, the indices were not encouraging and Nitti was honest enough to admit it. Inflation was rising faster than it had during the actual war, the lira was losing ground on international money markets, state spending remained stubbornly high, credit was hard to find and unemployment, worsened by the problem of men moving out of the army, was up. Italy confronted a severe economic crisis in which the nation would have to pay for the careless disdain of financial matters by Salandra and Sonnino when they had committed Italy to battle.[19] So parlous was the situation that, early in 1920, there was semi-official talk of bankruptcy. Throughout his term in office, Nitti, for all his thrift and care, could not see the economic skies lightening.

Moreover, any effort to make an accurate assessment of Italy's finances was certain to unleash the wrath of those who believed or wanted to believe that the war had provided a historic moment when a summit of national grandeur had been, or could thereafter be, reached. Nationalists feared that Nitti, with his accountant's mind so uncomprehending of military honour and achievement, had become Prime Minister to trade some hard-won territorial gain in the north-eastern border regions for 'food, coal and credits'.[20] As Giuriati put it indignantly, Nitti was the type who would 'abandon Fiume and all Dalmatia for a sack of grain'.[21]

Zealots of the nation constituted a minority of Italians (although in 1919 there were understandably more of them than usual). But Nitti was also limited in winning over those Italians who were not partisans of national expansion. To a public bruised so profoundly by the death and devastation of war, Nitti offered the austere slogan: 'produce more and consume less'.[22] No doubt it was an economically rational statement but his words had little traction in a country where, as also under Fascism, numbers of Italians would see themselves as living perpetually in *miseria* (poverty) and on the edge of starvation. Modern economic analysis may show that the income of those trying to prosper on dividends and rents and the salaries of civil servants were in the severest decline in 1919 and demonstrate that the real wages of factory workers and agricultural day labourers were slightly up[23] but many Italians began to think, during that summer and autumn, that the division between rich and poor gaped ever more balefully.

Was it the moment for socialist revolution? Numbers hoped or feared so. Party membership expanded almost tenfold from September 1918 to 1920 (24,359 to 208,974), while socialist branches increased from 998 to 2,815 during the same period. The advance was rendered more potent by the massive post-war influx into the union movement. Those enrolled in CGdL rose from under 250,000 in 1918 to more than 2 million in 1920.[24] In the elections which Nitti held in November 1919, Socialists won 156 seats, a trebling of their total at the previous poll in 1913, and 32.5 per cent of the total ballot. By that time the Socialist party could boast a majority in 2,126 communes (out of some 8,000) and in 26 provinces out of 69.[25] Socialism was strong in its appeal both to modern peasants and to the working class – industrial cities and their workforce had grown rapidly during the war, Genoa, for example, increasing from 295,000 inhabitants to 378,000 between 1915 and 1918.[26]

But what was Italian socialism for? There was the rub. Many leading party intellectuals prattled cheerfully about the complete overthrow of the existing social and economic order. Amedeo Bordiga, the son of a teacher from Portici near Naples, and himself a trained engineer who was destined for a time to lead the Italian Communist party, pushed an extreme line at the socialist congress held at Bologna in October 1919. There it was agreed that the Russian Revolution amounted to the 'happiest and most propitious event in the history of the [world] proletariat'. The storming of the Winter Palace proved without doubt that 'no ruling class has ever surrendered its despotic power unless forced to do so by violence'.[27] The Italian socialist movement, it was implied, must seize the citadels of the Italian bourgeoisie and do so now. Contradictions lurked, however. Giacinto Menotti Serrati, a maximalist who had been a pre-war patron of Mussolini, revealed that his *mentalité* retained messages from the past when he composed a 'Ten Commandments for the socialist soldier'.[28]

Antonio Gramsci, another revolutionary southern intellectual, did not always agree with Bordiga (whom he eventually succeeded at the head of the PCd'I) but he, too, was certain that the war had entailed 'the process of development of modern history which Marx summed up in the expression: the catastrophe of the capitalist world'. 'Only the working class can save society from plunging into an abyss of barbarism and economic ruin towards which the enraged and maddened forces of the propertied classes are driving it,' Gramsci wrote in an article in his Turin paper, *L'Ordine Nuovo* (The New Order). 'It can do this by organizing itself as the ruling class, to impose its own dictatorship in the politico-industrial world'. By May 1920 Gramsci's fervour had increased. 'In Italy at the present moment,' he argued, 'the character of the class struggle is determined by the fact that industrial and agricultural workers throughout Italy are irresistibly set upon raising the question of the ownership of the means of production in an explicit and violent form.' Gramsci was capable of pessimism, however, especially when he contemplated the 'backwardness' of Italians away from his adopted home of Turin. 'The revolution', he had mused on 15 November 1919 as Italy went to the polls, 'finds the broad masses of the Italian people, still shapeless, still atomized into an animal-like swarm of individuals lacking all discipline and culture, obedient only to the stimuli of their bellies and their barbarian passions.' He also feared the in-between classes, especially the petite bourgeoisie, in whose ranks 'there rot and decompose the indolence, cowardice and arrogance of the social debris and rubbish deposited by centuries of servility and the domination of priests and foreigners over the Italian nation'.[29]

A socialist song exhibited a somewhat crude definition of the purpose of revolution and, at least in its third verse, a frank sensualism

which, had they been confronted with its words, might have perturbed both Gramsci and the Soviet 'Great Headmaster', V. I. Lenin,
whom it otherwise invoked as the supreme revolutionary chief:

> Se arriverà Lenin faremo una gran festa;
> andremo dai signori, gli taglierem la testa
>
> Oilì oilà e la lega la crescerà
>
> Le guardie regie in pentola le fanno il brodo giallo,
> carabinieri in umido e arrosto il maresciallo.
>
> Oilì oilà e la lega la crescerà
>
> State attente vedovelle, che g'han firmà la pace,
> ghe vegnerà a ca' i zuven, ve baserà 'e cülate.
>
> Oilì oilà e la lega la crescerà
>
> Se arriverà Lenin faremo una gran festa;
> andremo dai signori, gli taglierem la testa
>
> Oilì oilà e la lega la crescerà.

(If Lenin comes, we'll have a great party and go to the bosses and cut off
their heads. Hi, ho and the union will grow. The Royal Guards we'll put
in a pot and turn into soup, the *carabinieri* we'll steam and their sergeant-
major we'll roast. Hi, ho and the union will grow. Watch out little widows,
now that peace has been signed, the lads are coming home and'll kiss your
fannies. Hi, ho and the union will grow. If Lenin comes, we'll have a great
party and go to the bosses and cut off their heads. Hi, ho and the union
will grow.)[30]

This revolutionary utopianism, with an undercurrent of violence
some thought always menacingly present in the Italian masses,
appalled moderate socialists. Events in Italy threatened to mimic what
had happened in Germany in the dark mid-winter of 1918–19, when

the Social Democrat first president of the Republic, Friedrich Ebert, summoned the 'Free Corps', freebooting bands of rightist soldiers working on their own or their officers' account, to put down the Spartacist revolt. The old reformist leader Filippo Turati, whose socialism had always been more ethical than activist, and the union leaders Rigola and Ludovico D'Aragona thoroughly disliked careless talk about imminent revolution. D'Aragona sternly denounced 'the sterility of maximalist method, which abandoned the realm of serious struggle to pursue quite impossible ends'. But, in late 1919, even CGdL, with the election on the horizon, felt impelled to declare that it stood shoulder to shoulder with the Socialist party in the intention of 'completely emancipating the proletariat from capitalist slavery'. In this battle, D'Aragona and Rigola now contended, it was not the moment to worry too much about the niceties of 'the anachronistic bourgeois conception of democracy' or grant respect to its verbiage about 'citizens' political equality'.[31]

For most Italians the real meaning of these comments was experienced on the ground, in their own villages and towns and in their workplace, be it in the fields or factories. In Turin, workers' councils from an initial base at Fiat were spreading rapidly into chemical and textile concerns, promising a Sovietization of Italian industry.[32] Outside that city, however, such bodies were rare. Omnipresent, rather, was social action expressed in strikes, lockouts and land occupations. In Tuscany, once, at least in the theory of the wealthy, a paradise of social harmony where sharecropping was the happy rule, a series of disputes culminated in the summer of 1920 with what has been labelled 'the largest agricultural strike in Italian history', one which was joined by 500,000 peasants and imperilled the entire local harvest. In July, the landowners of the region caved in and signed a new contract, allowing peasants to join a sort of management council for the estates which they worked and conceding an array of welfare provisions, most at the expense of the landowners.[33]

In Bologna, where the socialists won 63 per cent of the vote in the city in November 1919, a nationalist was left to bewail a world in which 'the province of Bologna is only nominally part of the Kingdom of Italy. The [socialist] Chamber of Labour rules and no one dare disobey its orders because everyone has become convinced that the government will not help anyone who takes the initiative in resisting the socialist tyranny.'[34] Even in San Marino, the local socialist party proclaimed that it stood for a line of all or nothing. Either the wealthy would reform themselves and disburse their property or it was time to 'finish' them.[35] In Venice, according to the tourist posters the most serene of places, waiters withdrew their labour, in September 1919 forcing the closure of Florian's, most sacred of bourgeois sites in Piazza San Marco.[36] So disgusted were the best people that a Fascio Giovanile Liberale (Young Liberal League) sprang up among wealthy youth.[37] In Ferrara, another successful strike resulted in the biscuit workers at a town factory carrying home a 50 per cent pay rise to the mortification of those who footed the bill.[38]

Even in the south, socialism seemed, at least in some places, to be capturing the future and remedying ancient ills. In Puglia, government statistics said that 210,000 day labourers made do on an annual income of 1,620 lire, earned in the 135 days when they could expect to find work, well below the 3,000 lire estimated as needed for basic sustenance.[39] Peasant boys were expected to labour from the age of eight (on half-pay) and were said to learn nothing from their growing up 'except to steal, to carry knives and to hate their employers'.[40] Would the war end this social tyranny? The peasants had heard Salandra, the leading Liberal politician of the region, say that, 'after victory, Italy will complete a great act of social justice. Italy will give land to the peasants with all the equipment needed so that each hero from the front, who has fought so bravely in the trenches, can become fully independent. This gift will be the compensation granted by the *patria* to its courageous sons.'[41] But there is little evidence that this ruthless conservative meant what he said. No wonder that the region in 1919–20 was scoured by urban and rural strikes – at Nardò near Lecce in April 1920 insurgents who thought they were making a local revolution held the town against all comers for nearly three weeks.[42]

In their utopian hope for justice the peasants were deluded and were soon paying a price for their error. Despite appearances and the frightened rhetoric of liberals, ex-liberals and a new right, the social-ist movement had not secured a majority in the country as a whole. In Sicily, for example, the social order, with its traditionally violent underpinnings, was feebly stirred by the currents of leftist revolution.

None the less, even there, the spectre of socialism stalked abroad. Before the end of 1919 a so-called Partito economico (the Economic party), led by Prince Pietro Lanza di Scalea, colonialist, Liberal and then Fascist minister and alleged patron of the Mafia, had already proclaimed that it would 'defend to the uttermost' the existing social and economic system and resist 'Bolshevism' by whatever means.[43]

On the surface, however, the greatest immediate rival to the march of socialism was organized political catholicism. On 18 January Catholics greeted the post-war period with the establishment of their own mass formation, the Partito Popolare Italiano (PPI). In the November elections this group won 100 seats and, in quite a few 'white' provinces, it dominated local administration. In Brescia, where the PPI's posture was decidedly conservative, the party out-polled the socialists by almost two to one.[44] As with the socialists, the political party was only part of the story; Catholics also sought a place of their own in civil society. In the Veneto and other white regions, the Catholic labour union, CIL, multiplied its membership even more dramatically than had CGdL, surpassing a million members in 1920, about 80 per cent of whom were peasants, sometimes but not always more peaceable and deferential than were the activists of Federterra.

Catholic power was not solid, however. The PPI was as riven by internal dispute as were the socialists. The party chief, Sturzo, and Alcide De Gasperi, his friend from the Trentino, who before 1915 had been a Christian Social member of the parliament in Habsburg Vienna and would survive to be Italian Prime Minister after 1945, anxiously steered a middle course between the Catholic maximalism of Miglioli or Don Minzoni, a radical priest based at Molinella near Ferrara, and the integralist conservatism and nationalism of Agostino Gemelli (1878–1959). This last was moving from his role as army chaplain to become in appropriate season an informant of the Fascist secret police and, still later, a forceful influence on the rightist factions of post-1945 Christian Democracy. For Gemelli and the bankers and businessmen of the PPI, talk about the age of the masses was all very well but any worthwhile politics had to be anti-socialist at heart.

If, in 1919, there was to be a further competitor to both the socialists and Catholics in 'new' mass politics, it seemed likely to find a base among the returned soldiers. In November 1918 a slogan was circulating among the troops that 'we, and only we, want to be in charge of our future'. As firing ceased, three million men lay still under arms. Plans for their demobilization were sketchy, although a Commission (soon derisively called the Commissionissima) had been pondering the matter since July. In November 1.4 million were released from service and another 500,000 between January and March 1919. The process then stalled until Nitti demobilized a further million in July–August. Schemes for soldiers' welfare and their integration into peacetime employment and life were vague but an association of those disabled in war (ANMIG) had been established in 1917 and it was from its ranks that, in November 1918, a league of returned soldiers was founded. It was named the Associazione Nazionale dei Combattenti (ANC). Its branches soon spread across Italy and, at least among those returning from the war, it outdistanced the socialists and Catholics, each of whom had tried to press demobilized soldiers into their own organizations and politics. The socialists launched a Lega proletaria fra mutilati, invalidi, feriti, reduci di guerra (Proletarian union of those maimed, disabled, wounded by or returned from war); the Catholics a Unione nazionale dei reduci (National returned soldiers' group). Neither did well. As one wounded warrior mused: 'Yesterday's parties have left no trace in our hearts. Our memory concentrates on the grey-green of the trenches and only that.'

The meeting of the first congress of the ANC in Rome on 22 June 1919 coincided with the collapse of Orlando's wartime government and with rumours that the King's cousin, the fiercely militarist Duke of Aosta, or a leading general, might mount a coup against parliament. Among the delegates, Francesco Giunta, a future Fascist minister, demanded that the ANC take up a political stance on the far right and accept the leadership of Mussolini or D'Annunzio. Ferruccio Vecchi of the Arditi was still proselytizing his own drastically nationalist (if Milanese) cause. Members of other currents had reverse ideas; Salvemini, by now an advocate of a radical liberal democracy, was one who wanted to take the ANC towards the left.

The Rome congress brought to the fore such southern intellectuals as Antonio Morabito, a lawyer from Reggio Calabria, and Nicola Favia from Bari, men not destined to make a major or longstanding contribution to national political life, perhaps because they still conceived their main task as favouring enough change to allow the old order to be restored. The ANC was embarrassed by requests that it bless land occupations; its leaders continued to declare that they wanted land distributed to the peasants, but even Salvemini disliked the violence which could easily bubble up when peasants took the law into their own hands.[45] Foreign affairs also posed many dilemmas with the ANC failing to proclaim Fiume a great national cause. Some ANC candidates stood in the November elections and they did well locally in Sardinia, for example, where, paradoxically, they allied with local autonomists.[46] However an overall tally of 3.5 per cent signalled failure and the launching in August 1920 of a Partito di Rinnovamento (Renewal Party) got nowhere. The ANC was not destined to rule in Rome. Protected by government subsidy, the movement lingered on until Mussolini dissolved it in January 1925.

The Sardinian radical and anti-Fascist, Emilio Lussu, left a memorable image of these years of alleged threat from leftist revolution, portraying 'the apprehension of a distant relative of mine, a big landowner, who, terrified that he was going to lose his property, kept repeating, "My poor children, how will they live?" As a matter of fact, he had no children, and still has none, so far as I know.' 'Imagination', Lussu concluded wryly, 'always plays a great part in times of political stress.'[47] It is well to be reminded that in 1919–20 quite a lot of the order established through the Risorgimento remained in place. In the November 1919 elections, the various liberal groupings, however factionalized in belief and however rent by their ties to rival patrons, occupied almost 50 per cent of the seats in the Chamber of Deputies (252 out of 508). Moreover, their opponents may have been singing victory but they were beset by evident divisions and the speed of their gains since 1918, too precipitate to permit serious education in the principles and purpose of the movements, betokened a superficial commitment of many of the rank and file to socialist or Catholic unionism. Similarly, the social order of Italy – respect for the patron and expectation of his benevolence, devotion to a hierarchical family, male supremacy over the female, a pyramid of prestige and alleged civilization rising from peasants in the countryside at the bottom to those with political, commercial or cultural wealth in Rome, Milan, Florence or comparable urban centres at the top – had scarcely crumbled into dust. Present political advantage was one thing. Firmly attaching a following through what Gramsci was to call 'hegemony', the control of information and common sense, was another. Nor had the war cured Italy's accustomed disunity. Regional contrasts remained great. Only ten socialists held seats in the south, only twenty-eight *popolari* in the north.

Yet a sense of comparison remains crucial. The social and economic crisis in Italy, if paralleled, for example, with the early travails of the Weimar Republic, may have been severe, but was not traumatic. No Italian had to propel a wheelbarrow of lire to the market to buy an egg; despite inflation, Italian pensions and savings had not been rendered worthless in the post-war economy; no revolutionaries seized power in an Italian city of the significance of Munich; no military-bureaucratic putsch of the style headed by Wolfgang Kapp was attempted in Rome; no foreign troops, stiffened with black colonial forces, occupied national territory. Despite the fondness of many Italians for racial stereotypes, especially about their Slav neighbours to the east – Giuriati, for one, deemed all 'Balkan peoples' as 'needing domination'[48] – an ideology of race could not with any conviction rally Italians against a great internal enemy. For all the equivocal nature of its gains, Italy had emerged a victor in the First World War. Although the rise of Fascism was violent enough and killed some 3,000 Italians, (of whom 425 were Fascists),[49] the level of political murder was lower in Italy than in Germany and in quite a few other Central and Eastern European states (though the social murder rate, for example in Sicily and Calabria, remained elevated by European standards). The swiftness of the Fascist rise to power in quite a few ways insulated Italy against the long-lasting effects of the post-war crisis and left it with a history in which compromise and contradiction were still possible. The imagination of Italians had been afflicted by the war and the immediate post-war crisis, but it was eventually clear, after the flutters of 1919–20, that neither the national culture nor that of the Italies had been wrenched out of joint. The softness, compromise, confusion or lack of rigour of Italian Fascism, compared with later fascist movements, were the result.

None the less, 1919 did see the rallying of a new right, which, although for the moment as factionalized as were the socialists, Catholics and returned soldiers, was determined to repel and liquidate what it saw as 'Bolshevism'. The most public cause of the right was Fiume, once the outlet of the Hungarian segment of the Habsburg empire to the southern seas. The right's leader, their *Duce* as his admirers called him,[50] was in retrospect the unlikely figure of the internationally lionized poet, Gabriele D'Annunzio. On 12 September 1919 D'Annunzio, having been enraged by a deal Nitti's government had arranged to internationalize the administration of the little port (it had a population of 49,000),[51] assembled a motley throng and, proclaiming himself the successor to Garibaldi, 'marched' from Ronchi near the old border at Monfalcone to Fiume (though actually D'Annunzio did the trip by car). Here was the Italian version of a *coup d'état*, a proxy seizure of power at an extreme periphery of the nation, yet with the potential to be transposed to Rome and so mounting an evident challenge to the entire political order. D'Annunzio and his followers remained in Fiume for more than a year, and their flamboyant 'poetic revolution' there was to have some influence on Fascist presentation and propaganda.

D'Annunzio was a remarkable personage, one who, in recent times, has been reinscribed into the pantheon of Italian national heroes, despite the part he played in the rise of the Fascist dictatorship. One of the most ironical moments in my own travels in Italy occurred at the tourist site of D'Annunzio's palace, the Vittoriale, at Salò, a building that stands guard over Lago di Garda, ready to repel the next German tourist or northern military invasion. As I marvelled at D'Annunzio's syncretic taste in architecture and furnishing, I had to squeeze past squads of Catholic schoolchildren on a patriotic outing. They were being tantalized with the magic of the poet's life by their supervising nuns. Just what the ghost of that D'Annunzio, who flaunted the fact that every one of his books was condemned on the papal index,[52] is making of this destiny of clichéd reverence from the Church must remain a matter of conjecture.

The future poet and celebrity had been born in 1863 at the Adriatic port of Pescara to a comfortably off family. Proud from an early age of his beautiful ears and flat abdomen, he liked it to be known that he gloried 'in being a Latin' and looked 'on all other races as barbarian'.[53] Something of a child prodigy, D'Annunzio rapidly became the most fabled figure in the ordinarily rather dull and parochial world of Italian literature. His sex life was designed to provoke shock, awe and envy. He let it be known that he favoured satanism and praised incest, at least when conjoined in the 'cause of Beauty'. After the war, he wrote with characteristically wide-ranging or disjointed sentiment: 'a greyhound or a well-trained racehorse, the legs of [dancer] Ida Rubinstein, the body of an Ardito fording the Piave, the form and structure of my highly polished cranium – these are the most beautiful phenomena in the world'. His secretary claimed that, on one occasion, D'Annunzio solemnly confided to his 'Legionaries', as he loved to call his following at Fiume, that he could levitate. When they reacted by bursting into laughter, quick as a flash he admitted that he had been joking.[54]

D'Annunzio boasted that he could never work at anything in an ordered or stock fashion, asserting that his best pieces were the result of an orgasmic frenzy of activity, even though his speed of composition may have been slowed by his studiously antiquated habit of writing with a goose quill.[55] He let it be known that he salivated a lot while penning his thoughts and kept four or five handkerchiefs ready on his desk. He had the Arditi slogan *me ne frego* (I don't give a stuff) inscribed in gold on a banner hanging from his bedhead (perhaps with ambiguous implication).[56] For all his studied impetuosity, he spent quite a bit of time polishing ties with such accommodating, wealthy and ideally generous patrons as Luigi Albertini, the scrupulously liberal editor of Italy's best-regarded paper, *Il Corriere della Sera*, and Oscar Sinigaglia, a leading entrepreneur who was another of Italy's patriotic Jews. Despite D'Annunzio's national reputation and his apparent fostering of nationalism, in practice he spent extended periods outside Italy, believing, as did most serious practitioners of the arts in his generation, that a man was nothing without the recognition of Paris.

Contemporaries were astonished by D'Annunzio and a fascination has lingered into our own era – in the early 1970s the Italian Republic printed a postage stamp honouring the poet's artistic achievement. Too open-mouthed an astonishment, however, is naive and unnecessary. Despite the many bizarre 'leaders' who have ruled over, and rule over, countries and regions in the twentieth and twenty-first centuries, a D'Annunzio successfully holding major office in a great power for a generation is hard to conceive. He himself made no bones about the fact that anything to do with economics sent him straight to sleep. Day-to-day administration was scarcely his forte.[57] Yet, between 1919 and 1922, quite a few significant and intelligent Italians viewed him as the logical chief of a new and post-war Italy.

How can they have been so admiring? Part of the answer lies, predictably enough, in the artfully outrageous charm of D'Annunzio's words. He, after all, was the ardent poet who, during the intervention crisis of 1915, had, with cheerful blasphemy, adapted the Sermon on the Mount to national ends: 'Blessed are those who return in Victory, for they shall see the face of the new Rome, its brow crowned again by Dante with the triumphal beauty of Italy.'[58] Sacramental contact with the poet, participation in his half-religious service, might leave his adepts convinced that the wars of the nation passeth all understanding. At Fiume, D'Annunzio soon established a *mise-en-scène* that, for a time, broke down what might be termed the fifth wall of the political stage by confusing theatrical drama and contemporary politics. While he could successfully suspend disbelief among his audience, D'Annunzio could play at being the head man; however tiny the set, it could seem to encompass all the world. There was music: the Arditi song, 'Giovinezza', now began its fame (soon it was to become the Fascist anthem). There was ritual. D'Annunzio engaged a number of choruses: returned soldiers, local women, other right-wing politicians, non-Italian fans visiting the place, in a dialogue which was enlivened with the war cry *'Eia, eia, eia, alalà'* and culminated in a bellowed *'A Noi'* ('the world belongs to us'). Each shout was soon to turn Fascist. D'Annunzio's Fiume coursed with high-flown words. He effortlessly coined phrases which sounded meaningful, which have continued to fascinate those who might otherwise be thought likely to be sceptical historians and to which postmodernism and the 'cultural turn' have granted a renewed significance. One such was the term *la città olocausta* (Holocaust City);[59] the poet had revived an adjective whose influence was destined to extend far beyond Fiume.

For all his nationalism, D'Annunzio could channel his flood of words towards foreigners – Croat nationalists, who disliked the Serb-led Yugoslav state, negotiators from the Irish Republican Army, colonial people in Egypt or elsewhere, groaning under the yoke of the British and French empires, a Japanese Italophile who was very likely the only Samurai in the Italian Army in the First World War.[60] There was also a foreign policy of a piratical kind; on 14 November Fiuman forces seized Zara, further down the Dalmatian coast. There were even *pourparlers* with an engineer named Vodovosoff, who said he represented the USSR, and D'Annunzio, genial and good-hearted when in the mood, did not eschew conversation with potentially friendly Italian socialists.[61] Similarly he dealt blithely with followers of Bela Kun, fled from the failed Bolshevik revolution in Hungary, and told an anarchist that, 'really', he stood for 'communism without dictatorship'.[62]

Despite this scatter-shot of non-Wilsonian internationalism to a global audience, D'Annunzio's greater and more malign impact was on Italy. In early 1920 the interventionist and syndicalist Alceste De Ambris, who had replaced the more respectable Giuriati as the poet's political secretary, was the major influence in drafting the Carta del Carnaro, a constitution which placed the cultural construction of 'new' men and women at its heart. Detecting too much meaning in its detail may be a mistake, but the Carta did express a sort of corporatism; one of its three electoral bodies (more than adequate for a town of Fiume's size) was to be based on sixty candidates, proportionately divided between different types of employment. Ten were to be industrial workers or peasants, ten employers, five schoolteachers and students, and five public servants. Mussolini's dictatorship eventually proclaimed that it was building a 'corporate state' and its own categories owed quite a bit to the terms pioneered by De Ambris. To be sure, the charter was, predictably enough, full of contradictions: it managed to preach decentralization and the virtues of localism, while crediting a major role to the charismatic leader. It also contained a number of references to the inscription of a 'new religion', while preaching the freedom of all existing faiths.[63] Rather than crafting a genuinely revolutionary society, beneath the fragile glitz D'Annunzio remained the incarnation of sensuality and self-indulgence. He was not alone – by 1920 the surviving legionaries, especially the more wealthy, middle or upper-class airmen, were alleged to relieve their tension over the continuing occupation and the town's diminishing food supplies through cocaine and rampant sexual promiscuity.[64]

The occupation of Fiume, the city's 'lyrical dictatorship', was moving not to a holocaust but to a less fiery and grandiose fall. In June 1920 Nitti's government collapsed and the new Prime Minister was none other than Giovanni Giolitti. The arrival of this 'neutralist' and 'arch-corrupter', the embodiment of that Italy which had existed before 1914, appalled all those seeking some form of new politics. However, Giolitti knew how to cope with a poseur like D'Annunzio. Nitti tried to treat Fiume as a domestic problem; Giolitti turned it into a matter of foreign affairs. His Foreign Minister, Carlo Sforza, was encouraged to open talks with the Yugoslavs, with whom improved relations were imaginable, the last Italian troops in Albania having been brought home in early August. By 12 November 1920 a deal was ready; Giolitti and Sforza had adroitly used British and French approval to obtain in the Treaty of Rapallo a generous border which assigned all Istria to Italy, plus four islands off the Dalmatian coast and Zara. Fiume became a free state, but one with a land connection to the *patria*.

In response, D'Annunzio tempestuously declared war on Italy, launching some raids on nearby towns or islands. But he could no longer rely on the sympathy of Italian military and naval forces stationed in the region nor on the local population, who yearned for a quieter life. He certainly could not hope to defeat Italy in war. In an event the right dubbed the 'Christmas of blood', the last Fiuman legionaries were expelled in a brief campaign, beginning on 24 December. Fifty-three died in the skirmishing; D'Annunzio, despite his reiterated boast that he stood for 'either Fiume, or death', did not.

In some historical accounts, at Fiume D'Annunzio pioneered 'modern politics'. Profound traces of the D'Annunzian style have been detected in 'the political behaviour of western society since the Great war', while, in his own estimation, D'Annunzio acted as a sort of 'John the Baptist' for Mussolini.[65] Each claim seems exaggerated. However, there can be little doubt that the alarums in Fiume did condition the behaviour of the more serious segments of the Italian right. One person from that zone, Benito Mussolini, the man who, in 1919–20, was still in the process of demonstrating that he was the new right's most ruthless and successful political operator, had to steer a careful course through the shoals which surfaced as a result of D'Annunzio's flamboyant but capricious actions. How had this other, soon to be greater, *Duce* and his Fascism been progressing through the turmoil of 1919?

Mussolini ended the war with an unnerving sense that his moment had passed. For all the vivacity of his paper, *Il Popolo d'Italia*, and the splash it had created in Milan and elsewhere, for all that by now a number of temporarily loyal clients acknowledged his leadership, Mussolini still could not compete with D'Annunzio and other ambitious new rightists as a public figure. He was not yet a celebrity; his charisma fascinated only a few. It was true that, during the latter stages of the world conflict, he had hit on the promising formula of rule by the *trincerocrazia* (the self-made aristocracy of those who had served in the trenches). 'Italy', he remarked optimistically in December 1917, 'is heading towards a two-party system: those who have been and those who have not, those who have fought and those who have not, those who have worked and the parasites.' With a pretentious re-evocation of his time as a Marxist, he foresaw in this division some possibility of 'the synthesis of the antithesis: class and nation'.[66] The other word that he now endorsed was 'productivism'; it sounded well to those industrialists at Ansaldo and elsewhere to whom Mussolini looked for financial backing.[67]

Despite his occasional yearnings for the comradeship of his socialist past, Mussolini had burned his boats with the movement in 1915 and thereafter unmercifully damned those who had stayed behind. He was equally to the fore in denouncing 'the horrors of Leninism' and its 'policy of terror'.[68] On 1 August 1918 he removed the word socialist from the masthead of his paper, replacing it with the phrase 'journal of soldiers and producers'.[69] But, with the coming of peace, just what might become a winning line was hard at first to see. On 23 November Mussolini announced that he wanted to set up a Fascio per la costituente (Union for a Constituent Assembly) to plan the new world. He did not refine its purpose except to proclaim intemperately that 'the old parties are like the corpses you keep as relics and it will not be difficult to drown them all'.[70]

An appeal to returning soldiers and talk of unashamed violence, both were set in his mind, although qualification about everything else was possible since, as he repeated, 'we are those who do not nurture political prejudices'.[71] This still-not-quite Fascism, in other words, was flexible about such basic matters as whether Italy should be a republic or a monarchy, clerical or anti-clerical and liberal or state interventionist in economic form. When, in March 1919, Mussolini addressed the meeting at the Piazza San Sepolcro, destined to be celebrated as the founding moment of Fascism (the hall in which the event took place was owned by the businessmen's group, the Alleanza Industriale e Commerciale), he was still open to persuasion in his ideological stance. His ambition, he stated, was first to conjoin those who belonged to 'the nation, the war and the Victory' and so 'to start with the interventionism' of 1915. As usual he directed a volley of hostile phrases at his socialist enemies, while hinting that he was not averse to their methods. 'We demand the right and proclaim the duty to transform Italian life, if it proves inevitable using revolutionary methods.' Any who tried to portray him and his friends as 'conservatives or reactionaries' were 'downright imbeciles', he maintained.[72] No wonder that a contemporary reported that Mussolini, when he spoke, was straining to say what his audience wanted to hear (it was a comment to be made frequently about a dictator who never renounced the value of tactics). His words, somewhere beneath their formal message, carried the hope that the audience would accept him as the 'Fascist' leader. Where he might lead them, or they him, could be left to the future to decide.

Reflecting this ideological pliability, those who came to Piazza San Sepolcro were diverse in their social base and cultural and political ambition. More prominent than Mussolini for the moment were the Futurists and their charismatic, if wayward, leader, Marinetti. Modern, adventurous (if sometimes silly) on social or artistic issues, they were likely to harbour an old-fashioned contempt for the masses and were therefore separated from Mussolini's hopes to bring the people into the nation. From December 1918 a network of *fasci futuristi* (Futurist cells) grew in urban centres from the predictable Florence, Venice, Milan and Rome to the less likely Palermo, Cassino and Cagliari. Among their members were such significant Fascists-to-be as Giuseppe Bottai, Olao Gaggioli and Piero Bolzon, this last an

Ardito officer with pre-war experience in Argentina, who, after Caporetto, had sworn vengeance on those who had reduced Italy to its defeat.[73] Similarly Vecchi, who actually chaired the meeting on 23 March, and the writer Mario Carli, another who liked to think of himself as a Futurist, were pondering ways to draft returned Arditi into a movement and had hit on the propagandist value of using their black shirts as a peacetime standard.[74]

The three hundred or so who approved the launching of the *fasci di combattimento* – their number was greatly multiplied when the official history of the movement was written after 1922 and their unity and sense of allegiance to Mussolini much exaggerated – were doing little more than again manifesting the sense among returned officers and non-socialist intellectuals that the cessation of war demanded a 'new' politics. Nine women attended, most significant among them Regina Terruzzi, a Milanese feminist, who sought to combine nationalist and humanitarian sympathies and who became an important, if embattled, figure under the dictatorship.[75]

In the aftermath of Piazza San Sepolcro, members did not flock in and the *fasci* established themselves slowly. By the end of the year there were thirty-one, with a total membership limited to 870, although the sort of ex-Ardito who liked to keep pistols on his desk and machine guns in his living room, and patriotic high-school boys, rendered feverish by the war's premature end, did join in some numbers. The opening of the Milan branch of the *fasci* was followed by the foundation of one at Genoa. Next came a number of other, generally northern, centres, including Turin. Naples, Trieste, Bologna, Cremona, Venice, Forlì and Zara opened membership lists from April. Rome and Florence had to wait for their founding until the summer. The trickle of Fascists can be contrasted with the flood of returning soldiers backing the ANC and its related organizations, which, at the end of 1919, were reckoned to have 20,000 members (they boasted 167 sections in Sardinia alone).[76] Even in December 1920, despite a noticeable growth over the last six months, there were still only 88 *fasci* branches, containing some 20,000 members.[77] Mussolini's home *paese* of Predappio did not open a proper party office until late September 1922.[78] Despite the troubles sweeping so many parts of Italy in the immediate post-war period, Fascism did not automatically and instantaneously locate a mass base.

The meagre number of these 'Fascists of the first hour', as they would be reverentially called after 1922, makes the assessment of early Fascist programmes a doubtful exercise. Any analysis is rendered more problematic by Mussolini's insistence that the movement must range freely in identifying its targets. In 1918 he had coined the slogan: 'the man who never changes his mind . . . is a blockhead'.[79] From the start, the *fasci* were most reliable in their definition of their enemy – official socialism and any who traduced the nationalist version of Italy's war. None the less, this early Fascism did often sound radical, even 'socialist', in everything except its foreign policy and reading of contemporary history (both in Italy and in Russia). In June 1919, for example, the *fasci* maintained that they wanted the voting age lowered to eighteen (Mussolini had frequently talked about youth bringing zest to anything Fascists might do).[80] Similarly the *fasci* demanded the abolition of the gerontocratic Senate and its replacement with a corporative chamber, staffed by those expert in 'work with their hands and brains, industry, commerce and agriculture'. Other initial *fasci* aims were the institution of an eight-hour day, minimum pay, participatory democracy on the factory floor and improved state insurance for workers. Landowners should be obliged to cultivate their land and any fields that were not utilized productively should be handed over to peasant cooperatives, with a preference for those run by returned soldiers. The army should become popular in its nature, with regular short periods of training for all. The *fasci* favoured progressive tax and the punitive review of war contracts and profits, as well as the seizure of the goods held by religious houses. State education (Catholic schools were to be eliminated) must be better funded and must aim to act as the disciplining academy of the nation. The bureaucracy must be purged and replaced by a more energetic and active staff. Finally, Italy, in its dealings abroad, 'must express national will and efficiency', moving forward with 'a dynamic policy, that is, one which does not tend to shore up the hegemony of the present plutocratic powers'.[81]

The programme was drafted, publicized and then left to gather dust. More important than any set of ideas was the response of the *fasci* and Mussolini to events. One paving a path to the future had occurred in Milan on 15 April 1919, when Vecchi, Marinetti and their friends had launched an armed assault on the offices of the socialist paper *Avanti!* This attack was inscribed in Fascist history as the birth of 'squadrism'. Mussolini did not accompany his social betters and their clients on the raid but he did justify their strong-arm action in an interview which he gave immediately afterwards to the conservative paper *Il Giornale d'Italia*. It was, he said grandiloquently, 'the act of a crowd, the act of returned soldiers, the act of the people, stuffed to the gills with Leninist blackmail'. 'We of the *fasci*', he added somewhat pretentiously, assume 'full moral responsibility for the episode'. In a further attempt to ingratiate himself with his wealthy and influential readership, he concluded with the enticing message to any who liked the idea of routing socialism that his movement had 'no political prejudices' and was open to all ideas.[82] To impress those Italians who carried weight in the nation, Mussolini began to steer clear of Marinetti who impoliticly treasured the neologism *svaticanizzare* (to de-Vaticanize), loudly demanding the expulsion of the sometime neutralist Pope Benedict from Rome.[83] Mussolini's more practical earthiness and his movement's general willingness to accept the real world, the coming *Duce* implied, could move beyond the *outré*, so self-indulgently favoured by the Futurists.

More complex a matter was the Fiume affair and the covert duel it entailed between Mussolini and D'Annunzio as the rival *duci* of the new right. Mussolini, chary of the poet's presently greater charisma, did not march with the legionaries to the Adriatic port, although he did, then and later, engage in correspondence with D'Annunzio. The editor of these letters has noted the way that Mussolini, until he was installed as dictator in 1925, astutely tailored his words 'to win over the recipient'.[84] Mussolini's first reaction to the expedition was that it would soon prove a flop and, when it did in time collapse, he quickly accepted the Treaty of Rapallo as a *fait accompli*. In between he tried to appear sympathetic enough to D'Annunzio so as not to blunt the nationalist and 'revolutionary' thrust the poet was embodying, while also staying sufficiently distant from the Fiumans' fondness for rhetorical and personal excess. Especially Mussolini tried to cash in on the destabilizing effect of the crisis, successfully reminding any who noticed of his leadership skills.[85] On 7 October 1920 he made a literally flying visit to Fiume – the short-lived first secretary of the *fasci*

(May to July 1919) was Attilio Longoni, a celebrated airman.[86] That trip allowed Mussolini to appear at the first national congress of the *fasci* in Florence on 9–10 October, dressed in a flyer's kit, proclaiming himself a new-style, modern, hero, who could brazenly challenge the heavens from his open cockpit. Mussolini was trying to fix his unstable movement's attention on the coming elections and yet again took the occasion to state, with staccato words designed not to hit a single target, that the *fasci* were 'not republican, not socialist, not democratic, not conservative, not nationalist' but rather 'a synthesis of all negations and all positives'. More tellingly, he pronounced that 'only the intelligent and the strong-willed' had the right to decide the country's fate.[87] 'Was there anyone more intelligent and strong-willed than he?' his audience was meant to ask.

For all Mussolini's cunning manoeuvres the elections did not go well. In his new home city, Milan, the aspirant *Duce* obtained fewer than 5,000 votes. *Fasci* candidates elsewhere did no better. *Il Popolo d'Italia* threatened to exhaust its credit and Mussolini talked about selling it and so abandoning his most important and still very personal political weapon. As 1919 came to its end, Italy may still have been lurching along in political, economic and cultural crisis. But so, too, were the *fasci di combattimento* and their leader.

5

Becoming a Fascist

If ever a word was in the air, then in Italy around the time of the First World War, it was 'Fascist'. *Fascista, Fascismo, Fascio*: each turned up on numerous occasions and in diverse settings. Doctor deputies, endeavouring to be a pressure group, formed themselves into a Fascio Medico Parlamentare as early as 1906.[1] More tellingly, those politicians who advanced from interventionism in 1915 to rouse a more strenuous war effort called themselves the Fascio parlamentare di difesa nazionale (Parliamentary union for national defence); the group embraced a range of politicians from Antonio Salandra to Leonida Bissolati, 152 of them.[2] In late 1918 the conservative Salandra talked enthusiastically about the idea of the war-time *fasci* staying together after the war; they would, he thought, constitute a hard-working and effective cohort (the word he actually used, *falange*, was destined to develop a history of its own in right-wing politics). Its ranks could be filled with 'men of good will'. The more astringently liberal Luigi Albertini, like so many others convinced that the world had changed irredeemably since 1915, suggested that the *fasci* 'from now on, must take over from the old parties'.[3] During the war, more radical elements, especially such syndicalists as Alceste De Ambris, Filippo Corridoni and Michele Bianchi, men with ties to Mussolini but by no means automatically yet under his sway, had called themselves the Fascio d'azione rivoluzionaria (Union for revolutionary action). In a more commonplace manner, a patriotic journalist hoped early in the conflict that Italy would be able to forge a Fascio balcanico among the Balkan states.[4] In 1918, another wondered why, historically, the subject peoples of the Habsburg Empire had not managed to unite in a *fascio* against their German and Magyar exploiters.[5] A

Fascio Wilsoniano d'azione fleetingly assembled those who thought the American president might usher in the national millennium for Italy.[6]

With the arrival of peace, the profile of the word was enhanced further. One careful historian has tabulated sixteen organizations that included it in their title in 1919.[7] They spanned the political stage from a Fascio liberale and a Fascio socialista comunista (an anarchist group) to a Fascio universitario dei partiti nazionalisti (for Nationalist students) and a Fascio degli studenti delle scuole medie (for middle school pupils). Railway workers could join a Fascio dei ferrovieri and post-office officials the Fascio rivoluzionario dei postaltelegrafici. At Imola, one of the smaller urban centres on the Po plain, the Fascio libertario imolese signed up a sprinkling of local libertarians. At Mantua, ex-interventionists, rallied by talk about the need to constitute a 'strong' state and re-impose 'values', formed the Fascio delle forze liberali e democratiche and began publishing a paper called *Il combattente mantovano* (The soldier from Mantua).[8]

Under the dictatorship this initial ambivalence in meaning was expunged from memory and the word Fascism was credited with just one significance and one long and glorious history. The key now became the Latin word *fasces*, the term for the bundle of sticks bound with rope and armed with an axe that the lictors (*littori*) had carried in procession before a consul (and archaeologists dutifully detected *fasces* among Etruscan remains in the Florence museum, for example).[9]

Lictors carried the sticks and axe with solemn ceremony in order to symbolize that the office entailed the authority to judge and condemn. In the hands of Fascist propagandists, the word Fascism became a vehicle of *romanità*; it expressed the boasted classical Roman inheritance of the regime. There was a linked modern meaning. The *fasces* pledged national unity above all; each of the sticks represented a sector of society, organically bound into the corporate system. No class, gender, regional or other form of division could weaken a Fascist state, locked together as it was, a proletarian nation, needing to end subjugation by the plutocratic, established, great powers, in a Darwinian struggle of the national fittest; one Italian people, one Fascist state, one *Duce* at the head.

In late 1919 this narrowing of sense had not yet happened. None the less, between then and October 1922, quite a few Italians began to think of themselves as Fascists; they became the self-conscious followers of Mussolini or the members of what in November 1921 changed from the relatively autonomous Fasci di combattimento into a single Partito Nazionale Fascista (National Fascist Party). Who were these early Fascists? What events and attitudes converted them to their creed? How, why and to what end did they wield axes, sticks, clubs, pistols, machine guns and castor oil? How violent, how intrinsically and viscerally violent, were these Fascists?

The elections of 1919 had scarcely dispersed the atmosphere of crisis that hung over the political world. Nitti's personality was still failing to elicit enthusiasm from Italian society or, despite his far-sighted recognition of the new global business and financial role of the USA, from foreign bankers. During the early months of 1920, the lira tumbled in value – it was worth 13.99 to the US dollar in January and 22.94 in April – and, as a result, international credit remained hard to find.[10] The appointment of the aged Luigi Luzzatti – a paternalist expert in local banking since the 1860s who first held office in 1891 – to the Treasury after a ministerial reshuffle in March, was a token of desperation and seeming proof of the exhaustion of Liberal talent. The collapse of Nitti's third government in June was unlikely to improve matters. The resuscitated Giolitti had a more distinguished political career than Luzzatti, as well as being a shrewder and more effective executive. But he was only just Luzzatti's junior and his neutralism (however qualified in reality) made him unacceptable to any who still deemed Italy's First World War a positive enterprise.

Giolitti talked of relaunching the economy and of defending social justice with a swingeing attack on war profits. Legislation to effect these measures swiftly won parliamentary approval. The devil lay in the detail, however, and any effort to collect monies from those who had benefited unacceptably in wartime soon languished. But Giolitti was now identified with these and other taxes on business, earning the ironic soubriquet the 'Bolshevik with the *Annunziata*' (the 'Collar of the *Annunziata*' was the senior royal honour). Giolitti was rather more successful in deregulating sectors of the economy that were still operating under wartime controls. Notably he eliminated the subsidy on grain, despite a decline in national production from 52 million quintals in 1911–12 to 38 million in 1920.[11] This effort to give bread a social price had helped drive the budget into severe deficit and, once the subsidy was cancelled, the national accounts did move back towards surplus. Even so, reconversion of the war economy was proving difficult and the implications became plain in the early summer when the great heavy industrial firms Ilva and Ansaldo had to be bailed out and restructured in drastically slimmed-down form. A prolonged rescue attempt for their chief financier, the Banca Italiana di Sconto, failed and the bank collapsed at the end of December.[12] Times were tough. GDP had fallen by 14.5 per cent in 1919; it declined by another 7.6 per cent in 1920 and by 1.8 per cent in 1921, before the graph turned upwards, in belated recovery from the war.[13] The cost of living, starting from a 1914 index of 100, had spurted to 264 in 1918, 268 in 1919, 352 in 1920 and 417 in 1921, before settling back to 414 in 1922.[14]

Accompanying this economic malaise was continuing and, for much of 1920, worsening, social disorder. Days lost to strikes by agricultural workers spiralled from 3,437,000 in 1919 to 14,171,000 in 1920 (eventually falling to 407,000 in 1921, a diminution which was testimony to the Fascist advance then occurring in the countryside). Factory workers had struck for 18,888,000 days in 1919 and that number fell only slightly to 16,398,000 in 1920 (7,773,000 in 1921). Peasants did well in 1919, the year of their union power, but by 1920–21 their real wages were in decline. Factory workers, by contrast, made huge gains in both 1919 and 1920 and thereafter held their own in 1921–2.[15]

The most dramatic event in 1920 was the so-called 'occupation of the factories', which, at the end of August, began at the Alfa Romeo plant in Milan, soon spread to Turin and Genoa and eventually involved 500,000 workers across the engineering sector. The metalworkers' union, FIOM (Federazione Italiana degli operai metallurgici), had been wrestling with employers throughout the year, while the union leaders, themselves mainly moderate in their politics, pressed for a 30 per cent pay rise. A bitter strike in March had been followed by the first major post-war lockout in April. The relative success of this latter act gave owners the impression that they carried national political weight. Many drew the lesson that, in future, they must depend more on themselves than on the army or police to protect their interests. Before 1914 Giolitti had stood for the idea that, faced with worker–employer conflict, the government must 'hold the ring', ensure that violence did not get out of hand on either side and engage its good offices to foster a settlement. This stance of apparent impartiality had never been a line that enthused all employers. In 1920–21 it seemed further proof that the Giolittian version of liberalism needed to be remodelled for the Spartan present and the toughly competitive future.

During the first days of September factory occupation went smoothly. Violence was avoided. The workers took pains to discourage drunkenness and disorder, any thieving was prevented or punished[16] and the factory councils, which had come into existence beforehand on many work-sites, proved capable of maintaining production. The interpretation by socialist party intellectuals of what the occupation meant, however, was more troublesome. Gramsci, hinting at an optimism of the intellect and a pessimism of the will, preached both cultural revolution and discipline: 'The material fact of the occupation of the factories, this act of authority by the working class which violates the sacred principle of private property and destroys the traditional schemas of social hierarchies, is in itself the origin and cause of new feelings, new passions, both in the consciousness of individuals and in the collective consciousness of the masses. Never have the most advanced worker elements needed cooler heads than at this moment . . . It is necessary for them to make every worker aware that he has become a soldier; that he has his orders; that he must be solidly inserted in the proletarian ranks, and that any defection, any weakness, any impulsive gesture, must be considered as open treachery and a counter-revolutionary act.'[17]

Among the employers, Giovanni Agnelli of Fiat was impressed enough by the occupation and the decorum and efficiency of the workers' initial management of production to contemplate adopting a version of mixed executive system in his company, resembling what came to be called worker participation. Fiat might be converted into some sort of cooperative.[18] In these circumstances, Bruno Buozzi, the reformist leader of FIOM, found all sorts of political figures and potential political figures anxious to discuss with him what the possible implications of worker rule might be. One person who expressed a willingness to adapt to a new industrial system was Benito Mussolini (despite his initial and characteristic statement on 5 September that the *fasci* must oppose with all their strength 'a Bolshevik experiment').[19] However, the longer the occupation lasted the more its purpose became blurred. Was it fundamentally an industrial dispute or was it the overture to full-blown socialist revolution? Giolitti, with his usual wiliness, gambled that only a few intellectuals contemplated the latter, even though he further alienated the more vengeful of the rich by telegraphing to the prefect of Milan the instruction that industrialists should not expect to be sustained by government, police or military support. Meanwhile, the details of a settlement began to be framed, and, on 25 September, the workers surrendered their control, having won a battle over pay and conditions but having lost the political war. Land occupations, which had been attempted simultaneously and spontaneously in parts of the south, resulted in even less advantage (and by now were being discouraged by the cautious leadership of Federterra).[20] From October 1920 the initiative in social action was passing to the possessing classes and so to a politics of the new right.

How had those who were to become Mussolini's henchmen been reacting to the ups and downs in the national story since 1918? In Cremona, Roberto Farinacci had had a good war.[21] In 1916–17 he served for a time at the front as a corporal in the Bersaglieri but, before long, either his skills as a railwayman or his lingering connections with Bissolati and Freemasonry gave him the chance for cushy work as a patriotic propagandist. Farinacci's paper, *La Squilla*, attracted enough credit to summon patriots to the cause, as its title promised. Farinacci also found time to lead a Lega patriottica (Patriotic league) and a Società Giordano Bruno, with the pleasing purpose of preaching the gospel of anti-clericalism. By now, Farinacci was a man who mattered at Cremona and one who let it be known that he marched the town streets, armed and ready (the story spread that he had shot out of hand two deserters who got in his way).[22] He did not confine himself to his own city. As early as October 1919 he expelled chattering socialists from the Caffè

Centrale in Florence, openly and without rebuke brandishing his pistol as he pursued them through the town.[23] Along with two sidekicks from Cremona, Farinacci had attended the *fasci* meeting at Piazza San Sepolcro and been acknowledged as a member of the new organization's executive. On 11 April he founded a branch of the *fasci* in his city. Its first members were the previous adherents of the Lega patriottica and the Bruno Association, their names swapped from one roll to another. Despite this opting for 'Fascism' (of some kind), Farinacci had not altogether severed his connection with Bissolati, for all the old reformist's readiness to compromise over the territorial settlement of the Adriatic, and was pleased still to call the town's most prominent politician his *duce*.[24] Under the Fascist regime, Farinacci would posthumously enrol his old patron as a backer of his cause in Cremona, tie him in spirit with Garibaldi and Mazzini and salute the reformist's heroism and self-sacrifice in volunteering for the front as a fifty-eight-year-old sergeant.[25]

The effrontery of this young man on the make, like that of so many other fledgling Fascists, knew few bounds. In the summer of 1919 Farinacci used his contacts to gain special entry as a veteran to a law course at Modena University, with its promise, after graduation, of wealth and status. Under the dictatorship Farinacci was to take his degree, seeing no problem in brazenly plagiarizing his final dissertation from another's work – Mussolini kept handy an incriminating copy in his office.[26] More patron than client, Farinacci enriched himself. For Farinacci, the first plank in his Fascism – by then it was clear – was personal upward social mobility. The second plank was violence.

Before the war ended, Farinacci, anxious to assert his authority in the province of Cremona, as well as in its capital, had made himself the spokesman for local middling peasants, hopeful of revising upwards their contracts with the larger landowners, while suspicious of the revolutionary socialism and Federterra membership of the day labourers. Farinacci was certainly no fan of social equality. As early as July 1919 he pulled Cremona railway workers out of the ranks of CGdL and campaigned aggressively against the call for a general strike. In November an early raid against alleged 'subversives' in the *paese* of Piadena threatened ruin, until Farinacci was rescued by the arrival of two armoured vehicles, one full of Fascists, the other of police. In natural (and frequently to be repeated) harmony, they quelled the peasant socialists.[27]

Farinacci's ties of mutual obligation to those with social, financial and political credit to spare were confirmed at the beginning of 1920 when he changed the name of his paper to the Mazzinian-sounding *La Voce del Popolo Sovrano* (The Voice of the Sovereign People); as a man pledged to social unity, he could now rely on more advertising monies than in the past.[28] In May 1920, at the *fasci* conference held in Milan, Farinacci was one of the few members of the original central committee of the movement to be re-elected (more than half lost their positions at this time).[29] By the summer of that year, fitting the rightward drift of the movement so obvious at the conference, he had become an active 'squadrist'. Now he and his followers, armed and motorized, launched raids throughout the province of Cremona with the purpose of subduing communist strikes and overwhelming the political and social infrastructure of both socialists[30] and Catholics; Farinacci remained the sworn enemy of Miglioli and his peasant union. The *ras* was especially ready to parade his power within Cremona's walls. On 5 September an affray occurred in the central Piazza Roma on a day when the Lombard *fasci* had gathered in the town to listen to a rousing speech by Mussolini. Two Fascists and two socialists died in the brawl, with Farinacci being briefly jailed until it was reported that ballistic tests had failed to prove that his gun had fired the fatal bullets.

Social violence and self-interest apart, were there any other features of Farinacci's ideology worth remarking on, except for his keen ambition and the fact that he came to Fascism after he had determined to make himself the boss of his town by whatever means (in late 1920, with lingering localism, he advocated each branch of the *fasci* pursuing its own line in the approaching administrative elections)?[31] Perhaps, despite what will be seen to have been his considerable ability under the regime to retain a certain independence as he sought to understand the world and his place in it, Farinacci did believe in his *Duce* (although he rarely called him such). But did such faith depend on Mussolini's star always tracking upwards? Probably. Farinacci was one Fascist who is not well explained by historian

Emilio Gentile's view of a totalitarian ideology inscribing a 'new state of mind' on its militant and crusading followers. The *ras* of Cremona, one of the first thirty-five Fascists elected to parliament in April 1921, was a man better understood as a rough and tumble boss than as a true believing fanatic. Farinacci did not so much strive to bring 'mythical thought to power'[32] as to enjoy the fleshpots available to those in authority and to win and retain them for himself, his family, friends and clients by whatever means necessary, even through the evocation of myth.

More polite in his origins and preferred image than Farinacci but equally murderous was Italo Balbo. This interventionist student, patriot, volunteer (and Freemason) had not begun service on the Alpine front until May 1917. There the young lieutenant was one junior officer of the Alpini among others, although he did brag of his intention to become an aviator. He was due to start a training course to this end in October but the crisis of Caporetto required his return to the front. In the event, his own battalion was wiped out by the Austrians before he got there. None the less, he did see service on the Tagliamento river and on through 1918, winning two silver medals and a bronze one for bravery in action and participating in the final push against the Austrians at Vittorio Veneto. Balbo was not formally demobilized until May 1920.[33]

In the interim, he took his law degree as well as one in social sciences, completing courses in which he had enrolled in 1914–15. His final thesis was written on 'the economic and social thought of Giuseppe Mazzini' and researched under the supervision of the patriotic historian Niccolò Rodolico. Balbo was a republican but he hated socialists, their unions and cooperatives. In his assessment, Mazzini's virtue lay in his idealism, in contrast to the sordid materialism of his opponents, including Karl Marx. Balbo also found time to marry advantageously; his wife belonged to a wealthy aristocratic family with origins in Dalmatia, a background which may have enhanced Balbo's already existing nationalist and irredentist slant on the border in the east. At university in Florence, Balbo was soon editing a paper, *L'Alpino*, in the cause of returned soldiers. He worked with Giunta on the anti-socialist right of the ANC, his political stance being that the nation must be defended and the victory maintained against any who sought to lacerate social unity. He backed D'Annunzio at Fiume with words and money, using *L'Alpino* to collect funds for the cause.

At the end of 1919, however, Balbo relinquished his editorship and returned to his home town of Ferrara, still unsure of his career. As he scribbled into a diary to be published in 1932 for the Decennale or tenth anniversary celebrations of the March on Rome, he had come back from war filled with a 'hatred for politics and politicians' (except, of course, for promising 'new' ones like himself). The 'shameful peace' and the 'systematic humiliation of all those Italians who tried to preserve the cult of the [wartime] heroes' disgusted him. Had he fought 'to hand back the country to Giolitti who sold off every ideal? No. Better to deny all, destroy all, renew all, from the base.'[34]

Within Ferrara and even more in its rural hinterland, the present enemy was not so much Giolitti as the socialists and their industrial and peasant unions. Already by 1910–11 the social situation of the peasantry in the province had become explosive, with landowners and their day labourers locked in radical and sometimes murderous disputes.[35] In 1919–20 compromise was even less likely. The local peasant league believed that its gains were now so sure that there was no need to preserve an alliance between the day labourers, who constituted the majority of its members, and various middling peasants, elevated in status and wealth by their rental or sharecropping arrangements with the owners. Such people, union chiefs argued, were objectively the agents of the great landholders 'in maintaining and prolonging their privileges and rule over the proletarian classes'.

Such an all-or-nothing posture stimulated anti-socialist forces to a counter-attack, especially after a massive land strike in August 1920 forced another landowner capitulation, despite active resentment being expressed by tenant farmers about the resultant terms and conditions. By October in Ferrara city, where a disdain for the countryside and especially for its poorer and allegedly rougher elements was axiomatic for many citizens, the local, once liberal, paper was sketching a solution to existing ills and displaying for all to see the typical limits of liberalism in times of trouble: 'A man', an editorial maintained, 'must arise' to stem the spread of social 'cancer' and arrest the Gadarene 'race to suicide'. He had no need to worry about parliamentary niceties or adopt half-measures. This individual could rely on 'the unanimous consent of the nation'.[36] At Ferrara, in other words, a preference for a more authoritarian and personal form of government existed before it was clear that Mussolini was to be the man and Fascism his ideology.

During the first months after the end of the war, those who were to become the local Fascists were still divided between syndicalists, Futurists and Arditi. Olao Gaggioli, a pre-war accountant and radical, who had been a volunteer and junior officer in the Arditi, had established the Ferrara Gruppo Futurista in February 1919. Although his presence at Piazza San Sepolcro is contested, by the summer of 1919 Gaggioli was the recognized leader of the local *fasci*. Over the next year, however, the group was beset by personal and ideological schism. The Ferrara *fascio* only resurfaced in the autumn of 1920, at last to become a serious force on the local political scene. Still led by Gaggioli, it could now rely on funds from the landowners and utilized its new wealth to acquire the trucks and weaponry of squadrist raids. Gaggioli explained: 'If someone is attacked by a man who demands his money or his life while a *carabiniere* near by remains unperturbed, he has no choice but to shoot at his attacker. With the *carabiniere* he can settle the account later.' Much as had happened in Cremona, on 20 December a riot in the main square of Ferrara cost the lives of four Fascists (promptly sanctified by the movement's propaganda as 'martyrs') and one socialist. The event united the local prefect and police authorities, liberals and the PPI against what they deemed the overweening socialists and, by March 1921, there were 7,000 enrolled Fascists in Ferrara, the second highest tally in Italy.[37]

Only now did Balbo join them. He had allegedly first noticed the *fasci* when some members marched past the elegant Caffè Estense where, as a wealthy and underemployed young gentleman, he was playing poker. He glanced up and asked cynically: *Chi paga?* (Who is paying the bill?)[38] Some months later, after dealings in a back room about the salary he might receive, in February 1921 Balbo emerged as the Ferrara *fascio* secretary. Dashingly handsome, with a hint of the Mephistophelean about him, none too zealous in his surviving republicanism, well connected both socially and financially, Balbo presented himself as a natural leader. The local prefect, Samuele Pugliese (another Italian patriot of Jewish extraction, a matter of importance at Ferrara given the city's wealthy and influential Jewish community), liked Balbo and sent approving reports about him to Giolitti.[39] After all, Balbo's Fascism at the time was patriotic and anti-socialist and little more than that. Balbo had been looking for an administrative job, having long marked himself out for politics of some kind. Perhaps his muted line on the complex local debates about the huge variety of peasant contracts or about what might be the precise ideological origins and intents of Fascism was further reason why Balbo emerged as the movement's chief at Ferrara. Certainly, his military career gave promise that he would be an active, intrepid and effective leader of the local squads on their aggressive raids into the countryside of Ferrara and beyond. As early as 26–27 April he joined an assault on the working-class redoubt of Castello in Venice and could boast that he and his men had wrenched down a red flag which had been fluttering insultingly on a pennon by the public gardens of that city. The attacking Fascists were for the moment repulsed from Castello, however, discreetly retreating before a hostile hail of stones and roof tiles.[40] Such ventures were in the main locally organized and were not specifically commanded by the movement's small central machine in Milan. As for Mussolini, although the two had met during the 'crusade' for intervention, any serious relationship only commenced after Balbo had assumed the secretaryship at Ferrara. The *Duce*'s charisma can scarcely be credited with making this Fascist.

In Bologna the conversion of Dino Grandi, a person whose values and actions bore quite a lot of comparison with Balbo, had occurred a few months earlier. Grandi, the aspirant anti-socialist but modernizing journalist of pre-1914, became a decorated captain of the Alpini in the war. By then he was already displaying a nimble awareness of the importance of contacts in this life when he moved close to a commanding officer, General Ugo Clerici, the King's adjutant – Grandi tried unsuccessfully to revive the connection during the political talks in the background of the March on Rome in 1922.[41] At the end of the war Grandi was another discontented ex-officer, who ranged across the world of returned soldier politics, joining the ANC and helping to organize a patriotic demonstration when Orlando reached Italy after his rebuff at the Versailles peace-making.[42] Still aiming to advance through journalism (and politics), Grandi took a university degree, in his case in political economy and law, writing his thesis on 'The League of Nations and Free Trade'. He later claimed to have felt sympathy for repressed Arabs, Indians and Irish, to have agreed that Italy was a 'proletarian nation' and to have set his heart on a 'new' politics, framed in a coalition between returned soldiers and youth. Proletariat and bourgeoisie, he thought, could be persuaded to march together in the national cause, just as, before 1918, they had done in the army. Grandi talked of identifying with D'Annunzio at Fiume, although he did not join him there.[43]

For all this familiar mélange of returned junior officer politics, Grandi gave little attention to the *fasci*. Briefly he seems to have wondered whether the Russian Revolution had a positive side, although by 1920 he had decided that Bolshevik practice was proving the pre-war theses of Vilfredo Pareto and Gaetano Mosca that every society soon falls under the control of its active elements. He noted cynically but with a hint of self-insight that intellectuals always worked for their paymasters and were, in reality, timid people, happiest with a quiet life.[44] Meanwhile his home city of Bologna and its surrounding countryside were beset by a social crisis similar to that in Ferrara. The sweeping socialist victories of 1919 prompted at the end of the year the formation of a body calling itself the Associazione Provinciale degli Agricoltori (Provincial Landowners' Association), that rallied associates in the city to forge an iron-hard coalition of 'all productivist forces'.[45]

Local Fascists in Bologna were led for the time being by the Bergamo brothers, Guido and Mario – revolutionary syndicalists, republicans and interventionists, self-consciously men of the left. They did not get far. One commentator claims that, at the end of 1919, the Bologna *fascio* had dwindled to six members.[46] Early in 1920 the brothers were driven out of the movement, with Guido Bergamo complaining that the *fasci* had become the pawns of the landowners and suggesting that their 'multifaceted and inconsistent' programme had switched to the reactionary cause, being above all designed to defeat socialism. Equally, Bergamo stated, the *fasci* gave rein to a violence, learned in the war. 'The pistol takes over from reason,' he warned sadly.[47] Certainly violence was not a form of behaviour to worry the new leader of the Bologna *fascio*, Leandro Arpinati (born 1892), another destined to have a major, if eventually dissident, career in the regime. Arpinati was an ex-anarchist, a friend of Mussolini in his socialist days, a railway worker and an interventionist. By 1920 Arpinati's politics were best defined as populist and opportunist. His entry to the *fasci* governing body in May 1920 also signalled a turn to the right.

Grandi viewed himself as being a cut above such people. His own arrival into Bolognese Fascism occurred suddenly after October 1920, when, at Imola, he was shot at by local revolutionaries. Moving his law office from that town to Bologna, he took the occasion to urge a united front against 'maximalist degeneracy'. Fascism, he argued, was a temporary matter, required only until the authority of the state was restored.[48] None the less, he began to write regularly for the new and successful local *fascio* paper, *L'Assalto* (The Assault) and, despite his formal allegiance to the law, legitimized squadrist violence, while never himself being active in the field (1,936 agricultural and industrial workers were officially recorded as being beaten up or subject to gun-shot wounds during 1921 in the province of Bologna, nineteen having been killed).[49] Grandi's entry into the *fascio* coincided with the so-called 'massacre of the Palazzo d'Accursio' in central Bologna. In the local elections, the socialists had just won 58.2 per cent of the vote in the city. The Fascists were determined to parade their rejection of this poll and, on 4 November 1920, they used the second anniversary of Vittorio Veneto to beat up any 'Reds' they could grab in the urban streets. Two and a half weeks later, they planned to oppose the installation of the new socialist mayor by occupying the town hall and tearing down the red flags exposed there. In the resultant mêlée, some hand-grenades exploded and there was firing on the crowd, with responsibility disputed between the socialists and the Fascists, the latter drawing assistance from attendant *carabinieri*. Nine died and a hundred were injured, but the only death that mattered to propagandists was that of Giulio Giordani, a rightist, who was shot inside the town hall. Through Mussolini's prose[50] and that of others, he was swiftly elevated to the status of an early Fascist martyr and the events of 21 November persuaded quite a few Bolognese, especially those in the respectable classes, that now was the time to rally to the *fascio*, given that, as Mussolini put it ringingly, 'the socialist party is a Russian army which has made camp in Italy'.[51]

In 1921 Grandi became one of the first Fascist members of parliament, winning a seat ahead of Arpinati and at first acting with studied intransigence; in the pages of *L'Assalto* he publicly endorsed a military coup. By 1922, however (he now nominated himself a 'Fascist reformist'),[52] Grandi was again a gentleman of a sort, contesting Arpinati's rumbustious local power.[53] Here was another Fascist who was possessed of his own mind and who had reached his own political position, a potentially transformable one, without special contact with Mussolini.

Farinacci, Balbo and Grandi were to play major roles in the dictatorship and to symbolize crucial aspects of Fascism. In the little history of the *fasci* movement in 1919–21, however, they were still competing against a throng of others for influence and authority. The secretary of the *fasci* from 1919 until November 1921, and so the second figure in the movement after Mussolini, was Umberto Pasella, a man who was to play little part in the regime after its rise to power, except as an elderly backer of the Salò Republic in 1943. Pasella was a syndicalist of relatively humble social origins. Born at Orbetello in southern Tuscany in 1870 and older than most Fascists, he was the son of a prison official and had led an adventurous life, having, for example, been a Garibaldinian volunteer in the successful Cretan rising of 1897 against Turkey. Less romantically, he spent some time as a travelling salesman, supplementing his funds by doubling as a 'theatrical illusionist', who, for payment, could divine the whereabouts of lost or concealed valuables. Searching for a different path to success, he worked as a socialist official in various northern centres, displaying his revolutionary commitment in the approved manner by serving periods in prison for crimes which included fomenting class hatred and insulting the army, religion and morality. None the less, in 1914–15, he swung to the cause of intervention and the nation and, in 1918, was reported to have ready, if needed, a secret committee which could pass government into more reliably interventionist and forceful hands.[54]

Here, then, was a possible candidate to have become a member of what historian Renzo De Felice called the 'emerging middle classes', a sort of Fascist 'new man', if rather a mature one. Pasella's politics within the *fasci* had a rough and ready side. He cannot reliably be placed on the more radical wing of the movement, however. In 1920 he expressed a preference for the monarchy against those party members who retained a yen for republicanism, for example. By then, Pasella was more willing than was his *Duce* (at least for the moment) to seek an electoral deal with the bourgeois parties.[55] Pasella was impatient with D'Annunzio's pirouettes at Fiume – perhaps he jealously preferred his own theatrical displays. Soon Pasella was distancing himself further from his and the *fasci*'s syndicalist origins. He enjoyed the prospect of power but did not countenance a full-scale Fascist reordering of society.[56] Nor did he forswear violence. As national secretary, he cheered news of squadrist action and, at times, fostered it.[57] Just as for young returned-soldier lawyers like Balbo and Grandi, so, too, for Pasella, the great task of the movement had become the dishing of the socialists, especially in the northern countryside, and, to achieve that end, any means would do.

In sum, Pasella's political itinerary was as circuitous as was that of those leading Fascists who were his social superiors. Yet he continued to see himself as embodying the myth of Garibaldi and the idea that a hero could change the world in an instant (even if daily complications evidently made political life in the longer term hard to define). Pasella's fall in autumn 1921 came after he flirted with Mussolini's opponents among the *fasci* chiefs during the debate about the 'Pact of Pacification', a proposed deal with the Socialists.[58] The *Duce*, confirming his own studiously savage personality, shrugged off Pasella's service and dedication without a backward glance.[59] A hint of treachery had lost Pasella any right to remain a Mussolini client.

Pasella's replacement, in what was now the position of Fascist party secretary, was Michele Bianchi (1883–1930), a Calabrian who, moving north, had commenced a political career as a journalist and political organizer before 1914 and was destined to hold on to the party secretaryship until January 1923. With De Ambris and Rossoni, he had been a leader of the syndicalist union, the UIL (Unione Italiana del Lavoro), which had broken away from the mainstream CGdL. Bianchi was not always the most popular or esteemed figure in leftist circles; at Ferrara, where he served as a socialist official for a time, he was held to have driven his Ferrarese wife to an early grave. He attracted accusations that he was both brutal and venal – city gossip said that he accepted bribes.[60] In 1914–15, in what was now becoming a hackneyed refrain for a Fascist, Bianchi opted for interventionism. He volunteered for war service, although, like a number of others, his abilities as a propagandist meant that he spent more time arousing patriotism than actually fighting. In 1919 Bianchi was an early proponent of the *fasci*, having, by October, been installed, according to his biographer, as Mussolini's 'closest collaborator'.[61]

As was the case with Pasella, the radical character of Bianchi's past did not mean that he was a zealot of left-Fascism, an advocate of its unions or of its ideas about a non-socialist redistribution of land and goods. Nor was he a critic of the *fasci*'s drift to the right. Instead, he was in the vanguard of those who favoured contacts with the old order. In October 1919 he suggested that the 'modern part of the Italian bourgeoisie', meaning especially those young men who had served at the front, could easily be won over to the *fasci*, given that the movement's programme was not yet curtailed by 'ready-made doctrines' but took its stand on issues 'according to whether the moment is ripe'.[62] It was predictable that when Bianchi died, relatively young, in 1930, it would be in the odour of religion. Despite his scandalous continuing affair with a grasping countess from his home region,[63] nothing had undermined Bianchi's status as a local notable. Bianchi, too, had converted to Fascism following his own road and with his own purposes and was not simply Mussolini's creature, even if, after 1922, when need be, he respectfully cast himself as a loyal client, expecting and deserving his *Duce*'s patronage and protection.[64]

Similar in background and policy to Bianchi was Cesare Rossi, a Tuscan born in 1884, who was first employed as a printer's assistant at Rome. Rossi was another lower middle-class figure, who moved through syndicalism to the more conservative wing of the *fasci*. By the time he had become deputy secretary to Pasella in May 1920, Rossi had acquired a reputation as the grey eminence of the movement, the key negotiator of secret contracts and deals. This role was compromised in 1921, when Rossi openly supported the Pact of Pacification, and ruined in 1924, when, heavily compromised in the flagrantly brutal murder of moderate socialist deputy Giacomo Matteotti, he tried to protect himself by blaming Mussolini for the affair.[65] After some brief months in exile, Rossi lived out the rest of the regime in the half worlds of prison, banishment and arrangements – real or plotted – with the secret police.

The biographies of Pasella, Bianchi and Rossi are not identical but they demonstrate that those who approached Fascism from a career in the pre-war left by no means naturally took up a position on the radical and leftist-seeming wing of the movement. Their behaviour was underpinned by their ambition, by their willingness to transform their ideals and attitudes, if such change could bring advantage, and by their ability to adapt and trim in the manner that they noisily criticized in pre-war liberal politicians. Did their nearness to the top of the *fasci* movement, however short-lived in some cases, make such men unusually cynical and manipulative? Perhaps the leaders of any movement, when their attitudes are scrutinized too closely, will turn out to have been as much moved by personal as by ideological desires. What happens when the spotlight is transferred further down into the rank and file of the *fasci*? Is it there that we can locate the true believers, the fanaticized adepts of a new political religion?

In this regard, a telling source is available in the diary of Mario Piazzesi, born at Cesena in the Romagna to a family that combined agrarian and business interests in a middling way. Between 1919, when a high school student, and 1921, when, still in his teens, he began an engineering course at Pisa University, Piazzesi was an active squadrist, devoted to the violent imposition of Fascism in Tuscany. After 1922 he held modest rank under the regime, which he followed to the bitter end at Salò. Still a Fascist following Mussolini's fall, he fled to Mexico (and it was from there that his diary was recovered).[66] In January 1943, despite the deplorable news from the front, Piazzesi wrote to Mussolini, expressing what he claimed had always been his sentiments: '*Duce*, I have served you in Fascism for twenty-two years as one does in a Holy Militia. For You, I have given my blood and my liberty. I am ready to give my life. *Duce*, in my history, there has never been a less than pure thought, a less than honourable action.'[67] Piazzesi's moralizing and his Victorian phrasing echoed ideals that the regime habitually preached to its subjects. What had motivated him to hold these views and what did they mean?

Piazzesi belonged to that cohort of European youth, regretful that the war had not lasted long enough to embrace them, of whom the most notorious exponent was later SS chief Heinrich Himmler.[68] In 1919 Piazzesi, still a schoolboy, rushed to join the Sezione studentesca of the Alleanza di difesa cittadina (Student branch of the alliance for citizens' defence) which, in Florence, where Piazzesi resided, had been formed under the sapient leadership of the well-connected Freemason and lawyer, Michele Terzaghi.[69] Piazzesi's initial diary entry recalls the religious awe inspired in him by hearing ripping yarns in the family apartment from decorated officers of the Alpini or Arditi about the heroic months of combat. At the same time, these guests shocked Piazzesi with their complaints about the Nitti government and their dismay at the Allied readiness to damn Italy as a 'pariah'.[70] In August 1919 Piazzesi was buoyed by news that the Alleanza was creating armed squads. He determined to join them. Initially he did not identify these groups with the *fasci*, given the latter's associations in literary Tuscany with Marinetti, whose anti-clericalism and exhibitionism Piazzesi deplored. He also disliked the Nationalist Association, whose members were older and positioned further up the class ladder than he was. Among the positives in his life were his version of the nation and his Tuscany, a region which he esteemed 'always in the lead, always first'. He contrasted Florence with the national capital – 'a filthy city, this Rome, unmanly, inert, without backbone, cowardly'. Rome was embodied in the Vatican, foreign embassies and *porchetta arrosta* (spitted roast pork).[71] By contrast, Piazzesi's trinity was composed of the Family, Tuscany and the Nation. These holy ideals steeled him against what he disdained as the wilful socialist policy of devastation and sabotage; Leonardo da Vinci and Cosimo de' Medici would turn in their graves, he stated, if socialists won the local elections. The 'red' curs had to be leashed; Italy must be saved from their 'Asiatic' Bolshevism.[72]

Still working for the local cause of the citizens' defence alliance, he and his patriotic friends began on their own behalf to sally forth against their perceived foes. Soon, however, Piazzesi concluded that he was a Fascist. Tuscan Fascism long remained proud of its verbal radicalism, even if the movement's first standards had been blessed by Countesses Capponi and Collacchioni, ladies from the region's 'best people' and richest landowners. Bruno Frullini, one of the first local squadrists, made some positions clear when he installed a spittoon in the movement's first branch office, ornamented with a rough drawing of Lenin in it.[73]

The social crisis in Tuscany came to a head in late February and early March 1921, when, in Florence itself, after the assassination of local communist chief, the evocatively named Spartaco Lavagnini, barricades were thrown up in working-class streets by a now desperate and divided left – the communists had split from the main socialist movement at the Livorno congress in January. This uprising prompted army intervention, a deploying of tanks and heavy artillery. In Tuscany, too, an alliance, whether open or tacit, was evident between the agents of government and the *fasci*.

But the most sensational action of the moment occurred at Empoli, down the Arno from the regional capital and, until then, a socialist redoubt.[74] On 1 March two truckloads of armed sailors arrived in the town, were mistaken for Fascists and attacked. A pitched battle ensued. Piazzesi and his squadrists reached the town two nights later, brushing aside what he claimed were faint-hearted Bersaglieri efforts to stop them – Tuscan Fascists had been accustomed for some months to receive their weaponry through contacts with the officer corps.[75] In the morgue, Piazzesi found nine corpses; one *carabiniere*, he claimed, had been emasculated in a way that replicated the barbarous behaviour of Ethiopian tribesmen after the Battle of Adua. Another had had his ear bitten off by a working-class woman, while he was being kicked to death by two other 'furies'; the alleged savagery and 'cannibalism' of communist women would be emphasized by other Fascist commentators.[76] Survivors, Piazzesi said, damned Empoli workers, their ideological leaders and local women by repeatedly crying out: 'They are not Christians, believe me, they are not Christians.' Piazzesi's mind, in other words, had readily united the stereotypes of imperial and gender war and inscribed them with class. He and his men determined to stay at Empoli and 'to give it a thorough cleansing', although in practice the terrified local 'reds' had fled into the countryside and hidden there until the incursion by the Florentine 'foreigners' was over.[77]

The events at Empoli had converted Piazzesi and his *camerati* (mates) to a Fascist faith. Whenever, in one raid or another, Piazzesi's squad suffered a loss, they sought to bury their 'martyred' colleague with due ceremony, solemnly bearing the corpse through Florence or some other centre and doing so while sporting their arms, wearing their black shirts and singing 'Giovinezza'. Their actions may have looked like adolescent mayhem. They were doubtless designed to reassert the control of the rich and possessing over the poor and socialist. But, Piazzesi was anxious to claim, they were more than that. This militia, he declared, was 'not in the hire or pay of anyone'. 'At times', he added, 'a force greater than us, guides us; perhaps it is our Fallen, perhaps the lament of so many mothers, and among them the silent cry of my own mother.'[78] By his own account, Piazzesi had become a Fascist fundamentalist, ready to sacrifice all to his 'holy' cause, if also vague in the extreme about what it might stand for once the present battle was done.

No doubt there were other rank and file Fascists who shared Piazzesi's view of the world, hated their socialist and communist enemies just as he did and knew that they must crusade for the nation. Fascist writer Luigi Freddi would similarly portray the 'barbarous' Bolshevik red flag as being the colour of 'menstrual blood' and so merge his misogyny with his anti-communism.[79] Piazzesi's venomous opinion of the women of Empoli was not original and can easily enough be located among the Freikorps, when they cleaned up Munich or some other hot-bed of revolution, or among those favourable to Franco in the Spanish Civil War, where, again, the working class were stripped of their humanity before, during and after they were massacred and their institutions were laid waste. In squadrists' minds, there was a war on, a conflict made more real by the failure of Piazzesi and his ilk to serve in the trenches. As in September 1919, another young *fascio* supporter had mused: 'for us, the great conflict just isn't over. Where there were external enemies, now there are internal foes . . . On one side real Italians, lovers of their country. On the other, their enemies, the cowards who seek to blow to pieces our national grandeur . . . Direct action is needed against them, energetic, decisive and courageous action. And we, the interventionists of the first hour, must accept the sacred task.'[80]

Tullio Cianetti was destined to be a leading Fascist unionist, eventually a member of the Fascist Grand Council. From his origins in the Umbrian middling peasantry, unlike Piazzesi, he became famous under the dictatorship. Cianetti began to comprehend the cause at Nardò, in the southern province of Lecce, in April 1920. Back from belated service to the nation as a junior officer during the last days of the war (he was born in 1899) but not yet demobilized, Cianetti decided that the Puglian peasants, who had tried to mount their own 'socialist' revolution, were misguided in their attempt to deny the nation. Yet, he admitted, they endured flagrant daily injustice at the hands of their landowners, men vastly more rapacious and exploitative than were their fellows in his home region. So troubled was Cianetti by his contact with social crisis in Puglia that he bought a copy of *Das Kapital*, hoping to learn from its pages why the world was so wickedly arranged. Before he got too far in his reading, however, another lieutenant, himself already a convert to the *fasci* and a ferocious and convincing critic of King Victor Emmanuel III, won Cianetti over to the idea of a 'new politics'.

For a time, Cianetti clung to the hackneyed soldiers' line that any deeds with a political motivation were ignoble and corrupting. The young officer's sense of military comradeship had to acquire a familial base. In March 1921 Cianetti at last left the army, returning to an Umbria swept by strikes and lockouts, although, as he remarked, 'his' Assisi preserved the calm of St Francis. Cianetti's younger brother, his high school friends and their teachers were already enrolled in the *fascio*, happy to serve their regional chief, Alfredo Misuri, while also having contact with the locally formidable Nationalists. Cianetti now crossed his Rubicon into politics: 'I, once a peasant and once an officer, newly aware member of the petite bourgeoisie, with white collar aspirations and a tradition of liberal and humanist thought, ended by fully embracing Fascism.' In his own mind, he did so to carry the victory in the war, won by the new generation, to its destined fruition at home.[81]

Cianetti, who had experienced the war only briefly, and Piazzesi, who knew it simply as myth, were young men who adopted Fascism at a somewhat different pace. But each chose it as a creed and as a guide to proper behaviour. After 1922 each willed that the ideology, its regime and dictator entailed a personal cultural revolution as well as one which they hoped would embrace the Italian people. Neither had actually become a Fascist because they had met Mussolini, been swept away by his oratory or were conversant with his writings. Rather, their Fascism grew from a complex of motives linked to the war and to the need to assert it as a triumph so great that it excised the Italian future from the Italian past. They knew they wanted to pledge their lives to 'Italy' (somehow defined) and must rescue the nation from the snares and delusions of socialism. Like Farinacci, Balbo, Grandi and many others who, in 1920–21, were learning to don the black-shirt and to mouth the slogans of the ideology it represented, Cianetti and Piazzesi had to a very considerable degree opted for a 'new politics', before that politics acquired the name Fascism. Each also found his manhood through his Fascism. Class, gender and ethnicity, each coursed through the two men's commitment to a militant and bracing novelty and to what they hoped were to be their lives of service, achievement and reward.

To a degree, then, they, and a number like them, were faithful Fascist converts, believers in the movement's growing array of rituals, men who imbibed through squadrism a spontaneous totalitarianism, in which they would move from the present task of liquidating the enemies of the nation to the greater travail of building a new state, inculcating a new spirit in the people and conquering foreign fields.[82] Yet, for other squadrists whose careers did not flourish and who did not have the occasion after the events to record or rework their attitudes, political motivation might be simpler. For them, the Fascist campaign constituted the violent way to assert their local power and to advance themselves and their families in wealth, status and authority. In the Fascist ranks of 1920–21, earnest ideals and a fondness for bullying (and murder) coexisted without rebuke, but rather with encouragement from the movement's leadership. If some Fascists believed, others aspired to gain.

The most notorious of the many Fascist thugs who will appear in our story was Amerigo Dumini, head of the squad that killed Giacomo Matteotti. Before 1914 Dumini returned to Italy from the USA to undertake his education and he was yet another who approved of the war. Indeed, he renounced his American citizenship in order to be able to serve in the Italian Army, where he rose to the rank of sergeant-major. He was wounded on Monte Grappa and decorated for heroism. Soon after the war, at least by his post-1945 account, having already associated himself with the Associazione Arditi d'Italia, he became a Fascist at Florence, where he had taken up residence. Thereafter, he joined with a will in Florentine squadrism, serving, like Piazzesi, in Terzaghi's Alleanza di difesa cittadina before it hardened into Fascism. From November 1920 he edited a weekly entitled *Sassaiolo fiorentino* (the title meant a Florentine stone-thrower), which proclaimed itself the 'paper of guerrilla warfare, *Arditi*-style'.[83]

Terzaghi, who fell out with the regime and served a term of *confino*,[84] eventually argued that Fascism had been 'a superficial court of obedience and discipline', whose members were actually in a 'permanent state of latent rebellion'.[85] Certainly Dumini liked to go his own way, so long as violence and personal benefit were involved. In autumn 1919 the Florentine *fascio* (it had already been 'founded' three times) pledged itself to the dictatorship of intelligence. More evident, however, was its members' liking for arms and action. From October 1920 Dumini's squad launched numerous attacks in the region, with the avowed intention of 'raising the Tricolour instead of the Red rag'. Any who objected would be beaten up or worse for their pains. Florentine Fascism was on its way. By April 1921 it could launch a five-day military-style raid in the province of Arezzo, where forty-three squads, each with a truck (often the lumbering Fiat model 18BL), were in action and where the arsenal included machine guns. At Arezzo itself, Dumini, dressed in a black-shirt and his old army coat, kidnapped and beat a local socialist member of parliament, marched menacingly through working-class parts of the town and invaded and devastated the Chamber of Labour. He and his men chopped its office furniture into pieces and piled up all the paper and files on a cart, which was then driven to the main square. In that public place the records of their foes were ceremoniously heaped into a pyre and burned.[86]

At Arezzo, as elsewhere in the region, such actions were greeted with relief by the local propertied classes and by many old liberals, including such distinguished landowning families as the Guicciardinis, Ridolfis and Ricasolis.[87] At the town of San Sepolcro, home of the Buitoni pasta concern, it was early reported that '"Fascismo" is . . . "Buitonismo"'[88] (after 1922, the Buitoni family continued to work hand in glove with the regime both at San Sepolcro and in the off-shoot family concern of Perugina at Perugia).[89]

Dumini's popularity among the respectable classes dipped, however, after a botched assault on the *paese* of Montespertoli and it was a good moment for him, not a real local, to move to Milan. There, although pursued by charges of arson and murder, he cemented a place as a henchman of Cesare Rossi. He also met and became a friend of Albino Volpi, a cabinet-maker, and Amleto Poveromo, a butcher, men who were to help him kill Matteotti.

Volpi's Fascism went back a long way but never lost its crudeness. He claimed to have been present at San Sepolcro;[90] he had attended, with Marinetti and Vecchi, in the cause of the Arditi movement which, with the other two, he had helped to found. The official record did not have him joining the Milan *fascio* until 1921,[91] that is, until after Marinetti and Vecchi's political prominence had faded. Volpi's record was studded with violent criminal acts, including, when he was engaged in the squadrist sacking of a suburban socialist party branch, the murder of a worker. Volpi, in other words, was an enforcer, a purveyor of 'protection', what Italians evocatively call a 'gorilla'. He began with Marinetti and Vecchi and ended with Dumini and Rossi and, behind them, Mussolini, because that was where the power had gone and because those who purvey protection need protectors. Volpi's record bears little relation to beguiling rhetoric about remaking society in accordance with the holy principles of a new political religion.

If Dumini, Volpi and their gang embodied the crudest and most rowdy element of Fascism (although they were scarcely unique in the movement), Elisa Majer Rizzioli, the founder of the women's *fasci*, reflected the movement's attraction for high society. Majer Rizzioli (1880–1930) was of the same age and from a similar class, ethnic and urban background as was Mussolini's wealthy and sophisticated patroness and mistress, Margherita Sarfatti. Her father was a Jewish businessman; her mother came from the Venetian patriciate. After her marriage to a notary in 1904, the childless Majer Rizzioli was swept into a life of patriotism. An irredentist and nationalist, she led Red Cross nurses to the Libyan war and was decorated for her further service in that capacity during the First World War. In the latter conflict she headed an Opera delle mamme (Mothers' aid) to collect and distribute clothing, food and funds to poor military families. In 1919 Majer Rizzioli marched with D'Annunzio on Fiume and thence organized a charitable trip for the children of the town to Milan. In response, the grateful poet coined the word *legionaria* (female legionary) to honour her and her friends. Majer Rizzioli's nationalism debouched into Fascism after she met Mussolini and was convinced that she had won him over to her Comitato di azione contro il lusso (Association against Exaggerated Luxury among Women). Her party ticket was ceremoniously dated to 1 January 1920 and she was published in *Il Popolo d'Italia*.

Four years later, Majer Rizzioli helped in the drafting of a new constitution for the Fasci femminili and she continued to edit a journal entitled *Rassegna Femminile Italiana*. Although her charity always possessed a bountiful side, patronizing towards poorer women, she did think that she was paving a Fascist path towards female liberation in service to the nation. She was wrong.[92] Among the squads the Fascist attitude to women was well displayed by the provincial weekly *La Vetta d'Italia*. In 1922 its editorialist feared that quite a few women were repelled by the violence of Fascist acts. They must understand, however, that killing was part of the mission to save Italy from the 'Bolshevik beast'. In any case, the writer added, in a recipe that would turn into totalitarianism: 'today a Woman cannot be Italian unless she is a Fascist . . . Any woman who wants to go beyond passivity must be Italian and so Fascist.'[93]

Alone among those early Fascists whose stories have been so far recounted, Majer Rizzioli, in her political journeying, was directly influenced by Mussolini, although her fascination with D'Annunzio and the nation does not make her choice surprising nor did she surrender her own understanding of life under the regime. But her meeting with Mussolini is a reminder that, while squadrists on the ground in Emilia-Romagna, Tuscany, Umbria, Puglia, the back streets of Milan and in such border towns as Trieste and Trento were brutally repelling their socialist, communist or, on occasion, Catholic, Slovene and German enemies, the *Duce* was operating in a more elevated world. In Milan and through the pages of *Il Popolo d'Italia*, Mussolini, however hesitantly at first after 1919, cut a superior line.

Whereas the squads were local in their make-up, intention and immediate purpose, he had a national and even potentially international
role – part of his claim to be a front-rank politician was bolstered by
his regular commentary on foreign affairs.

Mussolini, the daily expert on events, had a licence to roam.
Allowing that the *fasci* were too practical to be tied down by set programmes, their leader could be expected to hold a range of views. In
1920 he thus can be found celebrating the prospect that he was really
a reactionary, hailing Vecchi's *arditismo civile* as a potential school of
the nation and attacking the state for prolonging summer time, this
last in an article whose peroration read oddly for one destined to be
the artificer of totalitarianism: 'Down with the state of all types and
incarnations. Down with the state, yesterday, today and tomorrow.
Down with the bourgeois state and the socialist one.'[94] The choice
between Republic and monarchy, Mussolini counselled sagely, could
be left to the future to decide, bureaucrats should get a pay rise and
his movement's anti-clericals should not foolishly underestimate the
possible influence of a universal Church with 400 million followers.[95]
On foreign matters, the *Duce* was similarly expansive and similarly
nebulous. He stood for the annexation of Fiume and Dalmatia, he
announced in June 1920, as well as for a diplomatic posture that was
not subservient to the ungenerous allies but was instead open to ex-
enemies and to the successor states of the collapsed empires. He
favoured a colonial policy that avoided 'grotesque adventures' but
defended the national interest. He backed 'the revision of the
Versailles Treaty in those sections where it has demonstrated itself a
failure'.[96] Bolshevism, he knew, was not really a Jewish phenomenon
and the manifestations of anti-Semitism in current-day Hungary
could not be applauded. Yet, he reckoned, such responses should not
astonish. Even in Italy, where 'anti-Semitism is unknown and we
believe will never be known', Zionism was a troubling development.
It was to be hoped that 'Italian Jews continue to be smart enough not
to encourage anti-Semitism in the only country where it had never
been'.[97] In any case, for the present, it had to be admitted that Italy
needed peace. Somehow the Fascists were expansionists of a virtuous
kind; their views were not to be confused with the more captious and
aggressive imperialism of the Nationalist Association.[98]

As for home affairs, Mussolini sought similarly to be strident and brave, while dropping hints at worthy compromise and artful subtlety. 'We are not *a priori* for class struggle or for class cooperation. One or the other tactic may be adopted according to circumstances,' he advised opaquely. Anyway, he declared, there was evidence that all the other parties (except the socialists) were dissolving or becoming Fascist, 'that is, turning into temporary groups of men working towards a particular end'.[99] 'Fascism for the moment only has a history [back to 1915] and not a doctrine. It will acquire one when it has the time to elaborate and coordinate its ideas,' he promised.[100] In October 1920 Mussolini even alleged, after an outbreak of bickering in the Venetian *fascio*, that he did not seek to be 'the god the father' of the movement, which must cherish a breadth of ideas.[101]

Given the rise of agrarian fascism, one taxing issue was the charting of an ideal position on land ownership. Fascists in Ferrara sought to broaden their support among the middling peasantry with a policy based on the slogan 'we must give each man as much land as he can work'[102] and schemes for Fascist unions, which could foster social justice and class unity and simultaneously enhance production, were endorsed by Mussolini. In February 1921 he counselled judiciously that 'the dark, unstoppable and profound travail of the agricultural poor can find, through Fascism, a liberating solution', even though it might take time, given Italy's huge regional variety.[103]

Entrenched in his Milanese citadel, Mussolini did not just cogitate about suffering peasants and their possible relief through Fascist unionism. Rather, he and his friends and agents were talking to those who mattered in the national political world. There, it was announced at the end of February 1921, Giolitti intended to call a vote,[104] hoping again to 'make elections' as he had been accustomed to do before 1914. To that end, he was seeking to craft a national bloc, which could accommodate all those who opposed the socialist parties and the Catholics. A place in this grouping of men of good will could be found for the *fasci*.

Mussolini took the chance to accept Giolitti's offer of partial transformation to political respectability and yet proclaim 'without false modesty' that Fascism proposed 'to govern the nation'. The programme of the *fasci*, he added, still avoiding dangerous clarity, was 'that needed to ensure the moral and material grandeur of the Italian people'. The movement he headed eschewed dogmatism. 'We permit ourselves the luxury of being aristocrats and democrats, conservatives and progressives, those who follow legal process and those who do not, according to the circumstances of place and surroundings.'[105] Violence, he maintained, as the poll itself approached, 'must be reasoned, rational and surgical. It must not become an aesthetic or sporting game.'[106]

On 15 May the voting did not proceed as Giolitti had wished. The socialists dwindled in number but only from 156 to 122, with the communists of the new Partito Comunista d'Italia gaining sixteen seats from their rivals. The PPI went up from 100 to 107. The Blocco Nazionale won 275 but they were split and their successful candidates were anything but reliably loyal to Giolitti. Among them were ten Nationalists – in Salsomaggiore, an elegant spa near Parma, monarchist squadrists were doing the Fascists' work for them, while inveighing against Protestantism and looking forward to the disintegration of the British Empire (invoking Dante in this cause).[107] Such patriots of a kind were outnumbered by thirty-five Fascists (half of whom were lawyers). One new deputy was 'Prof.' Mussolini, who had topped the poll both in the Milan-Pavia electorate (where he secured 124,918 ballots) and in Bologna-Ferrara-Ravenna-Forlì (172,491).[108] Giolitti's days of carrying the fate of Liberal Italy securely in his hands were over. Fascism had taken a decisive step towards national government and Italy had been thrust into a political crisis, now even graver than it had been before.

6

Learning to rule in the provinces

The prominent role of Marxism in intellectual circles during the inter-war years and after means that there were many attempts to assess and define Fascism through class analysis. Palmiro Togliatti, Gramsci's successor as leader of the PCd'I and a refugee from Mussolini's dictatorship, had, in 1935, a dogmatic-sounding defini-tion ready in lectures which he was giving at the Lenin school in Moscow. The thirteenth meeting of the Enlarged Executive of the Comintern, he explained, had agreed: 'Fascism is the open terrorist dictatorship of the most reactionary, most chauvinistic, most imperi-alist elements of finance capital.'[1] The party line was that Fascists were mercenaries working in the cause of those commanding the ruth-less heights of the capitalist world. Fascists, when assigned a class position, so the vulgar Marxist view went, belonged to groups losing out in the historical process; they were petit bourgeois, unable to compete with the flourishing modern industrial capitalist bourgeoisie or with its destined replacement, the self-conscious and organized proletariat. Given the importance of the rural in the Italian economy, equally they might be middling peasants, the Italian equivalent of what Stalinism was damning as kulaks. Fascism might also attract the criminal lumpenproletariat and some greedy 'intellectuals', a social group able to float free in society and so wavering or unpredictable in its social slot.

As here expressed, this analysis is cruder than that actually favoured by minds as subtle and intelligent as those of Gramsci, Togliatti (who began his account with the Comintern definition and then used the rest of his lectures implicitly to enlarge on and qualify it) and other significant Marxist observers. None the less, the idea that fascism in general, and not just the Italian version, was the ideology of the *déracinés*, the uprooted, displaced and eventually to be defeated classes, has been a powerful and enduring one. When, from the 1960s, modern historians found the archives opening on the inter-war period and professional research into Nazi-fascism began, the Marxist concepts acted as a spur to much scholarship. The question 'just who voted for the Nazis?' became a vigorously disputed matter, with left-leaning historians endeavouring to demonstrate that the organized German working class, proud in its devotion either to the Social Democrat or Communist parties, resisted the rancorously anti-Marxist propaganda of Hitler. A rival school, which naturally enough had political motives of its own, was just as determined to show that Nazism was really an inter-class movement. If it lacked a simple class base, the theorem ran, it could not have been fighting in the cause of the bourgeoisie. It was anything but the reserve army of capital. Rather it nourished a greater hostility to liberalism than it did to socialism and communism.

The debates about Fascism were more muted, because Mussolini did not rise to power through a succession of electoral victories in the way that Hitler did and because material allowing for class definition was more fudged in relatively backward Italy. Nevertheless some evidence there was. Late in 1921, just before he left the movement's secretariat, Umberto Pasella engaged in a quasi-sociological analysis of the 151,644 members of the *fasci* (a swift and telling increase from the 20,615 who had joined by the end of 1920). Of those who held tickets in what was about to be formalized as the Partito Nazionale Fascista (PNF), Pasella estimated that 57.5 per cent (87,182) were returned soldiers; he did not enquire how many others, like Piazzesi, had not actually been to the war but still had their minds framed by it. But Pasella did try to provide a rough class analysis of those who had paid their membership dues. He reported that 24.3 per cent were peasants (of one kind or another), 15.45 per cent were workers, 13 per cent students, 12 per cent landowners, large and small, 9.8 per cent white-collar workers, 9.2 per cent traders and artisans, 6.6 per cent lawyers, doctors and other professionals, 4.8 per cent bureaucrats, 2.8 per cent big businessmen, 1.1 per cent teachers and 1 per cent seamen.[2]

The list allows some insight, although Pasella's categories may hide almost as much as they reveal. Just who the peasants and the workers were, how rich or poor, how self-conscious about their social position, how affected by education in the army or through other exposure to the process of nationalization, how dragooned by Fascist bullying in their *paesi*, remains imponderable. It is similarly unclear how practically or spiritually driven was each individual member. How lasting was each Fascism? Both the *fasci* and the early PNF had a rapid turnover, with up to half the members in 1922 not renewing their annual card.[3] All that is really clear from Pasella's detail is what was established in the previous chapter: from the moment in 1920 when poor peasant unionism began to face a counter-offensive from its enemies, the Fascist movement grew rapidly. Its attitudes and practice especially attracted ex-junior officers and other returned soldiers, disgruntled with their fate and that of their nation in the post-war and convinced that their generation must rule Italy in what should somehow be a new way.

Practitioners of this version of new politics were not at all averse to adapting the violence, first learned at the front, to uphold the cause of the nation or at least that part of it deemed worthy, as well as otherwise to benefit the more active, intrepid and ambitious members of their group. In class terms, Fascists were more likely than not to come from middling groups, all the more because they were a youthful movement, numbers of whom had not yet reached a secure social position, although they were typically anxious to rise. The final aspect of Fascist supporters was that, politically, they were above all anti-socialist. An occasional yen for syndicalism or some other nostrum about welfare through class collaboration and in the alleged interest of the nation doubtless lingered in some minds. So, too, Fascists could be contemptuous of old, complacent, 'slipper-wearing' members of the previous liberal elite and mock their flaccid appeasement of their class or ethnic foes. Yet such lambasting frequently came from the lips of the Fascist sons of liberal fathers. For all its sarcasm about the supine bourgeoisie, Fascism scarcely favoured an assault on property or the overthrow of the capitalist system that lay behind its maintenance in civil society. Rather than being the destroyers of the liberal world, Fascists wanted it to accept the tempering begun in the war and become slimmer, more efficient, less yielding and clement, more modern. They wanted to slough off the delusions of a lackadaisical past.

But class, and the ideologies which eddy about it, may not be the most instructive tools with which to analyse Fascism before its grasping of power in Rome. What about regional difference, so often a revealing matter in Italy? Apart from Pasella's tabulation, there is another breakdown of the *fasci*, this time from March 1921. Then there were 14,756 members in Trieste, more than 18 per cent of the overall membership of the movement. The next most numerous *fasci* were located in Ferrara (7,000), Milan (6,000), Bologna (5,130), Cremona (3,745), Verona (3,000), Naples (2,850) and Bari (2,809). By contrast only 581 Fascists had signed up in the working-class and socialist redoubt of Turin, 1,480 in Rome, 500 in Florence, 70 in Ravenna and none in the southern provincial capitals of Avellino, Benevento, Catanzaro, Cosenza, Foggia and Agrigento. Another tally exists for December 1921, when membership had spurted to 218,453, organized in 1,333 branches. Of this figure 62 per cent were located in northern Italy (135,349 in 817 branches), 13 per cent in central Italy (26,846 in 266 branches), 19 per cent in the mainland south (42,576 in 183 branches) and 6 per cent in the islands (13,682 in 67 branches). Five months later in May 1922 the pattern had shifted again but only a little. Out of 322,310 members (the largest total until then achieved by any Italian party), the PNF's biggest centres were in Cremona (31,400; Farinacci was indeed the boss of his town and a Fascist who mattered), Florence (20,880), Milan (13,967), Mantua (12,361), Bologna (11,773), Trieste (10,522) and Naples (10,395) but only 2,922 in Turin. Benevento still had no acknowledged Fascists (Mussolini's police chief, Arturo Bocchini, came from there, but at this time was still pursuing a prefectural career and anyway was never to view himself as an ideological Fascist).[4] The raw numbers fail to answer many questions about the character of the actual members. Yet the fluctuation across Italy deserves pondering. Why, for example, was Trieste such an early fortress of the *fasci* and why did it surrender its initial primacy to the cities of the Po valley and Tuscany? Why, too, were there so few Fascists in many sectors of the south and what might this absence reveal about the class and ideological character of the movement? After all, quite a few commentators at the time contended that, chameleon-like, Fascism assumed coloration from its immediate surrounds and often had as its ultimate purpose not so much national unity as the defence of specific local interests.[5]

Before 1914 Trieste rejoiced in being a flourishing and rapidly growing city, having assumed a place among Europe's top ten ports. The population expanded from 176,000 in 1900 to 235,000 in 1910, the majority of the newcomers being 'Slavs', that is, often Slovene, although sometimes Croat, peasants from the surrounding rural hinterland.[6] Some of the Italian-speaking population resented Habsburg rule, disdaining the growing presence of 'barbarous Slavs', although the number of active irredentists in 1914 did not much exceed fifty. In Trieste, as in similar centres throughout Europe, the socialist movement increased its profile, although ethnic politics threatened to divide the population into German, Italian and Slovene factions. In 1910, for example, nationalists could buy boxes of matches from local vendors with labels in the rival languages[7] and so flaunt their ethnic identity whenever they lit a cigarette in one of the city's elegant squares or *caffè*. Such tiny cultural wars could go beyond the symbolic. Sursum corda, an Italian patriotic association, from 1908 employed an armed squad to defend its office and prosecute its cause.

After 1915 the national claim to Trieste was the most significant war aim and fighting was vicious and prolonged on the Carso, the pock-marked low hills which separated the city from the border at Monfalcone and hinted at geopolitical change from the Venetian plain to the Balkans. Catholicism was a possible complicating factor of identity in the city and its surrounds (while Trieste was enriched by an ancient and influential Jewish community). During the war, the Catholic hierarchy complacently agreed that God stood on the side of the existing institutions. When, after Caporetto, the town of Gorizia was retaken by Habsburg forces, the local Archbishop compared Italian control to a Babylonish captivity and Bishop Karlin of Trieste pronounced that God had intervened to decide the battle of Caporetto, giving victory to Austria, 'the happy mother of all nations'.[8] Such postures needed to be explained away after 1918 when the Church rapidly displayed its ability at ethnic compromise by appointing Monsignor Angelo Bartolomasi, the wartime chaplain-general to the Italian armed forces, as its Bishop of Trieste. Religious travail was one problem. The war was also bad for Trieste's economy, since the long and narrow Adriatic was too exposed to naval attack to allow the port to prosper as the southern outlet for the produce of Central and Eastern Europe. After 1918 this loss of an economic role was confirmed when Trieste fell under Italian rule and further curtailed its ties to the north. Unemployment became a major problem in the city and the peasants of the region found their ordinary troubles worsened by the devastation of their fields in battle.

It was scarcely surprising that post-war Italian Trieste was a city in social, economic and cultural turmoil. In particular, it was a place where ethnic conflict brewed menacingly, while both Nitti and Giolitti talked in a softly liberal manner about permitting local autonomy but did so without offering precise policies that might, for example, rapidly revive the port. On its new borders, Italy was being afflicted by what has been aptly called an 'Austrian heritage',[9] entailing a set of vicious disputes over ethnic definition and role. More than 300,000 Slovenes lived under Italian governance, a fifth of their number anywhere. As if in proof of spiritual malaise, Trieste long led the nation in the number of psychologists operating there who thought of themselves as Freudians, and in the number of suicides.[10] More than any other part of Italy, the region of the Venezia Giulia and its capital city were swept by attitudes and behaviour that, in the rest of the ex-Habsburg world, were to be expressed as Nazism and the incorrigibly xenophobic little fascisms of Eastern Europe.

Events on other parts of the border exacerbated the problem of life in Trieste. Fiume lay fewer than eighty kilometres to the south-east and it was predictable that Nationalists would turn up in its streets to thunder about the need to expand Italian territory still further. As early as May 1919 Federzoni used a speaking engagement in the city to launch the Gruppo nazionalista di Trieste, expatiating on the virtues of production and a strong state as well as on the need for the nation to drive into Dalmatia.[11] However, from early 1920 Nationalists were outpaced by the *fascio*, now at the orders of Mussolini and Pasella, and led by Francesco Giunta, born 1887, a lawyer, volunteer and ex-machine gun brigade captain from San Piero a Sieve in the Tuscan

Mugello, one of the leaders of the ANC and destined to remain a prominent Fascist after 1922. Giunta moved the focus of the local branch from weighty discussions about the meaning of corporatism to a concentration on ethnic difference. As he put it bluntly: 'the struggle at Cremona is between factions composed of Italians; the struggle at Trieste is contested between Italians and foreigners'.[12] He was seconded by Piero Bolzon, Arditi chief, born in the same year as his *Duce* in Genoa to a wealthy family and now become a Fascist. For Bolzon, 'Slavs' constituted a 'barbarous' and menacing 'flood', people who were a prey to 'orgies' or to being utterly supine, primordially given to mysticism and murder. A crusade must be called to block their penetration of the *patria*.[13] Only then would the 'second Caporetto' that had unfolded since 1919 be converted into a new Vittorio Veneto and the medals that adorned every Fascist chest gleam with real victory.[14] Under his and Giunta's impulse, the Trieste *fascio* was tailored to harness the tension of the border. It was also designed for the pre-emptive strike and, in its ethnic battles, began to pioneer the signature Fascist method for dealing with enemies at home and abroad.

Under the dictatorship, Giunta maintained that the 'essence of squadrism' had come to the fore in the decision at Trieste to outmatch 'quantity with quality'. The double battle against 'communists' and 'Slavs', he explained, boiled down to a choice of 'either us or them'. If the victory won in the national war was to be defended, then compromise with such rabble was unimaginable. The contest was simple. As Giunta had put it in an article in his paper, *Il Popolo di Trieste*, in February 1922 (by which time the victory of 'frontier fascism' was largely won): 'We are neither clericals nor anti-clericals, neither Semites nor anti-Semites, neither Masons nor anti-Masons.' Such vexations, he urged, were a distraction from the major task of asserting Italianness against Fascism's internationalist communist and nationalist Yugoslav enemies. In this conflict a strong new state must replace the weak liberal one that, since 1918, had frequently proved itself disgracefully 'non-existent'.[15] Four months earlier Giunta had proclaimed at a stridently patriotic ceremony held on a local peak – which had been fought over in the war and was now heroically and spiritually climbed by 200 'sporting' Fascists – that Dante was the 'symbol of the race' (*razza*) and the sacred figure who had charted the national border distinguishing Italians from 'the eternal barbarian'.[16] On this as on so many occasions, the medieval religious poet, however falsified historically and ethically, was the handiest reference for those who viewed themselves as hot-gospellers of the national religion.

But what of the 'enemy within'? *Il Popolo di Trieste* had stated baldly that 'a Slavia inside Italian borders cannot be allowed to exist'. The ethnic minority could only be permitted to live, an editorial ran on, if it subsumed into Italian institutions and practices.[17] Mussolini was not behindhand in seconding this demand for total assimilation or some more drastic solution. On 15 June 1920 he found a metaphor with a future. Recent disturbances at Trieste had, he wrote, confirmed the virtue of the Arditi and the vice of the socialist party. 'We must energetically *cleanse* [sic] Trieste. To do so, we should start with what we ought to have done from the beginning: really *annex* the city.'[18]

Whether directly or indirectly, the *Duce*'s phrases unleashed the Triestine Fascists who became the first squads to take matters into their own hands and engage in what did amount to ethnic cleansing. In July 1920, relying on the active support of the local army command and marshalling his own forces in a quasi-military manner, Giunta led his *fasci* to the sack of the Narodni Dom, the headquarters of the local Slovene movement at the Hotel Balkan. The place burned for more than an hour and, Giunta boasted, 'the city paraded past the glowing ruin, with a light heart and the sense that an incubus had been lifted from their lives'.[19] He and his friends were not restrained by the fact that Bishop Bartolomasi, despite his own fervent patriotism, now publicly questioned Fascist 'threats and intimidation by force of arms, the savage torture and the physical injuries and ill-usage inflicted on [Slovene-speaking] parish priests and curates', counselling Pope Benedict XV to 'denounce the gross violation of justice and humanity' in the city and its surrounds.[20] Rather than being cowed by priestly anathemas, Giunta and his squad advanced to a general assault on any they deemed their ethnic enemies. In Trieste and its surrounds those who spoke for the Slovenes were beaten into silence. Ethnic cleansing was followed by political purge. In September Giunta's squad used the excuse of a local strike to crush the unions and their backers. 'Enemies of the nation' – no more precise definition was needed than that they could be accused of being communists and anti-nationals – were being liquidated and border fascism was framing a model applicable in other parts of Italy as the final solution to social disputes. In this 'holy' fight, fanaticism and cynicism could work in harness, since it was easy enough to label a foe wicked and personal vendettas could be readily cloaked with ideological attributes.

Following the strong-arm work in Trieste and its hinterland came a version of peace and an elevation of the leading Fascists to local 'men of respect'. In the 1921 elections Giunta and a colleague, Fulvio Suvich, yet another lawyer (by then in his mid-thirties and destined to be a key servant of the regime and a man in deep contact with the city's business sector), were successful at the polls. In April 1922 the Trieste court banned the use of Slovene in any local proceedings. Slovene schools began to be closed down: between 1919 and 1928 some five hundred of them ceased to function. Pleased by the general suppression of what it viewed as an irredeemably inferior culture, during the summer of 1922 a liberal paper remarked contentedly: 'Venezia Giulia, from being one of the most agitated parts of the country, has become one of the most tranquil.' Membership figures in the PNF stagnated because the major work was done. Trieste had become above all an Italian city. For Slovenes, socialists and any others who might not applaud national victory in the First World War, the peace now established was, in quite a few senses, that of the grave. Port traffic through Trieste in 1922 languished at less than half its tonnage in 1913 and, despite various patriotic initiatives during the next years, the city never regained the financial and cultural élan of the Habsburg era.[21]

In Friuli, away to the west of Trieste, the social crisis again possessed some distinctive characteristics. Despite the largely agrarian nature of the region, socialists could be found there, for example in the developing centre of Pordenone, and, in 1919–20, the local possessing classes participated with a will in the great fear among such people of 'Bolshevism and revolution'. The area also had to reckon with the time when it had been crossed by the front and so with the apparent readiness with which numbers of peasants and priests in 1917–18 had reconciled themselves to the loss of Italian rule. After Vittorio Veneto, Italian administration was stiffened by the presence of quite a few garrisons in the region, not to mention the first flutterings of what was to turn into the 'tourism of war', the organized visiting of what had been the battlefields. Already in May 1919 the patriotic Milan-based organ-ization, the Touring Club Italiano, committed to the nationalization of the bourgeoisie, advertised excursions into Venezia Tridentina under army patronage. Citizens who took up this opportunity were promised that they could live in tents like soldiers for a few days and join in a 'work of [national] poetry'.[22] At the same time, those who had fled with the Italians after Caporetto had to re-integrate into that local soci-ety which viewed them, and which they viewed, with suspicion. Just what should be the compensation or rewards of their patriotism? Friuli was another region where after the war nationalist fervour was hard to avoid even while its definition dissevered one citizen from another. For returning 'refugees', as they were called, to the fear of leftist revolt was added an uneasiness that, in the eyes of distant Rome, Friuli and its ter-rible wartime sufferings mattered little. A. M. Preziosi, the historian of these events, has claimed that the region was possessed by 'a sense of solitude in regard to the rest of the country, a knowledge of [other Italians'] profoundly unjust lack of interest'.[23]

As in most parts of Italy beset by post-war crisis, cometh the hour, cometh the man, the *ras* in the making. In Friuli, the new political chief was Piero Pisenti, the son of a doctor and himself a lawyer. Although Pisenti had avoided war service in favour of work as a pub-lic administrator, a dereliction his enemies in the PNF enjoyed under-lining,[24] in 1919, aged thirty-two, he set up the so-called Partito del Lavoro, with the aim of rallying anti-socialist and patriotic forces. He hoped that this 'Labour party' could appeal to 'the industrial lower middle class, shopkeepers, professionals, landowners and returned soldiers'. Pisenti, then, was yet another to manufacture his version of a new politics before they acquired the label 'Fascist'. By contrast, the local *fascio* remained small and split, with a boasted membership tally of just over a thousand.[25] In Udine, the regional capital, the first leader was Giuseppe Castelletti, a journalist employed by the city's liberal conservative paper. His Fascism combined anti-clericalism, hyper-patriotism and populist campaigns against anyone from the old elite who could be damned as an *Austriacante* (Austria-lover). In Pordenone, a *fascio* grew from its foundation in November 1920, with ticket-holders largely consisting of soldiers from the garrison who believed that they were camped in hostile territory and enjoyed skirmishing with their foes. Throughout Friuli, it was reported, the *fasci* appealed most to 'returned troops, bourgeois students and [returning] refugees from the lower middle and middle classes'.[26]

On such controversial matters as Fiume and the Treaty of Rapallo, the *fascio* of the region found it difficult to stick to a consistent line, however. To lessen the appearance of internecine wrangling, in January 1921 Pisenti, to the pleasure of most of the local respectable classes, was suddenly elevated to be branch secretary. He pledged to channel and discipline squadrism and so forge a wider coalition among all those not contaminated by socialism. Yet his own position remained shaky. In 1923 he obtained some notoriety through an anti-clerical outburst that, because of its crudity, prompted Mussolini to remove him from the administrative position he had been granted as the local PNF 'High Commissioner'.[27] Three years later, Pisenti was briefly expelled from the party while Farinacci numbered him among his foes. None the less, under Turati's secretaryship, in 1927 Pisenti regained his membership and thereafter served as a Fascist deputy until 1939. He stayed a Fascist till the bitter end, being a relatively moderate Minister of Justice under the Salò Republic. Despite the twists and turns in Pisenti's life history (he did not die till 1980 and had time in the post-war to write a memoir justifying the RSI or Salò as the 'necessary republic'), the bourgeoisie of his region had been quickly made content with the post-1921 settlement. As a local historian has explained, the elites 'had travelled along with the movement, supported it [financially and morally], moved away a little from it, and then, in the end, occupied it'.[28] In Friuli, what before the war had been called liberalism had restructured itself as Fascism.

In neighbouring Venice, a similar accommodation was occurring but it moved down a different path. Under Giolitti and then in the war, the rising figure in the city was the entrepreneur, financier and provider of services, Giuseppe Volpi. Volpi rejoiced in rewarding contacts with the Banca Commerciale, the royal family and Giolitti and had wires open in the Balkans, Turkey and the Germanic world or anywhere a profit could be turned. It was not long before Volpi would welcome Henry Ford to a Venetian holiday and together the two would survey the marshy site of what became Venice's golf course. During the First World War, the Nationalists had singled Volpi out as malign proof of Italian subservience to German (and perhaps Jewish) money. Even so, the sinuous Volpi rapidly adapted himself to battle and, in 1917, launched Porto Marghera as the heavy industrial centre which would grant Venice a 'modern' future and which immediately gave him lucrative government contracts.[29] Volpi was also involved in the Compagnia Italiana Grandi Alberghi (CIGA), a body seeking to attract a wealthy and cosmopolitan crowd of the best people to the city of dreamy canals and world-renowned art treasures.[30] In 1919 Volpi, by no means a single-minded and unimaginative nationalist, flirted with the idea of Italy entering a mooted economic union with France.[31]

There was every reason, then, for Volpi to be regarded as a bugbear by the first *fascio* in the city. The group fluttered into life in 1919 under the leadership of Pietro Marsich, one of the original members of the *fasci* directorate and, still in his twenties, confirmed in his position in May 1920. Marsich was a left interventionist, a volunteer and an officer in the Arditi, a syndicalist and republican, but also an elitist lawyer who scorned too crass a populism. Over Fiume, he proved a staunch fan of D'Annunzio but, until he was driven out of the party in May 1922, he remained the most open critic of Mussolini and the latter's fondness for cunning deals and ideological somersaults. In November 1920 Marsich almost pushed the party into schism over Mussolini's willingness to accept the Treaty of Rapallo.[32]

Volpi nurtured many interests in the Balkans and, however much committed to dousing the fires of Venetian socialism – in 1920 he and Archbishop Pietro La Fontaine launched the slogan 'the *Arsenale* for the Venetians' as part of a campaign to eliminate strikes in the local armaments and ship-building industries – he disdained D'Annunzio-style adventurism. Volpi took the occasion of Rapallo to cut the funding that, as a businessman's idea of a political insurance policy, he had been handing to Marsich's *fasci*. At the same time he improved his ties with another, more reliably conservative aspirant local Fascist, Giovanni Giuriati, born 1876 into the respectable classes.[33] In 1921, for a time there was a stalemate and the best people had to survive the social horror of a strike among gondoliers.[34] The spirit of the times was also expressed by a band of youthful Fascists returning from watching a Venice–Padua football game and beating up a young man in the shabby Via Garibaldi when he refused to doff his hat in salute at their passing.[35] Working-class Venice was not 'cleansed' by Fascism until after 1922, although, on the *terraferma* or mainland rural sector of the province, a squadrism was carrying all before it and ignoring the subtle ideological debates of the city. But Marsich's public announcement in August 1921 that 'we are not disposed to sacrifice Fascism to Mussolini' meant in the long run that he was not to have a party future. Throughout the Fascist years, the ancient port was to become the city of Giuseppe Volpi, Count of Misurata, Governor of Tripolitania, Minister of Finance, President of Confindustria, sponsor of the city's renowned Biennale, office-holder extraordinaire, the Pooh-Bah of his era and a man whom even the *Duce* of Fascism was happy to salute as the *Doge* of Venice.

By 1921 the heartland of Fascism lay not in the Veneto but in the Po valley, Tuscany, Umbria and the provinces of Novara, Vercelli and Alessandria in Piedmont. There the battle for social power was fought by the squads against the peasant socialism of Federterra and its leftist or sometimes Catholic backers in the various local capitals. Novara and its hinterland, for example, were the stamping ground of Carlo Gallarotti, the son of a liberal *sindaco* of Quarona in the province of Vercelli and the owner of a factory producing silver goods. Gallarotti, before 1914, earned a degree in accountancy from the small university at Novara but was better known as a sports fan. An officer in the war and POW, on May Day 1919 he was roughed up by socialists when dressed in uniform. In response, he formed a paramilitary force called I lupi della Valsesia (The Valsesia wolves), trim with their blackshirts and woollen tricolour cravats, working in the cause of the Novara *fascio*. On their raids, Gallarotti drove ahead in his Ansaldo model car, christened La Disperata (The Desperate one), with the *fasci littori* on its radiator and *Lupi della Valsesia* painted along its sides. By then, Gallarotti boasted, he was the Duca della Valsesia (the local Duke). He was five times arraigned for crimes including murder but always let off and was still raging across the province during the 1924 elections. In 1927, however, he was expelled from the PNF and reduced to managing the family silver factory. After 1943 he supported the anti-Fascist Resistance.[36] Under the regime, Novara's best-known Fascist was to be the once Nationalist Ezio Maria Gray, the fertile journalist who had led the campaigns against Volpi during the First World War, and who, possessed of a mind of paranoid cast, had then decided that every German tourist had been plotting an eventual invasion of the Italian homeland.

Although the tenor of Fascism could vary from one of these towns to the next, the movement always combined a lawless anti-Marxism with a bellicose desire to uphold the nation's recent victory in war. Much was expressed in the words of the squadrist anthem, 'All'armi!' ('To arms!'), although its music was surprisingly mellifluous and was to sound more so when echoing from bandstands in one elegant *centro storico* or another in the more tranquil years of the dictatorship:

> All'armi! All'armi!
> All'armi! Siam fascisti!
>
> Noi che del Fascio siamo i componenti,
> la causa sosterrem fino alla morte,
> e lotteremo sempre forte forte
> finché ci resta un po' di sangue in core.
>
> Sempre inneggiando la Patria nostra
> noi tutti uniti la difenderemo
> contro avversari e traditori
> che ad uno ad uno sterminerem!
>
> All'armi! All'armi!
> All'armi! Siam fascisti!
>
> Lo scopo nostro tutti lo sappiamo,
> combatter con certezza di vittoria
> e questo non sia mai sol per la gloria
> ma per giusta ragion di libertà.
>
> I bolscevichi che combattiamo
> noi sapremo ben far dileguare
> e al grido nostro quella canaglia
> dovrà tremare, dovrà tremare.

(To arms, to arms, to arms, for we are the Fascists. We who belong to the *fascio* will sustain the cause to the death and will struggle and fight so long as a drop of blood remains in our hearts. Always hailing our *patria*, utterly united, we shall defend it against its enemies and traitors, whom, one by one, we shall exterminate. To arms, to arms, to arms, for we are the Fascists. We all know what our aim is and we fight with the certainty of victory. We do this not just for glory but righteously for freedom. The Bolsheviks whom we fight we know how to disperse. At our war-cry that *canaille*, that mob, will have to tremble, to tremble.)

A variant set of lyrics added that the Bolsheviks were being opposed 'because they want neither Patria nor Family, because they are refuse and slime; they disgust us and must be cleansed from our streets. Always crying "Hooray for Italy" and "Down with all its renegades", let us hold high the tricolour, which is our eternal love.'[37]

Such menacing words were, frequently enough, turned into action – lynchings Italian-style. At Forlì, provincial capital of the Mussolini family, local Fascists kidnapped a communist worker, beat him up, tied him to a truck and dragged him through the town streets. He was then shot and his enemies urinated into his mouth ('reduced to a broken mess of bloody limbs and bones', he died the next morning at the local hospital).[38] On the outskirts of Fossombrone, a little further south, squad members armed with sticks and guns decided to punish a 'communist', Giuseppe Valenti, who had expressed open hostility towards the *fasci*. After Valenti resisted and shot one of the home-invaders, a local Fascist boss, Raffaello Riccardi, a future minister and respectable regime economist, determined on 'vendetta'. Riccardi collected a thousand armed men and purged the village, going from house to house on the advice of local sympathizers, sacking and burning. Valenti, who had fled the place, was tracked down some days later, bashed, tortured and forced to parade back to Fossombrone, where he was tied up outside the *fascio*'s branch office. The local police watched inertly as the victim was put through a kangaroo trial and then twice stabbed by Riccardi himself. Valenti was later taken to the cemetery and beaten and knifed to death. Again the police did nothing, while Riccardi evaded the feeble and fleeting attempts by the authorities to charge him for the crime by moving to Sicily for a short period and assuming a false name.[39]

Away from these zones of battle against poor peasants who had seemed overweening in their success in 1919, the spread of Fascism was more erratic, its purpose and social base not necessarily the same, although many of the patterns of its growth towards respectability and normality were constant. In Naples, for example, one of the few cities of the south that, already in 1921, rejoiced in an appreciable number of Fascists, the movement fragmented. There the first members of the *fasci* originated in left interventionism, identifying themselves as syndicalists or Mazzinians. Soon they found a charismatic chief in Aurelio Padovani (1889–1926), yet another of the Fascist generation and a professional soldier who, although he had only completed elementary school, through service in Libya and the First World War was promoted to captain in the Bersaglieri, while also being a fervent republican and Freemason. Married to a primary school teacher, Padovani was soon the father of six children.[40] Esteeming himself a 'tribune come from the people', Padovani judged as his special political enemies not so much the fledgling city socialist movement as the better entrenched Nationalists and so the established order and its traditional system of rule. However, these more evidently legitimate sons of Liberal fathers nourished their own pretensions to incarnate the war and the 'new politics' through a straightforward authoritarianism, shored up by the old world of patronage and 'corruption'. While contesting such forces with much populist rhetoric drawn from somewhere to their left, in 1921 Padovani viewed himself above all as a 'Mussolinian' and participated as such in the conflicts of that time. Seemingly on the winning side, he gained a place on the central committee of the infant PNF.[41]

Yet Padovani faced rivals. Also on the committee was Nicola Sansanelli, born 1891 near Potenza in the Basilicata, a lawyer, journalist and decorated and wounded returned soldier – he had been a lieutenant in the Bersaglieri. Sansanelli, unlike Padovani, was happy to reconcile Fascism with the monarchy and was soon accepted as a southern Fascist notable, heading the Naples *fascio* in 1921–2. In 1923–4 Sansanelli assumed the position of interim secretary of the party nationally but quickly retreated to his natural habitat in the south. From 1926 to 1929 he became the PNF's administrative chief, or *federale*, at Naples but ultimately had to be satisfied with such cushy jobs as teaching the 'history and theory of Fascism' at the local university.

More threatening to Padovani were those Neapolitan Nationalists who, before and after October 1922, deduced where the wind was blowing and sought accommodation with the *Duce*. In May 1923 Mussolini signalled that one of them, the retired general Paolo Greco, was his man in Naples. Padovani, still believing that he was the boss, resigned, lamenting that collaboration with Greco 'completely annulled the line followed by me and all the Fascists of Campania during three years of passion and faith'.[42] His complaint at the sudden disrespect with which he was being treated and his criticism of the *Duce* were bootless. Padovani had lost out as *ras* of Naples, although dissent lingered in local circles until, in a presumed accident, he fell to his death from a balcony in May 1926. Thereafter, when convenient, Mussolini, should he wish to strike a radical attitude, could regret his loss but Naples was secured by men who paid lip-service to Fascist revolution, while basking in the restored good life of their Liberal fathers.

In Sardinia, the established Giolittian order based on patronage was steeled by a military tradition that gave the Brigata Sassari (Sassari Brigade) renown among the national armed forces. The economic and cultural gap between landowners and the peasants or shepherds – these last numbered more than 10 per cent of the population – was huge, as was that between those who resided in the towns and those who did not. The state of the poor was so wretched that up to ten people lived and died in a single room. The ruling elite ended the war fearing that the lights of their system were spluttering out. Could alarmingly uppity peasants any more be deployed against the miners of Iglesias, when they or other local workers grew restless, for example? Casting around for an effective 'new politics' which might glue society back together, landowners and their agents wondered whether a Sard autonomist movement might not be the solution. In 1919 the ANC did well on the island. Yet, by the end of the year, the returned soldiers were split between the rival appeals of radicalism and conservatism, nationalism and localism, a strong and a weak state and, in January 1920, the foundation of a Sardinian Action Party, pledged to the slogan 'first Sards, then Italians', further complicated matters.

The journalist Paolo Orano, born 1875, a syndicalist, interventionist, volunteer and wartime officer (who spent his time crafting patriotic propaganda rather than serving at the front) had done best locally in the 1919 elections, without altogether clarifying whether he cleaved to the left or right. Orano signed up to the Milan *fascio* at the end of 1919 and when, during the spring of 1920, Sardinia was afflicted by strikes which, for a time, threatened to deprive Cagliari of its food supplies,[43] Orano and his associates decided to import to Sardinia the fresh ideas of the mainland. None the less membership of the Fascist movement on the island remained small and fluctuating. At Sassari, 100 members rapidly grew to 1,830 between April and May 1921 but then fell back to 610 by May 1922.[44] Some old Liberals and some new backers of the ANC resisted the *fasci*'s spread, and in 1922 the Action party acquired an intrepid leader in the war hero Emilio Lussu (after he escaped from Fascist jail in 1929, he outraged officials by immediately telegraphing his mother from abroad: 'I'm excellently well. Kisses. Emilio').[45] Lussu organized his own paramilitary group, the 'grey-shirts', countering Fascist intimidation with threats of his own. The impact of such resistance suggested that Fascism could be defeated in Sardinia since its roots were shallow there. The Fascist 'pacification' of the island had to wait until after October 1922, when a quasi-military campaign was directed against Lussu and his men. Lussu was one of the first to be imprisoned once the dictatorship set up its Special Tribunal to repress anti-Fascism in 1926. Local Fascism remained divided, with a radical fringe surviving and, from time to time, contesting the power of an old order which, with Mussolini's direct approval,[46] had largely been restored.

In Sicily, during the national or local election campaigns in 1919–20, strikes, peasant land occupations, Mafia murders and general social violence afflicted the island. Mussolinian Fascists made their first appearance at Palermo in April 1919 from a grounding in syndicalism and left interventionism but the branch soon collapsed. Established interests had set up organizations of their own, with Prince Scalea's Partito economico of 1919 turning into a Partito agrario in 1920, determined, it stated, to restore law and order (with whatever brutality and illegality required). Scalea's group regarded the hiring of protectors who were armed and on the alert as a natural accompaniment of politics; that was the Sicilian way and, as in quite a few other parts of Italy, there the 'squad' was scarcely a Fascist invention. The Nationalists were also organized on the island, made militant by a network of their own Sempre pronti (Ever ready) squads. By 1921 'Captain' Gennaro Villelli, a radical returned soldier from Messina, emerged as the Sicilian representative on the central committee of the PNF and the movement grew appreciably, even publishing its own satirical magazine with the suggestive title O Cattigghiu (Insecticide). Any potential radicalism could not last, however. After October 1922 the northern intellectual, journalist, Futurist, Alpino (he collaborated with Balbo on the group's post-war paper), captain of the Arditi and sometime activist in Trieste, Piero Bolzon was nominated as Mussolini's man on the island. By the next year, it had been decided that local Fascism needed a thorough purge, signalling the setting aside of any influence for people like Villelli, who was dropped from party lists, and the absorption into Fascism of Scalea and the by now more important figure of Gabriele Carnazza. This ex-democratic socialist held the helpfully lucrative Ministry of Public Works from October 1922 to July 1924 and his elevation to being Mussolini's 'virtual Viceroy' in Sicily[47] promised that the social structure of the island, its practices and world-view, its patrons and clients, would not be greatly altered, at least during the first years of the new regime.

In Calabria, the fragility of *fasci* was easy to see. In May 1921, at Catanzaro, the local prefect reported the sudden rise of a local Fascism. Its members, he said, were in large part secondary school boys (there was no local university) and returned soldiers, some of these last men with criminal records. They had taken to patrolling the main streets of the town, armed with heavy clubs and threatening all local 'subversives', even though, the prefect noted wryly, 'to tell the truth [their targets] so far have done nothing at all to disturb public order'. The Catanzaro squad was also ready to head out into the countryside and there deal with any socialist-administered communes upon which they happened. For the moment, however, official forces commanded the Fascists to surrender their arms, ordering them not to provoke incidents. 'The immediate and resolute intervention by the police convinced [the Fascists] that the warnings were not in vain,' a prefectural report ran. 'The result was that, in a few days, Fascism here disappeared and the national elections have occurred without the smallest incident.'[48] A year later the prefect was still convinced that the local possessing classes disliked outbreaks of political violence of any kind and, as a result, he found local Fascists promising that they would merely 'make propaganda in favour of *italianità* without any threats or brute force'.[49] In one incident thought worth recording at the hill *paese* of Rombiolo, the town band had prompted consternation in September 1922 by intoning 'subversive tunes' during a religious *festa*. As a result, local Fascists arrived the next day to remedy matters. The police were alert to their presence, however, and no brawling resulted, although the town band did play the royal anthem, the 'Marcia Reale', and, following that public acknowledgement of respect for the national institutions and themselves, the Fascists went home.[50]

The historian Pino Arlacchi has explained that, in any case, the social conditions of Calabria varied from one part of the region to the next. In the area around Cosenza, small-holding peasants could 'do without the market for the regulation of [the region's] economic relations and tended to discourage forms of permanent antagonistic conflict between the individuals and groups'. In that little world, the ancient 'dominion of relations of reproduction over those of production and exchange' survived. Wealth and poverty were still viewed as cyclical and established interests united effectively against 'the unmarried, the illegitimate, the wage labourer', each a hopeless outsider. For both winners and losers in such a social system, Fascism was, and remained, little more than noises off their stage, the preoccupation of those wayward and imponderable foreigners who lived beyond their town gates.

Other parts of the region were different, although often the political ramifications were the same. In Crotone, there was a rigid division between a ruthlessly oppressive group of landowners and an utterly repressed rural proletariat. In 1929, for all the alleged arrival of totalitarian social unity, 1.4 per cent of the population owned 78.1 per cent of the land. The landowners ruled by a system of 'naked authoritarianism', requiring no assistance from the modern state. Any whiff of peasant criticism and the landowners imported squads of unemployed labourers from other villages of the regions to take over what work and income there was available. Centuries of deprivation kept the peasants ten centimetres shorter than the regional average, itself well below that of the nation. Around Crotone, 'women beyond the age of thirty', one traveller commented clinically, 'are already in a full state of degeneration'.[51]

In Reggio Calabria, post-war politics were triply disputed between old Liberals, notably Giuseppe De Nava (in 1924 to be a Fascist Minister and long emphatic about his claim to embody the *patria*), self-appointed spokesmen of the Arditi, led by Silvio Tripepi, son of one of the two major pre-war political chiefs, and the *fasci*, who were headed by Giovanni Priolo, a technical school headmaster's son, destined for insignificance. Squadrist actions included the sacking of the local Chamber of Labour in November 1920, an event highlighted by the ceremonial dismemberment of a single red flag unearthed there and the bashing a few months later of a visiting socialist deputy in the foyer of the Albergo Centrale. Yet the socialist peril was feeble and that party's vote in 1921 did not reach 10 per cent. The result was again that the sun of Fascism shone wanly; in May 1922 Reggio and its provincial hinterland still only counted nine branches with 945 paid-up members.[52]

Some important Fascists, including Michele Bianchi and Agostino Lanzillo, originated in Calabria. The latter, born 1886 at Reggio, was a lawyer and intellectual, a syndicalist, if also one who readily divided the world into producers and parasites and an advocate of free trade, a troubled position for a Fascist by the 1930s. He worked with Mussolini on *Il Popolo d'Italia* from 1914 and has been praised by one historian as a Fascist leftist 'whose ideological position showed a certain consistency over the years'.[53] Perhaps. But Lanzillo is best understood as a southern intellectual, whose recognition as a *professore* was for him the chief guarantee that he would not be relegated to actually living or being forced to find his fortune in the south. As the humble client of his *Duce*, Lanzillo would eventually plead that a professorial position in economics he held at Cagliari be upgraded to one at Venice where, he believed, his *sistemazione* could become pleasurable, although he still hoped for an eventual transfer to more potent

Milan.[54] Lanzillo's preferences hinted again that the Fascist intention to unite the nation had scarcely shaken that structure of national life which persuaded every Italian and especially those who were southern intellectuals that their country was arranged in a strict hierarchy of 'civilization' and comfort, with the great cities at the top and southern towns and countryside at the bottom.

Any review of the Fascist presence in the south before 1922 must conclude that the movement imposed itself there very slowly, if at all. Only Puglia, where 'an organized and powerful peasant movement' stood in the field, committed self-consciously to revolution, was an exception. There, the battle between landowners and peasants had commenced before 1914, continued through the war and reached its climax in 1920–21. In January 1921 the prefect of Foggia reported to Giolitti that the owners had joined 'in an association in order to fight violence with violence'. The aim of this reaction, which conveniently donned the armour of Fascism, was to purge 'the countryside once and for all of the institutions, the symbols, and the leaders of the workers' movement'. Apulian Fascists marched to triumph, abetted by the 'massive collusion of the State apparatus in the region'.[55] Meanwhile the regional chief with the greatest profile under the dictatorship was Achille Starace, another who, like Bianchi and Lanzillo, broke free from his place of origin, in his case, Gallipoli, in the province of Lecce. There he was born in 1889 to a well-off local landowning and merchant family. Starace's rise in the greater world was all the faster because he could be presented as a loyal party technocrat, whether his job was to impose ethnic cleansing in the Trentino or to purge troublemakers from the PNF in Milan.

Lanzillo was acute or honest enough to agree about the diversity hidden beneath the name 'Fascism'. In early 1922 he observed: 'one Fascism does not exist but rather diverse Fascisms, which commonly don't even utilize the same name.' In more developed and industrialized areas (where he preferred to live), Lanzillo maintained that Fascism constituted essentially 'a romantic movement', devoted to the nation and its victory. In the countryside, he warned, it was 'the party of great and small landowners and of those who rent their land, thus a class party and it acts as such'.[56]

Yet, by the time Lanzillo expressed this opinion, the character of the *fasci* was again changing. In 1921–2, as the organization thrust towards power, its members became more 'Mussolinian'. In ironic parallel to the pyramid in which the cities and towns of the peninsula were arranged in Italian minds, a hierarchy, which led up to a *Duce*, anxious and determined to impose himself as their unchallenged and unchallengeable leader, was forming within the party. A crisis of a kind developed in the summer of 1921. To the dismay of some *ras*, Mussolini suddenly announced that he wished to frame a deal with those socialists who might be willing to treat, especially with their trade unionist wing, end the social war burning through the country-side and, by implication, look to the formation of a grand coalition of new mass parties and organizations in order to overthrow the liberal system, be it embodied in the parliament in Rome or in the institutions of civil society.

After all, the election in May 1921 had not brought the results that Giolitti expected. The Liberals did not reunite, their foes did not beseech 'transformation' and the old leader's magic in composing the parliament and the country no longer worked. On 27 June the Prime Minister resigned and was replaced by Ivanoe Bonomi, his Minister of War, a politician with guaranteed contact with the army and an independent ex-reformist socialist, who had publicly welcomed the spread of Fascism in his home province of Mantua. Mussolini brazenly took full credit for Giolitti's fall.[57] Furthermore, Italian communism, the *Duce* pronounced, writhed in its death throes, while the mainstream socialists, he predicted with typical rancour, 'tired of masturbating while awaiting the arrival of the millennium, are getting around to stretching out on the bed of collaboration with the bourgeoisie'.[58] While forgoing none of his boasted rudeness, Mussolini, as ever thinking of himself as more politically attuned than the *ras* of the provinces, was ready for a compromise, if doubtless one to be pummelled into the form which most advantaged him. On 2 August a so-called 'Pact of Pacification' was signed with four socialist members of parliament, three leaders of CGdL and Enrico De Nicola, the President of the Chamber of Deputies, the equivalent of the Speaker of the House. Among Fascist signatories were Mussolini, Pasella, Giuriati, Rossi, Sansanelli and the Turin war hero, officer and monar-chist, Cesare Maria De Vecchi.

Plenty of other Fascists were outraged at this supping with the socialist devil. Farinacci and Marsich had already announced their resignation from the *fasci*'s central committee. Marsich minced no words in damning what he regarded as a 'grotesque treatying', a pathetic engagement with 'sterile parliamentary practices'. Dino Grandi, in flagrant anonymity, arrayed Bolognese Fascism against the pact. 'Let's not joke, gentlemen,' he wrote. 'What we need today is not a ridiculous peace treaty but a solid, slow, military preparation for our revolutionary tomorrow, directed against the socialist State, which is ineluctably being ushered in.'[59] Seconding his words with actions, the young lawyer tried to beat up the elderly and respectable reformist socialist chief, Filippo Turati, in the parliamentary chamber.[60] Not to be outdone, Farinacci assaulted a communist deputy in the Chamber's toilets.

Other squadrists organized action of a similar kind in arenas beyond the usually genteel parliamentary forum. Marsich led a 'March on Treviso', a city which had not previously bowed to Venetian Fascism. Most celebrated in later Fascist history, in September Balbo, with some help from Grandi, arranged a 'March on Ravenna', timed to coincide with the commemoration of the sixth centenary of Dante, whose tomb lay in that city. Ignoring the prefect and the police, Balbo and his 3,000 men spent two days racking the local socialists while bivouacked in the town. Doubts about the lasting political utility of such paramilitary actions had been one of the reasons that had prompted Mussolini to put out feelers for a compromise. On 21 July the forces of the new Bonomi government blocked a march of five or six hundred Ligurian and Tuscan Fascists on Sarzana, an industrial town just outside the port of La Spezia. In the firing which ensued, eighteen Fascists died and thirty were wounded, many as a result of a manhunt in which enraged locals dealt with the invaders by pitchforking them to death or by stringing up any prisoners who fell into their hands.[61] Three days later, Mussolini warned in *Il Popolo d'Italia* that, regrettably, 'thousands of individuals had interpreted Fascism as no more than a defence of their own personal interests and as an organizer of violence for the sake of violence'. Such heresy must be rooted out and 'discipline' imposed.[62] Did his opponents in the movement really contemplate the liquidation of the two million socialists in the country and an opting for permanent civil war, he asked?[63] Their extremism was pernicious and naive. The time for too much local autonomy in the movement was over.

In reaction to such statements, through the late summer of 1921 many Fascists pondered their purpose and future, asking who might lead them. In the minds of Grandi, Marsich and Balbo, the alternative to Mussolini was none other than Gabriele D'Annunzio and, in August, Grandi and Balbo visited the poet at his estate overlooking Lago di Garda to offer him the chieftainship of the 'national forces'. D'Annunzio evaded their advances, however, stating that he must first consult the stars, unfortunately indecipherable that night since the skies were overcast.[64] The Fascists would have to put up with Mussolini as leader, although fans of the poet as 'the Genius of the Race' (*stirpe*) survived. After October 1922 one force to be visited by Fascist repression was the Unione Spirituale Dannunziana (D'Annunzian spiritual league); its branch at Lecce, for example, was sacked by the Fascists, commanded by later party secretary Achille Starace.[65]

More significant historically is the demonstration which the contact with D'Annunzio and Mussolini's subsequent revival give of the peculiar nature of Italian politics and of the complex relationship between the social arena where squadrism was socially cleansing swathes of northern Italy, without earning such prominent and potentially respectable men as Balbo, Grandi and Marsich a national profile and access to the world of high politics. The ambiguity in the bond between politics and society remains a major issue for any comprehension of the totalitarian ambitions of Fascism, which, if they meant anything, entailed a clear and precise domination by the centre (and Mussolini) over the periphery and so over the Fascists and the rest of the Italian people. Certainly in 1921, and arguably always, centre and periphery occupied different spheres, operating with diverse patterns, rhythms, assumptions and codes, no doubt needing each other but always retaining a flexibility and independence which makes it hard to ascribe the definitive presence of power to one area or the other.

Such issues will continue to mark our account of Fascism but, in 1921, Mussolini's authority as *Duce* was only briefly infringed. On 18 August his resignation from the movement's leadership during the dispute over the Pact of Pacification with the socialists was a gamble but also an intelligent one since Mussolini knew that, the wayward D'Annunzio apart, he had no rival as national head of the new right. Three days later, Cesare Rossi abandoned his own deputy-secretary-ship of the movement, spelling out more directly than the *Duce* his dismay at the drift of Fascism into being a 'pure, authentic and exclusive movement of conservatism and reaction'.[66] Ever the ruthless tactician, Mussolini, however, moving now to accommodate himself with the squadrists, found it helpful to be able to sacrifice Rossi as too stern a critic on the way. In November 1921 the third *fasci* congress assembled in Rome (the capital being still a zone where Fascism was weak). It was estimated at the opening that Mussolini could rely on the support of only a third of the delegates but it did not take long for the reality to be appreciated – there was no alternative to his leadership. A deal among the Fascists was stitched up and the now almost forgotten scheme to treat with the socialists was abandoned (on 22 October Mussolini had forsworn it as 'a pathetically insignificant episode in our history').[67] Simultaneously, the movement was transmuted into a party, the PNF (Partito Nazionale Fascista), expected thereon to pledge fealty to its *Duce* in a more disciplined manner. As a token of accord, Grandi, Marsich and Mussolini embraced before the cheering delegates; any differences between the movement's revolutionary and practical wings now seemed overcome.

A hug from a politician cannot always be relied on, however, and Marsich, shortly after, was driven out of the movement. Grandi became Mussolini's man. Farinacci sulked in his impregnable fortress of Cremona. Rossi had to accept the suppression of his paper, *Il Fascio*, as Mussolini exhibited a cynical skill at rewarding his enemies and rebuking his friends. All in all, those who mattered in Fascism now decided that they would move towards government, relying on Mussolini as their spokesman but with policies forsaking most of the movement's early radicalism and positioned ostentatiously far from Mussolini's own pre-war views.

Much fine print now came to light. Whereas once the movement talked a lot about welfare, now, as Mussolini expressed it: 'in terms of economics, we are overtly anti-socialist. I do not regret having been a socialist. But I have cut my bridges with the past. I have no nostalgia. I don't think about entering socialism but rather about leaving it. In economic matters we are liberals, because we believe that the national economy cannot be entrusted to collective entities or to the bureaucracy.'[68] Some Fascist unions might flourish but they must eschew strikes and other subversive acts, which were simply 'a pointless nuisance'.[69] Such business people as Gino Olivetti, honoured by Mussolini with the title '*duce* of Italian industrialists',[70] were pleased at the news and happily learned that Fascists in the Trentino had guaranteed that 'property is nothing if not man's first freedom; it expresses his first conquest and his first affirmation of his dominance over things'. Ownership of goods, these respectable Fascists thought, was a 'spiritual category no less noble than religion, no less grand than art, no less profound than political philosophy and practice'.[71] Whereas once the movement had flirted with feminism, now Mussolini required that female organizations focus on charity, 'to the exclusion of any political action which must be left exclusively to the party'.[72] Women, a female Fascist was moved to write, despite their instinctive dislike of 'brutality and violence, struggle and blood', must automatically second their men, applaud the *patria* and be unstinting in their devotion to Mussolini and the Fascist creed.[73] Whereas once the movement had been strenuously anti-clerical, now, in February 1922, the PNF welcomed the election of the new Pope Pius XI, who, before he obtained the pallium, had been Archbishop of Milan, with his own connection to Mussolini and his immediate entourage.[74] Whereas once the movement had scorned the lucubrations of effete intellectuals and devoted itself to strenuous and practical action, in January 1922 the monthly *Gerarchia* (Hierarchy) began publication under the editorship of Mussolini and Margherita Sarfatti, promising flexibility towards those in the cultural world willing to accept its aegis. Whereas once speeches about foreign affairs had been wildly expansionist, now Mussolini acknowledged that the nation had been made complete on its northern and eastern borders by its 'decisive' entry into the war.[75] Whereas republicanism had been an early and prominent plank in Fascist doctrine, now the party accepted the monarchy.[76]

What about parliament? Did it, should it have a future? The Fascist response to this fundamental constitutional dilemma was unclear.

Perhaps, Mussolini philosophized in April 1922, one day a 'March on Rome', a *coup d'état*, 'a violent revolution', might prove necessary, but, for the foreseeable future, it was better for the PNF 'to insert itself ever more intimately and profoundly into the life as a whole of the Italian nation'.[77] Lest the movement be thought to have become too flaccid, the *Duce* did not forget to endorse and justify successive armed attacks by the squads on Ferrara, Rimini, Andria, Viterbo, Sestri Ponente, Cremona and Novara.[78]

The appearance of Ferrara and Cremona on this list is proof of the lingering fluidity of Fascist authority in the provinces. A 'march' on a place typically harried local anti-Fascists, burning their offices, wrecking their printing presses, beating and humiliating their leaders and always implying that further opposition was useless. It was true, after all, that Italian socialism lacked big battalions to summon to its aid in the current emergency. Its rank and file were poor; their conversion to unionism was often recent and lacking in intellectual rigour. Happy to know this weakness, most members of the Liberal elite doubted that socialism possessed a legitimate place in national politics and society.

No doubt, hostility to Fascism could linger too. Yet, by the summer of 1922, the Fascist imposition of itself on the population of most of northern Italy was continuing to increase and the weakness of the government, from February 1922 presided over by the feeble Luigi Facta, was obvious. In July Balbo returned to Ravenna, liquidating any residue of socialist organizations surviving from his raid of the previous year. With that increasingly Fascist enthusiasm for ceremony, Balbo, after the socialists were bashed into submission, organized a public passing of the keys of the local *Casa del Popolo* (People's meeting place) to a mutilated returned soldier (and republican), R. Piccinini. Now Ravenna was not the only target. Rather Balbo's column acted like an army of occupation as it spread out through the Romagna, burning and smiting wherever it went, but meeting, Balbo noted frankly, little resistance.[79]

Trouble was still possible. Outraged by the socialists' opting for a so-called 'legal strike', on 4 August Balbo marched on Parma to find to his disgust that the local Fascists were locked in a factional conflict between followers of De Ambris and conservatives. Worse, the prefect was hostile and the local army commander had brought his own forces into the city, where they were hailed as deliverers by local socialists, who greeted the soldiery with shouts of 'Hooray for the proletarian army!' Balbo deplored this yielding to 'Bolshevism' but, by his own account, was buoyed by the appearance of still more Fascists from as far afield as Venice, travelling by car or train, and including Farinacci. Parma was again assaulted, this time street by street and with the aid of machine guns. An attempt at compromise by the local bishop fell on deaf ears and, by midnight on 5 August, the prefect had resigned and the army agreed to collaborate. In response, the Fascists demobilized but not before holding a victory parade through the main square the next day. Balbo rejoiced that 'the Parma raid was the biggest in which Fascism had so far engaged' (although historians dispute his version of events, arguing that Parma was the sole city where the Fascist assault of those days was not really successful).[80] Whatever the case, Balbo moved on to Ancona, took that city, too, and refreshed himself with some boysie nude bathing in the Adriatic.[81]

By October 1922 up to three thousand Italians had died in the political and social instability that had flooded the country since the end of the war. Contemporaries noted a rise in deaths by firearms in the north and, ironically, a diminution of killings in the south, perhaps because traditional society was to some extent modernizing there. At the time (and despite the appalling cost from 1915 to 1918 of the Liberal intervention in the First World War), the level of political violence was viewed as intolerable and a direct and immediate challenge to state institutions in a way that, given our twenty-first century knowledge of the appalling harvest of political deaths to follow, is a little hard to grasp. Compared with the toll in Weimar Germany, let alone in the USSR or in many of the successor states of Central and Eastern Europe, or in the failed states of our own times, Italians got off lightly in such sacrifice and, once again, this comparison will be worth remembering when assessing how deeply a Fascist regime impinged on Italian life.

None the less, by the autumn of 1922, there were quite a few Italians, especially among the political elite, who had concluded that the nagging political crisis must be resolved and the murders and mayhem in the countryside ended. Within the Fascist movement, similar thoughts obtained, with Michele Bianchi wondering in August whether the movement could retain the unity and sense of purpose needed to assume government. Time might be running out and it was hard to determine whether the insurrectional or the legal path was to be preferred.[82] This dilemma had also occurred to the *Duce*. Perhaps he and Bianchi deliberately played good cop, bad cop, when, that same month, they met Paolino Taddei, the Minister of the Interior and the most formidable figure in Prime Minister Facta's frail latest cabinet. Taddei found the often accommodating Bianchi impossibly 'fanatical', but Mussolini he deemed open to reason.[83]

Whether Taddei had plumbed a real division in the Fascist leadership may be doubted, but certainly, during the next months, Fascism strode towards office on two fronts, which were deliberately kept apart. In the countryside the squads and their *ras* daily took the field. In September the industrial town of Terni and the port of Civitavecchia, each only some hundred kilometres from Rome, were purged by Fascist bully-boys. In early October the Fascists, with Starace and Balbo in the vanguard, undertook the paramilitary occupation of Trento and Bolzano, pledging to convert any German- (or Ladin-) speaking peasants in the Alto Adige/Süd Tirol into Italians and forcing the resignation of the existing liberal authorities there. This raid re-emphasized the message from Trieste about the commitment of Fascism to ethnic cleansing. If, having vanquished national enemies, Fascism manned the frontiers of Italy, could Rome hold out for long against the squads?

Meanwhile, Mussolini moved with aplomb in the rarefied air of Italian high politics. Naturally he found it easiest to talk to such wartime leaders as the conservative Salandra, who was dreaming of a grand coalition of the right under his own leadership but was willing to let it be known that he considered himself an 'honorary Fascist'.[84] The eventual Mussolini cabinet included in its ranks Giovanni Colonna di Cesarò, Sonnino's nephew and political heir (as well as being the Nationalist president of the Pro Dalmazia association).[85] Until the very last moment, Salandra thought that Mussolini would accept junior office under his command. But the *Duce* and his agents had wires open to other places. The respectable Abruzzese Fascist,

'Prof.' Giacomo Acerbo, born 1888, a volunteer and decorated officer in the war, once an aspirant Giolittian, an economist and
Freemason, talked to Orlando; in another government under his leadership, could Mussolini be satisfied with the Ministry of the Interior
(Orlando suggested Foreign Affairs instead)?[86] There were hints that
the moralist editor of *Il Corriere della Sera* and occasional critic of
Fascist crudity and illegality, Luigi Albertini, could take the
Washington embassy in a new administration and there speak for an
administration which embraced Mussolini.[87] Discussions continued
with D'Annunzio, still a potential leader, although the feckless poet
was rendered immobile during the crucial weeks when, in August, he
injured himself after tumbling from a window in his *palazzo* on what
may have been another starless night. Even Giolitti, who, despite his
great age, was seen by many surviving Liberals and by Mussolini as
the most likely alternative Prime Minister, was engaged in talk and
may not have been enthused to learn from one of his senatorial contacts that 'almost all the sons of the Liberals are in Fascism, with their
fathers' consent'.[88] By late October not only these old politicians but
Nitti and Salvemini, the liberal democrats, Giovanni Amendola and
Luigi Einaudi, and the Catholic, Alcide De Gasperi, all were persuaded that Mussolini should be given his chance.[89] So, too, were the
King, the Pope, the army leadership and the nation's business chiefs.

Whether Mussolini possessed a set agenda in the wheeling and
dealing which preceded the March on Rome remains arguable. As he
often acknowledged, he was generally happier with tactics than with
strategy. What is clear is that, in autumn 1922, Mussolini had joined
in a political poker game where the other players thought themselves
able and experienced but where, either now aged or always second
rate, none could beat his ruthlessness and nerve.

October was to be the crucial month. According to Balbo,
Mussolini was stirred to act against Rome by the news of the successful March on Bolzano,[90] although De Felice is probably right to stress
that, even then, the die was not cast. It clearly was by the time the
party congress assembled at Naples on the 24th. A few days earlier,
first at Bordighera, where Balbo and De Vecchi took a prominent role,
and later at Florence, a plan for military insurrection was drafted.
Italy was divided into twelve zones and it was even suggested that a

temporary Fascist capital could be created in central Italy and that, from there, a Fascist government could negotiate with a Liberal rump in Rome.[91] Bianchi, Balbo, De Vecchi and retired general Emilio De Bono, born 1866 and thus elderly by Fascist standards, were pompously nominated the *quadrumviri* or four strong men to head the March on the Eternal City. By 28 October Perugia had become the assembly point for a push on Rome, although no more than 5,000 inadequately armed men were available.[92] Simultaneously, other cities were further 'cleansed' by Fascist assault: Trieste was again the object of a march by Giunta and his squad.[93] Three Fascists were to die in the half-hearted paramilitary attack on the capital.[94] Militarily there can be little doubt that the marchers could have been scattered by the battalions of the national army available in and around the capital. But the army leadership obeyed constitutional form and waited a government order that never came (while General Emanuele Pugliese, commanding them, sagely advised that the forces were loyal but it was most politic not to test that loyalty).

The Fascist campaign was enough to conquer, not so much militarily as politically. The March of 28 October was rapidly installed in Fascist legend, portrayed as the heroic summit of the 'revolution' – the entry in the Fascist *Who's Who* about the rather mild-mannered Acerbo, for example, stressed his commanding of a squad from his region which allegedly 'took Tivoli', just to the east of the capital, on that famous day. Yet the real achievement was Mussolini's and the major line of communication was his telephone in Milan, that personal citadel to which he had ostentatiously retreated. The *Duce* led less in the style of a conquering Caesar and more in that of a cool and natural expert in the haggling skills of the political market.

The last bulwarks of the liberal regime, Facta and the King, were frail reeds in the best of circumstances and now they bowed to what they perceived as the inevitable. Victor Emmanuel III was another to hide behind the constitution, while apparently most worried by dynastic squabbles. There were rumours that his cousin, the taller and more militant-seeming Duke of Aosta, was flirting with half-suggestions that the King should abdicate for a real man. Deciding that the imposition of martial law to block the Fascist advance was too radical a measure, the King yielded to what he viewed as the inevitable. The phone rang in Milan as the *Duce* had been certain it would. Mussolini was offered and accepted the prime ministership in a coalition government that rallied all but the socialists and communists and incurably purist dissidents among the other groups to its cause. On the evening of 29 October the *Duce* humbly took an ordinary sleeper on the scheduled express train south from Milan to meet the King. Only then did the erratically marshalled Fascist forces breach the gates of Rome. The squads' subsequent strutting was at its most violent in the working-class area around the Tiburtina railway junction and near the Basilica of San Lorenzo. It was a part of Rome destined to be bombed by the Allies in July 1943, when the populace would display a long memory, cheering the Pope and damning the tyrant Mussolini.

Then, it had long been plain that the 'March on Rome', however falsely glamorized by regime propagandists, had signalled a Fascist assault on and eventual takeover of the Italian state. In the complex of events in October 1922, this last conquest was not yet obvious. In some ways Mussolini's accession to office resembled any other government crisis and there was plenty of optimistically patriotic talk about restored consensus and unity. Nationalists, although, during the actual march, their so-called *Sempre Pronti* (Always Ready) squads had mobilized against Fascist revolution, were swiftly eager to embrace the new administration. *L'Alpino*, the journal of returned soldiers, for example, underlined its joy at a government that 'gives the nation back its soul, the soul of the war, the soul of victory [sic]'[95] The first press release of the *quadrumvirato* cautiously stated that 'the classes who compose the productive bourgeoisie know that Fascism wishes to impose a real discipline on the nation and to help all those forces which enhance our economic expansion and well-being'.[96] Rather it was the *Duce* who was now the militant. His justification to the newspapers of his trip to Rome proclaimed that he had 'three hundred thousand men in the country, organized and faithful to my orders'. He could count on their embodiment of the 'national will'. He would cut expenditure and make Italy respected abroad. And he would go to see Victor Emmanuel III 'wearing a black-shirt and as a Fascist'.[97] He would thus incarnate no mere political change but a social and cultural revolution. Alceste De Ambris, once D'Annunzio's philosopher at Fiume and a man who still thought of crafting his own revolutions, was not impressed. He wrote that Mussolini had reached office merely because of his 'cunning playing of wretched political games'; his efforts with the telephone in Milan meant that he was no more than a 'shirker, hidden away in his newspaper'. This pseudo-Garibaldi, De Ambris predicted, would, unlike the original one, 'die rich'.[98] No doubt De Ambris was a jaundiced observer. The *Duce* was installed in power but, on 30 October 1922, a large part of the historic meaning of Fascism was still to be established.

7

Learning to rule from Rome

Giustino Fortunato, the liberal shocked in 1917 to be assaulted by his peasants, was another to be sardonic about the news of the March on Rome, while reporting gloomily that even such luminaries as the liberal philosopher and historian Benedetto Croce were currently detecting some virtue in Mussolini. He himself, Fortunato remarked, retained the view that Fascism constituted the 'last post-war madness' and he prophesied that no good would come from it. In the south, he had been watching the triumphal progress of PNF secretary Michele Bianchi, until recently an activist resident in the north. Now Bianchi had reappeared in Calabria, gaily distributing present favours and future promises. A later scanning of the evidence can track what Fortunato was seeing. Local journalists eagerly expressed their fellow citizens' 'profound gratitude' to the PNF secretary for his success as an intermediary and patron, when, for example, in May 1923, he announced that the new government had set aside 111 million lire for public works in the region.[1] A reception in a small town for the distinguished visitor took care to offer him a menu crafted to mesh patriotism and the new order, with a meal composed of *Zuppa all'Italia*, *Vitello alla Vittorio Veneto*, *Pesca alla Fascista* and *Cassata 'Augusto Valerio'*. Bianchi reacted by publicly advocating state intervention which could generously provide 'water, drains, roads' and reliable electricity supplies for the place.[2] Results might be tardy, however. In Calabria, as one of Fortunato's correspondents told him, 'the world is as it was before'. Deputies issued *raccomandazioni* (letters of recommendation) with a will for any jobs going. The erstwhile opponents of Fascism swung over to its cause but always did so in their own interests. The peasantry, still the majority of the population, remained

184

indifferent to high politics; Fascism so far had not breached their world. Except in the Mussolini government's rhetoric, genuinely 'new men' were hard to find.[3]

No doubt Fortunato's cynicism fitted his character as a man whom history had defeated. Yet the thesis that change is occurring easily or completely in a society and that revolutions are automatically revolutionary should often be resisted. Alessandro Lessona, born 1891 in Rome, a decorated officer in the socially respectable cavalry during the war, a man with a law degree and contacts in the highest circles and a future Fascist Minister, claimed, when he reflected on October 1922, that, at that time, there was no thought of dictatorship. Mussolini, he maintained, had become the head of a parliamentary coalition that did not infringe liberal democratic practice and the best and brightest Fascists had not sacrificed 'many young lives' to impose a tyrant on the country. Rather, the task of the new government, soon to be achieved, was to restore law and order and, above all, turn back the 'Bolshevik' threat.[4]

Lessona protests too much. Yet it is true that, during the years from 1922 to 1924, the nature of what was to become the Fascist regime was not fully established. Its history commenced under the sign of the two faces of Janus, a god who looked forward and back. The government was composed of a coalition of Italy's most able, so long as they were not socialists, apparent proof that Fascism would not tear to pieces the belief systems of the Italian establishment. Mussolini took on the Prime Ministership, the Ministry of the Interior and the Ministry of Foreign Affairs, promising and achieving an activism that put memories of Facta or Bonomi in the shade. Other Fascists who grasped ministerial responsibilities usually came from the moderate side of the movement – Giuriati was Minister for Occupied Territories, Acerbo the *Duce*'s deputy in the prime ministerial office. Aldo Oviglio, born 1873, a lawyer based in Bologna where, as a Fascist, he contested the authority of Grandi and Arpinati, but was derided as a slipper-wearer by Farinacci, became the Minister of Justice. In this role he quickly issued an amnesty for those jailed for political crimes, many but not all being Fascists, and so continued the happy relationship between Fascism (despite its violence and illegality) and the law. Mussolini endorsed the decree by his fellow

Romagnole Oviglio, despite some worrying whether it was providing a stern enough example. Amnesty was enshrined as a typically qualifying and corrupting part of Fascist policing.[5]

Plenty of non-Fascists, people to be termed *fiancheggiatori* or fellow travellers, accepted positions in the government. Indeed, Salvemini, using a parallel to be repeated with greater notoriety about Hitler, for a time deemed Mussolini the tinny 'drummer' for established interests.[6] The two military ministries went to Armando Diaz and Paolo Thaon di Revel, the respective commanders of the national army and navy at victory in 1918. The conservative Catholic Stefano Cavazzoni held the Ministry of Works, while another rightist Catholic, Vincenzo Tangorra, was placed at the Treasury. His good offices were useful in persuading the government to smile at a bail-out of the troubled Banco di Roma, owned by Vatican interests. At the senior Ministry of Finance in any case was 'Prof.' Alberto De' Stefani, born 1879, a Fascist but one with a mind of his own and a well-regarded economist (equipped with a law degree and a doctorate in business studies), who preferred free trade to protection. A friendly historian has argued that De' Stefani was accepted as the leading party economist because he possessed the most interesting personality among those in the movement devoted to the dismal science.[7] Certainly De' Stefani worked hard and could count on Mussolini's backing in balancing the budget. In July 1923 the *Duce* told Goffredo Gobbi of the Associazione Liberale that Fascism and liberalism were not divided by any 'antithesis in programmes', even if they did deviate a little in method. Each sought 'the moral and material grandeur of the nation'.[8]

The Nationalist Luigi Federzoni took charge of the Ministry of Colonies and was soon engaged in arranging the merger of the Nationalist Association with the PNF, so adding its high-society profile and alleged expertise in diplomacy (and imperialism) to the Fascist amalgam. A number of observers have argued that thereafter ex-Nationalists frequently set the tone in Fascist policy-making. The Ministry of Education fell to the internationally acclaimed idealist philosopher Giovanni Gentile (1875–1944), by now a Fascist but an independent one with a conception of the movement that, in his mind, was elevated above the thuggery of Farinacci and the cruder squadrists. Among other key positions in the new administration's gift, the colonial governors, including Volpi in Tripolitania, stayed in office, as did Bonaldo Stringher, the long-serving CEO of the Bank of Italy, once a confidant of Giolitti. The commandant of the *carabinieri*, General Giacomo Ponzio, kept his post till 1925 when he was replaced by the noble Senator, Enrico Asinari di San Marzano. In sum, by most standards the Mussolini government was a distinguished one, presenting further proof of the way in which those who had belonged to the ruling elite of Liberal society willingly accepted an enhanced authoritarianism in their country's administration and suggesting that quite a few liberal 'freedoms' may be fair-weather causes.

How far change might go was, of course, the question and, in that regard, there was countervailing evidence from the moment the black-shirted Mussolini received the royal charge to become Prime Minister. It was true that the movement had forsworn its initial republicanism and anti-clericalism. Mussolini and King Victor Emmanuel were soon working together readily enough; the *Duce*, until 1943, undertook without complaint the duty of turning up at the royal palace, the Quirinale, twice a week, there to converse with the anything but loquacious monarch who, in 1923, murmured that he was glad the Prime Minister had won out against the 'low game of the parties'.[9] The Queen Mother, the less hide-bound Margherita, at much the same time passed on the message to *Il Popolo d'Italia* that she believed that 'Mussolini has saved the nation', adding that she had long revelled in the *Duce*'s commanding prose style.[10] Rumours eddying around that Victor Emmanuel would be replaced by his cousin, the taller, more kingly and more openly militarist Duke of Aosta, now ceased.

The new government's accommodation with the Church was equally swift. Just after Christmas Mussolini reverentially told a priest, who was interviewing him for the conservative paper *Il Giornale d'Italia*, that, contrary to previous impressions, 'I am a Catholic'. He also made clear his conviction that Catholicism must stay the state religion.[11] Early in the new year Mussolini met secretly with Cardinal Pietro Gasparri, the Papal Secretary of State – the venue was a senator's house with a front and back entrance[12] – and, by July 1923, Vatican pressure had persuaded the priest Luigi Sturzo to retire from the leadership of the PPI. Then and thereafter, nothing was done by the Church to save this party from dissolution.

Yet, in parallel to these deals with respectable and establishment Italy, Fascism was forming an institutional base which hinted that the new Prime Minister might be aiming not so much at a government as a regime. From December 1922, set alongside the Cabinet and contesting its authority, stood a Fascist Grand Council (Gran Consiglio), although its first formal meeting waited till 12 January 1923, when the *Duce* prophesied boldly that 'the Fascist revolution can last for a generation'.[13] In the new body there were jobs for such senior Fascists as Bianchi, De Bono, De Vecchi, Rossi, union chief Rossoni, Sansanelli and soon Farinacci, Giunta, Grandi, Pisenti and the rest. Aldo Finzi, a Jewish Fascist who was an airman associate of the *Duce*, and, on occasion, acted as his second in his duels, kept the minutes. Still more menacing was the announcement on 12 January of the intention to found a Milizia volontaria per la sicurezza nazionale (MVSN, Voluntary militia for national security), a paramilitary force which would rival the national army, absorb the Nationalists' Sempre Pronti formations and give Fascist squadrism national legitimacy.[14] Its grades, with their portentously classical names (a legion for a regiment, a century for a company), replicated those of the army and the MVSN was also granted its own welfare and health schemes and a *ufficio storico* or history office[15] to bond its past with a lasting future. The MVSN's establishment and that of the Grand Council hinted that the parliamentary coalition was a façade and a temporary one. Perhaps Fascism had come to Rome not just to play the liberal game but to rule by itself, of itself and for itself? Perhaps it was to be a revolution?

For the moment, the matter was not resolved. The installation of the *Duce* of Fascism as Prime Minister had not at once closed the gap between events in the national capital and those in the provinces. In Bologna, Cremona, Ferrara and other provincial cities and towns the squads remained primed and active, frequently being led by men with minds of their own, determined to impose their ruffianly version of 'revolution' on their localities and, as yet, unconvinced that they must always obey their Machiavellian *Duce*. To many, the triumph of the March on Rome seemed the moment for vendetta and pay-off, both against enemies and friends. As historian Salvatore Lupo has summarized it, then occurred 'an exasperated factional war, mainly directed at controlling local territory'. It was of unpredictable ideological character.[16]

In peripheral Catanzaro, for example, police reports immediately after the March on Rome tabulated a list of disorders. Fascists, their numbers swelling, were irrupting into peasant cooperatives, forcing their closure and ostentatiously recording the names of members for later retribution.[17] Anti-Fascist small-town mayors were being forced to resign under overt threats of beating.[18] A socialist Member of Parliament was prevented from leaving Catanzaro and driven to take refuge with friends after his home was invaded by Fascist bullyboys.[19] A Communist party branch in the city was attacked and the triumphant invaders carried off a table, four benches, some chairs, an acetylene gas container, some correspondence and propaganda booklets, even though the police reported primly that they already knew the contents of these last works.[20] In another *paese* in the province, Caccuri, the archpriest, and some sisters of Charity were the objects of Fascist ban; in Wild West manner, they were ordered to wipe the dust of the town from their feet and never to return.[21]

Mussolini, however, still needing to be the statesman one day and the revolutionary chief the next, could not risk openly endorsing hoodlums. As early as 8 November, at the second meeting of his Cabinet, he denounced a squadrist 'Sunday brawl' at Teramo in the Abruzzi. Such conduct was not genuinely political, he stated staidly, but sprang from 'shabby and partisan small-town passions'. He expected any outbreaks of loutishness to be restrained by 'the intelligence and energy of the local authorities'.[22]

But one word from the *Duce* did not yet bring automatic quiet and obedience and could instead prompt complaint. A primitive institutional Darwinism was easy to see. On 18 November Balbo wrote to Bianchi to express his disgust that Farinacci was being allowed to comment on the situation at Ferrara, when 'the only person really abreast of that subject is me'.[23] A year later Giunta was still trying to squash the bickering that separated one leading Fascist from another in too many provinces.[24] The most notorious example of Fascist rage in the weeks after the March on Rome occurred between 18 and 20

December 1922 at Turin. There the squads decided that they must impose their discipline on the working class of that city and its leaders and sacked the office of Gramsci's theoretical journal, *L'Ordine Nuovo*.[25] Running street battles resulted in which a score of people died. More perplexing was the fact that the leaders of the radical wing of Turin Fascism, Mario Gioda (an ex-anarchist) and Pietro Gorgolini (born 1891, with a law degree, a defender of the military role of Luigi Cadorna and destined to become a tame journalist of the regime)[26] were not those who led this raid. Rather it was headed by the ambitious and pompous *quadrumvir* De Vecchi, who, despite his love of the monarchy and his clericalism, was an open critic of Giovanni Agnelli and the chief capitalists of his city.[27] Just before the event, Mussolini had written to De Vecchi demanding obeisance to the *Duce*. Somewhat self-consciously, Mussolini also took the occasion to deny that he was in any sense a trimmer. During the March on Rome, he emphasized: 'I was on the barricades, ready to risk my life and I was not working for a parliamentary deal which at the last minute would sabotage and mutilate our victory.'[28]

It is possible that such words were read by De Vecchi as a green light for his cleansing of his city. If so, he was mistaken, or at least Mussolini was soon disassociating himself from the mayhem involved. De Vecchi found his own career in disarray and before long was sent to govern dusty Somaliland, remote from the levers of power and where a fiasco was always possible. De Vecchi's relegation suggests that Mussolini saw the founding of the militia as a way of harnessing the squads firmly to his own cause rather than to that of Fascist revolution. In September 1923 he instructed De Bono, whom he had put in command of the MVSN, to circularize members with the demand that they must above all be obedient to the party's central command. For all the 'utterly Fascist' character of the militia, discipline in its ranks must be 'purely and simply military'. Those who could not accept such rigour should strip off their uniforms and return to civilian life: 'It does not matter much if there is a reduction in the number of Black Shirts, even a considerable one. The more we limit the number of the Legions, the more they will be a splendid and reliable instrument in the hands of the government.'[29]

What, then, of this government's mandate and what, more generally, of its path between legality and illegality? From the beginning of his Prime Ministership Mussolini was thinking of holding new elections that could confirm his right to rule and expand on the thirty-five deputies who were still officially the only Fascists in the Chamber. Hitler would do the same (but much more quickly) and, since 1922, we have grown used to dictators justifying their seizures of power through rigged plebiscites soon after they obtain office. As so often, Mussolini was a pioneer in this behaviour and his actions retained a degree of ambiguity. The elections that he presided over and won in April 1924 were not merely a façade or, rather, they still reflected the practices of his Liberal predecessors. At the constitutional level, the poll was conditioned by the framing of the 'Acerbo law', designed, it was said in words which recurred at other moments of Italian history, to make the nation more governable. Under the provisions of this reform, a reward was to be given to that political grouping which garnered the most votes. This victor was automatically to receive two thirds of the seats in parliament. The remaining one third could be distributed proportionally. The idea was first Bianchi's and was bitterly and publicly opposed by Farinacci, who roared his dislike of the implication of old-style transformism in the implied creation of a grand coalition, detecting, rightly, that a corollary of the scheme was a dilution of the autonomy of the *ras*. The senior liberal politicians, Salandra, Giolitti and, after some initial doubts, Orlando, by contrast, all approved the Acerbo law, as did a parliamentary majority. A model of governance was being forged. Mussolini's regime was greatly to infringe the rule of law – the party secretary, Augusto Turati, in 1928 took it as read that 'a Fascist lawyer, in an essentially political case, cannot take on the defence of an anti-Fascist against a militant and worthy Fascist', demanding that all must think first of the 'nation and regime. In this dictatorship, every lawyer must place himself at the service of Fascist justice.'[30] Yet the regime did its best to avoid open illegality, preferring to have its actions approved and seconded by such constituted authorities as the upper courts or the Senate. The Fascist way was for the law to be taken over rather than openly hijacked into some revolutionary course.

In any case, the composition of the PNF was changing rapidly during the months after Mussolini obtained office. Membership ballooned from 300,000 to a temporary peak of 782,979 at the end of 1923 (in 1924 the number retreated to 642,246; in 1925 to 599,988, before there was a further rise, with the total surpassing one million in 1927).[31] The figures were complicated by the fact that quite a few of those early Fascists, who disliked the compromises of government or who, once Mussolini was in office, believed their patriotic task done and opted for other preoccupations, did not renew their party tickets. Similarly, it was also true that the administrative practices of the movement were always sufficiently flexible to allow the backdating of an individual's membership should that prove politically or socially useful. One advantaged in this regard was Alessandro Lessona;[32] another was Giuseppe Volpi, whose business skills may have assisted the granting of his party ticket which was paid for in July 1923 but dated to 26 January 1922.[33]

Once Mussolini had taken office, members flooded in from those southern regions which, previously, had been little touched by the movement and where local social problems had not seemed especially to need the ideology or the practice of Fascism. Their arrival suggested that Italians would be just as active in manipulating Fascism as the Fascists were to be in controlling them. All over the south, rival interest groups and competing patron–client networks sought advantage in their endless disputes by acquiring the gloss of Fascism. As a prefect reported from the Basilicata where, in January, armed skirmishes had broken out between groups claiming respectively to be Nationalist and Fascist: 'In reality in the Basilicata, neither Fascism nor Nationalism has existed or exists today.' 'Where there is a mayor and a communal council supported by personages from an old camarilla dressed up as Nationalists,' his report continued, 'Fascism will arise, or, in truth, another clientele will don Fascist clothes and found a Fascist branch.'[34] A slightly different situation was reported in the province of Reggio Calabria where the Fascist chief, Giuseppe Minniti, was charged with allowing anyone to join the party so long as they were subservient to him and to his factional interests. His egoism and corruption, it was said, were so blatant that they alienated genuine men of respect from the new government, reducing the politics of the region to a 'simply disastrous' situation.[35]

It was therefore unsurprising when, at the end of December 1924, the city of Reggio went into *festa* at a rumour that Mussolini had resigned. The popular reaction was as it might have been in 1860 at the fall of the Bourbons or as it was to be in 1943 with the arrival of the 'liberating' Anglo-Americans. According to one contemporary, 'in an instant, the city burst into celebration. Work was suspended everywhere and the shops were closed in sign of jubilation. A vast popular throng hailed the representatives of the opposition and carried them aloft in triumph. Those most compromised with Fascism made themselves scarce. Others now maintained that they were nauseated by the past regime and asked if they, too, could join the victory parade.'[36] As shall be seen, Mussolini was preoccupied with more serious matters at this moment and did not visit Reggio with condign punishment, although he did send Lanzillo to undertake an official investigation. This latter, protecting his own people as a patron should, claimed that the false alarm of a government change had been exaggerated by opposition figures, who indulged in 'vulgar and offensive speeches' to a crowd of three hundred. The citizenry, he decided, had not really applauded the news and, in retrospect, were openly critical of what had happened. In any case, by now the prefect had the town in hand and, outside Reggio, Fascism ruled serenely in the province. Nevertheless, Lanzillo promised to assemble the main Fascists and give them 'instructions, news and encouragement', read the riot act and ensure that the untoward events of 31 December were not repeated.[37]

The story of Reggio hints at the superficiality of the penetration of modern politics there. None the less, in the elections of April 1924, the PNF boasted stunning success in the country as a whole but especially in the south. The provisions of the Acerbo law proved unnecessary as the government ticket swept Italy. In a 63.8 per cent poll of eligible voters (up 5.4 per cent from 1921), the government-sponsored *listone* or big list won 66.3 per cent of valid votes. In the south their backing reached 81.5 per cent; it was 76 per cent in Central Italy, 69.9 per cent in Sicily and Sardinia and 54.3 per cent in the north. The socialists and communists, running as three separate groups, were cut to 14.6 per cent (29.2 per cent in 1921). The Catholics, who had already been abandoned by the Church hierarchy, gained 9.1 per cent (21.2 per cent in 1921) – clerically inclined rightist commentators had convinced themselves that Mussolini was another Bismarck but one

improved by a dose of 'Latin geniality'.[38] Various other small groupings, including Giolitti's half independent list of liberals, took the rest
of the votes.

In the new Chamber, 374 deputies out of 535 owed allegiance to
Mussolini.[39] Some equivocation survived. Michele Bianchi preserved
in his private papers a tabulation of how leading Fascists fared in
terms of personal votes on the electoral tickets of the various
provinces. Mussolini, in Lombardy, did best with 49.14 per cent,
being top of the poll in what had become his political home, the region
which, he boasted, best exemplified 'power, work and social equilib-
rium'.[40] Bianchi, in the joint regions of Calabria and the Basilicata,
was next best placed with 42.88 per cent and second position in preferences. Gabriele Carnazza won 33.06 per cent in Sicily (and was
third there), Pietro Lissia 27.97 per cent in Sardinia (fourth) and
Acerbo 26.38 per cent in the Abruzzi-Molise (sixth). Those who had
presented themselves in the north, despite the fact that Fascism had
deeper roots there and despite the flagrant violence of its deeds in that
part of the country, could not compete with the personal votes
achieved in the south. Balbo gained 16.09 per cent in the Emilia-
Romagna (and was seventh), the mutilated war hero Carlo Delcroix
12 per cent in Tuscany (tenth), Finzi 10.28 per cent in the Veneto
(eleventh) and the young intellectual Giuseppe Bottai 5.05 per cent in
Lazio and Umbria (fourteenth).[41]

These relatively low personal tallies suggest that the poll had been
won more in the way that Giolitti or his liberal predecessors,
Francesco Crispi and Agostino Depretis, had managed elections than
by some Fascist and totalitarian method. Much had depended on the
official actions of prefects and local police chiefs and the unofficial
functioning of patron–client networks. After all, although the government did act against bureaucrats whose loyalty it doubted with punishment through transfer or the sack (as earlier liberal administrations
had also done), it now went out of its way to urge its administrators
not to let local Fascists get away with brawling or corruption. As early
as January 1923 De Bono informed police that it was a mistake to
think that the government wanted 'unconditionally to protect the
Fascists, no matter what they do'. Six months later Mussolini urged
that 'the single and only representative of the government in each

province is the prefect and no one else'. Local Fascist chiefs must note the matter well, he added, and prefects must intervene where party members squabbled among themselves in a fashion that threatened good order. Police should move energetically to collect and sequester private arms. In sum, 'illegality of any kind, no matter who practises it, should be inexorably suppressed', the Prime Minister ordered.[42]

Too much propriety should not be read into these words. In the lead-up to the elections in Bologna, the ambitious prefect, Arturo Bocchini, suggested brightly to Mussolini that party members could be stationed inside local polling booths, where they could act as a stimulus to responsible voting.[43] In Ferrara, Balbo's electoral technique, at least according to the account of a colleague, was straightforwardly pre-emptive. Fascists could doubtless stand to attention within the booths. But, he added, not put off by the fact that he was still being pursued legally for his responsibility in the murder of Don Giovanni Minzoni in August 1923, the first voter should be made an example of: 'Let us take, therefore, this privileged elector and break his head open – even if he has voted for us, too bad for him – shouting, "Bastard, you voted for the socialists".' Such actions, he knew, would not be disowned by Rome: 'I would not take on certain responsibilities if I were not perfectly aware of the government's thinking.'[44]

To the violent repression of dissidence and the implied reward of any who did the government's bidding was added a tightening control of the press, another policy from which Giolitti and other 'liberals' had not refrained. In July 1923 the prefects were formally authorized to seize papers and fine owners, should their journals 'damage national credit at home or abroad', alarm and dismay public opinion and so disturb 'order'.[45] The looseness of the phrasing was evidently designed to embolden censorship and curb press freedom.

The plotting of elections aside, Fascism was finding a more populist and revolutionary way to bind its members fast into the emerging regime. Historians have spent much effort exploring webs of significance in the movement's liking for 'sacraments', growing, it is said, from the practices established by D'Annunzio at Fiume. This interpretation fails to admit that the more obvious example of a place where, in the early twentieth century, 'mythical thought' was brought to power, was Madison Avenue. The capitalist advertising of the virtue and appeal of consumerism outlasted and outperformed all its rivals and offered considerable direct challenge to Fascism. Yet it is true that 'Prof.' Mussolini, well before the March on Rome, was given to disquisitions on the need for Fascism to be 'above all, a set of ideas'.[46] This form of 'new politics', he maintained, must spawn a 'vast movement for the revision of all contemporary political values'[47] and indoctrinate the people with 'a religious concept of Italianness'.[48] Fascism, he instructed Bianchi in August 1921, must be armed with a developed philosophy: 'to equip the brain with a doctrine and solid convictions does not mean to disarm it. Rather it renders it stronger and more conscious in its actions. Soldiers who fight knowing their own cause are always the best.'[49] Rome, eternal Rome, was, he maintained in April 1922, Fascism's 'place of departure' and 'our symbol and, if you like, our special myth'.[50]

There was quite a bit of inconsistency in this, as in other segments of Mussolini's political thought, while he carved his cunning path between rational acts and a fanaticized and irrational deployment of myth. There were plenty of signs that the *Duce* hoped to win over both the hearts and the minds of Italians (including himself). As a youthful socialist, he had either read or made reference to the works of Gustave Le Bon, Georges Sorel and Vilfredo Pareto and knew of their theories that mass man (and woman) were not as likely to be marshalled by 'scientific' socialism as they were to rally behind myth, force and that dynamic individual who could be presented as embodying these matters. Nor was Mussolini the only operator in the Italian political world to be aware that many of his co-nationals lacked political sophistication. In July 1923 Salvemini commented bleakly that a maximum of 100,000 Italians were even remotely interested in politics; the other 39,900,000 could not care less.[51] Amendola thought that the fate of the nation lay in the hands of the educated, men like himself; trying to be too intellectual with other Italians was a waste of time, he advised.[52]

Backwardness played its part in the structuring of a Fascist response to mass politics but there was another reason why talk about myth readily surfaced in Italy. Reference to religion was not altogether surprising in the country which housed the Vatican and where so many identities (and the vocabularies in which they were expressed) were indebted to a version of Catholicism. As well as sponsoring a Fascist 'liturgy', Mussolini spoke readily about the 'wretched little socialist church' and the false 'theologians and preachers' which it spawned.[53] Imagining a new political religion was one thing, fully imposing it another. Belief under the dictatorship was always complicated by the relationship between Fascism and the Catholic Church. Fascist revolutionaries, unlike the Bolsheviks of Russia, never proselytized for an Italian 'League of the Militant Godless', committed to extirpate the previous religion in the act of birth of the new.

All such qualifications accepted, it is true that, from 1922 and, in some cases, even before, Fascism was providing its own ceremonial rites, its own hymns, its own dress – by the summer of 1923, Rome clothing shops were already offering special discounts to any who ordered job lots of black-shirts[54] – eventually its own calendar. In the minds of true believers, the meaning of Fascism became freighted with its own mystery and myth, to use words that were much favoured in its literature.

One early example was the Fascist 'anthem', 'Giovinezza', even though the song had a history of its own which was not without complication. The first lyrics were composed in 1909 as a male student song.[55] It was then taken over to become the special tune of the Arditi and, as such, was lauded by Mussolini in November 1919.[56] Thereafter 'Giovinezza' was gradually Fascistized and acquired many verses and a number of variants, including the eventual appearance of the Duce's own name in its lyrics, as well as a salute to Dante, the prophet who, allegedly, had marked out the national border on the Quarnero, the stretch of sea east of Istria.[57] The rise of 'Giovinezza' was sufficiently established by 1924 to persuade conductor Arturo Toscanini, who had initially favoured the fasci but now objected to the movement's tyranny, that he should publicly refuse to play the song at La Scala, already under Fascist administration. Toscanini stated angrily that the opera house was 'not a beer-garden nor Fascist propaganda territory'.[58]

The conductor's reaction should not surprise, since by then the lyrics did read as the best quick introduction to the creed of Fascism and to its ambitions to be treated as a political religion:

Salve, o popolo d'Eroi,
Salve, o Patria immortale!
Son rinati i figli tuoi
con la fe' dell'ideale.
Il valor de' tuoi guerrieri,
la virtù dei pionieri,
la vision de l'Alighieri,
oggi brilla in tutt'i cuor

Dell'Italia nei confini
son rifatti gli Italiani;
li ha rifatti Mussolini
per la guerra di domani
per la gioia del lavoro
per la pace e per l'alloro,
per la gogna di coloro
che la Patria rinnegar

I poeti e gli artigiani,
i signori e i contadini
con orgoglio d'Italiani
Giuran fede a Mussolini
non v'è povero quartiere
che non manda le sue schiere
che non spieghi le bandiere
del fascismo redentor.

(Hail, O people of heroes, hail O immortal *patria*, your sons are reborn with faith in the idea. The courage of your warriors, the strength of your pioneers, the vision of Dante Alighieri, today shine in every heart. In the Italy with its natural borders, Italians are remade. They are remade by Mussolini for the war to come tomorrow, for the joy of hard work, for peace and the laurel, for those who are renegades of the *patria* to be placed beneath the yoke. The poets and the artisans, the gentlemen and the peasants, proud of being Italian, swear faith to Mussolini. There is no poor part of town which does not send its formations, which does not spread the flags of Fascism, bringing us redemption.)

The chorus had remained the same throughout the song's vicissitudes:

> Giovinezza, giovinezza
> primavera di bellezza!
> Della vita nell'asprezza
> il tuo canto squilla e va!

(Youth, youth, springtime of loveliness. Your song rings out everywhere in the bitterness of life.)

Here, then, was an invocation of the youthfulness and the novelty of Fascism, a choral pledge that its triumph was bringing into the nation the 'new politics', as well as the thrusting energy of the young. Yet the musical victory was not necessarily total. What, it might be asked, was to be done with the 'Marcia Reale' or Royal March, anthem of the Savoy dynasty and of that Italy that had been made in the Risorgimento? At least until after September 1943, the answer was nothing damaging. Under the dictatorship, Italy boasted both a royal and a 'revolutionary' anthem, just as King Victor Emmanuel III remained head of state and so, despite the massive personality cult developed around the *Duce*, the bearer of a national charisma held in reserve. On public occasions, both anthems might be played, should propriety be observed with the senior 'Marcia Reale' being sounded first. Respect required that listeners spring to attention for the duration of each.

Rival ditties could appear. In the Venetian *Carnevale* of 1928 Edmondo Rossoni claimed to have written the stridently Fascist lyrics of a new 'Canto del Lavoro'. He persuaded Pietro Mascagni, once a socialist, always importunate to those in power – in 1926 he petitioned Mussolini for a state takeover of the costs of great music like his own and the establishment of a 'theatre worthy of imperial Rome' – and an artist of global fame,[59] to compose the music. This song, Rossoni pronounced, with its 'overwhelmingly Italian strain' (*musica italianissima*) must become the 'battle hymn' of the 'Fascist revolution'. It was duly premiered at the stylish Malibran Theatre,[60] but alas for Rossoni and Mascagni, the 'Canto del Lavoro' failed to inspire. Mussolini derided it with the comment that its music best suggested a 'hymn of a sitting worker'[61] and the orchestras of Venice soon returned to striking up the more mellifluous and familiar strains of Rossini, Verdi and Puccini and of non-Italian composers. Even though 'Giovinezza' was to be heard on innumerable occasions by Italians after 1922, musically speaking Fascist Italy was not destined to resound in a single way.

Fascist clothing was equally variable. Italy, even in the 1930s and during the wartime that followed, was never a rigorously uniformed society. It is true that the *Duce*, by the time he was locked into the Axis with Hitler, was rarely photographed any more in mufti. Yet he was known to work (and conduct his many interviews) in a comfortably battered blue suit, which he was wearing when, on a visit to the Quirinale, he was arrested on 25 July 1943. Photographs of ordinary life under the regime similarly show workers dressed as workers, peasants as peasants, women as women and bourgeois in *frac*; in other words, each with their class or gender (and sometimes their regional) markers, those being more powerful and accustomed than were party clothes. Fascist uniform, itself regularly varying, with different insignia, headwear and status, depending on time and occasion, was reserved by most for special 'party' occasions, even when millions of Italians had taken out membership. Advertisements for such dressage did none the less frequently occupy the pages of Fascist papers. In Starace's own *Gioventù Fascista* in 1933, for example, there were offers for the complete uniform of a Giovane Fascista at 21.50 lire, a Balilla's cost 12.25 and a Piccola Italiana could be equipped for 10.80, with extra reductions being available on multiple sales. More temptingly, the shop sold 'civilian and military uniforms, and everything for all sports' and only slightly spoiled its pitch by naming itself the 'Old England' store.[62]

By that time, Mussolini's militant-looking shaven head was becoming the most significant part of the *Duce*'s physical image and has passed a witting heritage on to present-day 'skinheads' who adopt it (and an unwitting legacy to those sportsmen who prefer their heads shorn). However, that style only emerged relatively late in the regime, having been prompted by a practical concern for Mussolini's early baldness and the fact that his hair had gone prematurely white, an ageing process needing to be concealed in an allegedly eternally youthful dictator. Perhaps out of respect, the hairstyle was mimicked by few other Fascists, although the pornographically racist Nazi, Julius Streicher of Nuremberg, sported the same cut, as did Gabriele D'Annunzio, whose premature baldness had long been thought, especially by himself, to signal his sexual potency.

The story of the Fascist calendar again combined revolution and tradition in uneasy mixture. In ironical half-parallel with that French Revolution which Fascism was pledged 'historically' to overcome, a new dating system gradually spread, to be given Mussolini's official imprimatur on 31 December 1926. It became the habit to tally years from the March on Rome, 28 October 1922. Under this system, December 1929 fell in Anno VIII; January 1936 in Anno XIIII (with a Latinist's punctiliousness).[63] The mathematical shifting caused some difficulty, however. Although, by the mid-1930s in tune with the new populism and more aggressive revolutionary cast which then characterized the regime, sometimes just the Fascist date would be given – that was the case, for example, in the Staracean *Gioventù Fascista* – mostly, Italian calendars used both systems. Books would say in their prelims that they had been published in 1934-XII and leave the reader to work out a more exact monthly date.

Similarly, Fascist festivals and holidays soon punctuated the year, the most notable being the 'Birth of Rome' (21 April and so a counter to any nostalgia for May Day) and the anniversary of the March on Rome. Yet, except for the suppression of anything that smacked of socialism, this calendar was grafted on to the existing division of time and was not designed to overthrow it. Fascist messages remained mixed. Thus the Fascist parades of 28 October were rapidly succeeded by All Saints and All Souls days (1 and 2 November), important festivals for the Church and its followers; 4 November, Vittorio Veneto Day, when the First World War was remembered in an atmosphere of national patriotism; and 11 November, the King's birthday – on both these last occasions Fascism had to share public acclaim with the monarch and his army. *L'Alpino*, for example, remarked in 1927 on how 28 October acted as a 'sentinel' to 4 November, adding a little mournfully that 'the day of the Dead' (2 November) was also appropriately near.[64]

Italian, national or party, holidays were countered by the cosmopolitanism of the great Church festivals, Christmas and Easter, but also by Epiphany (eventually to be partially harnessed by the party as the Befana Fascista) (6 January), San Giuseppe's day (19 March), Ascension (26 May), the celebration of St Peter and St Paul (29 June), the feast of the Assumption (15 August) and the Immaculate Conception commemoration (8 December). Local history, too, owned a special moment each year. Every *paese* cherished its *festa*, its one day of the year, and the festivities that then occurred predated and survived the dictatorship. The *festa* acted as the marker of the individual history and identity of a town or village as compared with its neighbour (even though a tincture of Fascism could be added to the ceremonial involved and, given the paradoxical growth of international tourism during the Fascist years, quite a bit of the 'invention of tradition' and 'sellebration' to attract and entertain visitors could condition and amend local practice).

Other Fascist insignia and ceremonial also spread into Italian life. Even before 1922 the movement had made much of any funerals held to mourn its 'martyrs', 'sacrificed' in squadrist battles. Black shirts, black flags, raids to seize socialist icons or to rescue Fascist symbols lost in a previous raid, became a natural part of the militancy of squadrist life and all undoubtedly conditioned the Fascist view of the world before and after 1922. These props of Fascism, for some, underpinned or confirmed their fanaticism. Historian Emilio Gentile has contended that squadrist raiders envisaged themselves as a 'communion' in the full sense of that word. He cites an article in *Gerarchia* in October 1922, whose author maintained: 'The banners fluttering in the wind, the black-shirts, the helmets, the songs, the cries of "alalà", the *fasces*, the Roman salute, the recital of the names of the dead, the official feasts, the solemn swearing-in ceremonies, the parades in military style, all of the rites which make those from the old, superior-feeling bourgeoisie shake their heads, work for us in demonstrating the power-laden resurrection of the original instincts of the race.'[65]

Perhaps. All societies, including liberal capitalist democracies, cherish rites and rituals of some kind. Yet, in the case of Fascist Italy, one impression can often be countered by another. Again in striking contrast to the root and branch revolution being attempted in the interwar period in the USSR, itself a place where social historians have demonstrated how frequently the intentions of the revolutionaries were derailed by the dogged traditionalism and self-interest of the peoples of all the Russias, Fascist rule left much intact from the past. This regime did not assault the family; it did little to alter the existing distribution of property. It remained constitutionally a monarchy and did its best to find accommodation with the Catholic Church. With that list of qualifications, its 'cultural revolution' could never be more than partial.

Doubtless, the dictatorship did become more radical during the 1930s, but for most of its history its revolution was not so all-embracing as to eliminate very many of the spaces where Italians crafted their existence and identity. After all, in September 1923 the Cabinet agreed that 'in festivals and other public events, the national and state flag must always take priority over party emblems'. Similarly, the *Duce* regularly emphasized that the authority of the prefect must outweigh that of the *federale* and other party bosses. Even on party occasions, the multiplicity of groupings could lead to complications and debate and gave contemporaries the chance to indulge in the familiar human game of asserting one individual's or organization's status over another. In December 1929 the party secretary Augusto Turati issued this advice to party members. In official ceremony, 'the following order of precedence has been established, except on occasions where, because of the circumstance or setting, there need to be variations: First [the representative of the] National Fascist party, [then] those with war-time gold medals', and so on through six rival returned soldiers' groups to the Fascist bodies. The most senior of these was to be the Associazione Nazionale Insegnanti Fascisti. After the teachers, Fascist post office officials were placed third, farmers fifth, bank officials eighth, those joined to the Fascist union for artists and professionals sixteenth, boy scouts or Balilla nineteenth and sportsmen twenty-first. 'Other associations', Turati concluded a little wearily, 'such as the Dante Alighieri, the Touring Club, the Navy League etc. etc. follow in the order that has been established by local custom.'[66]

Fascist fanaticism, Fascist fundamentalism, the theoretically selfless commitment to national revolution, were, it is becoming plain, an intricate and often contradictory matter. Among Mussolini's own henchmen, the great majority of whom established a party role before

1922 and, despite some ups and downs, did not surrender it until the regime collapsed, Balbo, Farinacci, Grandi and the rest, could not be relied on to endorse a single definition of Fascism. Their devotion to their *Duce* was frequently conditioned by self-interest and by a scepticism that half-promised to bring to the surface their doubts about his aims, methods and character, should his political star wane. If more credulous Fascist fanatics are searched for in the leadership group, then the best candidate may be the intellectual of the movement, Giuseppe Bottai. Born in 1895 and so, like many leading Fascists, the junior by about a decade of his eventual *Duce*, Bottai was the son of a wine-shop owner whose store purveyed its wares near Rome's railway station. Rising from that commercial background, in 1914 Bottai enrolled to study law at his local university. As was true for so many others, the war made him an interventionist, volunteer and junior officer, one who saw service at Caporetto and on Monte Grappa and was wounded. When demobilized, his self-conscious intellectuality made him flirt with Futurism but he was among the first to join the Rome *fascio* in August 1919, having concluded that politics mattered more than poetry. Perpetually adolescent in his attitudes and enthusiasms, Bottai was star-struck by his first meeting with the more experienced and worldly wise Mussolini. Even in 1946, when he claimed to be utterly disillusioned with the *Duce* and to be willing to arraign him for the revolutionary failure of Fascism, still Bottai recalled how the body of his erstwhile chief, 'although not large, filled a room', how his eyes fixed an interlocutor with an 'immense and unfathomable glance' and how his voice 'vibrated with echoes of the infinite'.[67] Throughout the history of Fascism, the poetaster Bottai was in love with his leader. Seemingly the most cultivated but, in practice, the most credulous figure in the regime, he was its version of an Albert Speer, with an added touch of Nikolai Bukharin, given Bottai's continuing preference for making a splash in the world of ideas.

Soon after the March on Rome, Bottai's special slot among the Fascist hierarchs was cemented with the founding of the journal *Critica Fascista* under his editorship and with the backing of an impressive number of other Fascist, Nationalist and syndicalist luminaries. The very title, with its echo of the great socialist magazine *Critica sociale*, expressed a platform and an ambition. Bottai, imbued with a true belief in the *Duce*, would work with other serious Fascist professionals (Farinacci's name did not appear among the supporters) to construct a philosophy that would outmatch Marxism and dazzle Italy and the world.

In his first editorial, Bottai talked about 'Fascism's urgent need to train a new ruling class to replace the old'. Polishing his clichés, he explained that 'a fervour for renewal was pervading all Fascism' when it contemplated its move from 'being an instrument of revolution and conquest to one of conservation and stabilization' in both the political and spiritual worlds. Despite that normalization, the movement, he advised, must never forget its origins in the spirit of 1919. Rather contradicting that radical-sounding line, the sometime syndicalist Sergio Panunzio, a southern intellectual from Molfetta,[68] expatiated on the then party view that Fascism and liberalism had much in common, asserting that 'Fascism is already a State, a western State, not an Eastern [or Bolshevik] one. The path down which Fascism is walking is not an Asian path but rather the path of law and of liberalism.'[69]

The second issue was buoyed by endorsement from Mussolini, who evinced his pleasure at Bottai's choice of title. Fascism, the *Duce* pronounced worthily, could only benefit from 'healthy, broad criticism, and not the cold, pedantic, apriori and so sterile, approach'.[70] By the third edition, Bottai had reached the conclusion that, although many Fascists had been attracted to the movement through their experience of the army, yet their beliefs could not be limited to being 'a barracks' ideology' (sic). Rather, the movement's base was religious: 'Religions as often conquer souls and spirits', he ran on portentously, 'with the solemnity of their ceremonies as with the prayers of their priests, and it is through these ceremonies that the mystical afflatus often enters their hearts. That is how it was for Fascism.' 'Yesterday's captains', he explained, entering dangerous terrain for one distrusted by Farinacci, were now reduced to being 'in great majority puppets who abuse the power they no longer possess'. 'Speculators, men on the make, the cynically ambitious' were making their plays. Their crude ploys must be blocked by an ever stricter Fascist 'discipline'.[71] Even boasts about 'Mussolinism', he wrote in December 1923, could not always be relied on. 'As far as we are concerned, Fascists have only one way in which they can be real Mussolinians and that is, to live the life of the party with intelligence.'[72]

Neither now nor later was Bottai given to naming the names of those not coming up to his standards. Rather, the campaigns of *Critica Fascista* were conducted in that opaque language of Nicodemism, which commentators have noticed became such a natural part of Stalinist life. No doubt being mealy-mouthed is necessary when undertaking some form of criticism in a modern dictatorship (and is not unknown in liberal democracies) but Bottai always lacked courage and was never short of vanity. *Critica Fascista* undertook a necessary task for the Fascist chattering classes, yet it should not be read as revealing much about life beyond that gilded circle. Back in his first issue, Bottai had admitted that 'the great majority of Fascists will, without grave effect, ignore our efforts', adding that he would be happy if 'ten' or 'a hundred' joined in the discussion which he was sponsoring.

Bottai's modesty may have been false but it was justified. Out in the country, Fascists in 1923–4 and after were not behaving with the purity and dedication that Bottai could conjure into existence in his study. For all the talk of religion and spirituality, Fascism had not sloughed off its rough and ready side. Some of its expression can be traced in Milan through police records, given the eventual fall of the local *ras*, Giampaoli, and so of his numerous clientele. One whose career indicates how Fascism operated on the ground was Giovanni Redaelli. This businessman of humble origins was in March 1929 sent to *confino* (compulsory residence) on Ponza (although he was amnestied after nine months). According to the police, his crimes over the previous decade amounted to a catalogue of greed and lawlessness, especially involving his directing of the company charged with running the Milan bus system, a lucrative job with its own opportunities to exercise patronage, which Redaelli had originally obtained through his contacts with Giampaoli. Redaelli had manipulated the share market, playing politics while doing so (he threatened official intervention against the staff of at least one company who had criticized his efforts artificially to lower prices by saying that he would have them arrested as 'subversives and troublemakers'). He ostentatiously broke currency regulations by exporting large sums to France and buying property there.

When challenged, he had his myrmidons publicly beat an opponent, Ugo Clerici, and the assault cost Clerici the sight of an eye. This
scandalous event took place at the Ristorante Savini in the Galleria,
fashionable social centre of the city.[73] Redaelli awarded high-paying
posts to his own clients, worried not at all by their probable incompetence and certain lack of qualifications. He acquired a luxury apartment in the prestigious Via Montenapoleone and lived the high life. 'A
lover of evening jaunts,' the police reported, 'he was well known in all
the more dubious nightclubs of the city, always to be found in the
company of the most ruffianly individuals in the Fascist movement.'
He owned three gleaming fast cars and drove around in the company
of his beautiful concubine. After he was expelled from the Fascist
party for 'being insufficiently aware of the duties that devolve on
those to whom the Party gives positions of command', Redaelli was
damned as a 'political opportunist', 'given to adopting opinions in
order to win credit from those from whom he was seeking to gain
protection and so a potential turncoat, essentially determined on business profit'.[74] Redaelli, it seems, despite his base in Milan and not
Sicily, might have been rehearsing the part of a local Godfather rather
than that of a crusading Fascist *milite*.

This parallel recurs when surveying further, humbler cases, which
came to light in the period after Giampaoli lost office. The Milan city
markets were another location where an unacceptable version of
Fascism had maintained its rowdy and violent course. Notable were
the Maurelli brothers, Leopoldo and Umberto, by 1925 the racketeers
who controlled the distribution of fruit and vegetables in the area
around Porta Vittoria. They cheerfully used 'blackmail and insult' to
reinforce their authority and lived ostentatiously, spending money in
the best places in the city as if there were no tomorrow. Like Redaelli,
the Maurellis had scant compunction in dealing peremptorily with an
opponent. They broke into one rival's house, beat, bound and gagged
him and then frog-marched him into their car, all in public view. They
sped off to their accustomed party meeting place, battered the victim
senseless, blindfolded him, put him back in the car, drove to a deserted
spot at the urban periphery and threw him out to recover or die.
Furthermore, two women accused Umberto Maurelli of rape.[75]

The brothers came from Fascist and squadrist backgrounds – each eventually penned an appeal to Mussolini emphasizing that his family was Fascist to its bootstraps, having expended sweat, blood and treasure in the revolutionary cause. Their only fault, said Leopoldo with injured innocence, was 'to have changed the political coloration of the zone around the Porta Vittoria using Fascist methods'. So significant and respectable a Fascist as Bottai would, Maurelli claimed, be willing to speak up for him. Furthermore, Maurelli noted sadly, his infant children and old mother were being unfairly damaged, both 'morally and materially', by his present cruel fate.[76] Separation from his brother was another ground for complaint. His relegation to a far-off *paese* in the province of Sassari in Sardinia showed that he was the unlucky victim of nefarious plots against his person. Even the police had to admit that Umberto Maurelli had been a lieutenant in the crack Alpini regiment and then a *capomanipolo* in the paramilitary MVSN. But that patriotic and ideological past did not mean, they stated, that the brothers and their associates had not in their corner of Milan acted like a 'criminal gang'.[77]

Another Milanese *confinato*, in 1929 sent briefly to Sardinia (but amnestied after only six months of his five-year sentence), was Ettore Biddau. He and his men had established what the police disapprovingly called a *squadretta d'azione*, which competed with the Maurellis for control over the suburban area around Porta Vittoria and Porta Romana. Biddau acted on occasion for Redaelli (he had a job at the bus company but lived well above his apparent income). When party officialdom began to attack Giampaoli, Biddau organized a demonstration in favour of the Milan *ras*. Mostly, his blackmail and threats were more simply directed to his own profit and expended in gambling, whoring and the rest.[78] To add to his misdemeanours, Biddau had regularly walked the city streets flourishing his extensive stock of unlicensed weapons, and, generally, had used his contacts with party bosses to place himself above the law.

In his defence, Biddau declared that he had been a 'Fascist' since 1914 (given that the movement did not come into existence until 1919, his selection of that date indicates the looseness of his definition of the term and the superficiality of his ideological commitment). Biddau had volunteered for the war and, he maintained, had been one of the first to buy and distribute *Il Popolo d'Italia*, returning decorated for his soldierly courage to a peace in which 'subversives' would not let him get on with his career, first as a pharmacist's assistant and then as a chicken salesman at the markets. Any wealth he currently displayed was merely the result of his tireless commitment both to that job and to his position as bus inspector. In any case, he had the care of his mother, who was now more than seventy, and the rest of his family and his solicitude for them drove his life.[79]

The police were not impressed. Their investigations revealed that Biddau had not volunteered and that his military service had not won him any credit for bravery. Nor had he been among those who had marched on Rome, as he had claimed. In fact, 'the medals and papers declaring that he had were granted to him through friends' (more evidence of the malleability of Fascist regulation and 'history'). Actually, he had not even joined the Fascist party until February 1923. When Giampaoli fell, Biddau had thought of fleeing abroad in a clandestine manner but had then contented himself with trying to block the best efforts of those party officials charged with cleaning up Milan.[80] In sum, Biddau, it seemed, was another undeserving and cynically self-interested Fascist, one whose 'religious' commitment to the movement was infringed by a desire for loot and whose sense of national unity came second to his desire to protect and advantage his family.

While Fascist factions competed for status and influence in Milan and Arnaldo Mussolini adroitly and piously cemented the Mussolini family interest there, in Sicily a battle had been launched against the Mafia, so plainly an economic organization or social structure which contradicted Fascist power. On 2 June 1924 Cesare Mori, a career official with years of experience on the island but most recently known for his doughty refusal to bow to squadrism in the Po valley, was appointed prefect of Trapani, with the task of dealing with local organized crime.[81] Over the next three years – in October 1925, with the backing of Federzoni, he transferred to the senior prefecture at Palermo – Mori became a very public opponent of the Mafia, eventually being permitted to publish an account of his work which depicted him as a sort of Fascist caped crusader, even a little local *duce*, sparring valorously and successfully for justice and the Fascist way. Although he was, of course, careful to emphasize that he acted on behalf of the real *Duce*, Mori undertook what he depicted as a successful campaign to win over the hearts and minds of Sicilians of all classes and so abduct them from Mafia influence.[82] He was not reluctant to use police dragnets and lengthy jail terms as a way of picking off middle-ranking Mafia operatives and simultaneously whittled away the power of Alfredo Cucco, the surviving local radical Fascist and Farinacci's man on the island.

By 1928 sweeping victory was proclaimed. Cucco had been expelled from the PNF and there was a major purge of the Palermo police, justice and administrative bureaucracy. In 1929 Mori retired a hero, even though his departure to a reclamation job in Istria may have been a little sudden. Similarly, his announced recipe for life, 'Vendetta is firstly a duty and secondly, a pleasure and a right', hinted at an iron realism or a cynicism which ill accorded with some of the more high-flown talk about Fascist new men and women. Sicily thereafter little preoccupied the regime and stayed relatively tranquil socially. Yet Fascism's triumph over both the Mafia and home-grown Sicilian party radicals had been incomplete. Cucco was readmitted to the party in 1936, by 1943 was a party vice-secretary and, during the Social Republic from September 1943 to April 1945, fortified by Farinacci's backing, he became Under-Secretary of Popular Culture. Nothing if not a stayer, from 1953 to 1968 Cucco was a deputy for the neo-Fascist MSI to the parliament in Rome.[83] Individuals apart, it may be true that, during the 1920s and 1930s, Fascist policies had curbed Mafia killings and exploitation for the short term but the regime's failure to do anything much to change the unequal social structure of the island or to alleviate its poverty meant that conditions were ripe for the Mafia to renew itself with American-led invasion after 1943. Mori's triumph had proved fleeting, more a matter of words than of deeds.

Sicily for a time was an exception but, on the whole, practical Fascism stayed out of the news (and out of subsequent historians' accounts) because it was so locally focused and because Mussolini, Bottai and the rest emphatically claimed legitimacy and purpose for their regime and its ideology by inscribing it into the plane of high philosophy, while not worrying overmuch about the relationship between theory and practice. However, on 10 June (fated to be an inauspicious date in Fascist history) 1924, the gangsterism of the suburbs manifested itself at Rome and so at the very heart of the regime. That afternoon, a squad led by Amerigo Dumini, still often an agent of Cesare Rossi and Filippo Filippelli, the editor of the pro-Fascist paper *Il Corriere italiano*, whose car Dumini was using and had helpfully parked the previous night in the *cortile* of the Ministry of the Interior, picked up the moderate socialist deputy and prominent recent critic of the regime, Giacomo Matteotti. He had been walking along the road which ran beside the Tiber in central Rome. Dumini, Albino Volpi and their gang, following a pattern established in other Fascist assaults, beat their victim to a pulp. So brutal was their attack that Matteotti died under their rain of blows. Exhibiting a certain inexpertise in the criminal life, Dumini's squad apparently then drove around for some hours while debating what to do, reaching no better solution than to scrabble a shallow grave for Matteotti, just off the road leading from Rome into the Sabine hills.

The outcome of this botched attack set off Fascism's greatest crisis. It took more than two months to find the body and the accompanying hue and cry almost did for the regime. The fullest Italian exploration of the murder has been conducted by Mauro Canali, who has no doubt that blame for it must be ascribed personally to Mussolini (although other historians are not altogether convinced). According to Canali, the real origins for the assault lay in the murky and corrupt business dealings in which the regime had engaged with American oil interests (Arnaldo Mussolini had been a key figure here), the Westinghouse corporation (where Aldo Finzi's brother, Gino, worked),[84] and Lithuanian arms traders (this time the major role was assumed by Balbo's brother).[85] As in the little world of the Maurelli brothers in the Milan markets, so, it is plain, at the summit of Fascist politics familism (and thuggery) flourished in a fashion that was not a world away from Mafia dealings in Sicily or New York.

In most liberal democracies it might be hoped that the kidnapping and killing of a leading opposition Member of Parliament would at once precipitate the collapse of a government whose chief, at a minimum, bore moral guilt for the death. In Italy in 1924, however, the government, after a reshuffle on 17 June which promoted the conservative Federzoni to the key post of the Ministry of the Interior in control of the police and prefectures, soldiered on. The King, the Vatican, the army chiefs, business, the academic world, all the old elites, contemplated the crisis and preferred not to swing decisively against the Prime Minister. The Stock Exchange briefly shook and then recovered.[86] Abroad, too, polite society preferred that the Fascist administration be allowed to go on 'saving' Italy from 'Bolshevism'. The London *Daily Telegraph*, for example, concluded that 'no sane mind' could blame the *Duce* for Matteotti's death[87] and, throughout the crisis, went on asserting that 'the public confidence in Signor Mussolini himself' was 'but little affected' by events.[88]

Within Italy the opposition was divided and the majority hamstrung itself by abandoning the parliamentary chamber in what, with that frequent Italian fondness for classical parallel, was called the 'Aventine secession' (from the occasion when the plebs had taken refuge from their patrician oppressors on one of the Roman hills). After an initial period certainly of confusion and perhaps of dismay, Mussolini once again proved his bravado as a tactician, riding out the constitutional crisis with aplomb.[89] The greatest threat to him, it was soon plain, came not from the liberals but from 'the Fascists'. Some were quick to pledge their constancy. Bianchi, on 16 June, recalled the 'faith, devotion and friendship which have bound me to you for so many years . . . and which continue unaltered and unalterable' and, as a reward for such constancy, sought Mussolini's urgent retribution against unnamed elements operating from the Ministry of Interior, who had been spreading malicious rumours about Bianchi's reckless womanizing.[90] A month later, Bottai wrote, in a rather stilted tone but with similar effect, of his own worries: 'We cannot hide that our substantial <u>faith</u> in your thought and methods prompts bitterness in seeing ourselves continuously misunderstood and sometimes even mistreated and boycotted by those who believe that they can yoke Fascism to their modish <u>chronic rebelliousness</u> [sic].'[91]

Whisper of rebellion there was. In Milan, Michele Terzaghi, a moderate who had been the chief spokesman of the Fascist deputies in 1921, was plotting against Mussolini's authority through the close contacts which he had retained with Freemasonry, an organization disdained by formal Fascism.[92] More threateningly, in the cities of the north those who looked to Farinacci as a leader and emblem grew bolder in their calls for an upturning of society. Their noisiest spokesman was Curzio Suckert, who, with Napoleonic bravado, took to calling himself Curzio Malaparte. The son of a German textile manufacturer in business at Prato in Tuscany (who married into the Pirelli family), just old enough to become a decorated young officer in the last year of the war, Malaparte was an intellectual whose eccentric track led from radical Fascism to Maoism. In between, he became the most vivid and independent of correspondents in the Second World War, if not necessarily the most factually reliable one.[93] For the present, Malaparte was rehearsing a role as a modernized and Fascistized new D'Annunzio, an activist theoretician of Fascist activism. In a journal he edited entitled *La Conquista dello Stato* (The Conquest of the State), Malaparte exploited the debate over how to deal with the Matteotti murder to proclaim that 'healthy Fascism now resides in the provinces [among people like himself]. There, its revolutionary spirit wants to conquer the state for Italy.'

During the following months the restiveness of the party rank and file increased, especially after the fatal shooting by his political enemies of a Fascist deputy, Armando Casalini, in Rome on 12 September. By the last days of the year, with Federzoni's efforts at the Ministry of the Interior to repress the squads being used as a malign example, Malaparte, Farinacci and others grew open in their dissent. Malaparte wrote an article asking 'Was Fascism against Mussolini?' and began by reminding the *Duce* that 'the point of view of the great majority of the Fascists of the provinces is this: it was not the Hon. Mussolini who carried the Fascists to the Prime Ministership, but the Fascists who brought him to power.' 'Their mandate', he urged, was 'revolutionary'. It must be honoured. The choice was now or never: 'either the Hon. Mussolini carries out their revolutionary will, or he resigns, even if only briefly, the revolutionary cause entrusted to him'. On the morning of 31 December, 10,000 armed squadrists, as if born like dragon's teeth from Malaparte's words, strode through the streets of Florence, pausing only to beat up any anti-Fascists they noticed. When that easy work was done, they threatened a second March on Rome, now to be directed against their *Duce*.[94]

Confronted by the danger that he was slipping into becoming the enemy of the Fascists, Mussolini acted. On 3 January 1925 he spoke to the Chamber of Deputies. The Aventine secession he denounced as unconstitutional. He himself, he added, was a 'man of reasonable intelligence, much courage and a sovereign lack of interest in filthy lucre'. When he asserted that no Soviet 'Cheka'-style secret police existed in Italy, he should be believed. Such a covert force could not, he implied, have sponsored the murder of Matteotti. In any case, that tiresome dispute no longer mattered. 'I declare here, before this assembly and before the whole Italian people, that I, and I alone, assume political, moral and historic responsibility for all that has happened . . . If all the violence in our country has been caused by a historic, political and moral climate, then I take that responsibility, too. This historic, political and moral climate I have constructed with a propaganda which has spanned the time from the moment of intervention in 1914–15 until today.'[95] With these dramatic and characteristically peremptory words, Mussolini announced the dictatorship.

8

Building a totalitarian dictatorship

It is frequently forgotten that the word 'totalitarian' originated in Italy. First applied to Mussolini's rule in May 1923 by critics who sought an extreme term to describe what they argued was a new situation, the title 'totalitarian' was taken up by the regime after 1925 and applied to itself. On 28 October that year, for the third anniversary of the March on Rome, Mussolini coined the formula that Fascism meant a system in which 'all is for the state, nothing is outside the state, nothing and no one are against the state'.[1] Throughout the inter-war period the one regime in Europe that regularly boasted of its totalitarianism was the Fascist dictatorship. The Nazis seldom described themselves that way. Critics of the USSR began to adopt the term during the 1930s, while radical Fascists, who were then wondering whether Stalin might *in pectore* be a (praiseworthy) Fascist,[2] did sometimes apply the term to the Soviet state. Less controversially, Italians used the word to link any other possibly friendly regime – the Austria of Dollfuss, the Spain of Franco, the Greece of Metaxas (before October 1940), even the Vatican – with the Italian original. But it was Mussolini's Italy that was said to have made concrete the meaning of totalitarianism.

Given the pervasiveness of the view that, in any era, Italians are always *brava gente* (nice people), a conclusion not without appeal especially to that Italy spun into praising the governance and culture of Silvio Berlusconi, the history of the modern political doctrine and practice most redolent of tyranny and death demands careful exploration. Mussolini's assumption of the dictatorship in January 1925, although not followed by full-scale revolution, did unleash a cascade of political and economic changes that, before long, were being portrayed by regime propagandists as the bases of its totalitarianism. They covered diverse tracts of Italian life.

On the afternoon of 3 January 1925 Mussolini and Federzoni telegraphed the nation's prefects with the order that neither Fascists nor anti-Fascists were any longer to be permitted to hold spontaneous 'meetings, assemblies, parades or other public demonstrations'. The police must act peremptorily to suppress all political dissidence and close down the branches of any groups which 'might be viewed as subverting the powers of the state', among them the liberal democratic Italia Libera (Free Italy). Communists and their allies should be arrested if they were a threat at all and resistance on their part should be 'repressed by whatever means possible'. Regular patrols should root out and seize any illegal arms caches. The dates of the dissolution or banning of other political parties varied but, from now on, non-Fascists lost all legitimacy under the Fascist system.

This first interdiction of political opposition was direct and savage. Mussolini and his government had endorsed squadrist terror from the past, promising that state terror would now be visited on any who dissented from the ruling party and its ideology. The building of a Fascist or 'totalitarian' state, however, proceeded under the cover of legal process. Laws were drafted, reviewed, approved by both Houses of Parliament and underwritten by the nation's senior courts. The process may have been dictatorial, the parliament tame, the courts (although scarcely purged) packed with friends of the regime, but the 'revolution', if that was what it was, did its best not to jolt out of shape its ties with quite a lot of the Liberal past.

One early step was more tightly to define the power of the Prime Minister, who, by the end of the year, was to be known as the *Capo del governo* (Head of government). Similarly, in local administrations, surviving autonomy was curtailed by the creation, in 1926, of the position of *podestà*, a mayor who was no longer to be elected but rather appointed for a five-year term. The office was to be unpaid, although prefects could decide on appropriate compensation where necessary.[3] Each *podestà* was, in other words, to be a mini-*Capo*, chosen by, and dependent on, the *Capo dei capi*, Mussolini. In this area there had been talk of experiment in female suffrage[4] but it was now revoked since, hereafter, the rights of both men and women to vote locally lapsed. In December 1926 the Fascist *littorio* (the bound *fasces* or lictors' rods) was acknowledged as the state symbol, its display was made obligatory on public buildings and the use of the title *Duce* was also formalized.[5]

Press freedom was subjected to a further diminution in a circular dispatched by Federzoni on 10 January 1925. Any sign of verbal sedition must be eliminated given the government's determination 'firmly to guarantee public order against any danger whatever of a disturbance'. Fascist papers, the Minister of the Interior's telegram continued, should exercise maximum 'discipline' and avoid any 'aggressive polemics'.[6] Mussolini could grow portentous by predicting to a correspondent of *L'Echo de Paris* that democracy would soon be succeeded by a beneficent 'superdemocracy', implying that was what was being created in Rome.[7] However, during the next months, the process of press control, already evident before 1925 – the editor of the conservative paper *Il Giornale d'Italia*, Alberto Bergamini, who was being persuaded to cede his position, had been assaulted at his home on 28 February 1924[8] – accelerated. The Ufficio Stampa or Press Office, which fell under the Prime Minister's ambit, saw its annual budget rise from 50,000 lire in 1922 to 438,000 ten years later.[9] Cesare Rossi, its first Fascist head, lost his position in 1924 because of the Matteotti affair, being replaced by the once liberal but pliable Count Giovanni Capasso Torre di Pastene, a journalist and decorated wartime officer. Four years later, Capasso was succeeded by the outright Fascist, Lando Ferretti,[10] a prominent sports administrator and propagandist from Bologna in his thirties and a journalist who had first made his way after the war on the editorial staff of *La Gazzetta dello Sport*. He could be relied on not to think too much.

By 1928 it had become compulsory for every journalist to be a registered Fascist and the regime was moving to achieve a uniformity, a dullness and a brevity, which is evident to anyone who scans the party newssheets of the 1930s. In the high years of the regime, petty interference in journalistic practice extended to banning reports of murders and other sensational crimes or of anything which might put off tourists (examples being the surfacing of sharks near Italian beaches[11] and inclement weather[12]) and imposing severe controls on the portrayal of a range of matters from the female body to the appearance of the *Duce* himself.[13] Ferretti complained that any exhibition of nude females would distract young males from concentration on their sporting lives and, in May 1930, Mussolini thought it worth his personal intervention to prevent any more gory and racially unsound publicity being given to 'monstrous births'.[14]

As totalitarianism took hold, the editorship of the main Italian papers was secured in safely Fascist hands. In November 1925 Luigi Albertini left *Il Corriere della Sera*, owned by the Milan industrial Crespi family, to be unsatisfactorily replaced by four editors in four years (Piero Croc. 925–6, Ugo Ojetti, 1926–7, Maffio Maffi, 1927–9, and then Aldo Borelli, destined to survive in office till 1943).[15] Alfredo Frassati resigned from *La Stampa* after this great Turin daily was banned by prefectural decree from 9 September until 3 November 1925.[16] In Venice, control of *Il Gazzettino* was disputed between rival Fascist factions, with Giuseppe Volpi steadily extending his financial and political domination which, however, remained incomplete until 1936.[17] More openly hostile papers like the communist *L'Unità*, the socialist *Avanti!*, the republican *La Voce repubblicana* and such liberal democratic organs as *La Rivoluzione liberale* of Piero Gobetti or Giovanni Amendola's *Il Mondo* were either sequestered or driven underground. Gobetti had been subjected to savage Fascist beating on 5 September 1924; his health was permanently damaged and, on 15 February 1926, he expired in Paris shortly after fleeing there. Before his death he had penned an acute summary of Mussolini, a man who, with 'his personification of self-confident optimism, his oratorical tricks, his love of success and of ceremony on Sunday, his virtuoso command of mystification and emphasis – all this makes him deeply popular with the Italians'. For Gobetti, the key to the *Duce*'s power and personality was (as it is, too, for some politicians of our day) an absolute lack of irony.[18]

Like Gobetti, Amendola, who had been one of the most active leaders of the Aventine secession, was another to be assaulted, in his case during a Fascist home invasion at Serravalle Pistoiese on 20 July 1925. He too sought sanctuary in France, dying an exile in April 1926. By the end of the 1920s the party line on press freedom had become what it was to remain. 'Discipline' over the news, it was claimed, worked in the interests of the nation. Luigi Freddi, in his own eyes a radical Fascist, thought all writers must now be *militi* first and foremost and claimed that Fascism revolutionized the way words were composed; authors' inexhaustibly ardent novelty was what prevented the regime from 'mummification'.[19] Ermanno Amicucci, a man who followed Mussolini from *Avanti!* into Fascism and rose to head the journalists' 'corporation' (their official bureaucratic organization), maintained with Fascist effrontery that press 'freedom' was a laugh in every country except Italy.[20]

The newer medium of radio was similarly yoked to Fascism. The notoriously corrupt Minister of Communications, running a new portfolio established in February 1924, was Costanzo Ciano, born 1876. Admiral Ciano, as he liked to be called, was a senior member of Mussolini's entourage and father of that Galeazzo Ciano who, in 1931, married the *Duce*'s eldest and favourite child, Edda, to become for a decade the regime's dauphin. During his naval career, the elder Ciano had won a quantity of medals in the Libyan and First World Wars.[21] A Nationalist in 1919, he set up a party called the Unione democratica without democratic intent in his home town, Livorno, but soon linked himself to the *fasci*. In 1921 he became one of their Members of Parliament. Following the pattern of Mussolini and of many Italian politicians in running their own dailies, the Ciano family acquired *Il Telegrafo*, Livorno's main paper. Exploiting the journalistic talent and moral weakness of the eventual editor, Giovanni Ansaldo,[22] the Ciano family made it an outlet of national significance as well as the purveyor of the Ciano line in politics and business. Costanzo Ciano's natural inclination was to prefer that the administration of radio fell into the charge of a generous private enterprise and, in December 1924, a group in Rome linked to the always patriotic and sometimes grasping inventor Guglielmo Marconi was granted a six-year monopoly. Its initial transmission ended with the playing of 'Giovinezza' and its programmes happily gave space to government propaganda to pep up the ordinary fare of music and religion.

Progress in the wireless world was limping, however; in 1926 only 27,000 radio sets, mainly in the north, could be tallied (Britons by then owned more than two million). In that year Mussolini, perhaps annoyed that his own first radio transmission of a speech on

4 November 1925 had suffered from technical difficulties, appointed new party secretary Augusto Turati as head of an investigating commission. The result of its deliberations was the establishment of the monopoly EIAR (the Ente Italiano audizioni radiotelefoniche), rejoicing in private finance but subject to tightening government supervision.[23] But, although Arnaldo Mussolini was to the fore in urging the spread of radio and in demanding that it preserve a high moral tone, the serious diffusion of propaganda by this medium had to await the 1930s and the era of 'going to the people'. Even then, progress was slow by European standards. In 1939 there were still only one million radio sets in Italian households and the percentage of the population with a radio licence grew haltingly from 1.28 per cent in 1935 to 4.10 per cent in 1942.[24]

An even better index of Italy's surviving technological backwardness was the telephone, which could be readily tapped by the regime's secret police because it remained such an elite product. In 1940 the total phone connections, including those of business concerns, tallied only just over half a million. Ten years earlier, only one in four lawyers and one in five doctors had phone connections.[25] The so-called 'white telephone' movies, as romantic films were known in the 1930s, where an alluring actress draped herself suggestively over her phone, had mass appeal because a conversation by such means was a luxury and not an everyday matter.

Film was another medium to attract Fascist interest. Before 1914 Italians had been prominent pioneers of the industry, with five hundred films having been produced by 1909. The war precipitated a crisis, however, and the number of Italian-made productions declined drastically to one hundred in 1921, fifty in 1922, seventeen in 1924, twelve in 1927–8 and still fewer in 1930.[26] Film-makers tended to spring from the more raffish sectors of Italian society but their product could be relied on not to be too unpatriotic. During the 1920s most of their appeals for government aid or good offices did not get far, although by 1926 Critica Fascista was suggesting that film was potentially the most Fascist art, healthily dominated by youth. None the less young director Alessandro Blasetti concluded in February 1928 that a state cinema industry could only aim at propaganda, asserting that such a focus would be certain to fail commercially, be boycotted by the public and – film, both in its markets and in its staffing, was often an internationalist concern – be rejected by foreign censors. Such comments were echoed by Bottai three years later and a major Fascist film industry did not develop until after 1933, when it was puffed by the backing of Mussolini's eldest son, Vittorio. In the more strictly defined realm of information, the Istituto Luce had been established in 1926 and granted government subsidy and supervision in the production of newsreels. Its possible monopoly was challenged by a rival Catholic organization, CUCE, and the Catholic Church also remained alert against what they, rather more than the Fascists, feared were likely cinematic infringements of public decency.[27]

Fascism admonished Italians to avoid pornography, labelling it another evil 'foreign' temptation.[28] Yet here, too, there could be backsliding. In 1929 an over-zealous *podestà* of Ariccia, on the outskirts of Rome, by profession a narrow-minded accountant, lost office after he obsessively exhorted the women of his town to lengthen their skirts. His edict had made him a laughing-stock, party officials were disturbed to learn, and had failed to have any effect on local fashions.[29]

At a more informal level, control of information came through the placing of a vast array of social institutions under the aegis of the PNF. In April 1926 the Opera Nazionale Balilla or Fascist boy scouts absorbed similar, previously loosely organized groups, aiming to give them a unique role in Italian society. Such totalitarian intention clashed with Catholic youth organizations. Furthermore the programme of fascistization and nationalization outraged some of the more upper-class monarchist and patriotic scouting leaders who had treasured the international aspect of their movement as the first reward for their own charity.[30] Until 1937 the chief of the Balilla was the tall, handsome, athletic, 'silent, tough and authoritarian' Renato Ricci. He had been born in 1896 to a poor but patriotic family from the anarchist redoubt of Carrara, where he soon became the *ras*.[31] After training as an accountant, Ricci had pursued a course of upward mobility as a volunteer, promoted lieutenant at the battle-front. In 1919 he joined the Liberal party at Carrara but he followed D'Annunzio to Fiume and, from 1921, became a radical, if self-interested and lawless, Fascist. Ricci's career in the PNF was made when he chanced to lead the armed guard on the train that was transporting the *Duce* to Rome after the March on Rome, and thus became known to Mussolini.[32] 'Captain' Ricci, as he was often called, could be relied on to mix populist rhetoric with studied deference to the dictator, accompanying him eventually to Salò. Ricci well fitted the *Duce*'s ideal of a manly if not exactly upright figurehead for disciplined youth.

If informers whose reports found their way into Mussolini's personal files could be believed, Ricci enjoyed the good things in life and was not too careful about how he got them, benefiting from a father-in-law, Cirillo Figaia, who was locally nicknamed 'the marble pirate' for the profits he ruthlessly carved from the main industry at Carrara.[33] It was Figaia's concern that was destined to provide the giant, eighty-metre stele, with MUSSOLINI DUX inscribed on it, marking the entry to the Fascist version of an Imperial Forum in Rome. Figaia (and Ricci) prospered while the larger Fabbricotti family firm, which had once employed Ricci's father but was tardy in bowing to the Ricci–Figaia axis, fell into terminal decline.

Ricci was not just a hard man in the business world. He also built up his segment of the party with energy and determination. The parades and assemblies of the Fascist scouts became the most obvious arena where young Italians rehearsed the ideology of Fascism, even if the rumours which eddied around Ricci, did, by the 1930s, make some more senior scouts wonder about the overall purity and dedication of the regime.[34]

The determination to control the scouting life is well embodied in the case of Giovanni Maria Concina, priest of the *paese* of Prata di Pordenone in Friuli. In late 1926 Concina was arrested after he clung to the cause of his branch of the *esploratori cattolici* (Catholic scouts) and allegedly punched a parent in the village who had pushed his son to join the Balilla instead. Concina was lambasted by aggrieved local Fascists as an erring soul who had refused a Te Deum to give thanks for Mussolini's avoidance of the Zamboni assassination attempt in Bologna in October 1926 and who was a friend of a pederast layman, guilty of making the Catholic scouts a 'hotbed of immorality'. The priest was arrested and jailed. Concina's own lengthy appeal against *confino* argued in justification that he had spent his life since his initial appointment in 1896 trying to elevate the economic and moral tone of his peasant parishioners. He had, he said, resisted Austrian occupation during the war in the joint interest of *italianità* and good order, though he had, earlier and later, also favoured Catholic unionism. His real purpose there, however, had been to defeat Bolshevism and he used capital letters to conclude his case that Catholic social organization in every instance 'AIMED TO INCULCATE CHRISTIAN CONSCIOUSNESS AND UNITE THE LAITY WITH THE ECCLESIASTICAL HIERARCHY TO PERMIT THE TRIUMPH OF THE REIGN OF JESUS CHRIST'. Concina never read political papers, he added in some contradiction, and he certainly had not abused the Balilla. Any village gossip about his habits was occasioned by the longstanding enmity of certain malign locals and was palpably untrue. Furthermore, his exile from the village would cause the death of his ninety-year-old mother. Concina's combination of stoutness and pathos had some reward. After being made a public example and placed under house arrest, he was soon amnestied.[35]

If youth constituted one of the categories that retained prominence in the Fascist version of identity politics, labour and work were still more significant matters. Fascism's jihad against Marxism had always contained a hint of ambiguity, given the profile of ex-socialists and especially syndicalists in the movement. By 1925 it is true that quite a few sometime leftists had either given up on the government led by Mussolini – De Ambris went into exile in France in 1923 and stayed there until his death in 1934 – or, like Rossoni, the union chief, were transforming themselves and their ideology in a conservative direction. But a pro-worker vocabulary was never altogether eliminated from the regime's discourse and it would resurface during the Salò Republic in 1943–5, when Mussolini frequently expatiated on the natural marriage between Fascism and a nationalized form of socialism. Chatter, then and earlier, about participatory or decentralizing totalitarianism and the eventual withering away of the Fascist party in a society become universal was all very well,[36] but how, by the mid-1920s, was the Fascist regime constructing a place for labour and for big business, rural toil and land-ownership, in its version of a state?

Tullio Cianetti, the young Umbrian peasant and returned soldier now become a party union boss, believed that the gap in his world between sharecroppers and other middling peasants and communist day labourers was far more profound than that which separated him from landowners. None the less, he reported that conversations with Rossoni proved to him that: 'To deny the existence of the class struggle is like denying the light of the sun.' Acceptance of such reality in his eyes, however, did not entail surrender to its negative effects on the nation. Rather, he explained in his memoirs, 'the fundamental essence of Fascist unionism is summed up in the single word: collaboration'.[37]

Mussolini's own definition of what social togetherness might mean remained flexible. He was relieved no doubt to find the commanding heights of Italian capitalism joining the great majority of the Liberal order and certainly most landowners in applauding the March on Rome. Thereafter he and De' Stefani were careful to present the new government as fiscally orthodox, preoccupied with cutting wasteful expenditure but willing to assist capital by the denationalization of the telephone network and the cancellation of Giolitti's investigation into excessive war profits, and determined to balance the budget. The Prime Minister found places for twenty industrialists in his *listone* and, in September 1924, went out of his way to promote figures from the business world to the Senate.[38] Spokesmen for industry still liked to maintain modestly that 'the genuine good businessman possesses, if not a horror, an aversion for politics. He interests himself in the matter for half an hour in the morning and half an hour at night, leafing through the papers. But during the day, all his thoughts are devoted to his work and to his business dealings.'[39] No doubt there was some truth in the celebrated comment by Giovanni Agnelli in October 1922 that 'we businessmen are for the government by definition'.[40] After all, the Liberal state had scarcely abdicated a public role in the economy. As Felice Guarneri, a Fascist technocrat with eventual ministerial charge of foreign trade, recalled, business was always locked into supporting the current administration 'because, in a country like Italy, . . . the state grasps the levers of command in so many sectors of the economy. [It controls] taxation and customs, domestic and foreign credit, imports, exports and international exchange value, tariffs, transport, public works, mining rights, water concessions' and much else. In 1922 Fascism, he contended, had been 'rather vague and uncertain' in its policy towards business. But the Italian way was for close linkage to be maintained between the economic and political orders at both a formal and an informal level.[41]

Yet there was always a qualification in the businessmen's desire to work with government. Italian industrialists, like their fellows in other places, for example in Weimar Germany, drew the line at the approach of Marxists and their trade unions to power. For quite a while they expressed concern about Mussolini, who, in a characteristically audacious and unprincipled search for (temporary) friends bringing tactical advantage, had not yet written off the 'practical' socialists of CGdL. No sooner had his team won the April 1924 elections than the *Duce* sought possible friendly contacts among those who seemed his union enemies, insinuating that there might be an opening in government for a unionist, who could view his role as 'technical' and not 'political'. This opportunity might extend to someone from Federterra and the cooperative movement so long as they did not insist on clinging to the socialist party.[42] Similarly Mussolini refused to commit himself either to Fascist unionists like Rossoni or to the more unbridled union-bashing segments of the PNF. In the *Duce*'s capacious mind, matters were often more complicated than such combatants saw. Rossoni, for example, was a noisy critic of what he regarded as the offensive greed of small shop-keepers, a social group with plenty of reasons to find some virtue in Fascism and by no means automatically liked by big business. None the less, in 1926, a restrictive shop-licensing system came into existence through the establishment of a Fascist Confederation of General Traders, favouring traditional retail methods over mass marketing. The Federation was destined to survive the regime, a fate helping to ensure that, even in the new millennium, Italy remains a country of small shops.[43] Such supermarkets as Rinascente, Upim (fifty-four of them by 1943) and Standa would open their doors to customers in a number of Italian cities by the 1930s but they remained the exception and not the rule for Fascist shoppers.[44] Housewives or, in many middle-class families, housekeepers and maids – Fascist papers regularly gave advertising space to the hiring of servants and the number of female domestic staff increased from 381,000 in 1921 to 585,000 in 1936[45] – found limits to the modernization permitted by Italian totalitarianism in what remained their daily marketing forays.

But the key arrangement in the labour practices of the developing totalitarian state came in October 1925 with the Palazzo Vidoni Pact. Endorsing its brief clauses,[46] the government took a large step towards the creation of what was to be called a corporate system, with business and labour accepting that each should bend to Fascist authority. With some reluctance, in December the membership of the big business league, Confindustria, agreed that it too must acknowledge that it was now Fascist.[47] Any surviving socialist or Catholic unions were liquidated. Ex-nationalist of reactionary bent, Alfredo Rocco, since January 1925 Minister of Justice, was the most public advocate of this simplification of labour relations and what he intended to be a disciplining of worker behaviour – in March 1925 there had been a rash of strikes, backed by the more unruly Fascist unionists. Although he did not forget to pay his respects to Mussolini's 'infallible intuition', Rocco proclaimed that the labour reforms, which followed the initial Vidoni Pact and which he drafted, amounted to the forging of a 'genuinely social', 'Fascist state', one led by a new ruling class, tempered in the war and bringing Roman-style discipline and hierarchy into all work. 'The Fascist state', Rocco announced in words designed to frame the meaning and purpose of totalitarianism, 'has its own morality, its own religion, its own political mission in the world, its own form of social justice, in sum its own economic arrangement.' 'Only through the state', he concluded, 'could a Fascist citizen find well-being and fortune.'[48]

On 3 April 1926, what is known as the 'Rocco law' on labour contracts banned both strikes and lockouts. True to the symbol of the *fasces*, which represented the vertical organization of society and rejected the horizontal, where bourgeoisie and proletariat were locked in struggle, now the regime established a syndical system that, in theory at least, bonded employers and employees. Boss and worker, each found representation in the several syndicates or corporations of industry, agriculture, commerce, maritime and air transport, land and inland waterway transport and banking, with intellectuals and artists being grouped in a seventh syndicate of their own.[49] The state pledged to act as the arbitrator in any internecine dispute through what became an ever-more complex hive of labour courts. Mussolini added the Ministry of Corporations to his vast array – at the end of 1926 he was additionally Prime Minister, Minister of Foreign Affairs, Minister of the Interior, Minister of War, Minister of the Navy and Minister for Air. The obliging Bottai, no real radical despite his fondness for philosophical lucubration,[50] took on the task of acting as his undersecretary, being elevated to the Ministry in September 1929.

The reform process, foreshadowed in 1925 at the Palazzo Vidoni, culminated two years later on 21 April, the dictatorship's Labour Day holiday, with the issuing of the so-called *Carta del Lavoro* (Labour Charter), then and thereafter inscribed as the fundamental expression of the nature of Fascist work and of the Fascist surpassing of class conflict. Through its provisions, syndicalist A. O. Olivetti maintained, the Fascist state had invented the economic system surpassing both socialism and liberalism. Its first clause ran: 'the Italian nation is an organism having a purpose, life and means of action superior to those of any individual or groups who are part of it. It is a moral, political and economic unit which integrally achieves the Fascist State.' Work, whether 'intellectual, technical or manual', the Charter explained further, was a 'social duty', from which no one was exempt. All labour was safeguarded by the state and so, although trade unions and professional organizations could exist, they must salute the primacy of the state in all their dealings. Entrepreneurship in business was still to be applauded and encouraged, since 'state intervention in economic production will only happen when private initiative is lacking or insufficient and when the political interests of the state are directly involved'. The employer should ordinarily undertake responsibility for the welfare of his employees but the state on occasion needed to intervene in order to provide extra assistance. Fascism wanted to explore means to improve insurance against injury in the workplace and to check 'involuntary unemployment', for example, while also providing youth training and welfare to women who juggled work and child-bearing.[51]

Rumour alleged that Rossoni was privately derisive of these changes, which, he lamented, were cosmetic, when the reality was that 'the government had handed over the working masses to the business world', but no channel now existed through which such dissent could be manifested. In any case, Rossoni was reported to have reconciled himself to the end of his version of socialism by privately acquiring a beautiful villa at picturesque Brisighella in the Apennines and extensive estates at the gates of Rome. In yet another display of Fascist familism, one deal was done in the name of his father, the other through the good offices of an uncle.[52] Meanwhile, for ordinary workers, real wages went into steep decline, falling by an estimated 10 per cent between 1928 and 1936.[53] When they came to pay the rent or the food bill for their families, members of the working class had few reasons to cheer the imposition of totalitarianism.

With their leadership, Fascist and non-Fascist, silenced or otherwise bought off, ordinary workers had to be content with such heavily publicized party bodies as the Opera Nazionale Dopolavoro (OND), codified on 1 May 1925. The OND's first national head was the reactionary Duke of Aosta. During its initial operation, this 'after-work' organization, the planning of which had been influenced by the paternalist schemes of Westinghouse and Ford,[54] made do on a meagre budget. Its centres rarely flourished in economically underdeveloped parts of Italy, where the concepts of sporting equipment, unused land and free time remained largely incomprehensible.

There was space for contradiction and paradox, too. Control from above was met by a rush of allegiance, often self-interested allegiance, from below. Throughout the sports world, there was a general wish to explain and justify activities in Fascist terms. Thus, the Associazione Colombofila Nazionale (National Pigeon Fanciers Association), which had been founded in 1904 and boasted a Count Alfonso Ayala Fulgosi as its president, was anxious to make it clear that, since 1922, it had thought of pigeon-racing as a practice useful to the national economy and national defence.[55] Similarly the improvements being carried out at the San Siro football stadium in Milan were ascribed to the personal skills and Fascist devotion of the *podestà*, Ernesto Belloni.[56] The weekly journal of Fascist artisans was sure that its members now played sport with a purpose and not like the *démodé* coffee-shop chatterers of old. Perhaps a hint of amateur values survived in *L'Artigiano*'s formula: 'know how to obtain victory without boasting and to be beaten without recrimination, to win with style and to lose with style'. But the journal urged all its members on to sporting endeavour.[57] Italian competitors did fairly well in the 1928 Amsterdam Olympics and did not forget to give the Roman salute in the march past.[58] In the succeeding 1932 and 1936 Games, the Italians were second and then fourth in overall results[59] and the national football team was to triumph in the World Cups of 1934 and 1938. The heavy industrial firm of Fiat, too, was anxious to be associated with organized leisure, claiming already in the 1920s that every factory had a 'perfectly equipped football team', while tennis was the preferred game of its white-collar workers, including the female ones.[60] Especially in the cities and the north, organized and apparently 'Fascistized' leisure became another important strand in the totalitarian mix.

If business thought that it had vanquished its enemies in the legislation of 1925–7, it was reminded that it was partially mistaken during a policy dispute that bubbled on during these years over the proper valuation of the national currency. What came to be called, in classically militant Fascist phrasing, the 'battle for the lira' was at the time the matter in which Mussolini engaged himself most directly,[61] committing his own prestige and that of Fascism in a way that allowed no backsliding, despite the nervousness of quite a few industrialists and bankers and, probably in his heart, of Giuseppe Volpi, who replaced De' Stefani as Minister of Finance in July 1925. Installed in office but not yet wholly expert in the ways of Fascist government, Volpi thought it rhetorically sensible to tell the Senate that classical Rome had reduced the value of its currency in the aftermath of its sack of Carthage.[62] Whereas in most instances since 1922 it could be maintained with some credibility that Fascism was a variant of liberalism, forced to be more activist by pressing immediate needs and by the continuation of circumstances, attitudes and methods which had first appeared in wartime, the quarrel over how strong the currency should be made it evident that Fascism could not always be relied on simply to toe a business line. Now the old elites learned that, in this dictatorship, economics might be subjugated to politics. As historian Roland Sarti has argued, the high valuation of the lira and the ardent way in which it was supported, foreshadowed the protectionist and state interventionist policies of the 1930s to be known as *autarchia* (autarchy).[63] Even though high finance had grounds to enjoy a heavy lira, rigidifying protectionism was a policy that once liberal businessmen could tolerate and work with for a time but never in their hearts treasure.

Business aside, after January 1925 the dictatorship was confronted by other, less economic and more directly political, organizations needing to be fitted into the new system of rule. Notable among them was the army and its officer corps. Mussolini did not need Mao Zedong to tell him that power came out of the barrel of a gun. Before 1925 Fascism had been as divided about what might be an ideal line on the military as it was on so many other matters. The more committed favoured radical reform, designed to streamline the army, give it a more genuine popular base and transform it into a sleekly formidable fighting force, eliminating those organizational, educational and social weaknesses which a number of critics claimed were to blame for the fiasco at Caporetto.[64] Dealing with the army was a priority for Mussolini in his new role as dictator.[65] His solution, however, was not of the sort that those who assume that dictators always confront and overwhelm all opposition might predict.

Instead, Mussolini fudged and compromised with the still largely monarchist and traditionalist army leadership, rather as he treated the institution of the monarchy itself. Reform was delayed or abandoned. On 4 May 1925 the *Duce* recalled to army leadership General Pietro Badoglio, born 1871 at Grazzano Monferrato in the heart of dynastic Piedmont. A trimmer and accommodator who, according to some, bore heavy responsibility for the defeat in 1917, Badoglio, avoiding the bitter debates about the army, the MVSN and the possible nature of Fascist war, in 1924–5 had been safely off the stage while serving as ambassador to Brazil.[66] Mussolini created a new supervising position (and a new rank) for Marshal Badoglio, who was elevated to be Chief of General Staff, as well as Head of the Army. Badoglio did not leave the senior position until driven to do so by the military catastrophe in Greece following the invasion of 28 October 1940. Prompted by his venal, procrastinating and doubtfully Fascist command, until 1943 and beyond the Italian Army remained more national and traditional than ideologically committed to Fascism. As a contact of Farinacci put it angrily, assuming that it was only possible to be a 'fiery Fascist' since a muffled one was a contradiction in terms, in the entire Ministry of War 'only two' real party men were gainfully employed. He was one.[67]

Accommodation rather than takeover was similarly the policy for dealing with that great Italian but simultaneously universal organization, the Catholic Church. From 1927 Fascism did successfully install its own spies in the Vatican, agents who included Pius XI's domestic chaplain.[68] The Liberals had paved this path by systematically intercepting papal diplomatic traffic during the First World War.[69] As early as April 1922 the then Nationalist Alfredo Rocco had defined Catholicism as an essential part of *italianità*[70] and, at that time, Fascism was also showing itself not averse to friendship with the Church. The public policy of polite dealings, which Mussolini had commenced on obtaining office in 1922, despite his own strident youthful irreligion and despite the profound anti-clericalism of such different members of the regime as Farinacci and the King (one of Victor Emmanuel's most cherished aphorisms was 'men who wear gowns have a long reach')[71] was soon amplified with more serious talks. Blessed by such important figures as Arnaldo Mussolini and Eugenio Pacelli, who would become Pope Pius XII in 1939 and was already a crucial power-broker at the Vatican, the treating eventually attracted the direct interest of Mussolini himself. The key negotiator on the Vatican's part was the future Pope's lawyer brother, Francesco Pacelli.[72] His attention to detail and the dictator's willingness to work into the wee hours resulted in the Concordat and other Lateran Pacts of 11 February 1929. They marked the formal end of the cold war between Church and State that had rumbled on since the Risorgimento.[73] Although spats could recur after 1929, although the completeness of the Vatican's control over what a Catholic historian has insisted remained Italy's 'churches', with their variation from one bishop's see to the next,[74] was incomplete and although Italians practised their religion in ways that differed by class, gender, age and region, none the less the signature of the Lateran treaties did mark the embrace of Fascist totalitarianism by the public forms of Catholicism. In the Risorgimento, there had been talk of *connubio* (marriage) between one grouping and another. After 1929 wedlock, or at least cohabitation, is a good way to understand official Church–State relations under Fascist rule. In 1930 Catholics throughout the world celebrated when it was announced that the old holiday of 20 September, the anniversary of the impious invasion of Rome by Italian troops in 1870, had been cancelled from the list of national holidays. Thereafter it was replaced by 11 February.[75]

Monarchy, army, church, business, labour, each was acquiring a distinct place in the hierarchy which was seen to typify Fascist Italy. Each could be portrayed as having dovetailed themselves to the now solidly united nation, expressed in the symbol of the *fasces*. But what about the Fascists, the old members of the PNF and especially the rumbustious provincial *ras* and their wilful and aggressive camp followers, those who had contemplated looking for some leader other than Mussolini during the last months of 1924? How were they being fashioned into the obedient subjects of a dictator and his totalitarian regime?

In the reordering of Fascist government after January 1925, the most surprising promotion was announced on 12 February when Roberto Farinacci took over the secretaryship of the PNF from what had been for some months a quarrelling directorate of fifteen chieflings. His story, in office and out (Farinacci lost the secretaryship in March 1926), can be read as a case study of the intentions and the limitations of the Fascist version of totalitarianism.

At first sight, given Farinacci's public rowdiness since the Matteotti murder – after Casalini's death he had urged in his paper, *Cremona Nuova*, 'if the broom is not enough, let us use the machine-gun'[76] – it seemed an odd choice to promote him to key office. Yet Farinacci's rough and tough approach to revolution was checked while the conservative Federzoni held the Ministry of the Interior (Federzoni remained in that post from June 1924 to November 1926, when Mussolini resumed public control over national policing). Farinacci could rail against critics of the Matteotti murder – in July 1926 he acted as defence lawyer for Dumini in his trial at Chieti and enjoyed publicizing the salacious imagination of a clerical paper which had alleged that Matteotti had had his genitals cut off and carried as a trophy to Filippelli[77] – but the extremity of his enthusiasm for Fascist revolution had its uses.

On assuming office, Farinacci spoke up at Cremona, as a favourite son might, about his new duties, proclaiming that 'Fascism must not give a rap about all those who support it with conditions . . . It must count only on the strength of its own cadres.' He followed up with speeches urging that 'Fascism is not a party but a religion; it is the future of the country', affirming that the movement had now 'really returned to its origins'. In August 1925 at Predappio, Farinacci declared that the nation was being hammered into shape by Mussolini, the son of a blacksmith, repeating the refrain that 'our party is a religion. Outside its ranks, a man is lost.' Back at Cremona, a couple of months later, the secretary concluded baldly: 'the Anti-Fascist cannot be an Italian'.[78]

Whether converted by this apparently fanatical totalitarianism or trimming their sails to the prevailing breeze, Italians responded to Farinacci's appointment by flocking into the party. The PNF's membership almost doubled under his leadership. Yet Mussolini's choice of Farinacci for the secretary's job was motivated by the ancient Machiavellian idea that a thief can catch a thief. The months of 1925–6 were filled not only with the legal construction of the totalitarian state but also the pervasive spread of a personality cult around the *Duce*. As Bottai, whose sensitive soul was often appalled by Farinacci's hooliganism, put it after the Cremona *ras* had been replaced as party secretary by the ostensibly proper Augusto Turati, Mussolini must always be acknowledged as 'dictator over the party'.[79] 'Fascism', Bottai wrote in 1927, 'is Mussolinism . . . Without Mussolini, Fascism would not exist and neither would we politically.' Now, he added, 'the Party is the political organization of the generation of Mussolini'.[80]

The *Duce*, after all, had felt impelled in September 1924 to instruct Farinacci that 'the time for threats is over'; Fascists 'should not refuse anyone' who evinced a desire to collaborate with them.[81] By opting for dictatorship in January 1925 Mussolini had not altogether thrown such caution or good sense to the winds and become a Farinaccian. From April 1925 the *Duce* kept in his private files, hanging like a sword of Damocles over the party secretary's legal and political well-being, the statement that plagiarism of a thesis should be punished with six months in prison.[82] Similarly, party members engaged in quarrel with Farinacci seldom forgot the faked degrees on which his rich career as the nation's most celebrated lawyer depended.[83] The

Duce himself scrupulously filed away a telephone tap in 1932, in which Farinacci boasted that his work as a lawyer was bringing him 700,000 lire in annual fees.[84] Thus armed against serious mutiny, Mussolini was soon urging the Cremona *ras* to calm his attacks on bankers lest national credit be damaged.[85] He also objected to Farinacci's brutal view that Fascism had been blooded in the Matteotti murder and had no need to apologize for it.[86] The task of the new secretary was not just to integrate the party into Italian society but simultaneously to discipline it, in other words to ensure that its cadres did not behave with too much independence or express too many heretical ideas. As Mussolini complained in May 1925, Fascism was troubled by a sad multiplication of too many qualifying adjectives. Words like integralist, revisionist or extremist were dissipating the meaning of Fascism. 'These distinctions are utterly cretinous and I completely reject them,' the *Duce* stated sternly. Fascism must continue to work like an army in which there were 'only leaders and followers'.[87] The rebellious *fasci* of Florence, Turin, Venice and Perugia no longer served a purpose. 'Squadrisms in the Holy Year' (the papal jubilee of 1925), he remarked in studied mockery of Farinacci's anticlericalism, 'don't preserve historic sense.' Farinacci should deal severely and now with any who still defined themselves that way.[88]

Nor did Farinacci mind acting as an agent of control. Mussolini had read his psychology well, for the undisciplined subordinate loved to exercise authority over others. With considerable irony, Farinacci's secretaryship marked a lessening of independence within the PNF, although it was left to his successor, Turati, to conduct a more rigorous purge[89] (to the previous secretary's disgust, among the victims were many of his erstwhile friends and Farinacci predictably swore vendetta on his and their behalf against Turati). According to De Felice, who admits that the reliability of the sociological categories is questionable, Turati also headed a party that had become more bourgeois and petit bourgeois than in the past, with a worker and peasant presence limited to 15 per cent. Although the membership was continuing to grow, many of these respectable new Fascists must have joined under Farinacci.

In a time of many ironies, the most delicious occurred in January 1926, when Farinacci got around to instructing party members to abandon their bad habits of indulging in 'certain forms of charity-collection that often resemble blackmail and so are harmful to the dignity of Fascism'.[90] Such righteousness was all very well but once his career as a party bureaucrat was over Farinacci remained entrenched as the boss of Cremona and local businessmen were ill advised not to seek his approval in any deal. On one occasion when intervening using a telephone tap to save the career of a troubled local schoolteacher, he commented, 'you know that I take to heart everything about Cremona'.[91]

Nationally, Farinacci retained a role as the leader of those who styled themselves the 'Fascists of the first hour' and so, should the truth be known (it could not be expressed), the opponents of too much Mussolinian guile. In 1943, at least in his own view, Farinacci stood forward as the potential successor to the dictator and most lusty Italian supporter of the alliance with Nazi Germany. The regime's secret police never ceased to take an interest in his activities, recording in July 1933, for example, with whom he had dinner on a visit to Milan and at what restaurant.[92] Yet Farinacci was anything but a fanatic of the type embodied by Hitler, Himmler and many Nazi leaders. Rather, Farinacci's ideological commitment to Fascism can easily be reduced to self-interest, if no doubt mixed with a frustrated anger at a wealth and glory never fully achieved and so to be expressed as a cheerful willingness to burn down the palaces which housed his betters. In sum, the Cremona *ras* was never quite a Fascist 'new man', for all the boasts of the regime that it was forging a different and true-believing style of Italian.

There was plenty of evidence that this revolutionist leopard never changed its spots. To provide examples – in September 1936 Farinacci drew the attention of Galeazzo Ciano, Mussolini's son-in-law and youthful and newly appointed Minister of Foreign Affairs, to his own son, Franco. The ex-railway worker boss of Cremona envisaged a more genteel and by no means fanatical future for his heir. Franco Farinacci had recently been awarded a law degree and was about to complete his military service. It would be nice if a career in diplomacy could beckon. So Roberto Farinacci begged a fraternal favour from Ciano. 'Could you [*tu*] find him some position linked to an embassy or some business seat of ours in which he can perfect his French and learn English?' 'If the thing is possible without breaking any existing regulations [*vigenti disposizioni*], fine'; 'otherwise', Farinacci, with apparent propriety but actual mockery, concluded, 'don't do anything'.[93]

Ciano got the message, perhaps assisted by his memory of an earlier missive from the Cremona *ras*, when Edda Mussolini's yuppie husband was still only Minister for Popular Culture (and in charge of regime propaganda). Ciano's task then had been to implement the newly populist intention of 'going to the people' and 'making space for the young', announced with fanfare by Mussolini and Achille Starace, the party secretary from 1931 to 1939, as imposing totalitarianism on the masses. Among the changes in behaviour meant to make Italians more militant and commanding was the abolition of the allegedly effete and foreign handshake. Thereafter, it was urged, Italians must greet each other with the 'Roman' salute. A Chicago doctor was cited as approving the resultant effect on the health of the nation. It must also benefit those politicians required to greet the people, as in the case of Herbert Hoover, who had recently been exhausted by shaking three thousand hands at a White House reception. The American president would have stayed fitter, Italians were told, had he merely raised his hand in the Roman salute. Starace urged that Fascists should lead by example in the matter 'among their families and in public'. 'It cannot be said', he ran on characteristically but with suppressed nervousness, 'that the Roman salute is being imposed out of false showmanship since it has not been dreamed up coldly by someone sitting at a desk or consulting books. Rather the salute has returned [from the Roman era] spontaneously, as a logical necessity in our epoch of squadrism.'[94]

While this loud campaign proceeded, Farinacci wrote formally asking the Ministry of Popular Culture not to cut the circulation of his paper, now re-badged *Il Regime Fascista*, but, he admitted to Ciano, the decision did not matter much. What he really wanted was just to impart his good wishes. 'And, since it is Good Friday [Farinacci was again flaunting his impiety] and so God cannot see us, and neither can Starace, therefore I send you a fraternal handshake which I shall transmute into a hug so long as this step does not infringe the existing regulations.' Farinacci's sardonic and repeated choice of words implied that a wise man knew that what was current and Staracean need not last forever.[95] Regulations, no doubt, were all very well for little and literal people but, for Farinacci and his friends, it was their flexible definition that counted.

For years, Fascist leaders had proclaimed that their regime was abolishing the *raccomandazione* (the confidential reference), just as they, hardy and manly legionaries of the revolution, had eliminated venality, jobbery and graft. In 1929 Turati instructed Fascist Members of Parliament that the practice must 'absolutely' cease, since it was a corrupt leftover of 'liberal [ideas] now rendered redundant'.[96] Mussolini had inveighed against it. The Fascist version of modernity was meant rigorously to eschew what were written off as 'Masonic habits', lingering from a less rigorous time, when liberal softness rendered the whole nation impotent. The new Fascist man and woman no doubt had to win their place in a society that was hierarchically arranged. But distinction in rank was meant to spring from Darwinian battle and a militant commitment and not from the furtive utilization of favour, connection and nepotism. Yet, bolstered by his father's support and contacts, Franco Farinacci was destined to engage in diplomacy. For a while he served the Fascist revolution in places as ideologically acceptable as Seville and Hamburg. However, his acquisition of English and the perfection of his French (and, it might be surmised, his failure to concentrate on German) had its value in the middle and longer term. In July 1943 Franco Farinacci chose the winning side, backed the monarchy and their Anglo-Saxon patrons and broke with Nazi-fascism. He did not leave Italian government service until June 1973, by which time he had risen to be a 'minister plenipotentiary, second class'.[97]

Roberto Farinacci, by contrast, was killed by partisans when the dictatorship collapsed in April 1945.[98] His Fascism, unlike his son's, did last to the bitter end. None the less, a scanning of the thirty-nine boxes of Farinacci's private papers reveals a world spanning the 1920s and the 1930s where the *raccomandazione* was an everyday feature of life, whether its preoccupation was political, commercial, social or even medical. The worst aspect of his loss of the party secretaryship, Farinacci made plain, was the punishment then visited on his followers throughout the country and especially in his old stamping ground of the railways.[99] Yet he abandoned none of his clients to their fate. Rather he was an assiduous patron, just as he clung determinedly to every honour that came his way – he demanded that Arpinati leave a boys' holiday camp with the title 'Colonia Roberto Farinacci', despite suggestions that he should avoid such vanity.[100] In Farinacci's world, a surgeon looking for a job[101] needed 'friends' in the same way as did a banker hoping for a financial concession[102] and a military man faced with an unwanted transfer[103] or a tardy promotion[104] or inadequate praise and reward on retirement.[105] Farinacci's help could be summoned and proffered to avoid categorization as a Jew,[106] to help local landowners avoid tax,[107] to reverse an expulsion from the Fascist party,[108] to get a son out of prison where nameless enemies had placed him,[109] to persuade a foreign fascist chief to pay for a contracted bust[110] and to ensure favourable reviews for a new history book.[111] Farinacci was a boss, a patron. By definition, he was possessed of clients and both he and his followers knew how and why their network functioned. The world was full of 'plots'[112] and 'vendettas',[113] in which malign enemies sought to cast down Farinacci or his clients or each through the other. Yet constant importunity could bring benefit as it did when in 1936 it was announced that the *Duce* had suddenly disbursed a special subsidy of 100,000 lire for welfare in Cremona from his secret funds.[114]

In this embattled world, Cremona stood as Farinacci's cherished home fortress. All railway workers in the town knew that, if they wanted to preserve their jobs, they must take out a subscription to Farinacci's local paper.[115] In 1928 Farinacci greeted the appointment of the self-consciously intellectual Giorgio Masi to the position of city school director with the surly comments that he had been surprised by the choice and had heard gossip that Masi intended to wipe the floor (*fregare*) with the local *ras*. But Masi must understand one thing: 'if, at Cremona, you don't do exactly what I say, I shall first break "what it is that you sit on" and then your nose'.[116] Thus instructed about his social place, Masi did behave in the way Farinacci wanted and was rewarded for his dutifulness. In 1937 unwise contacts with anti-Fascists who suddenly defected to France[117] brought down on Masi's head five years of *confino*. The complex plot had, it was alleged, entailed the assassination of Farinacci. Still, the Cremona *ras* intervened on Masi's behalf with a characteristically phrased note to the *Duce*: 'Masi is a philosopher and therefore a constitutional idiot. But in his soul he is quite incapable of harm. I am firmly convinced after knowing him for thirteen years that, even though his apparent attitudes can make him seem guilty, he is actually a complete innocent.' Masi served only three months. His wife was ill, Farinacci had added, his children potentially reduced to poverty. If he could be let off, 'I promise you [*ti*] that I shall keep him under my loving eye, and, if ever it proves necessary [again to keep him in line], I shall chop out part of his tongue.'[118] As Farinacci put it, in Cremona, as elsewhere, he carried weight: 'I never forget my friends.'[119]

If Farinacci sought to manipulate Fascism, at least while secure in his Cremona stronghold, not so much bowing to its totalitarianism as harnessing it to his own causes, other Italians were similarly eager to adapt the dictatorship and its rhetoric to their own interests. The beekeepers of the Trentino were an example. When an apiarists' school held a '*festa* of the bee', a local priest, the well-named Father Dante, homilized at Sardagna on the outskirts of Trento about the virtues of Mussolini, Fascism and the Lateran Pacts, while noting that bees were the natural model for Italians when they worked in perfect peace, harmony and fraternal love under their *Duce*.[120] By the end of the 1920s the apiarists' journal brimmed with their dedication to Fascism and was expansive on their delight in donning the black-shirt. They did not thereby renounce being a lobby group in their own interest, however. Rather, they were not ashamed to urge, they deserved special government support, given 'the great educational value of a colony of bees, characterized by comradely behaviour (*cameratismo*) and providing the classic case of cooperation'.[121] The presence of Italian bees, a 'superior breed' (*razza*), the 'best in the world', and their battle with intruding and inferior 'grey, dark' bees from the north, were proof that the lands watered by the Adige were fecund with *italianità* (Italianness).[122]

The survival of special interests among Italians, rich and poor, was not a matter much remarked on in the pages of *Critica Fascista* or in the other propaganda outlets of the regime as they peddled the gospel of totalitarianism. Turati, the PNF secretary from March 1926 to October 1930, a Fascist from clerical Brescia, who made much of his own dedication to a Spartan (and sporting) life,[123] was presented as proof of the new dedication to revolution. He took pains to emphasize that Mussolini incarnated 'the force of the race, the force of the idea' and proclaimed that the Fascist regime integrated 'state, nation and stock' (*stirpe*) into a mystical whole.[124] None the less, in a moment of half reflection, Turati admitted that 'for now', 'the inevitable deficiencies of men and institutions' meant that Fascism was a work in progress[125] and he himself was to provide some proof of lingering impropriety when he fell amid accusations of deviant sex. Before then, Turati did not forget to reward his own people. Under his aegis, Brescia could count on government subsidies for public works that were twice or three times higher than those accorded comparable cities.[126]

Mussolini, ever less able to shrug off his own profound cynicism, misanthropy and misogyny, needed little convincing that man is vile and must be driven towards virtue, that lies rule any discourse and that control mattered most. Back in June 1925 the *Duce* had stated to the Chamber of Deputies: 'We are not a ministry; we are not even a government. We are a regime', and one which intended to last.[127] The duration would be imposed, whether it was wanted or not. Just as surely as Fascism had risen with violence heavily conditioning its other messages, so, along with other features of the newly totalitarian state and its corporate society, went repression.

Following his proclamation of the dictatorship, the *Duce* was the object of at least four assassination attempts, with the last occurring at Bologna in October 1926. Then the presumed assassin, the teenage Anteo Zamboni, from a local family, was lynched by the enraged followers of the local *ras*, Leandro Arpinati. Although the case was never fully proven, Zamboni had probably fired at the *Duce* from the crowd assembled to cheer their dictator's visit to Bologna (he had been stirringly welcomed with a version of the 'Triumphal March' from *Aida*). As it flew by, the shot narrowly missed Mussolini's body. Such events prompted predictable calls for revenge from provincial Fascists – after the attack, Balbo from nearby Ferrara demanded the creation of 'Ferrarese Fascism's own secret police', which could deal with any 'subversives' it found.[128] It was not the *ras*, however, but the regime and the dictator that now constructed a system of repression, formalizing state terror. Building on an inheritance of police control of dissidence from Liberal Italy and from the army during the First World War, the Fascist state moved further into authoritarianism than had past administrations. In November 1926 a decree on public safety urged a tight surveillance of the smallest manifestation of dissent among the populace and did so with a breadth of definition that made the 'undeserving poor' perpetual targets of Fascist control. Anti-Fascists of whatever stripe could be punished with a system of warnings (*ammonizioni*) or of forced residence either at home or at some place, generally a village or island in the south, designated by the police (*domicilio coatto* or *confino*). The legislation also instituted the death penalty for attacks on the *Duce* or on leading members of the royal family.[129]

On 25 November 1927 repression grew harsher with the foundation of a 'Special Tribunal for the Defence of the State', which no longer needed to observe the niceties of liberal legal practice. During its first two years, 5,046 cases were brought before it. Nine hundred and four accused were convicted, perhaps a surprisingly low proportion. Lombardy provided 1,301 of those charged (261 condemned), the Emilia 689 (90), Tuscany 426 (119), Calabria 50 (7), and the Basilicata 3 (0).[130] Among those who now found themselves pent up in Fascist jail were such anti-Fascist leaders as PCd'I chief Antonio Gramsci (communists were always the most numerous of the regime's victims), democratic returned soldiers Emilio Lussu, Ferruccio Parri and Carlo Rosselli, and a number of socialists and republicans. Catholic leader Alcide De Gasperi was imprisoned in March 1927 but released eighteen months later, after the bishop of his home town of Trento intervened on his behalf. Thereafter, in a compromise which said much about Fascism, the Vatican and the relationship between the two, De Gasperi was allowed to go on living in Rome. The police did not interfere when he walked each day from his apartment to a temporary job in the Vatican library. His official task, perhaps appropriately for his future as post-war Prime Minister under the American imperium, was to recatalogue books in accordance with the system in use in the Library of Congress and, more covertly, to go on preparing 'alternative' Catholic politics should they be required after Fascism.[131]

By the end of the regime, the secret police had compiled dossiers on

130,000 Italians. Some 13,000 had endured the punishment of *confino* for terms which could in practice become life but could also, except for the most obdurate and ideologically informed anti-Fascists, be shortened by amnesty after apology or a successful plea for mercy on a victim's behalf by some influential figure. In peacetime, the Special Tribunal implemented nine sentences of capital punishment (tellingly five were imposed on 'Slav' nationalists), eight other recipients of the death penalty having their sentences commuted.[132]

These relatively low numbers may leave the impression that the Fascist regime offered a benign form of dictatorship and it must be accepted that, in its domestic policies, it was far less bloody than were the Nazis or Soviets or, for example, the more old-fashioned military version of authoritarianism embodied by General Franco after the Spanish Civil War. Fascism's secret police never altogether lost a ramshackle air – in 1926, when Bocchini became police chief in succession to the ex-prefect of Trieste, Francesco Crispo Moncada, his office was said to lack a telephone that worked.[133] After Bocchini's untimely, if raunchy, death in the arms of a young and noble mistress[134] brought the Neapolitan Carmine Senise, another career official, to succeed him, the secret police boasted only fifty-six functionaries, stiffened by 319 active agents and other staff. Senise did, however, find in the office safe an impressive stock of 21 million lire in thousand-lira notes, which went unrecorded in police budgets or other files.[135] Bocchini, it was plain, presided over a police force that was as expert at corruption as at violent repression. No Fascist fanatic, the police chief, neatly defined by Turati as 'the master of the triple play',[136] was as happy organizing the surveillance of party members as of anti-Fascists and, although he reported to the *Duce* on most days, he cheerfully added Mussolini's telephone to those his agents were tapping.[137]

Any implication that Fascist repression was a matter to be smiled at should be avoided, however. During the 1930s the police were estimated to undertake thousands of actions of a political kind every week; their interest could be as aroused by what was termed 'degeneracy' (the practice of homosexuality or abortion, for example) as by overt political complaint. Paralleling the situation in Nazi Germany and the USSR, they were backed by a huge set of voluntary informers, a number of whom retained their role after 1945. Perhaps the highest-ranking in their number was Agostino Gemelli, the magnificent rector of the Catholic University of Milan, who did not forbear to report on politically erring students.[138] One person in the know more bathetically revealed during the war that the newly appointed Senise had kept his sense of family alive by corruptly organizing the release of his nephew from a US prison and bringing him home to a high life with his Swedish mistress, an actress, and her young friends. Some 80 per cent of denunciations were anonymous,[139] indicating how unfree political systems of the Fascist type encourage the trickling down into society of their leaders' paranoid fears and cynicism. After 1927, if not before, individuals found that approaches to employment or even to the possibility of being granted welfare when in crying need were blocked by a political test. Passing it was a complex matter and sensible Italians were driven to arm themselves as stoutly as possible with patrons and friends of friends, each of whom might ensure that the test would prove 'unfair' and so surmountable.

Essential to the character of Nazi Germany, that regime which studied at the feet of Mussolini's Italy, and dominating its road to mass murder was an idea of race. The desire to extirpate 'Judeo-Bolshevism' drove Nazism to unparalleled fanaticism. In the formation of the totalitarian state in Italy, a Fascist version of racism can be detected, but neither in the 1920s nor later did it replicate the German version. Most racial theory, after all, was decidedly troubling for Italians, since it identified them as members of the 'Mediterranean' race, the third and least desirable of the groups who allegedly inhabited Europe, behind 'Alpines' and 'Nordics'. Like other Europeans, Italians frequently nourished racist assumptions about blacks, Arabs and 'Slavs' and, though those of Jewish faith or background were unusually integrated into Italian nationalism, anti-Semitism lurked in a number of Italian minds. But at least as powerful and perhaps more powerful were racial or quasi-racial assumptions about the gap between one Italian and another and especially between north and south. Cesare Lombroso, the northern criminologist who had competed with D'Annunzio for the palm as Liberal Italy's intellectual of greatest international stature, made his name by his mathematical and scientific separation of the types of crime committed by 'northern' and 'southern' Italians. The two regions, he maintained, were settled by peoples with utterly different ways of comprehending the world. Italy was sundered by a racial divide. Even as they waxed lyrical about *romanità*, those classical traditions allegedly refurbished in the Fascist empire, Italian historians and journalists usually accepted that Romans, Etruscans, Gauls, Samnites, Oscians and the rest had intermingled in the peopling of the peninsula.

These evident complications delayed and confused the imposition of a Fascist racism and made most local theoreticians fans of a spiritual (and subjective) definition of an Italian race, not one measured by blood and science. For all the drift into racial legislation and practice during the last decade of the regime's rule, neither the dictator nor the Fascists successfully ironed away the wrinkles in their racism. Yet, already on 10 December 1925, the regime had trumpeted the establishment of its Opera nazionale per la protezione della maternità e dell'infanzia (ONMI; National agency for mothers and children), promising greater help for the new-born, whose rate of survival remained humiliatingly below those of the countries of Western Europe. ONMI represented the triumph of a process that had been backed by reform-minded liberals and Catholics for some years and so was not specifically Fascist in its framing. This background may help to explain why the body was not suppressed until 1975. Its record under the dictatorship was mixed. Its pretensions to totalitarian control were never fully realized, while Catholic welfare agencies clung to their major presence in Italian society. Despite rising from 33 million lire in 1927 to 381 million in 1942,[140] its funding was never enough for ONMI to achieve what its leaders suggested it might and, as with all Fascist welfare, political interference could disadvantage those who were otherwise most in need. In 1934, despite the massive campaigns of the 'battle for births', only 11.8 per cent of women were assisted by ONMI when they had children.[141] None the less, ONMI was more active than any of its predecessors. Infant mortality did fall from 12.8 per cent in the first year of life in 1922 to 10.3 per cent in 1940 (although there was little sign of any catch up with the situation in France or Germany).[142]

Much of ONMI's work was worthy but humdrum and only indirectly linked to the preoccupations of the always highly patriarchal Fascist leadership. In his Ascension Day speech of 26 May 1927

Mussolini gave demographic and racial concerns a crucial place in the totalitarian quiver. He ranged widely with racial matters underscoring much that he had to say. Since border Fascism was still a spur, the *Duce* brightly argued that Bolzano (Bözen) in the Alto Adige (Süd Tirol) should be renamed Bolgiano further to emphasize its Italianness. Italians, he feared, his mind flitting on, drank too much – in his youth he had been the same, although he did not mention the matter – and, therefore, the government was cutting the number of retail outlets for liquor. 'We must rigorously watch over the destiny of the race [the word he used was *razza*], we must take care of the race, starting with mothers and children.' The need to be healthy and hardy meant that the Fascist state should discourage rapid urbanization. The spread of industrial cities, the *Duce* contended, 'led to sterility'. His Italy should be 'ruralized' and must fight and win a 'battle of the births'.[143]

The PNF secretary echoed his *Duce*'s voice or even set its tone, since in March 1927 Turati had already reflected on the need in the new Italy for all policies to hear the 'voice of the race [*razza*]', which, he maintained with a cloudiness that might have prompted envy from some German racists, 'is an expression of a will that can have an infinite number of forms and can be different today from what it was yesterday because the race, the basic stock [*stirpe*], I repeat, feels what is good and what bad and sometimes we don't ourselves listen to it'. Turati resolved his deepening rhetorical difficulties by allowing his argument to be overborne by his *Duce*; all dilemmas, he remarked, were resolved when he turned to 'A Man'.[144] None the less, in another speech, Turati revived these themes, spelling matters out more directly than Mussolini had done. 'The family', Turati urged, 'is the basic cell of the State, the Nation and the people. It is the only possible safeguard, the last trench for resistance against the corrosive action of the various amoral and immoral forces which cause social decay.' Along with family, the related issues of the 'problem of the race' and of 'female education' composed Fascism's 'fundamental matters of dispute'.[145]

The way Turati cast around for words that might seem to approach a question but actually were largely devoid of meaning hinted at a crucial contradiction in the Fascist construction of its control. Fascism had won many victories along its road towards totalitarianism. By 1929 almost all those political figures who continued to argue that it was possible and desirable to be an Italian and yet not a Fascist had been driven into exile or sat disconsolate in Fascist jails. In the plebiscite held on 24 March, 89.63 per cent of Italians voted, with 8,519,559 expressing their approval of the regime's works, 135,761 being brave enough to say 'no' and 8,092 opting to mar their ballots. Piedmont had the most recalcitrants (21,000), the Veneto, 20,800, Emilia Romagna, 14,600, but only 2,256 cast negative votes in Florence, 2,833 in Rome and 2,272 in Naples. South of there, hardly anyone manifested public dissent.[146] Bottai took the occasion to meditate on what he deemed the more real and profound meaning of the event compared with a democratic election. In Italy, he concluded, the reality was that Mussolini had become 'the *elect* of the Fascist people'.[147] The *Duce* in a literal sense incarnated the hopes and dreams, the force and will of the populace. The ballot had been surpassed; materialism had given way to a new mysticism.

When they review Italian behaviour at the onset of the 1930s, however, almost all historians accept that Italian minds had not really been wiped clean by Fascist totalitarianism or were passively waiting to be inscribed with the codes, rituals and world-view of the new order. The family remained the special object of Italian care and the setting where all sorts of ideas not at once reconcilable with Fascism survived and flourished. Fascist leaders may have talked about their hope in and solicitude for the family but those phrases did not mean that they had decided to take it on and bend it to their ideological will in the way that was then being attempted in the USSR (with uneven results) and would be essayed in Nazi Germany, at least where race was concerned.

One example of the rugged independence of the Italian family must suffice for the moment. The Zamboni family were stricken by the attempt of their teenage son, Anteo, to shoot Mussolini in Bologna on Sunday 31 October 1926. Not only did they have to endure the pain of Anteo's lynching but Fascist repression was pitiless in regard to them too. In the first days after the event, Mammolo, Anteo's father, a reasonably well-off printer, Mammolo's wife, Viola, his sister-in-law, Virginia, his brother, Lodovico, two of his other sons and their wives, a further son, Assunto, who was resident in Milan, and an eighteen-year-old cousin, Giulia, were arrested. Another son, Andrea, ill with heart trouble, was not dragged off to prison but his wife was. The police obviously thought that families mattered.

A number of the Zambonis were released after a week or so. But Mammolo had in the past displayed political interests, once anarchist and more recently Fascist, and his house contained copies of two pamphlets about the Russian Revolution, one about Fascist attacks on Freemasonry and a Beretta pistol. He stayed in prison. So did Lodovico and Assunto, Virginia and Viola. Their story as Fascist prisoners is highly complex and has been evocatively narrated by Brunella Dalla Casa. Mammolo, the printer who had wondered about anarchy and order, was given Samuel Smiles to read in prison and at once identified as a 'self-made man'. His life might not have been approved by Queen Victoria, however, since it turned out that, while married by civil ceremony to Viola, the mother of his children, he had had sex with Virginia. Although Mammolo could prattle about the way in which he had dedicated himself to 'Love and Work', urging the centrality of the family to his existence, he could as easily launch into tirades about the inability of Viola to understand him or otherwise be of use. These vagaries meant that the Special Tribunal pursued Mammolo and, still more, Virginia, with special malevolence – she was the last of the family to leave prison late in 1932. The sons clung to their own way of comprehending the world, with Assunto soon living with a Fascist spy, then marrying her and defining himself a Fascist true believer.[148] Throughout these experiences members of the family exchanged letters in which they displayed a breadth of interest in many matters, demonstrating that they were scarcely honed by Fascism into thinking only one way. All of the Zambonis, and especially Mammolo and Virginia, were, like the miller Menocchio memorably described by historian Carlo Ginzburg as doubting the Inquisition and its world order,[149] human beings who wanted to 'know for themselves'. Through this stubborn, if doubtless often confused, desire, they demonstrated that, after its early years of rule, the dictatorial regime, for all its propaganda and all its physical control and repression, had not yet successfully imposed a single and set knowledge on its subjects. For all the huffing and puffing of the official line about an infrangible national unity and for all the deification of the leader, the next years were not to bring radical amendment in this regard. Making 'totalitarian' a society as diverse as Italy's was to prove a Sisyphean labour.

9

Forging Fascist society

The Zambonis, despite their relative poverty, clung to deep and intricate ways of comprehending the world, both in Bologna and in prison. Other, mostly richer Italians dealt with the meaning of life under dictatorship in a more straightforward manner. What might be termed their everyday Mussolinism was, however, scarcely based on a literal application of Fascist totalitarianism. When their actions are reviewed carefully, it becomes plain that they by no means reliably believed, obeyed or fought, despite the regime slogan – *credere, obbedire, combattere* – insisting that they should.

Both Turati and Giovanni Giuriati, his successor as party secretary for a brief term from October 1930 to December 1931, swore that they would bring a more austere morality to the PNF. Giuriati, already a successful lawyer and president of the irredentist Trento and Trieste Association before 1914, was a Fascist of the most respectable kind, capable of considerable independence, having crafted his own path towards the dictatorship rather than being swept along with it. In office, Giuriati dreamed of the PNF as a Spartan force, an ardent and doctrinaire legion of the just. In his mind, it could even take on the supreme command of the armed forces and win.[1] Giuriati's 'totalitarian fervour', historian Emilio Gentile has noticed, was too passionate, his world-view too stringent for his *Duce*. Mussolini mocked the new secretary's determination to purge corruption from Fascist ranks, deplored his polemical battles with Azione Cattolica, the surviving Catholic lay organization, and eventually sacked him, rusticating him to the Senate and a sober life as a lawyer. In his memoirs, Giuriati none the less asserted his spiritual commitment to Fascism, reiterating his belief that Mussolini was 'the man predestined to unite in Rome, as Dante had prophesied, the two sacred symbols of the Eagle and the Cross'. Even after his political demise, Giuriati maintained that the *Duce* was destined to hunt 'not just from Italy but from the face of the earth, moral and civil disorder, heresy and war'.

In practice, however, Giuriati's ethics and religion had an unattractive side. He was pleased to recall that his own father, a zealous advocate of the Risorgimento, had rejoiced in 'a genuine racial instinct', directed against the Jews of his city, Venice, even though, in classic cliché, he counted some of them among his 'best friends'. It was a matter of physical repulsion, Giuriati thought it worth explaining; when his father saw Jews approaching in a *calle*, he would quickly pull on his gloves, since he knew that, as a gentleman, he would have to shake hands. Giuriati's credo similarly drove him to uphold the case, somewhere beyond a lawyer's usual line, that revolutionaries should be able to kill such opponents as Matteotti if they deemed it necessary.[2]

Giuriati's variety of Fascist fundamentalism is further evidence of the superficiality of any interpretation that argues that the most dastardly and dangerous Fascists were those, like Farinacci, who were thrusting upwards socially, elbowing rivals aside to establish themselves as members of an emerging middle class. Yet it is also clear that Giuriati's frighteningly intellectualized fondness for final solutions and his legalistic readiness to countenance illegality, were by no means typical of the Fascist movement. Among the rank and file of less gentlemanly bent, it is easy to find strong-arm work and the breaking of official and human law, but the motivation for such behaviour was more recognizable, more commonplace and far less 'religious' than that of Giuriati. The small histories of some people can be traced when, for one reason or another, they fell out with the power-brokers of the regime and found that their accustomed behaviour was rebuked and chastised, at least briefly. It is very likely that, for every individual expelled from the party and punished by the regime, many more were not but went on embodying corruption, brutality, patronage, familism and localism and being the little Farinaccis of the suburbs.

In Legnano, for example, Roberto Ciniselli and his gang took political opportunity by the throat. In 1927 Ciniselli had moved to this Lombard industrial town as a Fascist Commissioner, boasting, falsely, that he had seen heroic wartime service as a *bersagliere*. Rather than reforming the place and instituting the rule of virtue, he and such toughs as the chauffeur of his 'splendid Fiat 509', Giovanni Fiumi, had concentrated on 'exploiting women, carousing and wasting Party funds'. They ruled by blackmail and beatings. On one disgraceful occasion, Ciniselli dragged a local hotelier to party headquarters and had him roughed up merely because he had politely asked that one of the gang's loose women pay for her food and lodging.[3] Ciniselli and seven of his men were sentenced to terms of *confino* but were soon amnestied, Fiumi having argued that he was but an inexperienced youth who had been led astray by his natural 'obedience of, respect for, and faith in his *padrone*'.[4] A client who fully knew his place, he was implying, could transfer his loyalty to another – better – patron, if that was what times demanded. Fiumi's sentiments were scarcely Fascist but they were ones his contemporaries understood.

In and around Bologna, the fall of Leandro Arpinati, whose party future was torpedoed by Starace in 1933–4, revealed telling evidence of what 'everyday Mussolinism' had entailed there. To be sure, Arpinati himself was unusually purist in that, after he was purged, he refused to yield to the blandishments of the *Duce* to return to political life. Instead, he proudly refrained from appealing for special mercy, retaining his independence to his end (during the last days of the war he was murdered in murky circumstances). Casting aside his ideology without a backward glance, the ex-tough guy, in charming letters home, instead sought instruction on cooking – he was soon proud of his mastery of *spaghetti al tonno* and *riso al burro*. Prompting him further, his wife sent him a copy of Pellegrino Artusi's *La scienza in cucina e l'arte di mangiar bene*, Italy's version of Mrs Beeton, and urged him to try *gnocchi* by Christmas.[5] Perhaps preparation of that dish could ease the boredom of his exile on the island of Lipari where Arpinati, another unconvinced by chatter about national unification, lamented that the locals were 'somnolent poltroons'.[6] In more philosophical vein and opting for an iron realism which he shared with many of his contemporaries, Arpinati warned his son that, when you might expect 'loyalty and decency' in life, you were paid with 'envy' and 'hypocrisy'. 'Traitors' ruled the world, he advised, but he would never himself be one.[7] His Fascism may have crumbled into ruin but, in his own mind, Arpinati remained a man of honour, one of the better stripe of Italians.

But what of his followers, many of whom had risen socially in much the same way as Arpinati and so might typify those emerging middle classes sometimes depicted as constituting the social and ideological base of Fascism? One who lacked his patron's dignity was Gaetano Fornaciari. A devotee, according to the police, of gambling, a customer of bad women and, despite having no visible means of support, long ensconced in Bologna's commodious Hotel Astoria, Fornaciari bewailed his fate to his latest mistress, the Belgian Jeanne Ceci, by then a hotel resident again, but at the modish French resort, Le Touquet. 'You can imagine what *confino* is like,' Fornaciari expostulated from his exile at Calvello in the Basilicata. 'You find yourself alone in a *paese* thronged with unfamiliar faces and without the slightest hope of returning to your own family and loved ones.' His greatest fear was that he would 'die like a mad dog in these mountains'. Calvello 'lacked even the minimum of human comfort'. The locals were incomprehensible and brutal – already he had seen a seventeen-year-old girl gun down her seducer in the street.[8] Fornaciari may have been, as he claimed, a 'faithful soldier [*milite*] of the Fascist revolutionary cause' since 1920[9] but he was simultaneously that familiar Italian who knew in his soul that his country was multiform rather than homogeneous. In Bologna or Milan, he felt like a man. In the Basilicata, he walked among beasts.

Ettore Bartolazzi was another once poor ex-squadrist who, the police declared, had always displayed 'a limitless devotion' to Arpinati. In 1919 a railway worker, after 1922 he was soon promoted to management and at the same time took on a series of political jobs, including the administration of the local insurance office, dealing with those injured in agricultural labour. His pay for that post alone came to more than 20,000 lire per annum. Violent and with a vivid sex life, Bartolazzi had become a man who counted in Bologna. Arpinati's fall soon destroyed that apparent power. Bartolazzi was quickly reduced to being a simple clerk at the insurance office. Rather than accepting his fate, he continued to plot in the interest of the Arpinati faction. His punishment was two years in Matera province (although an amnesty released him after only two months).[10]

Another to fall with Arpinati was Marcello Reggiani, once an emigrant to the USA who heard his country's call after 1915 and became a sergeant in the army. In Fascist Bologna, Reggiani was wealthy and established, director of the restaurant of the Bologna Casa del Fascio and vice president of the city's businessmen's association. He was also proprietor of another restaurant, managed by his wife, in the hills above the city and there the Arpinati faction regularly dined. Reggiani, it was now contended, had been a socialist until 1921 and had only joined the PNF because of his friendship with Arpinati. Lots of jobs had been his reward, not only in the food trade but also in the local hospital administration and in the gas company. Reggiani was stripped of party membership on 28 October 1933, having earlier been removed from any employment linked to the party. He was eventually sentenced to five years' *confino* but amnestied after a few months, with his wife complaining that the family had already been utterly ruined.[11]

Still more salutary was the case of Settimio Arpinati, Leandro's cousin. Before 1922 he had been a socialist; indeed, the police reported that, when he realized that Leandro had become a Fascist, Settimio wondered whether it might not be better to discard his surname. None the less, after the March on Rome, Settimio Arpinati resumed contact with Leandro and benefit soon trickled down to him. Although only partially literate, he became the boss of the area around the town of Civitella di Romagna in the Mussolini home province of Forlì,[12] as well as shouldering responsibility for the company awarded a state contract to build popular housing at Bologna. A natural brawler, he played factional politics with a will, constantly sowing discord among local Fascists.[13] Found guilty by the regime's officers, Settimio Arpinati was relegated to a *paese* in the Basilicata, from where he was amnestied after just two months. In his defence, he played up his own illiteracy, denying that he had ever received a single favour from his cousin and ascribing his recent well-being to his hard work and devotion to his family. Whenever a task had been too complicated for one with his simple mind, he explained modestly, he had politely sought and automatically accepted the advice of the *podestà* of his home town.[14]

So much, then, for these sometime *militi* of the Fascist revolution, whose career paths led into the desert. According to those historians who argue that Fascism imposed a cultural revolution, the clients of Arpinati, just like the followers of Giampaoli, whose troubles were related in an earlier chapter, should have been crusaders for their ideology, perfervid in their devotion to its cause, true believers. Yet the evidence shows, rather, individuals who may have been Fascists but who, while they pursued the new politics, scarcely forgot the more longstanding themes of Italian or human history. They were violent, no doubt, and quite often their brutality was Fascist, as they sought to amend the political coloration of some area under their potential control, to benefit from any prosperity the party might bring in its train and to be hailed as a local chief. But the vast majority behaved as clients, family members, men of a certain age and *paesani* more than as vehicles of the new ideology. Their world was a textured place, not a simple totalitarian one. On occasion, they may have believed in the current 'revolution' but plotting a successful path through life caused such travail – being harried by malevolent enemies and traitors, by cabals and vendettas and marked by inevitable times of adversity – that scepticism was a natural and even key part of their personal armoury. So many matters that might seem fixed were actually negotiable. A press ticket, a guaranteed party past, a distinguished military record, speedy promotion, a beautiful mistress, the good life, all might come through friends, patrons and an individual's skill and ruthlessness. All could be stripped away in a trice, if a political moment passed, an enemy succeeded, a patron succumbed. For these Italians and for many of their fellow citizens, everyday Mussolinism was a matter of constant negotiation and frequent decision, its definition always liable to change. Quite a few people who strove to serve the regime (and themselves) were less revolutionary Fascist new men than old Italians.

Another Fascist with his troubles at the end of the 1920s and who ate the bitter bread of banishment was the Milanese Ernesto Belloni.[15] For him, the problem was that, although Italy might have been Fascistized, in his mind it was scarcely nationalized. After he fell to attacks from his enemies in the party led by Farinacci, this wealthy businessman and ex-*podestà* was sent into *confino* in the relative comfort of Vietri, on the coast near Salerno. Belloni was not happy, however. The little town, he complained, 'lacked restaurants, *caffè*, other shops and any outlet for pleasure where civilized people might like to enter and enjoy themselves'. Neither in the urban centre nor along the sea-front was there an inviting avenue or piazza where a man could walk without being affronted by dirt and rubbish. The locals, 'almost all of whom belonged to the most humble social rank', were not people with whom communication was possible. Even the local Fascist chief was crude and threatening.[16] Belloni, like many another, felt lost, reduced to being, in that telling Italian term, *spaesato* (taken out of his *paese*). The south was not his natural habitat. For Belloni, any drive towards a nationalization of the masses was blunted by a strict sense of hierarchy that knew the difference between a desirable location and one that was less so. In Belloni's understanding, Italy was split into happy places, where 'civilization' reigned, and sadly 'backward' regions, where 'barbarism' was the rule. The 'north' and the 'south' were simply not identical. It was all very well for intellectuals in *Critica Fascista* or other places to dream cleverly about how each Italian city could retain its own purpose and yet somehow avoid 'water-tight compartments', breed unity from diversity and hammer the nation into a totalitarian whole. Yet, whatever public words proclaimed, privately Belloni and many another were not convinced.[17]

After all, southern Fascism could retain a traditional air. Even party inspectors had to concede that there the personal was likely to outweigh the ideological. Take the case of two scheming doctors, Giuseppe Nicastri and Vincenzo Licata at Montemaggiore Belsito in the province of Palermo, apparently a pair of friends. Nicastri had once been a peasant boy whose family sacrificed much to afford him medical training. By the time Nicastri graduated in 1931, Licata, then fifty-seven and 'influential both because of his flourishing financial state and his high status as a doctor', had taken him under his wing. The relationship was not to be a simple one. Licata was a highly active participant in 'all the struggles and plots' in the *paese* – they roiled despite Fascist 'order' – and did not mind too much what methods he employed to achieve his objectives. Very early he taught Nicastri his techniques, persuading him, while still a student, to compose anonymous denunciations against a local *monsignore* with whom Licata was in dispute. In the meantime, Nicastri, who was intelligent and a good doctor, progressed in his own career.

By 1932–3, however, the two doctors had quarrelled, with gossip suggesting that Nicastri had tried to seduce Licata's much younger wife. 'From then on', the eventual police report ran, 'each began a pitiless struggle, one against the other, using any means and including legal recourse and informing the authorities about an alleged slew of plots and terrorist acts', planned by his rival. In 1939 matters came to a head amid anonymous rumours that Nicastri, once thought to have been a youthful promoter of a short-lived pro-Matteotti club, had set up a communist cell in his home village. As if to prove that bloody Bolshevik revolution was nigh, petrol bombs were thrown against both the Montemaggiore Municipio and the local Casa del Fascio. The police, however, denied any political intent in what they portrayed as a 'doctors' vendetta', as though medical men regularly took arms against each other. While judicial matters were proceeding, Licata suddenly died in custody, 'to the dismay of his numerous followers'. The police were inclined to believe that it was Licata who had actually been the better hater and the more committed practitioner of vendetta, as well as the organizer of the attacks on public property. They advised, none the less, that the older doctor's angry clientele could not tolerate an amnesty for Nicastri, who must be sentenced to *confino* (in the event he was let off after seven months spent in a *paese* in the province of Cosenza).[18] In Montemaggiore Belsito, patron–client ties and a politics of 'ins' and 'outs', noted by anthropologists as the common basis of southern political dispute,[19] flourished. There, 'men of respect', especially the doctors, lawyers, notaries and other professionals of the place, deserved and expected that title and their combat techniques were skilled and ruthless in adapting Fascism to their own causes.

The story of village rivalry is repeated in the tale of Francesco Giua, one of the handful of Catholic religious to be openly punished by the regime. A poor country priest from the *paese* of Oschiri in the province of Sassari, Giua was arrested for stating, one day in the summer of 1940 at the end of mass, to a group which included many local women: 'we simply must eliminate Hitler and . . . [meaningful pause]'. He went on to complain that the accounts of Italy's recent

entry into the war had not been worth reading owing to the seques-
tration for ten days of the Vatican's daily, *L'Osservatore Romano*,
'which is our paper'. Police investigations declared that, even before
Giua arrived in 1937, Oschiri was 'split into two factions, one of
which, and fortunately the more important, is headed by the public
authorities and Fascist chiefs. The other, composed mostly of women,
looked to the priest for leadership.'[20] Oschiri, in other words, had
long been a place of gender and political contest, poorly understood
as a simple battle between those for and against Fascist revolution.

The derring-do of this Sardinian village demonstrates how varie-
gated was the practice of Catholicism in Italy, for all the presence of
the Vatican in its midst. A proper social history of the subject is still
lacking and any survey of how Italians lived their Christianity under
Fascism can only be impressionistic. Mussolini, a raging anti-clerical
in his youth, for whom profanity was a joy (one contemporary commentator remembered Benedict XV in 1916 holding a service in Rome
in expiation of the blasphemies of *Il Popolo d'Italia*),[21] matured into
the canny politician who signed the Lateran Pacts. This agreement
was, in many ways, the moment when his regime's international prestige reached its peak – even the rationalist London *Observer* then
editorialized its approval. The 'temporal problem', which had dogged
Italy since the Risorgimento, had, the paper said, been solved by the
exercise of 'that lofty statesmanship which disdains to garble facts and
which looks resolutely to the future'.[22] Within Italy, too, there was
pleasure and relief at the deal. Anti-Fascist Catholic De Gasperi, for
example, condoned the regime's triumphant boasting with the
thought that, 'seen in historical and global terms', the Lateran agreements signified 'liberation for the Church and good fortune for the
Italian nation'.[23]

For a while, Mussolini and his regime were content to bask in the
glow of this success. There were prosaic occasions when the *Duce*
might evince pleasure at social recognition from so ancient and historic an institution as the Vatican. He did not disguise his gratitude,
when, on the marriage of Edda Mussolini to Galeazzo Ciano in April
1930, the happy couple and the new father-in-law were invited to a
papal reception, even if the *Duce* felt impelled to explain to others and
himself that he had not strayed too far from totalitarian purity. 'You

can't say we are really abroad,' he was heard to mutter. 'The welcome is utterly Italian.'[24] Similarly, in 1934, his missives to and from the Pope grew almost intimate as Mussolini lamented the crazy nature (*fesserie*) of Hitler's Church and racial policies and Pius XI replied that he recited an *Angelus Dei* every morning and night to the *Duce*'s guardian angel.[25] Even when State and Church squabbled, Mussolini was ready to take refuge in a dictator's little joke. In an ideal world, he mused somewhat disconsolately, Fascists would stick together in the same way that priests did.[26]

Mussolini's brother, Arnaldo, tried more zealously to unite Fascist and Catholic life. When Sandro, his eldest son, was dying of leukaemia, the *Duce*'s brother resorted to holy water blessed at Lourdes[27] and, after Sandro perished in August 1930, there were rumours that a hint had been dropped at the Vatican that the young man might be an appropriate candidate for beatification.[28]

Pope Pius XI, whose own propagandists were happy to depict as a bonny Lombard fighter the 'Pope of Intrepid Faith', was a hard man for whom 'mathematics' was the real 'poetry',[29] as well as a sportsman, the *Papa alpinista*, who clambering up a rugged peak could express his 'Latin courage,'[30] and the *Papa alpino*, who had natural empathy with crack troops.[31] But he was not ordinarily much given to reticence when he perceived Church interests being infringed. Ambassadors found that the pontiff would shout at them if crossed and, when the subject of Italy came up, Pius was not above reasserting the watchword of the lost papal state: 'Rome is mine'.[32] In 1938 he was gratified to be told that the Fascist government did not intend to erect a mosque in the Catholic holy city and national capital,[33] while regretting that the visit by Hitler in May meant that a banner was being unfurled in Rome with the swastika, a cross that was not Christ's, emblazoned on it.[34] The Vatican marked its disapproval of Nazi religious policy by petitioning successfully that the *Führer* be kept away from the Via della Conciliazione during his Roman sojourn.[35] The Pope was also doubtful of the sense and merit of Italian racism, although he turned one conversation about the need to avoid 'half-breeds' in Italy's new African territories into a demand that a firmer check be kept on missionary activity by 'Waldensians and Protestants'. 'Everywhere, each works in the service of Britain,' he remarked as though half convinced that Henry VIII still reigned in London.[36] To his death, Pius remained sceptical about the firmness of Fascist purpose, briefly telling the Archbishop of Milan: 'Mussolini has no money and therefore he will never make a [world] war.'[37]

Similarly, in such places as Malta or Croatia, where Catholic as well as Italian influence might be diminishing, Pius was more openly aggressive in language than was the Fascist regime itself. In 1939, with twenty-seven out of forty-six cardinals being Italian and nineteen out of twenty Curia officials the same,[38] an undercurrent of approval of Italian nationalism in the leadership of the Church was natural enough, although some contradiction was stored up in the decision to consecrate the first Ethiopian Catholic bishop at the Vatican in 1930. The anti-communism of the Church in general and the Pope in particular – he had been Papal Nuncio in Warsaw when Bolshevik armies were thrown back in August 1920 – was rather more deeply embedded than the Fascist version (and was hardened by a sort of Vatican imperialism which had never forgotten that the peoples of the Russias were schismatic Christians, needing for their own salvation to be brought home to Rome). In March 1930 Pius presided over an expiatory mass for the sins of the Russians.[39] Perhaps it was the pontiff's version of a joke when, in February 1932, Pius mentioned to Mussolini his hopes for 'Catholic totalitarianism', which, he fancied, might straighten out souls, just as the regime was steeling Italian bodies. In Fascism's postulates of 'order, authority and discipline', the Pope stated, he found 'nothing contrary to Catholic belief'.[40]

There were, after all, through the 1930s quite a few social and cultural zones of agreement between the authorities of the Vatican and of Fascism. It might be that the regime's harping on *romanità* and its invocations of the beauty of violence, the supremacy of the nation and the domination of the state (and, eventually, the centrality of the race) had a troublingly pagan side, much cherished by such regime anti-clericals as Farinacci and the more fanatical of new generation intellectuals and, on occasion if less reliably so, blessed by Mussolini himself. None the less, a 'clerical Fascist' strand was never absent from the regime's ideological discussions and collaboration was easy and fertile in a number of domestic fields. From the summer of 1936 the Spanish Civil War, with its lurid tales of 'Red' atrocities and with the steadily increasing Fascist intervention on the insurgent, Francoist and Catholic side, brought the rhetoric of Church and State into tight harness. Then, for example, a clerical paper in the pious Trentino could define all priests as standing erect, alert and armed in the 'Divine Falange of the Ministers of God' and regale its readers with such tales of alleged republican crimes as the burning of the religious alive and the subsequent sale of their barbecued flesh in town markets.[41] The paper also reprinted French Catholic reports that a seminarian at Lerida had been crucified for his faith and blamed the 'anarchist Sanhedrin' for the outrage, while urging that contemporary communism was merely the most recent apparition of the Devil who had earlier expressed his malignity through the somewhat motley crew of Manichaeans, Arians, Cathars, Protestants and Modernists.[42]

An alliance between Church and State could also flourish within the confines of Italy. Fascist administrators were happy to police Protestant missionaries, always the object of obsessive Vatican fear. Some insight into the gap during the dictatorship between religious history from above and below can be gained when scanning the records of those persecuted by the secret police for belonging to the Jehovah's Witnesses or other such sects. Especially during the deepening hostility of the later 1930s against heresies of any kind, no mercy could be expected for such people. Police accounts reveal a world in which the almost always desperately poor apostles of such faiths tramped the hills and mountains of the south or the city blocks of Naples, firm in their faith, clinging to the word they had found in their thin supply of books, most frequently with a personal or family connection to the USA and so guided by both a national and an international map of their own, which did not accord with any modernized, nationalized or Fascistized chart. A Neapolitan Pentecostalist was known to his disciples simply as L'Anziano (the Old One).[43] In Fascist eyes, he and his fellows' worst sin was their refusal of military service, sharpened by their view that 'the present form of government will lead humankind to destruction' and their belief that the militarism of Italy and other nations was not aimed at peace, as the official line made out, but rather at devastating war. As an official of the Questura (Police office) of Catanzaro explained with some insight about one case in his purview: 'The followers of such doctrines can be considered the real Anarchists of religion while they pursue biblical concepts [only accepted] by the raving or the sick in mind.'[44]

Fascist officials expected some pay-back for such policing of the frontiers of religion on their and the Church's behalf. In 1939 those in charge of party rural radio revealed that they had begun receiving complaints that their Sunday broadcast of a 'Country Hour' at 11 a.m., full of Fascist counsel, clashed with the typical hour of the mass. Of course, the account ran on, 'no regime more than the Fascist one wants every citizen to believe and to profess the religion of their fathers. Such a faith is the fount of belief in the *Patria* and in the family.' Yet, it was argued firmly, the transmission could not be changed. Priests were normally accommodating on any difficulties and, if the local one were not, then surely party officials could talk to him about the matter and win him around.[45]

At the more formal level, the issue of greatest debate between Church and State after the Lateran accords was what should be done with Azione Cattolica (Catholic Action). This lay body, just before the First World War and with the backing of Pope Benedict XV,[46] had united those who believed that their prime identity in civil society sprang from their Catholicism. Pius XI began his pontificate with a programme to revitalize and control the movement. In September 1923 Catholic Action was given a revised structure, placing its members under stiffer episcopal supervision than in the past. During the negotiation of the Lateran accords, the fate of Catholic Action was a point of dispute, with Pius XI making manifest his disgust at Fascist assaults on Catholic youth organizations. The church envoys thought that they had achieved a Fascist backdown on the matter and, amid the clauses approved in February 1929, article 43 seemed to guarantee regime recognition of the right of Catholic Action and its various associations to exist. In the meantime, the membership of Catholic youth groups grew from a claimed 600,000 in 1928 to 692,000 in 1930.[47]

The implied infringement of totalitarianism was soon the cause of further hostilities and, in May 1931, Mussolini moved to render Catholic Action youth organizations illegal. In deliberating the matter, Bottai's *Critica Fascista* remarked, with some obscurity,

'Fascism is totalitarian just as the Church is totalitarian' and each must be permitted to remain coherent in their policy of total control.[48] In counter to the Fascist line, Pius XI issued the encyclical *Non abbiamo bisogno*, its title implying that, given the eternity of the Church, there was no need to parlay with the petty actions of transient modern ideologies. In strong language, Pius condemned the 'out and out pagan worship of the State'. 'We do not wish to condemn the Party and the Regime as such,' he ran on resolutely, but 'we do mean to point out those of their policies which are contrary to Catholic theory and practice.'[49] In September 1931 it was announced that Catholic Action was founding a new organization for university students, a body destined to number among its members such later leading Christian Democrats as Aldo Moro and Giulio Andreotti and possessing special patronage from Giovanni Battista Montini, son of a sometime PPI deputy and the future Pope Paul VI (1963–78).[50]

Outraged Fascist purists ranging from Giuriati to Carlo Scorza, the squadrist destined to be summoned as PNF secretary in a desperate moment in April 1943, threatened a punitive response from party members and some Catholic Action branches fell victim to violent assault. However, the Jesuit Father Pietro Tacchi Venturi, frequently an emollient intermediary between the dictatorship and the Church, found ways to bring *Duce* and Pope together.[51] The regime was nearing its Decennale or tenth anniversary on 28 October 1932 and nourished grandiose plans for the celebration of the event. The Church, too, nothing loath at the idea of further spiritual and financial gain, had decreed that, commencing on 25 December 1932, a supernumerary Holy Year (*Anno Santo*) would be celebrated. Already pilgrims within Italy and from the wider world were planning their visits to Fascist and to papal Rome. Both the practical and the ideological suggested compromise. Catholic authorities drew comfort when *Critica Fascista* emphasized that 'the <u>Fascist family</u> is the essential objective of all Fascist policy' and defined the domestic hearth as one where there was 'no fusion between the sexes' but where rather 'the woman should return to being queen and *signora*'.[52] Was the Catholic family meant to war against such ideas? It was silly to bicker. Instead an accommodation was reached and Church–State relations in Fascist Italy settled into that wary toleration that would outlast the 1930s.

To be sure a level of mistrust lingered on each side. The Fascists continued to speak as though their civic religion was to be indoctrinated into every Italian and must arm the soul of the populace against any political, philosophical or religious heresy. The Church did not cease to preach its gospel and jealously counted the cases when the Mostra della Rivoluzione Fascista (Exhibition of the Fascist Revolution) outdrew the events of Holy Year.[53] In imperial Fascist Rome, the Vatican still lay there glittering and four-square across the Tiber. City planners, both Catholic and Fascist, may have agreed to build the Via della Conciliazione (Conciliation Street), which would open up St Peter's Square and flaunt its message of universal power in a way that Fascist aesthetics enjoined. Yet the new streetscape, destined to be incomplete when Fascism fell, left it to viewers to decide if it offered a path for a Fascist triumph over old faiths or the chance for the Vatican to dispatch its Christian soldiers on a mission into Italy and the world.

The message of history was easier to decode for any who studied papal business. The Lateran Pacts had brought great financial advantage to the Church, making Pius XI feel financially secure in a way that had not been true of his recent predecessors at St Peter's. The Wall Street crash, the Vatican's chaotic accounting processes and Pius XI's own fondness for making concrete his 'imperial papacy' in grandiose building schemes did prompt some worries during the early 1930s. But from 1937 the long-sighted Vatican administration and its clever chief financial agent, Bernardino Nogara, who, before 1914, had worked for Giolitti in the national interest in Asia Minor,[54] began heavy investment in US blue-chip stocks. In this financial strategy, the Church had picked the winner both financially and in foreign policy terms, as well as manifesting for those who cared to notice a precocious understanding that the use-by date on Fascism was fast approaching.[55]

At the height of the dispute over Catholic Action, Pius XI had maintained stoutly that 'the full and effective right to the education of the child belongs to the Church and not to the State'.[56] When the rivalry between priests and Fascists was translated to the classroom, practical cohabitation often resulted since 70 per cent of the teachers (*maestre*) in elementary schools[57] (and throughout the inter-war period only an elite of children – more boys than girls – progressed beyond the *quinta elementare*),[58] were women. These *maestre*'s own education and their traditional proclivities usually ensured that they were pious Catholics, convinced patriots and only lastly Fascists and then of a rudimentary kind. In Treviso, for example, in 1935 school-teachers were reported to be still more Catholic than Fascist and, it was lamented, children there collected saints' images more zealously than they did photos of their *Duce*.[59]

Throughout the country, the *maestre* mattered. In the 1920s *Il Corriere della Maestra* was reckoned to be the most widely read of women's journals.[60] The majority of *maestre* were lay teachers in state schools. Italy did not share the Anglo-Saxon fondness for private education, although Maria Montessori was one of the quirkier early enthusiasts of Fascism. For a time, she thought the new doctrine might shake Italians out of their traditional inertia and Mussolini was made Honorary President of the Opera Montessori (Montessori schools organization) established in Rome in 1924.[61] Her radical dreams of educational reform remained an illusion, however, and Montessori soon moved abroad. The *maestre* stayed. Like their male fellows in the *carabinieri*, they were expected to take their posting in a different region from their own, with a resultant loneliness and isolation and, perhaps on occasion, an impulse for them to nationalize the masses or at least make the children speak the same language that they did. Quite a few teachers in more ordinary schools were religious; the Church's tally of nuns almost trebled as Fascism took root, from 45,000 in 1911 to 129,000 in 1936.[62]

Fascist State and Catholic Church were generally in patriarchal concord about the proper place of women in society. When Turati primly instructed party branches in 1930 that young female Fascists should always be escorted by an older woman 'of absolutely guaranteed seriousness' and that they should also be banned from military parades and unbecoming sports,[63] priests did not demur. They might not fully have endorsed the phrasing but they were also unlikely to quarrel much with Mussolini's private recipe on the women's question: 'Either children or beatings'.[64]

The Church, after all, was still convinced that, left unchecked, the temptation of Eve could fracture most resistance. Priestly training under the dictatorship remained typically closed. While his vocation was being established, a trainee priest, the Church authorities demanded, must engage in a *fuga mundi* (flight from worldly things), avoiding the sexual threat latent in sport and the cinema and the potential diversion from the holy which might arrive with any unwatched contact with the man's family, too many of whom might be young and female.[65] In this instance of priestly training, a matter that was especially dear to it, the Church was more ready to take on the family than Fascism usually was. Church speakers did not hesitate to make plain their view that a calling to the priesthood had to be treated as a sublime event. Family doubts in such cases must perforce be set aside. Fathers, mothers and all relations should acknowledge that 'the sacrifice imposed on the Priesthood is the most divine and fertile, eclipsing all others [notably the case of soldiers killed for the *patria*]. The priest renounces his own family in order to embrace the great family of the poor, troubled and meek, and so of all the suffering members of the body of Christ.'[66] Church propagandists were also sure, when Pius XII succeeded Pius XI in 1939, that 'the Pope does not die and does not change. The Pope never goes away and, if he does, he immediately returns because the flock cannot survive without a Shepherd, the people without a Father.'[67] Some Fascists may have thought of themselves as tough and militant crusaders for a new civic religion but their dedication and their sense of self-worth rarely surpassed that of the Catholic Church.

The Church was indeed confident that it knew what was best for women. For both it and the State, abortion entailed a special sin since it transgressed what were thought to be the rules of God, the nation and the race. Sharing this view, in 1931 the dictatorship enhanced its penalties for this crime and for other forms of birth control, just as the debate over Catholic Action reached its angry apogee. The encyclical *Casti connubi* had formalized the Church's disapproval of contraception of any kind the year before. ONMI officials then estimated that 20 per cent of conceptions in Italy were terminated illegally.[68] That same year, Fascism banned female beauty contests as demeaning to the *sposa e madre esemplare* (exemplary wife and mother).[69] A bachelor tax had been introduced in 1926, although the Fascist leadership, with the notable exceptions of Mussolini (and King Victor Emmanuel III), was scarcely prolific.

In theory both of Church and State, society should rejoice when women breed, cook and worship. A Fascist paper, entitled *Stirpe Italica* (The Italic Race) and with the caption 'We are the best' on its masthead, celebrated a peasant woman who, it alleged, turned up at a *comune* to register her son the day after he was born, while explaining that she was a little late since she had been up earlier to cook her husband's breakfast.[70] But this vision of the dutiful wife and mother may have existed rather more in the eyes of party or priestly observers than in reality. For all the easy words expended by the Church and by Fascist bosses, to ordinary Italians, under the stress of family life in an economy stuttering after the Wall Street crash, abortion remained a normal, if agonizing, part of life. A case study of a *paese* in the hinterland of Monza has shown, for example, that the villagers not only resented the arrest in 1928 of a local doctor as an abortionist but also demonstrated their hostility to the persecution that he was suffering. Their complaints in turn produced an official climb-down, the release of the doctor and the turning of a blind eye to the peasant women's actions.[71] With something less than Fascist or Catholic stringency, officials must have decided that he and the women knew best how to manage their reproductive lives.

In what might seem the more modern setting of urban Turin, working-class women could not usually afford dealing with doctors and so, when in need, often applied knitting-needles on themselves – one reported to an oral historian that a friend had aborted herself six times in this fashion (she eventually died of cancer of the uterus). By the end of the 1930s a series of trials in that city tabulated an inventive range of methods of terminating a pregnancy. They included: 'falling off a bicycle, subjection to heavy work, immersion in fast-flowing water up to the stomach, imbibing large quantities of purgatives (bitter salt, laxative pills, taurine tablets, castor oil, manna [a mould on rye], senna and herbal concoctions such as the well-known Sabina and laudanum leaves, quinine on its own or mixed, for example with saffron and iron); then there was the use of mechanical means (bone crochet-hooks with the head removed, knitting needles, parsley stalks, bone hairpins), taking hot baths and various kinds of douches, inserting pessaries of abrasive substances into the vagina'.[72]

This split between the world of the rulers and that of the people deepened further when race threatened to become a preoccupation. In 1935 Federico Marconcini, an economist with teaching appointments both at the state-run University of Turin and the Catholic University of Milan, brought the obsessions of Church and State about reproductive matters together in a lengthy study entitled *Culle vuote . . . sviluppo – cause – rimedi* (Empty cots . . . development – cause – remedy). For Marconcini, unless the contemporary demographic catastrophe was turned around, then Italy, even if not yet so sick with 'germs aiming to destroy it' as was France, was facing 'suicide'.[73] At base the issue was not a material but a spiritual one, a matter of will. The desire not to have children was stimulated by the excessive growth of cities, destructive places where a 'slow, inexorable, human physical-psychological collapse and so morbidity, immorality, prostitution, murder, madness – the satanic other face of the beauty of every metropolis in all time and throughout the world' could be diagnosed. A fine modern apartment, Marconcini pronounced portentously, was the sworn foe of children.[74]

But the real enemy in the economist's mind was the modern woman. Feminism, he warned, pushed females into such male professions as 'the law, journalism, teaching in middle school, the bureaucracy'. Down that slippery slope there followed 'full freedom in choice of reading, the freedom to flirt, to smoke, to cut short their luxuriant locks, to wear masculine-looking clothes, to engage in violent sports like football, fencing, javelin-throwing and skiing'. D'Annunzio, D. H. Lawrence, Marcel Proust and Hollywood should take responsibility for this lamentable loss in female decorum and dedication to procreation, he charged. Only if feminism were opposed, with 'reasonable' strength, as Marconcini put it ambiguously, could the 'principle of authority' and of 'virile discipline' be restored to contemporary society, permitting it to regain its 'divine sense of life'.[75] For the inspiration of this catalogue of reactionary ideas, Marconcini gave thanks to Mussolini but also contended that the Catholic Church wholeheartedly endorsed his view of the gender order.[76]

In less academic prose, Fascist newspapers often excoriated the vices of the modern *donna crisi* (twitchy woman), thin, neurotic and very likely sterile, as distinct from the virtues of the traditional *donna madre* (woman and mother), stocky, large-hipped, big-bosomed and, above all, fertile. The new populism of the PNF under Starace increased the publicity devoted to large families. From 1934 Mussolini in annual homage received a couple from each of the nation's ninety-two provinces and handed out a purse of five thousand lire to those chosen to meet their *Duce*. By 1937 a special party organization was created to provide increased welfare for large families. Two years earlier a *Giornata della madre e del fanciullo* (Mother and child day) had been added to the list of annual party celebrations when medals – bronze, silver and gold – were distributed to those with six, eight and ten children. The imitation of military procedure was deliberate since these were births for the nation and the ceremonies now always saw the dictator himself in uniform and in a military setting, for example, at a parade in front of the Victor Emmanuel monument, with its altar of the *Patria*, in Rome.

Once again, somewhere beneath the din and glitter, contradictions lurked. It was the Catholic Church and not the PNF that first sponsored an Italian Mothers' Day. Most of the more ostentatious measures in favour of demographic growth were not instituted until after 1933, that is, until after Fascist Italy was being influenced by developments occurring far more quickly and thoroughly in Nazi Germany (although Scandinavian social democracies were also busy intruding the state into the functioning of the family and into eugenics – more than 60,000 sterilizations were carried out in Sweden in the years after 1935).[77] Italian authorities were generally suspicious about this Northern European (and North American) confidence in a 'scientific' control of births, another reason why Italian racism, when it began to flourish openly during the later 1930s, usually took pains to be spiritual and 'voluntarist' rather than material and 'scientific'. Eugenics was not a science with many paladins in Italy.

Moreover, contrary to some legend, Italy was not an especially prolific society. Its birth rate at around 23 per 1,000 inhabitants per annum by the late 1930s registered steady decline (it had been above 30 before 1914) and this fall was not checked by the new policies then adopted. The Italian marriage rate fell below that in the UK and Germany, where, in the latter country, the imposition of Nazi rule inspired rapid increase.[78] Despite a rhetoric about 'ruralization', fostered by the *Duce*'s contention in 1927 that the nation must pursue such a policy even if it took 'billions' and 'half a century' to complete[79] and his Green-sounding demand that Italian youth must learn 'a love for the woods, fount of spiritual and physical wholesomeness which will remove adolescent Fascists from corrupt and enfeebling suburbs',[80] Italian cities and especially Rome continued to grow. The population of the capital, staffed heavily by state and party officials, sped past one million in 1931, tallying 1.4 million a decade later. From 1921 to 1936 Rome's population expanded by 74 per cent, ahead of Milan 36 per cent, Bologna 32 per cent, Florence 14 per cent, Palermo 3 per cent, Naples 1 per cent, while, during those years, Catania surrendered 7 per cent of its inhabitants.[81] In these statistics, an observer can detect signs of that post-Fascist nation where, during the 1950s and 1960s, so many Italians transferred from south to north. Fascist policy condemned internal migration and did act as some brake on it, but even under the dictatorship, for all the talk about preference to the countryside, the number living in communes below 10,000 stayed in major decline.[82]

One organization which was meant to stem migration and harness peasant and female virtue for the party and state was the Federazione Nazionale Fascista delle Massaie Rurali (Rural Housewives Association), founded in February 1933, made a branch of the Fasci Femminili (the Women's Fascist group) a year later, and so yet another institutional product of the Starace years. Many Italians were still peasants; on official figures they composed more than 40 per cent of the population in the early 1930s, although their contribution to national income declined from 38.3 per cent in 1921 to 29.8 per cent in 1940. The Massaie Rurali were utilized in regime propaganda to assert that the regime was virtuously transporting its special variety of welfare, modernity (and Fascistization) to the poorest and most backward segments of Italian society. By July 1942 the Massaie Rurali counted more than 2.9 million members, a tenfold increase since October 1935.

The movement's leader was Regina Terruzzi, born 1862, a feminist and once socialist schoolteacher, who had been won over to the nation through interventionism in 1914–15. Befitting her years but with somewhat ambiguous implication, she was proud to call herself 'the mother-in-law of the Fascists' and she did refuse to be cowed by the more dimly patriarchal *ras*.[83] Under her inspiration, the Massaie Rurali displayed some flair in penetrating the peasant world, especially in northern Italy, with a diet of propaganda combining the nationalist and the useful. Yet the silly was never far away. During the Ethiopian war, members were regaled with a recipe for a patriotic green, white and red omelette[84] while, when the Second World War raged, women in southern Apulia were told they should revive the 'traditional art' of weaving coats from ground sea-shells.[85] Moreover, the finances of the movement were always constrained by the nation's deepening economic difficulties and neither Terruzzi nor other leaders, most of whom were bourgeois or aristocratic 'charitable women' rather than peasants, were able to resolve Italy's massive regional and class differences. Even in the north, in some isolated rural *paesi*, it was reported, there were women who had never heard of Mussolini.[86]

It is easy to forget how ubiquitous poverty remained in Italy, a country where the occasional peasant protestor might still cry out 'Down with those who can eat!' as a way of protesting about poverty.[87] In Trieste, in February 1933, the main square suddenly faced an irruption of boys from poor families who stoned the pigeons clucking there. City worthies were appalled and tried to intervene against this inhuman game. But, according to an account threaded with the ancient 'respectable' Italians' fear of the plebs, they were frustrated because the boys' mothers emerged from their horrid lairs, 'crying, howling and cursing with the news that they had sent their sons on the killing mission because their families were dying of hunger'. The police arrived but, believing that it was better not to confront such furies, did not act.[88]

Even in Rome, poverty was never far away. In 1934 inspectors worried that, in some suburbs, everyone seeking welfare could not 'be satisfied because the agency concerned lacked the means to deal with requests'. In Trastevere, for example, such distribution happened only on Saturdays and involved the handing out of 250 grammes of bread, 60 of pasta and 50 of beans. But supplies regularly ran out and the accustomed crowd was left unsolaced and unhappy.[89]

On the southern Adriatic, Bari was the home from 1930 of the annual Fiera del Levante, hailed, a little self-consciously, by local regime spokesmen as offering the port 'a sign of power and a challenge to destiny' that could surely raise the city to the near equivalent of Milan. In its devotion to trade display, the Lombard capital faced west, it was explained. The whole gorgeous east lay in the potential fee of Bari.[90] Mussolini himself came on a touted visit there in September 1934, with propagandists boasting that any survey of the Puglia region demonstrated that the 'southern question' had been resolved. 'Progress' in Bari, 'the Fascist city *par excellence* in appearance and spirit', it was said, was 'stupefying'.[91] Yet official statistics admitted that local culture might still be thinly spread – Bari libraries tallied only 13,092 books as read in the year of 1933 for a population of more than 187,000.[92] By the early 1930s, in this Fascist showcase for the south and fastest growing city in the peninsula apart from Rome and Milan, 42,000 out of a then urban population of 170,000 lived more than four to a room; 62 per cent of dwellings lacked a separate kitchen, 52 per cent were equipped with electric light, 44 per cent could rely on running water, 42 per cent rejoiced in some form of toilet, while only 4 per cent possessed a bath and 1 per cent central heating. Employment remained precarious in this urban setting. Very many sales jobs were still ambulatory. The pressure on them was so great that in 1938 the regime tried, unsuccessfully, to restrict the posts to those with 'proven merit in war or political life'.[93]

As the cases in north, centre and south illustrate, for quite a few Italians life and subsistence remained synonymous terms. Any review of the vocabulary of those poor who, from time to time, were arrested by the police at once uncovers cases of both the socially marginal and more ordinary workers and peasants being doubtful as to whether they and their families could survive from one day to the next. Especially among the impoverished in the countryside, wages were declining – for day labourers, a social category disliked by the regime, they slumped from an index of 100 in 1928 to 72 ten years later – and food consumption similarly fell.[94] According to the great oral historian Nuto Revelli, in the mountain country of Piedmont, by no means the poorest part of Italy, conscription to the Ethiopian war was welcomed since young men knew that, in the army, the soldiers' diet included meat.[95] In Calabria in 1939 the local *federale* admitted that the word *miseria* (utter poverty) summed up the lives of the great majority of those whom he administered.[96]

Throughout the 1930s the problem of poverty was exacerbated certainly because of the impact of the world depression and perhaps because of the damage incurred through the regime's faltering management of the economy. Italy's economic troubles had been hidden for quite a while, unlike the parlous situation in the USA and Germany, and at the beginning of the decade some learned economists even wondered whether the 'corporate state' might not offer a universal recipe to avoid economic busts.[97] Fascists were themselves eager to find reasons for the collapse of American wealth. In *Critica Fascista*, one writer was sure that it had happened because this New World society lacked a unifying 'race, stock and history'.[98] In 1932 Bottai greeted the Decennale with the pronouncement that all capitalism lay deep in crisis, a great contrast with ordered and productive Italy, the only nation that had located the 'right road'.[99] When Franklin Delano Roosevelt took over the presidency of the USA in January 1933, Italian commentators often depicted him as a Fascist in spite of himself, driven towards an interventionist and corporate state as the only rational exit from the Depression.[100] As the leading journalist Luigi Barzini (senior) put it in typical phrasing, events in the world economy were proving that 'Italy is [always] right'.[101] Starace's journal, *Gioventù Fascista*, even claimed in January 1933 that a once wealthy but now wretched American immigrant had turned up in Naples trusting in 'the hospitality of our people and the generosity of the *Duce*'.[102]

Yet there was plenty of countervailing evidence that the Italian economy was by no means escaping the general crisis. Gold reserves had been diminishing since 1927. Already in 1932 Felice Guarneri had detected a 'profound crisis' in the nation's finances, assailed by collapsing production, unemployment and a balance of trade in dangerous deficit. Later in the decade and now the head of the new Ministry of Exchange Controls, Guarneri was warning the *Duce* of the imminent threat to Italy's ability to fund its international commerce. By 1938, horror of horrors for men about town, coffee was not always available in urban bars.[103]

Even on official figures more than one million Italians were without work in 1932 (up from about 300,000 in 1929), and recovery thereafter was tardy and partial. Through the 1930s the contribution of Italy to West European production fell from 8.2 to 8.0 per cent.[104] The national growth rate at 1.9 per cent (1922–38) stayed below the West European average of 2.5 per cent, despite what might have been thought the likelihood that Italy could catch up with the more developed economies. Whereas in the Giolittian era, Italy (narrowly) outperformed Germany (2.7 per cent to 2.6 per cent), between the wars the Italians lagged well behind the Germans at 3.8 per cent and were much inferior to social democratic Sweden's 4.1 per cent.[105] In 1934 the annual deficit had expanded to 6.6 per cent of GDP (it was 16.1 per cent in 1936 and 28.2 per cent in 1940 as aggressive war took its financial toll). In 1934 military expenditure still only amounted to about two thirds of the monies disbursed on public works, education and other social arenas. In 1936 preparation for war took more than all domestic spending, in 1940 three times more. Despite such outlays and the 'planned' aggression they promised, Fascist stockpiles and the other economic preparations for war were 'totally insufficient'.[106]

For the moment, however, these battles lay ahead. Instead, while the world economy buckled and the Nazis rose towards power in Germany, the Fascist regime concentrated on polishing its image and infusing the themes of its propaganda into its subjects' minds. In 1932 the new party secretary, Starace, presided over a change in the constitution of the PNF, which emphasized that the party should act as a 'civil militia at the orders of the *Duce* and in the service of the Fascist State'.[107] The personality cult around Mussolini grew luxuriantly. Soon after he became PNF secretary, Starace ordered that a solemn ritual 'Salute to the *Duce*' occur at the beginning of every meeting (it was first used at the Palazzo Venezia on 12 December 1931). He also suggested that letters be signed off with a 'Viva il Duce' rather than with the more accustomed forms. Fuelled by such sacramental acts, the party, he hoped, could become the nervous system of the body politic.

In every way the party claimed to be favouring the betterment of Italian citizens. In July 1932 the Bologna still dominated by Leandro Arpinati – he had just joined Benito Mussolini and a distinguished local intellectual in being accorded honorary citizenship of the city – knew what a Fascistized world meant. In Bologna's suburban blocks, it was reported confidently, a Fascism of the everyday entailed a 'continuous devotion to spreading the party gospel, to civic education and to practical matters, [a policy] requiring sacrifice, faith and passion' on the part of local party members. Their commitment ensured that 'wise doctors offered free medical assistance, while trustees not only were ready with advice designed to calm disputes and resolve a gamut of problems but even worked to relieve unemployment and to help the needful'. As if that were not enough, the local party branches kept a watchful eye on emerging sporting talent, useful for the city's teams or those of the nation and 'all sections of the party organized a range of recreations as well as providing legal support, when required'.[108]

The great showcase of the regime was its Decennale or tenth anniversary celebration of Fascist rule and especially the Mostra della rivoluzione fascista, which opened its doors on 28 October 1932 in Rome. Those displays would not close for some years and the Exhibition's organizers eventually boasted it received almost four million visitors, at a rate of some 5,000 per day. It was even said to have turned a profit,[109] although accounting procedures may have been complicated by the various lures offered to Italians to visit the Exhibition and the Eternal City (and to participate in the concurrent Catholic Holy Year). Railway discounts reached 70 per cent and cases came to light where accommodating hoteliers and guides used a single visit to the Mostra to justify a group claim for a travel refund.[110]

There had been an earlier Decennale in 1928, the tenth anniversary of the end of the First World War, warmed by victory parades and speeches from both Mussolini and D'Annunzio. Then, too, there had been a careful link made between what was called 'Fascist martyrology', the record of 'our brothers fallen on the *piazze* of Italy', and the war dead. The alleged tally of 3,000 party victims, it was emphasized, must be seamlessly added to the half a million fallen sacrifice in the war.[111]

Preparation for the second and greater Decennale had begun almost immediately after the first, with the chief organizer being Dino Alfieri, a respectable bourgeois Milan ex-Nationalist, who had his delay in converting to Fascism cleaned up through the familiar but disconcertingly non-purist manner of acquiring a backdated party card.[112] Then and later, Alfieri moved in the elegant and gilded circle of Galeazzo Ciano, the *genero* (son-in-law), as he was coming to be known. Mussolini himself was always anxious to cut a figure in intellectual circles and, in a different fashion, so were Ciano and Alfieri. The Decennale turned into a time of philosophical display when the new cohort of intellectuals, so long as they did not mind being defined as the 'generation of Mussolini', could expect enhanced status and gainful employment. The regime gave its backing to the massive and sometimes scholarly project of the *Enciclopedia italiana*, where the *Duce*, assisted in his prose by Giovanni Gentile, put out a 'definitive' short article, explaining the meaning of Fascism.[113] The historian Gioacchino Volpe celebrated the completion of the work in 1937 with the cryptic statement that each article carried the philosophy of Fascism in every line and the whole was simultaneously 'relatively perfect' from a 'scientific' viewpoint.[114] Now was the time of the flourishing of what one historian has acutely termed the 'patron state'. In 1933 the so-called artists' syndicate had 1,865 card-carrying members; six years later, this total had expanded to 4,526.[115]

In *Critica Fascista* and other such places, it became easy to find portentous justifications for what was happening at the Mostra and throughout the regime's expanding set of cultural events. Perhaps it was now that texts or, more likely, performance and display, became a social laboratory in which the totalitarian regime successfully manufactured the new mass subject. Yet one analyst has underlined sceptically how the regime utilized 'promises of creative autonomy and state subsidies' in order to 'domesticate and normalize intellectuals while giving them the illusion that they worked within a pluralist system'.[116] It was equally true that urban and generally bourgeois intellectuals, more or less accepting of Fascism, succeeded in enhancing Mussolini's and some other leading politicians' longstanding assumptions that ideas and will mattered more than material concerns and so assisted the general drift of the dictatorship to be 'on display' in all its actions. In this sense, Fascism in the 1930s became a sort of relief organization for a slew of otherwise potentially unemployed intellectuals. By boosting the intellectuals' self-importance and anchoring the Fascist regime more firmly to words than to material matters, Mussolini, Bottai and the rest were deepening the unreality, later to be exposed so dramatically in the war. They were not so much controlling culture as allowing culture or its veneer to occupy the centre of Italian life and to become Fascism. The unreality of this project, impossible wholly to overlook, in turn deepened the dictatorship's longstanding nervousness, its half-expressed fear that things were not what they were said to be and therefore its glimmering of recognition that the regime and its ideology were not built to last.

Even when Fascism sought most visibly to occupy any space available, contradictions abounded. The attempt to provide a mass culture through government and party action gave advantage not just to creative intellectuals. Throughout the 1930s Fascist Italy continued to breed new state and para-state so-called *enti* (quangos). Where the territory of one overlapped that of another, the most frequent solution was to create a third, with the task of harmonizing any conflict that had arisen in what was by definition a world of struggle. In 1928 Mussolini located a further lapidary phrase when he pronounced that the regime would definitively resolve the 'problem of the bureaucracy'. Only a year later, however, he had backed away from this irksome task, admitting he could not hope 'from outside, to amend, reduce and thin a state service largely constituted by the southern middling classes, whose adhesion to Fascism is known to be purely formal'. In 1933 Starace, recalling that any deployment of the *raccomandazioni* had been banned in 1924, in 1926, in 1927, again in 1928, and always with no effect, confessed that the lack of a Prussian spirit among the nation's bureaucrats and the similar absence of real authority in the Fascist state meant that the *Duce* was reduced to placating state officials with 'an elaborate set of little gold and silver medals, armed with ornately coloured ribbons'. The result, says the historian of this social group, was anything other than a brave new world. Rather, by the Second World War, clerks in the state administration were too anxious about their status and pay to care much about a dedication to Fascism or to the nation.[117] At least in this sector of the economy, there had been little progress towards the people, little spiritual conversion, little cultural or social revolution. As Italian leaders tried to work out the best position for the nation in a dangerously fraying world order, corporate society remained more myth than reality.

10

Placing Italy in Europe

Unremarked by most among the citizens of Fascist Italy was Eugenio Bellemo, a priest, born and trained at Chioggia, a fishing port south of Venice. His fall, in 1932, was caused by his attempt to run a foreign policy of his own (one tailored to help Chioggia but judged by Fascist authorities as harmful to Italy). His story can round out an account of how the Italian dictatorship sculptured a place for the nation in Europe's diplomatic world and will suggest that Italians' international dealings were rather more complex than they might seem if paying attention only to formal diplomatic documents and elite speechifying.

A poor boy, so the *carabinieri* would get around to reporting, Bellemo had signed up at the Chioggia seminary during the 1880s. But, the police ran on, 'full of life, he tolerated the restrictions of the priestly discipline grudgingly, and sought a way out for himself by concentrating on studying problems to do with fishing, being sure that he would thus make his fortune'. He left the seminary soon after ordination and, 'curtailing his priestly vocation to one daily mass', he took with a will to the lay life. He enjoyed a relationship with two local women and, after they died, set up with a third, who, in 1932, still resided at his Chioggia house. In the decade before 1915 he filled a series of administrative roles for the local fishermen, who were just beginning to organize as a lobby in a modern or semi-modern fashion. In one incident, he managed to persuade 3,000 locals to demonstrate against the government for failing to provide appropriate insurance against what remained a perilous way of family subsistence.[1]

When the First World War made fishing in the Adriatic still more problematic and ruin loomed for many of the poor, Don Eugenio 'was quite prodigious in extracting government subsidies for the fishing families'. By then he was widely recognized as the 'leader of his community'. He could even be dubbed the town intellectual since he published articles about fishing matters in *La Gazzetta di Venezia* and *Il Resto del Carlino* and then a whole book, *I Mercati del pesce in Adriatico*, in 1924. As official acknowledgement that he was the man who most mattered in Chioggia fishing circles, in 1908 he had been elevated to be a *Cavaliere*, in 1911 a *Cavaliere Ufficiale* and in 1925 a *Commendatore*.

The onset of Fascism raised troubling questions about Bellemo's position, especially because, accustomed to his successful ways, he evinced no eagerness to identify with the new movement. By 1926 a Fascist fishermen's syndicate or union had opened in the town but it fared poorly from a combination of maladministration and the open criticism of its leaders by Bellemo. The result was that, for eleven months in 1928–9, as a sensible-sounding compromise if one with a tang of old-fashioned *trasformismo* about it, Bellemo himself was put in charge. Before long, however, the priest was sacked, the official excuse being that he had still not joined the party but really because he had not ceased to think of himself as his own man (the police did admit that he always lived modestly and, lacking brothers and sisters, made no effort to siphon off reward for family gain). He did not hold back from exercising authority. In his days of domination, it was said, no fishing licence could be obtained and no other government activity begun or expedited without his personal intervention.

His power had its challengers, however, especially while a conflict bubbled on between the fishermen and the wealthier boat-owners (most of the latter resident in easeful Venice), with Bellemo being perceived as swinging adroitly from one side to the other according to the tactical moment.[2] The Fascist syndicate, meanwhile, continued to languish in a way that dismayed those government inspectors who, from time to time, reached Chioggia. By the early 1930s Bellemo's name was linked with the tough and perhaps violent local notable, Marcello Teodoro Boscolo. This owner of two boats, who austerely denied himself the delights of life in Venice, was urging the Chioggia fishermen to keep up their traditional and profitable, if illegal, habit of clandestine fishing. Their treasured site for such labour lay in those parts of the Adriatic now defined as Albanian waters[3] and so under the modern control of the regime headed by King Zog, then regarded by Italian and Fascist diplomacy as a dutiful enough client.

Matters came to a head in spring 1932, when Bellemo led Chioggia into a sort of mini-fishing war. One of his methods of combat was surreptitiously to telegraph to the press the news that rival fishermen to those of his town were launched on an expedition to breach the sea border of Albania. It was this small effort at treachery, however helpful to Chioggia, which alerted the police to his case. Bellemo's policy was deemed 'anti-national' because the resultant publicity hampered Italian consular officials who were trying to negotiate fishing rights and other commercial matters with the Albanians at a national level.[4] Bellemo, the Italian authorities declared severely, had known exactly what he was doing in inserting himself and the interests of his followers into government business. So Bellemo, Boscolo and their men were sent off to *confino*. Some variety of Fascist totalitarianism was imposed on Chioggia and those 'Italies' that Bellemo embodied gave ground to Italy (and Albania) and to the homogenizing processes of modernization and nationalization.

Affirming and expanding the borders of Italy's place in the world had, after all, been a keynote of the Fascist agenda from the movement's earliest days. In November 1921 the new PNF had sculpted into its programme the determination to reaffirm 'Latin civilization in the Mediterranean', to impose 'Italian values' on any non-Italians within Italy and to defend 'Italians abroad', wherever their place of emigration. The state, the military and the diplomatic service, resolute to overcome past Liberal weakness, must, the party pledged, become the agents of Italian 'grandeur' throughout the globe, expressed both 'materially and symbolically'.[5] Individual Fascists saw few reasons to gloze their tongues about this thrust towards some form of world power. Francesco Giunta, while still a 'border Fascist' in Trieste, bade his country resume what he saw as its natural role as 'the first nation in the Mediterranean', which meant, he added still aglow with the saga of the Roman Empire of two millennia before, 'to dominate the world'. The young Dino Grandi was similarly happy to proclaim the Fascist movement fundamentally 'expansionist', although somewhat obscurely he contended that it was simultaneously not at all 'imperialist'.[6]

When, in 1921, Grandi expressed this line he was trying to separate the modernity of what were still the *fasci* from the more traditional platform of the Nationalist Association. Certainly the Nationalists were not reticent in urging a great power role on Italy and in demanding more authoritarian policies domestically to ready Italians for the imminent and necessary international struggle. For Enrico Corradini and his confrères, the First World War had been insufficient or, rather, the advantage promised through Italy's victory in it had been eaten into by parliamentary weakness and socialist treachery. Fascism might be stained by crudity, such Nationalists reasoned, but its rule was needed to build a real state, one which could move forward and conquer.[7]

Quite a few business people similarly emerged from the First World War with the belief that Italy must press aggressively ahead with a colonialist programme as part of a more general assertion of national power in the world. In January 1920 the Turin industrialist Luigi Ferraris was sure that 'Italy needs colonies in order to publicize its level of civilization but above all to integrate its industry and increase its wealth at home'. One approach, he suggested lightly, might be to meddle gainfully in the current Egyptian revolt against their English overlords.[8] At around the same time, Oscar Sinigaglia, another industrialist of Jewish heritage, if an unusually modern one since he had been trained as a civil engineer, pushed Italy to accept a possible mandate in Georgia, arguing that an advance there could ease Italy's deficient energy supplies[9] and implying his support for an eventual further move from Tbilisi to the oil-producing regions nearby. Sinigaglia was the patron of many Nationalist causes, holder of ticket number 602 in the Fasci di combattimento and sponsor with Giovanni Giuriati of a body called the Lega italiana per la tutela degli interessi nazionali (Italian Association for safeguarding Italy's national interests). It aimed to unite 'all Italians in a single family, a real family'.[10] Class divisions and parliamentary debates, Sinigaglia complained, were what hindered the nation from assuming its proper place in the world and thereby enriching itself.[11] Fascism, he was sure, was the best available means to achieve the ends he desired.

Nor, contrary to Fascist legend, was nationalism absent from other segments of Italy's elite. A Liberal like Vittorio Scialoja, Foreign Minister in Nitti's second government in 1919–20, deemed emigration a 'plague and a national shame', which must somehow be curtailed or amended.[12] Nitti affirmed that the expansive demands made in 1915 during the negotiation of Italy's war entry were actually 'exceedingly modest'.[13]

Talk about national expansion and a new social discipline designed to achieve it, in other words, did not fall into Fascist discourse from a clear blue sky. None the less, some historians maintain that Mussolini was, from start to finish, a fanatic who thirsted for war and lusted to tear down the existing world order. In such interpretation, the *Duce*'s foreign policy lay at the heart of the Fascist revolution. In this view Mussolini was, even before 1922, the rogue leader of a rogue movement, a madman with whom no truck could be had except at the expense of his interlocutor.[14] Yet the more credible line is that Mussolini reached office without having settled on a 'programme in regard to foreign policy' and that, as late as 1933, he had not at all succeeded in framing a genuinely independent position for Italy among the powers, let alone a revolutionary one.[15]

To be sure, the *Duce*, a journalist ready with an opinion on anything, had regularly commented on international events since before 1914. A trawl through his voluminous writings and speeches in these years can find comments which range from backing Irish republicans in their 'utterly just' cause against the English[16] to claiming that the appropriate diplomatic role for Italy was to work for 'balance and conciliation between the [European] powers'.[17] Similarly, his elevation to the prime ministership at once prompted him to tell an interviewer from the establishment paper *La Stampa* that he stood simply for a 'dignified line, without weakness or threats', a studiously mild contrast to what he proclaimed was his radical willingness to control the internal situation 'with machine guns'.[18] The *Duce*'s first diplomatic note to France and Britain pledged that the new government would watch over national interests while reconciling them with peace and justice, but was also emphatic that Fascism embodied the 'full Italian meaning of Vittorio Veneto'. Armed by the spirit of victory, the nation must now receive the rewards that should have been its due in 1919.[19]

For a decade and more after 1922 the international ramifications of Fascist government in Italy remained unclear. There was a vast amount of sabre-rattling from the *Duce* himself and from an eager crew of commentators about foreign affairs. Plangent rhetoric about injustice in need of urgent and aggressive amendment could colour almost any policy. When, for example, in July 1925 Mussolini announced that the country was engaged in the *battaglia del grano* (battle for wheat), his phrasing was both military and xenophobic: 'The battle for grain', he bellowed, 'entails freeing the Italian people from their slavery to foreign bread.'[20]

The dictator was not the only Italian with such habits. The Fascist historian Gioacchino Volpe drew a salutary-sounding lesson from the Corfu crisis in August–September 1923, when Mussolini aggressively ordered his fleet to bombard and occupy the island as retribution for a Greek government deemed responsible for the murder of an Italian general in Albania. (King Victor Emmanuel was said, after the occupation, to have advised his young Prime Minister to 'play hard' there).[21] Britain and France, Volpe wrote in the PNF ideological journal *Gerarchia*, were the wealthy nations. Britain, he added, especially since 1918 had strayed well beyond its accustomed ruthless protection of its interests and was now malevolently campaigning against 'the young, poor, prolific and expansionist nations'.[22] Among these last, he knew, Fascist Italy was the natural leader and he did not bother to underline the customary Nationalist corollary that Germany and Japan (and sometimes the USSR) fitted the definition of those eventually bound to shrug off the hegemony of the rich and tired. In the still more intellectually ambitious *Critica Fascista*, Fascists and Nationalists reacted to the crisis over Corfu by lambasting English perfidy and greed and deriding that 'traditional friendship' which sentiment claimed to have married Italy and the UK since the Risorgimento.[23]

Not all futures were clear, however, and many Fascists rejected the idea of scanning distant horizons. In the aftermath of the squabble in the Adriatic, a journalist in *Critica Fascista* undercut the idea that Fascism was somehow universal, singling out 'the followers of Hitler in Bavaria' as laughable examples of people perversely reliant on 'brain storms' rather than a real comprehension of the originality of Fascism. Mussolini's movement, the writer knew, was 'an exclusively Italian phenomenon'.[24]

By contrast, at around the same time the young Tuscan intellectual Alessandro Pavolini thought that Fascism might have an international profile. Its compelling ideas, he predicted, were likely to spread most swiftly in Latin countries, where the national stock was most comparable to the Italian, but must eventually penetrate all Europe and the world beyond, although the Italian model would, of course, never surrender a jot or tittle of its primacy.[25] Another journalist detected that Japan was a potential seed-bed for the ideology. The best elements in imperial society were, he stated, already disciplined and nationalist, anti-Bolshevik and warlike, potential Fascists in spite of themselves.[26]

Whatever the possible place of Fascism in the philosophy and politics of the world, aggressive-sounding phrases were rarely avoided for long in the regime's militant vocabulary. Fascists took with a will to deriding those who believed in global conciliation. Woodrow Wilson earned an impolite obituary in *Critica Fascista*, where an anonymous reviewer berated him posthumously as a fatuous prophet of false promises and false teeth (Fascists often thought that Anglo-Saxon teeth were deplorably caried compared with Italian), whose liberal internationalist plans and ideas had no future.[27] In 1926 the old Nationalist Corradini, another happy to ridicule the League of Nations,[28] stated bluntly that 'Fascism wants the death of its foes'. In its open approval of force, he added, it embodied something new and positive in Italian and international history.[29] Italy's still unsatisfied 'rights' in Dalmatia, another writer in *Gerarchia* declared threateningly, had been blocked by 'the biggest international swindle of the century'.[30] A forward move, he implied, was a natural and positive step, should diplomatic or military opportunity beckon.

War plans there were. In the formal arena of diplomacy during the decade after the Corfu incident, Mussolini and his aides often gloried in their belligerency. In July 1927 the dictator, who nine months earlier had twice urged Badoglio that 'there was not a minute to lose' in arming Italian soldiers with 'an aggressive and offensive mentality' towards Yugoslavia,[31] reacted to further tension in the Balkans. There, the Kosovo dispute between the Yugoslavs and Italy's (importunate) client Albania was only one spur to ethnic tension and plotted terrorist acts. In heated response, Mussolini suddenly ordered his military to prepare a war plan against Yugoslavia and, for good measure, simultaneously to draft a blueprint for an invasion of France, Belgrade's patron in the Little Entente. At around the same time, Italy negotiated a treaty of friendship with revisionist Hungary, a state with its own blatant hopes in the destruction of Yugoslavia. Both militarily and diplomatically, Italy might be read as preparing itself for aggressive war.

The historian Macgregor Knox, convinced that the Fascist dictatorship was irredeemably rogue, has characterized such policy as 'relentlessly provocative' and systematically war-mongering.[32] Back in the 1920s French Foreign Minister Aristide Briand called Mussolini a 'madman', although he did consider that the *Duce* could be 'humoured'.[33] The qualification which Briand here expressed should not be forgotten. Whether humoured or not, Fascist Italy did not attack either of its neighbours until 1940–41 and then in very different circumstances from its 1920s' plan. Rather than collapsing into war, Italo-Yugoslav relations to 1941 followed a jagged course no doubt, but one where there were moments of rapprochement and even dalliance between Mussolini's regime and that in Belgrade. Fascist backing for the Croatian nationalist Ante Pavelić was considerable. It included financial aid and the offering of safe havens for the followers of this murderous terrorist in Italy itself (although Badoglio and others had seen advantage in backing Croat separatism as early as 1918[34] and the more frequent recipients of Italian largesse were groups like the paramilitary Heimwehr in Austria and dissident soldiers in Spain where any revolutionary political élan was muted by social reaction).

By 1932 the Ustasha were enjoying payment of 70,000 lire per month from a secret Foreign Ministry fund.[35] Yet the patronage was never wholehearted. Its most active agents were such relatively junior figures in the regime as the ex-Nationalist Roberto Forges Davanzati, with Mussolini on most occasions loftily refusing to involve himself directly.[36] In 1934 the *Duce* even advised that all contact should be broken with 'this useless and dangerous band' (although his advice was not followed).[37] The charge that the *Duce* did not act in 1926–7 because an attack on Yugoslavia for the moment was 'ruled out' by Italy's 'economic and military weakness' sounds like an over-simplification.[38] Certainly it could only be accepted after a full-scale investigation of the meaning of 'planning' during the Fascist years.

What, for example, should be made of the dictatorship's mainly friendly dealings with Great Britain at a diplomatic level (despite occasional press spats) and with the United States commercially? As early as 1924 Mussolini, perhaps a little crassly, asked Washington to choose as its ambassador to Rome 'a major financial expert or a great industrialist or an eminent politician with a profound knowledge of the American economy',[39] and one historian has suggested that, throughout the 1920s, Italy is best viewed as an international client of J. P. Morgan and the other US banks (if, on occasion, a verbally wayward one). In 1930 Dino Grandi, by then Minister of Foreign Affairs, hailed the USA and Britain as 'the two great peoples of the world' and there was no sign that his *Duce* demurred.[40] So sober was the *Duce*'s image among the British ruling elite that, after Hitler began to rise, they warmed themselves with the thought that, whatever the extremity of the *Führer*'s ideas, they were bound eventually to calm down on the Mussolini model.[41]

What, too, is to be thought about the Italian dictatorship's deeply realistic relationship with the USSR, even while the Italian domestic vocabulary was full of the evils of bolshevism and the need to stem it wherever it might be found? One of Mussolini's first diplomatic notes called for general applause at the victory of Fascism over the 'spiritual epidemic' of bolshevism.[42] Five years later, when in 1927 Britain broke off diplomatic relations with the USSR and war seemed imminent between the Soviet state and Europe's leading capitalist country, Mussolini expressed his pleasure to London, promising that 'I shall profit from the first opportunity to do likewise'. After all, he added in words that must have been music to British conservative ears, 'I have always been convinced that the Soviet regime constitutes a permanent danger'.[43] Yet Fascist Italy did nothing to organize a crusade to the East and there was no break in relations either in 1927 or at any other time before 1941. Rather, the Fascist regime quickly sought to normalize its relations with the USSR (and thereafter did its best to win some commercial gain from them), even if Grandi typically ordered his ambassador in Moscow not to become too loyal a friend of the Soviets.[44] Whereas Nazi anti-communism was visceral at home and abroad and war in the East was its natural denouement, the Italian rejection of the Soviet system, at least on the international stage, was tactical and rhetorical rather than active.

Assessing other chatter about plotted aggression during the first decade of Fascist rule is an equally perplexing task. Throughout his life Mussolini had something of a love–hate relationship with France and there were moments when he seemed to flirt with war against the country long lampooned by Nationalists as the Latin *sorellastra* (stepsister). Only a couple of months after taking office, in February 1923 the *Duce* suddenly told the Minister of the Navy, Paolo Thaon di Revel, that he ought to have a plan ready to seize Corsica in case an anti-French revolt broke out there.[45] A few months later Mussolini asked War Minister Armando Diaz surreptitiously to commence enrolling exiled Corsican patriots in a potentially irredentist foreign legion.[46] Yet neither plea was followed up and Franco-Italian relations settled into a course that was at times uneasy but was scarcely out of kilter with past Italo-French relations.

On another occasion the *Duce* talked petulantly of imminent conflict with Turkey but his concentration on the matter soon waned and nothing serious eventuated. Mussolini can certainly be charged with restlessness in foreign policy but, for the moment at least, there continued to be a gap between the words of his regime and its acts. If real violence and murder are to be located in Fascism's international dealings before 1935, they surface in Libya and the so-called pacification being ruthlessly pursued in the empire inherited from the Liberals. To be properly understood, the drastic actions there, which bordered on genocide, need to be set within the general context of European imperialism, while the most brutal perpetrators, however much operating in a cruel atmosphere endorsed by the *Duce*, were officers in the royal and national army, whose Fascistization was partial at best. As Emilio De Bono, general, governor and ex-*quadrumvir* explained, no atrocity claims in that part of the world really mattered in European chancelleries because all gentlemen understood that anything was better than lingering as a nomad.[47] The willing executioners of empire were, in sum, as much Italians (and Europeans) as they were Fascists.

Another issue deserves clarification. Just how much were the foreign policies of Fascist Italy really Mussolini's own? It is easy enough to find the *Duce* warning off those he deemed his more ham-fisted party colleagues, such as Farinacci, from commenting too expansively on foreign affairs,[48] although, in that press which he controlled, Farinacci continued to discuss the international scene, automatically grovelling when Mussolini was mentioned but not always concealing his own ideas. Dino Grandi, the Fascist whose career prospered best in the diplomatic arena – he was allowed to be Foreign Minister from September 1929 to July 1932 – rarely forgot to kowtow to his all-seeing and all-knowing leader. In one typical report, Grandi told his Prime Minister that real diplomacy was Mussolini's personal invention, 'another creation of Your Art of government, through which You [*Tu*] are educating the new ruling class'. In case that absurd hyperbole was not enough, Grandi prefaced these comments with the fawning hope that the *Duce* was 'not cross with his pupil'.[49] On another occasion, Grandi hastened to apologize to the dictator after an incident in which he had solicited and received press praise from Farinacci, with Grandi, never averse to Machiavellian ploys tailored to his own advantage, endeavouring to bring a bitter smile to Mussolini's face by calling Farinacci a 'buffoon' and damning his paper, *Il Regime fascista*, as 'flashy and loud'.[50] The voluminous Grandi–Mussolini correspondence remains a case study of the posturing and lies which accompany dictatorial rule (and not only that) and which are expected both of the minion (sometimes aspiring to a higher role) and the chief (needing always to flaunt his infallibility, however incredible the claims may be).

While beset by such leadership, the professional diplomats frequently lamented that their new chief did not observe due form and proper practice in the way they had been trained to do.[51] In 1927 Mussolini and Grandi proclaimed that they were engaged in a root and branch Fascistization of the staff of the Foreign Ministry and would hereafter insist that all diplomats and consuls were warriors for the Fascist revolution.[52] After the Second World War those who had once served Fascism (but mostly proceeded with their careers under the Republic) were anxious in their memoirs and in those histories produced by orthodox diplomatic historians to plead that they bore no responsibility for the eventual disasters of Fascism and had not really countenanced the aggression involved.

They protest too much. Any genuine Fascistization of the diplomatic service was incomplete and it can be argued that the professionals were better at duchessing certainly Grandi and perhaps Mussolini than the Fascist chiefs were in revolutionizing the diplomats. Moreover, nationalism of the sort which had been expressed in the ANI was deeply entrenched in the minds of the Italian diplomatic service and, for much of the time, Fascist dealings abroad, as led by Mussolini, were more reticent than those sketched by Nationalist writers. Even at the policy level, it is possible to find cases when an old Nationalist was anxious to galvanize his *Duce* beyond what actually happened or, at a minimum, to gain approval for present or later advance. In September 1926, for example, Prince Pietro Lanza di Scalea, Sicilian landowner, Nationalist and conservative, who had occupied the post of Under-Secretary of State for Foreign Affairs in a succession of Liberal administrations before 1914 and was Fascist Minister of Colonies in 1925–6, hailed a deal which had been reached with the Imam of Yemen. This arrangement, he informed the *Duce* in the nervously envious language of the moment, was proof that Italy did not intend to 'be imprisoned within the territorial limits and the resources of its existing colonies' but rather should turn the whole Red Sea into 'a zone of our influence'.[53] Similarly, lesser officials (and ones failing to perceive the coming Holocaust) highlighted the presence of Jews scattered over the Mediterranean, quite a few of whom possessed Italian citizenship. Adroit subsidy and cunning deployment of these 'splendid instruments for the spread of the Italian spirit', one diplomat advised from Cairo, might help Italy undermine the authority of its rivals throughout the Mediterranean littoral.[54] It was Raffaele Guariglia,[55] youthful Nationalist sympathizer and then Badoglio's Minister of Foreign Affairs after July 1943, who, in 1932, was the first to plan an Italian takeover of Ethiopia. 'War', that is, aggressive war, he concluded (and his meaning may be complex), was justified, given the national need for empire. 'You achieve nothing great unless you are willing to soil your hands with blood,' he counselled.[56]

During the 1920s Italy, in other words, was a country that accepted peace with reluctance and on occasion pined for general disturbance. In 1928 the *Duce* may have signed the Kellogg–Briand peace pact forever renouncing war (shortly after publishing in *Gerarchia* a sarcastic attack on the whole idea from a now Fascist, once Nationalist, journalist), but Fascism was not a reliable paladin of the Geneva spirit.[57] Rather, all news reports and oratory in Fascist Italy were deeply coloured with the memory of the last war and the allegedly attractive prospect of the next. Rather than being able to pinpoint a moment before 1935 when Mussolini or his regime were hell-bent on European conflict, it is better to emphasize how hard and long the dictatorship worked to spread a certain type of militarism among its subjects. Until the late 1930s Italians at home (and, in a different way, the subjects of the empire inherited from the Liberals) were the first and main targets of Fascist aggression.

The totalitarian state had, after all, created a network of youth organizations in which all Italians of the so-called 'generation of Mussolini' were meant to muster. In June 1939 the regime proclaimed that it had enrolled 1,355,575 in the Figli della Lupa (children aged 6 to 7), 1,576,925 in the Balilla (for boys 8 to 13), 1,501,834 in the Piccole italiane (for girls 8 to 13), 756,236 in the Avanguardisti (for boys 14 to 17) and 387,321 in the Giovani italiane (for girls 14 to 17), 745,608 in the Giovani fascisti (young men from 18 to 21) and 378,140 in the Giovani fasciste (young women from 18 to 21). A further 98,834 had signed up as members of the university-based GUF (Gioventù Universitaria Fascista). The total was 6,701,639.[58] From their creation in 1926 until 1937 most of these organizations were led by Renato Ricci, in practice one of the more overtly corrupt of Fascist bosses, but in appearance an athletic-looking soldier. His elevation to head the so-called ONB (Opera Nazionale Balilla) had been prompted by the need to get him out of his home town of Carrara where quarrels among local factions had become embarrassing – at least one of his opponents had found Fascism no protection against a term of *confino* sparked by too aggressive a lingering social radicalism.[59] Ricci's pretensions to modernity had received further justification in 1926, when he took out a pilot's licence, earning himself a note of congratulations from the aerial-minded *Duce*, who rejoiced that such an example would 'bring gain to the efficient war-preparedness of the nation and the moral health of the party'.[60]

Official propaganda made much of Ricci's good looks and

seconded his demands that even the tiniest members of his scouting organization must think of themselves as soldiers in the making. In 1930 Ricci publicly requested the provision of every Balilla gym with arms, since exercising with them was what really made a child a man.[61] With every passing year of dictatorial rule, photography and newsreel concentrated more insistently on squads of children, uniformed, marching or in serried line, courageous and audacious little legionaries of the new Italy. One treasured ceremony, repeated in many town *piazze* across the peninsula, had a Giovane Fascista passing a rifle to an Avanguardista and then to a Balilla and even a Figlio della Lupa, with the strident message that they were handing on the torch of militant life (and of certain death to Fascism's foes). Any excuse could justify a Fascist parade, initiate a military drumming, require a military air.

Yet parades, no matter how totalitarian they were pronounced to be in the official press, could carry more than one message. The fact that girls, too, could expect to attend such events (although in smaller numbers than boys) carried a greater infraction of accustomed family life than did most aspects of the dictatorship. The ideological effect was, however, varied. The opportunity to dress in natty uniforms, to drill but also to play sport and to walk to Fascist functions alone or with a female friend of the same age, brought a breath of modernity into the lives of quite a few Italian girls. This was especially true of those young women who, from 1932 onwards, joined the Orvieto Academy of Physical Education, the most prestigious place to be trained as an active female Fascist. When he tried to set out the 'essence of the GUF', its Fascist chief, Fernando Mezzasoma, decreed ambiguously that girls could indulge in sport – the 'graceful' activity of archery was a good example – but must eschew 'useless and dangerous over-competitiveness', since the real aim of all education for young women was to perfect the 'healthy and vigorous mother'.[62]

It was not only girls who could adapt Fascist pomp to their own hopes and understandings. I still remember a school visit I made during the 1970s to Griffith, an Italian emigrant centre in southern New South Wales, to speak about Fascism. After the lecture, I talked to an elderly immigrant Calabrian about his memory of the dictatorship. His eyes lit up as he recounted just how short the skirts of the

Fascist girls had been and how he and his mates had always gone to a parade with an arsenal of small stones that they then endeavoured to flick meaningfully on to, or between, the girls' legs. At least if his remembrance was correct, for youngsters like him a Fascist rally was where he could dream of sexual conquest more overtly than was possible within the confines of his family home.

During their time as scouts, boys and girls could expect to spend one vacation and often more under Fascist canvas; by 1942 officially there were 5,805 Fascist campsites, with an annual enrolment of almost a million children.[63] At such places, sports and other leisure activities were meant always to have a militant, pugnacious and xenophobic purpose. There was quite a bit of marching, sounding of trumpets, roll-calls and other conduct mimicking that of real soldiers. Even children's literature was the object of totalitarian intrusion, although with erratic results. In 1933, historian Volpe published a schoolchild's *Storia dell'Italia e degli italiani* with emphasis on heroes and grandeur and pushing a 'warlike, nationalist and expansionist consciousness',[64] although a review of the matter has concluded that such works did not succeed in ousting more romantic and less directly militarist children's reading and play.

Especially under the influence in the 1930s of the fanatical Party Secretary Starace, the regime was persistent in trying to adapt play to the preparation for war. In a society where the gifts of the festive season often had possessed particular regional histories, the Befana Fascista (Fascist Epiphany) of 6 January assumed a national and nationalizing role and allowed Mussolini and his wife, Rachele, and other leading Fascist families to tout their own charity. The sanctions campaign during the Ethiopian war stimulated demands that Italian toys should go to Italian children and encouraged claims that, in the artisan field as in every other, a national primacy had long existed.[65] When autarchy became the accepted national economic line, it was maintained that any decent Figlio della Lupa, Balilla or Piccola Italiana would react with horror if they learned that their parents were purchasing toys not made by Italians. In such a case, it was suggested, they would 'not feel really Italian and not worthy of growing up in the Mussolini era'.[66] By 1937 Roberto Melli, a Fascist writer, went a step further to argue that 'toys must be at the service of the

State. They must help the modelling of a special type of nation and become an instrument in the hands of a legislator who really wants to mould and quicken the conscience of his people at a fundamental turning point in history.'[67] Fascism, it transpired, according to the newly populist phrases of the time, stood for the 'democratization of the toy', since the regime deplored foolish luxury, preferred practicality and aimed at a situation in which every child should receive the comfort, pleasure and stimulation of a gift each year.[68] The national cast of Fascist giving should, for example, help Pinocchio to repel the challenge of Mickey Mouse or Topolino, as he is known in Italy, that repulsive creation of 'Taylorism' and a too rational brain.[69] So much was theory. In practice the *Topolino* comic went on being read by an estimated 140,000 Italian children each week, including those in the Mussolini household. Its distribution did not cease until February 1942, weeks after Italy and the USA were at war.[70]

Unabashed by such details, regime journals continued to link play and war. In May 1938 customers were informed about an excellent new toy, manufactured by the firm of Zuccarello at Treviso. An artisan from that place, it was announced, had constructed a 'really interesting machine gun destined to delight both young and . . . old. This gun is the perfect replica of the real version. It can be moved and managed and actually works, even if without harmful effect,' it was added reassuringly. Made of wood, the gun could be turned, focused and then suddenly fire 'thirty little projectiles each to a distance of ten metres'. For early Befana shoppers that year who neglected this purchase, there were other models of similar allure and purpose, including a submarine crafted by an artisan from Brindisi. After partial submergence, this vessel could rise from the water and 'set off shots against an invisible enemy from a little cannon, placed on its deck'.[71] Family cats, it might be surmised, had a hard time as the decade drew towards its violent end.

Yet neither rhetoric nor practice reliably hardened the young (or the mature) in the way that some fire-breathing enthusiasts favoured. Not long after Melli wrote his aggressive piece, another commentator thought more expansively about the philosophy of the toy. For Enrico Serretta, it was a happy prospect that children came home from parades, doffed their party uniforms and began innocently to play.

'The truth is', he stated, 'that there are toys for all ages, because in every era, human nature needs something which embodies leisure, a "pass-time", a distraction from the daily grind and a satisfaction of the urge for luxury, caprice and vanity.' After all, he went on in words which fit many stereotypes about Italian males but which scarcely brimmed with Fascist rigour, why did 'mature men' insist on 'possessing a doll, a live doll and do all they could to enjoy her, discounting expense to see her elegantly dressed, or to let her tool around in a car and to have her look beautiful, seated in the best stall in a theatre'?[72] The permanent and ubiquitous desire to play was his only answer.

A further complexity in the dictatorship's training of youth arose from the longstanding Italian disavowal of the corporal punishment of children. In spite of much ranting to the contrary, Fascist scouting had a gentle side. The Balilla boasted loudly that it made boys 'strong, courageous, intelligently prepared and militarily organized'. That was what being a Fascist entailed.[73] Their commander, Captain Ricci, insisted on it. Yet, according to the movement's propaganda, he was not a cruel or unfeeling chief. As one Fascist scout summoned from the border region of Bolzano to admire 'imperial' Rome remembered in words which might today sound overly innocent: 'He, the head of the Balilla, caressed the curly blond or brown hair of one youth or other, tired by the morning exercises and ready to go to sleep. And He [sic] smiled, with his face shining with a youthfulness of his own. Then we felt ourselves not so much standing before our Chief as in the company of a Friend, a dear Friend, who was there to console us in those moments of camp life when we felt homesick.' Weary as the boys were and in urgent need of their siesta, their Fascist vim revived, the narrator of these events maintained, when Ricci regaled them with gripping yarns 'about the sacrifices which our infantrymen had made on the stony Carso to liberate their brothers from the yoke of foreign oppression' and, he inevitably added, the Fascist oblation of blood during 'the fratricidal struggle' before the March on Rome, which had allowed party men to 'save our *Patria* from the Bolshevik flood'.[74] Wide-eyed, at least according to the official account, the boys artlessly imbibed the echoing message that the national war in 1915–18 and the party and ideological battle from 1919 to 1922 were the same in nature, purpose and value.

The same themes predominated in Fascist schools, although with some nuance. In such places the Roman salute may have been made compulsory as early as 1925[75] and subsequently pressure may have grown to train Italian children in a 'Fascist manner', with Fascist text-books (notoriously some smuggled party indoctrination into mathe-matics problems) and teachers who, on official occasions from 1934 onwards, were compelled to sport a party uniform, assembling them-selves and their charges in militant ranks, pedagogues and pupils of the revolution.[76] The Fascist philosopher Giovanni Gentile served as Minister of Education from 1922 to 1924 and, thereafter, from this or that key cultural podium, did not cease to demand that Italians be engrained with a sense of the strong state and devote and sacrifice themselves to the nation, infusing it with a will sadly absent among previous generations. Yet, throughout the schooling process, repeated indiscipline was not met with a beating as it would have been in the Anglo-Saxon and Germanic worlds but merely with suspension or expulsion.[77] Rich bourgeois (the Fascist founder of the Buitoni pasta business remembered that he and his four brothers were regularly horse-whipped by their father in Perugia)[78] and poor peasant fathers may have been ready to slap their children brutally across their faces in what had long been the private family manner but the official method of child-raising disliked such habits, opting instead for ten-derness, tolerance and even indulgence, especially while the child was young.

Another ambiguity was present in what, during the early 1930s, was the greatest publicity story of the Fascist moment, that of the deeds of flying ace and Minister, Italo Balbo. This clear-eyed, anti-socialist killer of squadrist days, now in his thirties, had matured into a debonair figure in the mondaine life of the dictatorship. His hand-some character was affirmed in his two crossings of the Atlantic, over Christmas/New Year 1930–31 to Brazil and, during the summer of 1933, to the USA, a country he had earlier visited with enthusiasm in 1928. On each occasion Balbo flew as the chief of what was called an 'armada' of planes. These events were given huge play in the Fascist press, with admirers materializing in throngs among the emigrant Italian communities of the New World, in Italy itself and in the other places visited. In an account of his trip, also published with official subsidy in English, Balbo spoke of the 'weird ritual' whereby the Sioux of Chicago inducted him as 'Chief Flying Eagle' and admitted that, along with Augusto Rosso, the diplomat destined in 1941 to be national ambassador in Moscow, he sloped off to Luna Park, where 'we danced, we shied coco-nuts and patronized the shooting-gallery' and where incognito was pleasurably impossible to preserve.[79] Back in Italy, the journal *L'Alpino* suggested in hackneyed parallel that mentioning Balbo in its pages was like evoking a saint in church.[80]

Boosted as a Fascist celebrity, the touring *ras* felt free to pontificate about the limitations of the New World. 'The individual in a city like New York', Balbo maintained, 'is utterly submerged by the mass mind. The individual in that capital toils, suffers and enjoys himself collectively.'[81] That fate might be good or bad in a Fascist estimation, depending on the moment and the definition. But the first message of Balbo's trips was of the regime's showy dedication to modern technology and its accompanying fascination with aspects of the US mission in the world. Until very late in its history, Fascism did not reliably place the USA among its certain foes. Moreover, the Balbo 'raids', as they were termed with customary militant ring, constituted another occasion when there was something of the military – what were planes for in the final analysis but war? – but also something of the more simply modern. Yet, somewhere in their hearts, many Italians doubted whether Italy had really become more modern than the USA. They rejoiced no doubt that a young party hero had won a national victory but, like him, they simultaneously registered what peasant emigrants had always maintained, that the USA was the infinitely wealthy 'land of cockayne'. Its films and its popular culture were penetrating Italian souls and were by definition countering with consumerism any attempt by the dictatorship to control its subjects' dreams.

There was, however, one who was cynical about the whole affair and he, predictably, was Mussolini. From the press fanfares Mussolini drew a traditional politician's message. Balbo was acquiring too much glamour which might cast a shadow over the *Duce*'s charisma. The spectacle over, to his expressed dismay Balbo learned that, from New Year's Day 1934, he had been posted to hot, dusty and far-off Tripoli, there to vegetate as Governor of Libya.

In sum, a review of Fascist training and the picture it reveals of

Italy's place in the world has multilayered results. Read literally, Fascist words told obsessively of the coming war, its glory and duty, of male heroism and female sacrifice. The dictatorship blithely spread a ready-made vocabulary of abuse, available for rehearsal against any foreign nation with which Italy's relationship became troubled. They painted in loud tones an image of a dictatorship that was perpetually teetering on the edge of aggressive war. They harped on an Italian 'primacy', that favoured Fascist word (allegedly an inheritance from Vincenzo Gioberti's Risorgimento work, *On the Moral and Civil Primacy of the Italians*, 1843), urging that leadership was or urgently must be achieved in every field, by force if need be. The 'cultural revolution' and the 'civic religion', read literally, amounted to a gospel of assault and demanded a commitment to Fascist fundamentalism from every Italian. Yet not all the accompanying unspoken assumptions meshed easily with the bellicosity of this discourse. Despite its bragging about totalitarian uniformity, the Italian dictatorship was interlaced with many histories and, away from the threatening power and ideological defiance of its speeches and statements, it harboured many diverse ideas and, for much of the time, a practice by no means reliably focused on instant and permanent war. Beneath the verbal swagger, some sense of hollowness, fear and even some practicality lingered.

For much of its international life, at least until the attack on Ethiopia in 1935, what was most significant about Fascists' and other Italians' placing of themselves in Europe and the rest of the globe was not so much the insolent phrases of assault as the ultra realism and cynicism which underpinned many Italians' world-view (those of Chioggia fishing expert and priest, Bellemo, for example). Disbelief was often a more basic force than belief. Even in the Liberal era, Antonino Di San Giuliano, the Sicilian aristocrat who was Italy's Foreign Minister 1910–14, had been impatient with the idea that diplomacy should prefer ideals to the concrete. When he was upbraided by the British ambassador for breaking international law through Italy's continued 'temporary' occupation of the Dodecanese islands (a control to be made permanent by the Fascist government in 1924), Di San Giuliano replied brazenly that there was no reason to worry. 'There were', he pronounced, 'continual new developments in international law.'[82]

Earlier Italian leaders, despite their liberalism, did not discountenance force should it prove useful. Cavour, the diplomatic architect of Italian unification, talked of setting 'fire to the four corners of the world', asserting boldly that 'we Italians have conquered the world before and can do so again',[83] (although this politician of many parts was so given to speaking with multiple voices that the meaning of his phrases should not be assumed to be literal).[84] A generation later, Crispi more feverishly contemplated unleashing a world conflict, if benefit for Italy (and himself) could be wrung from it.[85]

No doubt the Liberal flirtation with war was not the same as the Fascist one, but, whatever the dictatorship's inheritance from the national past and whatever the influence on Italian practice of the structures of international life from the nation's standing as the least of the great powers, in most instances after 1922 a driving cynicism about the practice of international life outweighed revolutionary dedication. One telling area was the use and the discussion around it of the most obvious weapon of mass destruction in inter-war Europe, poison gas. In June 1925 Mussolini joined his nation to twenty-four other countries by signing the Geneva Convention, swearing never again to deploy chemical or bacteriological weapons in battle.[86] Here was one of those curious moments when the Fascist regime, despite its regular disquisitions on the fatuity of the League of Nations, participated in that organization's activities in a fashion hard to distinguish from other member states. Endorsing an agreement was one thing; accepting its provisions was, however, another. As early as January 1928 in its campaigns to restore 'order' in Libya, Italy did use gas. It continued to do so. In 1935–6, during the invasion of Ethiopia, Italy unleashed an estimated 317 tonnes of chemicals on its hapless and defenceless black enemy,[87] with its propagandists having the effrontery to claim that the real poison gas was being let off by the 'preachers' of Geneva.[88] So blatant were the Italian actions that France, in April 1936, and Britain, in July, began to stockpile their own supplies of gas as precaution.[89]

The Italian willingness to bomb with chemical weapons, although denied by patriotic post-war historians, was not much hidden at the time. In June 1927 the semi-official monthly *Esercito e Nazione* (Army and Nation) published an article arguing that gas was a weapon no different from any other. Leonardo da Vinci had allegedly foreseen its value and its abolition was pointless.[90] The first attacks in Libya were accompanied by commentary in a major air journal, exulting in the success of bombing and strafing there.[91] Balbo, when Air Minister, had rhapsodized about the 'natural marriage' between the sky and chemical warfare.[92] Giulio Douhet, the apostle of air *Blitzkrieg*, was sure that the bomber would always get through and grew notably sarcastic at the suggestion that there were limits to the means of modern war. Believing in the power of peacetime legislation over the matter was, he pronounced, simply 'puerile'.[93] The employment of gas and the whole armoury of chemical weapons was inevitable.[94] Some years later, the Italian manoeuvres in May 1935 included a display of 'chemical warfare' that was appreciatively watched by Mussolini, Starace, Federzoni, Bottai and Badoglio. Mustard gas, phosphorous and more conventional smoke bombs were utilized for both defence and attack and the *Duce*, naturally first among the official party, was given the chance to hurl his own gas bombs. According to newspaper reports, the distance he achieved provoked spontaneous applause from the numerous audience, with the dictator evincing 'visible satisfaction at the effect of the power and the invisibility of the means being used'.[95]

Similarly, after Ethiopia had been invaded, it is easy enough to find Fascist journalists applauding the deployment of gas against the 'barbarous' enemy, with their ready, if unconvincing, moral counter being the charge that Italians were being killed by 'dum-dum' exploding bullets.[96] Earlier in the 1930s Fascist writers were also free to argue publicly that gas ought to remain in the national arsenal and to deny that its use was more atrocious than were other means of warfare.[97] The journal of the Air Ministry argued in time for the Decennale celebrations of 1932 that 'chemical warfare can be considered inevitable since a belligerent will never deliberately renounce a weapon which could prove influential on the duration and result of a conflict'. In its time, the writer reasoned, gunpowder had been regarded as a terrible weapon and one that could not be defeated.[98] By 1940 the dictatorship had laid down a considerable stock of chemical weapons, although, for reasons that may be debated, they were not actually employed in Fascism's Second World War.

In much of the historical literature, it is simply assumed that the brutal dictator, Mussolini, bears the responsibility for the production and deployment of gas as a weapon. 'Absolute terror', the *Duce* advised in his flashily rancorous way, was the best approach to governing Ethiopians.[99] Yet matters were not so simple. In the empire, the blame for the utilization of chemical weapons must be shared between Mussolini, his Fascists and the traditional Italian Army officer corps, especially those colonialist officers typified by Graziani and Badoglio (with some context provided by the fact that, at least before 1925, Britain in Mesopotamia and Afghanistan and France in Morocco had similarly not forborne to employ methods of state terror on 'tribesmen' opposing their control). It is telling, after all, if depressing, to find that the self-consciously modern and well-educated air force officers were the most directly involved in gas attacks.

Yet the more significant matter is the way in which the dictator, his henchmen, journalists and military men were possessed by a common *mentalité* about chemical weapons. Until the outbreak of the Second World War, those Italians involved in military discussion and schooled by Douhet[100] agreed that the atrocious could not be prevented and, as one put it in regard to bacteriological war, the 'end justified the means' (sic).[101] Even though they allowed the anti-aircraft protection of Italian cities to remain minimal, they concluded as a corollary of their imagining of coming battle that the civilian populations of cities devastated by conventional bombing were not to be distinguished morally from those who fell to an onslaught from chemical weapons. Killing, they reasoned, naturally found the shortest and most effective way to success. Any further moralizing about the matter was both hypocritical and pointless. The morality of war and peace, in other words, was simply that there was no morality.

Fascism, with its habitual use of the language of aggression – not for nothing did Mussolini regularly rejoice in his own savagery, seeing himself as a cat who walked by itself at night ready to scratch, claw and kill – deeply tinctured such thoughts and assumptions. Yet Fascism did not by itself create its bleakly Darwinian view of the functioning of the international system. Perhaps the relatively weak are automatically inclined to doubt the moral preaching of the powerful and to seek any way to gain ground, whether metaphorically or literally. The conclusion that we live in a wicked world is, after all, one that frequently does seem to fit the state of humankind.

In any case, from 1930 onwards, in the day-to-day world of diplomatic dealing, developments outside Italy, although to a degree influenced by the Fascist story, began to play a searchlight on the regime's position in Europe and so require that the fudging and contradiction possible until then be abandoned or adapted to changing circumstances and opportunities. In September 1930 the National Socialist German Workers Party, under the Austrian-born demagogue Adolf Hitler, suddenly won more than 100 seats in the German Reichstag. In the two elections of 1932 it more than doubled that total and, on 30 January 1933, the Nazi *Führer* was invited to become Chancellor of Germany. From then on every aspect of European politics was rendered unstable because of the menace of Nazism.

For Fascist Italy, there were a number of immediate ramifications in Hitler's rise. Hitler was a most unusual German nationalist and racist because, in a rare example of the infringement of his fanatically (pseudo-)scientific beliefs, he numbered Italy as among the natural friends of his new Germany.[102] Having outgrown his youthful view that one mediocre Wagner performance was worth a hundred Verdis and that Italian opera plots were full of 'knavery and self-deception' because that was the way of such a people,[103] Hitler treasured Mussolini's March on Rome as the act that had allowed him to glimpse the path to power. Italy he admired as the fount of the art he loved, the place of blue skies, Botticelli, Michelangelo and Raphael. A breathless contemplation of the 'greatness' of Italian painters, lasting in his view unchallenged 'from the fourteenth century to the seventeenth', could fill his table talk as late as June 1943. When his work was done, the *Führer* dreamed of touring Tuscany and Umbria: 'my dearest wish would be to be able to wander about Italy as an unknown painter'. To justify his Italophilia, Hitler had to convince himself that 'northern' Italians were somehow racially Aryan – 'from the cultural point of view', he once remarked, 'we are more closely linked with the Italians than with any other people'[104] – and that the veins of Mussolini, Dante and other heroes pulsed with no contaminating blood from the inferior 'Mediterranean race'.

According to most other racial theoreticians, Italians fell far short of the Nordic ideal. Moreover, Italy's betrayal of its Germanic allies of the Triple Alliance, feebleness in losing at Caporetto to Germanic armies, insatiability in demanding at the Paris peace-making that the German-speaking peasants of the South Tyrol be surrendered to its rule and harsh denationalization campaigns in such territories once Fascism had obtained power were more immediate proof to Germans that Italians were primordially and permanently inferior, a 'traitor people'. Hitler's pledge in 1938 that 'the question of the Alto Adige does not exist and will not exist while I am alive'[105] and that a population exchange should proceed despite its unpopularity among those moved off their ancestral land[106] had a double edge to it, given the implicit admission that it was only the *Führer* who stood against a more aggressive Nazi policy to match blood and soil wherever Germans lived. It is easy to forget that, for mainstream German nationalists, Italy, as much as Poland or Czechoslovakia, was a false victor of the Great War, a state that must be forced to disgorge the territory it had greedily swallowed in 1918–19. 'The whole Teutonic nation', a more orthodox commentator alleged, was committed to saving the people of the South Tyrol from their present fate, blighted by Fascist insistence on excising German-sounding names from tombstones and on cutting down German-style Christmas trees.[107] President Hindenburg was said, on his deathbed, to have warned Hitler against getting too close to the Italians.[108]

Italo-German bickering over Fascist Italianization policies in the Alto Adige had been one of the features of the 1920s and, especially in 1925–6, there were moments when the bilateral relationship seemed about to break down. Among almost all Italian policy-makers, there was one fundamental geo-political conclusion to the border dispute and that was that an *Anschluss*, a fusion of Germany with the post-war rump state of Austria, must be avoided. Such a union would return the full power of Germandom to the Brenner frontier and at once offer more direct and inviting sanctuary to any German-speakers in the province of Bolzano who dreamed of going home to the Reich. As Dino Grandi, then Under-Secretary for Foreign Affairs, told his diplomatic staff in 1927, Italy could never willingly accept an *Anschluss* and, he added with the habitual realism of Fascist and Italian diplomacy, borders must be defended with soldiers and guns, not treaties. This, he maintained, was a policy decision from which Italy 'would not retreat even a millimetre',[109] although four years later with Nazism on the rise[110] he thought more pessimistically that Italy's credible task was to delay the union of the 'Germanic race' as long as practicable. Well after the Nazis were entrenched in power, a reflex of Italian nationalist hostility to Germany can be detected in Fascist circles. In May 1935, for example, Giovanni Preziosi, the racist writer and client of Farinacci, complained noisily about alleged 'Pan German' plots in Bolzano. Everyone, he stated, knew that German policy from 'Barbarossa to Frederick [the Great] to Hitler . . . is one of the constant violation of pacts'.[111] In 1938 Massimo Magistrati, the Italian chargé in Berlin, warned that German interests still controlled the hotel industry of the Alto Adige and therefore its economic life and were working assiduously to preserve the local sense of German identity to Italy's present damage and later jeopardy.[112]

If Hitler's fondness for past masterpieces deflected what might otherwise have been a natural German hostility to post-war Italy, then the ideology of Fascism caused similar complications in regard to Italian reactions to the Nazi rise to power. As the 1920s came to a close, the debate about the universal merit or potential of the Fascist revolution grew. The meaning of an aphorism of the *Duce*'s that Fascism was 'not for export'[113] began to prove complex. The Nazi advance was one encouragement to think universally. The numerous retreats from the Wilsonian mixture of parliamentarism, liberal capitalism and benign nationalism (self-determination), which, by October 1938, left not a single liberal democracy surviving in all Europe outside its western fringe, were similarly influential in stimulating Italians to think that generic fascism might be 'the doctrine of the twentieth century', as the *Duce* took ambitiously to calling it. Mussolini's own brother Arnaldo, seeking cloudily to find means to persuade Italian youth that it was still manly and unflagging in its determination to change the world, was an early proponent of such ideas. He was joined by Giuseppe Bottai, always anxious to highlight some intellectual importance in Fascism (and himself), and by a number of younger journalists, of whom the most theoretical was Berto Ricci, from 1931 until its suppression in August 1935 editor of a journal entitled *L'Universale*. Then and later, until his death in war in 1941, Ricci, once a youthful prodigy in mathematics and a glamorous figure in the regime's literary scene, urged the creation of 'a coherent and intransigent Fascist totalitarianism'[114] which could 'absorb the whole man and all reality' and whose formulae would, with arithmetical precision, carry the same implications for all peoples. The Japanese, he was sure, in the clarity of their vision and the 'wise brutality' of their foreign dealings had much to teach Italy.[115] Certainly their approach was to be preferred to that of the feebly luxurious D'Annunzio and the silly Marinetti – Ricci, in his capacity as leader of a new generation, vented his sarcasm on the preciousness of the *Futurist Cookbook*.[116] Yet, for Ricci in his more benign moments, the present was seeing the death of both nationalism and Christianity; Fascism's destiny was to save Western civilization in what he foresaw as an osmotic process where other people naturally bowed to the ultimate greatness of Rome (and Mussolini). Such unlikely comprehensions of the world encouraged the formation of a Fascist 'International', which, after some years of discussion, was launched in 1934.

Most of its foreign members – such people as the Dutchman Simon Ooms and the Belgian Paul Hoornaert – were not destined to stun the world. A key lesson of the history of this International is that a relatively weak power is likely to find an international clientele that is similarly weak and uninfluential, while all the more urgently hungry for sympathy and subsidy. Yet one of the mostly unspoken targets of Fascist universalism was Nazi Germany. Italian backing for the International was designed to reassert the primacy of the Fascist revolution over its competitors and, more implicitly, anxiously acknowledge that the Germans were going further, faster and higher than the Italians had managed to do. From 1933 onwards it was no longer possible to be a 'fascist' in the same way as before.

In these circumstances of the need to conceal an actual loss of independence and significance, it is not surprising that direct Italian commentary on the Nazi rise was textured in character, emitting more than one message. Roberto Farinacci, with his habitual bravado at claiming Italian significance which, in October 1931, prompted him to argue that Mahatma Gandhi had something of the Fascist in him given the Indian pacifist's 'profoundly mystical soul' and his historic role as 'the most formidable enemy of the Empire which English history records',[117] oscillated in attitude. When, in September 1932, it seemed possible that the Nazi star might be waning, Farinacci wrote at some length on the differences between the two movements. The Italians were more intelligently anti-socialist than were the Nazis, he explained knowingly, and understood Catholicism and its universality better. It would be good if the Nazis did obtain power in Germany, he still supposed, because they had pledged their friendship for Italy. Yet these Germans had a lot to learn. In any case it should be remembered that they were no more the identical twins of Fascism than the now defunct dictatorship of Miguel Primo de Rivera had once been in Spain.[118]

When Hitler did take office, Farinacci welcomed the triumph of such 'healthy' and 'energetic' elements, praiseworthily determined to root out 'the subversives',[119] but, rather than repining too much on the matter, his attention soon switched to the Four Power Pact or the Patto Mussolini (a plan to establish a directorate of Italy, Germany, Britain and France and engage in a review of the Europe which had resulted from the First World War settlement) as Farinacci knew it must be called in Italy. This diplomatic arrangement, allowing revision of the provisions of the Versailles peace-making, was, he claimed, a victory both of realism and of Fascist idealism and was, Farinacci may not have been especially chuffed to know, openly approved by the Vatican.[120] It was proof that 'a new Word and Spirit [Verbo] are of their own account spreading in the world, the Spirit of resurrection, life, harmony, development, order and civilization'.[121] It demonstrated that, through yet another Mussolinian miracle, Rome was now 'the centre of international policy'.[122]

Farinacci's bombast is as it may be but the interpretation of the framing of the Four Power Pact remains an issue of debate among historians. For those who see Mussolini as recklessly embarked along a superhighway to war, it is the talk about treaty revision and the likelihood that the Duce was seeking to cover his back before assaulting Ethiopia which matters.[123] For those who instead detect Realpolitik in the line pursued by the Duce and his counsellors, the treaty constituted a sensible effort at compromise and it is to be regretted that neither Britain nor France made much effort to run with it.[124] One American historian even wondered whether the Pact might not have been a sort of NATO before its time.[125]

Certainly the treaty was a failure and some token of the Fascist understanding of its now exposed position to a Germany on the march was evident when, in September 1933, following an earlier commercial deal, Italy signed a new friendship and non-aggression arrangement with the USSR.[126] Surveillance of favourable expressions about Nazism within Italy, for example among German expatriates, now increased in zeal.[127] That the times were tricky was further demonstrated during the next year in Hitler's first and demonstrably unsuccessful trip to salute Mussolini at Venice in June and then, dramatically, in the vicious slaying by local Nazis of Austrian chancellor Engelbert Dollfuss in July, while his wife and children were house guests of the Mussolinis at Riccione.[128] Fascist authorities reacted by rushing troops through Italy's own German-speaking lands to the Brenner frontier but found that no other European power was as ready as they were actively to block an *Anschluss* (even though Hitler for the moment forswore his Austrian friends). The xenophobic journal *Stirpe Italica* set the tone for the moment with a cartoon of a Balilla kicking a monster with a swastika on its back over the border.[129] Even in March 1935, journalists, still equipped with an anti-'Hun' vocabulary much used in the First World War, were stating roundly that the 'German mentality' was unchanged in its 'crudity, discourtesy and brutality'.[130]

At a more practical level, to a Fascist mind but perhaps also to an Italian one, the message was plain. With the Nazis at large, the world had become a realm in which the devil would take the hindmost. Ideas half-thought, an ideology half-framed, plans half-sketched, ambitions half-repressed, had come into their own. In December 1934 Mussolini committed his regime certainly to the dismemberment and perhaps the total conquest of Ethiopia. A border was transgressed both physically and conceptually. From 1935 the Italian dictatorship would pursue, and sometimes lead, the path to aggressive war.

In mid-May 1935 a French zoologist provided a token for these new times. At that moment, most of the Fascist press still wrote as though Italy were the friend, all things considered, of Britain and France and, whatever the divergencies in their ostensible ideologies, the three Western powers were virtuously working to contain Nazi German fanaticism, especially when it was directed against Austria.

The trip by French Foreign Minister Pierre Laval to Rome in January and the Stresa meeting of the leaders of Britain, France and Italy in April, supplementing the not-quite-forgotten Four Power Pact, although naturally depicted in Fascist circles as the result of Mussolini's toughness, farsightedness and genius, seemed to express a Europe which had not yet opted for diplomatic revolution. As a sign of the recent rapprochement with Italy's 'Latin sister', France, M. Bourdel, the director of the Paris zoo, followed his political chiefs to Rome. There, along with the directors of such institutions at places as potentially antithetical to Fascism as Prague and Barcelona, he attended a ceremony with the *Duce* himself, who, accompanied as so often by Bottai, congratulated himself on the expansion and modernization of the facilities at the Rome zoo. The place – party rhetoric maintained with some lack of originality – was another masterpiece of Fascist order and modernization. The Frenchman had brought a present to celebrate such progress and especially the improvements prompted by the Decennale in the ape and monkey cages.[131] In retrospect, however, it might be thought a more resonant gift than Bourdel and its recipients had understood. It was a gorilla.[132]

I I

Going to the people

In July 1932, as if in reaction to the huge Nazi gains in the recent German elections, there had been a major reshuffle, pompously called a 'changing of the guard' by regime propagandists, in the Fascist government. Grandi lost the Ministry of Foreign Affairs, and was shortly afterwards to be sent as ambassador to the court of St James in London, where he would seek to ingratiate himself both with his hosts and with his *Duce*, an increasingly tricky task. Fulvio Suvich, before the war an irredentist and later a nationalist and natively suspicious of Germany and Hitler, was promoted to become Under-Secretary. His new Minister of Foreign Affairs was Benito Mussolini.

As the years passed, external affairs were destined to intrude more and more inescapably into the functioning of the Italian dictatorship. Yet, for the moment, as important a signal about the behaviour and purpose of the regime was the change at the Ministry of Corporations. There Giuseppe Bottai was dropped from command. Instead, the *Duce* assumed ministerial control over what Bottai and other Fascist propagandists were portraying as the dynamo driving Fascist development, while at the same time making Italy a fairer society, one where all workers and peasants were watched over and safeguarded by government. Mussolini was to take charge while the corporate state was finally cemented into place. As Bottai, even out of office, explained it, corporatism constituted 'the revolution in the Revolution'. It was, he wrote, 'perhaps the principal element determining the perennial, permanent and inexorable' character of Fascist rule. Philosopher Giovanni Gentile agreed that corporatism demonstrated that a genuine democracy had been installed in Fascist Italy, no longer a prey to corrupt and 'anarchoid' politicians but in real touch with the people.[1] It ensured that the party was 'the centre of national life'. It pledged Fascist democracy, Fascist equality, Fascist social justice and, according to one expert whose internationalist enthusiasms would allow him to convert to Christian Democracy after 1945, might even prove the ideal recipe for the world economy.[2] The corporate state signalled that the dictatorship had overcome 1789 and all that; it lay at the heart of the Fascist revolution.

The corporate state was also the quintessence of totalitarianism. By the end of 1933, with the framing of a new law on corporations to be promulgated on 5 February 1934, an observer could no longer find 'any political, economic and cultural activity which the party did not back, encourage and control, directing to the farthest sectors [of Italian life] the hot breath of the Fascist spirit'.[3] In 1935 Bottai was again urging that corporatism must penetrate every business, industrial or rural, since otherwise Fascism 'will never have a corporative economic policy'.[4] With the invasion of Ethiopia in its final planning, Bottai scorned those who wanted to draft too accurate a budget on the matter. Italy, he pronounced, was acting out of its revolutionary will. 'The party branch, which is the principle and instrument of political unity, and the Corporation, which is the means of social and economic unity, are what inspire our drive towards power.'[5]

Anti-Fascists in exile at the time and most economic historians since have dismissed such claims as mere verbiage. They have contended that the corporate state was little more than a sham, at best a work in very slow progress since the Chamber of Fasces and Corporations, which had long been slated to oust the outdated parliamentary system, did not actually do so until 1939 and then with considerable ambiguity. In his classic study *Under the axe of Fascism* (1936), Gaetano Salvemini poked fun at the long succession of announcements from Mussolini, Bottai and others that the 'real' corporate system was about to be born. Such talk, he argued, amounted to 'the great humbug'; in truth there was no genuine corporate state. In the Italian economy, any advantage always and automatically went to the bosses. 'Don Quixote attacked windmills as if they were real monsters; Mussolini', Salvemini judged, 'deals with real monsters [those who own the means of production] as if they were windmills.'[6]

Who, then, was right, Salvemini, or Bottai and the regime propagandists? Certainly the law of February 1934 did give official birth to twenty-two corporations, each meant to express the needs and contribution of a different sector of the economy through a vertically structured alliance of employers and workers. Although the clauses of the 'Law on the formation and functions of the Corporations' were careful to leave space for the authority of the dictator and his appointees and the new system was no revolution impelled from below, none the less the reform did proclaim that the corporations had now taken over the management of much economic life. Wages, conditions, production, the settling of any labour disputes, all fell to them.[7]

Just how much was the cherished freedom of finance, business and property being infringed? One organization whose history may help to answer this question is the Istituto per la Ricostruzione Industriale (Institute for the Reconstruction of Industry, IRI), set up in January 1933. Favoured by such regime technocrats as Alberto Beneduce, trained as a statistician, a former southern client of F. S. Nitti who had readily adapted to the dictatorship (but only joined the PNF in 1940), and Guido Jung, the Sicilian Jew who was Minister of Finance from July 1932 to January 1935, IRI was created to bail out those banks which had stumbled into deficit because of the world economic crisis. Through its provision of credit, IRI was soon appointing managers over a wide range of the national economy. The companies in its charge included car manufacturer Alfa Romeo and many banks, as well as those heavy industrial concerns most closely linked to the preparations for war. This state intervention was initially conceived of as 'temporary', necessary simply because the Istituto Mobiliare Italiano, founded under Beneduce in 1931 to channel funds to business, had proved inadequate as the economic slowdown worsened.[8]

The 'temporary' soon drifted towards the permanent, however, since no real financial recovery eventuated in Italy. The cascade of conflicts in Ethiopia, Spain, Albania and the Second World War washed away any path that might lead towards economic normality. Adventures abroad ensured that, during the second half of the 1930s, the national economic line became autarchic, that is, rigorously protectionist, seeking external trade through barter rather than some free arrangement which might have been approved by Adam Smith.

IRI can thus be read as an attempt at totalitarian control over the economy (and a telephone tap did hear Agnelli complaining that, through such a body, businessmen would be driven to help the government rather than, as was more meet and proper, being helped by it.)[9] The alternative view of the matter is to see IRI as an accidental umbrella under which Italian owners found it convenient to shelter from the rigours of free competition. Certainly business showed little sign of wanting to be weaned from the state nourishment it was receiving. IRI did not close in 1945; even in the 1960s it was still esteemed in some circles the best explanation of the economic miracle of the new Republic.

The prominence and pervasiveness of IRI also allowed industrialists and bankers to draw profits from Fascist aggression, without taking or seeming to take responsibility for such policy. This cover, which might in time prove useful, may help to explain why, in their official statements, most Italian businessmen went along with rapturous regime accounts of the way corporatism bound Italians together in a Fascist whole, contented bosses and workers alike, eradicated selfishness and terminated any need for special interest groups. None the less, somewhere in the recesses of the business mind, suspicions lurked that, while the dictator grew ever more insistent about 'going towards the people', the state might yet become too 'social'. Fascist intellectuals, as they polished their own ideals either out of fanaticism or the more commonplace desire to appear acute and avant-garde, might countenance the serious infringement of individual rights to private property. Those with a head for business needed to be alert against such heresy.

One place where worries about over-zealous government surfaced, however much in Nicodemic or indirect phrasing, was the journal of the building and real estate industry, *La Proprietà Edilizia*. A scanning of it provides fine evidence of the way in which special interest groups survived in Fascist Italy and sought to adapt the rhetoric of totalitarianism to their own advantage. *La Proprietà Edilizia* was edited by the economist Bernardo Attilio Genco, with help from the *nobile* Enrico Parisi, an aristocrat who held the post of Commissioner of the corporative Federazione Nazionale Fascista della Proprietà Edilizia (nobles retained quite a presence in Fascist power elites).[10] Through

the 1930s Genco and Parisi tried to laud the triumphs of the corporate state and yet cling to more liberal-sounding ideas about the
sacred nature of private property and the undesirability of too strict
government controls over it. Genco welcomed the announcement in
December 1930 of a nationwide 10 per cent cut in rents as the economy slowed (proof that the unfreezing by the regime, still attracted to
liberal economics, of wartime controls in 1926 had not been a success
socially).[11] Genco underlined the discipline with which proprietors
had accepted their loss to the general benefit to the nation, buffeted by
the world economic crisis. He did, however, add the humble suggestion that interest rates might now also be lowered and sedulously cited
his *Duce*, when Mussolini promised in his abrupt but not always consistent fashion that 'the State, in the future, will abstain from any further intervention, whether direct or indirect, in rental contracts'.[12]

Parisi drew a sentimental portrait of the marvellous moment when
Mussolini addressed industry spokesmen amid the luminous
surrounds of his new office at Palazzo Venezia. He did not, however,
forget to highlight the message that 'freedom to negotiate rents is now
consecrated as the unbreakable basic principle of Fascist housing policy'. 'Nostalgia for tied arrangements,' he ran on, with his own views
by no means abandoned to the apparently overweening dictator,
'whether half-concealed or for special purposes, has received the most
categorical condemnation. So a demagogic rump, always ready to
cabal, are silenced.'[13] Some months later, the Federazione's journal
published another swingeing attack on what it sarcastically deemed
the *animus garibaldinus* of tenants. Such people liked to moan about
landlords who had found ways around the 10 per cent reduction
when the likelihood was that the thrifty owner was still waiting for
the 90 per cent owed him.[14] As he lobbied in his industry's favour,
Genco did not forget to summon the ghosts of great men past to the
cause of property-owners. Arnaldo Mussolini was one *grande Estinto*
in his armoury of apposite citation,[15] Enrico Corradini another.[16]

It was true that prominent Fascists, like the Procurator General,
Senator Silvio Longhi, sounded of some menace when they defined the
essence of corporatism as being that 'the state recognizes and safe-
guards individual property rights so long as they are not being exercised in a way which contravenes the prevailing collective interest'.

Under-utilized land in the countryside, for example, so listeners to the party rural radio broadcast were informed, could be expropriated where need be. It was not, the party spokesman hastened to add, that Fascism in any way 'lacked respect for property and for private initiative'. It was just that corporatism required that all Italians put the overall interests of the nation first.[17]

Mussolini usually did his best publicly to distance himself from what might be read as the threat implicit in such language. In his 1933 meeting with the industrialist Alberto Pirelli, who was acting for the association of Italian shareholders, the *Duce* acknowledged that Fascism rested on the ownership of property and, having overthrown socialism, was adamant in rejecting all types of collectivism.[18] It was thus not so vexing for Genco to pilot a satisfying verbal path around the problem of the Fascist stance on property by maintaining that the role of the state in the corporate system was not a malignly bureaucratic and redistributional one. Rather, 'in the field of business', Fascism 'avoids licence on the one hand and coercion on the other'. Private initiative was not 'mortified' but helped to see its own interests, as 'bound into those of the nation'. The real purpose of corporatism, Genco argued in the phrases of the lobbyist down the ages, was efficiency and productivity, since Fascism demanded above all the end of petty quarrels between interest groups.[19] Proprietors were not to be pushed around by the state but encouraged to be active participants in national economic growth. Fascism, it was claimed, had nothing to do with 'rigid and intransigent protectionism'.[20] As the industrialist Ettore Conti similarly averred in words which would soon need swallowing, Italians and Fascists were too practical a people ever to be seduced by the idea of a closed economy. 'Even the Chinese behind their Great Wall were not really autarchic,' he declared. 'Of genuine practitioners of autarchy, history only knows cavemen and hermits in the desert.'[21]

But, with the passage of the years, the drift to autarchy was difficult to deny. In the summer of 1934 rents were again lowered by government decree,[22] and in March 1937 Parisi had the task of justifying a rent and price freeze. It was all a matter of the special moment, he explained, and could be accepted given that Italy had the blessings of 'a strong government, the Fascist one, which can rely on its huge prestige and its massive means for propaganda'. But he still found space to warn that, should movement develop in the rest of the economy and something like normal times return, then a prolongation of the freeze could only harm the whole building industry.[23]

Yet normality was far away. As early as 1935 the real estate industry journal published an ominous piece about how best to build safely and securely in an age vulnerable to aerial bombing. The author not altogether comfortingly urged that key industrial and military sites should be scattered around a city, made indistinguishable from apartments and so able to fool an eager bomber, while adding that it should be obligatory to provide an air-raid shelter in each building, capable of giving sanctuary to twenty or thirty people.[24]

Words and deeds bounced uneasily off each other. For all the drift towards a war economy, Fascist writers still felt obliged to argue that Mussolini's regime was based on the private ownership of property. The prominent journalist Corrado Masi said as much during the summer of 1937, when he contrasted the comfort and safety of home, where the individual right to property provided the foundations of 'the grandiose edifice of the new Italian Civilization', with the bestiality of 'red' Spain, where commissars indulged their savage and dystopian will against the property-owning classes.[25] In the privacy of his study, Mussolini might on occasion dream of 'social Fascism' and, after 1943, hope to preside over a real social revolution. Until then, however, Fascism held back from launching a full-blooded assault on individual ownership. Corporatism, although it may have sometimes constrained Italian business and although autarchy may have dragooned rich Italians in ways they disliked, entailed no serious leap towards a collectivized economy. If Italian society and culture were, by the late 1930s, being jostled out of some established grooves, the change was coming not through permanent Fascist economic revolution, as Bottai for one liked to claim, but rather from permanent Fascist, Italian and Mussolinian war.

Economic life doubtless had its special style and rhythms but conditioning all activity in Fascist Italy was charisma. The spell-binding power which allegedly emanated from Mussolini, the infallible, numinous, ubiquitous, transcendent and, by the later 1930s, ever more bellicose dictator, meant that rationality could never dominate thought for too long. The longer the regime lasted, the more its hired pens pumped out an endless stream of words, which mattered, or were said to matter, more than any facts.

The process of constructing an imagined dictator, an empyrean *Duce* beyond all others, had begun very early in the dictatorship, with the approval and assistance of Mussolini but not through his work alone.[26] Words were not the only building blocks of this dictator's image. Photographers clicked away at the militant and now frequently helmeted warrior-chief. Mussolini's baldness was made to shine with masculinity, determination, aggression and combat, in direct contrast with the luxuriant locks which Fascist fashion demanded for the female head. The threatening nakedness of the *Duce*'s pate is perhaps the only place where his posthumous charisma outshines that of Hitler. The *Führer*'s prim toothbrush moustache, so brilliantly mocked by Charlie Chaplin, droops by comparison.

As the personality cult inexorably spread, the first purpose of all pictures and words was to heighten the leader's mystical charm. In 1939 a lexicographer published a 'Mussolinian dictionary', plugging it as a 'manual of practical use for every private and para-state business', since it allowed a reader to recover the dictator's endlessly profound thoughts on anything.[27] Just mentioning the leader's name was enough, according to prominent journalist Ottavio Dinale, since 'Mussolini' had universal resonance. The Decennale Exhibition had been summed up in 'Him' (the use of the capital letter in such reference was now *de rigueur*), Dinale maintained. 'The Revolution is Him. He is the Revolution.' Similarly, *Duce* and his capital city were but one whole. 'Rome is where the *Duce* is, it is in Him, with Him, in His divinations, in His struggles, in His torments, in His will, in His many creations.'[28] Another more downmarket writer deemed Mussolini eponymous with the century, 'a GENIUS. He is the GENIUS who brings good fortune to the Italic people.'[29]

Just who consumed this portentous guff, apart from Mussolini and his tame intellectuals, must remain doubtful – neither then nor after 1945 were Italians great readers (Bottai on one occasion noted unctuously that acquiring a taste for reading was a 'delicate and mysterious' matter[30] and so unlikely, it was implied, to be a matter for everyone and everyday). Myriads of photographs and newsreels were undoubtedly more powerful than books in illuminating the leader's divinity. Perhaps the most effective verbal means of inscribing the *Duce*'s charisma were the regime's quiver of slogans: 'Better to live one day as a lion than one hundred years as a sheep', 'we go straight ahead', 'book and rifle, perfect Fascist', 'let's arm ourselves and you go and fight', the almost comically Freudian 'it is the plough that makes fecund the land and the sword that defends it' and, most commonly, 'Believe, obey, fight', 'Mussolini is always right' and 'the world belongs to us'. Such jingles, in themselves no sillier or falser than those that capitalist consumerism was spreading from Madison Avenue, well suited the PNF in the age of Starace. Under his aegis, membership rocketed up to record levels, reaching the two million mark in 1937. This mass party could now scarcely aspire to be a disciplined vanguard commanding the nation towards a united destiny. Instead it was a dumbed-down flock, chanting party patter, content with circuses and some bread, offered ambiguous hope through corruption and war.

The domination of the dictator's image might not be helpful for the transmitting of Fascist ideology into Italian hearts and minds. In many circles, Mussolinism began to outweigh Fascism. Despite the modernity of its propaganda means, the personality cult confirmed the ancient lore of the good king, waylaid by bad counsellors, guilty of the world's continuing injustice.

Even if warmed by his own charisma, for the most part Mussolini remained a careful politician. To bolster the rodomontades and the advertising, the leader took pains to employ a personal secretariat, which received correspondence from hundreds of thousands of Italian citizens. With his deepening cynicism, the *Duce* employed a 'reserved' section of this office to store near at hand multiplying accounts of the corruption and vice of his oldest followers and closest friends. Any dipping into the secretariat's 'ordinary' files, by contrast, reveals an Italian public which, at first sight, seems won over by the Fascist religion, happy to pray to and so petition the *Duce* as they might to God. A vast number of correspondents begged no more than a signed photo of their leader, as a holy image, the icon watching over their home and happiness.

Yet a hope among ordinary people that they could control and manipulate their own lives had not been suppressed and it peeps out from these files too.

During the Second World War, Margherita Vivarelli, for example, the wife of a Sienese lawyer and Fascist who had been killed on the Yugoslav front in April 1942, initially requested just a signed photo. She approached the *Duce* through the president of the local bank, the Monte dei Paschi di Siena, and the local prefect, who charitably noted that she was of 'unblemished political and moral conduct' and reiterated Lavinio Vivarelli's distinguished career as a Fascist, his untimely death and the present struggle of his surviving family, rendered harsher by the fact that the Vivarellis were 'declined members of the local patriciate'. The result was that Signora Vivarelli received a special subsidy of 25,000 lire, for which – it was the summer of 1943 – she politely gave much thanks: Lavinio Vivarelli had passed on to her and their children 'a pure and lofty faith' and they were 'ready and resolved to serve the Fascist cause with all our passion so long as we live'.[31] Her gratitude was reasonable since the sum granted was fifty times the monthly widow's pension that was her formal due.

Those from further down the social order did not always possess the verbal finesse that Margherita Vivarelli could summon to explain her conduct nor could they rely on the contacts that guaranteed her virtue and smoothed her path to monetary compensation. But a canny search for financial gain was present, too, among the poor and meek. Some sought employment: Emilia Torcellan, a jobless Venetian mother of two, not married to her unemployed waiter companion and portrayed as hot-headed and given to careless talk about herself going to Rome directly to beseech her *Duce*, was told that she could register with the prefect and so soon expect her ideal reward, a cleaning job at the city casino.[32] Enrichetta Petronio, from a village in Istria and described as belonging to a family in desperate poverty, sought and received funding to buy a new sewing machine and so amend her present status as an unemployed seamstress.[33] Giuseppe Bonasoro, a father of twenty from Brindisi (only ten of his children were living), writing in 1927 when Fascist demographic policy was just getting under way, requested either a subsidy or a signed photograph. Despite his pledge of possessing a 'purely Fascist soul' and a profound admiration for Mussolini's 'work for the nation', Bonasoro had to make do with the photo. His further petition in 1936 for tax exemption got nowhere. Perhaps he should not have expatiated in his original appeal about his limitless devotion both to the *Duce* and to King Victor Emmanuel III and all the royal family?[34]

Italians were not the only ones endeavouring to ingratiate themselves with the dictator. Eric Campbell, the leader of the New Guard of New South Wales but too minor a figure to star in the Fascist International, in 1933 expressed gratification at the signed photo that he had received, promising to have it 'suitably framed'. Helped by a *raccomandazione* by Oswald Mosley, who introduced him as 'the chief of the Australian fascists', Campbell had drawn from a recent visit to Italy, he noted respectfully, 'knowledge and inspiration'. 'The New Guard', he felt obliged to add, 'is entirely Fascist in its endeavours to solve the moral problem which confronts the people of the Continent [of Australia], but its politics are necessarily adapted to the needs and psychology of our people here.'[35] Another foreigner to rejoice in his receipt of a signed photo, in his case an extra large one, was Jiang Jieshi (Chiang Kai-shek), head of the Nationalist forces in China, in 1934 still viewed as a natural friend of Italy.[36]

Those who wrote to their *Duce* had, it is clear, many different motives but each correspondent was impelled by the belief that he or she could arouse the dictator's personal interest. The letter-writers reckoned that Mussolini was a potential weapon to be deployed in the everyday battle for life and in contests with their neighbours. They approached the great man in some awe, no doubt, and in some belief in Fascism. Yet it was neither a credulous belief nor a frozen awe. Rather, as they made contact with Mussolini, these ordinary Italians sought to wheedle the dictatorship into serving them. Each man and woman was making his or her own Fascism, one where the pay-off was always more important than the belief.

A simpler way to adapt Fascist governance fruitfully to individual and family advantage was through crime and fraud, a choice that can be located in other dictatorships. Sheila Fitzpatrick has written incisively about the role of 'tricksters' in Stalin's USSR,[37] those who, like the Ostap Bender portrayed in Ilf and Petrov's picaresque set of short stories,[38] aimed to make hay no matter how dimly the Soviet sun might shine.

It is easy to locate similar cases in Fascist Italy, individuals who, in hope of enhancing their fortunes or status, let it be known in this bar or that hotel that they were agents of OVRA (the Fascist secret police),[39] were secretly helping some other police section[40] or, in deep cover, were acting for the party in one capacity or another. At Savona, the down-and-out Alcide Landini tried to make a splash with claims of the rich rewards given to secret agents, among whom, he intimated incredibly, was himself.[41] More elaborate was the scam attempted by three Neapolitans who, during the summer of 1936, toured the hinterland of Modena looking for what they said were contributions to the cost of forwarding gift copies of the *Scritti e discorsi di Benito e Arnaldo Mussolini* to offices of the Fasci all'estero. They kept the money, and failed to appease their arresting officer with the plea that only the prolongation of sanctions had prevented them from posting the books abroad as they had promised.[42]

Rather more ambitious and, for quite a time, more lucrative was the scheme of Anita Fabbri, a pensioner from Rocca San Casciano in the Romagna. Through her elaborate con-job, which worked productively for over four years, Fabbri extracted hundreds of thousands of lire from her business clients by boasting close personal contact with Rachele Mussolini. She invented a person known as 'Rosina', who spoke on the phone to her gulls in a heavy local accent, the better to prove that she was an intimate of the *Duce*'s wife, bolstering her claim that she had regularly visited the leading family at their Villa Torlonia in Rome. Her success demonstrates how eagerly Italians believed that the Fascist system, belying its words about purity, could be corruptly manipulated for their gain through contacts and *raccomandazioni*.[43] The Fabbri file also offers an intriguing glimpse into Italian gender and religious histories. In September 1935 Anita Fabbri confessed her financial misdeeds to none other than the knowing and well-connected Jesuit Father, Pietro Tacchi Venturi. At least according to the police report, Tacchi Venturi advised this erring daughter of the Church to confess all, first to her husband. But Signora Fabbri could not bring herself to do that and it was the police who, at the end of 1935, caught up with her.

A more bathetic effort to augment his local importance by alleging contact with the Mussolini family was made by Giuseppe Sturano of

Rho. This youthful insurance salesman and member of the town band was to the fore in local Fascist events. However, he received a year's *confino* at Agnone in the Molise after he was heard boasting that he had been a personal guest of the *Duce* at the Villa Torlonia. He stated that he had found the leader aged and suffering from diabetes, but welcoming. After all, he added ambiguously, Mussolini had met Sturano's mother when the two were together in Zurich (at about the time Sturano was conceived).[44]

It must be assumed that Rachele Mussolini knew nothing about the Fabbri stratagem and that Benito Mussolini had not bedded Signora Sturano. But, in another case, financial chicanery can be traced near to the *Duce* or at least to his son-in-law, Ciano, and his family. Giovanni Gastone Conti, during the late 1930s, earned fame and respect as a man-about-town in Bologna. Conti, who had begun as a poor cobbler in Verona and had left his original family there, lived like a gentleman in his new city. His improved lifestyle was financed through his widespread reputation as a mediator. A number of local businesses regularly paid for his services. His spiel was to say that, as an old party member and sometime squadrist (the police would dispute these claims), he rejoiced in contacts in the highest places. As proof, he was given to letting his clients glimpse his two notebooks, crammed with the personal phone numbers of the regime's elite. He could also exhibit a file of appreciative letters, which, he alleged, guaranteed his network.

The game was to extract quite a bit of money in Bologna and its surrounds, with Conti asking to be paid for his necessary expenses in the current deal and for a generous *pourboire* beyond that. Spheres where promises were typically made were in regard to military and civil service transfers (as ever Italians felt the need to be alert lest they were obliged to serve somewhere lacking in civilization). Advantage might also be won over government contracts, especially when involving rule in Africa Orientale Italiana (AOI – Italian East Africa), where government expenditure was great and the contracting process opaque. Eventually the moment came when Conti and client travelled to Rome and met, in his impressively opulent office, a lawyer, Giovanni Colmayer, who happened to be the uncle of Massimo Magistrati, himself the brother-in-law of Ciano and a diplomat long stationed at Berlin. Colmayer's role, in a scene which seems drawn from some *commedia dell'arte* play or from Ben Jonson's *Volpone*, was to lament that the mediation had, after all, not worked and to hint that, you never knew, but with more time and more generous funding, it still might.[45] The police report on the matter was severe but Conti only received two years' *confino* and that in Avellino province, not very far to the south. The problem, officials at the prefecture noted, was that despite the public hostility aroused by the scandal, Colmayer, 'who bore the greater responsibility in the matter', had been let off with a warning.[46] The police did not commit to the record their explanation as to why leniency might have been granted such a personage as the uncle of the brother-in-law of the son-in-law of the *Duce*.

A poorer and less adroit manipulator of contacts on high was Vittorio Contarini, whose wife, Velia Tartagni, was 'niece to the cousin of Signora GUIDI, Augusta, the sister of Her Excellency Donna Rachele Mussolini', as the police report politely put it. Contarini was a clerk who had built a friendship with his wife's older cousin, the warmth of the contact not being hampered by the fact that Augusta Guidi was 'all but illiterate'. With the outbreak of war, tightened employment regulations prevented Contarini from moving to what he deemed a better job. His answer was to type a letter, emphasizing Augusta's support for his cause and bearing a postscript: 'Signora Guidi is the sister of Her Excellency Donna Rachele Mussolini'. Contarini chivalrously declared that, in so doing, he had acted without Augusta Guidi's knowledge but admitted that he had in any case sent her a cheque for two hundred lire as a thank-you. His punishment was harsh, compared with that dispensed in the cases so far reviewed – three years on the bleak Tremiti islands. He was still serving there in July 1943.[47] Contarini had crossed into territory too far beyond the legitimate borders of his 'family'. In his case, if not in that of Colmayer, Fascist law obtained. It did so as much because of Contarini's naivety and ignorance in 'placing' himself, as because of the totalitarian control over Italian life.

These endeavours by various paths, gainful or not, to imagine and to harness a useful Mussolini from below do not mark the end of the complications a historian can trace during the Fascist dictatorship in the people's absorption of the leader's charisma. Mussolini's image may well have penetrated Italian dreams but, whatever their fervour in reciting a Fascist liturgy, Italians cleaved to some other Gods but Him. Until 1943 Italy remained a monarchy. King Victor Emmanuel III may have been too parsimonious and wordless a figure to attract a surfeit of popular attention and love. Cannily he may even have resisted the temptations of nationalism in 1935 when he transferred much of the family funds to Hambros in London.[48] Yet inevitably he was often present at ceremonial events and journalists seldom forgot for long that the *Re Vittorioso* (the ever-victorious king; his name might be a standard for the nation)[49] embodied Italy in his own way. In 1925, for example, the town folk of Bergamo were said to have been overwhelmed with emotion at a royal visit, while the King was alleged to have mentioned his own happy memory of the trip at a later reception. All in all, this event, so a local account ran, demonstrated that 'our city, if not at the top, is certainly able to compete with the most attractive and impressive of urban centres'.[50] The monarch's charisma, in other words, could mysteriously affirm Bergamo's own past, present and future; it may have been inferior currency to that of the *Duce*'s but it did possess some potency.

As the regime tightened its control over national life, the monarch did not vanish as a source of meaning. In the Trentino in 1930 the local scouts were, it was hoped, enthralled by a lengthy tale of Italian heroism in the First World War embodied in two boys, one called Vittorio and the other Emanuele.[51] In 1935 *Il Legionario*, the journal directed at Italians abroad and edited by Piero Parini, the head of the Fasci all'estero, called for a general hurrah, a *Viva il Re!*, for Victor Emmanuel III, 'because he is the King of Victory, the heroic and wise King who, every time the *Patria* has been threatened by tragedy, has had a sublime pride in his people's *virtù* and a serene intuition of the strength and genius of his men. He is the King before whom all flags wave. The black-shirted people of Italy venerate him.'[52] Victor Emmanuel's birthdays – especially when he turned sixty in 1929 and seventy a decade later – occasioned florid articles in the press, placing him, where constitutionally to 1943 he was, at the summit of the nation, even if journalists usually remembered to ascribe the active greatness of his victorious era to the *Duce*.

The royal family was numerous. Queen Elena was statuesque and, despite what the snobbish claimed were her rustic Montenegrin origins, was not out of place at the opening of fashion shows and other high society events. She duly presided at the fifth Mostra della Moda, which began receiving visitors at a slightly inauspicious moment in April 1935.[53] *Il Legionario* transmitted to its readers an image of Elena as 'the Pious Samaritan', 'because the Queen, from the height of her throne, has always known how to kneel in mercy towards the humble and weak so that her sweet name, despite its connection with much intellectual work, is, for the whole nation, covered by the mystic aureole of her mercy and goodness'.[54] The Queen was much to the fore at charitable ceremonies, even though her penny-pinching husband grumbled that she was far too generous to those whom he viewed as the undeserving poor.[55] For schoolchildren, Elena's birthday, 8 January, was a holiday which, only two days after Befana (Epiphany), the usual time of present-giving in families, could readily be linked to the Queen's charity. It was true that, by the 1930s, the regime talked about the Befana Fascista and children were encouraged to exalt their *Duce* as the greatest gift to the nation. But an eclectic comprehension of bounty survived in one little girl from the Trentino, who ornamented her room with photos of the King, the Queen, the Duchess of Aosta, Mussolini and the local hero, Cesare Battisti.[56]

Umberto, the son and heir of Victor Emmanuel and Elena, was tall and arguably good-looking – one colonialist journal deemed him 'the handsomest prince in the world'.[57] By the 1930s the Prince of Piedmont, as he was titled, was a regular and much photographed presence at military parades. Umberto's wife, Maria José, a Belgian (at their marriage in 1929, Fascist federations were instructed to send them appropriate gifts 'in an absolutely voluntary and spontaneous fashion'),[58] was beautiful and fecund. It was reported that Maria José was a concert-standard pianist whose playing had been praised by Paderewski.[59] Her short and boyish haircut was viewed critically by the more patriarchal Fascists as too encouraging to female liberation.[60] Her stylishly slim and athletic appearance was, however, imitated enthusiastically by such other young women as Edda Mussolini-Ciano, anxious to modernize their looks, bodies and lives. Queen Elena's tresses, by contrast, remained traditionally long and luxuriant, allowing experts to follow their fancy in designing appropriately regal hairstyles on public occasions. For her part Maria José did her bit for Fascism and propriety by allowing herself to be photographed for ONMI breast-feeding.[61] In so doing, she gave an example to better-off women to behave as their social inferiors had always done and helped favour the sonorous, if not always successful, Fascist campaign firmly to regulate Italian mothering techniques.

Victor Emmanuel's daughters were in their time ready to marry and a catalogue of royal rites of passage punctuated every year. The phrases used reverentially to describe the royals did not differ markedly from those ascribed to the *Duce*. Fascist rural radio hailed the birth of Princess Maria Pia in 1934 by talking about the 'profound veneration' for the infant among the whole nation and calling down 'the most elect blessings of heaven' on her.[62] The arrival of little Victor Emmanuel, grandson of the King, in February 1937 stimulated more elaborate phrasing: 'From the ancient trunk of the Savoys has sprung forth a branch, a promise, from the millennial oak a gem is revealed, the one highest and nearest to heaven, because He is the Prince of the Empire, the first to be born an Emperor.'[63] In *Il Legionario*, Piero Parini replicated the sentiment but added a Fascist gloss: 'The royal baby is born today under the sign of Empire. The cot that today we watch over is bathed in the light of Empire. The future of this baby, who is born for us, we measure against the Empire. Not for vain pride, but with a clear and precise sense of reality. We can do so because Benito Mussolini created this Empire and did so on the totally secure and invincible basis of the Fascio Littorio.'[64]

Amedeo Savoia-Aosta, from the cadet branch of the family, was another prince to make a splash in Fascist government. He, late in 1937, was nominated the 'third Viceroy of Ethiopia'. In a curious half-acknowledgement of the traditional engagement of the royal family and its immediate circle in national imperialism, he was destined to govern in Addis Ababa until the collapse of the short-lived empire. The press, in announcing this nomination, combined accounts of Aosta's 'aristocratic distinction', popularity and alleged linguistic brilliance – he was said to speak both Piedmontese and Sicilian like a native – with the claim that he drew on a 'pure Fascist faith', enlivened by his 'profound and affectionate admiration' for the

Duce.[65] In this and other moments, mention of empire was difficult without some reference to royals.[66]

No doubt Victor Emmanuel III largely accepted his subordinate place in the power structure and propaganda campaigns of the dictatorship. Yet, until July 1943, all public buildings continued to display a photo both of the King and the dictator, reflecting the survival of Italy's constitutional dyarchy. Victor Emmanuel III and Mussolini were in many ways the regime's odd couple, rubbing along in their frequent dealings, the one and the other grumpy and cynical, the King, despite his thriftiness with words, always able to be malicious, Mussolini, a prey to jealous pique if the monarch's charisma showed and willing to talk on occasion about getting rid of him but never doing so, not until after he was sacked by the King in July 1943. Before that last stage of the war, the marketing of the monarch and his family's alleged virtues and significance to a deferential public, often with a phrasing replicating that used about the god-like *Duce*, did not cease. Most subsequent commentators have ignored them but the Savoys were an integral and valuable part of the Fascist regime's manipulation of history and its invention of tradition as Mussolini and his men strove to nationalize the masses and to stay in office.

Throughout the Fascist decades, Italy, site of the Vatican and mainspring of the universal and Catholic Church, was home to another more powerful and historic and much more charismatic monarchy, the Papacy. Although the Lateran Pacts subdued most overt conflict with the Fascist state and Catholic authorities were patient in putting up with such crass and inapposite Fascist utilization of Christian parallels as the depiction during Easter 1937 of the conquest of Italian East Africa as a resurrection,[67] the Church had scarcely abandoned its rituals or hidden its mystical power. On Italian children's school reports their results in religion were still listed first.[68]

Mussolini's personality cult, however strident, scarcely overbore the accumulated spell of the hundreds of Popes, the nation's scores of current bishops and the myriad of saints, still loved by individual Italians and summoned to be their protectors or the protectors of their *paesi* in times of joy and trouble. When, in April 1934, returned Alpini (soldiers from the First World War), their travel facilitated by a host of discounts to trains, restaurants and the Vatican museum, celebrated their annual meeting at Rome, they naturally marched past King and *Duce*, stationed together on a platform at the Colosseo. But they also took mass in the Vatican, where Pius XI's homily evoked their memories 'of the little church in their home village, prayers learned at their mother's knee and, above all, their real fear of God, making them strong and conscientious, ready to undertake the most difficult tasks in life'.[69] The next year, just as propaganda about the need to invade Ethiopia was building to a frenzy, listeners to Fascist rural radio were told that May was the Marian month. Then, it was explained with an old-fashioned emphasis: 'Catholics of the Roman Church revive our cult of the Virgin Mary just as surely as dawn summons the sun . . . Hail to Mary, at dawn and at dusk, on the street which rises and that which descends. Hail to Her in that Europe which builds temples, sows the furrow and favours progress. Hail even in the East where, eventually tiring of the fanaticism and superstitions, they will shatter the lying idols and accept the embrace of the one true god.'[70] Mary, like the Pope, was still a powerful presence in Italian minds.

For a great many Italians, their saint's *festa* was the one day of the year and cherished more heartfully than 21 April, 28 October or 4 November and the tinsel party and national celebrations. The devotion a local saint could rely on from below was never successfully ousted by the numerous Fascist attempts at the invention of tradition from above as, for example, when they sponsored ersatz medieval or Renaissance festivals at Florence and other Tuscan towns.[71] Rather, Fascist organizations tried to bolster themselves by invoking local saints. In the Trentino, the paper directed at the local Balilla moralized about children's duty to love their grandmothers by citing the case of Santa Massenzia, the saintly mother of the chief local saint, Vigilio.[72] Fascist overlooking of such figures, by contrast, could unleash popular fury. In 1937 a jeering crowd of about a thousand demonstrated at Rocchetta San Antonio, in the province of Avellino, after the *podestà* and town council stingily refused to provide the usual level of finance for the *festa* of St Anthony.[73] Order was restored only after *carabinieri* were rushed in from a larger nearby town and the police were soon complaining that a full investigation was blocked by the pervasive sullen *omertà* that stopped locals from informing on the ringleaders.[74]

In the spring of 1939 a more complex dispute broke out at Tires, in the province of Bolzano. There, on 23 April, the feast of St George ended with an evening march by peasants whose singing of 'Tirol ist Mein Heimat' was applauded by their fellows but then ended by the police, who outlawed further appearances by the village band. The result, according to an eventual report, was 'widespread discontent', led by peasant women. Carolina Rogger, the wife of the sacristan, set up a new band, using her four children, their friends and some stray musical instruments. On 30 May, after mass, they began playing from an orchard next door to the Roggers' house, to the 'delight of the female element and the population of the place'. An appreciative crowd formed. Again the police intervened and trouble threatened when about a hundred peasants, mobilized by speakers of German, a language the *carabinieri* could not understand, assembled. There were many arrests but eventually the prefect of Bolzano intervened with amnesties, 'in harmony', as he noted, with the accord recently reached between Nazi Germany and the Fascist regime for a population transfer of ethnic dissidents from the Alto Adige.[75] Hints of national rivalry and incomprehension marked the Tires story but so, too, did a popular version of Catholicism. When contrasted with the Church's charisma, expressed in whatever language, any magic emanating from the *Duce* could sometimes seem flimsy and ephemeral.

The royal family and the fraternity and sorority of the saints could be further backed up by local heroes. One who gave a mixed message from his grave was Cesare Battisti, the martyr irredentist hanged by the Austrians in 1916. In Battisti's home region of the Trentino, few public events could occur without his spirit being evoked. If San Vigilio was the region's Catholic saint, Battisti was the prime model of virtue for lay adepts of the nation. When, for example in June 1935, a monument, designed by Fascist architect Ettore Fagiuoli and looking rather like a spaceship, was opened on the Doss Trento hill commanding the provincial capital, the ceremony had a civic religious air but one that was as local, military and royal as it was Fascist. A semi-official provincial journal, *La Rivista della Venezia Trentina*, described the event with somewhat predictable phrasing as 'the apotheosis of Cesare Battisti'. A parade had been led by the King, whose face, it was reported, 'shone more than ever with the light of triumph and joy'. As the hero's remains were carried in a coffin towards their new resting place and the crowds poured down rose petals from their windows, Battisti, the journalist maintained, 'took on life and movement and, summoned by the high and solemn sounding of all the bells from [the city's] Italian towers, appeared magnificent and luminous, like the figure of Christ'.[76] With or without Church and party approval and with whatever religious meaning, Battisti was securely numbered among Trento's saints (and would survive in the role beyond Fascism).

Italian homes may have contained images of the *Duce* but portraits of the Popes, Mary, Christ and the holy saints, the King, the other royals and a slew of not reliably Fascist lay saints, of whom Garibaldi was the most loved and widespread, could also be found on apartment walls. Stalin and Hitler went far in their personality cults to focus on themselves the glow and illumination of any charisma that might be around. However noisy and bright Fascist audio and visual propaganda may have been, it was far from achieving a similar monopoly.

None the less, the Ethiopian campaign has been widely seen as a period when the dictatorship won the greatest consent from the populace and certainly a case can be made that the years from 1933 to 1936 were tough for those who tried to keep aflame a torch of anti-Fascism. The regime remained committed to the instant repression of political opposition. The other face of Mussolini's regular visits to the King at the Quirinale was the almost daily presence at the Sala del Mappamondo of Arturo Bocchini. The police chief's job was to reassure the always anxious *Duce* that the anti-Fascists had been harried into silence. They had. However, as so often in the Fascist story, there was something telling in Mussolini's need to be endlessly and therefore ineffectually reassured. In the dictator's mind, the inexperience, superficiality and unpredictability of Fascism were never completely erased.

There were quite a few reasons for the relative disarray of political anti-Fascism by the mid-1930s. Predictably, not all those who objected to Mussolini's dictatorship found it easy to be in accord in their understanding of Italy's past and in their diagnosis of Italy's present and likely future. The movement called Giustizia e Libertà, established in Paris in 1929 under the leadership of Carlo Rosselli, just after he, Emilio Lussu and Francesco Fausto Nitti, nephew of the ex-Prime Minister, had succeeded in a bold escape from their imprisonment on Lipari, best embodied a left interventionism. Rosselli's elder brother, Aldo, had died as an officer in the First World War and his mother always remained a patriot and moved in Fascist circles. In 1919 Rosselli had still talked of his hope in a *fascio formidabile* of the best people in Italy but he demanded that any such group place the needs of the nation first and, from 1923 on, disdained Fascism as corruptly serving sectional interests. He was also a sort of hereditary republican (Mazzini had died in the family house in 1872),[77] while simultaneously being a natural European, easily at home in London (he had an English wife) and Paris.[78]

Rosselli and his friends in the movement favoured an ideological meeting between socialism and liberalism but did not necessarily convince other anti-Fascists about this alliance. The much more conservative liberal, Benedetto Croce, who stayed inside Italy and was not prevented by the regime from expressing his views nor from receiving his acolytes in his family palace at Naples – it housed more than 80,000 books[79] – always maintained that any opposition outside Italy possessed limited value.[80] Croce on one occasion told a young admirer with a haughtiness in which his junior found a 'religious air': 'You see that I do not occupy myself at all with the lands I own. My brother, who inherited from my father the necessary qualities, does that. But I do not for a moment think of selling my property. If I got rid of only a single hectare, you would see all my ancestors rebel against me.'[81] Somewhere in his mind, Croce feared that the increasing activism of Rosselli and his associates could stain the lofty ideals and social comfort of liberty with the darker levelling effects of equality.

Ideology, class and history, especially as recalled from the war and the bitter social struggle from 1919 to 1922, all could dog unity of action between liberals of any kind and the largest body of active anti-Fascists, those who belonged to the Communist party. They, in turn, had to reckon with the tyranny of Stalin, announced in that dictator's fulsome fiftieth birthday celebration in 1929. Bocchini's police continued to arrest communists but party members' activity and purpose were always in considerable degree guided by whatever happened to be the current Comintern, Soviet and Stalinist line (an estimated 200 party members in exile in the USSR perished in the purges).[82] That freedom to think for themselves which, in the late 1920s, still allowed the Sicilian communist Girolamo Li Causi to ridicule what he called the 'Cadorna tactics' of continually sending communist missionaries back into Italy to certain arrest,[83] was steadily curtailed. The PCd'I's most original thinker, Antonio Gramsci, himself used by the party as a sort of national saint after 1945 and archly called by an American historian 'the Marxist you can take home to mother',[84] maintained his independence because, from November 1926, he was safely pent up in a succession of harsh Fascist jails – the regime let him out in time to die at a Rome clinic in 1937.

Class difference had not been altogether expunged from the PCd'I. Giorgio Amendola, communist son of the sometime Liberal Minister of Colonies and gentleman-intellectual, Giovanni Amendola, found, when he was sent into *confino* at Ponza, that rank and file prisoners were suspicious of the intellectualizing of their social betters in the party. Worker and peasant communists, so abstemious and so bound to their families that they could save half their meagre prison stipend (meanly cut in 1930 from ten to five lire per day) to transmit to their loved ones back home,[85] often had more in common with their jailers than with such party leaders as Amendola. One dissident Fascist, condemned in the 1920s to Lipari, where pigs still cleaned the town street of rubbish and other detritus, has recalled that the islanders viewed the intellectual political prisoners of the time as a 'species of nabob, with fabulous personal incomes'.[86]

Culture could be an even more powerful marker of class than was money. The memoirs of relatively educated prisoners often underline the way that their guards automatically addressed them as *professore* (as Stalin, with a hint of menace, did to Togliatti, Gramsci's successor as party leader)[87] or *professoressa* and regarded the ideological contest which had sent them to their current fate as not necessarily permanent and their political views as no more imponderable than was the current ruling ideology of Fascism.[88] According to Camilla Ravera, the nuns at her prison in Trani were convinced that she had gone to her present damnation as a communist anti-Fascist because she had learned to read. They themselves scrupulously eschewed that sin.[89]

Regional difference also marked the story of the Resistance. The communist Cesira Fiori, a Roman *maestra* whose communism had been nourished by the bleakness of her father's life as a fruit and veg man at the city markets,[90] was struck by the way the *carabinieri* in her escort to prison spoke dialect and leafed through pulp literature if they read anything; certainly they were studiously ignorant of Fascist texts. They were also no believers in a single Italian nation. She recalled one pointing out to her a village away in the distance on a hill in the Basilicata and remarking that there the local women never spoke. They were clothed in an antique garb, the *carabiniere* confided fearfully, wore a dagger in their hair and were not afraid to use it. They belonged, the policeman added dolefully as he hurried along the road below, to a 'race of brigands'. When confined at Maratea, up country from Potenza, she herself was disconcerted to see that any burden that needed to be carried was hoisted aloft by the women; men only lifted their 'squeeze-boxes and their whips' and, as far as she could see, spent most of their days slicking down their hair with vast quantities of oil.[91]

Despite their militancy and sacrifice and despite their claims after the war to have constituted the only active opposition to Fascism, the communists on occasion displayed some ambiguity about the dictatorship, while it was pursuing its more populist policies and winning a seemingly massive degree of consent. In his clever 1935 lectures to the party school in Moscow, Togliatti insisted that Mussolini presided over a genuinely mass regime, even if it was a reactionary one. Party chiefs within Italy were also ready to counsel a line which could be summed up as 'if you can't beat them, join them'. Party faithful might find it rewarding to become active in the *dopolavoro*, PNF scout and sporting organizations, communist chiefs could muse, there to locate active workers who, after ideological nudging, might be persuaded to convert from Fascism to communism.[92] Only the outbreak of the Spanish Civil War ended this half flirtation with the regime.

Other anti-Fascists were similarly capable of mistaken political analysis. The socialist leader, Pietro Nenni, predicted in April 1935 that the coming conflict in Ethiopia would be much harder and would go on for much longer than the government expected. Interpreted generously, Nenni may well have been right but, when in May 1936 he declared that the war in Africa would soon spread to Europe and that the current Fascist triumph would prove hollow,[93] he sounded mistaken and petty, a party hack easily dismissed as cavilling against the nation.

The space created by class, regional and gender differences in turn allowed variations in the ways anti-Fascists experienced their punishment, which do not always accord well with the theory of totalitarianism. To be sure, prisons could be brutal and judges unforgiving. The more intellectually sophisticated or committed anti-Fascists were especially likely to confront the fact that their terms of *confino* were prolonged from an initial five years towards infinity by crude administrative fiat, often directly exercised by the *Duce* himself, in a way that mocked proper legal process. The poor and committed were even more likely to find the regime cruel and unforgiving – in a typical case a peasant from the hinterland of once 'red' Empoli received four years' *confino* for the crime of tying three red ribbons to a tree on a back road.[94] Fascist officials were ready to allow ill prisoners to perish before granting them proper medical attention. For those who survived, the files are full of examples of the police refusing to give approval to requests for shoes – as one put it, why, on the Tremiti islands, did a communist need shoes and underwear without holes in them?[95] Mussolini, in 1927, had already employed that most terrifying of metaphors of the twentieth century when he demanded that anti-Fascists be eliminated from 'circulation, in the way that doctors isolate those with contagious diseases'.[96] Places of imprisonment could be found all over the country but were likely to be in such southern communes as Pisticci in the Basilicata, Boiano in the Molise or on islands off southern coasts.[97] The Fascist prison system did not constitute a holiday camp.[98]

Neither, however, was it a Gulag Archipelago nor an Auschwitz. Guards could on occasion be humane, ignoring or flouting regulations, not unsympathetic to those they saw as 'poor Christians' like themselves. The regime could bend and back down. An attempt to institute the compulsory use of the Roman salute on the Tremiti islands was abandoned as a bad job after prisoners refused to comply.[99] On Ponza, for a while, prisoners ran a flourishing anti-Fascist funded and managed mini-market, offering goods at a better price and quality than the town grocer and attracting a clientele including the local police. It functioned for some months before the authorities in Rome realized that it was something of a bad advertisement for Fascism, dictatorship and tyranny.

With the outbreak of world conflict, a number of foreign residents and Italians were interned, 19,117 of them by April 1943. In the accustomed Fascist manner, the Geneva Convention was frequently ignored and the military police talked about instituting a 'radical and totalitarian' line against any real or potential dissidents.[100] Yet words were not always translated into deeds. A detailed study of activities in the camp at Ferramonti di Tarsia during the war has indicated that the commandant, irritated and humiliated by the inability of his sergeants to pronounce the foreign names of interned Jews, began to cut the number of the compulsory thrice-daily roll-calls, eventually abandoning them altogether.[101]

Another complication arrived with the longstanding tradition that wealthy prisoners, if their families were willing to pay the bills, could buy themselves a better diet, better clothing, better furniture and bedding, better reading matter, and a better lit or sunnier cell, one which excluded other prisoners. The diary of liberal democrat Ernesto Rossi is graphic in this regard. Loneliness and political drive eventually pushed him into sharing his prison cell with some communists and he claimed to enjoy their company, however much disliking their factiousness and recognizing that they held him to be irredeemably bourgeois. He was left to tell his mother bleakly in 1931 that Italy was a bedraggled place: 'Cavour was really an Englishman, born by mistake into a Balkan country.'[102]

Money apart, prison life could also be ameliorated, especially for those whose political commitment was not adamantine, through influence and favour. The archives are filled with letters to Mussolini (and on occasion to Rachele and Edda or to King Victor Emmanuel and Queen Elena) asking for a special case to be recognized. Fawning apology frequently brought benefit, with the *Duce*, who always found time in his busy schedule to deal personally with the political prisoners, regularly allowing early release, the reduction of a sentence, its conversion from one level of severity to a lesser or amnesty. Here was another instance where regulations did not always mean what they said and where merciful corruption could reign. One young Fascist taken on as a clerk at the party office in the Mussolinis' home provincial capital, Forlì, reckoned that 80 per cent of his mail dealt with *raccomandazioni*.[103]

In sum, under Bocchini and his secret police's weather eye, there were multiple reasons why formal political resistance to the regime when it was readying to invade Ethiopia and conquer an Italian empire had dwindled. Yet the commitment of the Italian masses to Fascism, their bowing to its pretensions to be genuinely totalitarian and so to reduce them to being atomized individuals, slates wiped clean on which the dictatorship alone inscribed its will, remained highly doubtful. Rather, the novelty of Fascism, only partially concealed by the vivacity of its advertising machine, left most of its subjects with world-views that carried knowledge and understanding and so histories from a vast array of other places. The Church, the family, the locality, the gender order, migration, these and many other matters helped to keep open a medley of mental paths which Italians used to negotiate their world and to appease or to manipulate the powers that were. Whatever else was happening to Italians under Fascist dictatorship, they had not surrendered their ability to be active in managing their own lives and in telling stories to themselves about their fate and character. To demonstrate this reality, one little but emblematic story may suffice.

On the evening of 27 March 1933, in the *paese* of Maranzana, some thirty kilometres south of the Piedmontese provincial centre, Alessandria, a group of four male residents, so the police reported, decided to enjoy each other's company. Armed with bread and salami, they sauntered out of Maranzana town and repaired towards a hamlet called Ghini, where the youngest of their number, Antonio Gabeto, owned a storehouse containing a stock of wine. Drinking wine, after all, was a recommended Fascist activity, with *Il commercio vinicolo*, an organ of the industry, proclaiming that demographic tests proved that wine consumption favoured reproduction: 'A generation of non-drinkers or of enemies of wine', it pronounced, 'cannot be a generation of good Italians and fervent Fascists.'[104] Unaware of this learned reasoning but eager to imbibe, the four friends trudged on, meeting on their path a local builder's labourer, the resonantly named Lorenzo

Boccaccio, and his peasant friend Antonio Tornato. They invited their fellow *paesani* to join them.

The hours passed convivially. The six Maranzanesi consumed the food, washing it down with 'about twenty litres of the wine' which Gabeto was providing, although the quantity involved would be debated. Giovanni Benazzo, a very poor peasant from the village, whose family (including an aged father reduced to semi-blindness through an accident in his rural labours) was trying to make do with share-cropping a three-hectare lot mortgaged to the town notary, remembered that he and his friends had broached a demijohn of thirty-five litres and consumed the great majority of it. Gabeto estimated only about ten litres of that draught were left undrunk.[105] In any case, rather than measuring their alcoholic intake too closely, the *paesani*, to celebrate this pleasant moment of male community, sang 'popular and country songs'. Spring was in the air and Easter was at hand. It was a time to be sociable.

About one o'clock the next morning the six staggered out into what must have been the crisp night air. By that stage, Tornato could scarcely stand, let alone walk. Somehow the other five helped him back to his house in Maranzana, outside of which the jolly group burst into a special Easter song. Their serenading stirred Tornato's wife from her solitary slumbers. After reclaiming her husband, she issued the still thirsty surviving singers with a further two litres of wine. Soon only three of the original party were left, Boccaccio, Gabeto and Benazzo. They lurched their way down Maranzana's Via del Littorio (Lictor Street), singing, perhaps a little boisterously, as they went.

The end of their drinking night was not to prove as sweet as its beginning. Boccaccio, according to his own later account, found himself alone in the street. Perhaps momentarily mournful, he sat down abruptly on a wooden plank just outside the Municipio and fell asleep. Some time later he rolled off the bench he had created for himself and fell heavily to the ground. He woke with a start and stumbled off to his own house after the town piazza clock tolled 4 a. m.

Other townsmen, who were interviewed by police, had different versions of the events. One witness had only heard Boccaccio, Benazzo and Gabeto intoning the words of 'Nella risaia', 'an old socialist song', celebrating peasant unionism in the rice-fields of that part of Italy. But another informant was sure that the three friends had actually been singing the 'socialist anthem', 'Bandiera rossa' ('Red Flag'). They had done so for at least 'five minutes'.[106]

This charge was enough to bring down the weight of Fascist law upon them. Gabeto, who was not yet eighteen, got off with an *ammonizione* (warning). But both Benazzo and Boccaccio were sentenced to *confino*. In Boccaccio's case, the sentence was three years to be served at Grassano in the province of Matera. In the event Boccaccio was amnestied within the year. The local police were more charitable in their rating of Benazzo. That perhaps grasping town notary had been around for more than twenty years and, it was implied, was not too gentle in his dealings with ill-educated and gullible peasants; the wretched Benazzo, it was noted, apart from his elderly parents, had in his charge five sisters, at least one of whom had recently returned to the family nest, having lost her job as a hairdresser.[107] The suffering Benazzo had his sentence commuted to an *ammonizione* after seven months.

The prefectural report about Boccaccio was more severe, if also a little vague and predictable. Boccaccio had been born in 1888 and so was old enough to have been Gabeto's father. He had done military service both in Libya and in the Great War but had not covered himself with soldierly glory. Rather, he had been taken prisoner by the Austrians on the first day of the battle of Caporetto and only returned to Italy in 1919. He had not been an active socialist in the years before Fascist 'good order'. Yet, the official commentary noted, he was suspected of having harboured 'socialist sentiments'. Moreover, after 1922, he had neither joined the Fascist party nor displayed enthusiasm for the regime's festivals and achievements. Evidently still restless, he had, on three occasions, emigrated to France. He had most recently returned from there in March 1932. All in all, declared the Fascist police (who were as much police as Fascists), using a phrase which is common in their prose, Boccaccio was '*poco amante del lavoro ed è dedito al vino*' ('no lover of work and much given to drinking').[108] Boccaccio belonged to the undeserving poor: 'He is a dubious figure morally because, although married and the father of four children, he has never looked after them properly. Rather, when he has any money, he spends it on parties and loose women, ensuring his family remains in need.'

In the official assessment, Boccaccio deserved his penalty. Perhaps countering this judgement was an appeal to the *Duce* some months later from Lorenzo's eldest son, Luigi, suggesting that, whatever his wasting of his family's love, Lorenzo Boccaccio had not exhausted the stock of their loyalty. Luigi asked that his 'unhappy father who is suffering in some far-off place and so makes his family suffer, too', be returned to his accustomed hearth.[109] This eighteen-year-old peasant youth added that his request should be listened to since he was a fully paid-up and participating member of the local branch of the Fascio giovanile and had proceeded into that movement through the Balilla and Avanguardisti. Another matter in his favour, at least the police believed, was that he had only just returned from treatment for kidney disease, obtained at public expense at the hospital at nearby Acqui because of the family's 'poverty of the most squalid kind'. Boccaccio, too, ought to be let off, since, it was urged, when the crime was committed, he and his friends had been 'in a state of perfect unconsciousness, given that they were extremely drunk'.[110]

It is a tiny story, but how much history and how many histories are contained within it! In its detail lie insights into the world of Italian rural male sociability, gender relations, food and drink, public health, the family, religion, formal and popular, and migration. Also displayed are Fascist policing, both ideological and practical, the willingness of some of the dictatorship's subjects to inform on their fellows, the urban geography of Fascism and its marshalling of space, and the ambiguity of the Fascist nationalization of the masses, given that a *confinato* was dispatched to somewhere undesirable but in Italy. Such places were usually south of Eboli, beyond which local peasants would tell the Turin intellectual Carlo Levi when he was sent into internal exile, Christ and modern politics had not penetrated. Yet Fascism had beset Maranzana, despite its remoteness. The main street was called the Via del Littorio. Villagers listened from their windows to the parody of politics being engaged in by Boccaccio and his mates. Some in that hidden audience were ready to inform against their neighbours. We cannot be sure what mixture of fanaticism, self-interest, malice or fear prompted *paesani* to such denunciation. But we do know that there were village spies of an autonomous and so largely spontaneous kind and that villagers were aware that the police would be interested in something as simple and innocent as the choice of a song.

There are other matters worth attention. At Maranzana, it is plain, men's work retained a natural primacy over anything females might do and, in reward, men accepted that they needed time by themselves to bond with their male fellow villagers, away from their families. Yet families were also manifestly strong and durable. Despite his apparent limitations as a father and husband, Boccaccio was defended to the uttermost by his son.

Also present is the history of the foreign policy of the Italies as distinct from that of the nation-state, Italy. In 1933 the dictatorship had not yet gone to Ethiopia or indulged in its other wars in Spain, Albania, Greece and the rest. None the less, from the very beginning, Mussolini had pronounced that Italy must always be recognized as a great European power and, during the 1920s and early 1930s, he, or rather the Royal Italian Army, engaged in brutal and even genocidal acts while restoring control over Libya. In Maranzana, it may be surmised, the locals did not care much about who ruled in Tripoli and Benghazi. They were also unlikely to have been preoccupied with whether Austrian Chancellor Engelbert Dollfuss or Albanian King Zog were acting as dutiful clients in that part of Europe which Fascist bosses had marked out as their sphere of influence. The *paesani* had not been reliably programmed with 'eliminationist' anti-Arabism, anti-blackism, anti-Slavism or anti-Semitism. Rather than rallying behind national foreign policy, people in Maranzana knew instead about France, perhaps Belgium, even the United States and the rest of 'America'. In a basic sense, despite Bottai's pledge that Fascism was imposing a new unifying geography on all Italians,[111] they rejected the modern, rational and scientific maps printed and taught by the Italian nation-state, its academic geographers and party ideologues, let alone those being magnified by Fascist imperialism. They did so because they still possessed maps of their own, charts of the mind which were more practical, more comprehensible, more useful and more theirs.

The holes in these peasant maps extended into the Italian peninsula. Luigi Boccaccio, by his own account a regular at Fascist parades, knew where local migrant centres in France were. The family map in that regard may well have been quite detailed. By contrast, he was ignorant of Grassano in the Basilicata, except that he believed it to be far off, beyond village ken. In his mind and in the imagining of many Italians whose family had engaged in migration, such an alien part of Italy may well have been further off and more imponderable and alien than was America.

Finally, in the story of the Maranzana three, there is a hint of resistance or dissent and so further small, fleeting but significant evidence about the perpetual inadequacy and superficiality of Fascism. In 1933 *paesani* in a small town of the province of Alessandria, some with memories which went back before the dictatorship but at least one of whom was only a small boy when Mussolini took over, still knew the words and the tune of 'The Red Flag' (as did their secret listeners). They could sing it as a demonstration of (drunken) brotherhood and of implied insult to Fascism. When wine brought out the truth in them, they, like many another subject of the dictatorship, knew they were much more than simply Fascists.

12

Dictating full-time

If, by the early 1930s, men and women at the bottom of Italian society still cherished a complex set of identities, what had a decade of Fascist rule done to Benito Mussolini, the *Duce*, to his personality and character? To be sure his image in Italy was ubiquitous, his authority unchallenged, his rule seemingly complete. In the summer of 1932 a typical party report admitted, with what might be read as a disconsolate air, that, throughout the south, the people were 'strangely fixing themselves with ever greater tenacity on the *Duce* and displaying a steadily weakening attachment to Fascism, which is comprehended through local feuds and the seldom or never exemplary behaviour of party bosses'.[1] In that part of Italy, it had to be said, 'Mussolinism' now outweighed any lingering attraction offered by the party and its ideology.

But what was this object of so much love and approval actually like? Was Mussolini still the same person who had orchestrated the political seizure of power in 1922 and the conversion of his government into a regime and his own Prime Ministership into a dictatorship after 1925? Was the *Duce* really the man of granite that propaganda endlessly claimed him to be? What, too, about his power? It might be untrammelled in theory but how did it work in practice? How were decisions made in the Fascist state and how were the ideas of the leader converted into action? Was he, in sum, a strong dictator or a weak one?

At first glance, this last question might seem absurd, a non-issue. What is the point of being a dictator, it might be remarked, unless you dictate? Yet a literature has flourished for decades wondering about the possible weakness of Adolf Hitler and probing the limits of his rule (or attention span), while at least one historian has stated that Stalin, too, was in some sense a vulnerable chief. By this analysis, the Soviet 'man of steel' could not rely on his writ running without challenge across the diverse population of all the Russias. In response, it has been suggested, Stalin felt an immense frustration at the circumscribed reality of his power.[2] Given the Italians were also plainly not yet forged into diamond-hard Fascist beings, how was the *Duce* reacting to what some might see as his anticlimactic 'revolution'?[3]

Though blotted out by the trumpeting of his glory, a precariousness can indeed be detected in Mussolini's biography. In 1925, for example, the decision to opt for full-scale dictatorship had apparently taken a psychological toll on the *Duce*, as perhaps had the whole Matteotti affair. Whether or not he was directly guilty of ordering the socialist's death may still be debated, but Mussolini, unlike Stalin or Hitler, did not plume himself on murder, despite his addiction to the praise of violence. One of the oddities of the story of the Matteotti crime is how the *Duce*, after the event, paid what very much looks like blackmail money to Dumini and the other killers. Furthermore, by the 1930s, the dictator, prompted by Bocchini, went out of his way to provide financial help to Matteotti's widow and children. The Matteotti family joined the long and erratic list of those receiving unofficial subsidy from the dictator's private secretariat. Perhaps guiltily and certainly uneasily, Mussolini, in one of his last interviews in 1945, returned to the matter, again denying that he had ordered the murder.[4] Such protestations do not lead to pardon, however. In the case of Velia Matteotti, the dictator's motives may have been mixed. Her accommodation with his regime – she eventually allowed her children to receive a state and therefore a Fascist education – can be read as the result of carefully plotted corruption. The cash was designed not so much to aid her as to besmirch her husband's reputation and that of his surviving admirers.[5] Yet other dictators of the twentieth century seldom saw the need for such a devious approach to the leftovers of their terror. Rather they had a short way to ensure that there were no leftovers.

If the death of at least one of his enemies arguably left nightmares in his mind, the *Duce*, again distinguishing himself from the two other 'totalitarian' chiefs, was not given to killing his friends. No Night of the Long Knives or Great Purge blighted the twenty years of Fascist rule. Rather, the henchmen of 1919 mostly remained the henchmen of 1939. Roberto Farinacci, the most restless and outspoken of Fascist underlings, did lose office after 1926, never to return, and he did have his every subsequent move tracked by the secret police. Both Bocchini and the *Duce* enjoyed preserving a bulging file of salacious evidence about Farinacci's affair with Gianna Pederzini, an opera singer. Expensive presents,[6] champagne dinners, overnight stays in adjoining rooms at the best hotels,[7] public[8] and private quarrels[9] and offers from friends to find Pederzini work in Rome so that she could be near her lover, exhaustive descriptions of such matters went into the record for the *Duce* to flick through when in the mood.[10] Equally, Mussolini grew used to shrugging his shoulders at secret reports that Farinacci was causing scandal in the PNF through his 'pretended puritanism' and 'mania for scandal'.[11] Greed, hypocrisy and a love of gossip, the *Duce* believed, were what made humans human (and so lesser beings than himself, putty in his hands). Yet, despite the *Duce*'s deepening misanthropy, until the latter stages of the war Farinacci was right to claim that he remained his leader's friend. The rowdy *ras* of Cremona could address the *Duce* as *tu* and even, to some degree, tell him the 'truth'. The human ties between the two were not sundered.

Only with Mussolini's overthrow in July 1943 and his return two months later as little more than a Nazi puppet in the Social Republic did the Fascist revolution start devouring its own. In present-day Italy it is becoming common to hear that 'Mussolini never killed anyone' and was therefore not at all comparable with Hitler and Stalin. As the evidence marshalled in this book persistently illustrates, any attempt at the whitewashing of Fascist rule amounts to a disturbing misreading of the dictatorship's pernicious history. Yet it is true that Mussolini, despite his regular urging of mayhem and his perpetual studied savagery, was not directly steeped in blood. He may have persistently talked about warring against the world but, on quite a few occasions, in practice he avoided drastic action.

Certainly in 1925 the *Duce*'s avowal that he was a hard man in every circumstance showed some cracks. In the early morning hours of 15 February, immediately after he had made the calculated but risky step of handing over the secretaryship of the PNF to Farinacci,

Mussolini collapsed at his bachelor flat in the Via Rasella in central Rome. He coughed blood and his alarmed housekeeper, Cesira Carocci (like many of his personal staff, a fellow Romagnole), urgently summoned medical help.[12] The *Duce* was diagnosed with an ulcer, an illness which would dog him thereafter, both on its own account and because much of the treatment accorded to it seems to have been wrong. In January 1927 Federzoni recorded meeting his leader when he was suffering so 'atrociously' from stomach pain that he could scarcely speak.[13] Matters seem to have improved somewhat over the following years. But, especially once Italy embarked on its Second World War and the threadbare character of the Fascist revolution was exposed for all to see, Mussolini was frequently sick.[14] How often the bad health was the result of physical woes and how much it was psychological may be debated.

Unlike Hitler, although similar to Franco and Saddam Hussein to name but two other dictators, Mussolini was a family man. His private life did on occasion peep through into the public arena, with Mussolini managing to be a patriarch, Italian-style, and, on occasion, a bemused father and hen-pecked husband. The radical young Benito had begun living with Rachele Guidi, his eventual wife, in a humble room at Forlì in early 1910. They were then companions in the socialist manner and, on 1 September, produced a daughter, Edda. Although the ménage moved together to Milan after Mussolini became editor of *Avanti!* in late 1912, the *Duce*-in-the-making scarcely confined himself to a single partner. One statistically minded commentator has reckoned that Mussolini had sex with at least 400 women in the course of his life[15] and, during his time in Milan, he did not allow life with what he laughingly called his 'domestic tribe'[16] to restrict his predatory range. It was then that he began his lasting relationship with Margherita Sarfatti,[17] while he also pursued a perhaps unconsummated affair with Leda Rafanelli, Arabist, anarchist, libertarian and woman of artful *belle époque* mystery.[18] Rafanelli and Sarfatti were each Mussolini's seniors, while also above him in class, intellectual status and worldly confidence. Rachele, by contrast, was seven years his junior and from a poor peasant background; more than one of her sisters remained illiterate throughout their lives.

In December 1915 Mussolini, no longer a socialist, married

Rachele in a civil ceremony. Nine months later she produced a first son, the appropriately named war baby, Vittorio. It was just as well that the relationship was solemnized because army officialdom believed and historians are nowadays inclined to agree that Mussolini, some months earlier, had contracted a marriage with Ida Irena Dalser, whom he had met at Trento before his move to Forlì. Dalser had produced a son whom she named Benito Albino in November 1915. This probable bigamy and certain complexity were kept hidden from public view, although Mussolini continued to fund Dalser, with his younger brother Arnaldo distributing the sums involved in this as in so many other covert deals in the Fascist story. In 1926 Dalser was confined to a lunatic asylum in her home province of Trento (though anti-Fascist sources claim she was perfectly sane) and she died in 1937. Mussolini never saw his putative son, who in turn after having been declared mad seems to have perished during the Second World War.[19]

In 1918 Rachele produced a second male child, Bruno. By then she had established herself as Mussolini's legitimate wife. With her husband's rise to power, further conventions needed to be observed. In December 1925, whether possessed by a sense of mortality after his illness, already plotting the deal with the Vatican that would be ratified in 1929, or just reflecting his drift towards social conventionality, Benito Mussolini wed Rachele Guidi in church and simultaneously legitimized his children in religious terms. Two further offspring, Romano in 1927 and Anna Maria in 1929, completed the Mussolini household, which also included a family cat. The *Duce*, it was remembered, was happier stroking it than cuddling his children and he kept a photograph of it but not them in his office.

Edda was eighteen when her younger sister was born and by then she was doing her best to be a bright young thing, Fascist-style. Just before her parents' church wedding she had been enrolled in a private school for young ladies at Florence where the majority of her classmates were aristocrats or the daughters of wealthy industrialists. It was thus somewhat unnecessary for Mussolini to urge the institution's authorities to treat her exactly the same as they did their other pupils.[20] The Santissima Annunziata College was scarcely a place where 'revolution' figured prominently on the curriculum. Mussolini was not the only politician (or successful and upwardly mobile human being) to take out this sort of social insurance policy for a favoured child, but Edda, even after she became Signora Ciano in 1930, remained an ambiguous symbol of the new generation of Fascist womanhood. She did have three children, with a younger son being named Marzio (Mars), as crassly Fascist a name as was Gallo (Cock), her term of endearment for her chubby husband. However, Edda Ciano was also slim and fashionable, ready to party with film-stars and Mrs Simpson and fond of an alcoholic drink (while also one of the first Italians to consume Coca-Cola). Her smoking as a teenager brought sententious advice from her father to stop, as he had done once his time as a soldier was over.[21] In her modishness, Edda Ciano was much more a European bourgeois than she was a Fascist *donna madre*. Edda was certainly not a peasant in her heart and mind.

Rachele, with her squarish build and five children, fitted the official image of the Fascist woman much better, but in her case too equivocations could be detected. From 1925 the canny Rachele, always a woman with an eye to gain, accompanied by what might be read as an ingrained peasant suspicion that good times did not last for ever, especially for people like her, bought land near Forlimpopoli, in her part of the Romagna. The Villa Carpena thereafter became a place of family residence, although the *Duce* took pains not to be portrayed as having risen to become a local squire. Throughout the dictatorship, Rachele seldom appeared at official events but she was active in her own region and established a reputation there as a 'woman of respect', a good patroness on occasion but, if riled, a tough and relentless enemy. Under her prompting the family kept extending its holdings in the Romagna. In 1927 the *Duce* accepted the gift from a grateful nation of the Rocca delle Caminate, above Predappio.[22] This mouldering medieval castle was now modernized into a liveable dwelling and the family did pass time there. They also acquired the rights to a beach house at Riccione, the Romagna's premier resort, if scarcely one that could match the charm and elegance of the Venice Lido, Forte dei Marmi in Tuscany (seaside vacation choice of the Cianos), Capri, Lerici and quite a few other holiday sites. It was at Riccione that Mussolini was photographed powerfully cutting a path through the waves as though wanting to dictate to them too. Just down the coast at Rimini, Claretta Petacci, the *Duce*'s last mistress, took up residence for a while at the Grand Hotel. In the still halcyon summers of the late 1930s, the two lovers, surmounting the evident family and privacy difficulties involved, sometimes managed to stroll on the beach together beneath a romantic moon.[23]

Such sexual delights and family complications lay in the future when, in November 1929, the Mussolinis were reunited in a formal sense in Rome. Now the *Duce* was granted, for a peppercorn rent, occupation of the palatial Villa Torlonia, just outside the Michelangelo-designed Porta Pia, on the eastern outskirts of the Eternal City. If today tourists stroll down a couple of blocks from the Aurelian wall, they can still view the place, now with the house in ruin, despite longstanding talk of its refurbishment as some sort of museum, but with its estate a public park. In the deal that brought the Mussolinis to the Villa, there were the customary hints of a limit to a too ardent Fascist assault on ancient wealth. The Torlonias were princely landowners, whose administration of their peasantry has been portrayed as among the harshest and most rapacious in Italy.[24] If the Torlonias were generous to the *Duce* in the rental of their Roman villa, their expectation was that the dictatorship would look favourably on them and keep any uppity peasants from trying to win some form of Fascist equality from the Torlonias or their bailiffs.

During the dictatorship's second decade, the functioning of the Mussolini family continued to be a side-issue of the regime. Vittorio and Bruno, dutifully photographed as party scouts or athletes but not starring intellectually at their Rome high schools, were growing to gawky manhood. In his twenties, Vittorio Mussolini did manage to cut a figure in the cinema business, so often an arena that appealed to the young, wealthy and devil-may-care. Bruno, who, in the manner of dictators' sons, liked boxing, fast women and faster cars, eventually became a test pilot and was killed on the job during the war in August 1941. Perhaps the best sense of the Mussolini elder boys is given by reading Vittorio's account of the Ethiopian war (his father was officially overjoyed that his sons enjoyed bombing),[25] which was brutal and racist in content and laddish in style.[26] Neither Vittorio nor Bruno gave much sense that they could be groomed for a leading role in a Fascist future. The *Duce* was heard calling his eldest son a cretin and, although Bruno's sacrifice to the nation prompted Mussolini to compose a booklet entitled *Parlo con Bruno* (I talk with Bruno), implying timeless intimacy between the two and so curiously mixing Fascist, Catholic and familial piety,[27] in truth the father had scarcely enjoyed a close relationship with his second son.

When Fascism was finished, it was the third brother, Romano, who did best, making a name for himself in the Italian cultural world. Romano Mussolini became a talented jazz pianist and his CDs are still available for purchase by fans. What Hitler was accustomed to anathematize as a negroid and degenerate form of music was an ideologically impure choice for a Fascist youth, if one that united Romano Mussolini with the vast majority of his generation of Europeans. One of the droller scenes of the Second World War occurred at Munich during the family reunion in September 1943, when the teenager was found playing boogie-woogie in the presence of SS men. Heinrich Himmler did not take to Romano Mussolini. Although his own school reports were no better than his brothers', Romano, more teenage rebel than upright party *milite*, was ready publicly to deny and shame his father when the *Duce* bragged, falsely, that he was reading the Greek citations of Nietzsche in the original.[28]

The youngest Mussolini child, Anna Maria, had the cruellest destiny. In the summer of 1936 she was diagnosed as a victim of poliomyelitis. Her incurable illness struck her father hard, although he ignored the reminder in her fate of human hubris as he combined deep sorrowing for her with lightly approving Fascist intervention in the Spanish Civil War.[29] Colleagues did none the less notice him at the time, dishevelled and with red eyes, not quite his usual ebullient self.[30] Among the henchmen, Farinacci sounded the most sincere and personal in expressing regret.[31]

If there was a hereditary prince within the family, it was Galeazzo Ciano, bright, happy, shallow, while the sun of the Fascist imperium shone secure at the top of Fascist society through his marriage to Edda. Ciano's diary remains one of the great texts for any who seek to understand the Fascist regime[32] and its author was a man of some wit and talent, if one easily overawed by his father-in-law and achingly anxious to display both his cleverness and his thrusting Fascism. When he doffed his black-shirt and engaged in private life, however, Ciano outdid his wife in soft bourgeois habits, looking to play the doubtfully Spartan game of golf[33] most afternoons. With the passing of the years and his youthful promotion to become Minister of Foreign Affairs, Ciano, through his greed and corruption, attracted public notoriety and, beneath his studied ruthlessness, the lightweight character of his Fascism meant that party enthusiasts took to blaming him rather than his father-in-law for the yawning limitations of the 'revolution'. Rachele, rarely forgetful of her part as a woman of the people, did not hide her contempt for the yuppie who was so feckless that he allowed Edda to find contentment or lovers in an agreed 'open' marriage. Neither to his mother-in-law nor to himself was Ciano a convincing revolutionary. Yet, in a fashion that is psychologically telling, Mussolini did go on liking his son-in-law at least until the betrayal of July 1943, when Ciano was among those members of the Grand Council who voted Mussolini out of office.

Within the Mussolini household, then, the new generation scarcely fitted snugly to the official model of new men and women, hardened by a cultural revolution and joining in worship of the party's civic religion. In any case it was a figure from the older generation who mattered more than they did. Until his premature death in December 1931, aged forty-six (the same as his mother, Rosa Maltoni), Arnaldo, the *Duce*'s younger brother, was the most significant member of the clan. Arnaldo Mussolini had enjoyed more formal education than had his brother, as well as having become a junior officer after he was conscripted into war service, proof of his superior social status to that of Benito. Yet, ever since Mussolini had broken with the Socialist party, Arnaldo had become his de facto chief political agent. 'Mussolini the little', as he was reconciled to being called, the 'good one' as distinct from the 'mad',[34] from 1919 to 1922 was an ever-present shadow[35] while the *Duce* crafted his subtle course through the foothills that led towards power. Arnaldo, who in 1914 was commencing a career that promised a life as a small-town administrator, now coped with aplomb with the tangled accounts of Mussolini's personal newssheet, *Il Popolo d'Italia*.[36] Amateur lawyer, accountant, businessman and journalist, Arnaldo had to display many skills. In every eventuality, he must prepare the way for Benito and, after his stormy passage, smooth over the wake of his brother's course to glory.

The Prime Ministership won, after 1922 Arnaldo Mussolini was quickly appointed substitute editor of *Il Popolo d'Italia*, the organ which both sentiment and self-interest made crucial to the *Duce*'s every act. With the one resident in Milan and the other in Rome, the two men stayed in regular telephone contact, a call typically made each evening around 10.30 p. m. after formal work was done kept a check on the many informal matters that linked the Mussolinis.[37] Arnaldo handled the most pressing areas of family finance, remaining assiduous, for example, in securing the newspaper's line of credit, still slender enough to cause preoccupation in 1926.[38] He also assumed the role of an electoral agent, being adroit and cynical in accepting that southerners who joined the *listone* (pro-government electoral slate) in 1924 might themselves be motivated more powerfully by interest than by ideology.[39] Mixing the public with the private, Uncle Arnaldo simultaneously kept a watching brief over Rachele and the children, assisted by the fact that, for much of the time, the two families lived in apartments near to each other in Milan. A careful man in most of his arrangements, Arnaldo Mussolini rapidly established himself as an influential member of the elite of his city, centre of the nation's stock market and fulcrum of national finance, industry and trade, the place where 'real business' was done by contrast with showy Rome, where politicians speechified, tourists thronged and dictators dictated. Arnaldo Mussolini became the person in the family with the best contacts and the necessary membership cards. Despite doubts about the fervour of their revolutionary commitment, the Milan branch of Rotary and the Touring Club Italiano, the latter being the city's most respectable and national private organization, were glad to count him on their books.[40]

Arnaldo Mussolini's ventures in the banking world extended beyond Italy. By 1924 he was deeply involved in secret and probably corrupt dealings with American companies, including Standard and Sinclair Oil, each of which set aside romance about democratic values as they advanced their causes in what they deemed a well-run dictatorship. According to the historian Mauro Canali, author of a number of very detailed accounts of Fascist policing, in June 1924 Matteotti intended to bring the sordid plots between the American companies and the Fascist elite into the open. The socialist was silenced for ever so that Dumini, and behind him the *Duce*, could lay hands on the dossier on corrupt practices which Matteotti was allegedly carrying when he was kidnapped.[41] Arnaldo Mussolini's decorum at the time as a good citizen of Milan was, in other words, only skin-deep. When violence was called for in the family interest, he saw no problem in its surgical exercise. Matteotti might not have been the only person prompting a need for Arnaldo to marshal armed backing for his brother's government. While the result of the Matteotti crisis was still uncertain, in December 1924 Arnaldo was said to have been working with Mario Giampaoli silently to establish a further secret paramilitary force, primed to defend Benito and his team from unnamed attacks.[42]

Once the dictatorship was safely installed, however, Arnaldo Mussolini distanced himself from such louts as the *ras* of Milan and soon played a major role in Giampaoli's downfall. He similarly evinced his disapproval of Farinacci and was much pleased when the more respectful (and Catholic) Augusto Turati took over as party secretary. He continued to bless the career of the obedient Achille Starace. Once his brother ruled as dictator, Arnaldo Mussolini thought that a man of respect should observe the conventional niceties. One reason for Arnaldo's disdain for the impious Farinacci was that the younger Mussolini had never indulged in the cheap anticlericalism of Benito and their socialist *mangiapreti* (priest-eating) father, Alessandro. The brother of Arnaldo's wife was a priest and the younger Mussolini was a natural advocate of, and player in, the negotiation of the Lateran Pacts. None the less his Catholic piety could readily slip into a Fascist one in what was Arnaldo's jumbled philosophy of life. By the early 1930s Arnaldo saw no inconsistency in combining his Christianity with 'Fascist mysticism'. He was an early advocate of universal fascism and patronized such young party radicals as Berto Ricci.[43] This fondness for high-flown phrases did not eliminate the mundane, however. Just before his death, Arnaldo commented ironically to his brother on the way in which he was besieged by petitioners and their *raccomandazioni*.[44] The young brother had mastered a revolutionary vocabulary when its usage seemed appropriate but he remained staunchly practical should reality intrude.

Benito Mussolini was the last person to be worried by his younger brother's intellectual and ethical confusions and contradictions. Instead, Arnaldo, while he lived, was the *Duce*'s only reliable rock in the swirling seas of life. At a bleak moment in 1945, the dictator was still bewailing the too early loss of his 'lightning rod to the people'. Arnaldo, he conceded sadly, was the only man he had ever trusted.[45]

The relationship between Arnaldo and Benito Mussolini was, it is plain, an emblematic one. The ambitions of the Fascist revolution to change the cultural map of Italians rarely assaulted the family and certainly did not undermine the familist assumptions of the Mussolini brothers (nor, indeed, those of the numerous siblings, uncles, cousins and other relations of Italians, Fascist or not, who turn up in this book's pages). It is not an established approach to it, but as telling a way as any to summarize Fascist rule until 1931 is 'The Mussolini Brothers Inc.'

After Arnaldo's death the *Duce* was bereft. He shed public tears and spent a night watching over his brother's bier in Milan, before composing a memorial in his honour[46] and arranging for Arnaldo's writings to be posthumously collected and published. Arnaldo was speedily promoted to join the party's saints and martyrs; he was proclaimed a journalist without peer and, thereafter, any anniversary was likely to unleash a doting piece about him in the tame press.[47] Although Benito Mussolini could readily enough label some underling a 'friend'[48] and may have still been able to give something of himself to Farinacci, Ciano and his daughters and sons, the mobile and smiley dictator of the 1920s gave way to an ever stiffer semi-deity. With his brother gone, Mussolini transmogrified into a shaven-headed (his hair went white within a year of Arnaldo's death), uniformed and grim figure. To public view he now became a sort of (in-)human, stoney-faced, Easter Island monolith, legs akimbo, chest puffed out, chin jutting and bellowing an order to any underling around (since, for such a mighty chief, one homunculus who crossed his path was indistinguishable from another). Trusting no one, the *Duce* now assumed that no one trusted him and his cause and took for granted that the world was a harsh place of battle without quarter. Without Arnaldo's softness and religiosity it was easy for Benito Mussolini to think what he had always known, that Darwin and the Social Darwinians had got the meaning of life right.

As if to confront this cruel universe, it was now that Mussolini boasted to one of the throng of press men and women who wanted an interview that he had become an automaton: 'I have organized my activity through a division of labour, and a struggle against the dispersal of energy and other time-wasting. It is this that explains the volume of work I get through and the fact that I am never tired. I have turned my body into a motor, which is under constant review and control and which therefore runs with absolute regularity.'[49] The phrase 'mathematical certainty' began to stud his prose, with the *Duce* claiming infallible knowledge and foresight (if, when the cases involved are reviewed by the sceptical historian, they very frequently demonstrate the reverse). Already in September 1929 Mussolini had transferred his office from his old quarters in the Palazzo Chigi to the grandiose Sala del Mappamondo in the Palazzo Venezia. Huge and brilliantly decorated, the room gave visual confirmation of the dictator's impetuous and bursting force, his grab for world power, but also made him into an emperor from Byzantium, set far above the human world. Photographs today may reveal the image of a man dwarfed by the baroque furnishings and the immensity of his surrounds, a littleness enhanced by the ostentatious lack of clutter on the dictator's desk and by what may be imagined as the remorseless ticking of a clock the *Duce* had placed there to warn his guests against overstaying their welcome (if there was one). In the 1930s, however, for true believers and party propagandists, it was the dictator who dominated the place. His body may have been small and visibly ageing, his clothes rumpled (in his private labours Mussolini preferred a battered suit to official dress and needed reading glasses, which he vainly discarded when a visitor arrived),[50] but his spirit, his 'ether', was meant to overwhelm all.

Was Mussolini, then, becoming, as has sometimes been alleged, the prime victim of his own propaganda?[51] Was he drifting into being the most credulous and convinced believer in himself? Perhaps. Yet the *Duce*, whatever his other failings, was not stupid. It is possible that he still followed his star but, as his term in office wore on, he became ever more cynical about the human condition and notably about the party, the ideology and the revolution. Now he was ready to write off humankind in general and his underlings in particular. They were, as he put it in telling metaphor, mere worms that could only flourish in the carcass of a great animal (he had his live self in mind).[52] Italian businessmen he damned as avaricious rogues at heart, universally anxious to defraud the exchequer.[53] The King was tedious and useless, the people undisciplined, lazy and in need of the whip,[54] Franklin D. Roosevelt a sad paralytic,[55] Pius XI was unmanfully incontinent,[56] even Hitler was no more than a muddled small-town conjurer, should the truth be known.[57] Women were of value only in bed, but there they defrauded their lovers since sex satiated them but left the male 'empty'.[58] Hitting on an adequate subordinate was about as unlikely as winning the lottery.[59] Even Christmas was a bad joke and, he would grinchily urge, it should be suppressed.[60] Mussolini's catalogue of grievances was endless and all-embracing.

How, then, did this Timon-like hatred of those around him mesh with the high and even utopian ambitions of the Fascist 'revolution'? Did the profundity of Mussolini's contempt for his fellows and his people reflect a surfeit of power or, instead, a deepening and, in its way, sensitive recognition that, despite the clangorous fanfares and the infinite glory, the *Duce* still did not rule Italian lives? After all, as he confessed to a starstruck young Fascist in a moment of depression in 1938, he had, he feared, while ostensibly a peerless dictator, become 'a prisoner' of himself, 'of others, of events, of hopes and illusions'. Today, he went on, in words which tyrants and other bosses normally avoid mentioning: 'I must often think what I do not say, and say what I do not think. Yes, there is a real gap between the two Mussolinis. Sometimes it is profound and terrible. Perhaps, one day, one of the two will beg an armistice, break his sword and submit. I still don't know which one.'[61] Why, it should be asked, might he have felt so weak in his sway? How, by the mid and late 1930s, did the government of this *Duce* work?

Contrary to patronizing legend, Mussolini was a full-time dictator. History, especially in the Anglo-Saxon world, mainly remembers his speechifying and implies that the dictator was so busy orating that he had little time for anything else. In practice, however, the *Duce* was, most of the time, an assiduous bureaucrat, fond of fine print and anxious to display his mastery over it. Details, he remarked on occasion with some affection, were the fleas of an executive's life. They made you scratch your head and get weaving.[62] Even at the darkest moments of the Second World War he liked to comment sarcastically on the errors he picked up in newspaper reports.[63] It was true that, from time to time, the *Duce* did depart on trips around the country where speech-making was mandatory, although quite a few of the dictator's declamations to provincial audiences were short and had little further aim than to warm the hearts of his listeners now that, for a moment, they had their chief in what he too agreed was their beautiful, unforgettable, historic and Fascist town. Major homilies were surprisingly few, with his Ascension Day effort of 1927 and its applauding survey of the totalitarian features of the regime, its yen for ruralization, its possible foreshadowing of racist legislation and its heartfelt praise of the police, being the most stark.

The speeches may have seemed spontaneous. The way charisma was inscribed on to the *Duce* meant that he had to be a spiritual vehicle of the nation and its revolution. For such a superhuman being, ratiocination was too tawdry and ordinary a matter. A *Duce* did not reason; he inspired. He did not counsel; he spell-bound and overwhelmed his worshipping crowds. Yet it is known that Mussolini did in fact prepare himself for his appearances at the microphone well beforehand and tried very hard to keep his emotions and his text coolly under control.[64] If he conveyed as much through gesture and tone as through his formal argument, as regime propagandists, and notably the blind but still awed ex-soldier and celebrated war hero Carlo Delcroix were eager to contend,[65] he did so knowingly and through study and practice.

But once he took office, oratory was more a hobby than the act of every day. Mussolini was a hard-working dictator. When he laid claim to labouring through a sixteen-hour day at the office he exaggerated but perhaps pardonably since he could often be found at his desk. Not for Mussolini, Hitler's bohemian habit of very late rising nor the *Führer*'s time-consuming love of pointless chat. Not for the *Duce*, Stalin's liking for drunken parties with his cowed colleagues, late into nights full of icy menace. Especially as the regime lengthened into its second decade in office, Mussolini eschewed any social contact with his colleagues and, perhaps oddly for an Italian, tried hard to avoid their physical touch. The *Duce* was not the sort of boss who exhibited his popularity by walking arm in arm with his juniors on a *passeggiata* or who kissed a guest on both cheeks. More sedately, in the Sala del Mappamondo, Mussolini conventionally and briskly shook hands with a visitor, ignoring Starace's exhortations about making the Roman salute the only form of greeting.

In his attention to business, there was a grain of truth in Mussolini's pretensions to be a bureaucratic machine. When a young socialist, he had been taken in hand by a sophisticated and aristocratic Russian comrade, Angelica Balabanoff. She taught him philosophy, a subject he would never cease to evince a fascination for, and assert a mastery over, by making out lists, that simplest way of instructing those who cannot really understand.[66] Risen to lead his country, the *Duce* retained the desire to keep his administration neat and tidy. What he required from his staff was 'the clear chronology, the able synthesis, the telling detail, the essential reference'.[67] Then, often using a coarse-nibbed black pen, held with a very firm hand, he could minute 'Yes' or 'No', just initial 'M' or perhaps jot down a peremptory marginal comment and so trace his path successfully through mountains of paperwork. When matters became more taxing and a policy line rather than an administrative fiat was required, Mussolini liked to make abrupt lists of his own, each point ideally reduced to a few words and very rarely extending to more than a sentence. It was almost as though in his mind's eye really a Fascist Caesar, he was chiselling dicta in marble or in bronze.

Succinctness in command can be a virtue but it also leaves vast space for underlings to interpret just what the ringing words 'really' mean. So it was in the power structure of Fascist Italy, where Mussolini frequently held numerous ministries at the same time and always interfered even more aggressively in those not directly under his aegis. When policy had to be converted to fact, a lapidary phrase, a bout of aggressive language, were often, if not the end of government, only its beginning since the *Duce* made very little attempt to work out how words might be converted into deeds, rather regarding such day-to-day matters as well below him. Charisma of the sort Mussolini was meant to incarnate has a connection with the history of those celebrities who nowadays fill our television screens and newspapers and, especially in the Italy of Silvio Berlusconi or in those places where actors of stage or screen have become political actors too, threaten to bewitch our minds and trash our democracies. Celebrities, beneath the glitter, are often people of no account. Only their dazzle matters. Similarly, the Mussolinian way of ruling was meant to be so charged with Fascist dynamism that it could allow no turning back and gave little time and less justification to any ponderous surviving view that a modern state to be properly ruled might above all need a clear decision-making process and a regular method for transmuting plans into action. But the *Duce* was too overwhelming to be expected to sift through memoranda carefully setting out alternatives and explaining the difficulties of a particular project. His rule was rapid or it was nothing.

Revelatory in this regard is Mussolini's typical daily activity – the interview, confined to fifteen minutes by that ominously ticking desk clock. Most mornings were fully occupied in this fashion and the programme could extend into the afternoon as well. At least if one of his young admirers is to be believed, Mussolini, getting the mathematics palpably wrong, towards the end of his life would recall having held hundreds of thousands of such meetings during his dictatorship.[68] Here, too, the method of dictatorial rule has its replica in today's world. For much of the time Mussolini was foreshadowing the behaviour and the intellectual processes of the chat-show host, as first this person, then that, then another, here an Italian, there a foreigner, here a young party philosopher, there a grizzled veteran seeking family support, here a pretty woman, there a family member, minister, party chief or military officer, were ushered in and out of his grandiose office. Like a good journalist, and Mussolini was one, he liked to know beforehand whom he was meeting, what they were likely to say and what he should reply.[69] Since vanity was hard to forgo and even an all-conquering *Duce* did not enjoy days chock-full of quarrelling, it was best to please (although bullying could never be ruled out) and the surest way to get through any meeting was to tell the listeners what they wanted to hear and to confirm what they already knew. The new book was brilliant, the scheme ideal, the movement well crafted, the subsidy forthcoming. Attentive observers had already noticed that, somewhere beneath the bravado, Mussolini, throughout his career, had been fond of stating the obvious and the agreeable, given to tailoring his words to what he had divined others expected and always himself well attuned to the attitudes and prejudices of his interlocutors.[70] But, by the 1930s, much of the government of Fascist Italy was done this way, at great cost to efficiency, regularly blocking meaningful change and, above all, preventing any serious criticism of deficiencies and any assessment of how they might be overcome.

The great problem with the system is that what was usually happening was a dialogue of the deaf. The *Duce* had not really mastered the subject he was discussing so vibrantly but so briefly. The interlocutor was not really told how to make concrete the agreed decision; that issue would have to be puzzled out later (or just avoided). This government by words and image, by spin, ensured that, over many important matters, there was no government at all.

Yet there were times when Mussolini did overtly and dominatingly impose his own views about policy. It has already been noticed how the *Duce* charged forward in the 'battle for the lire' and used the valuation of the national currency to teach the nation's bankers and industrialists that they now must bow to him and to Fascism. Without being asked to explain his policy but responding aggressively to the merest hints of disapproval from his minister Volpi, and from others in the financial elite, Mussolini urged that it was his 'infallible intuition' which had pointed the way to the so-called *Quota novanta* (accepting that 90 lire equalled US$1).[71] This statement, with its in retrospect whimsical confidence that economics, too, were 'all in the mind', marked the moment in which the old liberal elites knew that they were living in a dictatorship and were to be governed by what is best labelled 'applied charisma'.

Many of the other policies of the 1920s, however, were not Mussolini's alone. The razzmatazz of the regime, its advertising jingles and propaganda, came from many sources and their texts and dressage were accepted by the *Duce* rather than being the result of his initiatives. Most of the legal framework of the totalitarian state was drafted by ex-Nationalists and bore more of their philosophy than it did that of Mussolini or of radical Fascists. The Lateran Pacts, most widely hailed triumph of the regime, were equally by no means thought up and turned into practice by the all-seeing dictator alone. It is true that, during their last stages, he joined in the negotiations with a will and was ready to labour hard and long – night after night in his

1. Piero Bolzon, officer, gentleman and Fascist.

2. An early squad.

3. Pius XI inaugurating
Holy Year, 1925.

4. The complexity of salutes
in Fascist Italy, Rome, 1926.

5. Mussolini smiling
and striding (with
Achille Starace),
Rome, 1927.

6. Mussolini and Edda becoming respectable in the Borghese gardens, Rome, 1927.

7. Victor Emmanuel and Mussolini in civvies at the harvest.

8. Mussolini meets peasants in the Pontine marshes.

9. The athletic Renato Ricci and his boy scouts, Rome, 1930.

10. Boy scouts from Bolzano at Rome zoo, 1930, admiring an elephant and not a gorilla (see page 306).

11. The Sala del Mappamondo with a very small *Duce* at a desk in the corner.

12. Dante and Battisti joined as ghosts, Trento, 1935.

13. Fascist scout piping, 1935.

14. Fascist boys on holiday, 1935.

15. Teenage Mussolinis as toughs.

16. Roberto Farinacci.

17. 'Liberated Tigreans' and the Fascist white man's burden, 1935.

18. Little migrant Fascists in Melbourne, Australia, 1936.

19. A seventy-six-year-old lady named Camilla donates her wedding ring after fifty-six years of marriage, 1936.

20. Cesare De Vecchi di Val Cismon as Minister of Education, 1936.

21. Giuseppe Bottai being scholarly.

22. Fiat in Ethiopia, 1936.

23. Vittorio Mussolini's wedding – the Mussolinis in high society, 1937.

24. Queen Elena, being statuesque, 1937.

25. Achille Starace, the King and small children,
Rome, 1937.

26. Princess Maria José and baby prince Victor
Emmanuel, 1937.

27. Mussolini, Italo Balbo and small migrant Fascists in Libya, 1937.

28. A Caesarian trio for 'the New Roman Empire', 1937.

29. Camelized troops outside the Victor Emmanuel monument, 1937.

30. Church and State in the rain, 1938.

31. Galeazzo Ciano as Fascist pin-up, 1938.

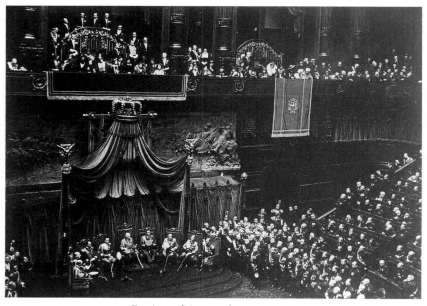

32. Fascist and Savoyard ceremony, 1939.

33. The Axis licked.

34. Italians pleased to become POWs, Calabria,
September 1943.

35. Schoolteacher partisan, Val d'Aosta,
1944.

office well past midnight – to refine clauses, pleasing to all. The Mussolini who now worked in sensitive collaboration with colleagues, courteously sought the approval of the Vatican's agents and was ready to overlook rumours of loud complaint by Pius XI, himself notoriously ready to let anger be his guide, resembled more the sage politician than the fanatical ideologue bent on hell-raising. It was this adroit Mussolini who increasingly disappeared from view during the following decade.

None the less, there were also occasions when the *Duce* emerged from the ramshackle administrative practice of his dictatorship to take the lead directly and carry an idea into practice himself. From the end of 1934 it was the *Duce* who decided to wage war on Ethiopia and the *Duce* who gave the conflict its blatantly Fascist cast. Some disagreement may be possible about the other battles in which the regime had engaged and would engage but this invasion was 'Mussolini's war'. Mussolini determined on action. Mussolini ignored the feeble and ill-conceived efforts by the British government to dissuade him from military attack. Mussolini set aside nervous worries from such people as Volpi, Acerbo and the King about risking African adventure when Hitler and the Nazis had reduced Europe to being a tinder-box. Mussolini drove his doubtful generals into brutal attack and persuaded them to sweep on to Addis Ababa, in what turned out to be the only successful Fascist version of *Blitzkrieg*. Mussolini (perhaps with the occasional doubt) rejected all compromise and demanded conquest. Mussolini brought empire back to 'the fatal hills of Rome'.[72]

So much was short-term triumph. Yet the dictator's victory would prove fleeting and, when it is studied with care, Mussolini's administration of imperial war, somewhere beneath the sweeping gains, had not really overcome the difficulties and absurdities of charismatic rule. In assessing his governance, a handy yardstick is available, given that the Fascist venture into Ethiopia, three years prior to the outbreak of the Second World War, bears considerable resemblance to the Liberal attack on Ottoman Tripoli, three years before the First World War began. In each case, Italy was an unrepentant aggressor that had to put up with moral condemnation from such great and powerful friends as Britain and France. In 1911–12 Prime Minister Giolitti was determined to tough out any querying of his nation's act by the European powers and, if his style was not Fascist and he was eager and willing to negotiate with any worth talking to, he decided early to annex the entire territory of what became Libya and refused all counsel to retreat from this choice. Giolitti was much vaguer about what the expansion of Italian empire was for and, once the Turks had surrendered, he was happy to leave the new colony as much to its own devices as was practicable. The Liberal Libyan War was more a matter for domestic consumption in the peculiar circumstances of Italy's fiftieth anniversary celebrations than it was a carefully placed milestone towards further foreign and imperial advance.

Fascist aggression sounded different and war in Africa was soon succeeded by other small conflicts within Europe. Yet, away from the headlines, much of the pattern of Mussolini's colonial war repeated that of Giolitti. The *Duce* did press on to total victory but he, like his Liberal predecessor, scarcely solved the dilemma of what African empires were for in the twentieth century. He, too, had no war plan in the fullest sense of the term. Both the Liberal and Fascist leaders were, in their different ways, imperialists, absent-minded not in fomenting war but in thinking through what peace thereafter might entail. As shall be outlined further in the next chapter, Fascist imperialism did leave a considerable mark on the regime and its people (and it did kill tens of thousands of Ethiopians). But, once Addis Ababa was conquered, Mussolini himself seems largely to have lost interest in the matter and certainly never visited his new territory.

As for the other foreign policy initiatives of the 1930s, most were in some part Mussolini's own. They were not, however, only his. The intervention in Spain[73] and the attack in 1939 on Albania were organized in the first place by Ciano and his entourage. The Axis with Germany developed a force of its own and, although Mussolini certainly hitched his star and reputation ever more closely to it, he made the functioning of the German alliance, which grew to penetrate many sectors of his regime, another area of government which was not reliably under his direction and definition. By the late 1930s, in almost every eye, Mussolini was reduced to being 'Dictator Minor', a lesser being compared with the *Führer* and his frenetically active Nazis. They, not the *Duce*, moved headlong to war.

In these years of a regime beginning to turn sere and yellow, the practice of administration was departing further and further from the hopes that Fascism could conjure into existence, through its 'third way', some steely modern form of *buon governo*. In 1922 one of the key institutions of the new state was meant to be the Grand Council, that assembly of party notables which might act as a Cabinet, Fascist-style, where an ideologized decision-making process could reach its pinnacle. As time went on, however, the Council did not bloom. Instead, it gave every sign of withering away, from 1923 to 1929 meeting almost twenty times per year, from 1930 to 1936 ten and from 1937 to 1940 only six.[74] Once the war began it did not assemble at all, although it was never formally abolished, and in July 1943 was resuscitated to become the vehicle for the *Duce*'s overthrow by his fellow Fascists.

It was true that in 1939 the Chamber of Fasces and Corporations finally ousted the old Chamber of Deputies in what was boasted to be the jewel of ideologically driven constitutional reform. The sociologist Didier Musiedlak has demonstrated that this new forum for debate and decision had a changed character from the old, with the once predominant lawyers, for example, now outnumbered by party officials and by economists, engineers, agronomists and other technocrats on the rise.[75] The meaning of such careers may be rather more problematic than Musiedlak is willing to contemplate, however. He deals with simple categories and makes no attempt to investigate how many state servants still bore training in law and jurisprudence even if they did not directly practise as lawyers. There are reasons to be careful before accepting Musiedlak's conclusion that his evidence shows an enveloping 'totalitarianism' that, by 1939, may have been 'special and imperfect' but was 'nonetheless real'.[76]

It has already been noticed how the major student of the functioning of the bureaucracy under Fascism has contended that public servants exhibited an india rubber-like ability to absorb and deflect the more interfering of Fascist initiatives and preferred their patterns of behaviour to move with their own rhythms and understandings rather than those of some notional revolution.[77] In this view, the tally of more than 260 new *enti* or semi-autonomous concerns that had come into existence by 1943[78] is not proof of a totalitarian state spreading its tentacles like an octopus. Rather, in its latter days, the Fascist state was a frayed one, where there were plenty of fields to conquer by the ambitious and ruthless at a secondary level, so long as they made proper obeisance to Mussolini, but the purpose of their activity was rarely and accidentally connected to the national good and had little in common with any understanding of 'revolution'.

In his concluding paragraphs, Musiedlak utilizes the word 'monocracy' to talk about Mussolini's way of ruling by the 1930s and it may be useful as a term that is fresher than some of its competitors. Memoir accounts of these years recall a *Duce* in his office, holding his endless interviews and giving his for the most part hollow commands. But they also depict the busy anteroom of the Sala del Mappamondo, where, since interviews, unlike mainline trains, did not reliably run on time, Fascists, respectfully awaiting their *Duce*'s attention, crowded around. The anteroom was a place where gossip and malice swirled, personal advantage was plotted and alliances, trustworthy and lasting or not, were framed. Just being admitted to see the *Duce*, to emerge unscathed and clutching a paper that might indicate that a decision had been made, was the great aim of most courtiers of the dictator. The job thereafter was to convert the seeming blessing from on high into something that mattered among the *enti* or in the party or out in the business world. To a considerable degree, an underling, after seeing his *Duce*, was vested with power, so long as he was ruthless or smart enough to use it.

Fascism liked to display its modernity and underline its achievements by publishing impressively scrupulous-seeming accounts of works done and outlays accurately estimated. Yet, in a purist sense, the Fascist state had no national budget since Mussolini's private secretariat was a law unto itself and, as Musiedlak has helpfully demonstrated, most other leading Fascists sought and received personal funds over which accounting processes were vague or non-existent.[79] When, after 1940, the leaders of Fascist Italy proved even less able than their Liberal predecessors to manage a war economy, one reason was because corruption or, rather, flexible accounting, were rusted on to Fascist life.

In no part of administration were such assumptions more natural and more pervasive than in regard to the police budget, where

Mussolini perpetually smiled and turned his gaze from any idea of public or party accounting. As Mauro Canali has shown in his exhaustive archival account of informing and other forms of surveillance in Fascist Italy, Bocchini and his leading associates were allowed to be a law unto themselves under the dictatorship, with Bocchini acting as a generous patron and being rewarded in response with his men's full loyalty.[80] These agents had generally known the police chief earlier in his career and their commitment was to him, their office and themselves much more than to some ideology. Although relatively small in number this group was able to weave a spider's web of control across Italian society. This process was not normally one of torture and death, as the more sensational histories of modern tyranny might suggest, but rather of venality and perfidy, of anti-Fascists lured into dishonour and betrayal and of ordinary men and women persuaded to spy and to tell. Prodding the process along was cash – unbudgeted cash – monies that the dictator allowed to his police chief and Bocchini to his staff, with no questions asked. At least 815 'confidential agents' – one informer of German descent rejoiced in the name Carlo Marx – were, at one time or another, added to the secret police payroll and stationed throughout Italy and abroad although quite a few did not stay the course in this form of employment. Bocchini brooked no interference in regard to their choice of quarries but he did accept *raccomandazioni* from party colleagues in regard to hiring. Among the most assiduous of his courtiers in seeking out jobs for their friends and relations were Starace and long-term Under-Secretary of the Interior, Guido Buffarini Guidi.[81]

In the history of Nazi Germany, one of the most notorious features of life in Hitler's dictatorship is agreed to have been the rise of the 'SS state', the creature of Heinrich Himmler. This state was a cancer spreading through both Germany and the NSDAP (Nazi party) and threatening, by the end of the war, when it could boast its own factories, economy and (bizarrely international) armed forces, the Waffen SS, to devour all. The SS state may have had a mind of its own but deep within it was inscribed ideology and race. The SS state was simply the most fanatical efflorescence of Nazi fanaticism.[82] It had no direct equivalent in Italy. Yet Canali has brilliantly implied that, in the activities of Bocchini and his men and in their regular blessing by Mussolini, the dictator, who always put a meeting with his police chief at the top of his agenda, can be detected an Italian version of this variety of informal state.

Policing mattered a very great deal to Mussolini. In no area of the alleged exercise of his power is it easier to find him interfering. He insisted on personally handling the censorship policies of his regime, although with erratic effects which remained mostly reconcilable with the narrow cultural line then pursued by the Catholic Church. None the less, all writers and journalists in Fascist Italy understood that the dictator was perpetually looking over their shoulders and acting as a sort of bullying editor for the nation.[83] Similarly, almost every one of the 13,000 of his subjects punished with *confino* had their penalties initially decided by the *Duce* and any amnesties thereafter were similarly his choice. Bocchini and his successor, Camillo Senise, knew that every aspect of their work during an interview might grab the dictator's complete attention. Yet here too there were curious limits to the tyrant's power, constraints that were simpler than the psychological issue of why the dictatorship could never be safely installed and why its chief must forever imagine plots primed to overthrow him.

But, for all their cruelty, the secret police of Fascist Italy were not agents of the revolution and so were radically different in their effect on Italian society from the SS's impact on Germany (and New Order Europe). If the SS state embodied Nazi evil at its worst, the Fascist police offer a countering case, a more 'normal' specimen of the bleakness of dictatorial rule, if also a deeply troubling one, especially since, after 1945, reform was visited slowly on this part of national Italian life. Himmler believed in the weirdest Nazi mysteries; Bocchini believed in nothing except a satisfying coitus and a succulent lobster. Nazi policing sought to be a killing machine, whirring inexorably on following scientific principles to cleanse the world for a racial utopia. Fascist policing sought to foster human weakness in order to allow a tranquil life for those in charge and because, in the policemen's minds, the old Adam outlived any rhetoric about revolution and modernity, would outlast the impact of any stirring paeans to the *Duce* and dictator and continually mocked clever ideologizing. The SS sought to take the world to a future that was even more Nazi than that being achieved at Auschwitz and on the Russian front. The Italian police sought to winnow away Fascist ideals. Not for nothing was Bocchini at permanent loggerheads with Starace, who dreamed on occasion of establishing a PNF secret security organization, separate from the state body. He did not succeed.[84] Somewhere in the fine print of Fascist administration, 'Mussolini's Italy', as it was so easily called, was, under police guidance, being reduced to cynicism and, in that depressing fate, was meshing itself with the ever more cynical dictator in the wasteland of his personal and intellectual life.

The best symbol of the dictator's decline during the last decade of his rule was his relationship with Claretta Petacci, the young woman who, from about 1936, became something like the regime's *maîtresse en titre* – in 1942 Bottai would lament tartly that the regime was '"Pompadouring" itself and with what a wretched quality of "Pompadour"'.[85] Born in February 1912, Petacci was two years the junior of Edda Ciano and almost thirty years younger than her lover. She was also anything other than the 'new woman' of Fascist legend. Her father, Francesco Saverio Petacci, was one of the Pope's doctors; Signora Petacci claimed that she was a distant relative of Pius XI[86] and certainly did her best to facilitate contact between her daughter and the dictator. Whatever their past, the Petacci family were about as bourgeois and as Roman as a family could possibly be and in their softness and greed well embodied the sort of Italians whom Fascist rhetoric constantly excoriated as the enemies of the revolution.

Claretta Petacci herself had none of the intellectual zest of Leda Rafanelli or Margherita Sarfatti (this latter was by now a fading figure in the regime[87] although, after the introduction of anti-Semitic legislation in 1938, Mussolini did personally assist her emigration to the USA via pro-Fascist Portugal).[88] Scarcely a possible companion for Mussolini the thinker, Petacci was rather an airhead of the most predictable kind, a character who had been foreshadowed in Alberto Moravia's great novel about the emptiness of her sort of bourgeois life, *Gli indifferenti* (1929) (*The Time of Indifference*, 1953). Her route to Mussolini's bed was emblematic. When still a girl she had been starstruck, not by some he-man from Hollywood but by her *Duce*. She papered her bedroom in the upper bourgeois suburbs of Rome with his image and posted a gushing poem to her hero.[89] The two actually met in 1933 when Claretta was eighteen. Her father had given her a sports car for her birthday (not the present a peasant girl could expect on such an occasion). She drove it to the beach near Rome and it was there she happened upon her leader who was himself tooling around with little or no escort. Mussolini took her phone number and was soon in contact, although the affair did not fully blossom until three years later. By then Claretta had been married to Riccardo Federici, in a nuptial which was personally blessed by Pius XI. Federici was posted to Tokyo as air attaché and he conveniently remained in Japan until 1945. His young wife stayed in Rome.

There, with her family's connivance, she became a regular visitor to the room in the Palazzo Venezia, just off the Sala del Mappamondo, that Mussolini reserved for naps and other forms of leisure. Petacci gave no sign of any interest in Fascist mysticism or the rest of the regime's big ideas. When briefly imprisoned in August 1943, she concentrated her reading on *La Gazzetta dello Sport*, one of Italy's inimitable sports dailies,[90] although she did scribble her other thoughts, full of self-pity and exhibiting a complete lack of awareness of the disasters all around, into a jejune diary. While times were happier, her mind focused on such matters as whether her breasts and teeth were the size and shape they should be and how she could still manage to smoke, when the *Duce* disapproved of her habit. Historians have access to love-talk between the two – it was lamentably banal – through the curious habit of the police in tapping the phone connection between Petacci and the dictator.[91] The *Duce* gave her minks and jewels, although the more catty of Rome's social set maintained that nothing could overcome the deficiencies of her bearing and dress sense.[92]

The love affair, in sum, has little of interest in it and might be as easy to ignore as Mussolini's other sexual deeds (by all accounts, they were nasty, brutish and short and, contrary to the *Duce*'s own lucubrations about coitus, presumably unsatisfactory to his female partners) were it not that Petacci, unlike all the rest, lasted. In 1945 she died at her lover's side. Moreover, with her promotion to be a figure who counted in the dictatorship, so her own family began to play a part in the regime and to afflict its reputation.

In that regard, too, the story is banal but its banality is that familiar in regard to the entourages of most dictatorships and is completely lacking in the fervour and fanaticism, the totalitarianism, that was meant to have become profoundly rooted in the minds of the subjects of this regime. By the late 1930s the Petaccis became people who counted. F. S. Petacci published a semi-racist attack on abortion, hailing Fascism for the alleged way that it had purified young Italian womanhood.[93] Such sentiments, however hypocritical they seemed from Claretta's father, may have just been Catholic and did not provoke a major stir at the time. Rather more scandalous were the activities of Claretta's two siblings, the younger sister, Maria, and her brother, Marcello Cesare Augusto Petacci, whose Christian names bespoke the imperial pretensions of the Roman bourgeoisie well before they became subjects of a Fascist dictatorship.

Like many who have had a toe-hold on fame and fortune, Maria Petacci, born 1923, tried to make a splash in the entertainment industry, first as a singer and later as a star of risqué movies. With some inevitability she married a sprig of the aristocracy and took the stage-name of Myriam di San Servolo.[94] Neither professionally nor in her choice of partner did she remotely resemble a *donna madre*. She survived the world conflict.[95]

Marcello Petacci, destined to be in Claretta's company in the fatal days of April 1945 when the two would die with the *Duce*, had, during the late 1930s and in the war, proved a scapegrace too. The example of his professional success as a surgeon must suffice. In May 1938 young Marcello had contacted Mussolini's private office with the announcement that, 'following the desire of the Chief', he intended to take his *libera docenza*, his full degree qualifications, in surgical pathology, with the intention of serving in the armed forces. In order to secure his success he sent along a list of names of eminent university doctors, who 'could easily be summoned to be part of my examining commission'. In response, the relevant officials set about preparing a letter of recommendation to some of these experts. The phraseology was direct enough: 'Dr Marcello Petacci is well known for his background in politics and for his scientific record which he has gained despite his youth. It would thus give great pleasure if Dr Petacci could achieve his wishes and we recommend him to you very strongly in any dealings which you will have with him.'[96] Someone then minuted drily on this draft: 'I doubt if it is a good idea to make reference to his scientific record with these professors.'[97] And so another, briefer, letter was written, urging 'all possible interest' in Petacci receiving 'kind treatment'. For the brother of the mistress of the dictator, a *raccomandazione* could not be gainsaid. He passed his exam. However, perhaps to the good fortune of serving soldiers, few, if any, seem to have faced his ministrations in war.

Back in May 1933 David Low, the brilliant cartoonist enlivening the pages of the London *Evening Standard*, drew a sketch of the Four Power Pact, then preoccupying European chancelleries (in Italy it was still called the Patto Mussolini). The caption of the cartoon sardonically compared the diplomatic deal with a film studio: 'They have imposing façades but no rooms behind. They are meant to be looked at but not lived in.'[98] It is a comment that can also be applied to the way in which Mussolini, then and thereafter, was getting through the day as a dictator. At a public level he seemed a god. More privately, even perhaps to himself, he was rather too mortal. It was all very well for one Fascist propagandist, who must have believed that he could still hear echoes of the classical Roman empire, to remark that the *Duce* spoke in the same way that Julius Caesar did.[99] But the events of the second decade of the dictatorship were to show that its dictator had feet of clay and his regime would prove unable to surmount the terrible tests awaiting it. Now all that Fascist talk about war would have to adapt itself to real conflicts, be they in Africa or in Europe. They would bring some short-term victories but, within a decade, disaster.

13

Becoming imperialists

On 2 October 1935 massive Italian forces invaded Ethiopia, one of the two areas of Africa that, until then, had not succumbed to European imperialism. The military invasion had been prepared over the previous nine months, with some 100,000 troops sent to Eritrea and the Italian Somaliland, bolstered by a huge volume of stores. At home, the regime mounted its most obstreperous propaganda campaign to justify Italy's unilateral act. The attack on Ethiopia, Mussolini and his tame journalists maintained, expressed Fascism to its uttermost; Italian legions would be modern, efficient, pitiless and unstoppable. Joining the invasion, young Fascist intellectual Indro Montanelli maintained more carelessly, was the equivalent of 'a long holiday, granted by Santa Claus in compensation for the tedium of being stuck at a school desk for thirteen years'.[1]

Whether convinced by such messages or by other matters, many Italians welcomed the invasion, viewing the creation of a 'real' Italian empire as a cause for present national sacrifice and eventual national rejoicing. The majority were buoyed by pride and pleasure when on 5 May 1936 Italian armies entered the Ethiopian capital, Addis Ababa, from which the Emperor Haile Selassie had just fled in confusion and defeat. Four days later, Mussolini announced: 'Italy finally has its own empire. A Fascist empire, a peaceful empire, an empire of civilization and humanity.'[2] The *Duce* spoke for nation and regime when he saluted 'a date in the revolution of the black-shirts which will never be cancelled', the time when 'the Italian people held firm and did not bow' to the 'fifty nations' of the League in Geneva which had enviously tried to stop them through international sanctions.[3]

Yet somewhere in this triumphal tale questions lurked for Italians, just as they had for Mussolini's personal rule. Had the victory really been Fascist and modern, an Italian foreshadowing of the Nazi wars to come? Or, rather, was it national and traditional, a belated grab for Africa by the least of the great powers, where not far beneath the fanaticism of the regime's rhetoric the old imperial motivations of 'glory, God and gold' lingered? What sort of imperialists were Fascist militia and other officials, Italian soldiers and civilians, men and women? In Africa Orientale Italiana (AOI, Italian East Africa), as the three colonies of Ethiopia, Eritrea and Somalia were now referred to, did Italians conquer and kill as 'Mussolini's willing executioners'? Did they act because they had been indoctrinated by the regime's teaching (or by that of Liberal Italy) with imperialist fervour? Or were Italians reluctant imperialists, at least in those places marked out for them by the state? How lasting and how profound was the enthusiasm of 1935–6 or was it as fleeting as the exultant shouts which greet some national sporting victory and then quickly subside as real life returns?

When troops crossed into the territory of Haile Selassie and when Italians back home heard the news in press, radio or newsreel report, it may be surmised that some of them were whistling the catchiest tune of the day, a ditty entitled 'Faccetta nera' ('Little black face'). This song so took the nation by storm that, according to one commentator, 'there was a period of time when, in the whole country, no one sang anything else'.[4] Soldiers were proud to report that 'natives' also learned the words and tune.[5] Its first verse went:

Si mo dall'artopiano guardi er mare,
moretta che sei schiava tra le schiave,
vedrai come in un sogno tante nave
e un tricolore sventolà pe te

Chorus
Faccetta nera,
bella abissina
aspetta e spera
già l'Italia s'avvicina.
Quando staremo

vicino a te

noi te daremo un'antra legge e un antro Re

(If from the plateau, you look down on the sea, little black girl, who are a slave among slaves, you will see, as if in a dream, lots of ships and a tricolour waving for you. Little black face, pretty Abyssinian girl, you wait and hope, and already Italy is approaching. When we are there in your company we shall give you a different set of laws and a different King.)

It did not take long for the regime to become unhappy about this song and its sentiments. Its lyrics contained no direct mention of Fascism and worse was the idea of love between the liberated Ethiopian girl (however patronized) and the arriving Italian soldier. Soon after the conquest, the regime began busily to construct its own version of apartheid in its empire. Even buses were segregated.[6] Now it was no longer possible to contemplate the sophistication and tastiness of Ethiopian cuisine, as one colonialist journalist writing in a magazine sponsored by the Ministry of Colonies had been innocent enough to do a few years earlier.[7]

No wonder, then, that the official line became that 'Faccetta nera' was 'stupid'. Its inciting of a mixed race family was deplorable, all of a part with the sad trade in pornographic images of African women. These photos, a journalist remarked severely, despite their ban under Fascist law, circulated in millions throughout the peninsula. The ignorant peasants and workers who lusted over them failed to understand that black girls sweated and stank and were riddled with disease. Harsher repression was needed and, in the interim, no sensible and sensitive Italians, no real Fascists, should again sing 'Faccetta nera'.[8] But still in 1938 two rival records went on sale, one employing the state-financed symphonic orchestra and choir of EIAR for its sound. So popular had the song been that it prompted many alternative versions in various dialects, apart from the Neapolitan in which it had begun. Whatever the wish and will of Fascism, in the Italian memory of a short-lived empire 'Faccetta nera' retained a place.

The historian Renzo De Felice read the Ethiopian war as the high moment of popular consent to the Fascist regime.[9] But the history of imperialism and its effect on Italians under the dictatorship were more complex than this summation allows. In Liberal times, too, some Italians had wrestled with the meaning of empire. To be sure, pre-Fascist Italy could scarcely claim to be even the least of the great imperial powers. During the 1880s Liberal politicians had acquired control over Eritrea and part of the land occupied by the largely nomadic Somalis – the ports of Djibouti, Zeila and Berbera and their hinterlands, however, fell into French and British hands. Although the empire was not acquired absentmindedly, it did not yet promise a high national destiny. In 1881 Assab, the first base for a penetration of Eritrean territory, boasted, according to a solemn survey prepared by the Italian consul, a population of 160 (11 Italians, 55 Arabs, 93 Danakils and one Indian).[10] Italian expansion met with regular checks, the calamitous defeat by Ethiopian emperor Menelik II at Adua in March 1896, which overthrew Crispi's schemes to build his own AOI, being the most grievous disaster (5,000 Italians died).

This military and political humiliation was succeeded by the withdrawal of Italian forces, with almost all socialists and quite a few liberals proclaiming their distaste for imperial adventure. The classic question became: why should Italy invade the territories of others when its own southern provinces were so backward and poor? Yet a thirst for empire had not really been slaked. Among the educated classes, the hope that Adua could one day be avenged and the belief that Italy could only acquire proper political and cultural respect and commercial advantage through territorial expansion lurked in quite a few minds. An earlier defeat, that at Dogali on 26 January 1887, where 'five hundred' died, was, for example, converted into a lasting nationalizing propaganda device by Ruggero Bonghi, a Liberal worthy, who held such offices as Minister of Education and president of the patriotic Dante Alighieri Society. In justifying the cause in Africa, Bonghi deployed blatantly nationalizing phrases to a parade of those who returned alive: 'For the first time, because of your acts, the workers of the countryside, the workers in the city, have felt deep down in their hearts that the fatherland for which the soldier dies, for whose future he sacrifices himself, is not the town of his birth or this or that region of Italy from which, before now, we took different names, but it is Italy itself, the whole of Italy, which has had so many glories in the past and, barring a failure on our part, will have as many in the future.'

It would be rash to assume that Bonghi spoke to the whole nation or that, with such words, he was politically engaged in anything more than the nationalization of the bourgeoisie. Yet that process was a significant one. When their wounded came back to such cities as Perugia,[11] the Dogali veterans were greeted by crowds, and town-planners in Rome patriotically named the square outside the city's main railway station the Piazza dei Cinquecento (Square of the Five Hundred). Middle-class boys voraciously absorbed the works of Emilio Salgari (1863–1911), with his images, spread across 105 novels, of an imperial other, needing European help to modernize but also naked, wild and seductive. In so doing, they mimicked their fellows in Northern Europe, breathlessly reading Kipling and Haggard or the frontiersman tales of Karl May – the young Adolf Hitler became the best-known fan of that last writer. So, too, middle-class Italians rejoiced at the 'national' victory in the 1907 Peking to Paris car race. The winning team was tellingly composed of Prince Scipione Borghese, the owner of the car and an aspiring Liberal politician, his peasant driver and the journalist Luigi Barzini (senior). Barzini's vivid descriptions by telegram of the strange worlds the 35 h.p. Itala car traversed sold many papers back home.[12]

The greatest informal impulse to empire, however, was the new nation's alleged inheritance from classical Rome. The claim to constitute the 'Third Italy' (after the empires of the Caesars and the Renaissance) was well established in Liberal times and, although the matter is rarely noticed, permeated Italian minds long before Mussolini was portrayed as the *DUX* and Germans decided they should build a Third Reich. Before 1914 no Italian child in middle or high school could avoid a bath in the 'greatness that was Rome' and it was entirely predictable that Italian archaeologists should press ahead of the government in suggesting a return to places in North Africa or Asia Minor that had once heard the tread of Roman legions. *Romanità* (literally 'being Roman', and so the translation to present circumstances of the philosophy and practice of classical times) had many faces. When, in 1911–12, Giolitti, of all undemonstrative politicians, seized the Turkish *vilayets* of Tripolitania, Cyrenaica and Fezzan, he found it natural to call the new colony Libia (Libya), the name which it had last borne in classical times. Similarly, Giuseppe

Piazza, a Nationalist journalist writing in 1914, knew that 'Rome was always a conquering place' and demanded that the Third, Liberal edition of the city become more active in carrying out what he saw as the mandate of history.[13] In 1919 Federzoni, yet another with Caesarian ambitions, similarly proclaimed that 'the word "Rome" says to the world that Italy cannot tolerate the slightest infringement of its national rights'.[14] A decade later and now a Fascist, Federzoni drafted an extraordinary plan for an expanded African empire which would take Italian rule to the gulf of Guinea,[15] a dream which exceeded any ambitions nourished by the *Duce*.

Not all contemporaries went as far as Piazza or Federzoni but members of those social groups who, before and after 1915, were joining the Touring Club Italiano and devouring the carefully tabulated information and alluring photographic images that it provided of the wider world were true believers in European imperialism. They were possessed by a vaguely formulated hope that Italy, too, could bear its burdens. They may not have booked to go but they felt more stoutly Italian when, in a 1908 number of the TCI journal, they learned that camping trips were now possible under club auspices in Eritrea. At Asmara, the Albergo Menghetti was said to be a place where 'relatively speaking, all desired <u>comforts</u>' were available and where gentlemen's wearing in the evening of *lo smocking* was de rigueur.[16]

The TCI's advertising material was always emphatic about the organization's commitment to 'peace' and improvement,[17] even though one of its writers discerned that the 1914 war was 'in essence a racial conflict'.[18] Mussolini was not the only Italian in whose mind Social Darwinism reigned. However, as Italy drifted towards Fascist dictatorship, it was the Nationalist Association or ANI whose upper-class supporters were the most convinced and aggressive advocates of imperialism. Already before the war, a Nationalist like the aristocratic Luigi Medici del Vascello could proclaim that the Mediterranean was a *mare nostrum*, needing to be preserved from British or 'Slav' control, whatever might be Italy's current alliance arrangements. Syria and Palestine, he blethered in a speech of 13 April 1915, 'trembled with the memories and the language of Italian traditions'. 'Remember, gentlemen, that Constantinople was built by a Roman Caesar on the gorgeous banks of the Bosphorus, . . . and, while the call of the *Muezzin* rocks the Turk in his fatal torpor, the Galata tower sighs imploringly still to its Genoa: come back Italy!'[19] War only enhanced such luxuriant views. In 1919 the Nationalist journal *Politica* took it as read that 'the contest for empire' was 'the iron law' of humankind, insisting on acknowledgement across the political spectrum that a country's foreign policy must surmount petty domestic squabbles.[20] So, too, it was the ex-Nationalist journalist Roberto Cantalupo, who, under the dictatorship, knew automatically that 'colonialism is a process of an unstoppable political and spiritual expansion which will also give grandiose economic benefits'.[21]

Mussolini himself came from a very different background and was often happy to polish his sarcasm on the Nationalists' pretensions and lack of a popular base and understanding. Quite a segment of the Italian left carried the principles of anti-colonialism as central to their creed. The young *Duce* exhibited his objection to the Giolittian attack on Libya in public demonstration resulting in his own arrest and imprisonment. The more securely intellectual Salvemini contemptuously disdained the national seizure of a North African 'sand-pit', drawing pleasure in exposing the falsity of the analogies which Nationalists kept dragging up from the classical past. Catholics had a more ambiguous attitude towards empire; after all it was the leadership of their Banco di Roma, including members of the Pacelli family, who were to the fore in pressing for the seizure of Tripoli. None the less, in the Church, too, currents critical of imperialism ran free and Pope Benedict XV was aware of them. Then and later, the imperial preoccupations of a universal church were not always quickly reconciled with the expansionism of the petty nation-state, Italy. In its missionary guise, the Church bore moral and religious responsibilities in the world colonized by the great industrial powers. Simultaneously it sought to win a religious contest against such heretics and schismatics as the Copts of Ethiopia or those in Russia who believed that the third and true Rome had moved to Moscow after the fall of Constantinople.

Whereas cooperation in AOI between the papal and Italian Romes might not be too difficult to arrange, the politics of Eastern Europe were beset by many dilemmas, with the issues made tenser by the regime led by Bolshevik revolutionaries who believed that all religion was a retrograde and irrational opium of the masses. Pius XI's and Pius XII's Vatican became a more intransigent fount of hostility to the inter-war USSR than was the Fascist government, although Church campaigns clung to a verbiage about saving an erring sister religion from itself as well as from godless and, some churchmen did not forbear to note, Jewish Marxists. Inter-war Europe saw neither a political nor an ecclesiastical Eastern Locarno.[22] For all the normality of Fascist–Soviet diplomatic deals, a religious war smouldered not far below the surface of events to the east and was fuelled in part by the Vatican.

As far as Fascist fans of an African advance were concerned, any hint of anti-colonialism, be it socialist, Catholic or some other popular form, was deplorable and treacherous. In 1926 Pietro Lanza di Scalea, now Minister of Colonies in a totalitarian government, claimed that the dictatorship had rendered anti-imperialism obsolete for Italians. Once, he wrote, hostility to national gain had been stirred up in malign plots by 'parties which found their existence endangered by any national revival' and which 'believed that victories over barbarism were not necessary for the development of our civilization', attitudes which made the most perverse exalt 'the sterile anarchy of primitive regimes'.[23] But now no more.

Scalea's words appeared in a book published in honour of the silver anniversary of the reign of King Victor Emmanuel III. Italy, like other European monarchies, was a country where the impulse to empire was seamlessly linked with myth-making about the monarchy. Umberto I (1878–1900) had been as involved as Crispi in sponsoring those policies that led to Adua.[24] Other royals were easy to find in the Fascist Italian empire. Mussolini made a well-publicized trip to Libya in April 1926, his nose bandaged from the shot fired at him by the Irish-born attempted assassin, Violet Gibson (who was politically declared deranged and hustled out of the country). However, propagandists magnified the glory of his peregrinations only a little more than they did the King's travelling to Tripoli in 1928, Eritrea in 1932, Cyrenaica in 1933 and Somalia in October 1934. The young and sporting Crown Prince Umberto made his own publicity splash in Eritrea and Somalia in 1928.[25] Another member of the royal family,

Luigi, the Duke of the Abruzzi, younger son of the militarist Duke of Aosta, ran a model estate in Somalia. There in March 1933 he died, a lonely bachelor, because, it was rumoured, Queen Mother Margherita, most authoritative of the Savoys, had forbidden him to marry his lifetime love, Katherine Elkins, the wealthy and Jewish daughter of a senator from West Virginia.[26] The Duke had varied his dashing imperial exploits with cooler but equally intrepid mountain climbs within the Arctic circle and Mussolini felt obliged to give a eulogy at his funeral, where Fascist geographer Giotto Dainelli grovellingly saluted the Duke as 'the last great Italian explorer'.[27]

This link between imperialism and the heights of Italian society deserves remembering when assaying the violence and murder that stained the history of the Fascist imperium. Most Italian historians have been anxious to argue that Fascism, despite its leadership's vagueness and confusion about the virtue or vice of empire before 1922 – D'Annunzio at Fiume at times almost turned into a crusader for what came to be called the Third World – marked a change for the worse in Italian colonialism.[28] In so obscuring a more widespread national responsibility for killing, they are scarcely alone. Conservative Australia is united in hating what it condemns as 'black armband history', indulged in by any who seek to account for the shredding of my country's Aboriginal population after white settlement. Other societies have also been loath to admit the deadly aspects of their imperial rule. Yet the negative face of liberal imperialism should not be obscured. Italians in their empire killed as much because they were European imperialists as because they were Fascists.

Of their domain, the first to receive a distinct impulse from Fascism might be thought to have been Somalia, which had the small fortune to welcome the ex-*quadrumvir*, bristlingly moustachioed Cesare De Vecchi, as governor (in disgrace after his too murderous sack of Turin) from October 1923 to May 1928. Despite his brutality and braggadocio, De Vecchi was, among leading Fascists, the one with the best contacts in high society, a monarchist and increasingly pious Catholic, destined to be the first Italian ambassador to the Vatican. In regard to the genteel face of imperialism, he was a not inappropriate choice as colonial Viceroy. De Vecchi got around to composing an account of his tenure. Immodestly he used Julius Caesar's *Gallic Wars* as his model, composing his ostentatiously staccato phrases in the third person. Somalia, he contended, constituted the 'Southern Thule of the Mediterranean peoples'. If the legions of the first Rome had not trod its friable soil, Greek colonists had established themselves along its coasts. The Somalis, he conceded, were a little too treacherous to be entirely relied on but they were 'good fighters' and might best be comprehended as 'Africa's Irish'. In any case, by his own estimate, it had only taken a few months of effort for De Vecchi to turn around an administration that he had found in a state of collapse. On 2 February 1924 he issued a peremptory order disarming local clans and thereafter moved successfully to impose Italian rule throughout the colony. In his assessment, by January 1928 Somalia was fully prepared to welcome the visiting Crown Prince, who was photographed in pith helmet elegantly leaning on a post marked 'the Equator' and beside a pole from which an Italian flag uneasily drooped.

Other accounts are not so sure about the completeness of De Vecchi's boasted Roman triumph nor about the permanence of Italian pacification of the colony. Some Somalis may have welcomed the *Governatore*'s establishment of a mixed race police force or *Corpo zaptié*.[29] Others were doubtless attracted to the financial gain that could be won from enrolment in the Ascari or black colonial brigades of the Italian army. Such fighting and police formations, even in 1935–6, played an important military role in the empire. These soldiers of the king could be celebrated. In the early 1930s, the children's writer 'Marga', whose typical prose combined Fascism and Victorian-style moralizing, imagined a meeting between a Fascist toddler and a loyal and brave Ascaro, wounded by an Austrian dumdum bullet in the First World War.[30] In 1936, despite the deviation from Nazi-style European racial purism that such reliance entailed, Giorgio, the son of Cesare Maria De Vecchi and a young man who underlined his dedication to his *Duce* and his King, still was ready to compare black Somali soldiers with white Arditi, holy crusaders of the nation, in their dedication, discipline, fighting qualities and alleged popularity among ordinary Italians.[31]

But, in practice, the clans were clans and, for all such honied words and despite the erecting of some Fascist architecture in the capital, Mogadishu (Muqdisho), including a Siena-red Casa del Fascio,[32] life for most Somalis continued to be more conditioned by the arrival of the monsoon in the towns and locusts in the countryside[33] than by the fruits of Italian modernization. Somalia did not become a colony of settlement. In 1935 an estimated 250 Italian civilians resided in the capital, ten of them being women and three or four children. At least retrospectively Antonia Bullotta, a female resident, observed that the Somalis often mocked Italian pretensions to rule. She stressed that, in 1940, world war overwhelmed colonists who knew in their hearts that they could trust neither the Somalis nor themselves. After AOI proved a military joke and the Italian empire was routed by a small British imperial force, the Italians of Somalia split into factions, each seeking its own advantage, unable to find national commonality, despite the evident crudity of such Allied commanders as a 'New Zealander in a state of semi-savagery'.[34] At least if Bullotta's retrospective is to be believed, official claims that the colonists had been mustered into Fascist new men and women of empire had proved wide of the mark.

Bullotta's account of Somalia has one gaping omission. Nowhere does she mention the concentration camp at Danane, on the coast four kilometres from the Mogadishu town centre. In the second half of 1936, the *lager* – erected at the end of 1935 for Ethiopian POWs but over the next months left largely empty because the Italians, operating in the sector of the Ethiopian war commanded by Marshal Rodolfo Graziani, seldom bothered to take prisoners – began to fill. Along with another such installation at Nocra in Eritrea, the camp received some 6,500 Ethiopians, who had refused subjugation to Italian imperial rule and were carelessly dismissed by Graziani, now imperial Viceroy of all AOI, as 'elements of little importance but none the less harmful'. According to Ethiopian figures, almost half the prisoners died between 1936 and liberation in 1941, falling prey to a variety of diseases, occasioned by dirty water and poor or non-existent food supplies. Angelo Del Boca, the major Italian historian of empire, argues that a death toll of over three thousand may be exaggerated but is willing to concede that Danane was 'a sort of Dantesque mad-house'.[35]

Yet, here, too, contradictions appeared in a fashion that the constant repetition of the horrors of Nazi rule does its best to excise from the fretful history of humankind. In August 1937, shortly before Graziani was replaced as *Vicerè* by Amedeo, the new Duke of Aosta and the sort of royal imperial governor who would not have looked out of place in Nairobi or Canberra, the camp acquired in Colonel Enrico Mazzucchetti, from a Lombard military family, a fresh commandant. Mazzucchetti was horrified by his initial inspection of the place when he was confronted by a naked, skeletal body, reminding him, he said, of a piece of *baccalà* (dried cod), lying out in the open, awaiting burial. He noted in his diary with military briskness: 'There is much to do here.' He was soon petitioning the government for 180,000 lire in extraordinary funds and, when he was fobbed off with 8,857, took revenge with complaint that the administrators of Mogadishu and Addis Ababa were inept and malign, sadly lacking a genuine 'imperial mentality'. For all his charity, Mazzucchetti had not 'gone native'; he continued to think of Ethiopians as 'dirty' and in need of beatings from time to time. But he was a Fascist imperialist who hoped that he was bearing the white man's burden with propriety.[36] Similarly, even in the ferociously racist pages of *La Vita italiana* in 1938, a commentator who foresaw a population of three million white settlers in AOI within fifty years also believed that the native population would steadily increase in number and, under a beneficent Italian imperialism, rejoice in an improved standard of living.[37]

One part of the Fascist empire where the story of Italian rule is not wholly bleak was the Dodecanese islands, that naval booty which Italy had acquired somewhat accidentally while warring against Turkey in 1911–12. Liberal and then Fascist politicians refused to hand the islands to their national Greek rulers on the grounds that Italy was the sort of great power that should never yield advantage unless accorded greater gain. As with all of the Italian empire, the definition of national progress was dubious. Although Fascist rhetoric occasionally expatiated about the strategic possibilities of the Dodecanese group in the eastern Mediterranean,[38] the islands were always a charge on the Italian exchequer.

As for the islanders, they were occasionally troubled by Italian rule. De Vecchi succeeded the long-serving ex-Nationalist Mario Lago as governor there at the end of 1936 and was soon talking tough about language use and religious practice. In July 1937 local schools were forced to adopt identical programmes to those in Italy and, in 1938-9, anti-Semitic legislation was enforced at Rhodes, much to the dismay of its ancient Jewish community.[39] None the less, in retrospect, Fascist Italian administrators were recalled by all but self-consciously Greek-nationalized, middle-class islanders as more human and humane than were the Germans, British and French who had had occasion also to rule them. Many islanders believed further that the Italians had been more helpful masters than were the agents of the Greek government based in Athens that finally took national control after the Second World War. With a somewhat ironical acceptance of racial categories, *una faccia, una razza* (one common look, one race), men and women of the Dodecanese recalled the Italians as people after their own heart. The Fascist garrison and Italian officialdom, it was thought, had been chivalrous towards local women and kind to children. They were the skilful builders of 'beautiful things'[40] and, better still, pleasingly easy to manipulate by the crafty locals whose Greekness encouraged them to boast that Ulysses was their ancestor.

Italian wartime rule of mainland Greece has left a more negative history and other sectors of the Fascist empire cannot have their story painted in the heart-warming tints of the Dodecanese. Until 1935 the nation's most significant area of colonial rule, if always an expensive one in treasure to Italy and in blood to the natives, was Libya, where 10,000 locals died during a first revolt in 1914-15, a toll largely hidden from the national press.[41] The First World War further exposed the thinness of the original conquest. Soon after 1918 the liberal democrat Minister of Colonies, Giovanni Amendola, moved to amend matters. In August 1921 Giuseppe Volpi, the man Amendola had appointed as governor, reached Tripoli. Volpi had been instructed to restore Italian rule, achieve law and order and locate a means to draw profit from the colony. While engaged in these burdensome tasks, he proved himself the accommodating patron of the colonialist soldier Rodolfo Graziani, born 1882. They had met a few years earlier in Turkey, where Graziani, now retired disconsolate from the army after the war, was trying to revive his fortune by selling carpets.[42] In his memoirs, Graziani avoids comment on that part of his life but does claim that, in 1905, he entered the officer corps after surmounting a resonant exam request 'to demonstrate how Nations, although fallen into ruin, can rise again while maintaining their honour and love for liberty and independence'.[43]

Graziani's comprehension of these words was eventually to prove contradictory. But, after October 1922, Volpi readily accepted that he had become a governor in a Fascist government, being allegedly pleased at Mussolini's rapid insistence that his Fascists must now display 'absolute discipline'. In a series of military campaigns, exacting an official death toll of 6,500 Arabs and 620 Italian soldiers (some of them being Ascari),[44] Volpi imposed the appearance of peace on Tripolitania. He also presided over some modernization, at least of a public kind. Tripoli's cityscape was updated, with a special feature being the Lungomare Volpi, elegantly skirting the sea. The financially adroit governor even balanced the colony's budget, although he needed all his skill to do so. By contrast he was none too careful of Arab sensibilities, seizing land without compensation, imposing taxes and separating the European, Jewish[45] and Arab communities, one from the other.[46] Meanwhile he encouraged Graziani to range free in the interior; his military man liked to think of himself as a Roman coping as a Roman might with barbarians and was not squeamish in his dealing with rebels.[47]

In August 1925 Volpi was replaced by the martinet ex-*quadrumvir* General Emilio De Bono, while, from November 1926, the neighbouring colony of Cyrenaica welcomed as governor Attilio Teruzzi, another former soldier with African experience, as well as an early Fascist, if one regularly the butt of Mussolini's sarcasm because of what the *Duce* deemed his ineffable stupidity. In January 1929 the two colonies were united and given a single governor, Pietro Badoglio, who did not cease being Chief of General Staff. This rash of military men, some more directly Fascist than the rest, even though each hated the others and saw as his first task the contesting of his predecessor's rule, meant that Libya was becoming an increasingly militarized territory. Resistance by the original inhabitants, notably the religious order of the Senussi in Cyrenaica, had not been blunted by Fascist assault so far nor by a legislative loss of equality for Arabs in the new general law promulgated for Tripolitania and Cyrenaica in 1927.

In reaction to this lingering resistance, Italy embarked on what has been called a policy of genocide. Leading it were Badoglio, who urged his men to be 'ferocious and inexorable' in carrying out their raids, Graziani, who was the actual commander in Cyrenaica, Federzoni, who talked of the need for massive Italian immigration there,[48] and Mussolini, who, as ever, demanded that one act of savagery be surpassed by the next. Together they embodied much of the coalition that ran the Fascist empire, expressing the alliance that existed there between traditional imperialism and the dictatorship's new ideology. The actual perpetrators of the killing were similarly as likely to be upper-class technocratic airmen or ordinary Italian soldiers, some of the latter being Ascari, as fanaticized Fascist militia. The three cruellest acts in the campaign were the capture and hanging, after a desultory trial, of Arab leader Omar al Mukhtàr in September 1931, the bombing of the holy city of Cufra and other places, including the oasis of Taizerbo, inhabited only by shepherds and peasants, with canisters of poison gas,[49] and the penning of some hundred thousand people from the interior in concentration camps near the coast. These *lagers* were serviced with such deliberate lack of care that about half of the prisoners – men, women and children – died, while a Fascist expert described events in malignly hackneyed metaphor as a 'cleansing'.[50] Yet a more dreadful continuity was reflected (according to the tabulation of a Fascist journalist) in the fall of Libya's native population from 1.4 million in 1907, to 1.2 in 1912, 1.1 in 1915, 1.0 in 1921, 850,000 in 1930, and 825,000 in 1933.[51] Some of this loss may be explained by internecine killing and by nomads finding sanctuary in the French or British Empire across the border. But in no circumstances can the tally suggest that Italy, under either Liberal or Fascist flag, ruled Libya benignly.

Once the army had done its work of suppressing overt rebellion, it was time for civilians to take over and in January 1934, to Graziani's disgust, the next governor of Libya was announced to be Italo Balbo, once a callous squadrist chief but by now a more handsome figure, *persona grata* with the best people, Italian and foreign. Although Balbo was appalled by the thought of his new posting[52] – a reaction which underlines the perpetual peripheral character of empire in many Fascists' understanding of the meaning of their regime and its 'revolution' – he proved an energetic governor. In 1933 only a few thousand Italians were resident in the vast tracts of Libya. One unreliable settler was Amerigo Dumini, Matteotti's murderer, who ran the Azienda pastorale Dumini in Cyrenaica, backed by a bottomless government subsidy; officials in 1939 reckoned that Dumini had milked more than 380,000 lire from the exchequer during the previous decade.[53] Under Balbo, however, these small examples of the regime's ability to park its difficulties in a distant clime would be overborne by a serious attempt at mass colonization.

Ruthlessly seizing land in the Cyrenaican plateau and elsewhere, Balbo maximized the publicity potential of a migration scheme, translating to the colonial arena the skills and image which he had displayed as the dauntless leader of his aerial raids across the Atlantic. Soon this Fascist celebrity, second only to Mussolini in his public appeal, had even foreign observers talking about a 'sober gold rush', wherein poor and numerous Italian families – each was required to count a minimum of eight members – were transported to a colonial El Dorado. Libya was renominated the *quarta sponda*, the national 'fourth shore', its promise to enclose the Mediterranean at last rendering a genuine *mare nostrum*. If some admitted that the migrating peasants evinced a fatalistic air about their adventure, contemporaries hailed the public works, achieved or promised – Balbo took care to please any adventurous tourists who visited Tripoli by opening a splendid archaeological museum there in 1936 – and lauded the housing of the migrants. As one British journalist related: 'Uniformity is the most impressive feature. The houses might all have been cast from a single mould (as, indeed, they virtually were) and set with mathematical precision in farms ruled out on a drawing board . . . Behind each house is the same little concrete-walled yard, flanked with barn and byre and storeroom in identical order. Each has its haystack of uniform shape and size, and – in the villages west of Tripoli – its identical round cistern for irrigation and domestic water supply.'[54]

The Minister of Colonies, Lessona, had envisaged 500,000 immigrants settling in Libya but the number who came was far fewer, the largest group leaving Italy on 28 October 1938 in what was heralded as the migration of the *Ventimila* or 20,000 (really about 10,000). The experiment was soon overwhelmed by the onset of the Second World War and, in any case, the colony was struck by drought in 1940.[55] At the end of 1941 Libya counted 8,426 surviving colonists and that number halved in 1942, when the battle for North Africa raged over the very places Balbo had chosen for farms. The costs of the state intervention were high; from 1937 to 1942 more funds were expended on the colony than in its previous twenty-six years of Italian rule. The scheme certainly had a modernist Fascist air to it; from the numbers involved to the apparently mathematical precision of the planning, it could be read as an example of what Fascism called *bonifica* or 'scientific' reclamation. Whether the peasant immigrants were especially Fascistized or even nationalized as Italians during the process must remain doubtful, all the more because its time of ordinary functioning was so brief. Such reports as exist do display the arrivals' delight at houses where, for example, a family of ten, which in Italy had to make do with two beds, now obtained a separate sleeping space for each member.[56] Although the intrusion of Fascist bureaucracy meant that the immigrants did not merely compose chains linking a *paese* to the world in what had been the traditional manner of emigration, they did none the less travel in family groups and their identities remained as centred in their family life as in a grandiose Fascist 'revolution'. In any case, given the massive volume of Italian emigration before 1914 and again after 1945 – from 1946 to 1965 more than 280,000 Italians left for an external destination each year[57] – Libya always possessed an ersatz quality as a colony which might resolve the issue of Italian expatriation.

At least as problematic were Fascist attempts to colonize Ethiopia after the victory there. The Ethiopian empire contained a welter of class, ethnic and religious differences, which bureaucrats and colonists jostled rather than radically amended. Despite thoughts in the metropolis of large-scale settlement – the Pope was said to have believed that five million Italians could settle during the first decade of Italian rule – in 1941 there were only 3,200 functioning European farms in the whole vast territory.[58] Even that derisory total was bought at a heavy price in state expenditure and AOI became a plaything of the military, which provided most of the real administration in a never wholly pacified territory. At times contesting authority with the soldiers, at times collaborating with them were a group of voracious entrepreneurs, usually middlemen with good contacts to someone in the Fascist leadership, seeking gain through government contract or other forms of feather-bedding.[59] Marshal Badoglio, basking in his reputation as the soldier who had conquered the empire,[60] set an example of a kind by accepting elevation to the title Duke of Addis Ababa and, as a *pourboire*, half the funds he unearthed in the occupied city's main bank.[61] Farinacci commented sardonically, after hearing that Pavia university was granting the Marshal an honorary degree, that the only honour which still escaped Badoglio was to become a Cardinal or to be canonized.[62] Like many another in the Fascist years mindful of his family, Badoglio was said to have encouraged his sons to maximize profits in military contracts and other colonial affairs,[63] while in 1937 Lessona organized three million lire as a government gift towards the building of a palatial Rome villa for the humble soldier's family, then debating whether the Duchy of Addis Ababa was hereditary or not.[64] Ruled in this cavalier manner, an empire that under Haile Selassie had been self-sufficient now had to import food.[65]

The impact of Italian immigration on the inhabitants of Ethiopia remains a subject that needs further research. Italian chroniclers, with an insouciance they share with some other metropolitan historians of empire, have not bothered to tally the dead in the military conflict of 1935–6 and its aftermath. It is likely that tens of thousands of Ethiopian lives were sacrificed in those years and that there were further brutal killings in 1937, after the Ethiopian resistance wounded Viceroy Graziani in an assassination attempt. For three days Fascist militia were encouraged to rage through the 'native' quarters of Addis Ababa in an expanded colonialist version of a murderous squadrist raid. The casualties at that time numbered in the thousands, perhaps tens of thousands. Ethiopian historians estimate the total dead from Italian wars and governmental actions as above, even well above, 300,000.[66]

Another cruel feature of Italian rule was state racism, with legislation passed in 1937 banning physical congress between whites and blacks. The rigour with which Italians in the colonies practised such apartheid is contested in the literature, where it is easy to find memoir accounts emphasizing that what was drafted in Rome was not easy to fit to 'real life' and so was not fitted. In Ethiopia, white women were rare.[67] In this circumstance, Italians, who thought of themselves as expert in the ways of Africa, did not refrain from transgressing the official line and some of the more celebrated figures in the colony continued relationships with local women.[68] Up to 10,000 mixed blood children were sired in AOI between 1936 and 1940.[69] In October 1938 the royal Viceroy, the Duke of Aosta, admitted that 'effectively separating Italians and natives, in the actual housing situation [in the colony] is utopian'.[70] Matters were further complicated by the colonial version of 'institutional Darwinism', since army officers knew that they were different from Fascist militia, civilian bureaucrats were anxious to distinguish themselves from both and the few real colonists clung to their own identities and behavioural patterns.

A more shadowy form of resistance to the stentorian shouts of Fascist colonialism can be tracked in the archives. Even in 1935–6, when national consensus seemed to be complete, some indiscreet Italians mouthed ideas that had once been espoused by socialism or by the Catholic Church and were punished for their pains. One was Abele Zanichelli, a water-melon seller of the province of Reggio Emilia (before and after Fascism, a socialist or communist redoubt). On 4 September 1935 at the village of Vezzano sul Crostolo, he told his customers that 'you need a big-head like the *Duce* to go into a war. His real aim is just to have the Italians die in war and of hunger, since now they will say we must tighten our belts.' Anyway, he added, 'the Abyssinians are in the right because we are the ones who are breaking into their homes'.[71] Another hostile to empire and the conflicts it might spawn was a leading railwayman of Forlì. Aurelio Amici was arrested for declaring, while enjoying a coffee at a local bar, that Italy was mistaken in bringing down the wrath of Britain on itself. 'That nation', he advised, 'should always be feared because it succeeded in subjugating Napoleon Bonaparte, William II and others' and was vastly rich compared with Italy.[72]

A third doubter was Italo Valesani of Feltre. He had gone out to Eritrea in June 1935 as a worker whose task was to pave the way for the military. However, he soon returned and was arrested after remarking at a Feltre *caffè* that Assab was a 'cemetery'. 'In those sorts of places,' he said, 'white men can't survive.' Malaria and other tropical fevers were endemic and inescapable.[73] In yet another case of dissidence, this time from the province of Ascoli Piceno, the Concettis, father and son, were punished for their deviant views of the war and their guileless sense of family solidarity. After the father started wrangling with other citizens of the town of Falerone about imperialism, Francesco Concetti, until then a young Fascist with a wholesome political record, weighed in with approving comments about Malthus and added his view that 'the head of government is neither a superman nor a semi-deity'. When Mussolini was dead, Concetti argued with a surviving sense of historical decorum, 'then we shall see whether he was great or not. For the present it is better to keep quiet.' The *Duce* was not a real philosopher, Concetti maintained boldly, at the cost of a five-year sentence to *confino* (he and his father were amnestied after twelve months).[74]

When the invasion began, one who continued to question national military prowess was Ferdinando Belli, a reasonably well-off shopkeeper in his forties from Cremona. In the local paper Farinacci may have been thundering about how the war was a conflict between 'barbarism and slavery on the one hand and civilization on the other' and have urged that any who disagreed 'offended, and engaged in aggression against the white race, demeaning themselves to the equivalent of slave-traders and professional bandits'.[75] But not everyone had heard. In late November 1935 Belli, returning from a hunting party with friends to dinner at the Osteria Transvaal at Acquavigna Cremonese, moved the cruet around to demonstrate that, in practice, Italian forces had so far occupied a tiny proportion of Haile Selassie's empire. 'In any case,' he said, 'in its previous wars, Italy only managed to seize a few stones and some sand and that's what it will get with this one, too.' The British had justice on their side in their imposition of sanctions, he added. Belli, it turned out, had been decorated for courage in the First World War and had enrolled in various Fascist organizations, while not actually taking out a party ticket. None the less, the police explained that Belli 'was habitually ready to launch into criticisms and negative appreciations of government measures and so no one who knew him was surprised by his arrest'. The official appraisal was typical but double-edged, since it implied the existence of a discourse of criticism at Cremona. A sceptic might suspect that it would not be stilled by Belli's punishment of three years in the hinterland of Reggio Calabria.[76] In the frequent pattern for 'apolitical' victims of Fascist policing, Belli was amnestied within a year.

The national victory won and the grandiose celebrations of the proclamation of the empire over, a current of dissent resurfaced from time to time. Stefano Vassallo, a poor thirty-three-year-old mattress-maker from Ventimiglia on the French border, was arrested in August 1936 for expostulating while tipsy: 'Cowardly Italians. You have killed 80,000 Abyssinians in order to drag liberty into the mire. We are the real barbarians.'[77] Equally troubled was Luigi Luciani, a forty-two-year-old peasant from Brugine to the south of Padova. Luciani interrupted a conversation at the local inn to ask: 'What have the Moors [sic][78] done to us that we should go off to their country to kill them?'[79] More salacious were the ideas of Filippo Torquati of San Benedetto del Tronto, a barber in his early twenties. While waiting in line at the local brothel, Torquati declared: 'Italy, without any serious reason, invaded Abyssinia and conquered it, unfairly stripping his empire from the Negus. Our soldiers broke into the *tukuls* [of the Ethiopians] and demanded the favours of Abyssinian women. When they were refused, they killed them.'[80] Under cross-examination, Torquati, a poor man who had joined the PNF in December 1936 and had 'no political precedents', also suggested that the regime, before going off to Africa, 'would have been better off first to think about civilizing the Italians'.[81]

In sum, the acquisition and subsequent rule over Ethiopia, though endlessly hailed in the Fascist media, left intact traceable doubts among Italians and doubts that had a long history. Some clung to the view that invading a foreign country or seizing the property of others was a sin and an error. Others worried about the cost of imperial adventures for a nation that evidently had not solved its own problems of poverty and 'backwardness'. There were even those who deemed Mussolini and his aides headstrong or corrupt, maladroit in both their diplomacy and their war-making. The Fascist journalist Giorgio Pini remarked in 1937, with what seems in retrospect studied irony: 'Fatto l'impero, dobbiamo fare gli imperialisti' ('Having made the empire we must set about making the imperialists').[82] Pini's words confirm the suspicion that quite a few Italians remained unconvinced that a Fascist 'cultural revolution' was converting them to whole-hearted Africanists. Three years later, a grandiose Mostra delle terre d'Oltremare (Exhibition of overseas territories) opened at Naples. It was not a popular success.[83] A more recent commentator has under-lined how uneasy most Fascist monuments about empire were and how unimaginative their placement in Italian cities; they were, she says, 'visually pedestrian, neutral, disembodied affairs'. Their shabbi-ness belied the inordinate expenditure of the years from 1936 to 1939, when the empire exhausted a quarter of all government monies, and so gives the first explanation of Fascism's dismal military performance in the Second World War.[84]

On Good Friday 1939, Italian forces crossed the Adriatic to dethrone King Zog of Albania and seize his lands. They thus engaged in what might seem a fanatical Fascist act to spread their revolution within Europe. By June that year, it was announced that Albanians were being marshalled into a local Fascist party and the country's new administrators were soon passing legislation confirming other key fea-tures of the corporate and totalitarian state. Analysing the meaning of the invasion and the subsequent Italian imperial rule over Albania is made difficult, however, by the fact that Zog's country was already in most ways a de facto Italian protectorate before 1939 and because the motivation of Ciano, who was the chief proponent of the attack, com-bined a thirst for financial gain and resentment at the way that Nazi Germany had already added Austria and most of Czechoslovakia to its Reich. Locating a more popular enthusiasm for ruling Albania is not easy. In most Italian eyes, it remained a 'far off country of which they had seldom heard'; its acquisition had not been driven by any mass movement or by any novel ideological fanaticism.

For all the global dreams that, on occasion, sparked Fascist ambi-tion, the locality, like the family, remained throughout the dictator-ship the focus of a great deal of Italian thoughts and actions. Yet, in its empire-building in Libya, AOI and the Balkans, Fascist Italy, fre-quently following a path marked out by its Liberal predecessor, sought imperium in places which lay well outside the knowledge charted in the mental maps of ordinary Italians (as distinct from the small group of Nationalists, colonialist experts and other Africa fans). Daily life and imperial aggrandizement ran along tracks rarely des-tined to meet.

The inhabitants of this other, pre-national Italy had long been pur-suing a *Weltpolitik*, rather grander in its span, more successful in its achievement and more evidently beneficial than anything achieved by Fascism. This global policy or set of policies were traced by the nation's world-spanning emigrants. Here again a massive difference existed between Fascist Italy and Nazi Germany in regard to the relationship between regime policy and what might be deemed a popular will. When the Germans struck east and brought Austria, the Sudetenland, Danzig and the *Volkdeutsche*, wherever they might be found, home to the Reich, they were pursuing what could credibly be explained as a national policy. In their Third Empire, all Germans would live and all non-Germans might die or be reduced to helots in a national final solution, an ethnic cleansing of an ultimate kind. But Fascist foreign policy did not assume this pattern (except in wartime Yugoslavia). Mussolini's troops dallied in African climes where, despite occasional extremist voices favouring genocide, mostly the issues paralleled those of other imperial European states gone to a continent where hundreds of millions of Africans lived. Yet the emigration that had been so massive from the 1880s to 1914 and threatened to resume its old course after 1918 siphoned Italian citizens not to these colonies but to the permanently foreign soil of New York and Buenos Aires. If a 'total' Italian nation was to be built, then how was the Fascist regime to deal with these emigrant Italians in need of redemption? What should Fascism do with those men and women who, before 1922, had abandoned the *patria* in a spontaneous and independent action of the Italies and not one markedly framed by the nation-state?

As in so many other matters, Fascism, in its early days, had only an approximate ideological answer to emigration and its problems, even though that massive process had carried an average of almost 600,000 Italians out of their country each year between 1906 and 1915 (after curtailment in the war, in 1920 the figure jumped back to more than 610,000).[85] Again it was members of the ANI who were most preoccupied with the loss of blood that they believed rendered the body politic anaemic; the sociologist Robert Michels maintained that the USA and other receiving countries had nefariously sucked out from the migrants the 'red corpuscles' needed to stiffen their societies.[86] Moreover, migration was a matter that affected different parts of Italy differently. Fascism's determination to convert socialist provinces meant that the party's operations were most aggressive in those parts of the country where emigration was lowest. Marxism had preached that migration was an international conspiracy benefiting the possessing classes, demanding that socialist cadres should stay home and fight the bosses there rather than seek wealth in flight from their homes and factories. Fascists in Bologna and Ferrara had little reason to concern themselves with migration, because emigrants were flooding out of the Veneto, Sicily or Calabria and not from the Romagna.

Although it was natural for fledgling *fasci* to start appearing in some emigrant centres – it was estimated they totalled at least 150 by February 1923[87] – Mussolini initially appeared something of a liberal on the issue, accepting in May 1924 the task of presiding over an international migration conference in Rome. He did talk early and characteristically, however, about greater state intervention to amend the chaotic situation of the past.[88] In December 1924 he told the Chamber of Deputies that it would be 'better for Italians to work their own lands rather than those of others', yet he still thought that migration to Brazil, among other places, had positive effects.[89] It was only with the formation of the totalitarian system that Fascism formalized its hostility to emigration. By 1927 Grandi had declared that this last word should be banned from Italian vocabularies.[90] Italy under Mussolini's regime, prompted by the virtual closure of the USA against immigrants from what was viewed there as racially inferior Italy, became a place from which it was relatively difficult to migrate and the world economic crisis of 1929 and after did not make migration an easy option for any potential host country. From 1926 to 1935 the annual average exit fell to 149,000; in 1936 a meagre 42,000 left Italy.[91]

At the same time the dictatorship worked much harder than had its Liberal predecessor to preserve and establish the sense of being Italian among the nation's global diaspora and, while engaged in that process, pursued the task of forging new Fascist men and women in emigrant communities. In 1932 Grandi urged that migrants be persuaded that they belonged to a 'little *patria* understood as being Fascist to the core'.[92] Regime journalists were soon declaiming (inaccurately) about the way their nation had won the international gold medal for demographic increase over recent generations, insisting that classical Rome offered the model for spreading influence abroad. As the journal of the Fasci all'estero (Fascists abroad), a body first organized in 1923 after taking over a liberal organization, put it windily, the Eternal City was truly universal and transcendental: 'In so far as Rome is concerned time does not exist and neither does space.'[93] A little more practically, propagandist Mario Appelius contended in *Il Popolo d'Italia* that emigration, once a weakness, had already been harnessed by Fascist dynamism into a source of influence for Italy and was 'infallibly' destined to become 'a factor of power'.[94]

The Fasci all'estero were given a prominent position in the dictatorship's bureaucracy and, from 1928, placed under the wartime pilot and journalist Piero Parini, born 1894, once a junior to Mussolini on *Il Popolo d'Italia*. Parini pledged that he would 'defend *italianità* in past and present' and, under his prompting and helped by subsidy from Rome, before long most migrant communities boasted their own *dopolavoro* (after-work) clubs and Balilla (scouting) groups. Their officers, where necessary commanded by local Italian consulates, did their best to join in national and Fascist celebrations – the Birth of Rome, Vittorio Veneto Day, the Befana Fascista – and rallied emigrants through film and speeches to share the euphoria of the invasion and victory in Ethiopia, for example. Nor were the police absent from the emigrant world. Anti-Fascists were kept on as tight a supervising leash as they were in Italy, especially because the host countries usually had a freer press than did the Fascist dictatorship and so anti-Fascist papers could survive, despite the regime's anxious financing of pro-Fascist journals in every centre. Embarrassing incidents were always possible; on Christmas Day 1928 the vice-consular coat of arms in the Queensland sugar town of Innisfail was stolen by an intrepid anti-Fascist and hung on the public toilet further down the street, an act the local Italian authorities treated as a serious affront requiring formal complaint to the Australian government.[95] Consuls were not above encouraging local Fascists to assault emigrant anti-Fascists and otherwise made life miserable for any who dared to doubt Fascist achievement.

Historians remain divided about the meaning of these attempts to Fascistize emigrants. There is plenty of evidence of migrant communities extolling Mussolini as a great leader and of their members donning black shirts, giving Roman salutes and accepting the accoutrements of the Fascist cultural revolution. Doubts remain about the profundity and ubiquity of the conversion, however. After all, with the onset of the Second World War, there were few instances of emigrant Italians deciding that they must serve their old Fascist *patria* rather than their new one; historians of Italo-America see the conflict as the moment when Italo-Americans became American patriots. Over the last two decades, while communities have looked to play victim politics, both in the USA and in Australia, a literature has developed arguing that the internment policies towards Fascist activists, doubtless very crudely implemented by the host countries, was another of those parts of the war for which governments should be expected to apologize and pay compensation.[96] Such claims do not acknowledge that quite a number of emigrants did look like Fascists in 1939–41, even if their uniforms really signalled not Fascist fanaticism but merely an enhanced national spirit and one where self-interest played a major role. Fascist consuls could be generous to ostensible sympathizers with the regime, at a time when Anglo-Saxons did not hesitate to relegate Italians to a position far down their list of racial virtue and so to block their political and commercial advantage and restrict their social mobility in their new societies. None the less, the claims of diplomats like Dino Grandi,[97] once he had become ambassador to London (and had his own self-interest to consider), that the 'community' in Britain was fully Fascistized and radicalized, cannot be taken at face value.

As was true of the people in large tracts of Italy, migrant communities were braided with many histories and did not necessarily constitute united and single groups. Class, gender, time of departure, region and many other factors apart from politics continued to fracture the migrant world. So many matters were not yet systematized. In 1939 Emma Orlando, a teenage girl from the Abruzzi, left her home *paese* of Casalbordino on a family migrant chain to catch a boat plying to Australia. At Naples, she recollects in her memoirs, she first saw the sea.[98] Yet the Adriatic is plainly visible some twenty kilometres down the hill from the main *piazza* of Casalbordino. How can the peasant girl's blindness be explained? The answer is, of course, by historical change. After residence in Australia, 'sea' meant many things to Emma Ciccotosto (as she became after marriage): the move from Italy, the fishing which employed many fellow Italians in the port of Fremantle, employment and leisure. None of these meanings had yet been imagined in Emma's world when she was still a peasant child, leaving behind the swaddling bands in which she had been wrapped as an infant. The girl Emma had never been to the seaside, although she may have heard stories of pirate raids or of other fabulous maritime adventures. But a 'modernized' sea was not yet part of her history and her identity. Aged thirteen, Emma Orlando was not a fanatic for empire, not a Fascist, not an Italian, not a modern woman; she was, however, a peasant girl from Casalbordino, comforted and strong in her family life.

Other complications in the ways Italians understood the travails of the world and its peoples can be displayed in a very different case from nearer the summit of the regime's life. Piero Parini had gone on being a true believing Fascist. During the Ethiopian war he made a bathetic attempt to enrol a Fascist-style international brigade that welcomed returned migrants joining the crusade for empire (its military utility was slender).[99] Parini was so charged by this imperial prospect that he urged Mussolini, in one of the most extreme expressions on record of Fascism, to accept a death toll of up to a million Italians (and who knows how many Ethiopians?) to carve out an empire and avoid the humiliation of further emigration.[100]

Yet, like many other Italians, Parini had a family member, Friar Alberto Parini, in the priesthood. This cleric earned a footnote in history in 1946 for helping to conceal from police the corpse of Benito Mussolini, stolen from its unnumbered grave by some Fascist nostalgics. Then the Franciscan seemed, like his relative, an unreconstructed friend of the regime and a backer of its hope in resurrection. However, 'charity' and 'belief' were words complex in their definition in the history of Fascism and Father Alberto Parini retained an ability to design his own highly idiosyncratic track away from and towards totalitarianism.[101] By so doing he may stand for many Italians caught up in the curious history of Fascist empire.

In early December 1942 Friar Parini fell foul of the dictatorship and was sentenced to five years' *confino*, though he was amnestied within a fortnight. His crime was that, on more than one occasion, he had publicly attacked the *Duce*'s demand that, to become thoroughgoing Fascist warriors, Italians must learn to 'hate their enemies'.[102] That phrase, the priest had argued, not mincing his words, constituted a 'gross blasphemy'. 'Those who want to regulate the lives of others', he had cautioned with evident unkind reference to Mussolini's own disordered personal behaviour, 'would do well to regulate their own.' It was also not a good idea, he added, to let yourself be seduced by huge headlines or by what the party transmitted in radio broadcasts. Such false news was in practice 'no more than an irritant to the poor people who today are so oppressed but who will one day rise to throw off those who presently oppress them'. Whatever the future might hold, on all occasions Parini urged, returning to his chief theme, we must remember to pray for our enemies.[103]

When asked to speak in his own defence, Father Parini protested that, despite the sound of his words, he was a patriot. A ringing speech he had once given at Dongo in the not-far-off province of Como (where Mussolini was destined to spend his last night) had led to his being offered honorary membership in the Fascist party. He explicitly repeated his rejection of any idea that Italians should hate their enemies. But he also declared that an adjutant of the Duke of Aosta and Piero Parini could be summoned to act as guarantor for him. In fact the *raccomandazione* preserved in the archives was from Farinacci. The *ras* of Cremona wrote to Senise, the new police chief, with initial heavy sarcasm: 'I want to profit from the occasion to get into Heaven. Is there any hope, do you reckon? But, if you can do anything for [the friar], I shall be grateful.'[104] Parini was amnestied the next day.

Fascism was a violent, aggressive and imperialist tyranny, with too many killing fields on its conscience. By 1942 it was also an openly racist dictatorship, not by accident the partner of Nazi Germany as that supremely horrendous regime implemented its final solution. Yet, the cases of Emma Orlando and Alberto Parini, of Ferdinando Belli, Filippo Torquati and many another, in their different ways suggest that not all Italians automatically bowed to the official Fascist view of empire or the party line on human and national identity. Neither in AOI nor in Albania nor anywhere else did the dictatorship excise the contradictions which separated the notions of an empire uneasily made by Italy the great power from that more informal imperium which has allowed traces of a diaspora from the Italies to amplify and enrich so many lives in so many countries today.

Yet it is important not to become too sentimental. If the worst violence in Fascist Italy came from above, especially in the empire, a harshness can easily enough be located below. Galliano Conte, the municipal dog-catcher of Treviso, was ill-advised enough to tell a local woman in May 1938 that he longed to employ his techniques for disposing of unwanted canines on Hitler (then visiting Italy) and Mussolini.[105] Virgilio Stucchi, a Neapolitan drunk, in spring 1941 looked forward to an English victory as the occasion on which Mussolini and all his family could be boiled in oil. Actually that might not be bad enough for the *Duce*, Stucchi reasoned; Mussolini should get some even worse special treatment.[106] With scarcely less charity, a number of irritated factory or peasant women called down 'cancer' on their leader.[107] Poor on poor killings did not disappear under Fascist order; such events were simply not reported in the tamed press. Furthermore, the many contradictions of Fascism fostered a popular cynicism and a desire to win by any means possible which scarcely rendered Italy an Arcadia. Italians may not, for the most part, have been fully fanaticized *militi*, but they were not simply 'good people' either.

14

Embracing Nazi Germany

The swift success of Italian arms in Ethiopia took the world and many Italians by surprise. Despite the mobilization of 500,000 soldiers, fewer than 3,000 Italians died in battle, less than half those killed at Adua in 1896. A retired Italian general earned a salute from his *Duce* when he crowed over the discomfiture of foreign pundits and remembered that there had been a similar absurd moral outrage in 1911–12 when the Liberal regime seized Libya.[1] There was a downside to the victory, however. The brutality of Italian methods of combat and the truculence of Fascist diplomatic dealing and press comment stimulated a widespread view outside Italy that Mussolini was the worst and least restrained of European dictators. He was, in the language of the time, the one capable of a 'mad dog act', the tyrant master of a barbarously aggressive campaign;[2] in more current words, the unappeasable rogue leader of the most rogue of states. The use of poison gas, the London *Times* editorialized, was quite beyond the pale. Worse might follow. 'Whenever the League [of Nations] fails to check one dictator in his disregard of treaty obligations, there is – and always has been – a direct encouragement to others to follow his example.'[3] Fascist Italy, the paper was soon adding, had reached 'zero in the scale' of international 'turpitude' in its murderous and treacherous assault on the Ethiopians.[4] An English Jesuit paper deployed more predictable metaphor when it damned the invasion of a sovereign state as 'nothing short of brigandage and murder on a large scale'.[5]

Public opinion heard of the wickedness of Mussolini and his regime in other ways as well. In 1935–6 the topic of Italy sold books and accounts of the dictatorship poured from the presses. It was now in the USA and UK that Salvemini's *Under the axe of Fascism* and George

Seldes' *Sawdust Caesar* found an appreciative readership,[6] with the latter being especially influential since its sardonic account matched many existing Anglo-Saxon stereotypes about Italian braggadocio and inferiority. G. L. Steer, the London *Times* reporter, published his experiences of the war under the sarcastic title *Caesar in Abyssinia*. Forgetting Britain's ruthlessness in its own imperial past and present, Steer described Fascist attacks in acid phrases: 'For the first time in the history of the world, a people supposedly white used poison gas upon a people supposedly savage. To Badoglio, Field Marshal of Italy, must be attributed the glory of this difficult victory. Some [Ethiopian casualties] were blinded . . . Others saw the burns spread upon their arms and legs and felt the increasing pain, whose source and end they could not understand and for whose cure they had no medicine.'[7]

It was now, too, that unflattering portraits of the *Duce* sketched by his old political enemies found a translator; a sometime writer for the British Labourite *Daily Herald* summed up the Italian dictator as the traitor-thief, the 'Barabbas', of the socialist movement.[8] In Africa and the rest of the world, the stirrings of black nationalism were quickened and, although Mussolini was not viewed as the only white racist, he did qualify as the worst.[9] In New York in June 1935 Joe Louis's knock-out victory over the Italian and Fascist Primo Carnera in a much-publicized heavyweight boxing match was hailed joyously by one black writer: 'What had started out as an Alp looked about the altitude of a chicken croquet by the time Joe got through with him.' When the news of the result spread, black youths were reported to have run through Harlem streets shouting: 'Let's get Mussolini next!'[10]

Among Anglo-Saxon elites, an admiration for Mussolini had almost always been qualified by the thought that the *Duce* was good for Italy because Italy was Italy and Italians were Italians but, for a self-consciously sensitive gentleman like Anthony Eden, Mussolini, in bringing on the Ethiopian war, was proven the 'gangster' on the international block. When the time was ripe this malign *Duce* should be blackballed from civilized circles. As the least of the great powers, Italy had often been thought to pester the world order established by its betters. Hereafter the Fascist dictatorship appeared not just pestiferous but menacing, not just demanding but criminal.

Back home, the overwhelming victory in AOI and the ringing statement that empire had returned to the 'fatal hills' of Rome pushed the dictator and many other Italians, puffed with national pride, towards ideological extremism and practical aggression. Gennaro Mondaini was Italy's leading academic colonialist, an expert geographer, historian and economist, by now in his sixties, who had been in his time secretary of the Istituto Coloniale Italiano, a Liberal lobby group which was the harbinger of a planned and popular national imperialism. Now, in a semi-official journal, Mondaini blessed the Fascist achievement of empire, fashioning Mussolini's victory into a legitimate part of a national aspiration which had begun in the Risorgimento, if not before. 'The conquest of Ethiopia,' he wrote, was owed to 'the political genius and firm will of Benito Mussolini, the military strategy of Pietro Badoglio and Rodolfo Graziani, the heroism of Italian troops (national [white] and colonial [black]), and the unanimous enthusiasm and admirable social unity of the whole Italian people.' In 1911–12, he lamented, imperial expansion had been opposed and demeaned by the anti-colonialist faction. Ethiopia had been different. It was 'the first extra-European war felt by the nation as a given, a sad but necessary step in its millennial existence'. The achievement of empire, Mondaini argued, entailed a leap forward into a genuine world policy, signalling Italy's escape from the 'Mediterranean and from the colonial tutelage' of Britain. By displaying the 'cohesion' of its people, the 'efficiency' of its military and the 'adaptability' of its corporate economic system, Fascist Italy had at last shouldered the white man's burden. Now it could proceed to raise its Ethiopian subjects, who, under Haile Selassie, had groaned in the 'last fortress of barbarism', towards 'civilization'. The taking of Addis Ababa, Mondaini concluded proudly, marked a milestone both in the glorious history of Italy and the praiseworthy story of European colonialism.[11]

Mondaini, in other words, still read the proclamation of the empire through lenses which were both Liberal and Fascist; he was more an old-fashioned imperialist than evangelist of a revolutionary new order. Other observers drew less temperate lessons from the victory of Fascism and its *Duce*. Giovanni Gentile glorified the triumph of Mussolini, the 'Man of All Times and Seasons'. The dictator had not just prospered on a foreign shore, Gentile mused; he had 'created a new Italy'. Now opposition was impossible. 'All doubts and uncertainties, derived from focusing on detail, from shabby resentment, from inveterate prejudice or just because it is hard to win, dissipate like fog in the wind.' Now and for ever, Gentile stated, Italy had no meaning unless it was coupled with Fascism. The subjects of the dictatorship could rejoice in belonging to a new and totalitarian state and in absorbing an ideology which amounted to 'a faith, a total conception of life'. Through its African conquest, Italy had demonstrated that there was no decline in the West and would not be in the future so long as all were ready to bow to Rome and its primordial might. Yet, Gentile implied, in this wicked and dangerous world the time of battle was not over. 'When Mussolini again raises his great voice', the regime's senior philosopher proclaimed in semi-biblical language, 'and calls us to the harvest, he must find tomorrow, as today and yesterday, ready hearts, just one heart, with the same thought, the same political line.'[12]

But were there any lurking adders, any snares and delusions, in this seeming paradise? The nervous pessimism which was so deeply implanted into Fascism and which was a permanent part of the project of the Italian nation catching up with its more powerful neighbours naturally suggested that there were. One who admitted them openly was the young journalist Indro Montanelli, who hid his own profound conservatism and banality beneath a devil-may-care persona, a recipe which would serve him well in the post-war Republic. Montanelli had volunteered to fight in Ethiopia but after his arrival found time to report on certain deficiencies which, he feared, lay deep in Italian hearts. He was happy, he announced sardonically, to leave European-style racism to the blue-eyed and fair-haired peoples from north of the Alps. But all Italians must hurry up and learn a more 'African' racism. If 'millions' of Italians were to settle in the Tigré region, as they should, they must migrate girded with a pronounced sense of their superiority. 'Racial dignity', Montanelli decreed, was the beginning of colonial wisdom.[13]

With the military success, Montanelli's preaching continued. The new migrants must come to Africa as soldiers and possess an iron discipline to be imposed on themselves and, more menacingly, on others.

'Owning a colony entails an examination in life, one that can easily be failed,' Montanelli remarked with some uneasiness. No doubt Fascist soldiery had 'embellished the reality of war with squadrist poetry, undertaking combat as a beautiful adventure'. That was good and great. Yet now there must be a new seriousness, one that could not be based simply on academic learning.[14]

In the radical pages of the Farinacci-sponsored *La Vita italiana*, war similarly deepened anxieties about the role of race for Italians. The Ethiopian conflict had brought to the surface the requirement to think harder about a 'totalitarian vision of the complex Jewish problem'. The noisy and fatuous opponents of Italy's campaign, the journalist continued, based in Geneva no doubt but actually inspired by London and Washington, were either Jewish or 'Puritan'-Protestants. In each case, these lies and heresies at war with 'Roman truth' sprang from 'identical ethical-religious principles and concepts'. Italian Jews, fortunate in their experience of the marvellous assimilationist skills of Rome, cleaved to the Fascist revolution. However, outside Italy, Fascism and the 'Jewish movement' stood 'poles apart' and the 'mean materialism' of the Jews was inimical to the spiritual elevation of Fascism. Furthermore, Italy now ruled 'millions and millions' of Arabs and must safeguard and sustain their interests. Italians should be pleased by the loyalty and patriotism of their own Jews but their geniality should not obscure the deepening requirement to oppose the global spread of Jewry.[15]

Empire and the Italian version of a world policy, relations with Nazi Germany, the advance of the varieties of fascism within Europe and the problem of an Italian Fascist line on race became the key areas for policy resolution by Mussolini and the dictatorship in the years following the occupation of Ethiopia. Already in May 1935 Mussolini had openly told the Chamber of Deputies that Italy could not allow itself to be 'petrified' in its defence of Austria. The Austrian question, he contended, might be a great problem but it was not an issue for Italy alone. Europe also must acknowledge its significance.[16] What the *Duce* was signalling was a rapprochement with the Nazi regime, based perhaps on ideological affiliation and certainly sponsored by the familiar dictum that the enemy of my enemy is my friend.

The campaigning in East Africa was therefore accompanied by a warming flirtation with the Nazis. By January 1936 Mussolini was telling German ambassador Ulrich von Hassell that Italy could accept an Austria working 'in parallel' with Germany, adding that the Stresa grouping with Britain and France was 'dead for ever'.[17] Despite dissent from Suvich, Triestine Under-Secretary for Foreign Affairs, who asked that any dealing be 'psychological' rather than 'material', since the Germans, once invited to the Brenner, would not stop there,[18] the *Duce*, during the next month, made it clear that Italy would not object when Germany remilitarized the Rhineland, as it did on 7 March.

The drift of Europe into rival blocs accelerated after 17 July 1936, when the Spanish army, in league with the Church, the landowners and the rest of the conservative world and with the enthusiastic backing of the small local fascist group, the Falange (a movement whose social base at the time was largely confined to students and taxi drivers), rose in revolt against its Popular Front, left-leaning government. The Falange's young and self-consciously 'poetic' leader, José Antonio Primo de Rivera, son of the military dictator of the 1920s, was soon executed and by 1937 General Francisco Franco had emerged as the leader or *Caudillo* of the insurgent cause. Unwilling to be relegated to a mere onlooker of such events, Fascist Italy, with every passing week, became more embroiled in the bloody civil war which enveloped Spain and threatened to spill beyond its borders.

Before 1936 Italian funding for the rightist Spanish opposition and their plotted terrorist attacks on the Republic flowed not to the Falange nor the numerous other local fascist-inspired groups but rather to dissident generals, although they did not then number the politic Franco in their ranks. The initial Italian engagement in Spain was not so much part of some global aggression as an act prompted half by accident and half by the foolishness of Ciano, who had returned from the masturbatory experience (in his words) of bombing unarmed Ethiopians to be made Europe's youngest Foreign Minister.[19] In his callow way, Ciano sported on his coat a lucky amulet to display to friends and admirers,[20] but it did not guarantee him and his policies permanent good fortune. Instead, once having entered the Spanish quagmire, Italy became ever more bogged down, sending massive treasure and numerous 'volunteers' to the battlefront. By February 1937 almost 50,000 Italian troops (some 29,000 from the

MVSN) were fighting there and, in the following month, they added to the list of notorious national military defeats at the Battle of Guadalajara, when the victorious Republicans, including some anti-Fascist Italians, rallied in the International Brigades. Some Italians noticed and drew a less than Fascist message from the news. Balbo was said to have stated publicly that the rout was all that could be expected: Fascist volunteers fought for double pay, while the reds were impelled by genuine ideological belief. Balbo also deplored the slaughter out of hand of POWs by Fascist militia chiefs and grew sentimental at the thought of a political system based on elections.[21] Despite such mutinous mutterings, the thick-skinned Mussolini offered frequent and unwelcome advice to Franco on the surest means to become a 'real' Fascist; a single party, militia and union structure, he reckoned, were enough to do the trick.[22]

The wily Franco took the aid and ignored the presumptuous Italians, be they the dictator himself or the party and army men who turned up in Spain. By the war's end, Italy had suffered far more casualties (officially the total was 3,819 dead and 12,000 wounded) than they had in Ethiopia, had wasted 759 planes, 157 light tanks, 6,791 trucks and 3,436 machine guns and spent a reported eight and a half billion lire.[23] The regime's paranoia may have exaggerated the matter but there can be little doubt that anti-Fascist hopes were lifted by the news that filtered through from Spain. Previously unpolitical Italians now fell foul of the secret police because they burst out over Guadalajara 'at last they [the Fascists] have been beaten'[24] or because they were found with a copy of a pro-Republican tract.[25] In very many ways the intervention in Spain inflicted grave damage at home and abroad on the image of the nation and regime, not least through the callous and well-publicized cruelty of some Fascist officers. Mussolini notoriously ordered the killing of prisoners, especially ones identified as Italian anti-Fascists, although, as so often, he did little to follow up his outburst and Farinacci came back from a piece of personal diplomacy in Spain full of stereotypes of his own about the dark and bloody nature of the Spanish of whatever ideological stripe. They had a more Stygian mind-set, he believed, than happy Italians.[26]

Italy's ally during the long and bitter battles in Spain was Nazi Germany, although Hitler was much more ruthless than Mussolini in ensuring that his nation benefited from the experience, through hard bargaining over mineral rights, for example. Rather than sacrificing German soldiers as cannon fodder, the Nazis preferred to provide 'clean', brutal and deadly aerial assistance, a prefiguring of the policies of the USA and NATO in some recent wars, when politicians have feared to report the death toll in their infantry to domestic audiences. Hitler apart, the Germans predictably evinced little admiration for Italians at the front. The nationalist Minister of Finance, Hjalmar Schacht, was still heard to repeat the northern European truism that 'we know . . . that Italy is never a completely reliable ally'.

The collaboration in Spain with the Nazis continued to lock Italian foreign policy into the German orbit. On 1 November 1936, after a visit by the then eager Ciano to Berlin, Mussolini announced in sometime Germanophobe Milan that henceforth Germany and Italy were joined in an 'Axis'.[27] Collective security and other Geneva peace plans he denounced as an absurdity and, in December 1937, the regime joined Germany and Japan in leaving the League of Nations. A few days earlier, Italy, abandoning its earlier Asian policy of making Jiang Jieshi its client, signed the anti-Comintern pact with the two other revisionist powers.

By now one die was all but cast. Throughout 1936–7 there were increasing signs that Italy was abandoning its objections to an *Anschluss*. Italians began to point out that, after all, the Austrians did not like them. In February 1937 the crowd in Vienna booed the Italian national team and then pelted its players with rubbish and empty bottles when they arrived for a football match. The vain Ciano let it be known that his last visit to Austria had been received coldly; those attending diplomatic banquets did not burst into the sort of spontaneous applause he believed his due.[28] People like that, it now began to be said in knowing circles, were not worth defending.

In March 1938 the Nazis completed the job they had botched in 1934 and occupied Austria (to the apparent delight of all but the local Jews and Marxists). The *Anschluss* was achieved. Despite some frowns in the elite and his own scarcely veiled glumness at the news, Mussolini had to accept the arrival of Germanic armies on the Brenner frontier, which, with surprising care, his regime busily fortified in the months that followed.[29] None the less, Italy gave every appearance of seconding German aggression against Czechoslovakia over the summer of 1938. During the Munich conference in September, the *Duce*, despite propaganda efforts to portray the eventual agreement as his personal triumph and the worryingly unmilitant welcome to the outbreak of peace given by vast sections of Italian opinion, seemed to be replaying the role once cast for Austria-Hungary as the ally of imperial Germany during the First World War. It was all very well for Grandi to observe fawningly from London that 'the great victor' at Munich was 'Mussolini. To Mussolini, and only to Mussolini does the world owe its salvation.'[30] The *Duce* himself might seek to out-trump Ribbentrop with his 'one hundred per cent' commitment to an alliance, aimed at changing in short order 'the geographical map of the world'.[31] Yet, somewhere beneath the aggressive phrases, Italy was becoming less the 'first ally' and more the dutiful cupbearer of the racist and fanatical Nazi state, ready to accept the rapid German betrayal of the Munich accord and its seizure of the rump of the Czech state in March 1939.

On their own account, the Fascists now opted for naked aggression. With what sometimes seemed an Italian parody of Nazi behaviour, over Christmas–New Year 1938–9 propagandists launched an unbridled campaign demanding that perfidious and degenerate France 'return' Tunis, Djibouti, Nice, Corsica and more to their 'natural' Italian owners. The racist anthropologist Guido Landra began publishing pseudo-learned accounts of the existence of an Italic race – he thought its members could be called the *Littoriali* – who covered most of southern and western France and should one day come home to an Italian Reich.[32] Such fantastical extremism was hard to convert into policy and, rather than invading France, on Good Friday Fascist forces annexed Albania to their empire. This last step was partly a spiteful reaction to the German failure to notify Rome about their decision to occupy Prague, although back in May 1938 Ciano, who believed that he could gain political prestige and financial advantage through the invasion, had already explained to Mussolini that the Balkan country was 'really rich', despite appearances to the contrary. Racial theoreticians were not behindhand in pronouncing the Albanians the all but pure descendants of the Pelasgians whom Homer had called divine.[33] Ciano, who after his marriage had been briefly sent to work at the Italian embassy in Beijing, none the less did admit that the current poverty of the populace reminded him of what he had once seen in 'Chinese villages'.[34] The national illiteracy level was a dismal 85 per cent, roads were non-existent and, by every index, Albanian peasants, the vast majority of the population, subsisted in grinding poverty.

The Germans were not put off by their ally's gain nor by the fact that Italian governance of Albania, despite the immediate introduction of the visible paraphernalia of Fascism, was soon evidently based on corruption, patron–client networks and the cohabitation of Italian and Albanian elites in a fashion that scarcely followed what were to be the rules for the treatment of 'inferior' peoples in the Nazi new order. Leading Albanians were granted membership in the Italian senate and, at least in theory, more ordinary people acquired identical civil rights to Italians, including the ability to purchase property in Italy and to reside there.[35] Italian propagandists were left to console themselves with the unlikely claim that their invasion had been greeted by 'the adhesion to a man of the Albanian people' and with the pious hope that the area inland from still tiny Valona (population under 10,000) was a 'Lombardy run wild'.[36] Vatican officials blessed the annexation with the somewhat greedy thought that the conversion of Albanians to Catholicism was now certain to accelerate.[37] In retrospect, however, Francesco Jacomoni, the young nobleman about town who was Ciano's special agent in the country, agreed that the ideas and institutions of the Albanian Fascist party scarcely penetrated Albanian society. The pompous renaming of the local parliament as the Consiglio superiore fascista-corporativo (Fascist corporative upper council) was, he admitted, 'premature'.[38]

In May 1939 the two dictatorships joined in the so-called Pact of Steel, a defensive and offensive diplomatic and military deal, implying that the regimes would march shoulder to shoulder in any coming war, one that the Germans at least understood lay not far in the future. A letter from Mussolini to Hitler, which, when read closely, contained a hint of embarrassment, hailed the 'inevitable' war but then hedged about when Italy might be fully ready to fight it.[39]

This studied positioning of the regime as the friend and ally of Nazi Germany, the Francoists in Spain and the ambitious Japanese was emphasized by the drift of Italian economic life. In October 1936 a de facto devaluation of the lira by over 40 per cent from the rate established in the heady days of 1927 was pushed through with a minimum of publicity.[40] The imposition of sanctions by the League of Nations states during the Ethiopian war, banning trade with compliant states, had augmented Fascist determination to pursue *autarchia* and the turning of the economy in on itself through outright protection or commercial arrangements based more on bureaucratic-controlled barter than free trade. Propaganda waxed loud about the wisdom and virtue of this line. Autarchy was depicted as a natural accompaniment of the planting of the 'corporate state', further proof that Fascism was charting a third way between the opposed but equally dated and ethically detestable programmes of socialism and capitalism.

The Ethiopian war had in any case entailed a radical reordering of national trade. Victory only increased the tendency of the empire to swallow a large proportion of national production; exports to the colonies multiplied tenfold from 248 million lire in 1931 to 2.5 billion in 1937.[41] Within Europe, there was also a telling readjustment. In 1932 Germany took 11 per cent of Italian exports, the same total as Britain, with France absorbing a further 8 per cent. By 1936 Germany received 20 per cent, Britain and France combined 6 per cent and, two years later, this latter figure had only recovered to 9 per cent, with Germany now up to 21 per cent. In imports, the tallies were more striking. In 1932 Germany provided 14 per cent, Britain and France combined 15 per cent; in 1936 Germany 27 per cent, a total repeated in 1938, Britain and France 3 per cent, rising merely to 8 per cent in 1938.[42] Despite the war build-up, over half a million Italians, on official figures, remained unemployed in early 1940.[43]

By the time of the Munich conference, another trade was binding Italians to the Nazi regime. The overheated Nazi economy was demanding labour in a fashion which, in a bizarre twist to Nazi ideology, made Germany a more multicultural country with every passing year of Hitler's rule (even if, after 1939, many of the immigrant labourers worked, often to their deaths, as slaves). In 1937 the Fascist and Nazi governments began amicable discussion of an experiment which, during the next year, transferred more than 37,000 Italian peasants – they were almost all *braccianti* or day labourers at this stage – to employment in the Reich.

There was plenty of irony in the deal on the Italian side too, given the regime's fervent if belated hostility to emigration to foreign lands. Much of the rhetoric justifying the expansion of the Italian empire had been emphatic that a conquered Ethiopia or a properly mastered Libya could absorb the nation's surplus hands and end the demeaning leakage of Italian blood to the New World and to the more industrialized parts of Europe. As the worker-exchange scheme with Germany continued – in 1940 just short of 100,000 Italians left for the north, 50 per cent of them now industrial workers; in 1941 more than 228,000, with the total emigrants in the end numbering almost half a million[44] – the Fascist authorities felt obliged to cover the reality of renewed emigration with much regime fanfare, solicitude (and spin). Those departing were bade farewell with parades and singing. Fascist trade unionists were sent along with them, charged zealously and impartially to watch over worker welfare.

The reality was bleaker, however, or, rather, it replicated many of the usual lights and shadows of guest-worker migration. German labour rules were harsher than Italian but work conditions were often better and were certainly more modern and productive – in January 1942 a critical Nazi expert reckoned that the Italian economy functioned at 25 per cent of its capacity.[45] Spies were soon reporting that the labour scheme was deeply besmirching the image of Fascism. If the emigrants were unhappy, they blamed the regime for sending them to Germany; if they were satisfied with their working lives, they drew unfavourable contrast with the conditions back home. Nor did the Germans love Italians. During the war, Carlo Scorza lamented that they viewed all emigrant workers as 'draft-dodgers'; a tougher selection policy, he argued, must in future send only 'the most vigorous and vital elements of Italianness, that is, . . . the representatives of the New Era, willed and created by Benito Mussolini'.[46]

The complaints or otherwise of individuals, be they party officials or the workers, were unlikely to alter policy, however. With its trade in blood, the Italian government was each year further ensuring that it was impossible to uncouple its foreign policy from that of Hitler. Already in 1938 Pope Pius XI had warned against the migration, expressing a fear that the guest workers would come back to Italy with their souls stained by the Nazi determination to cancel true religion from men's hearts.[47] If, in 1939 or 1940, Italy did twist and turn with the approach of Nazi war, in practice the dictatorship's room to manoeuvre was narrowed by the tens of thousands of ordinary Italians who, as a result of their migration, had become potential hostages in Nazi hands. Here was a major unspoken assumption driving Italy sooner or later into the Second World War on the Axis side. As an Italian historian has ably defined it, already in 1939, in its economic and financial life, Italy had become 'the first satellite of the Reich'.[48]

Another aspect of the Axis was cultural exchange. Massimo Magistrati, whose job in the Italian embassy meant that he often had formal charge of such matters, recalled how the diplomatic rapprochement between the two states fostered a tremendous volume of contact, if, he added, one where rivalry could be as evident as genuine friendship or ideological association. In his prim way the *Führer* had been disgusted to find that a travelling art exhibition had been stacked with the works of Boccioni and other Futurists, lauded in Italy but perceived as decadent by the German dictator.[49] In less controversial mode, artisans from the two countries began exchanges almost immediately after the Nazis took office. In February 1934 Vincenzo Buronzo, the editor of *L'Artigiano*, was received by Hitler. After presenting the *Führer* with a bronze copy of the Perseus of Pompeii, Buronzo saluted the German chief with a *Heil Hitler!*[50] A swapping of apprentices began thereafter.[51] A little later, Fascist rural radio held a combined transmission for schools, using the broadcasts to foster personal contacts between children through mutual stamp-collecting or pen-pal arrangements. As one Italian boy listener was alleged to have written in October 1938: 'I am proud that my people are friendly with yours, because nowadays our two people are strong and decisive and are destined together to dominate the world.'[52] Some months later, a special programme, *Voices from Germany*, was launched on this medium, aimed at further uniting Nazi and Fascist youth.[53]

Mussolini himself blessed these developments, telling Hans Frank, the leading Nazi lawyer, in September 1936 that, 'among the Nazi and Fascist leadership group, we must favour direct ties, above and beyond those of official diplomacy'.[54] The *Duce* and the *Führer* began regularly to exchange personal letters and visits. The first such trip in

June 1934 to dreamily artistic Venice had notoriously been a fiasco, the low point in relations between the 'fascist' regimes. However, Mussolini's stay in Germany in September 1937, despite including such diversions as the *Duce* having to watch Göring play with his colossal toy train set,[55] was serious and public proof of the tightening of the Axis.

Hitler came again to Italy in May 1938. Constitutional propriety had the King and not the *Duce* greet him at Rome railway station and the *Führer* was appalled to discover that he must stay in the stuffy and scarcely Germanophile surrounds of the royal Quirinale palace. Hitler was happier at the Uffizi art gallery in Florence, although his academic guide noted a marked difference in the aesthetic appreciation and the personalities of the two dictators. The *Führer* wished to be regaled with full details about the works of art, Mussolini preferred more sweeping commentary and was palpably anxious not to have his ignorance revealed. The *Duce* was, however, capable of hinting at a residual scepticism when Hitler burst forth with generalizations that the beautiful deportment of the women on the Via Veneto in Rome was explained by their customary carriage of family goods on their heads.[56] From London, Grandi, as ever going out of his way to ingratiate himself with his leader, claimed that local reports of the visit had expressed 'limitless admiration, without doubt or reserve, about the organization and splendour of the *Führer*'s reception' and the formidable character of Italian military preparedness which had then been displayed.[57] A pattern of what later was to be termed 'summits' was being established; in 1944 the *Duce* and *Führer* would meet for the sixteenth time.

The dealings with Nazi Germany were all very well and there were some Fascists who clung blindly to the Axis, at least for the moment. Yet, if a new cultural influence was spreading in 1930s Italy, it was more evidently that of the USA and its consumer capitalism. Edda Ciano, trying hard to be a modern woman, was reputed to spend her spare time flicking through American magazines (her husband, by contrast, was thought no reader of anything much and the couple's luxurious villa did not possess a library).[58] Films from Hollywood were taking their audiences by storm in Italy as elsewhere, with Fascist cinema unable to contest their popularity. In 1938 American movies earned almost three quarters of ticket sales[59] and, even if thereafter import controls were imposed, many Italian directors still looked to Hollywood formulas to frame and sell their films. Young Italian writers similarly modelled their works on the winning approach from across the Atlantic and, in their hearts, New York began to supplant Paris as the place where they longed secretly to be. With the onset of war, Bottai's cultural journal, *Il Primato*, complained about the corrupting effect of American culture, praising instead the Nazi film industry, purged of Jews and genuinely revolutionary in its cultural commitment, but the young stars of the 'Mussolini cohort' were not fully convinced.[60] Rather, many nurtured a rival world-view, that long cherished by the nation's emigrant masses, where 'America' was the modern paradise and guide.

One seductive feature of American life was mass sports but, in Italy, leisure was meant to be totalitarian in purpose. Notoriously, Starace exhibited his bursting virility by having himself photographed jumping through a fiery hoop and leaping over phallically erect bayonets at the party hierarch games. He did so in the presence of a *Duce*, who, although keeping his feet on the ground, turned out in sportive gear. Starace's journal, *Gioventù Fascista*, directed at university youth, argued that rugby was the most Fascist of games, asserting that it had been introduced to the Welsh by the legions of Julius Caesar.[61] Sport and empire, Italians began to be instructed with some unoriginality, went together. A journalist in *Gerarchia* warned with a Victorian sternness: 'above all, Italians must face up more to their physical responsibilities'. 'Fascism', he advised, 'has never thought of sport as an end in itself. Rather it has always considered and still considers it a means of collective physical education, fundamentally assisting the physical and moral elevation of the race.' The Italians, he added in the newly thrusting language of the moment, had established a primacy in every 'mass sport' and were elbowing past the English, who foolishly treated games like 'tennis and crickt' (sic) as innocent Sunday pastimes and preferred undertaking sporting endeavours with traditional phlegm rather than inserting 'bellicose instincts into the pure soul of a sportsman', as Fascists took pains to do. The only other nation which shared insight into such training for the morrow was, he noted, Nazi Germany.[62]

A more informal glimpse into the Fascist sporting world comes through an incident at the industrial town of Sesto Fiorentino. There, Wais Mattiolini, a big man in his twenties, was the star boxer but he refused all invitations to join the PNF, despite having no direct allegiance to any formally constituted anti-Fascist group. In 1938 he decided to give up boxing and moved to Florence. It was ill-advised of him to return one day to Sesto, however, where he was followed around by a bunch of Fascist toughs who, it may be assumed, abused and ridiculed him. When he picked up a hammer from a garage bench in response, he was set upon by the Fascists and severely beaten (he needed six days in hospital to recover). He was also arrested, labelled an anti-Fascist and sent for a two-year term of *confino* to a mountain village in the province of L'Aquila.[63]

If the sporting life was meant only to be Fascist, language was another territory to be marshalled in a totalitarian manner as the demand grew to purge the national tongue of foreign intrusions and borrowings. 'To speak foreign languages in Italy is a piece of idiocy, a crime,' it was urged. 'To speak Italian abroad is a basic duty, a Fascist requirement.'[64] Enhancing such xenophobia, Starace presided over a campaign to eliminate the allegedly flaccid and Spanish-derived, polite, third-person use of the word *Lei*, to be replaced by the allegedly manly, second-person *voi*, though with mixed effects on Italian speech. One ex-squadrist fell foul of the secret police by publicly ridiculing Starace's campaign and by maintaining that the '*voi* absurdity' was the final proof that 'Fascism today is completely different from what it was in 1920'.[65]

During the Ethiopian campaign, the brand names of state-produced cigarettes and cigars changed from Kentucky and Britannici to Tigrina and Fiume.[66] Trifle or *zuppa inglese* was now baptized *zuppa Impero* – Empire instead of English soup.[67] In such border areas as the Trentino–Alto Adige, where the assertion of *italianità* was habitual, there had long been an insistence that tourism speak 'with an Italian voice'.[68] Now, throughout the country, hotels which preferred that word to *albergo* in their title were told to amend their names – every Grand Hotel was meant to become the *Albergo Grande* – and an effort was made to detach the entire tourist industry from its natural cosmopolitanism. The campaign for linguistic purification provided an opportunity to cut a figure in the intellectual world. Experts now reviewed the words used by commentators to describe football[69] or boxing[70] and were alert to any alien note they could turn up in the technical terminology of the sciences.[71] Achieving refinement nevertheless remained troublesome. In the summer of 1940 the Associazione italiana del brigge (Italian Bridge Club) sought for their favourite pastime acceptance of the spelling *brigge* rather than such alternatives as *bricc, brigio, brisia* or the dismally literal *ponte*. *Brigge* it was to be in the new order, despite the cavilling by some purists that Italian did not usually favour a silent 'e' at the end of a word. Other doubts about the Fascist virtue of the (decidedly bourgeois) card-game, attacked during the sanctions crisis as both foreign and effete,[72] were countered with the argument that bridge's origin was not English but Russian, a claim which might have passed muster in 1940 but would cause trouble in 1941.[73]

Yet, as so often in Fascist Italy, somewhere beneath the rhetorical flourishes, pragmatism lingered. Despite the fondness for absurd renaming, some experts acknowledged that spoken language changed slowly and that popular usage was unlikely to be amended at a stroke by a party decree. The processes of public discourse, one linguist explained, moved at a pace that was fifty or a hundred times slower than that of politics.[74] Verbal autarchy was anyway conditioned by the survival of the nation's 'very many, very much alive and very widely spoken dialects' (as well as by surviving class distinctions in speech). Reformers had an unenviable task. There had been pressure to replace the word *garage* with *autorimessa* but the suggestion had not been well received in Bologna where a dialect term, *armessa*, meant loss or damage. No wonder, this analyst concluded, the most enthusiastic political advocates of reform were now giving up the battle (and so, it was added optimistically, leaving space for the real experts to move at their own rhythm and with greater effect).[75]

If the pursuit of linguistic totalitarianism had some limits, there were similar difficulties in making every parade the same. Under Starace's orders the regime's iron discipline was to be expressed by the armed forces, Fascist or national. Each was now expected to use the goose-step at all formal ceremonies, geese being the creatures who had, in Livy's story, saved the classical Capitol from invading Gauls.

In case there were any stray thoughts that the Italians were mimicking Prussian traditions, the march was dubbed the *passo romano* (Roman step) and among its public fans was the protean Dino Grandi, as ever trying to express the spirit of the moment.[76] From London, he wrote to his *Duce* that a Fascist parade was 'not the Anglo-Saxon "ballet", it was not the Teutonic "catapult". It was a single block of steel, a powerfully weighty mass quite like the German, yet not of cast-iron but of vibrant metal. It is the most powerful instrument of popular pedagogy which you have ever created.' More resistant to such outrageous grovelling, the army refused to give up its traditional salute and go over to the Roman one. When Hitler reached Rome railway station in May 1938, he was saluted in the old manner by the King and in the Fascist way by the *Duce*.

In June 1935 the new Ministry of Popular Culture (called by everyone wryly 'Minculpop') had opened to administer the ever more thunderous and pervasive propaganda campaigns. It was expected that the public would be readier to accept the preaching since, at much the same time, the regime instituted the so-called *sabato fascista* (Fascist Saturday), with businesses and shops being forced (sometimes reluctantly) to allow their employees the afternoon off. Minculpop's first chief, until he left to bomb Ethiopians, was Ciano. The following year, Bottai reflected tellingly in his diary about the meaning of the regime and its cultural revolution: 'Political propaganda. Propaganda policy . . . The centre of the matter is this: the advent of the masses into political life occasions the same needs and demands, the same advertising techniques, as in the business and banking worlds.' Once a leader could get by through the astute manipulation of elite contacts, Bottai reasoned. Now no longer. Rather, 'in a mass regime the chiefs can only be made known with bold strokes, in a fashion that impresses millions of hearts and imaginations. You have to impose the physiognomy, the gesture, the vocabulary, over and over again through photography, film and photography once more. You have to repeat once, twice and again, over and over. Just as in commercial advertising. Any political idea which thinks it can spread via the book, the newspaper article, the conference, via culture, with lots of home-work, is deluding itself.' Mussolini, Bottai mused, had understood the matter and so had

Ciano. Publicity campaigns, he concluded with a hint of understanding or of malice, 'launch some terrific products but, unfortunately, also some useless ones'.[77]

By the second half of the 1930s, Fascist Italy is indeed best understood as a propaganda state, a place where spin conquered (almost) all. Yet, despite postmodern theory, men and women do not live by words alone. The conquest of an empire and accounting for it could not be a visual or verbal matter only. With its taking of Addis Ababa, the regime had opened the floodgates of race in Italy or at least had placed the nation in a situation where its racial practice would begin to converge not just with the imperial racisms of the white men of Europe but with the anti-Semitism and the strictly 'scientific' racism of Nazi Germany.

As so often in Fascist Italy, one explanation for this new line was the insecurity present in Mussolini's and the other leaders' minds. Anxieties about the superficiality, inconsistency and meretriciousness of Fascism resurfaced after Italian armies advanced to victory. Whether Italians were worthy of the white man's burden became an insistent question that lurked not far below the surface of the boasting. Montanelli was not alone in wondering whether Italians would prove too racially casual to cope with their at last being the masters in Africa. Italians, a semi-official journal urged in the summer of 1936, just had to accept that some peoples were naturally inferior and could never reach European standards in their behaviour or their laws.[78] Fascists, a party historian added, must eschew any thought of assimilating their new subject peoples and especially avoid any sexual congress. The fate of the nation depended on the observance of a sharp racial distinction between blacks and whites.[79]

Following words came deeds. Fascist administration of Ethiopia was soon underpinned by legislation, intruding the categorizations of race into everyday life. From 19 April 1937 it became illegal for blacks and whites to marry. The plans for grandiose urban development in the empire were based on a rigorous segregation of native peoples from their white masters. As an engineer put it in classically racist phraseology: 'We must ban natives from any access to our cities unless we can force them to pass through a sort of station of human reclamation [he used the redolent Fascist word *bonifica*]. In a perfect colonial city, the destruction of bugs and the disinfection of clothing must be carried out in a totalitarian fashion.'[80] As other imperial powers had done to their indigenous populations, so in Ethiopia the Fascist government rapidly took over the best local land and distributed it to Italian immigrants.

There were deepening ramifications at home too. In a way that the literature of the Holocaust does not always predict, anti-Semitism sprang more directly from the Italians' racism towards their black and Arab subjects than from a passionate and primordial hatred of the Jews. Since the Risorgimento, Italy had not seemed a very anti-Semitic country. The liberalism, rationality and anti-clericalism of the makers of the nation had extended to the Jewish question and leading Italians derided the absurd and vicious religious anti-Semitism of Pope Pius IX, for example. National unification entailed the closing of the ghettos and the granting of full civil rights to all citizens, regardless of religious belief or inheritance. The matter was clear at the opening ceremony of the Victor Emmanuel monument in Rome. For the patriotic fiftieth anniversary celebrations of 1911 the mayor of the capital was a Jew, Ernesto Nathan, who still spoke an Italian heavily accented by his English family origins. A few months earlier, in March 1910, one Prime Minister of Jewish heritage, Luigi Luzzatti, succeeded another, Sidney Sonnino. At that time, of a total of fewer than 40,000 Jews – assimilation made an exact figure difficult – twenty-four had won a place in the Senate and quite a number refreshed Italian intellectual life; 8 per cent of university professors were in some way Jewish.[81]

The combination of patriotism and middle-class social position ensured that Italy's Jews played a prominent part in the rise and rule of Fascism. There were five Jews at Piazza San Sepolcro, three were 'martyrs' to the party cause before 1922 and 230 were officially inscribed as having participated in the March on Rome.[82] By the 1930s it is estimated that about a quarter of Italy's adult Jews belonged to the PNF, well above the average membership of some 10 per cent of Italians.[83] Aldo Finzi, the Under-Secretary of the Interior closely involved in the Matteotti murder, Guido Jung, Minister of Finance in 1935 (the Ethiopian war precipitated his conversion to Catholicism), and Margherita Sarfatti, patroness and lover of the

Duce, all were Jewish in background. As late as October 1937 Mussolini still awarded a medal to Alberto Liuzzi, a volunteer MVSN 'hero' killed in Spain, who happened also to be Jewish.[84]

The most extreme case of a Fascist Jew was Ettore Ovazza of Turin (he had joined the local *fascio* in June 1920) who, in 1934, set up an anti-Zionist paper entitled *La nostra bandiera* (Our flag). Ovazza zealously separated the universal Jewish religion from what he believed was Italian Jews' overwhelming commitment to Fascism and derided Zionists as a deluded and minuscule minority. He disliked Nazism but opposed boycotts of German goods on the grounds that nothing should be done to interfere with the 'fertile peace work' of the magnificent Mussolini.[85] In 1938 Ovazza launched his own variety of a squadrist raid to burn down the office at Florence of a Zionist journal. In 1940 he explained away the racial laws as tactical; they would, he maintained, be abrogated as soon as Italy won the empire it deserved.

Not entirely dissimilar in attitude and demonstrating that those who objected to anti-Semitism could themselves be racists of a kind was Oscar Sinigaglia, the Nationalist financier of Fascism. In July 1938 he wrote to Mussolini, disgusted that a lifetime of dedication to the *patria* was to be thrown away. 'Is it really possible', he lamented, 'that I must feel separated from my *patria* and made to belong . . . among Mongols and the Negroid?'[86] Sinigaglia, who had cancelled himself from Jewish communal lists in 1931, formally converted to Catholicism during the war, which he survived, only to die in 1949.[87]

The shock and horror which filled Sinigaglia's letter was the greater because he, like so many of his fellows, had never believed that the barbarous attitudes of Germans could take root south of the Alps. In his memoirs depicting his own life as a 'fortunate Jew', Dan Segre, born 1922, could recall no instance before 1938 when his Fascist friends and teachers discriminated against him on ethnic or religious grounds. 'I was convinced that being Jewish was a treat no different from Cirio jam,' he says, 'the more so because I was the constant object of jealousy among my school friends for being allowed "for religious reasons" to be absent from the boring lessons' of the high school priest.[88] Although it was true that a number of leading anti-Fascist exiles were of Jewish background, among them the

Rosselli brothers, murdered in France at Ciano's behest in 1937, and that this equation was sometimes noticed by leading Fascists, including Mussolini, from 1926 to 1938 only 151 Jews followed the Zionist track to Palestine.[89] Fascist Italy also gave sanctuary to foreign Jews persecuted elsewhere, among them the Russian family of historian Alexander Stille[90] and the German one of George Mosse.[91] In manic response, in the 1920s the Nazi theorist Alfred Rosenberg denounced the vices of the 'Judeo-Fascist regime', entrenched in world-polluting Rome.[92]

Yet all was not quite as bright and simple as this account has so far suggested. Currents of anti-Semitism did eddy through Italian life, in the Church and among its most conservative sustainers, some of whom quickly surfaced in 1938, claiming biblical and patristic justification for persecuting Jews,[93] as well as in the Fascist party. Two important and fertile journalists, Telesio Interlandi (Mussolini once warned equivocally that Interlandi was, in family background, 'a Sicilian and a Sard, two lands where madmen grew')[94] and the defrocked priest Giovanni Preziosi, regularly raged against the Jews. In September 1921 Preziosi deplored how Palestine, 'that land of Jesus, meant to be the symbol to all of union and peace, now amid general silence, has become the seat of wars and bloodshed, because the crucifiers of Christ have decided at any cost to make it their national home'.[95] Other, less paranoid nationalists were inclined to dislike Zionists as people trying to have 'two fatherlands'.[96] Victor Emmanuel III, in his mean-spirited way, did not hide his distrust of any 'foreign Jews' who settled in his kingdom.[97]

Among the Fascist leadership the situation was mixed. Balbo rejoiced in his power base at Ferrara, a city with a considerable Jewish community, one that was by tradition highly patriotic and frequently treated their *ras* as a favourite son. In 1937 Balbo talked openly about having had three best friends in his life, all of whom were Jewish. By this time Balbo was offstage in Libya, a colony with its own special Jewish community. There the local Jews endured some ups and downs with Fascist administrators but they welcomed Balbo's appointment. He viewed them as natural allies in his plans for modernization and development, even if legislation that closed shops on Sunday and enforced their opening on Saturday paid no attention to Jewish susceptibilities. In 1938 further laws placed Libyan Jews below the Arabs whom they had traditionally viewed as rivals and inferiors. But Balbo did his best to obfuscate and procrastinate on the most severe provisions of the racial laws and historian De Felice has concluded that the local situation of Libyan Jews in 1939–40 was not too bad.[98]

In London, Dino Grandi did his serpentine best to win personal advantage from events back home, telling Ciano of his profound admiration for the 'toughness and crystal-like transparency' of initial government efforts to push the anti-Semitic line.[99] Soon Grandi was writing about the 'Jew Blum' (the French Prime Minister) as a natively 'sinister person'.[100] As ever he was not so good at understanding that others might not be as cynical as he was and, according to one memoirist, was shocked when a Jew in Bologna did not greet him. 'Ciao, Sacerdoti,' he said from what he saw as the high moral ground. 'How come you don't recognize an old friend?'[101] Ciano's home town of Livorno was another with a traditional Jewish community and the Ciano who enjoyed a mondaine life did not look like a fanatical anti-Semite. In February 1938 he told Margherita Sarfatti that he possessed 'moderate views on the subject'.[102] None the less his diary a few months later reports the enveloping anti-Semitic agenda with no suggestion of doubt or opposition.

Starace as party secretary was a leader of the racial campaign. It was he who, in July 1938, had Ciano distribute a circular to Italian diplomats stationed around the world, stating the official line on race. Actually, he contended, Fascism had been campaigning for the 'quantitative and qualitative improvement' of the race since 1922. Current developments merely reflected the usual method: 'first action, then doctrinal formulation, one which must not be thought of as academic or as an end in itself but rather as the last determinant of a precise political action'. 'With the creation of the Empire', Starace explained, 'the Italian race came into contact with other races. Hence it had to guard itself against hybridity and contamination.' So, he concluded, racial laws were already drafted and applied in Italy's imperial territory. As for the Jews, matters were not entirely finalized but it was plain that they had always held themselves apart from real Italians and also constituted the 'General Staff of anti-Fascism'.[103]

The most evidently anti-Semitic Fascist chief, apart from Starace and the scambling Farinacci, was the intellectual Bottai. Balbo, Grandi, Ciano and Farinacci favoured anti-Jewish policies out of a cynical desire to curry favour with their *Duce*. Bottai, more earnestly, believed or sought to believe. His journal, *Critica Fascista*, was soon proclaiming the originality and profundity of Fascist racism, defined pompously as 'eminently spiritual, even if it sprang from purely biological data'.[104] The party, it was urged, must take a pre-eminent role in explaining racism to the populace. Then they would understand that the anti-Semitic laws had not been copied from Nazi Germany but rather were the natural expression of three thousand years of Italian 'history, thought and art'.[105] Italians must learn how to be coldly objective on the race question, acting with a 'surgical intransigence in the Mussolinian sense'.[106] So meticulous and so petty was Bottai that, as Minister of Education in June 1939, he demanded that universities ensure the full segregation of the races during the oral exams being conducted that summer.[107]

Just how intransigent the *Duce* was on the race question remains a matter of dispute. There can be little doubt that, in 1937–8, Mussolini took the lead on the race question and stood directly behind the writings on the matter of such ambitious young intellectuals as anthropologist Guido Lantra.[108] During this campaign, such racists found it easy enough to locate apposite quotes from the younger *Duce*, allegedly proving that he had always harboured racial understanding.[109] Yet, it is just as possible to find Mussolini saying the reverse – De Felice noted his comment before the March on Rome that 'Italy has never known anti-Semitism and, we believe, will never know it'.[110] Throughout his life, Mussolini was given to peremptory summaries of the national character of Jews and many other peoples. His observations were often cast in forceful terms; they did, however, tend to fluctuate in content depending on the moment and audience. In this arena, too, the *Duce* was enough of an ordinary politician frequently to say what his listener wanted to hear. Furthermore, a part of Mussolini's habitual racist vituperation was concentrated within Italy, since he was quite capable of talking of Neapolitans as belonging to an inferior race and Lombards and Romagnoles to a superior one. He could also attack the inhabitants of Faenza, the next town along the railway line from his home in Forlì, where he had been mistreated at school, as though they constituted an incorrigible and alien race.[111] Similarly, after 1938, Mussolini seems to a considerable degree to have lost interest in the persecution of the Jews and to have stopped patronizing Lantra, either bored with or confused by his lucubrations. Certainly neither race in general nor anti-Semitism in particular ever moved the *Duce* in the fanatical way in which they drove Hitler.

When surveying the racial practice of the dictator and his subjects – from October 1938 the Church connived at a widespread sale of back-dated baptismal certificates[112] and most Fascists, with Farinacci in the vanguard in excepting his own secretary, wanted to define their friends or clients as special cases – it is tempting to slip into stereotypes about *brava gente*. According to secret police reports, the city population of Milan, for example, reacted to the Nazi pogrom of *Kristallnacht* with horror, complaining that the Germans were proving as 'barbarous' as were the 'reds' who sacked churches in Spain.[113] Yet racist practice there was and most Italians actively or passively condoned it. In a set of laws promulgated between August and November 1938, Jews, with few indications of serious popular opposition, were banned from being teachers or scholars in Italian schools and universities, from having Christian staff, from serving in the armed forces and from marrying Christian 'Aryans'. Foreign Jews were expelled from the country, with a vicious backdating debarring any citizenship that they might have been granted since the First World War. There is no evidence of direct Nazi pressure to justify such policies. Rather, Fascist anti-Semitism took wings from the belated adoption of racist ideas in their empire, assuming a different pattern from British or French colonial racism largely because Italian rule came so late and happened to coincide with an anti-Semitic moment, not just in Germany but in Poland, Romania and other European states with which Italians had religious or national ties. Fascist racism is not thereby any easier to forgive. Rather, in its medley of racial themes, its knitting together of prejudice against Jews, Arabs, blacks and Slavs, as well as in its cynicism and corruption, Italian racism may contain more subtle and powerful lessons for those of us who come after than did the mad and single-minded Judeocide at the heart of Nazism.

The determination to be racist was fuelled by one other factor, the widespread ongoing fear among Fascists that, somehow, their revolution was not yet real. As Giorgio Almirante, a young man destined to lead Italy's neo-fascists for decades after 1945, put it in the new journal *La Difesa della Razza*, anti-Semitic 'racism can be the decisive factor clarifying us to ourselves'.[114] The new campaign, he argued, amounted to 'the biggest and most courageous recognition of itself that Italy has ever attempted'.[115] The main political backers of the new legislation – Mussolini, when he was concentrating, and Bottai, who urged all teachers to subscribe to *La Difesa della Razza*, to read it and to foster its message among their pupils and friends[116] – agreed that a dose of racism could smarten up the new generation. It could at last stiffen Fascist revolution and make it genuinely permanent.

Hopes may have sprung but achievement remained problematical. One Fascist who was racist in his time and in a more general sense incarnated the textured character of the regime's cultural and social revolution was the Sardinian (aspirant) intellectual Edgardo Sulis. He was in many ways a man to whom may be awarded the ironical title of the Unknown Fascist Soldier. His story is worth telling at some length as a case study of (the limits of) Fascist racism, Fascist fanaticism and Fascist revolution.

The first claim to fame of Edgardo Sulis is that in 1934 he published a book with perhaps the most egregious title of all the starstruck accounts of the *Duce – Imitazione di Mussolini*. In its pages, this Thomas à Kempis of Fascism set out the basic tenets of what he labelled in somewhat hackneyed phrase 'the new political religion'. In the articles of this totalitarian faith, love of country, of nation, of *Duce* and potentially of race fused in mysterious fashion. Mussolini embodied all that mattered to those who served the revolution. As Sulis preached in his peroration: 'You should imitate Mussolini alone; you should have no other example in life except him.' This 'imitation' amounted to a 'love which pervades every thought and action, sometimes unconsciously so and then you are sublimated . . . [into] perfection'.[117]

Nor, with the passage of the years, did Sulis resile from this position. Rather, he continued to publish essays, afire with Fascist fervour, effusive in their commitment to a radical restructuring of society. In 1937, writing in *Gerarchia*, he urged that the torch of revolution be passed to a new aristocracy and suggested, at least by implication, that the time of tired old noblemen and the flabby Savoy dynasty was over.[118] Two years later, he returned to his theme in a work entitled *Rivoluzione ideale* (Revolution of the mind), dedicated to his father, a 'volunteer in life and in death'. Delight in Fascism could readily slip to lauding Mussolini. 'Fascism', Sulis urged, 'is Mussolini'; the *Duce* was the bearer of a 'new civilization'. 'Fascist law, Fascist legal practice, the Fascist constitution, the new idea, all today possess only one name: Mussolini.' Whenever they thought about anything, Sulis explained, all Fascists naturally wanted to centre their mental processes on and in the *Duce*, holy vessel of the Fascist revolution. The dictator's refulgent glory illuminated Sulis himself. In his preface, Sulis highlighted a report by the Agenzia Stefani (the Fascist press agency) that Mussolini had graciously granted him an interview. It was then, Sulis recalled, that he had been visited by the divine afflatus that now stimulated his prose.

When grovelling was done, Sulis did make some other points, though they amount to a mixed bag. The Fascist revolution meant above all else the substitution of unworthy men by those who believed to the bottom of their souls. Under Fascist rule, the father, the Head of the Family, had his power and authority refurbished. In his own sphere the father replicated the role of the *Duce* and so ensured women's healthy devotion to maternity and household cares. Then, too, there was the question of private property. Everyone had a right to it, of course. But, wrote Sulis, the sternly revolutionary legionnaire, individual wealth should not be allowed to become an obsession. The new aristocracy being tempered by the Fascist revolution must not yield to the material but, rather, should be ready to sacrifice its goods as well as its being to the holy mission of the *patria*.[119]

After all, Sulis added in an edited work entitled *Processo alla borghesia* (Trial of the bourgeoisie) and also published in October 1939, when Fascism was grappling with the problem of war entry, the foe was identified and should now be arraigned – it was the bourgeoisie, that class which the *Duce* had charged with being the 'enemy number 1 of the Revolution'.[120] Sulis proceeded to indict it on a number of counts. Rather than being heroic in the manful Fascist manner, the bourgeoisie was in its fundamental nature womanishly weak. Sprung from a sordid union between the 'daughters of Luther' and the misguided paladins of 1789, its creatures could not rise above a life of ease. They served no *patria*. They were wedded to money and brought forth no offspring except their own self-interest.[121] Now, their doom had sounded. Whatever might eventuate at the front, Fascist Italy must rage against bourgeois feebleness, excising it ruthlessly from Italian homes,[122] exposing and destroying its lingering influence on national education.[123] A genuine Fascist revolution could do none other. If his words are to be read literally, Sulis endorsed a brand of Fascism that seemed determined to thrust Italian totalitarianism into every nook and cranny of life and dominate the people's very souls.

Nor did the war cool Sulis's ardour. Editing two new works became his chief and cushy wartime activity (he was no volunteer for the front). In one, Sulis argued that the conflict in which the Axis was engaged amounted to a 'civil war among the European people'. In its epic battles, a new civilization was seeking to overthrow an old. Fighting could take its course but on the domestic front of this struggle to the death certain issues must be clarified. Corporatism, Sulis admitted, was still in practice only 'a point of departure' but it must continue its development within the Fascist state. The Catholic Church might also need some reformation in a fully Fascist world since, Sulis argued intransigently, 'for us God is not a nightmare nor a teacher but rather a reckoning'. As ever, Sulis's revelling in the bloody destruction of the old order was checked by the need to salute the *Duce*. War showed that there was one sure fortress in time of troubles – Mussolini. 'Fascism', Sulis emphasized in now familiar sentiment, 'does not originate in an idea but rather in The Man who is the vessel of the idea.' 'No one is perennially new and eternal as He is.' In sum, the *Duce* was 'the Man of tomorrow', as well as of today. 'The people . . . need Him as they need air and bread; a people can believe in itself because it believes in Him.'[124] After September 1943 Sulis rallied to the Social Republic, rising to be head of the press office of the Under-Secretary to the Presidenza del Consiglio and, in March 1945, offering to set up a Gruppo Rivoluzionario Repubblicano to propagandize the trinity of Italy, Republic and socialization among a still reluctant public.

Yet another side to the Sulis story is traceable in the archives. When his hometown background is revealed, it turns out that the radical

Fascist ideals contained a strong dash of self-interest and that Sulis's devotion to a totalitarianly united Fascist nation was studded with the more down-to-earth and divided history of the Italies.

Edgardo Sulis was born in April 1903, being in other words a decade younger than most prominent Fascists. His father, Antonio, had based himself at Villanovatulo, a small inland *paese* on a back road in the Sardinian province of Nuoro. In this remote place, so off the national track that it was deemed by the dictatorship unwelcoming enough to receive *confinati*,[125] Antonio Sulis did well for a time, backing the Fascist revolution, sustaining it locally (at least by his own later account) during the troubles which followed the murder of Matteotti (it was then that Edgardo first signed up as a member) and serving as a centurion in the party militia, the MVSN.[126]

The Sulises prospered in the wake of their family head's political choice. By the end of the 1920s they rejoiced in the ownership of a palazzo in the *paese* and land and an old country house in the hills outside it, real estate to a value of more than 100,000 lire.[127] The decision by Antonio Sulis to construct a palatial new edifice at Villanovatulo, however, caused comment. Just as life blossomed, Antonio, defined by those who were not his friends as 'turbulent and quarrelsome', began to cede to others the various official positions he held in the town. Soon he was left merely as the combined secretary and cashier of the small local Istituto di Credito Agrario per la Sardegna. Blasted by a newly hostile wind of fate, the Sulis family were now beset by rumours that they were living beyond their means and station. Worse, anonymous letters and whispers in the piazza charged that all was not well with the administrative practices of Antonio Sulis at his credit bank.[128]

Such calumny signalled an approaching crisis for the Sulises. Whatever their devotion to Fascism – and one malicious authority judged Edgardo at the time 'apolitical' rather than fervently Fascist[129] – they now counted the party *podestà* of Villanovatulo an enemy. As if in proof of the ill wind swirling around them, a government inspector turned up to audit the books of the *paese*'s credit bank. There he found a deficit of 42,000 lire and evidence of forgery. In outraged or desperate response, on 16 May 1932 Antonio Sulis committed suicide, leaving a widow and three sons (one of whom was a friar) weighed down by dishonour and debt. Assunta Sulis, a *maestra*, had recourse to a small government pension but that was scarcely sufficient to repay the family's many pressing creditors.

Edgardo Sulis now initiated a stubborn endeavour to restore his family's fortune and reputation. As he saw things, his father had been 'a staunch Fascist whom terrible mistakes in local politics brought to ruin'.[130] Before ending his life, Antonio Sulis had taken the trouble to pen a farewell letter, emphasizing that he had died a believing Fascist and restating his commitment during the 'tough times' of Fascism's rise.[131] In this assertion lay the potential for an improvement in the family fortunes, the most promising means through which Edgardo and his younger brother, Italo, could resume their places among their town's elite (and even seek to go beyond it in the way that Antonio Gramsci, himself a Sardinian, argued was typical of 'Southern intellectuals'). Whatever had been his father's actual relationship with the dictatorship and its revolution,[132] now was the time for Edgardo Sulis to affirm his ideological rigour. History, the little history of Villanovatulo and its intersection with the great history of Fascism, might yet be on the family's side, especially if Edgardo Sulis could be its chronicler. The Sulises might possess a usable past which could offer opportunity for well-rewarded connection with that greatest of patrons, Benito Mussolini, and his Fascist state.

To be sure, Edgardo took a little while to embark on the path that led his family to a new *sistemazione*. At first he tried to organize a rumour campaign, denigrating his father's enemies and, notably, the *podestà* and his lieutenant, the secretary of the *comune* of Villanovatulo. Sulis naturally rallied to his cause his own friends and partisans, presumably once themselves the clients of Antonio Sulis and now ideally his own, at least if he could affirm his inherited role as a man of respect. However, that tactic proved barren, since a number of further official probes did nothing to damage the *podestà*. In some desperation, Edgardo and brother Italo opted for action. As a police report put it, in phrases loaded with traditional assumptions about life and so with attitudes which make Fascism seem a superficial short-term event fleetingly surfacing above the ancient structures of the Italies: 'Exploiting the discontent which more or less openly always eddies through the population of a place like this, both because of a native riotousness and the profound hostility elicited by any demand for payment by the communal authorities, the Sulis brothers, on 21 August [1932], secretly organized a demonstration which seriously disturbed law and order at Villanovatulo.'[133]

Although the brothers themselves refrained from physical action, they incited their followers to break into the offices of the *comune*, shouting against the *podestà*.[134] In the Fascist dictatorship, retribution for infractions of public peace was swift. Edgardo and Italo Sulis, deemed responsible for the demonstration, were arrested, found guilty and sentenced to *confino*, in their case to a mountain *paese* in the Molise on the mainland. As far as the prefecture of Nuoro was concerned, Edgardo Sulis was a bad hat, a young man overwhelmed by 'vanity and megalomania'.[135] Not even a pious letter from Assunta Sulis, pledging that her sons had really not committed any crime and underlining that their actions had been in response to the family's money troubles,[136] seemed likely to salve the deteriorating fate of the Sulis boys.

But Edgardo Sulis had an ace in his pack. He had written a book. It was entitled *Imitazione di Mussolini* and was a work which could persuade the Nuoro authorities that the young man was not a loopy subversive but someone of 'outstanding intellectual qualities, devoted to Fascism and the *Duce* and so meriting encouragement and help'.[137] Sulis had managed to get a letter through to Mussolini's private office, an epistle in which he humbly requested that the *Duce* compose a preface, naively appending a note about the personal motivation which had prompted him to write: 'my dream is to try to repay the family debt either in part or in whole through my efforts [as a writer]. It is the honourable thing to do and I place all my hopes in a better future when I can restore splendour to the memory of my poor father. It is a holy work.'[138]

Whether won over by the account of the Sulis family tragedy or by the book's content and title, the secretariat reacted favourably. Publication could proceed. Being an approved writer had immediate advantages. In November 1932 Sulis formally appealed on behalf of his brother and himself to have their term in *confino* cut short. He was, he explained, the author of a book in the process of publication, entitled *Imitazione di Mussolini*.[139] Though not all the authorities were convinced, the tactic worked and, late in 1933, Edgardo and Italo Sulis were permitted to leave the Molise.[140] The *Imitazione* was already at the printer's; it reached a presumably grateful public in February 1934. Three months later the sentence that had been imposed on the brothers was formally revoked.[141]

Now that he had become an intellectual, a brave new world opened for Edgardo Sulis. The radical writer Berto Ricci accepted him as one of the editorial team on his journal, *L'Universale*. Some of Sulis's musings were published by *Il Popolo d'Italia*.[142] Along with Ricci and other journalists, in July 1934 Sulis was granted the useful favour of an official audience with Mussolini.[143] Better still, the government put him on a monthly stipend extracted from the *Duce*'s secret funds. It eventually totalled 72,000 lire. From the same source, Sulis received a special gift of 56,000 lire and, thereafter, he continued to have his life sweetened by smaller bonuses.[144] Shrugging off his troubles with the law and his father's disgrace, Sulis had risen to be a man of presence among the Fascist elite. Here, it might seem, was a member of the emerging middle classes, doing well from doing good for the dictatorship.

His motivation for this new course remained complex. Despite his new social status, his residence in Rome in an apartment on the redolently named Via dei martiri fascisti (Fascist Martyrs Street) and the tracts he wrote with their revolutionary fervour, Sulis had not forgotten Villanovatulo and the family finances. Even as he imagined a new and revolutionary Italy forged by Mussolini's blessed hand in the crucible of Fascist revolution, Sulis cherished a *mentalité* rooted in the Italies. When he was not composing fiery expressions of his Fascist faith, Sulis spent time trying to extract the maximum possible benefit from his clientship to the *Duce*.

A prosperous existence was such a taxing matter, especially for the son of a father who had died in financial and social disgrace. The generosity of government payments to him could never quite overcome that original sin and its wages. Impelled by the need to confront the wickedness of a world where creditors did not know the meaning of mercy, Sulis kept asking for more money – from the *Duce*'s office, from the Ministry of Popular Culture with its overseeing role in Fascist journalism and from Mussolini himself. As Sulis put it in a moment of desperation: 'Do with me what You like, order me as You will, since Your command and only Your command has the force of goodness.' If only a new subsidy could be paid, Sulis added, in a rapid four months he could finish the book that, he claimed, Mussolini had ordered him to write (and which turned into *Rivoluzione ideale*). 'At the bat of an eye-lid', the *Duce* could force Sulis's greediest enemy, based in a business concern in alien Milan, to 'see reason'.[145] Mussolini's assistance could rescue poor Sulis from all his troubles, begun in the 'sad times' of family disgrace and caused by 'capitalism'.[146]

On this occasion, Sulis did get the money he requested and by March 1939 *Rivoluzione ideale* was approved by Minculpop as 'a stimulating work, likely to foster lively discussion about the political and spiritual matters which it treats'.[147] But financial assistance and a guarantee of publication were not enough. What Sulis really wanted was another chance to meet Mussolini personally,[148] an encounter which he hoped would confirm his place as a specially privileged client and which would alert his patron to the likely benefits of continuing munificence and sympathy. If his request was now refused, could he the following year formally present the *Duce* with the copy of the book when it appeared?[149]

Any occasion would do. As he urged in March 1939: 'I am very embarrassed to disturb you yet again. But as the father of a family I have a duty not to let myself go under. In my present condition, only You [*Voi*] can help me.' His record, he explained, was impeccable. He had always worked for Mussolini and for Mussolini alone. He was grateful, of course, for the exceptional payment he had received some months ago but what he really wanted was a regular pension for his wife and children. If he could not repay the family debts, he would have to sell his house and land and drive his old mother out to a cruel fate. Such an act would create scandal in any situation but it would be made worse by the fact that, in Sardinia, he was known as a journalist who worked for *Il Popolo d'Italia*. His wife, who was regularly pregnant in the way a Fascist woman should be, was frequently sick and her illnesses were another expense and a strain on his nerves. He had knocked at every door in the kingdom but nowhere did there seem to be *sistemazione* for 'a revolutionary political writer'. 'Help me', he begged, 'and You will never regret having done so.'[150]

A year later he wrote again, signing himself 'with intransigent faith'. Still his career had not flourished as he had hoped it might. More paternal debts had fallen due. His situation was 'very urgent'. If only he could see the *Duce* face to face he was sure that he could tell him things that others concealed from him.[151] The outbreak of war offered opportunity. Sulis expressed the wish to publish a journal to be entitled *Asse: della nuova civiltà* (Axis: a new world order), proselytizing the view that 'the Axis is not just a relationship between one state and another but a meeting of two Revolutions, utterly hostile to all other conceptions of contemporary civilization. Here lies the power of the Axis and the certainty of it lasting.'[152] Again Sulis was left to complain sadly that the authorities had rejected the scheme, despite his record, the plight of his four children and the fact that so many papers actually remained redoubts of 'bourgeois and foreigner-lovers', men who lacked his own 'coherent faith'.[153]

Alas for Sulis. Although, as has been seen, he did retain a presence in wartime journalism to the bitter end, he still stubbornly sought to gain another meeting with the *Duce*.[154] A last recorded attempt in November 1942 carried a special sense of desperation, with Sulis promising that, once secure in his Leader's presence, he would reveal 'a substance which could block the radio reception of foreign programmes and so at a stroke eliminate the problem of enemy propaganda penetrating the Italian people' and release 'a new fount of energy, practically inexhaustible, activated by a new magnetic force'.[155] As Italian Fascism slid to its ruin at the front, Sulis was drifting from the nostrums of radical revolution to those of popular science, perhaps destined to be a more secure hope in that Americanizing culture which was soon penetrating Sardinia. But again, sadly for Sulis, Mussolini was neither moved to assay Sulis's mysterious knowledge of warfare nor to grant him an interview.

They must have met at Salò when Mussolini dispiritedly slipped into the oxymoronic condition of being a puppet dictator, although the last days of the Repubblica Sociale were not an ideal time for any seeking lasting *sistemazione*. However, Sulis did not fall victim to the popular vendettas in 1945 nor did his Fascist fanaticism drive him to seek his own death in coincidence with the demise of the revolution and its *Duce*. Rather, changing his shirt with apparent aplomb, within a few years Sulis began writing for a Catholic journal entitled

Orizzonti.[156] On his new horizon, the cross of Christian Democracy perhaps now matched the allure that the *fasces* had once held for him. He did not die until 1989. Edgardo Sulis, it is apparent, was a Fascist, a racist, a fanatic and yet also a son, a father, a Sard and a 'Southern intellectual' and so, contrary to some assumptions about those who work for a dictatorial cause, a recognizable human being. In this medley of fundamentalism and the everyday, Fascist passion and Italian dedication to his family, he was not different from many of his contemporaries.

15

Lurching into war

Not all young men avidly seeking fame and fortune through their ability as wordsmiths were as fortunate as Sulis or were as starstruck as he was and had cause to be with Fascism. Ruggero Zangrandi, for example, a middle-class Roman, although he was the high-school friend of Vittorio Mussolini, the dictator's eldest son, and, like him, moved in the wealthy, wanton world of cinema, lacked serenity. Were his talents and those of his friends as recognized as they should be, he asked? The depressing answer was that they were not, even though, as he explained stiffly in *Gerarchia*: 'Finding a proper job (*sistemazione*) for a medico, lawyer, engineer or doctor in philosophy is not the easy matter it is for a carpenter, a mechanic or an agricultural labourer.' For such ordinary workers, he believed enviously and also with a marked sense of class superiority that in theory ought to have been dispelled by Fascist social unity, the regime could 'do much and often all'. For the former group, aid was less forthcoming. Bottai, the Minister of Education, had tried hard, Zangrandi conceded. However a more radical and 'surgeon-like' (that dangerous metaphor again) solution was needed. One answer, perhaps unlikely to be popular with his younger friends, was to fail more students while at *liceo* (high school) and so curb the number of importunate university graduates.[1]

It was true, after all, that in 1938 the authorities counted 119,000 employed teachers and some 100,000 unemployed ones. Whereas once Gentile had wanted secondary and tertiary education restricted to an elite, the populist policies of the 1930s brought quite a few more Italians to schooling (although post-Second World War Italy still counted over 10 per cent of its adults as never having been to school and almost half as not making it through the five primary classes).[2]

During the 1930s, however, the regime was deficient in providing the new graduates with jobs commensurate with their qualifications. In a figure that throws glaring light on the hypocrisy of Fascist disquisitions about modernization, it is estimated that in 1935 about half of engineering graduates were not working professionally. A few years earlier the Fascist doctors' union maintained that the country needed 900 students to finish their degrees each year when 2,000 were doing so.[3] Under the dictatorship one out of every hundred law graduates was actually admitted to the bar.[4] By contrast, those in government service shot up from fewer than half a million in 1930 (a lower total than in 1922) to not far short of three times that number in July 1943.[5]

Zangrandi was trying his wings as an intellectual of the new generation, one of the 'cohort of Mussolini', as it was called. From 1933 he and his friends experimented with something they called *novismo* (new-ism). It meant, in truth, a flirtation with any ideas that could bring them benefit in status and wealth and, more importantly, deliver self-worth and social purpose. Zangrandi eventually recorded his memories of the 1930s, charting his 'long journey through and out of Fascism'. With an appealing honesty he recalled the ingenuousness with which a well-off youth could mingle curiosity about the USSR and a hope that Mussolini was being frank when he expatiated on the determination of the dictatorship to achieve social justice. Zangrandi, in other words, was a young man comfortably enough off to look for a way both to understand his world and to change it. Prevented by his bad eyesight from the orgasmic experience of conquering Ethiopia,[6] Zangrandi believed that the solution for himself, Italy and Europe was to be found in the crafting of words and so in a cultural revolution. This great change must be implemented by him and his friends rather than by Starace, the crass party chief, who, to Zangrandi, was the evil counsellor from whom the good *Duce* needed rescuing.

For other young men and some young women of the 1930s – the lingering gender order of Italian education is indicated in the fact that at Bologna in 1932 boys occupied more than three quarters of *liceo* places in the city[7] – the ideal arena where they could craft a credo for the next generation of Fascists was the annual Littoriali (youth) games.[8] This competition had been instituted to bring together the best and the brightest from Italian universities

(Starace affirmed that they would also be the most warlike),[9] and it did uncover a galaxy of talent. Almost all who were to matter in Italian culture through the two decades after 1945 cut their teeth in the activities of one year or another of the Littoriali – later communist politician and thinker Pietro Ingrao, for example, won the prize for 'Poets in the age of Mussolini' in 1935. The programme steadily widened its themes, by the end embracing sport (later Christian Democrat Aldo Moro was honoured on the perhaps unlikely but doubtless Catholic theme of the 'physical regeneration of our people').[10] As the war approached there were some doubts about the steadiness of the games' focus; by then, there were thirty-five separate titles for men alone.[11] The palm, however, was still awarded to those who applied themselves to mastering philosophy and the other great disciplines of high culture.

The full games were held at a different city each year but they were preceded by qualifying rounds at each of the nation's twenty-six universities, rousing great interest and debate among talented youth. Student journals and other newssheets of the Fascist student organization GUF avidly reported the qualifying rounds, while simultaneously trying to take the lead in identifying the issues of moment. Bottai, who became Minister of Education in November 1936, replacing the tediously pugnacious De Vecchi, took great care to present himself as a generous and open-minded patron. Whereas De Vecchi looked hidebound in his requirement that pupils display proficiency in religion before being promoted, and in his demand that secondary school teaching of the subject always be done by priests,[12] Bottai presented the Littoriali games as a showcase of Fascism's special modernity.

Bottai loved to reiterate that Fascism fused thought and action. His School Charter of March 1939 stated emphatically that university programmes should be 'scientific' in character. Tertiary courses, Bottai pronounced, must be spurred by a sense of 'high political and moral responsibility', even though simultaneously they should not forget the practical.[13] He saluted the beneficial reforms associated with Giovanni Gentile, but now, he stated, the regime must go further, crafting a 'modern humanism' that expressed the genuineness of the Fascist revolution. Italian youth were so fine and so committed to the regime that they should have their influence in the 'cultural, tourist and sporting sectors' steadily augmented, both nationally and inter-nationally.[14] 'In the field of culture', the Minister proclaimed, 'Fascism excommunicates no one' (although, he added in immediate contra-diction, Jews must accept their 'appropriate place' in the national system).[15] Bottai's flexibility also had its limits on gender questions, where, as Minister, he was as opposed as his predecessors had been to women undertaking lifetime careers as teachers, even though the female presence at Italian universities increased from 13 per cent to 21 per cent during the 1930s.[16] Bottai, something of a sensitive, new-age guy, did flirt with Fascist-style ecology when, after Italian entry into the war, he countered the requisitioning of school iron gates and fences with the happy thought that educational establishments, inside and outside, could be 'given a more gentle aspect with displays of plants and flowers'.[17]

A recent oral history has recounted the different fates and different memories of members of the Littoriali. Some ex-contestants under-lined the inspiration they had drawn as teenagers from their ideology: 'Fascism', said one, 'meant something that made men better, purer, more honest and generous, happy to serve the Country and ready to fight from one moment to the next.' For another, Mussolini was the key: 'I thought him just, incorruptible, in love with Italy . . . His oratory, especially in its moments of smiling irony, gave me profound spiritual and intellectual pleasure.' Yet doubts could creep in. A con-testant at Palermo in 1938 was dismayed to find a *Duce* old, lined and with a limited attention span, grumpy among those who wanted to stand tall as young revolutionaries. Other party bosses were more easily mocked. One competitor was aware that he could not make out what De Vecchi was saying in a speech at Venice and then realized that he could therefore more readily ogle the girl Littoriali. In retrospect, Starace was deemed a cretin, Ricci corrupt. The proclamation of the Empire was a time of euphoria, the *Anschluss* a moment of doubt, the war itself a delusion. In North Africa, Littoriali found that nothing worked; during the summer of 1940 men laboured in their under-clothes because they had been provided only with stores of winter garments.[18]

The most telling matter, however, was that each contestant among the Littoriali remembered his or her own version of Fascism. Belief might often be ardent; lively and wide-ranging debate with others possible. Yet youthful ideas about Fascism remained flexible and partially formed while the generation of Mussolini waited for the rigours and reality of life. And compromises kept surfacing. Membership in GUF, the party's organization for university students, brought a 50 per cent discount in the purchase of cinema tickets, even for newly released films. If, in addition, a sage male student joined the militia, present on every campus, he got three months off his eventual period of conscription and was exempted from any other compulsory pre-service parades.[19] Adolescents may have tried to believe in their own purity and that of their nation and regime but practical advantage, when offered, was hard to forgo.

As the world descended towards war, the gamut of opinions of those attending university reflected the many contradictions present in this dictatorship still so nervy about its meshing of theory and practice, its choice between a human face and more straightforward tyranny, its balancing of tradition and 'revolution'. Sexual matters tormented some, all the more since the health of the race was being newly emphasized in regime propaganda. Anti-homosexuality campaigns – partly fostered by the Church, where Pius XI's encyclical *Casti Connubi* of 1931 had anathematized any sex not directed at procreation – reached a new level of fervour. At Catania – of all ironical places given that the 'Greek' resort of Taormina, just up the coast from the provincial capital, had had its modern tourist industry largely created by Baron Wilhelm von Glöden, pioneer photographer of the young male body and aristocratic gay – homophobia boiled over.[20]

With the Baron at last dead, Molina, the *Questore* of Catania, almost foamed at the mouth as he railed against an abhorrent 'homosexual plague' that, he lamented, was now worse than it had ever been (a conclusion which, if true, said little for a decade and more of Fascist sexual totalitarianism). 'Today much spontaneous and natural repugnance is set aside and, sadly, anyone can view for himself coffee shops, dancing halls, bathing establishments or retreats in the mountains where, depending on the season, young men of all social classes publicly meet their [gay] friends,' Molina expostulated. A 'wave of degeneration' was sweeping over Catania. Erect in his Fascism, the

Questore had intervened 'to stop, or at least to contain, such grave sexual aberrations which offend morality, damage health and limit the improvement of the race'. The police, he added, most despised those individuals who, at the beach and other places, appeared 'tricked out in an almost female way, attitudinizing and gesturing in the most repellent manner'.

Molina was not merely worried by homosexuals; he was neurotically alert to any form of sexual misconduct. He reviled the behaviour of Vittorio Grillo, a young barber who, with a group of friends, had taken to parading themselves 'perfectly shaved, their hair brilliantined and dressed in the latest fashion' in and around the best *caffè* and cinemas of Catania. When women walked past, 'alone and even when they rejoiced in a male companion', the gang harassed them by 'bold and even sometimes obscene phrases, allusions, attitudes and gestures'. When Grillo went so far as to annoy the young wife of the colonel in charge of the local airport, the police stepped in and, to Molina's pleasure, Grillo was punished with a sentence of six months in the back blocks of Catanzaro (he served three).[21]

Just before this dashing fellow went to his fate, a Fascist dragnet picked up fifty-six homosexuals in Catania and its surrounding region and dispatched them to *confino* on the Tremiti islands.[22] Another two hundred and fifty from elsewhere in the country were similarly punished. From Tremiti, Bocchini, the police chief who liked to boast genially that he was a Fascist only from the waist up, received a report from some more measured jailer than the *Questore* of Catania, declaring the homosexual prisoners still on the island had behaved well and should be amnestied. They were.[23] In pursuit of its homophobia, the regime never pushed matters to the extremes reached in Nazi Germany, where castration became official policy.[24] But the events at Catania made plain that, in Fascist Italy too, homosexuals were not welcome in the political, racial and gender order.

When De Vecchi had sought a way to define the basis of the militant training of the new generation while Minister of Education, the predictable word he hit on was *bonifica* – reclamation. In a typically pompous diatribe he asserted that Fascist culture was so revolutionary that it had not just penetrated 'every aspect but even every fount of life'. That was no more than could be expected of 'the most profound Revolution . . . history has ever known'. Yet, for all its depth and span, he had to admit, the process was incomplete. 'Blows with the pick-axe' were still needed 'to cut the academic out of the Academy'.[25] De Vecchi's phrases were trite and hypocritical – words, words, words. But the task of reclamation was a regular theme of Fascist government and some grandiose works of drainage and land improvement were begun and completed. The loudest fanfare concentrated on the Pontine marshes outside Rome, an area which had for centuries resembled the Third World. A communist historian underlined how malaria-ravaged families there subsisted 'in straw huts, just like those in Ethiopia, without any provision of water or of schooling'.[26] Fascism was determined to erase this poverty which so mocked empty phrases about the new or imperishable *romanità* of the Eternal City.

In 1936, in a proclamation of another battle won, the regime sponsored the translation into English of an account of its land improvement policies throughout the country. Cesare Langobardi began decorously with an apposite quote from his *Duce*, placing high on the national agenda a commitment 'to reclaim the land, and with the land . . . the race'. When Langobardi turned to examples of the regime's victories, it was only natural that he should chronicle the draining of the Pontine marshes and the construction of the town of Littoria (after 1945 renamed Latina) and other new settlements. Unalloyed triumph was his message: 266 km of roads and 150 km of light railway built, a main canal of 28 km dug, fed by 'over 700 kilometres of secondary affluents', five million cubic metres of soil moved, in 1934 alone almost eleven and a half million work days expended. The new farms, Langobardi contended, at once produced bumper harvests, the ancient scourge of malaria was at a stroke eradicated, the collaboration between public and private enterprise was universally happy and efficient and the migration to the region of Italians from elsewhere was of general benefit.[27] In the Pontine marshes and in similar efforts at *bonifica* in Sardinia or Sicily, on the Piave or near Brisighella, Langobardi concluded, his analysis underpinned by twenty further pages of illuminating quotes from his *Duce*, Italy was being wondrously modernized and reclaimed for Italians.

Historians surveying these events have been as sceptical about the claims as they should be about the assertions of a totalitarian reclamation of youthful morality. Despite Fascist boasts about their own foresight and uniqueness, the effort to defeat nature through modern agrarian technology was a long-running one, in which the policies of the dictatorship were by no means special. Here, as an *Annales* historian might say, was a 'structure' and not an 'event', whose history is best recounted over the *longue durée*. Yet Mussolini's regime did bring its peculiar imperfections to the efforts at land improvement. Contrary to fulsome rhetoric about a united people, poor Venetan migrants to the Pontine region, often day labourers or *braccianti*, distrusted by the regime for their past socialism, were persuaded to leave their home region to the benefit of existing landowners there. Public money was converted into private gain, with little benefit to the real poor, whose meat consumption, for example, fell through the 1930s. Once the peasants got to the Agro Pontino, they were met with hostility by the locals, troubled by what they considered the loose morals of northern women who, despite the patriarchal nature of their families, ventured out to dance and rode bicycles. Employment for both men and women was as likely to be piece-work as anything more lasting. Neither conditions nor pay were good. Moreover, the migrants had to meet the expenses of their move, and frequently left more indebted than they had been in the past. The land itself was slow to become genuinely productive and, in compensation, the regime was driven to pay a 'camouflaged wage' to keep the 'pseudo-sharecroppers' on their farms. Throughout the process, the migrants blamed local Fascists and those bureaucrats with whom they came into contact for their travails. In their eyes, Mussolini, a species of 'good king', remained a hero above the ruck of life. Rumours circulated that he came on anonymous and gift-bearing visits at night, as a saint might have done (except that the beneficent *Duce* was thought to ride his motorcycle). In more practical vein, it was said that the newly installed peasants did their best to circumvent official regulations, for example exhuming the corpses of diseased cattle and eating the meat.[28] Such beliefs and actions, with their embedded traditionalism, yet again reflected complications within the Fascist project of modernizing and homogenizing the population.

The Fascist fight against malaria was similarly less successful than regime spin contended. In its campaigns against this debilitating disease, the Liberal authorities had progressed unevenly but when Fascists took up the matter, their approach was notably 'top-down and bureaucratic'[29] and unalloyed authoritarianism alienated popular support. Some incremental gains in health were made but they were fading by the 1930s and were quickly eliminated by the Second World War. Any serious check on the depredations of malaria across Italy had to await the arrival of the American armed forces with their supplies of DDT.

The regime may have hoped that its land reclamation policies would attract the greatest acclaim but plenty of other public works figured in Fascist policy and propaganda. The national railway system was a cherished part of the project of bonding Italians, all the more because Farinacci had been prominent in pushing railwaymen early into a Fascist union. 'Mussolini', it was said, 'made the trains run on time' and improvements did occur over the two decades of dictatorship. After all, in 1915, the Chiusi–Florence sector of the main Rome–Milan line was still single track and resulting bottlenecks had severely hampered transport during the First World War. In 1936, leading propagandist Paolo Orano hailed the regime's achievement in typical phrases of the time. The mustering of the Fascist syndicate, he wrote, proved that 'every public service needs its specific military guarantee and the permanent attention of responsible authorities mobilized and made completely alert by the armed representation of power'. Both 'in peace and war', he argued militantly, 'the railways hold the country in a state of perpetual mobilization, a mobilization of business, trade, entrepreneurship, intellectual exchange, all acting as an infallible help to that unifying will on which the incredible national conquests have been securely based'.[30] Talk was one thing, however, reality another. When the national transport system was tested a few years later by the Second World War, the Fascist railways showed little advance on the Liberal ones and the transport of goods, especially south of Rome, remained a serendipitous affair.

Road-building offered a similarly bumpy record. In the 1920s much was made of the opening of a 'super highway' from Milan to Como. The economic turmoil of the next decade required some restraint, however. In 1933 the *autostrada* from Florence to the sea was the last to be inaugurated under the dictatorship, while plans for an underground railway system for Milan were sketched that same year but the system was not destined to open until 1963.[31] Swathes of the south remained isolated by unpaved tracks, still more readily traversed by donkey than by wheeled and motorized vehicles.

None the less every Italian city still bears the architectural and urban planning hallmarks of the two decades of dictatorship, with Giampaoli in Milan and Arpinati in Bologna presiding in the 1920s over the opening in their cities of new football stadia, capable of holding the crowds of spectators who were beginning to flock into the weekly games. The national capital, Rome, was, football ground included, to a great degree rebuilt by Fascism.

Any tourist wanting to survey the aesthetics and social intention of Fascist architecture in the national capital might start with four sites. The ambiguities of the regime in its early days, still coloured by a Liberal and D'Annunzian inheritance, are vividly displayed at the Piazza Mincio, just beyond the Viale Regina Margherita and not far from the Mussolini family residence at the Palazzo Torlonia on the Via Nomentana. Here, apartment blocks are ornamented with mosaics of scenes from Dante and look for all the world like the Victoriana of Dante Gabriel Rossetti and Edward Burne-Jones transposed south.

More manly and imperial was the design pursued in the area around the Victor Emmanuel monument, where, as confirmed in a masterplan for the city gazetted in 1931, medieval buildings were bulldozed to allow the construction of the Via dell'Impero (now the Via dei Fori Imperiali) through to the Coliseum.[32] The myth of Rome hung heavily over the area, with the ruins of the Forum, Palatine, Trajan's forum and Nero's Golden House systematized to preach a gospel of untarnished and imperishable glory inherited from the classical empire. The most blatant sign in this regard was the set of four maps of Rome, the Urbs (Great City), traced from its tiny start until it ruled the known world, which were appended to the walls dividing the broad new thoroughfare from the Forum. (Sardonic contemporary passers-by were reported to have joked that any meaning transmitted to the present depended on which way an observer was walking.) A later commentator has complained that the long-term victor in this and much Fascist urban planning was the car, perhaps scattering the occasional group of gawping tourists but in practice left to roar down the otherwise empty 'imperial' roads in a central Rome deprived of Romans.[33]

Another telling site is the Foro Italico, once called the Mussolini or Imperial forum, out to the north of the city and near that Milvian bridge over the Tiber where the great Constantine, on 28 October 312 in his March on Rome, saw and marked the sign of the cross and so conquered the forces of his less pious or perceptive rival emperor, Maxentius. This Foro was begun as one of the major sites of the Decennale in 1932. Here, huge naked male statues of athletes surround a running track, while, marking an avenue headed towards the stadium, a series of concrete blocks commemorate Fascist victories in campaigns at home and abroad – triumphant battles for the lira, grain or birth-rate, for Ethiopia and empire. There, mock classical mosaics chant *DUCE, DUCE, DUCE* or *A noi*, even if some of the more ample promised features such as a racetrack were never built. Equally absent was a characteristically boasted 'large car park, of sufficient size for all those participating in any way in the sports on offer'.[34] After 1946 the new administration left this monument as it was, except to add further blocks welcoming the defeat of Fascism and the voting in of the Republic. The area, doubtless appropriately, was used during the Olympic Games of 1960, as well as, in more humdrum fashion, today providing the public who trudge in to watch the two expensive and erratic local football teams, Roma and Lazio, with space for their mindless sportive graffiti.

The most redolent site, however, is the Fascist model suburb of EUR, planned for the regime's twentieth anniversary celebrations or Ventennale in 1942 but completed after liberation. All Italian historians know the area well, since the state archives are housed in a white travertined and columned Fascist building, with high ceilings and echoing halls. Since Mussolini's days, EUR has not weathered well, becoming the most soulless part of Rome, with wide streets, rushing traffic, ponderous official buildings and little else. Some of the fault lies with post-Fascist construction in the 1950s and 1960s, such disastrous decades in capitalist architecture, with ugly utilitarian glass and steel ministries varying the more grandiloquent Fascist structures. But it is hard not to conclude that EUR well exemplifies the dead heart of Fascist planning, with its remorseless overlooking of human difference and its ludicrous desire to brag. However much, on most occasions, Fascist city planning did not fully break the continuity with the past or manage to impose a genuinely revolutionary vision, at EUR the regime did invent a city which, worse than the coldly authoritarian planning in nineteenth-century imperial Paris and Vienna, did not work for human beings and, in its sterility, survives as a Fascist lesson in how not to foster urban vitality.

An American historian has contended that the typical Fascist cityscape aimed to combine 'surveillance and spectacle'[35] and much about EUR testifies to her case and to the character of the regime by the 1930s as a propaganda state. She also hints at the fundamental survival of class difference in Fascist town-planning, never overcome despite constant claims to the contrary. As a special outpost of *italianità*, Trento was another natural object of Fascist solicitude. With a population of only 20,000, the urban centre taken over from the Habsburgs did not even boast reliable drains until 1925. Thereafter the city was much reworked with 'unhygienic' and 'overcrowded' medieval houses pulled down to make way for the Piazza del Littorio (now the Piazza Battisti), for example. New apartment buildings were also constructed, varying in size depending on whether the occupants were thought likely to be from the middle class (especially public officials) as opposed to the workers, whose blocks were carefully organized to have a controlled exit and entry. Trento was a city whose housing bespoke class difference and social control at least as powerfully as it did parades and party pomp.[36] In its cementing of class hierarchy, this Fascist city looked back as much as it looked forward.

To be sure, the dictatorship advertised itself as a kind of welfare state, whether by its efforts to improve the lot of mothers and children through ONMI or by its provision of national insurance through INPS, the latter body being established in 1933 with alleged autonomy to give social security to all Italians. Again a gap separated theory and practice. ONMI was very slow to get properly underway and its functioning was always torn by regional difference. Even in 1936 one third of the country's provinces lacked ONMI service except on paper. Similarly, the holdings of INPS were regularly plundered for more immediate regime needs. Fascist charity generally came with strings attached and was directed at the 'deserving poor' (in Fascist terms), either the docile or families with contacts and influence rather than those most in need. Political checks were facilitated by the fact that, since 1933, all workers had to carry *libretti di lavoro* (job books). Since the Church had not abandoned its own charity, Fascist social services were scarcely firmly 'totalitarian'. As a fine analysis of the matter has concluded: welfare under the dictatorship amounted to 'a re-vamp of old-style charity', concentrating on those already in the fold rather than those outside it.[37]

But what of the Fascist state and war, especially given that, by the later 1930s, the regime's expenditure on defence and related matters was pushing the country towards bankruptcy? Was Italy in 1939–40 militarily prepared for a modern conflict? What, in particular, had happened to the Italian Army under a dictatorship which often sounded as though fighting was its game?

At the top, there had been much stability. Pietro Badoglio, the son of a Piedmontese petty bourgeois local mayor, had been promoted Chief of General Staff after Mussolini assumed full dictatorial powers in May 1925.[38] Thereafter Badoglio was laden with honours, promoted Marshal, in 1929 granted the Collar of the *Annunziata*, with the right to address the King as cousin and, after the acquisition of the empire, elevated to a hereditary dukedom of Addis Ababa. Badoglio proved a bonny (and greedy) defender of his own and his family's cause, swiftly ridding himself of any who opposed his primacy in military administration. None of the celebrated changes of the guard, which Mussolini enjoyed imposing on his civilian henchmen as he moved them from one ministry to the next, afflicted the army. Badoglio was no special fan of Fascism, being openly sarcastic about Starace's *voi* campaign, for example,[39] and he jealously protected the army officer corps from party interference. Under his command, the military remained a sector of national life where there was a survival of personnel, of *mentalité* and even of weaponry (in 1940 equipment included artillery captured from the Austrians in 1918 and rifles that were even more antiquated) from the Liberal past.[40]

This officer corps was scarcely aglow with the white heat of modern technology. In October 1940 General Mario Roatta clamoured his objection to suggestions that the cavalry be abolished.[41] In 1941–2 the army was to dispatch 20,000 mules – they were ill adapted to the freezing cold but sometimes useful as food – to the Russian front but failed to provide its men with sleds.[42] Despite the fashion triumphs of the national leather industry, neither in 1940 nor later did the army manage to equip its forces with boots that could last through the workaday. The wealthy wife of one party boss thought wartime charity required her to tour the shoe shops of her city, buy up their stock of six or seven hundred pairs and urgently dispatch them to her husband's brigade on the Greek front.[43] Conscription functioned poorly. In September 1939 official accounts of mobilized soldiers in Genoa spoke of bewildered, half-dressed and half-fed men, wandering disconsolately around the port city, without orders or purpose.[44] Where more elevated military learning was involved, Badoglio saw no reason to waste time on the tactics of tank warfare, suggesting in the summer of 1940 that there would be plenty of opportunity after the conflict to study the German handling of such weapons.[45] At no stage in the war did industry manage to produce a serviceable tank, capable of taking on the Soviets' T-34 or even its English rival.

In sum, despite the usual chatter about totalitarianism, the officer corps remained a caste resentful of and largely impervious to party interference. Nuto Revelli, one of the great reporters of Italy's war, who was converted from an enthusiastic young Fascist athlete into an anti-Fascist by his experience of it, has recalled entering officers' school at Modena in September 1939, there to be sarcastically nicknamed 'the German' because of his efficiency. In his training, he found not so much Fascism as a devotion to the King, not so much a modern fighting force as a coterie of gentlemen loyal to that Piedmont which had set a military tone in 1848. Although, as he would later recognize, he had never seen a tank, he had been Fascistized in the sense that he was utterly confident that Italy would win any contest, since its armed forces were the last word in sleekly contemporary warfare. However, when Revelli was placed in command of his first training marches, he noticed that half his men lacked serviceable boots.[46]

Despite Fascist (and Nationalist) propaganda about how the navy expressed 'a fundamental aspect of the vitality of a people taken in its most ample sense', with national naval power straining to assume 'a leading role in the new historical cycle commencing in the Mediterranean',[47] in 1939–40 Italy proved as unready for modern maritime warfare as it was on land. At a moment of euphoria in early 1936 plans were mooted to build what was called an 'escape fleet', designed to smash the bonds of British and French superiority and allow the Italian navy to sail beyond the inland sea. However, the programme was planned to take twenty-four years before readiness could be achieved and was not pursued.[48]

During the late 1930s Italy did spend huge sums on defence and, in June 1940, possessed 113 submarines, second in the world behind the USSR.[49] But their effectiveness was conditioned by the fact that these vessels were not only technologically antiquated but life-threatening to their crews with their tendency to leak poisonous fumes from their engines. Italian mines were 'woefully outdated' and anti-submarine equipment was also sub-standard.[50] Rather contradicting the ideology flaunted in the anti-Comintern pact, the Italians had contracted in 1934–5 to build patrol boats for the Soviet fleet and they were in time delivered, the last in 1939 with the fast destroyer *Tashkent*.[51] Perhaps the money received in payment was envisaged as assisting the war effort but the sham of Italian naval preparedness was rapidly displayed in combat. Successive engagements off Calabria in July 1940, the loss of three battleships at anchor at Taranto in November and a further defeat at Cape Matapan in March 1941 sank Fascist Italy's maritime cause. The propaganda boast that the navy exemplified 'the fertilizing course of the nation's vital tissue'[52] could scarcely have been further from the truth.

The air force was yet another fine symbol of the fissure between talk of war and its reality. The Aeronautica had been the darling of the regime and, as in other countries, was treasured by those in the bourgeoisie who viewed themselves as modern. Fascist propagandists loved to recall that Italy set 110 flight records between 1927 and 1939 and, in that latter year, held 36 out of the 84 such titles recognized in world aviation.[53] Air force officers were likely to be both well educated and to come from the upper strata of society. Air force journals were inclined to mix their Fascism and nationalism with a sort of expert internationalism, a pilots' fellowship. A typical piece in *L'Ala d'Italia*, a fortnightly published by the Air Ministry, enthused about Balbo's 'raid' in 1932, with a salute to 'the great international of the air', uniting the Fascist Minister and the American and Australian

airmen, Charles Lindbergh and Charles Kingsford Smith.[54] Bert
Hinkler, another Australian air pioneer, was buried in the Florence
cemetery with Fascist insignia and the semi-official mourning of *L'Ala
d'Italia*.[55] Momentarily, Fascist sexism could even be set aside when
celebrating Amelia Earhart with the somewhat unlikely claim that
'nothing seduces women as flying does' and it was noted admiringly
that in China women pilots went off to war.[56] In more complacently
masculine vein, the reactionary modernism of early flight, where
open-cockpit men simultaneously managed a machine and challenged
the gods, had prompted an equation between flying and fascism in
many places. Göring, Mosley, D'Annunzio, Balbo, Finzi and the *Duce*
himself, who still in the Second World War loved to take control of a
plane, were only the more obvious examples.

Despite this boosting of the air as a realm where Fascism soared
into the future, Italy failed to resolve the problem of aircraft production. Its planes may have been swift but they had not overcome basic
technological deficiencies. In the fighting in North Africa, they were
frequently kept on the ground by the absence of serviceable filters
against sand. In September 1939 the air force had only stockpiled six
weeks' petrol supplies.[57] Fiat's open-cockpit G-50 has been hailed as
the least effective monoplane fighter of the war, while historian
Macgregor Knox has recorded how 'the Piaggio [heavy industrial]
firm gleefully falsified test results after falling under suspicion because
its engines routinely failed in flight. The air force took the matter to
Mussolini, but Piaggio continued to produce engines so sloppily manufactured that they were dangerous.'[58] The two most notorious statistics of the Italian war effort were that the number of aircraft ready
in 1939 was actually 840 (and quite a few of them could not fly),
rather than the 8,528 claimed,[59] while by 1943 Italy was managing to
produce fewer planes in a year (about 1,600) than the USA could
manufacture in a week (their annual total was 85,898).[60] Despite
Douhet's reiterated press campaigns about the next war being decided
from the air, in 1940 Italy was not equipped with worthwhile shelters
in its cities against aerial bombardment and sketched no plans to
organize its civilian population when bombers struck. In the spring of
1939 Ciano typically displayed his savoir-faire in having mastered foreign terms (and thus his disdain for Fascist linguistic purism) by jot-

ting down that Italy's military power was *molto bluff*, warning a few weeks later that economic expert Felice Guarneri was reporting that, if bankruptcy was to be avoided, the regime must put '*lo stop* to its imperialist policy'.[61]

In sum, technologically speaking, the combined military forces of the dictatorship scarcely justified national pretensions to be the least of the great powers. Furthermore, the national economy was mineral-poor, autarchy having done nothing to remove the urgent requirement to import a vast array of key primary products, up to 80 per cent of its raw material. To go to war it was estimated that 150,000 tons of copper were needed, of which the nation produced 1,000.[62] The problem of energy supplies and the utter dependence on imported coal, which had troubled Liberal Italy before 1914, had never been resolved. The oil that lay just below the Libyan sands had not been exploited. Moreover, the armed forces remained poorly equipped with drivers and mechanics; Italy was not yet a genuinely motorized society. The honorary degree that Mussolini was awarded in chemistry in 1939[63] could not conceal the limitations of Fascist science, in turn further damaged by anti-Semitism, given that Jews had been prominent among the professoriate in physics and mathematics. Cheap talk by Malaparte, when still in his Fascist phase, in the journal *Il Selvaggio* (The Wild One), that modernity was 'bastardly, international, superficial, mechanical – a concoction manipulated by Jewish bankers, pederasts, war profiteers and bordello owners'[64] was not a good recipe for a society preparing for a modern and global war.

By 1939 war it was to be. The Pact of Steel signalled its imminence. Perhaps the Italian leadership did believe that the Nazi gearing up for battle was merely tactical.[65] Certainly the German ambassador, with more than a touch of his nation's natural sense of superiority over Italians, reflected in his diary in late May 1939 that Mussolini 'must know that Italy cannot fight a world war, either militarily, materially, or morally'.[66] As the weather brightened and tourists, if fewer in numbers than in the past, thronged the main resorts, *Il Popolo d'Italia* celebrated the first broadcasting in an experimental way of television with an entirely local content, boasting that the whole business was further proof of 'Italian labour and genius, come to the fore under a severely autarchic economic system'.[67] Luckily the world was to be saved from Mussolinian TV. Rather than staying at home and tuning in, the *Duce*, a few days later, turned up at a performance of Verdi's *La Forza del Destino*, staged outdoors at the Baths of Caracalla, to flaunt a dictator's humility by seating himself in the 'popular area', declaring the view and acoustics excellent before departing for an assignation with his mistress, Claretta Petacci.[68] In his swagger and levity he ignored the malign destiny which might have already been detected in the wings of the arena.

While the Fascist and Nazi governments were treatying with different purpose and intention about marching shoulder to shoulder towards a revolutionary new order, an undercurrent of discontent peeped through among Italy's own German citizens. In a typical case uncovered by the secret police, in May 1939 Francesco Anrather, from the hinterland of Trento, was relegated to the Tremiti islands for five years because he had sung the 'Horst Wessel Song' in public and greeted a friend with a *Heil Hitler!* Anrather, the secret police maintained, had explained that the song asserted that 'today we have Germany in our hands; tomorrow it will be the world'.[69] Here, then, was evidence again of the possible national or racial conflict which might sunder the Axis between the Nazi and Fascist regimes. On the German side there had been further thoughts about the matter since shortly after the *Anschluss*. Göring, who was just the man to enjoy regular trips to the fleshpots of the south, was the first to come up with the idea of a root-and-branch population transfer which historian Götz Aly views as the benign enough prototype for the genocidal Nazi ethnic cleansing to come. The Italians were at first doubtful of thus confessing that they had not assimilated all their people to Fascist rule, but in October 1939 an exchange did commence, with some 185,000 German-speaking ex-citizens eventually preferring the Reich and 82,000 choosing Italy as home.[70]

In one curious case illustrative of the precariousness of ethnic identity, Bruno Grillo, an 'unpolitical' hairdresser from Merano, and his sister Elisabetta opted for Germany, 'despite being of Italian race and language'. Once under Nazi rule, however, they grew unhappy and soon returned to Italy. Unimpressed by the claim from the two that 'really' they had been trying to escape the clutches of their violent and drunken father, the Grillos were punished for their ambiguous patriotism with five years' *confino* at Spezzano Albanese in the hills of Cosenza province, ironically a *paese* with a populace of Albanian descent. They were amnestied on 28 October 1942.[71]

A world away from the Grillo siblings, the man technically in charge of Italian foreign policy was Galeazzo Ciano. Yet the *genero* was another whose Fascism was not limpid in character and purpose. Ciano had been born in March 1903 and in the early 1920s was a brilliant student at his upper bourgeois *liceo classico*, soon gravitating to the fashionable Caffè Aragno in Rome where he hung out with gilded youth more interested in literature (and sex) than in politics. He penned some poems and short stories, with the themes of his juvenilia being death and fate.[72] He was later inscribed as a member of the self-consciously radical Disperata squad and a participant in the March on Rome. But neither was true and he was another to have his Fascism backdated through contacts and the need for good appearance.[73]

Ciano emerged politically in 1931 with his marriage made in a Fascist heaven to Edda Mussolini. The *Duce* had for a while ear-marked Costanzo Ciano as the person to replace him as head of government should an untoward event occur. But during the 1930s Galeazzo Ciano moved into position as the dictator's dauphin, rising effortlessly from a diplomatic posting in China to Under-Secretary of Press and Propaganda in September 1934 to Minister (journalists found him a congenial figure with whom to deal), then, after his stint as a bomber, Minister for Foreign Affairs. Once in office, he followed a staffing track not unknown to his predecessors and successors by doing his best to eliminate from influence any diplomats who had been close to Grandi, while he, Grandi, was Minister. Ciano was reported to have viewed the by now ambassador in London – who was his like in many ways in class background and reckoning with the world – as 'the enemy number one of Fascist foreign policy'.[74] By contrast, Ciano got on well with Police Chief Bocchini, who must have savoured the *genero*'s vanity and realism.

Despite or because of the fact that, in his innermost being, Ciano was 'a good bourgeois, a conservative . . . by instinct, tradition and education',[75] from 1936 to 1939 the young diplomat led national foreign policy into violence, aggression and murder, being, as has been noted, the architect of intervention in Spain and the occupation of

Albania, the patron of the killing of the Rosselli brothers and the loud fan of the German alliance, even if he whispered to his friends that it was best if the Nazis were placed in thrall to their Italian superiors and made to work for Italian ends. None the less, in his speeches and diplomatic dealing, Ciano repeatedly hailed Italians and Germans as the young and dynamic newcomers, destined to oust the fossilized existing powers. Conditioning any ideological fanaticism, however, was a high society lifestyle, featuring an appetite for oysters and pheasant at the best restaurants[76] and much sexual dalliance – he was said to have combined this interest with his sporting life by having sex with wanton starlets in the rough of the Acquasanta golf course in the capital.[77] Neither of these latter forms of athletic endeavour nor the very public installation of an exercise bike at his office in the Palazzo Chigi stopped him from rapidly looking puffy, hardly the model of a honed Fascist male body, straining in its readiness to jump through fire and brimstone for the regime.

Somewhere beneath the exhibitionism, Ciano was an intelligent, if flighty, young man, capable of insight about his own country and about others and anything but anxious to touch off a real world war. Contemporaries remembered his brio as a conversationalist, at least in his father-in-law's absence (he was said to have been in strict privacy an excellent mimic of the *Duce*).[78] The portrait of Ciano by a Romanian diplomat as a 'lucid young sensualist' is both succinct and accurate.[79] Even when examined in the most cursory manner, Ciano was anything other than a *milite* of the Fascist revolution. Instead, his personal habits and world-view were shared by many other politicians in countries ruled by regimes which did not harp on about totalitarianism. Perhaps the dictator himself liked and protected him (up to a point) as a reflection of the respectable side of Fascism and of the *Duce*'s own half-latent social (and intellectual) ambition. In very many senses, Ciano, the *genero*, and Farinacci, the *Duce*'s old and never altogether renounced 'friend', stood as the 'two faces of Mussolinian Fascism'.

What, then, did Ciano make of the world situation during the summer of 1939? Although never failing to salivate at the temptation of victory, gain and personal triumph, Ciano did now at last open his eyes to the fact that the Nazis were for real. Without any equivocation or possibility of compromise, Nazism meant war. On 11 August Ciano, a Daniel hoping not to burn, arrived at Salzburg to meet Hitler and the odious Ribbentrop, to reveal that, contrary to so much sabre-rattling, Fascist Italy did not want battle.[80] In his diary, Ciano reported that the implacable Hitler was determined that the timing and character of the conflict will be 'decided by them and not by us' and that the only ghost of a bargain Germany was willing to offer its partner in the Axis was 'a tiny hand-out'.[81] To a friend and client, Ciano remarked in dismay: 'they're madmen; they want all-out war', moaning piteously that Nazi brutality and bloodiness had given him a sleepless night.[82] Not even a happy jaunt to his fiefdom in Albania could dispel the clouds which hung over the *genero*; that place, he for once admitted, was insignificant when face to face with the grand crisis.

Turn and turn about was still possible as Ciano greeted news of the Ribbentrop–Molotov pact as a 'master coup', stimulating momentary hope that a diplomatic revolution might yet bring easy 'booty' to Italy.[83] But, indeed, it was to be a full-scale conflict and not even the sudden Italian request urgently to be sent an enormous volume of primary material imports could halt the Nazi war machine.

Confronting this horror, Ciano wanted out. Even the *Duce*, despite the reams of verbiage pledging his commitment to his ally and the public meshing of his charisma with the destiny of the *Führer* and despite his hatred of the thought that Fascist Italy in 1939 was going down the road traversed by Liberal Italy in 1914–15, agreed. Mussolini's frequent personal letters to Hitler drifted towards admitting that Italy was not ready.[84] By 1 September it had been decided that Italy would stay out of the 'war for Danzig' and leave the future to resolve itself. The next day Ciano reported happily that 'public opinion', that is, those subjects of the dictatorship in the *genero*'s ken, had reacted 'with absolute faith in the decisions which had been taken'.[85]

Italy, then, had become not neutral as at the start of the First World War but, lest the structures of history seem too visibly to overbear ideology, non-belligerent. It remained so until 10 June 1940, that is, for 273 days as against the 296 of the *intervento* in 1914–15. There was one difference, however. In the first conflict, Italy used the period of neutrality to transfer from the side of its allies to that of its 'friends'.

In 1939–40, Italy, lacking 'friends' except its ally, was destined to march with the terrible Nazis.

Why and with what immediate effect become the obvious questions. How did Italians confront their months of watching from the sidelines a second great, if doubtless not yet world, war, when for so long propaganda had assured them that Italy would be there? How was caution to be reconciled with the carelessness of the easy victories in Ethiopia, when the propaganda agreed with Starace, exceeding himself in oafishness, in maintaining, 'for me, making war is like eating a plate of macaroni'?[86]

Back in late December 1938 Rino Parenti, then the *federale* of his city, had found a splendidly arch phrase to define the state of Milanese opinion. The city, he wrote to Starace, evinced a 'totalitarian-ness' that was 'relative, indeed very relative'.[87] In the country at large it was not difficult to trace heretical thoughts; the secret police were on the lookout for them. In the spring of 1939 Silvestro Fiorioli della Lena, a Roman pensioner in his sixties,[88] was sceptical about the likelihood of an Italian stroll to glory in a coming war. He told a line of people, waiting to buy lottery tickets, that 'England has gold; France has it, too. But Italy only has paper.' The *Duce*, he predicted, must soon fall from power since it would become clear that he was no more than a swindler. 'Mussolini has spent so much money on the armed forces in order merely to look important in the world,' he explained.

Also troubled by the idea of a conflict with Britain was Umberto Cleva, a skilled ship-worker from Muggia. He was denounced for telling his fellows, as they laboured on the battleship *Vittorio Veneto*, that 'the British fleet is superior to the Italian one. Our sailors are just no good and, if there is a war tomorrow, they will be unable to compete with the British.' Cleva had never been a cause of political concern for the authorities before, although they did note darkly that he was thought to mix with bad company. His penalty was three years' *confino* at Ruoti in the Basilicata but he was amnestied within the year.[89]

Another who suffered for his admiration of the Anglo-Saxon world was Vincenzo Cinalli, a poor peasant from Montedorisio in the Abruzzi, aged fifty, who had only recently repatriated from the USA, where he had long been an emigrant. In June 1939 Cinalli had announced in English at the local *dopolavoro* or party after-work club that the British would emasculate Mussolini 'and accompanied his words with a meaningful gesture of his hands'. Hearing his words, the locals hurried Cinalli out of the room, presumably in an attempt to save him from himself. However, he was denounced after 'rumour' and 'surprise' in the *paese* alerted the *carabinieri* to the matter. Under cross-examination, Cinalli added that the *Duce* had still not paid the Americans properly for loans underwritten during the First World War. He was sure that, if there were a new conflict, British forces would rout the Italians. He said all this 'smilingly', while maintaining that, 'in such a war, he was ready to fight for Italy and the *Duce*'. The police decided, not altogether unreasonably, that Cinalli was 'mad' but he was sentenced to three years at the penal colony at Pisticci anyway.[90]

Along with esteem of the English enemy, another common theme was mistrust and dislike of the Italians' overbearing Axis ally. Giovanni Re, a Milanese clerk and piano teacher in his forties, told a couple of workers at the local Alfa Romeo factory in September 1939 that 'the Germans are a horrible lot, while the British and the French are gentlemen'. Sooner or later, he added, the Nazis would be sure to want to grab Trieste and anyway they were 'overweening backers of every disorder and loved provoking war'. They were also certain to lose. Re had been decorated as an officer in the First World War and had volunteered to fight in Ethiopia, although his service had not been required there. His wife, a language teacher, was a party member and his sons were enrolled in the Fascist youth organization, Giovani italiani del Littorio.[91]

A different but related tack was taken by Ambrogio Nini, the owner of a printer's shop in Milan, arrested in the first days of the New Year, 1940. Nini had loyally undertaken his military service, exhibiting no previous political dissidence. He was, however, a pious Catholic. The Germans he had always disliked because, in his mind, the nation of Italy had been united against their wishes and they had never ceased to be a threat. Worse, the Ribbentrop–Molotov pact had brought the two major international evil-doers together and it was unimaginable that Italy would fight a war in harness with them. Nini was so upset that he had printed copies of a single-page pamphlet en-

titled *I boia del 1939* (The killers of 1939). It stated that 'Italy would
be covered with infamy if it had to send a single man to help out barbarians who never hesitate to launch themselves against smaller
peoples, driven on by their false ideas about domination.' Every serious country had an interest in seeing the destruction of the 'terrorist'
communist and Nazi states, he declared.[92]

Not all Italians were yet convinced that their nationality and party
allegiance meant the same thing. Enrico Gianrossi of Sarzana was a
salesman, nearing fifty, who, during the tense days of August–
September 1939, taunted people he called 'you Fascists' with the
statement that they could scarcely fight so rich a people as the English,
when 'Italians don't possess a drop of coffee or a grain of sugar and
also lack uniforms and boots for their soldiers'.[93] Police investigation
showed that Gianrosi rejoiced in a good previous reputation, both in
his employment and as a citizen. He had served and been wounded
in the First World War. He had not, however, sought membership in
the PNF.

If Ciano had possessed the desire or the will to listen to Italians outside his immediate circle, he might, in other words, have detected
many doubts among the little people about how their masters were
going to pilot the nation through the shoals of the international situation. The regime elite was itself divided and uncertain. Mussolini, to
adapt a comment he was said to have made about Hitler when they
first met in 1934, sounded like a gramophone with its needle stuck in
a single groove, automatically mouthing phrases about an iron solidarity of the Axis between the two fascist revolutions and growing
incandescently Germanophile at any hinted parallel with 1914–15.
Yet, for all this fury, and Mussolini was very fond of furious decla-
mation, what government action there was did not suggest precipitate
entry into battle. The dilemma confronting Italy was profound. As
Ciano mused after a visit to Hitler in mid-October: 'every Italian in
Germany hates the Germans from the bottom of his heart. But without exception they are all convinced that Hitler will win the war.'[94] In
November the Italian embassy in Berlin engaged in a minor subversion of ideological purity, obeying instructions from Rome to be generous with entry permits for Jews and Poles.[95] Ciano, always a
bourgeois somewhere in his being, gave his self-interested heart to

'poor little Finland', dreaming of ways in which Italy could provide military backing against the wickedly Bolshevik USSR, even though, and because, the communists were presently Germany's ally. The *genero* had also had the by no means stupid thought that Italy could just stay out of the war and grow rich from trading with both sides.[96]

In most instances, however, it was best to wait and watch developments at the front since, over the winter of 1939–40, fighting was frozen into the 'phoney war'. It was time to make a major or major-seeming change at home. On 31 October the ministry was reworked and among leading figures only Ciano, Grandi, who, after his return from his London embassy, had become Minister of Justice only four months earlier, Bottai and Paolo Thaon di Revel, the Minister of Finance, retained office. The too frankly pessimistic Guarneri lost his position over exchange controls, being replaced by Raffaello Riccardi, a corrupt and bloody old squadrist, now turned theoretician of a European-wide corporate and autarchic economy.[97] But the greatest alteration to the regime's image was the sacking of Starace, replaced as PNF secretary by Ettore Muti, a youngish (born 1902), soldierly and athletic, sometime squadrist from Ravenna, renowned neither for his intellectual strengths nor his financial probity.[98] Ciano boasted that it was 'his' ministry and predicted that Muti would prove 'child-like' in his willingness to follow wherever Ciano might lead. Perhaps there were opportunities of a different kind, since, Ciano noticed cheerily, job hunters, each waving an indispensable *raccomandazione*, crowded around.[99]

Muti took over a party which now counted 21,606,468, half the population, as members or as participants in related organizations.[100] This huge number signalled the elephantiasis which had long beset the party and, during his first days in office, Muti set to with vim to eliminate some of the overlapping that confused relations between one *ente* and another.[101] But it was soon evident that he lacked the needed stamina for the job. In the confusion of finding a credible line about the war and simultaneously raising the PNF's drooping profile, propaganda grew, if anything, shriller; words once again mattered more than deeds. In *Gerarchia*, Fernando Mezzasoma banged on about the new selectivity which was to feature in the training of party cadres. The best young men would display for all to see their 'silent and knowing discipline, their readiness to obey without which they will not merit the privilege of command, their intransigent faith, the force which alone can "move mountains", their acceptance of sacrifice as the indispensable means to every conquest . . . their joy in combat as the supreme end of their existence', he maintained.[102] In *Critica Fascista*, journalistic cogitations veiled policy confusion with the assertion that the need for treaty revision and its mismanagement by the old powers had 'carried Italy perforce on to Germany's side', while simultaneously pronouncing that the nation always pursued its own interests. All in all, it was argued, Italy was the 'master of the situation' which was 'fluid and replete with every possibility'.[103] In so far as the domestic situation was concerned, Bottai's journal greeted the dropping of Starace with a reiteration that 'the Party is the central motor of the life of the Regime; the Party is the backbone of the Kingdom'.[104] Economic matters received an occasional mention but the constant line of this and other organs was that 'quality' and 'belief' were what really mattered on every front of any coming fight.[105] 'Will' overbore the need accurately to count planes or produce boots with waterproof soles. Meanwhile, the most drastically anti-Semitic papers pressed on with their campaigns, with Preziosi characteristically proclaiming in January 1940 that 'the policy of His Britannic Majesty is the policy of Jewry'.[106]

Military policy similarly did not illuminate what might be Italy's intentions. National GDP hardly increased (and, alone of the combatants, it would continue to fail to do so once Italy entered the war).[107] Stockpile deficiencies were not repaired; energy needs were not filled. In February 1940 a special appropriation gave more funds to the frontier fortifications still being erected on the Brenner and so potentially against Germany than the combined total earmarked for the French and Yugoslav borders.[108] That same month, Bocchini spoke of his preoccupation that food supplies were dwindling alarmingly[109] (women, more anxious to defend their families than serve the nation, had reacted to the threat of war by hoarding basic foodstuffs). Although commercial negotiations with the suspicious British marked time, at the end of May 1940 Italy was still delivering armaments to France. It also sold four destroyers to neutral Sweden.[110] Around that time, Carlo Favagrossa, who led the General Commissariat for War

Production, an organization born in the Ethiopian campaign to enhance efficiency but destined never to work effectively, complained that Italy was now worse off than it had been in 1939. Once the war began, Favagrossa would tell Ciano graphically that Italy's situation in regard to material reserves and possible credit was like a 'bath, with the taps blocked and the outlet open'.[111]

In all probability, in assessing why, on 10 June 1940, Fascist Italy entered the Second World War as the 'first ally' of Nazi Germany, none of this activity, be it actions or words, mattered much. Rather, Italian entry was decided because, when it overran Norway, the Low Countries and France, Nazi Germany had won or gave every appearance of having won the war. Ever since the Risorgimento, the structures of Italian history suggested to the nation's most astute minds that Italy, to sustain its pretensions as a great power, must join the winning side in a war and do so when the result was all but plain and the demands to be made on the country were not too onerous. That situation existed in early June 1940. As the Fascist unionist Tullio Cianetti later recalled in his gullibly honest way: 'almost the totality of us Italians in a few days [in May–June] were engulfed by admiration and enthusiasm for the astonishing German victories'.[112] A secret police account from Milan on 28 May agreed about the population's rising enthusiasm, 'because the view is now widespread that, in entering the conflict, our sacrifices will be limited'.[113] In Rome, a week earlier, it was said that a general impatience could be detected among the popular classes and a profound happiness at the prospect of dealing in short order with the arrogant English.[114] Students were reported to be especially ardent in favouring the war,[115] while on 16 May the Vatican was stated to have accepted that Germany was destined for total victory.[116]

Since the war turned out to be not victorious but humiliating, not brief but long, not gainful but barren, there were innumerable reasons why, after the event, Italians who counted in the admittedly opaque decision-making processes of Fascist Italy sought to ladle the entire blame on to 'one man alone' – the dictator. Mussolini's verbal savagery made it all the easier to pin the responsibility on him. But if the dictator's words are decoded and placed in proper context, their relative significance is reduced and it becomes plain that all the post-

Risorgimento national elite helped to prepare the national course in 1940.[117]

Yet there was much that would prove Fascist about the Italian version of the Second World War. To be sure, fitting the pattern also in France and Britain, national casualties would prove relatively light, less than three quarters of the dead from 1915 to 1918, despite battles now lasting fifty-eight months against the forty-one of the First World War. Italians also undoubtedly killed fewer foreign soldiers under Fascism than they did under Liberalism, although, befitting the new times, they slaughtered far more civilians in the Nazi-fascist 'crusade' than in the earlier combat.

The nature of the Fascist 'new order' will be explored in the next chapters. What first must be stressed, however, is the way the war swiftly brought to the surface the contradictions and ambiguities of the Mussolini 'revolution', with its combination of levity and anxiety, aggression and spin. On 10 June the regime and most of its fellow travellers had decided to close their eyes and think of their version of Italy, hoping and expecting that the battle was won. Italy had no war aims, except to participate in a brazenly brutal Fascist fashion in the campaign and then half-plan to derail or muddy German hegemony at a peace conference. The Fascist leadership was made up of politicians with a 'short-war illusion', making that which is better known among European leaders in 1914 – when they believed the First World War would be over by Christmas – seem trifling or prescient in comparison. The Italian armies mobilized slowly and ineffectually and inflicted no significant damage on France by the time the Republic's leadership surrendered – it was on 15 June, five days after the Fascist declaration of war, with the Germans already in Paris, when Paul Reynaud first proposed an armistice. With Pétain having in the interim taken over, the French laid down their arms a week later.

In the empire, there was a brief and much heralded raid on British Somaliland, which fell to Italian forces, stiffened by local black and Arab auxiliaries in August[118] – Hitler, perhaps made malicious by the sight of such racial impurity, sent congratulations and a simultaneous query as to when the Italians intended to move forward elsewhere.[119] The victory at Berbera proved a fleeting triumph. From February 1941 a motley Anglo-Indian imperial force swept through the paper-thin defences of AOI. Addis Ababa fell at the beginning of April. Some sporadic resistance lingered for the next six months but the much-glorified Fascist empire had melted as if the Alpini, unlucky enough to be stationed in the tropics, there defended the realm of a snowman. Even in Libya, Italian generals, no matter how ostensibly 'Fascist' with Graziani in command, were hesitant in thrusting against British rule in Egypt. In December 1940 it was instead a British imperial force under General Archibald Wavell that attacked from the east and, over the next two months, drove the Italians back to Benghazi, destroying a Fascist army that was six times larger than its rival. Already, by 7 January 1941, Wavell reported that 57,000 Italian POWs had fallen into his army's hands.[120] Earlier, on 28 June, nervous Italian anti-aircraft gunners had shot down a plane as it approached Tobruk. They did not notice that it was a trimotor of unique national design and had not flown towards the port from the enemy direction.[121] On board was Italo Balbo, the governor of Libya and the first elite casualty of Italy's war. If any further proof were needed of the limits of Fascist war, back home that autumn tens of thousands of peasant soldiers were demobilized since they were needed to get in the harvest.

Opinion which, in the days immediately following 10 June, was agog for a triumphant Italian Fascist *Blitzkrieg*, rapidly revived its earlier doubts, suspicions and fears. The citizens of Milan, Genoa and Turin reacted timorously to their first bombardment from the air,[122] with the Milanese being both terrified and annoyed at the lack of anti-aircraft defence.[123] There and elsewhere, the secret police busied themselves with 'defeatists', even if they were frequently persons whose real crime was to be picked up for saying publicly what everyone believed. Alfredo Marletta, now in his thirties and a plumber from Catania, for example, was arraigned for his open condemnation of Germany. He and his friends were said to have bought the Vatican's paper, *L'Osservatore Romano*, each day and there found information that eventually led Marletta to express his hope that the war would be lost so that he could 'see the end of Fascism and Nazism'. Marletta, it was rumoured, had vaguely Republican sympathies.[124] Angelo Lucantoni, who ran a *rosticceria* in Via Sella in central Rome, was another who thought it a bad joke to claim, as the Fascist press did, that the British were afraid of Italians. He added that the outcome of the Axis, should it prove victorious, would be that, in any post-war arrangement, Italians would be forced to become Germans. Lucantoni, informants stated, was yet another to have been long known for maligning the Fascist regime.[125] Cosimo Lassandro, an elementary teacher who had begun training as a Jesuit but did not stay the course and now resided at Bari, had, it was said, also made himself politically suspect because of his reiterated criticism of the Axis. A PNF member since 1933, he was arrested and sentenced to two years' *confino* after he told customers at a local *caffè* that Britain would be 'a tough nut to crack' and predicted that Italy and Germany would lose the war.[126]

Gaetano Conte, from Lecce and now a postal clerk in Milan in his fifties, who, according to the police, was notorious for chatting at his workplace about the inadequacies of the 'totalitarian states', concurred. In his view, 'the French and the English are more civilized peoples than are we and the Germans. They keep their word when given, unlike the Germans.' Conte predicted that the Nazis might at first seem to be helping their allies but they would eventually 'swindle them'. It would be good if the war were lost, Conte concluded, since, then, 'Fascism and Hitlerism will be eliminated'.[127] For the housewife Adele Rossi of Cuneo, the problem simply was that the Italians were trying to 'rob the English' by attacking them. Mincing no words, she looked forward to the day when she could 'cut off the Head of Government's balls . . . because his caprices had killed so many fathers of their families'.[128]

The expression of another familiar theme brought two years in *confino* to Giuseppe Biasini, a travelling salesman in his thirties. In a *caffè* at Chiari, a town near Brescia, he chided the government for making 'bombastic speeches saying that we are ready and yet anyone can see that those called up are not given lodging, food or uniforms. This was true not only at Chiari but also at Brescia and Cremona as I have seen for myself.' Biasini, under arrest, added that he loathed the Germans and the Axis. 'It will be a real disaster if Italy and Germany win a war.'[129]

Ideas about the sin of armed aggression had not vanished. Umberto Rossetti, a poor curate from the province of Reggio Emilia, doubted if God was on the side of the Axis. He told some local landowners that 'so long as we have in government a man who does not possess a clean conscience, because together with his Hitler he has blood on his hands, things will go badly. We shall never win the war. They will say that we are winning victory after victory but really that will just be chatter. The best proof of the matter is that they keep boasting about their successful bombardment of Malta and yet they never conquer it.' The investigating police were worried by Rossetti. Perhaps he was mad, they speculated – cases of suicide could be traced in his family. On the other hand most of his relatives were well off and respectable and Rossetti himself had not earlier been noticed expressing doubts about the Fascist regime.[130]

For all the flurry of war and dictatorship, in the countryside a traditional world had never been fully lost. According to communist Cesira Fiori, when they heard the broadcast across the village square at San Demetrio in the province of L'Aquila of Mussolini's speech declaring on 10 June 1940 that Italy had entered the Second World War, the women of the place repaired to the local church. There the priest explained what they now must do, and soon, whether at his behest or their own, they were purchasing stocks of flour and other essentials in the pessimistic (and justified) view that shortages would not be long in coming.[131] Peasants had long seen war as one of the great natural and unnatural disasters, a time when they must think of themselves and seek to outwit and outmanage the nation-state. Their pessimism remained unchanged by Fascism.

By any index, then, Fascism was not proving sleekly fitted to fight a modern war. Yet the die was cast and Mussolini's nervous talk about waging a parallel campaign rather than one that was completely integrated with the racial battle of his ally needed some justification. The minds of Ciano and others in the leadership were turning to Greece, ruled, it was true, by the semi-fascist regime of General Ioannis Metaxas, a politician who, like Franco or Dollfuss or Antonio Salazar in Portugal, had often enough been regaled with patronizing advice from Mussolini about how to arm his regime with Fascist social steel.[132] Although there was the Corfu incident to savour in the past, Greece, unlike France and Yugoslavia, had not been an eminent target of official outbursts of xenophobia. In September 1939 Mussolini had told his ambassador that Italy had no intention of attacking

Greece, either then or later.[133] Not to worry; in autumn 1940 an invasion from Albania was prepared or anyway ordered for 28 October, the eighteenth anniversary of the Fascist assumption of power. Four days before the invasion was due, Ciano convinced himself in discussion with military experts that 'one hard blow' and Greece would 'utterly collapse in a few hours'.[134] Over-confident and insouciant, on 26 October he leaked the news of the planned attack to friends as they were chatting in the comfortable surrounds of Acquasanta golf course.[135] A March on Athens, Ciano and his father-in-law surmised, would prove no more arduous than had been the seizure of Liberal Rome. They did not yet know that their subjects would soon be lamenting that Fascist Italy had engaged itself in 'a second and worse Caporetto'.[136]

16

The wages of Fascist war

When, after a trumpery three-hour ultimatum, Italian troops violated the Greek border and opened a new front to the Second World War, they were encouraged to sing of combat without the equivocations once present in 'Faccetta nera'. The first tune to acquire a degree of popularity was entitled 'Vincere' (Winning). Its lyrics, a pastiche of the *Duce*'s words that had become the regime's slogans, went:

> Temprata da mille passioni
> la voce d'Italia squillò
> 'Centurie, Coorti, Legioni
> in piedi che l'ora suonò!'
> Avanti gioventù!
> Ogni vincolo, ogni ostacolo superiamo!
> Spezziam la schiavitù
> che ci soffoca prigionieri nel nostro Mar!
>
> *Chorus*
> Vincere! Vincere! Vincere!
> E vinceremo in cielo, in terra, in mare!
> È la parola d'ordine d'una suprema volontà!
> Vincere! Vincere! Vincere!
> Ad ogni costo! Nulla ci fermerà
> I nostri cuori esaltano
> nell'ansia d'obbedir!
> Le nostre labbra giurano:
> o vincere o morir!

(Steeled by a thousand passions, the voice of Italy cries aloud: 'Centuries, Cohorts, Legions, stand to attention because now is our moment.' Forward youth, together we shall break every bond and overcome every obstacle. We shall smash the slavery that is suffocating us as prisoners in our own Sea! Win! Win! Win! And we shall win by sky, land and sea. This is the military order of a supreme will. Win! Win! Win! At any cost! Nothing can stop us. Our hearts exult in our desire to obey! Our lips swear that either we shall win or we shall die.)[1]

The bitter truth, almost instantaneously apparent in Greece, however, was not victory but defeat. Rather than crumbling as the Fascist leadership had expected – Mussolini envisaged a lightning drive to Thessaloniki[2] – Metaxas's regime, itself authoritarian in intent and ramshackle in reality, a 'third-rate power' as a military historian has testily rated it,[3] was easily able to withstand *Blitzkrieg*, Italian-style. Within weeks, Greek forces had pushed the front back over the Albanian border and by mid-November no Italian troops remained in the country. The war was a disaster logistically. Although Badoglio had tried procrastination with airy talk of needing 'three months' preparation,[4] the generals had only been given a fortnight's notice about the invasion. If the mobilization was confused, Fascist failure was more glaring when it came to coordinating technology and men. It was said that only a hundred or so of Italy's light tanks (Macgregor Knox sardonically calls them 'useless' 'tankettes')[5] out of an allegedly available total of 1,750 reached the front.[6] In any case, the mountain terrain and the lack of roads in an Albania that had scarcely been modernized by King Zog or by the new and inexperienced Italian occupiers made mules as potentially useful as were mechanized vehicles. But the commissariat could not even provide these animals reliably. Italian ports functioned with a maximum of inefficiency, being typically obstructed by rival authorities, each more anxious to cling to its immediate power than speed the cause of the regime or nation. Everywhere there were stories about boots with cardboard soles and men, dressed in summer uniforms, expected to fight in the freezing cold.

The disaster in Greece was so manifest that on 6 December Ugo Cavallero, thought to be a more militant figure and a soldier who was close to Farinacci, replaced Badoglio as Chief of General Staff, an office which remained in his hands until July 1943. Farinacci, who had been bombarding his *Duce* with advice that, in the more wisely and strenuously governed USSR, Badoglio would have long ago been shot along with a number of other generals *pour encourager les autres*, was pleased.[7] The reaction of public opinion is harder to gauge, although informers were insistent that popular cynicism about the quality of party bosses flourished.[8] Somewhat surprisingly, signs of nostalgia for Badoglio surfaced. Even a year after his sacking, it was possible to be picked up by the secret police for suggesting that not he but 'Someone Else' was responsible for Italy's military woes. One lingering fan was Terzilio Anzaghi, a book-binder from Perugia who was a *mutilato* from the First World War. Anzaghi had only joined the PNF belatedly in 1939 but, with the usual Fascist administrative flexibility, as an old soldier he had been granted backdated party tenure from 3 March 1925. His sin in talking about Badoglio's alleged competence had been worsened by a discussion with a friend about the increasing presence of Germans in Italian towns and the cry that Italy was being reduced to no more than a creature of Germany.[9]

More straightforward in character was the reaction of the Turin manager Carlo Giretti, now over sixty, who at his office grumbled with a sense of local patriotism about the sacking of the Piedmontese Pietro Badoglio as Chief of General Staff. Giretti could not bear talk of Badoglio's 'treachery'; he knew in his bones that a *monferrino* could never be a traitor. Italy's position in Greece was appalling, he acknowledged, but whose fault was that? The Germans were likely to take over and they had no intention of rewarding Italy with more than scraps from their table. Mussolini was smuggling money out to Argentina, Giretti added daringly, and 'they say he does not occupy himself with policy any more but spends his time on two women whom he keeps at Rome'. Sooner or later, in this atmosphere of enveloping disaster, Giretti prophesied, there would be a 'revolution'.[10]

Such mutterings may not have meant much. But neither did Mussolini's initial promise to Cavallero to eliminate 'Muslim-style vacuity' among the general staff and ready it for victorious war. Rather, matters soon returned to usual, with Cavallero bewailing the low level of troop and officer morale in Albania and attacking the regime's failure to provide restorative periods of furlough to frontline soldiers.[11] The only hope lay to the north, where there might be the humiliating prospect of aid from the Nazis. Italian expectations in that regard were, to say the least, extensive. Late in December the Italian Army leadership transmitted to the *Wehrmacht* a list that went far beyond that of August 1939, then described by Ciano evocatively as 'enough to kill a bull'.[12] The Italians now asked for 'almost 8,000 trucks, 750 ambulances and specialized vehicles, 1,600 light anti-aircraft guns, 900 88m anti-aircraft guns (with tractors, searchlights, rangefinders, sights, and munitions), 800 medium tanks, 300 armoured cars, 675 anti-tank guns, 9,000 mules, 300 medium- and long-range radio sets, 20,000 rolls of concertina wire, half a million engineer stakes, 10 million sandbags, and numerous lesser desiderata'.[13] The request – the mules were a nice touch – dramatically demonstrated the dismal failure of the Fascist regime to tie its economy to war in the way expected of a modern state.

According to tough general Mario Roatta, throughout the conflict troops received half the clothing ration that had sustained their fathers in the First World War.[14] Italian soldiers frequently resented the arrogance and questioned the brutality of their Nazi German comrades but they just as often envied the German army as embodying an equality unimaginable in their own. Nazi soldiers, they believed, ate well. They did not.[15] Ordinary Germans were furnished with waterproof boots. They were not. German officers understood technology. Italians did not.

The percentage of the Italian GDP directed to the war effort peaked at 23 per cent in 1941, a derisory figure for a relatively weak economy, especially when compared with Germany's 64 per cent (in 1942), the USSR's 61 per cent and Britain's 52 per cent.[16] The breakdown of the initial Greek offensive was confirmed by another failed assault there in March 1941. In Libya, matters were, if anything, worse. Two thirds of troops transported across the Mediterranean were lost to the British between December 1940 and February 1941, 130,000 Italian POWs being captured while Allied forces suffered only 550 deaths.[17] Mussolini had talked glibly about Italy's running a 'parallel war', distinct in nature and purpose from that of his ally, and had invaded Greece without apprising the Nazis of his plans (if that is the right word for them). But, in the winter of discontent of 1940–41, Fascist

Italy showed itself incapable of carrying through its own military ambitions and, thereafter, even when the situation at the front improved, remained clearly subordinate to the Nazis, never the most accommodating or rational of friends or allies.

In December 1940 Goebbels jotted down his view that the Italians had proven themselves millstones around German necks, underlying that even the Italophile Hitler had bemoaned their 'matchless amateurism . . . The Italians have brought the entire military prestige of the Axis crashing down in ruins . . .' 'The Italians are, after all, a Romance race,' Goebbels concluded sarcastically or malevolently. The Nazi Propaganda Minister had just 'read a memorandum from the South Tyroleans directed against Italy. The blood rushes to one's head. Reason tells us that nothing can be done, but the heart says otherwise.'[18] As ever the phantom of a Germany that was not an ally but an enemy haunted Italy.

For the moment, the current war was bad enough. According to Knox, the leading analyst of the battles, in early spring 1941 'Italy and the Fascist regime lay at Britain's mercy' and only a tactical error by Churchill, who failed to order a final push in North Africa, kept the Fascist state in the war.[19] The military record was and remained dismal. Yet harping on it can distort analysis of Fascist politics and society at war. Italy did fight on and, in 1941–2, there were quite a few occasions when German (or Japanese) victories and British, American and Soviet defeats played a reflected glow of success, even over Fascist arms. Italians were doubtless junior partners, even very junior partners, but they were associated with German triumphs in the Balkans after April 1941 and in North Africa under Erwin Rommel, whose forces between March and May that year carried Axis power over the Egyptian border. After June 1941 Italian soldiers did join the fight on the Eastern front, where the initial thrusts presaged swift and overwhelming victory; following Pearl Harbor, Italian propaganda did cheer the Japanese advance towards Australia, even if, among worldly wise Florentines, secret reports revealed, an undercurrent of suspicion existed that the news of these gains was designed to camouflage Axis losses in Africa and Russia.[20]

At the highest level of diplomacy the dictatorship counted for something in the German-led plans for a 'new world order', strategic, economic and racial. In Greece, Yugoslavia and southern France, Italy did govern a wartime empire which, whatever may have been its future had the Axis won the war, did exist and was ruled by Italian methods and with an Italian purpose. What, then, was the Fascist version of a new order?

In June 1940 Italy had entered the war without a plan, a deficiency that was never completely overcome. None the less, thoughts about a fresh arrangement of borders did soon occupy Italian minds. As early as 26 June Ciano tabulated a wish-list envisioning the annexation of Nice, Tunis and Corsica, French and British Somaliland, Aden, Malta, Iraq and the Holy Places. These annexations were to be bolstered by some sort of Italian overlordship over 'independent' Cyprus, Egypt, Syria, Lebanon and the rest of Palestine. The prospect of eventual Italian control of the Ticino and the detail of national oil supplies, Ciano added modestly, could be left to future study.[21] Then there was the issue of Yugoslavia, which the *genero* and Hitler agreed should soon be liquidated. After the war, it would be estimated that between 1.5 and 1.7 million Yugoslavs had died under German and Italian occupation, 11 per cent of the pre-war population.[22] The character of that deadly collaboration is still properly to be explored by historians, but in 1940 the *Führer* was happy to invite his ally to rule the Adriatic, although he did add a little brusquely there was no need for German forces to ask for Italian assistance in what he saw as the imminent triumphant landing in Britain.[23]

Gradually the euphoric thoughts of the first days of the war dissipated. For all Italy's expenditure of men and treasure in the Spanish Civil War, Franco continued to resist blandishments, even from the *Duce* himself, to enter the conflict on the Axis side.[24] The Spanish dictator and his Falangist Minister for Foreign Affairs, Serrano Suñer, were unmoved when Mussolini told them in February 1941 that Stalin was 'out of the game'. The Soviet chief was, the *Duce* claimed, 'too smart' to fall under 'the influence of the Jews', adding that the temporary Italian defeats in North Africa and AOI did not matter since Italy's relationship with Germany was 'clear, rectilinear and intimate' and the two friendly regimes were marching to total victory.[25] Whenever battles were won, Spain might flirt with full participation in the Axis but months passed and no consummation resulted.

In the Balkans, too, even after the Germans swept aside Yugoslavia and Greece, Italian domination was not easy to achieve. A PNF inspector reported optimistically that the Slovenes to a man and woman were delighted to become subjects of the *Duce*'s beneficent rule, but the Germans, it turned out, had their own interests in the region and were scarcely content to work for Italian supremacy.[26] Those locals who had volunteered for or been persuaded to associate with the Axis were also often unreliable in Italian eyes. Despite years of Fascist backing,[27] Pavelić and his Croat Ustasha were at least as inclined to ingratitude as were the Spanish and studiously curried German favour to evade Italian control.[28] The Nazis persevered with their alarming fondness for doing whatever they wanted while ignoring Italian wishes and needs. In the early hours of 22 June 1941 Mussolini was given fifteen minutes official warning about the commencement of Operation Barbarossa, even if, a week earlier at a meeting with Ribbentrop in luxurious Venice (a dinner at the Palazzo Volpi, which featured servants in black velvet with buttons of glittering, if fake, diamonds, mosaic pavements and a gorgeous art collection), Ciano, with his usual brightness, spotted that the Germans were raring to assault the USSR and wipe the Judeo-Bolshevik evil from the face of the earth.[29]

When the *Wehrmacht* rolled eastward, Mussolini was left to maintain to the *Führer* that he had long favoured this choice, adding that old party members were overjoyed at the chance to extirpate communists abroad as once they had done at home.[30] Italy, he promised expansively, on every front would march with the Nazis to 'the very end'. With its hint that yet another war would soon be added to the general conflict, Hitler's raving that the US government was in the 'hands of the Jews' elicited no cautionary counter from the Italian side.[31] German racial fanaticism should be let to run its course. Timidly, Italian officials counselled patience and understanding when their German counterparts demanded that the authorities ensure that there be no racially defiling mixed marriages between Italian workers in Germany and local women,[32] or when a Nazi pointed to a photo of the *Duce* and sneered: 'Look at our *Gauleiter* in Italy'.[33]

Amid the tumult of battle, by November 1941 the Italian government had slipped into accepting the inevitability of open conflict with the USA. On 3 December the *Duce* formally told the Japanese ambassador that Fascist Italy had not the slightest objection to a Japanese attack on the USA and, after Pearl Harbor, he added the traditional mecca of Italy's emigrants to Fascism's formidable list of enemies.[34] Out in the provinces, the choice was explained as inevitable given Anglo-Saxon greed and aggression. However, in Bologna, the official announcement that Italy was at war with 'paradise' could draw only a dispirited crowd of 3,000 to the main square, with police reporting that they displayed 'indifference, coldness and a complete absence of any support except that ordered' by the regime.[35] During the next days, despite the Japanese victories, informers spoke about popular disorientation with the new front and deepening perturbation at the likely length of war.[36]

Italian policy-makers found it hard to look beyond the Mediterranean. Ciano, as ever making little effort to tighten his own belt, reported his pleasure at meeting a Göring in notably good form (the Nazi's girth proved that food supplies were not lacking at his table either). The *genero* had shrugged his shoulders when Göring prophesied savagely that twenty or thirty million Soviets must die that winter.[37] Even so, Mussolini now began a reiterated, if hopeless, attempt to persuade Hitler that, after the defeat of the USSR, the epicentre of the war should move to Egypt and the Mediterranean where, in his view, it belonged.

Any escape from the horrendous barbarity of the war in the east was now out of the question and Italy was also implicating itself directly in the final solution in Croatia, where the Ustasha leadership, still registered in Rome as clients, if ones prone to stray when permitted too much independence, let slip 'with a smile' that the total of Jews in the area under their command had diminished from 35,000 to 12,000 souls.[38] A few months later an Italian official put the number of survivors at 6,000 out of 40,000, with the rest, he informed Ciano euphemistically, 'wasted' by the Croat authorities.[39]

Hardly any Italians rejoiced at news of such brutality; it was easy for them to complain about the barbarism of the Croats. The Fascist government's own wartime practice of anti-Semitism remains a matter of debate.[40] Certainly, both in Yugoslavia and in France, military men and state and party officials were unhappy with the extremity of what they began to discern as not just Croatian but also German policy. In response, they refurbished the ancient bureaucratic arts of procrastination and obfuscation to hamper the baleful 'productivity' of their allies. Even Mussolini, with some equivocation, was not a fan of the Nazi line and tried at a minimum to shut his eyes to its terrible effects.[41]

None the less, while the war proceeded, the persecution of the Jews within Italy continued – the complex array of anti-Semitic legislation was not to be repealed by Badoglio until January 1944.[42] From May 1942 Jews were obliged to engage in forced and public work; in Rome, they laboured under the 'very windows' of the Vatican on the Tiber embankment.[43] Categorization as a Jew carried disadvantage or worse as the patriotic young historian Mario Toscano, sometime Fascist deputy *podestà* of Novara, found to his regret. Toscano was armed with numerous distinctions and counted on plenty of friends willing to intervene on his behalf but all to no avail. In the eyes of the wartime regime, he was indisputably Jewish.[44] For him, Fascist war meant the loss of his job and status but not his life.

Menacingly, in June 1943 plans were afoot to confine all Jews, whose number and places of residence had already been tabulated by state officials, in four work camps but the process of collection had not got far when the scheme was deflected by the events of 25 July and the first overthrow of Mussolini. Yet, within Italy, as in the territories under Fascist occupation, anti-Semitic measures were not carried into practice with the fanaticism of the Germanic world and Eastern Europe. To quite a degree the persecution of the Italian Jews was left as an intellectual matter. Not distracted from debate by the war effort, Preziosi and Farinacci, on the one hand, and the respectable Abruzzese Fascist Giacomo Acerbo on the other, engaged in arcane wrangling about whether or not Italians could or should pretend to Aryan racial status.[45] Such appalling publications as *La Difesa della Razza* were offered to the public with official approval and subsidy. Bottai led the way in zealously expelling Jews from anything to do with education and culture. Yet Italian 'experts' divided over whether 'blood stocks' or 'will' constituted the key explanation of racial difference and no final victory was ever won for (pseudo-) science in Fascist circles.

Similarly, Italians continued to gag at too open an adoption of eugenics, even while they heatedly condemned miscegenation.[46] Lacking a drive to a mathematical resolution, Fascist anti-Semitism retained much in common with other racisms – anti-black, anti-Slav, anti-Arab – in Italy[47] and elsewhere. Under the test of war, that X-ray which so often illuminates the bases of a society, Italian racism survived but was little different from what it had been before 1940 and what it would continue to be after 1945. The killing of the Jews never became the central motivating factor in Italy's war. Of the 7,495 Jews to be deported east (610 survived), all left after September 1943, when German control was much more direct than before.

Italy's occupation policies in the territories which German good grace or lack of immediate interest allowed Fascism to rule uncover a similar pattern of ferocity, limited and conditioned by incompetence and half-suppressed doubts about the value and sense of murder. Wartime totalitarianism announced that the dictatorship must conquer *spazio vitale* (living space) for new Fascist men and women to strut in[48] but the mimicry of Nazi phraseology did not mean a replication of German administrative style and practice. Even in Dalmatia and Slovenia, the official line of colonization or forced Italianization suffered from practical limitations. In the province of 'Lubiana', annexed on 3 May 1941, there was talk about 'disappearing' the inferior or even non-existent culture of the Slovenes, even possibly removing the Slovenes themselves.[49] New party secretary Aldo Vidussoni's background as a second-generation border Fascist made him especially ready to be brutal to the Slovenes, whom he suggested could be 'exterminated'.[50] Nor were army leaders much more tender. In April 1941 Mario Robotti informed his men that every Slovene hated Italians and demanded that his men return the hatred with interest.

Yet, in the complexity of Italian rule, qualification soon proved necessary. Schemes to force Slovenes to speak Italian stagnated. Throughout Italian-occupied territory, more than one force stood in the field. Were the real enemy the communists, the local nationalists (of one brand or another), the Jews or the Germans? Each was a threat of a kind, although those partisans who killed Italians were the prime foe. As Mussolini vaingloriously advised Roatta in August 1942: 'we must substitute the terror of the partisans with that of our own. We must end the Slovenes' conviction that the Italian people is composed of those who are weak, artistic and pathetic.'[51]

Who, too, was in command? The Fascist party boasted of its 'totalitarian' presence but in practice was rarely sighted. Mussolini, as ever, led the way with savage words, trying palpably to impress Hitler with the view that Axis administration in the Balkans should be based on 'extreme decisiveness' and the liquidation of opposition.[52] Yet he also complicated matters with his interference over petty details and his erratic patronage of this figure or that, each anxious to build a small empire while warmed by the *Duce*'s smile. Mussolini's administrative style remained inconsistent, with a firm line often being enunciated in Rome but with little obvious follow-up and no regularized method for implementation. The army, too, was scoured by factions. Officers had trouble making up their minds whether, in the new order, they should, as tradition decreed, behave in a gentlemanly fashion towards a fallen enemy. The men they commanded remained in their eyes imponderable and inferior beings; communication with them was often a dialogue of the deaf, with each literally speaking a different language. Then there was the issue of those locals who could claim Italian support. They, too, were beings from an alien world. In Kosovo and Macedonia, Italian occupiers often stood aghast at the drastic ethnic cleansing inflicted by their friends on non-Albanian peasants[53] but lacked a language of command to stop them.

The horror of the Italian occupation in Greece was similarly alleviated by its incoherence and inattention to detail. Both their German partners and the embattled Greeks were reported habitually to dismiss the Italians as *macarondes* (macaroni lovers). Not even the early arrival of Volpi in Athens in May 1941 could secure Italy the leading place in the local economy or check German arrogance and sadism.[54] As elsewhere in the Balkans, Italian financial or development schemes were by definition detached from reality, given the automatic seniority of the Germans. Under Axis care, Greeks were soon perishing from starvation and both German and Italian occupiers let them die. Italian troops, however, rarely enjoyed their dominance, which, unless they were constantly stiffened by a German presence, soon became precarious. By 1943 it was reported that 12,000 out of a Fascist force of 93,000 were ill with malaria and the generals in charge were vociferous in their complaints about the non-arrival of supplies and reinforcements, the inadequacy of equipment – in Crete 40 per cent of Italian soldiers were reported to lack boots – and the absence of any overall strategic plan.[55]

Meanwhile, for all the battles won in Eastern Europe, the Pacific, the Balkans and even, for a while, in North Africa, an Axis knock-out blow did not come. Malta did not fall. It was useless in June 1942 for Mussolini to petition Hitler to send more petrol and diesel south, with the promise that the Italian air force and navy could then sweep the Mediterranean free of Axis foes.[56] The *Führer* was more interested in prompting the Italians forward into Egypt, telling the *Duce*, not altogether comfortingly,[57] that 'the goddess of battle only appears once to a real *condottiero*'. Worst was the Eastern front. In August 1942 the Italians were being assured and seemed to believe that the occupation of Stalingrad was imminent.[58] Yet the Red Army resisted and, by December, in the light of events on the Volga or the Don, some Italians were beginning to wonder, with never abandoned Machiavellianism, whether a compromise with Stalin's 'totalitarian' (a word with the potential to sound better than communist) regime might not be the best policy. If the USSR could be deflected south, it might relinquish some European territories to the Germans and so allow the Axis to concentrate where it should, that is, in the Mediterranean against the 'enemy number 1 of the "New Europe", the Anglo-Saxons'.[59]

While gigantic battles were fought out in Russia and the Ukraine and threatened to spill further west, with every passing week of late 1942 and 1943 it grew plainer that Fascist Italy's war was lost. It was all very well for clever young Fascists to suggest that the commitment to accompany Nazi Germany to the bitter end did not necessarily mean following where the Germans led.[60] But now was not the moment for brittle cunning. Mussolini preferred the accustomed formula of changing the guard. In February 1943 the demotion of Ciano from the Ministry of Foreign Affairs marked the end of an era. In a gesture either of bravado or hopelessness the *Duce* resumed the ministerial title but left the real work to the new Under-Secretary, Giuseppe Bastianini, who was thought in some places an Anglophile and who, with pointless propriety, set about drafting belated memoranda on what might constitute Italy's war aims.[61] The *genero* went as ambassador to the Vatican, where, a prey to despair,[62] he was not especially active, yet where he must have been intended to seek peace or sanctuary for Italy. Attention began to switch to the domestic situation. There, leading Fascists, as well as other men near the King[63] and the officer corps, searched for means to rid themselves of their *Duce* and so, by implication, shrug off Hitler and the whole German alliance.

How, then, had Fascist Italy fared as a wartime society? What level of totalitarian control and hardness did Mussolini's administration impose at home on the Italian people? To what extent did the dictatorship foster a Fascist 'people's war'?

In February 1940 the army leadership had raised the question of the ordering of civilian life in a coming conflict. Mussolini replied with some asperity that the matter was already in hand: 'the civil mobilization of citizens . . . demands an appropriate organization that is united and permanent. It will rally the whole populace available to work just as an army does. It would be quite pointless to create a new body of this kind, because it already exists and functions with perfect efficiency. It is the PNF.'[64] Certainly, with the onset of war, membership of the party continued to rocket up. From 2.6 million members in 1939, it bulged to 4.77 million in 1942.[65]

At its top, Starace's recent replacement, Ettore Muti, had never warmed to the bureaucratic tasks of party secretary and on 30 October 1940 he was permitted to resign, so that, a fighter among men, he could attend the Greek front. His replacement was Adelchi Serena, born in 1895 at L'Aquila, a southern Fascist with a law degree from Naples and considerable administrative training. Serena also boasted extensive experience in party welfare, having long worked with Fascist women's groups, and was anxious for Fascist women to play a more prominent role in the war effort, especially in bringing aid and comfort to those suffering from bombing or whose families had otherwise fallen victim to war. In office, he endeavoured more generally to rally the party organization and rework its relations with the masses. He was soon prompting correspondence from Farinacci, as ever determined that his 'friends' be treated well in any circulation of jobs.[66]

Serena did not last long as PNF secretary. His activism made him powerful enemies among the other Fascist bosses and on 26 December

1941 he was replaced by Aldo Vidussoni, born just before the First World War in Habsburg Trieste. Serena, with a dignity unusual in the Fascist story, retired into private life, rejected the RSI, helped the partisans and, after 1945, remained mum about his life under the dictatorship. The new secretary did not replicate the older one's decorum or ability, however. During his tenure, Vidussoni's proved to be an appointment that bore some comparison with the horse that the Emperor Caligula once elevated to a consulship. A stripling in his twenties and dim to boot, Vidussoni, whose chief claim to fame was that he was a maimed ex-volunteer from Spain where he had sacrificed an eye and a hand for Fascism, never showed the slightest sign of mastering his brief. His only experience for office had been a brief spell as *federale* at Enna where he was said to have learned merely that 'every Sicilian is a traitor'.[67] As PNF secretary, his tosh about a fresh burst of 'de-bureaucratization' in order to bring to the fore the new spiritual purity of youth[68] remained words on paper or in thin air, doing nothing to arrest the steep decline of the PNF's prestige and influence in Italian society.

By September 1942 it was reported in Bologna that 5,000 and more had refused to renew their party tickets and half of those youths invited to join had disdained the offer.[69] Two months later, Farinacci lamented that the party had 'exited from Italian life', with the new generation having become utterly cynical about the meaning of Fascism. Despite his own flaunted lubricity, Farinacci now had the gall to complain that youth leaders were more interested in their sex lives than in ideological purity and commitment.[70]

For all the chatter about a new openness to youth, by 1942–3 168,000 young Italians were avoiding the draft through their alleged commitment to university study, up from 85,000 in 1939–40,[71] and this demonstration among the coming elite that the better part of patriotism was discretion survived Mussolini's determination to convert university youth into combatants.[72] During the conflict, 960,000 Italians found the means to be exonerated from military service and gossip suggested that the process in this regard was anything other than open and fair.[73] Furthermore, around the end of 1942, more than 1.5 million of those under arms were serving within Italy, outnumbering the 1.2 million abroad.[74] In these circumstances, official boosting of Vidussoni as proof that a new generation, the 'cohort of Mussolini', was stepping forward, steely Fascist crusaders, armed and ready in the hour of trial, convinced no one. Bottai noticed that the party secretary had trouble reading those reports which he was meant to deliver at major meetings, either because of deficient literacy or because he went into a panic at the frowns of the more senior men to whom he was talking.[75] The only possible advantage of Vidussoni's period in office was that he became the focus of most discontent among the *Duce*'s henchmen, who, in mocking him, for a time diverted their mutinous thoughts about their fate, the war and Mussolini.

It was while Vidussoni shuffled his limited concentration between boxing matches and parades that a series of depressed jokes began to circulate widely, eventually coming to the annoyed attention of the *Duce* himself. Picked up as the unlikely ringleader of heretical humour was Leonardo Patanè, a forty-year-old born at Giarre in Sicily, but by the war years a hairdresser in Milan. The secret police arrested Patanè in February 1942 for possessing a printed list of current film titles, each decoded as carrying a political message.[76] Among these latent meanings were *I miserabili*, to be translated as 'The Italians', *Paradiso perduto* (Paradise lost) really meant 'The Empire', *L'eterna illusione* (The eternal illusion) was the proper rendering of the slogan 'Vincere' (Winning), *Non è una cosa seria* (It's a joke) should be comprehended as 'Fascism'. Hitler was *Il pirata sono io!* (I am a pirate), Churchill, *L'eroe del giorno* (The hero of the day) and Mussolini, *Un'ora sola che vorrei* (An hour is enough with you). England was concealed under the title *Terra d'oro* (The land of gold), the Russians were *I nostri parenti* (Our own relations), the Axis, *Dopo divorzieremo* (Later we shall divorce) and the war, *Un caso disperato* (A hopeless affair).

Police investigations revealed that these jokes had spread swiftly around northern Italy, being eagerly related in Milan and among soldiers stationed at Udine, for example. In this latter place, one of those caught with the list was Sergio Rodomonte, the Fascist son of a wealthy furrier, who had typed out an extra copy at the local party office.[77] The titles were still circulating in Sicily in September 1942. Mussolini intervened to demand the harsh punishment of Patanè and quite a few others. Before being consigned to San Vittore prison and then his place of *confino* in the Basilicata, Patanè was, in the Fascist manner, beaten up at a suburban Milan party branch, losing two teeth and suffering three broken ribs for his pains.[78] He was, however, amnestied after only seven months in the south.[79]

Other 'defeatists' had themes of their own. At the beginning of 1941, Pietro Sommavilla, an unpolitical travelling salesman from Belluno, turning fifty, who lived at Turin but was staying at a Fossano hotel, blamed military failure in Greece and North Africa on the squabbles which he knew endlessly fractured the army proper and the Fascist militia. After all, he remembered, as so many of his fellow citizens did, when the call-up occurred, there were not enough uniforms to go round. Wars, he concluded, were useless; they only changed things so that they could remain the same. A peaceable life in civvy street was the ideal, he declared with a notable lack of Fascist rigour or passion, and who would want to surrender it to go a-soldiering?[80]

As the war dragged on and victory did not come, the plight of Italian forces on most fronts led some to suggest that Mussolini himself was in decline. For Domenico Bassi, an unpolitical hospital worker in his fifties from Trieste, the key evidence of this wasting of his dictator's powers came in the way the *Duce* gave continuing office to 'that stupid cretin, Ciano . . . merely because he was the son-in-law'.[81] After all, even the most assiduous propaganda could not hide the humiliatingly complete nature of some defeats. Rachele Traverso, a housewife of Ventimiglia, down on her luck, disturbed Empire Day celebrations at her home town on 9 May 1941 by wandering around the flag-bedecked shops and asking querulously 'what, now that the empire was almost entirely occupied by the British, were all the flags for?'[82]

So many reports in the media could, on occasion, be read against the grain. The death of Mussolini's second son Bruno, a test pilot, in August 1941 occasioned much official mourning.[83] Not all Italians comprehended these events in the way intended, however. Ivo Gianrossi, a mechanic in his thirties from La Spezia, bemoaned the way 'the newspapers carry on and on about Bruno Mussolini while, when one of us dies, they don't even bother to publish the name'.[84] More generally but certainly not alone, Antonio Immovili, a builder's labourer from Rome, stated that military communiqués fibbed and

talk about imminent victory could be discounted.[85] Cesare Milani, a
Rome plumber, born 1907, similarly understood that, if the Fascist
papers acknowledged ten dead from an air raid on Naples, this admission meant more than a hundred had actually perished.[86] Also able to
read propaganda with the opposite meaning to that intended was
Achille Clerici, a day labourer from Novara and a decade older than
Milani. Clerici, when drunk, yelled that Italians had no hope in the
war because 'the English eat four times a day whereas we can't even
manage half a meal daily'.[87]

The opening of fresh fronts compounded the regime's dilemma in
justifying its military campaigns (all the more because, despite the
propaganda barrage, national war aims remained at best vague). The
Nazi attack on the USSR prompted Renato Ghidoni, a driver from the
province of Mantua, to suggest that the Germans were now combat-
ing a people as barbarous as they were. No good, he prophesied,
could come to Italy from their battle.[88] Following the Japanese assault
on Pearl Harbor, Fascist Italy set the regime's fate against the knowledge of so many Italians who, whether directly or indirectly, had registered the fact from the migrant experience that 'America' was the
wealthiest country in the world. An early example of the resulting
clash of attitudes came at the small *paese* of Raviscanina in the hinterland of Caserta. There, on Christmas Day 1941, some peasants
were lunching at the dilapidated local inn and listening to the news.
When one of the company repeated the official line that Italy would
'soon give a proper lesson to the English and Americans', the elderly
returned emigrant, Basilio D'Abbraccio, who had two sons still in the
USA (and a brother in the *carabinieri*) and who was rumoured to have
prospered from his years away, leaped to his feet and cried out: 'Italy
makes war by big talk. Up America! Down with Italy!'[89]

Before the USA came into the conflict, Maria Ciocca, a comfortably
off baker's wife from the *paese* of Vinovo, outside Turin, herself born
in New York in 1895, was another who comprehended the world
through her emigrant experience and contacts. For a number of years,
but especially in recent months, she had told any who would listen,
when she went shopping or was out for a stroll, that she was a convinced sympathizer of Britain and the USA. Repeatedly, it was now
remembered, she had 'denigrated the Axis powers and persuaded the

ignorant in her town that the war would be lost'. The police, troubled by their unchivalrous pursuit of a 'respectable' woman, noted that her son was serving loyally in the national army and her husband led an irreproachable life, politically speaking. Ciocca, they thought, was not dangerous but they did agree that her constant malicious chatter tended to depress local spirits, especially among other women. Perhaps the explanation, they ventured weakly, was that Ciocca drank too much?[90]

Still more suggestive was the tale of Angelo Rossi, an itinerant musician from Rome and a member of those 'dangerous classes' likely to attract police attention in any society – although now in his fifties he possessed no previous record. In December 1942 Rossi was playing his squeeze-box and gossiping with local women at the village of Affile near Subiaco (just next door to the home of Fascist General Rodolfo Graziani at Arcinazzo Romano). When offered a glass of wine, Rossi complained that at Naples you now paid eighteen lire a litre for a drink (Vidussoni himself had lamented the failure of the regime to curb the price of a tipple).[91] 'The war would go on for another three years,' Rossi confided knowingly and, seemingly emboldened, added in his version of a traditional rural news service that 'the *Duce* has an ulcer. It could kill him. Italy is finished. It has lost the war. After the war, money won't be worth anything any more.' At least according to the police, one listening peasant, fearing that this talk was dangerous, quietened Rossi with the boast that the Italians would win in Europe and then go to the USA and wipe it out.[92] Rossi's story nevertheless provides significant insight into a rural world, with rural attitudes, flourishing at the very gates of Rome, despite two decades of 'modernizing' Fascist propaganda. Rossi and his audience retained a knowledge of their own, an understanding of present and future that was nearer the truth than that retailed by Fascist officials. Rather than being forged by a generation of Fascist propaganda, Rossi and his kind still made their own news.

Pointed gossip about corruption in high places was especially hard to suppress or deny and stimulated thoughts of class difference that should have been excised by Fascist rule and Fascist social 'justice'. Theft and influence-mongering had been a habitual part of the Fascist story but their impact was augmented in war when people were dying for the regime and the nation. Army chiefs, Fascist bosses, the rich of any kind, all were thought to cheat and to lie. According to one hostile or envious Fascist source, Badoglio's Roman villa had cost twenty million lire from secret Ministry of the Interior funds (he did not add that the Minister had been Mussolini) and the Badoglios were alleged not even to have paid for the family towels.[93] Once combat began, Acquasanta golf club house, haunt of Ciano, Bottai and many younger bourgeois Fascist chiefs, was only one among such places to pay no apparent attention to rationing.[94] A typical secret police account claimed that Manlio Morgagni, a close journalistic associate and personal friend of the *Duce* and the head of the national press agency (Agenzia Stefani), was given to Lucullan entertainments of fellow newspapermen, with no expectation that he or his guests should present their ration cards.[95] High-class restaurants, especially in Rome, similarly ignored the restrictions formally imposed with rationing.[96]

Fascists were not the only alleged sinners in this regard. Marshal Ugo Cavallero was reported in January 1942 during the victorious weeks following Pearl Harbor, to be utilizing three government cars for his personal benefit. His wife and daughter-in-law (his son, a major from the staff, was on long and comfortable leave from active service) occupied two with daily shopping trips to the city. (A telephone tap revealed a similar willingness to evade petrol rationing among ladies in the circle of the Agnellis, whose menfolk were rebuked for similarly setting a bad example in purchasing land with no worry about its price).[97] Of the three chauffeurs who waited on the Cavallero family, two were brothers, each with official military rank, one a sergeant, the other a corporal. Despite their officially onerous military duties, they found time to run the family butcher's shop at a village just outside the capital and, as a result, the Cavalleros ate well.[98] Mussolini himself evinced a traditional urban view of the cunning of *contadini*, when he told Göring, of all obese people (it was odd how Italians on more than one occasion ended up talking to him about food), that the nutrition problem in Italy was only a matter of interest for those sixteen million out of his forty-six million subjects who were not peasants. Those on the land, their supplies unaccounted for, dined well, the *Duce* believed, with a profoundly cynical and false understanding of how life worked, little altered by two decades of totalitarianism.[99] Minister Riccardi's boasts that any control of consumption in a Fascist war was belated, because the economy functioned so richly and was rigorously directed at social justice, read as hollow indeed.[100]

When Grandi suggested to Ciano that severe penal sanctions should be introduced to strike down tax evasion, the *genero* replied that such swingeing approaches could never work in Italy.[101] He himself did not lead the way in the matter and rumours of massive tax avoidance by Farinacci and other leading hierarchs in land deals on the outskirts of Rome were common.[102] Grandi, another for whom self-sacrifice rarely seemed to possess much attraction, was left to bide his time and, as Minister of Justice, pointlessly to plan prison reform, inevitably defined as *bonifica umana* (human reclamation).[103] With ministers otherwise occupied in one way or another, Italy, alone of the combatants, did little to amend its taxation system in war and government receipts fell 20 per cent between 1939–40 and 1942–3.[104] Ciano's reputation for corruption was so notorious that by the summer of 1942 one young Fascist, Felice Chilanti, was picked up by the secret police after he and his friends began semi-serious plotting of a violent removal of the *Duce*'s son-in-law, a scheme, it was rightly suspected, concealing a deeper sense of malaise among the more believing of the new generation.[105] A few months earlier, a Jesuit priest from Bassano was arrested after his preaching about the virtue of poverty slid into using the example of Costanzo Ciano as a billionaire who yet had been forced to meet his Maker.[106]

At the time, there was tittle-tattle, too, about Rachele Mussolini, despite her contempt for Ciano and her 'honesty' or bluntness of a kind. Her close friend, Ferdinando Boattini from Predappio, was charged by a naive *carabinieri* officer with gambling offences. The policeman, whose lot was not to be a happy one, found that his case did not prosper and, in retribution, he was peremptorily transferred from his home region (he came from Castrocaro in the province of Forlì, a spa where Rachele had many dealings) to Cefalù in Sicily.[107] The gap between the world of the great and the world of the little gaped.

Rationing had been introduced in Italy soon after the war began and propaganda was soon endeavouring to persuade Venetian women that they could sparkle in a coat made out of tabby cat fur,[108] but food was the greater issue. As early as April 1942 official reports admitted that about 40 per cent of the population were suffering from hunger 'in the full physiological sense of the word'.[109] The production of pork, such a basic part of the diet of those Italians accustomed to eat meat, fell by almost two thirds from 1940 to 1942.[110] The bread ration, already low and on occasion simply unavailable because of failures in production and distribution, was further reduced in March 1942, an announcement which prompted a rash of hostile demonstrations, often led by women peasants.[111] The not wildly observant ex-Futurist writer and painter Ardengo Soffici noticed that bread supplies were already doubtful in usually spoiled Florence as early as May 1941. The authorities, he added, knew all but did nothing since they were too involved in their own internecine battles.[112]

Another assault on public morale was bombing, which worsened from week to week as the front neared Italy. A total of 9,719 male and 8,657 female civilians perished from bombing raids between June 1940 and September 1943. The casualty lists expanded in 1943–5, when a further 22,363 civilian males and 19,057 civilian females were killed.[113] Reactions were mixed. Even if scarcely suffering in the way that was destroying so many lives on and behind the other fronts, Italians, even of moderate cast, were ready to complain that the Anglo-American bombers were 'inhuman, indiscriminate' and willing to massacre 'women and children',[114] although they were equally ready to lament the regime's inefficiency in failing to provide any functioning anti-aircraft defence. Other values surfaced as a result of the bombing, notably a surviving regionalism. When the citizens of Milan heard the news of the raid on Rome on 19 July 1943, secret police reported them to be 'decidedly pleased'. In one public house a man spoke for all when, putting into words many Italians' dislike of the national capital and its inhabitants, he expressed delight and relief at the thought that, at last, the Romans were feeling the war on their own skins.[115]

In Sicily, the regime's failures and inadequacies were especially striking. Gaetano Zingoli, a Fascist memoirist who in 1941 took responsibility for the functioning of the corporate state there, recalled that even basic transport had broken down. The citrus harvest rotted in train trucks, while the sea crossing from Messina to Reggio Calabria functioned badly or not at all. By 1942 fertilizer supplies were nowhere to be found and the black market, despite anathemas against it by prefects and *federali*, dominated the exchange of goods and services.[116] Medicine disappeared; in the absence of quinine, malaria again took its prey. The failure to provide soap supplies meant that a scabies epidemic swept through schools and villages. Hunger stalked the lives of all but the richest, most ruthless or subtle – the official ration offered Italians a calorie intake about the same as that in German-occupied Poland.[117] To get the harvest brought in, Zingoli had to pay three times the official wage and peasants had various means of circumventing government control, through hoarding and the forging of tickets approving milling or secret night-time labour to their own benefit. Zingoli even claimed that copies of the *Gazzetta Ufficiale* were failing to reach the island, an absence that could justify the ignoring of many decrees. As elsewhere in Italy, anti-aircraft defences did not exist, and at Catania ordinary men and women took to hiding in the ruins of the classical Roman amphitheatre when they heard American bombers approaching.[118]

In its endeavour to combat popular depression and alienation caused by these glaring deficiencies in its war effort, Fascist propaganda was stuck in a familiar groove, its heightened fervour suggesting a fever was striking down the regime and hollowing its ideology. Songs such as 'Battaglione M' (Battalion M – for Mussolini) clung to that Fascist mysticism, which, according to some intellectuals, had been all the rage during the 1930s but now had very doubtful appeal to any but those most committed to the party. Its chorus, almost in parody of that poetic fascism which in Spain and Romania had hit on the not always alluring slogan 'Long live death', ran:

> Battaglioni – della morte
> battaglioni della vita
> ricomincia la partita,
> senza l'odio non c'è l'amor.
>
> Emme rossa – uguale sorte
> fiocco nero alla squadrista,

noi la morte l'abbiam vista
con due bombe e in bocca un fior.[119]

(Battalions – of death, battalions of life, let's try another round of battle. Without hatred, love cannot be. The red M, the same fate, with our black tassel, squadrist-style. We have faced death with two bombs in hand and a flower at our lips.)

Similarly the great party organs hammered away at old refrains, if with diminishing conviction and effect. In *Gerarchia*, young Luigi Meneghello, born in 1922, destined to be a partisan and, after 1945, a distinguished and anti-Fascist novelist, hid his immaturity with talk of how 'for the best of us, there can no longer be a separation between Fascism and our individual consciousness . . . Our pains, our hopes, our needs, are all summed up in the word "race". They are all expressed in our customs, traditions, history. They spring from Fascist Doctrine. We must live in Fascism and so make Fascism a guest in our hearts, breathe it with our every breath, live in it and for it.'[120] For his part, the racist anthropologist Nicola Pende offered deep thoughts on Fascist feminism. A 'science of woman', given a proper place in universities, he reasoned, could nurture a fuller knowledge of the 'neuro-endocrine temperament [sic] of every female', allowing girls to display a greater dynamism than that of the accustomed *sposa e madre esemplare* (exemplary wife and mother).[121] Not to be outdone, Edgardo Sulis was again dreaming of a real social revolution, still in January 1943 perplexingly scarcely begun;[122] it must, he proclaimed, prevent Italians from being swamped by the massification of pseudo-democracy or bolshevism and permit them to stand tall and united as self-conscious individuals.[123]

Although Giuseppe Bottai was beginning to waver in his Mussolinian fervour and entertain heretical thoughts about the leader's revolutionary limitations,[124] the journals under his aegis likewise stuck to familiar themes but, in wartime, with a more nervous impulse than in the past. In 1940 *Critica Fascista* predictably deemed the conflict 'a religious act', one which 'assumes in itself the mystic power of our faith' and which therefore could permit a 'collaboration with Germany' precisely because no identity cemented the Axis allies.[125] The proud, arrogant, ignorant and insular English, 'barbarians' not far beneath the mask of their modernity, were destined, readers of the journal learned, to hear the curative 'tread of Legions on their sad and monotonous roads'.[126] Italo-German forces were moving to their certain victory over the 'materialist "civilization" of the Anglo-Saxons and Jews'.[127] Italy, it was stated with an unexplained promiscuity of racial prejudice, must not be allowed to fall into their 'negroid hands'.[128]

In Bottai's new outlet, *Il Primato*, cherished as the mouthpiece of the best and the brightest, Italy's war was justified on its own 'revolutionary' and 'spiritual' account and with scant initial reference to the Nazis,[129] although by 1941 Bottai was maintaining obscurely that *romanità* and Germanness had worked in harness across the millennia.[130] The war, he repeatedly told his intellectual audience, was to be decided as a contest between philosophies; at heart it was a battle between intellectuals. In his journal their ambitions should have free play.

Some heresies could be discussed – a writer in a university journal in May 1941 sounded like an Eric Hobsbawm in the making when he averred that nations were 'a historic and therefore contingent political form' and added that, personally, he looked forward to a time when all people on earth would become one.[131] *Il Primato* itself promised some liberality in dealing with subject peoples; even in Slovenia they could retain their 'cultural and historical individuality', one editorial argued charitably.[132] Yet the party line, in all its force and mutability, was hard to evade for long. When it came, the attack on the USSR was portrayed in these circles as proof that there always had been 'a fundamental, pre-destined and utterly violent antagonism between Fascism and communism'.[133] Bottai contended that now the corporatist permanent revolution could wash over other countries in a grandiose battle between 'gold and blood'.[134] Under such curative cleansing, the real Europe could emerge, purged of its past divisions.[135] The Molfetta philosopher Sergio Panunzio suggested that a 'third wave' of Fascism must sweep aside the communists, who were quailing at the prospect of combat with a regime that stood not so much for 'social justice' as for 'moral justice'. Victory was nigh because, for a generation, Italians had been 'living Mussolinianly'.[136] Pearl Harbor signalled the happy commencement of a genuine 'world war', *Il Primato* pronounced, even if it underlined, with some ambiguity, that Italy was fighting for 'Europe'.[137] Possible 'racial' contradictions in the Tripartite Alliance with Japan could be ignored since, by the summer of 1942, the final battle was all but won. Victory was ascribed to the Italian and Fascist fighting spirit, with Bottai maintaining that Nazism amounted to nothing without the inspiration it received from Rome.[138]

During the next months, however, the war situation grew steadily grimmer and Bottai's ideological quiver had no rhetorical arrows left in it except to urge young Italians to cleave to the party, the *patria* and the dictator. Thereby, he hoped, they could summon up the blood and stiffen the sinews of their 'racial reserves' to surmount the test of war. Even the soft middle-class intellectual readership of *Il Primato* was assured with desperate populism that Italy's traditional peasant poverty and resultant natural toughness were qualities that would repel Britain and its cruel bombers, with their pitifully 'ignorant pilots, the sons of sheep-farmers in Australia and New Zealand'.[139]

While he moralized about an austere peasantry, Bottai did not give ground on his principle that philosophy mattered most. In November 1942 he was still proclaiming that 'ideas judge men, not men ideas' and, in such a contest, he was sure the revolutionary purity and coherence of Fascism was destined to triumph.[140] Six months later, despairing about the battle front, Bottai self-indulgently opted for nostalgia as he reviewed the two decades of *Critica Fascista*'s existence and its harnessing to the regime's cause of 'every critical energy that was also of sure revolutionary temper'. The party, he argued mechanically, remained 'the indispensable tool giving cohesion and direction' to the people. Beyond it stood the *Duce*: 'the Olympian Mussolini, with his sovereign certainty of having foreseen and set up the new century, the Man who, with his incredible intuition, is always alert to the way history is going'.[141] The 'fortunes and misfortunes of battle', Bottai, clinging to his anti-materialism, pronounced again, 'decide nothing of substance'. Only ideas conquered.[142] The portentous words kept rolling out but their conviction had been blown away by the winds of constant and humiliating defeat and the reality of material and organizational failure.

Bottai remained a Fascist-style gentleman and scholar but some of his fellows were cruder in their expression. Radio journalist Mario Appelius did his best to back the official advice that Italians must 'hate their enemies' by mocking English women. They were, he said, 'dames with big feet, boxers' hands, leathery skin, sharp elbows, the stride of Scottish soldiers and voices that sounded like a broken record'.[143] In Venice, the local paper similarly rejoiced that the grand hotels no longer had to put up with 'false barons' and 'false talk' of a 'false cosmopolitanism'. Best was the absence of the English, 'those angular wandering skeletons, with their half-French hair-dos and make-up, and their vulgar horsy laughs from mouths much worked over with the gold of London dentists'.[144] The disappearance of their pet dogs was also cheering. It had been the English, after all, who, 'with the excuse of leaving in Venice Byron, Browning, Ruskyn [sic] etc., took us for incurable idiots and acted like masters [*padroni*] in our house', it remembered petulantly.[145]

Anti-American propaganda focused on the 'madness' of Franklin D. Roosevelt, allegedly a side effect of his paralysis, the country's insatiable greed and limitless naivety and the 'hidden hand' of the Jews there. *Il Mattino*, the Naples paper, found a sure omen in the sum of the fourteen points of Woodrow Wilson and the eight of the Atlantic Charter. Twenty-two signalled 'The Madman' in a pack of tarot cards![146]

Yet, whether in high or low cultural mode, it was hard not to conclude that, well before July 1943, regime propaganda was reduced to going through the motions as it awaited the inevitable end. Certainly, despite totalitarianism, Italians knew of ways beyond the party to comprehend the world. One counter to the regime's phrases was the Catholic Church, an institution of enhanced significance given that war, in Italy as in other combatant societies, stimulated piety, increased attendance at mass and underscored the priest's traditional role as a possible defence in times of trouble. The Church, always armed with *occhi lunghi* (the ability to see and prepare in the long term), had never forgone its right to contemplate life after Mussolini and after Fascism. Its comprehension of the *longue durée* was well displayed in the counsel by a missionary priest to a migrant worker in Germany, blessed with twins and wanting to christen them 'Benito' and 'Adolf'. 'Better to choose also a second name', the advice came.

'Why?'

'Because some time in the future a second name could be useful to them.'[147]

While battles went well and even as they palled, the spokesmen of the Catholic Church did frequently evince sympathy for the Italian war effort, with the effort to eradicate 'godless Bolshevism' being particularly applauded.[148] On Sunday, 2 February 1941, for example, churches throughout the country held patriotic ceremonies in which there was much priestly praise of 'totalitarian participation'.[149] In May 1943 the Cardinal Archbishop of Venice was still expressing solidarity for Italian troops, preaching that nations could not die.[150] The future Pope John XXIII deemed the war a conflict between the poor and the rich, the worker and the capitalist and imagined, with a dim understanding of the economic base of modern battle, that a 'giant' could still slip on a 'banana skin'.[151] Angelo Bartolomasi, again chaplain-general to the armed forces, during the ill-omened days of July naively reported on the alleged enthusiasm of Corsicans for Italian rule, even if, on most occasions, he was as primly worried by the men's habitual indulgence in blasphemy and their fondness for sexual incontinence as he was by political matters.[152] A meeker image of those who gave spiritual comfort to Italian arms, however, was supplied by a barefoot Augustinian friar trying on the Greek front to teach illiterate soldiers – he estimated they were about one eighth of the complement – by utilizing a blackboard and chalk he had gleaned from some friendly nuns.

Another glimpse of Italian society at war comes from the Gargano, a superstitious region where Padre Pio, destined to be the nation's most publicized holy man after 1945, was already known for his sanctity (and anti-communism). Around the *paese* of Rodi Garganico, Rosalba Valente began predicting her own death, an event she said was destined for 14 May 1942; it would be heralded by an earthquake and 'a reign of grace'. Hearing this prophecy, with its implication of the end of the war and the overthrow of the social order, the countryside was swept by religious enthusiasm. Crowds flocked to see the saint in the making and *Il Corriere di Napoli* spread her gospel throughout the south. When 14 May passed, however, and Valente lived on, she and her supporters faced trouble and the police moved in to arrest those they believed had managed events to their own benefit.[153]

For all this failure of religious mystery, the people of the Gargano, in their pious hopes and fears, remained a world away from Rome and the official line or lines. In regard to the Vatican's dealing with the war, there has been an absurd and lengthy debate whether or not Pius XII was 'Hitler's pope', a warrior who de facto served the German side of the conflict.[154] Of course he did not. The Church authorities judged Nazism before and after 1939 an ungodly movement. It is fairer, however, to see Pius and the hierarchy over whom he presided as fellow travellers or outright sympathizers with Mussolini and Fascism. In what they perceived as this wicked world, the Vatican liked most of what they saw in Fascism and, should the truth be known, preferred it probably to liberal democracy and certainly to socialism and communism. All in all, the Church's wartime stance towards the dictatorship was not very different from that prevailing among businessmen and landowners, who thought that Fascism, despite its eccentricities, was fine for them until it became obvious that it was going to lose its battles on every front. Similarly, even if Farinacci from time to time remembered to mock priestly sins and arrogance, maliciously drawing his *Duce*'s attention to De Vecchi's and Federzoni's increasingly craven habit of confessing their sins to the Pope himself when any parish priest would do,[155] Mussolini and his regime remained happy to prolong their cohabitation with the Vatican and its agents. The Fascist new order bid fair to be an old arrangement in so far as Church–State relations were concerned. The contradictions of Fascism in this realm were well instanced in autumn 1942, when Roosevelt was able to send his agent, Myron Taylor, for talks in the Vatican, passing through the streets of Rome, despite his country being then locked in battle with the Axis.[156] It is hard to imagine Hitler or Stalin being so accommodating to a visiting foreign agent.

Despite the charity of the Church to Fascism and despite the regime's efforts to puff its cause, public opinion recovered with difficulty, doubt and hesitation from the setback in Greece. Already in December 1940 police reports remained frank about popular laments concerning the unavailability of 'oil, dried fish, tuna, rice' and the scarcity of flour and coal.[157] In the summer of 1941, despite it being high season, fruit had disappeared from the Bologna markets.[158] Ciano, Farinacci and Starace – only in Lecce province, still dominated by his clientele, was Starace's sacking from the MVSN regretted[159] – were widely disliked and the *Duce* was deemed a leader past his prime.[160] Momentary victories were well and good but was not Italy ever more destined to fall under the hegemony of Germany, even if the Axis won the war?[161] Maybe the conflict with Yugoslavia was felt by the people as other Fascist battles had not been and with some parallel to the national war of 1915–18,[162] but whatever might happen there the family could not be fed without recourse to the black market. Injustice stalked the world and Fascist lies lost their lustre.[163]

The popular malaise and the profound detachment of the majority of Italians from the regime or at least from its war effort became plain in March 1943 when a rash of strikes swept Italian workplaces. Commencing on the 8th in some small workshops in Turin,[164] spreading spontaneously to centres in the north and involving Milan and the textile town of Biella a fortnight later,[165] the refusal to work reached as far south as Pistoia in Tuscany. The extent of worker participation and the support the strikers frequently received from the owners took party officialdom by surprise and, at a minimum, was proof that many Italians had given up on Fascist war. Their complaints focused less on ideology and more on pay and conditions, but these last became a preoccupation because the regime had been so inefficient at feeding its people and was now proving so doubtfully able to defend them. It goes without saying that, throughout the conflict, Fascist unions showed themselves feeble and directionless, anything but the vehicle of revolution on which Bottai, Sulis and the rest had set such store.

Fascism was nearing its end. By March 1943 and with increasing frequency thereafter, rumours of plots and counter-plots, involving Ciano and Grandi, the Papacy, the King and his entourage, Senise, his secret police and the industrial world became commonplace. The great industrialist Alberto Pirelli, who in his time had tried to put a human face on Fascist business, encouraging young experts to look beyond national borders as members of the Istituto per gli studi di politica internazionale (Institute for the Study of International Affairs), the training ground of a generation of historians, had had enough. In his diary, he spelled out his hopes and fears. An easy solution was hard to discern. Mussolini demurred when Pirelli raised the prospect of a deal with the Anglo-Saxon powers, with the implication of an eventual joint attack on the USSR or some form of colder war against the communists. The King did not see how he could move, given that the people still applauded their *Duce* and civil combat was the worst of eventualities. Bastianini was being too clever when he suggested that Pirelli contact the English and so expose himself to possible retribution in an atmosphere growing more menacing or desperate. The Vatican's financier, Bernardino Nogara, was ready to be a middleman but to what precise end remained sketchy and would not the Germans react quickly and terribly to betrayal, that word which could so readily spring to mind from a hostile examination of Italian history?[166]

Meanwhile, within the PNF, a last throw was attempted to reunite a Fascist people and war. On 19 April 1943, the squadrist Carlo Scorza, born 1897, a second-ranking old Fascist who remained transported by his *Duce* – in a lengthy piece of grovelling in 1933 Scorza had concluded that every Italian should say a daily prayer to God for the gift of their leader[167] – became party secretary, with the slogan 'everybody and everything for the war'.[168] The corrupt *ras* of Lucca was capable of some honesty or frankness, at least by comparison with Vidussoni. On 7 June he tabled a devastating report on the state of the party and nation, with the populist message that the only hope lay with the lowly social sectors that ran from 'the petite bourgeoisie to the little people' (*popolo minuto*).[169] The party itself, Scorza charged, was now too big to act as a vanguard and its leaders were too blatantly corrupt to retain any credibility, even if some young people and some old fighters were still worthy of their chief. In the state bureaucracy, the divisions of the wider society repeated themselves, with the top figures never having been Fascist and only the lower ranks being genuinely committed to the ideology and revolution. The same was true of the armed forces where no serious central organization had ever functioned. Laxity and confusion characterized the entire war effort so far.

The people as a whole, Scorza admitted, had not warmed to their Nazi German allies, even if they did fear them. Italy's pressing task was to convince its Axis partner that the Fascist regime was making a serious contribution at the front, something that the Germans had never conceded. In this and every other issue, Scorza concluded, it was time for more discipline, a greater radicalism and a determination to deal harshly and swiftly with enemies on high. Yet, by any serious measure, it was too late for a line whose populism was cheap and contestable. Scorza's report began to gather dust.

The crisis came on the evening of 24–25 July at the 187th and last meeting of the Fascist Grand Council. Those who look for mathematical portents might have noticed that 187 is 200 minus thirteen, and it was indeed to prove an unlucky moment for Mussolini (and many of his underlings). Back in 1922 the Grand Council had been hailed as a key element in the Fascist revolution, the summit for its discussions and decision-making. Over the years, however, the Council was another agency with more promise than achievement on its record. During the second decade of the dictatorship its meetings dwindled, and in July 1943 its members had not convened since before the war. Now, on a hot, still, Roman evening, with thunder somewhere in the air, the *ras* of once upon a time re-assembled, richer, paunchier and more flaccid than in their squadrist youth. The feline Grandi, the studious Bottai, the peppery De Bono, the brutal Scorza, the wealthy but unsatisfied Farinacci, Ciano, too, of course, and such more recent arrivals into the highest echelons of the regime as Enzo Galbiati, the chief of the paramilitary MVSN (a Fascist martinet who thought he had a wire open to his *camerati*, Himmler and the SS), all turned up at the appropriately named Sala del Pappagallo (Room of the Parrot) in the Palazzo Venezia.

The henchmen most in the know, Grandi being their chief, were edgy as the Roman night drew on. For months they had talked behind their hands of getting rid of their *Duce*, given his manifest inability to run a successful war. Now was their moment; now or never, given that the Americans were already strolling through Sicily without stern sign of military or popular opposition. Each petty *gerarca* (boss) clung to the illusion that it might actually be his moment, above all. Grandi, in particular, envisaged a Grandian Fascism which, under a Grandi-led government, would keep the authority held by the best people and the resultant discipline over the feckless masses but would also, in some totally unexplained fashion, magically render Italy's war happy not sad. Grandi was the most pompous and deluded but, should the truth be admitted, he, like his colleagues, was worried less about matters of high strategy than about the present. For two generations and more the *gerarchi* had lived in Mussolini's shadow and flourished in their public and private lives despite their leader's not infrequent raging about their incompetence and corruption and his fondness for moving them peremptorily from one post to another. They knew about the modus vivendi of being a Fascist, and each and every one had grovellingly pledged his deepest fealty to his *Duce* on very many occasions.

Now they were planning to change the rules of the game. What if Mussolini had foreseen their plots (he certainly had good information about them)? What if, when challenged, the Italian dictator proved as bloody as the German and Soviet tyrants were? Were the *gerarchi* about to find themselves cut down in an Italian equivalent of a Night of the Long Knives or Great Purge? Or, by dislodging the dictator from his office, were they replaying in modern form the roles of Brutus and Cassius, destined to fall victim in their turn to some communist Mark Antony ready to employ a populist rhetoric that would hunt them to their deaths?

While the ghosts of Fascisms past circled, the henchmen sweated and the meeting dragged on interminably. Mussolini himself droningly spoke for more than two hours, trying to remember or to forget his wife's robust parting advice that he should arrest them all. His tone was uneasy, with much pleading that, if the war was a disaster, it was not his fault, overlain with an old man's tiresome desire to prove that he still had an 'iron memory' for (often irrelevant) detail. When the dictator finally ran out of words and self-excuses, his critics preferred the tangential to the direct, with De Bono expatiating on the army's heroic history and so intimating that the blame for Italy's present condition could not be placed there.

At midnight, Mussolini, perhaps recalling that he would turn sixty in four days' time and was certainly not at the peak of his physical condition, suggested the meeting be adjourned. Grandi, fearing that the critics of the *Duce* were potential marshmallows should they face the heat of any attack or delay, objected successfully to the curtailment of discussion. After a thirty-minute pause, when the dictator took some mineral water (throughout the meeting he had grimaced at the pain coming insistently from his stomach ulcer), talk resumed. Eventually

Grandi put his motion, requiring that the task of running the war effort be formally returned from *Duce* to King. It carried nineteen to seven, with Giacomo Suardo abstaining and Farinacci petulantly declaring that he would vote only for a motion of his own. 'Gentlemen,' Mussolini said with some surviving aplomb, 'you have opened the crisis of the regime.' It was 3 a.m. when the Grand Councillors dispersed on to the war-darkened and cooling streets of Rome.

Still the result was unclear, or could have been. But Mussolini, after dragging himself home to a presumably sarcastic reception from Rachele, the person who was now openly thought to have the most balls in the family, slept briefly and was back at his desk on the morning of 25 July, seeing first Scorza and then the Japanese ambassador. At 5 o'clock in the afternoon, the dictator kept his accustomed biweekly appointment with the King at the Villa Savoia, just across the city from the Mussolinis' Villa Torlonia. Victor Emmanuel III, too, had been driven by the calamity afflicting his Italy to act. Mussolini, he told his battered interlocutor, must face the fact that he had become the most hated man in the country. Ex-military chief (and Piedmontese) Pietro Badoglio had been chosen to replace him as Prime Minister. Though the words were not uttered, the *Duce* was under arrest and was hurried away with an armed escort to the highly ironical fate of *confino* on the island of Ponza, where he was housed in an ill-maintained building once used for an Ethiopian prince who had stood up to the invading Italians in 1935.[170]

The event was sudden and public opinion had not been prepared for it. When the news began to be broadcast over and over again on state radio that the King had appointed Badoglio, the great majority of listeners rejoiced, if only because, mistakenly, they thought that the war was now over. As their early modern predecessors might have done at a moment of political change, they rushed out on to the streets of Italian cities to cheer (and, if opportunity was there, to loot). The shattering of Fascism preoccupied the population less than did the hope that killing had ceased and food supplies would return, proof that belief in the ideology had evaporated even among the *popolo minuto* long since. When war beset their families, Italians of all classes were quickly ready to disassociate themselves from the imponderable actions of the Great.

For a generation, propagandists had noisily preached the gospel of a new civic religion, a modern mass politics and the fixing of a novel national and ideological code into every Italian soul, but at this moment of crisis the impact on popular belief was demonstrated to have been superficial. Under the stress of military defeat and with the apparent opportunity to be released relatively lightly from war, Italians turned to their families and home towns, to friends and patrons and to the Catholic Church, as though the dictatorship and its ideology had been but a bauble. In so doing they behaved as the subjects of authoritarian regimes often behave: they were ready to bow to a dictator while he grasped the levers of power but felt free when the time was ripe to slough off his rule as a skin which never quite fitted and was never deemed likely to last. In July 1943 that always denied but never defeated nervousness of Mussolini and other Fascist bosses as to whether their outpourings of rhetoric since 1922 really meant what they said and their half-expressed doubts about whether Italians really loved them proved justified. Under the test of war, unlike Soviet communism in 1941–2 and German Nazism in 1944–5, Fascism was incapable of marching to the bitter end.

The last act, however, had not been played. During the 'forty-five days' of its power in Rome, the Badoglio government fumbled change. In its heart not a world away from Grandi's thoughts about the best solution for a post-Mussolinian Italy, the new administration was hesitant in abandoning many of the social (and racial) controls that Fascism had imposed. Former Fascist papers found it hard to amend their phrasing when, for example, *Il Gazzettino* of Venice congratulated the citizens of that city on their worthily 'totalitarian adhesion' to the new politics.[171] A fug of negotiation obscured the path to a peace through some sort of accommodation with the Anglo-Saxon and Soviet allies, themselves astonished by the speed and totality of the collapse of the dictatorship.[172] The King and Badoglio could not even agree where to hide Mussolini securely, despite the ex-*Duce*'s depressed acceptance that his political career was over. As summer came to an end, a cascade of disasters swept over Italy, tumbling it towards a more real and tragic war than the one Italians had until then experienced. On 3 September negotiators in Portugal approved a separate peace and, five days later, the matter was made public. The eighth of September, however, has lived as a day of infamy in Italian memory. Certainly it was a moment when a still partially Fascistized state collapsed and the ruling elite, as embodied by Victor Emmanuel III and Badoglio, cravenly abandoned their capital, their armed forces and their people to the Germans, thundering down from the north before the Allies could muster themselves effectively in the south. Bereft of politicians and law, Italians were left to fend for themselves. On 9 September, it seemed, Italy had not just ceased to be a dictatorship or a country governed by its social elites; it had also demonstrated that, under by no means the most strenuous of examinations visited on the combatants in the Second World War, Liberal, Fascist and any other form of nation-building engaged in since the Risorgimento had failed. With some parallels with the fate of France in 1940 or that of Humpty-Dumpty, the nation of Italy had fallen. How, it must be asked, could it be put back together again?

17

Losing all the wars

In June 2004 US President George W. Bush went on a state visit to Rome, with the hope of his neoconservative friends and allies that his presence would enhance the vote for Silvio Berlusconi and his governing coalition in the European elections. While there, Bush was taken to a site that still resonated with the national past of Fascist dictatorship. It was the Ardeatine caves, outside the Aurelian Walls, a place where, on 24 March 1944, 335 Italians (including 72 Jews) were shot out of hand. They died in reprisal for a partisan 'terrorist' attack on German soldiers the day before as they marched down Via Rasella where Mussolini had, during the 1920s, rented a bachelor flat in central Rome. By some definition, the thirty-three who perished were actually Italian since they belonged to the 11th company of the 3rd regiment of the so-called Bozen SS, recently recruited in what had been the Alto Adige. The ten for one Nazi policy of reprisal explains the number executed at the Fosse Ardeatine. The journalist Robert Katz has evocatively described the horrid scene: 'With their hands tied behind their back, and linked to one another in small groups, the prisoners were herded into sealed meat trucks and driven just beyond the ancient walls of Rome. There, on the Via Ardeatina, the trucks stopped at a labyrinth of tunnels among the Christian catacombs of the Appian Way. Inside these man-made caves, the Germans lighted torches and forced the Italians to get down on their knees and bow their heads. They proceeded then systematically to slaughter them by discharging 9 mm bullets at the base of their necks at an angle that passed through the brain and the top of the skull. Sixty-seven SS platoons laboured into the last hours of that day to complete their work.

When they finished, German engineers blew up the entrance to the caves, hoping to seal their contents for all time.'

Soon the carnage became common knowledge. After liberation on 4 June, the bodies were located in two mounds, '335 individuals from every branch of human society: workers and artisans, diplomats and chauffeurs, lawyers and trainmen, municipal clerks and pedlars, physicians and mechanics, professors and students, musicians and shop-keepers, generals, waiters, bankers, industrialists, shoemakers, pharmacists, sailors, farmers, butchers, landlords, postmen, boys, Jews, and a Roman Catholic priest'.[1] Eleven of the victims were not Italian.[2] All were men. The Germans, it seemed, murdered with a populist and not a class agenda.

This massacre was not the only one to disfigure the Italian peninsula as the front moved slowly north after 8 September 1943. During the last decades, there has been much historical re-exploration of the more notorious killings, acknowledging the divided nature of memory about them. In June 1944 in the Val di Chiana near Arezzo,[3] at Guardistallo south of Livorno,[4] or in September and October around Marzabotto on the outskirts of Bologna, the Germans responded to partisan attacks by slaughtering civilians, male and female, young and old, more than two hundred in the Val di Chiana, forty-six at Guardistallo (plus eleven partisans) and 771 at Marzabotto. Both at the time and later, especially in the Tuscan cases, *paesani* were affronted by the destiny which had picked their families out for death and were likely to blame those fighting against the Nazis for bringing on the shambles.

Such attitudes are perhaps predictable and the more significant evidence coming out of the stories may lie elsewhere, although it has not been much remarked on by historians perturbed that the existing record was too simplistically 'anti-Fascist'. At Civitella di Val Chiana, for example, the Fascism which had existed in 1922 had long faded, and in 1944 both those who had favoured Mussolini's rise and those who opposed it were united as victims but above all as *paesani*. When they confronted a terrible end these Italians exhibited identities nurtured by their families and their home village more strongly than by Fascism or by any competing ideology. At Guardistallo, the local community in its hour of trial looked inwards and sought sustenance from the wisdom and charity of the local priest. Illuminating the superficial nature of more modern ideologies and the failure of their authority as well as the fragmentary social base of the Italian nation, Don Mazzetto Rafanelli, it has been claimed, stood as 'the only person representing in some institutional way the community'. He was 'the defender of the *paese* and the custodian of its inhabitants, their guardian against both the Germans and the partisans and above all the person who embodied the social and community solidarity of the village'.[5]

George W. Bush was not escorted by Silvio Berlusconi to Tuscany. Instead, while the other leaders of Europe were readying themselves to commemorate the D-Day landings in Normandy and claim (with a predictable overlooking of the horrendous but determining battles on the Soviet front) that the Second World War was won in the West, the 'Leader of the Free World', as the pro-American Italian press was still given to calling him, engaged in his ritual moment of mourning and celebration at the Ardeatine caves. Yet here, too, memory has been contested, as the oral historian Alessandro Portelli has evocatively shown. The belated trial at Rome of the former SS captain Erich Priebke brought back from Argentina in 1994 and sentenced to life imprisonment in 1998, kept the massacre in the news. Before and since, disputes raged over whether the partisans should have attacked the Germans and whether it was morally right for them to have risked civilian lives – one casualty on the Via Rasella was an eleven-year-old boy, Piero Zuccheretti, blown to pieces by the explosion. Post-war Fascists sought to promote their own accounts, where communist conspiracies and murder bulk large. Portelli, by contrast, takes pains to underline diverse contexts and so other civilian killings by the Germans in and around Rome. Notorious were the ten women shot after being found guilty of stealing bread from a shop in the Ostiense;[6] or those slain or wounded by the Allied air raid on the working-class San Lorenzo area of the city on 19 July 1943.[7]

But for Bush and Berlusconi and also, ironically, for Portelli, a historian who places himself on the contemporary left, the SS's terrible deed has transmitted a different message. The Fosse Ardeatine is a 'national monument'; it ennobles Rome, the often despised capital of the nation; it unites Italians. According to Portelli, in an outburst of populist urban pride which might offend survivors of the 'barbarization of warfare on the eastern front', amid the horrors of the Second World War the killing was 'the only "metropolitan" massacre, the only cold-blooded mass execution perpetrated in the space of a big city, in which the variety of the victims synthesized the complex stratification of life stories in a metropolis . . . The Fosse Ardeatine is the symbolic maelstrom in which the space of the city and a century of its stories come together.'[8]

If this conclusion is to be believed, the Ardeatine caves constitute a monument to the nation, the virtuous nation as victim. The massacre becomes therefore a sort of Italian Holocaust, an equation further emphasized by the high proportion of Roman Jews who died in the hail of Nazi bullets. When Bush stood in silence not far from the catacombs, he was burying any suggestion that, during the frightful years from 1943 to 1945, Italians were murderers too. The history he appealed to remained what it had been in Roberto Rossellini's beautiful but escapist and exculpatory film *Roma: città aperta* (1945) (Rome: open city), when Italians, whether priest or communist, man, woman or boy of the people, Fascist or anti-Fascist, were *brava gente* and the killers were the ultimate 'others', officers in the SS and homosexuals to boot.[9]

Yet, if history is to serve its best purpose as 'criticism . . . criticism, again criticism and criticism once more' (a definition springing from the anti-Nazi cause in the Second World War),[10] the story of the last twenty months of combat in Italy is too serious a matter to be left to such sentimentalization. After 1943 quite a few Italians killed with a will (as they had already done during the rise of Fascism, when obtaining and controlling the national empire and when building the Axis new order since 1940). Furthermore they now set their nation on a course that, following a Nazi-fascist victory, would have entailed a bloodbath that can scarcely be imagined. The contemporary desire to market history as happy 'sellebration' should not be allowed to obscure the terror of the Salò Republic and the nightmare its role as a victorious partner of Nazi Germany would have entailed.

What, then, happened in Italy after the country was cut in two by the presence of Allied and German armies? Militarily speaking, the events of 8 September did not signal the end of the war, rather its resumption. Between September 1943 and the calming of civil society at the end of summer 1945 as many Italians died as had perished in the campaigns from 1940 to 1943 while Mussolini was still *Duce* of a united nation, the majority, 200,000 of them, being civilians. The collapse of 8 September meant that, thereafter, Allied and Nazi military forces fought each other with bitter determination across the convoluted mountainsides of Italy, south of the Po valley. They did so on the backs of the populace, triply split between the contending forces of Fascism and anti-Fascism and a greater number who hoped to wait out the combat and survive.

Bombers now rained down their cargoes on Italian railway junctions, industrial sites and cities. Since the Allies generally had command of the air, mostly the threat came from the south. The historic and tourist treasures, which dotted almost every Italian town and which could appeal to the learning and the hopes of leisure of Germans and Anglo-Saxons alike, led to talk of agreements about 'open cities'. Rome, for one, with its further advantage in housing the Vatican, was lightly bombed compared with other European capitals or with Milan, Genoa and Turin. Yet even the Romans did not escape aerial attack. In 1943–5, although the level of brutality never reached the pitch that was commonplace in the Balkans and further east, Italians felt the Second World War as never before. They lived in a country which was very partially their own, the south in the hands of the liberal capitalist Allies, the north under the sway more or less of Nazism.

At the end of 1942 the German leadership had begun examining the potential defection of Italy from the Axis and in May 1943 Himmler knew of 'not very secret plans for a coup' from groups near the King and army. Planning in Berlin envisioned pushing the border near to Verona, where it had been for the Habsburg empire before 1914. None the less, the events of 25 July came as a surprise and the unprepared Germans had involuntarily to accept Badoglio's initial announcement that the war was continuing. Within Italy, some German soldiers were reported to have joined the crowds applauding Mussolini's fall. The Nazi authorities were not reduced to credulity, however. Within three days, Rommel had been ordered to draft an

'Operation Alaric' to blot out what was left of this paper Roman empire and push the front with the Allies as far south as possible. In mid-August four army corps and eight divisions of German troops began moving into Italy and, by the signature of the deal between Italy and the Allies on 3 September, 'the German occupation of Italy was already a *fait accompli*'.[11]

On 12 September the military commander of these forces, Field Marshal Albert Kesselring, instituted German military law throughout the areas controlled by the Nazis and, for the remaining months of battle until his desperate transfer to the Western front in March 1945, he was the prime ruler of these territories. In the Nazi manner, a veneer of power-sharing ensued, with Rudolf Rahn, the ambassador of the German state and the most regular contact with Mussolini, frequently acting as the first spokesman of German policy. Rahn had transferred to Italy from Vichy on 30 August and in his memoirs recalled a mutually duplicitous meeting with King Victor Emmanuel at 11 on the morning of 8 September. Thereafter Rahn stationed himself at Verona, with the sapient words of his *Führer* ringing in his ears: 'it is a real tragedy that the Roman Mussolini has as his followers almost *in toto* merely decadent Italians . . . Only a virile state can found an empire and Italy is not virile. The excessive warmth of family relations there overwhelms all the rest.' Whether primed by Hitler or not, Rahn noticed how divided the champions of the Salò Republic were.[12]

Kesselring and Rahn were not the only Germans to count in occupied Italy. Albert Speer, Alfred Rosenberg and others in the Nazi leadership sent their own men to the peninsula in hope of advantage in their perennial internecine disputes. The SS, under the orders of General Karl Wolff, an official who boasted of being Himmler's right-hand man,[13] pursued their lethal course across the country. Their fighting men of the Waffen-SS included non-German fanatics and mercenaries picked up on other fronts and transferred south. The Nazi authorities also moved to a practical annexation of swathes of northern Italy, combining the provinces of Bolzano, Trento and Belluno as the Voralpenland, under the Austrian Gauleiter, Franz Hofer. Further east, the provinces of Udine, Gorizia, Trieste, Pola, Lubiana and Fiume were denominated the Adriatisches Kustenland

and placed into the hands of Friedrich Rainer. To all intents and purposes, a Nazified version of the Habsburg empire was put back in business in this part of Europe, with Goebbels echoing German nationalist thought since 1915 when writing furiously of his determination that the inferior race of Italians must pay and pay heavily for their treachery and levity. They were, he pronounced, 'a gypsy people gone to rot'. Nazi policy on gypsies did not make it a comforting parallel.[14]

Badoglio and the King had fled Rome without leaving clear orders to their own troops, notably those garrisoning parts of Greece, Albania and Yugoslavia, about how they should react to armistice with the Allies and what in particular they should do about their angry German ex-comrades. The result was military disintegration.[15] Italian soldiers long recalled their 'humiliation, rage, pain, worry for their families and bitterness over the sad end of their *Patria*'.[16] Already on 10 September the German high command confirmed their ancient prejudices with a succinct communiqué concluding that 'the Italian armed forces no longer exist'.[17] Up to 700,000 Italian military personnel fell into Nazi hands, most being carried off to captivity in Germany, where some would be eventually retooled as fascist soldiery but where the majority were destined to work as slave labourers for the Nazi war. A further 500,000 came under Allied control and were returned only slowly and reluctantly by those benefiting from the work they had been able to do. On the Ionian island of Cephalonia, a full-scale battle erupted between Nazi and Fascist forces lasting a week and, on 24 September, after a victory made inevitable given their mastery of the air, the Germans proceeded to liquidate over 6,000 ordinary soldiers and sailors and the great majority of surviving Italian officers, these last shot against a wall in blocks of four, eight or twelve over a four-hour period, in what has often been read as a foreshadowing of the terror the Nazis were to inflict in Italy itself.[18]

In the south, the Allies botched any chance they may have had of occupying much of mainland Italy. They had crossed to Reggio Calabria on 3 September, and on the 9th made a major landing at Salerno, 50 km south of Naples. There they met the Germans, who offered fierce resistance. Allied forces did not reach Naples until 1 October, having been assisted by an uprising within the city that, during four days of bitter contest, brought down vicious Nazi reprisals on the Neapolitans. Thereafter the advance stalled. A landing at Anzio on 2 January 1944 did not lead to the rapid freeing of the populace of what had once been the Pontine marshes. Instead it took five months of pitiless air raids for German defenders to be expelled from the Benedictine monastery of Monte Cassino, commanding a hill-top south of Rome. This redoubt was not abandoned by its defenders until May. Around Latina, the Germans, before leaving, criminally broke the dams, allowing the mosquitoes and malaria back into the marshlands and mocking the brief achievement of Fascist *bonifica*.

Rome was finally entered on 4 June 1944, with Florence falling on 3 August, again after days of bitter dispute and with the destruction of all the bridges over the Arno, except the Ponte Vecchio. Still not routed, the Germans and their RSI allies thereafter successfully defended the 'Gothic line', running from the Tyrrhenian to the Adriatic Sea south of Bologna and the other gateways to the Po valley. That richest part of Italy was not liberated until the last days of the war in April 1945.

Political and social power, especially in the areas south of Rome occupied by the Allies, soon returned to the old elites who had ruled society before 1922 and who, thereafter, had fellow-travelled contentedly with the dictatorship. With the Cold War waiting in the wings to replace the hot conflict against Nazi-fascism, anti-communism, in Allied eyes, provided the key index of political worth and liberals, landowners and even Mafia chiefs could readily enough be rebadged in that regard. Fascism, in other words, disappeared at a stroke from public view in this part of Italy but anti-Fascism faded faster and more fully.[19] Croce's cosy view that the dictatorship had been no more than a parenthesis in national history was partially explained by the fact that he had been able to endure the regime's more drastic measures in some comfort while residing in his Neapolitan palace. Meanwhile, contrary to his interpretation, the more conservative aspects of Fascism's spirit and the social exploitation that underpinned them were by no means removed from the old kingdom of Naples-Sicily. Post-war neo-fascism was to find a greater following in southern than in northern Italy.

In the north, the outline history of the new Social Republic is quickly enough told. It began with an act of will, albeit one riven with contradiction. On 12 September Mussolini was rescued from his prison at the ironically named Campo Imperatore by an SS troop under Otto Skorzeny, an Austrian, who took care in his memoirs to recall that, personally, he had never forgotten or forgiven the 'loss' to Italian rule of the Germanic South Tyrol.[20] The *Duce* was flown off to Bavaria, where he met members of his family (including Ciano, back-pedalling from his role in the plot against Mussolini in July) and some other Fascist chiefs. Hitler had personally rejected suggestions from Farinacci that the *ras* of Cremona should be put in charge of that rump of Italy in Nazi-fascist hands, although Farinacci's was the first voice surviving 8 September to be beamed by the Nazis to Italy. In the *Führer*'s priggish view, Farinacci, for all his flaunted racism and revolutionary fervour, was a bounder and vulgarian, unthinkable as a regular interlocutor of his fastidious self.

The result was that when, on 18 September, Mussolini, with hesitant voice and uncertain morale, made his initial broadcast back to Italy, he announced that, already for three days, he had resumed control over the country. The regime over which he presided, he stated, 'will be national and social in the fullest sense of the words. It will thus be Fascist in a way that takes us back to our origins.' The traitors of July, he ran on, must be inexorably eliminated. 'We shall liquidate the parasitic plutocracies and finally ensure that work lies at the heart of the economy and is recognized as the fundamental basis of the State.'[21] After two months' subsequent debate in which the titles Stato nazionale repubblicano (National Republican state) or Stato fascista repubblicano (Republican Fascist state) received some backing, it was finally decided on 1 December 1943 that Mussolini's new government should rule the Repubblica Sociale Italiana (RSI or Italian Social Republic). The new regime carefully avoided the word 'Fascist', opting instead for 'social' as a signal of its revolutionary commitment to a 'new order' at home and abroad. In popular discourse, its name was often abbreviated to the 'Salò Republic', after the small town overlooking Lago di Garda, the sometime Gardasee, where a number of its ministries were situated. It lay next door to Mussolini's own headquarters at Gargnano. Salò's other claim to fame lay in the grandiose and eccentric villa, the Vittoriale, where, until March 1938,

D'Annunzio had lived out his disconsolate if luxurious last years as the Principe di Monte Nevoso. In anti-Fascist vocabulary, those who favoured the RSI were called *repubblichini* (little republicans and so distinguished from the more worthy old-style Republicans, the *repubblicani*).

The PNF, renamed the Partito Fascista Repubblicano (PFR), was, with due formality, placed from 15 September under the secretaryship of Alessandro Pavolini, born 1903, a gilded youth from an academic family in Tuscany, who boasted twin degrees in law and political science. Pavolini's mother had been one of the first of the respectable classes (her husband was a distinguished professor) to bless the rumbustious *fascio* in her city.[22] Pavolini's colleagues went on thinking of him as very 'Tuscan' and writerly in nature.[23] Too young to fight in the First World War, Pavolini took out his frustration with class hatred against the socialists and served as a teenage squadrist. In 1925 he earned further ideological merit by leading a mob of middle-class students who howled down Salvemini when he tried to teach non-Fascist history at the local university and drove him into exile.[24]

As *federale* of Florence after 1929, Pavolini moved in the same circles and behaved in the same way as Ciano. He led a comfortably worldly life as a cultural agent of the regime, even if he preened his intellectual self with 'staging Fascism for the masses'. In association with the 1934 Littoriali games, he put on a grandiose event, called '18BL' after its somewhat ambiguous 'hero', a Fiat truck, portrayed as rolling forward unstoppably to political victory in the world war and to social triumph in squadrism. Unsurprisingly this crude piece of propaganda was costly and unpopular; even cultural historians admit that it was a 'colossal failure' and 'embarrassment'.[25] It was not repeated. The thick-skinned Pavolini moved on to purveying more traditionally high cultural fare at the *Maggio musicale* (Florence's annual spring music festival) to a cosmopolitan clientele. Although he volunteered for Ethiopia and boasted about his military prowess there, treasuring all the while a photo of an updated Fascist Madonna and child, waving a skull and crossbones flag,[26] initially Pavolini was no special fan of the Axis.

With Ciano's backing, the Florentine was promoted to head Minculpop from October 1939 to February 1943. From that office he became involved in a scandalous affair with the riggish actress Doris Duranti, to whom, if rumour be believed, he gave fur coats, five at a time, and three million lire in shares in a cinema company, while secret police noted his car (complete with its chauffeur) waiting patiently outside Cinecittà during the day and parked beside her luxurious city apartment in the wee hours.[27] Pavolini, for all his bouts of fervour, did not seem an ideological purist by nature. However, whether on the spur of the moment or not, in July 1943 he fled to Germany and, although still the target of manic attacks from Preziosi, who was appalled that his brother had a Jewish wife,[28] Pavolini, now a 'super-Fascist', became a crucial figure in the bloody history of the RSI.

Matching Pavolini and inevitably his rival was Guido Buffarini Guidi (eight years his senior), another Tuscan, this time from Pisa. A volunteer in the First World War, who graduated with a law degree in 1920, Buffarini Guidi made his name in 1923 as mayor of his city, cunning in steering a middle course between two violently opposed local Fascist groups.[29] He subsequently rose as a Fascist administrator of cautious mien, being Under-Secretary of the Interior and the holder of many secrets, from May 1933 to February 1943. In the July crisis, Buffarini Guidi voted for Mussolini, breaking with Ciano, who had long been his patron, although he was also thought well of by Donna Rachele Mussolini. As early as 18 September Buffarini Guidi, in Rome as was Pavolini, was given charge of the Ministry of the Interior and so of the state – as distinct from the party – police. He retained the office until February 1945, despite being ready, with the right audience, to mock the *Duce*'s absurd words about modern Italians bearing the heritage of imperial Rome and ridicule the radical-seeming ideological impulse of the RSI.[30] His eventual fall may have been precipitated by his open complaint to Mussolini in January 1945 that everything the Salò government did, or sought to do, was methodically denigrated and blocked by the PFR and that too many envious informers and more or less secret agents interfered with ordinary administration.[31]

The Ministry of the Interior was a post that Mussolini, in his pomp, had only once before not kept to himself. In the dangerous aftermath of the Matteotti slaying, the Nationalist Luigi Federzoni had assumed the Ministry as a surety to the King that Fascism did not stand for murder. In the RSI, the failure of the *Duce* to be Minister of the Interior demonstrated his declining powers and his desire to play that part of puppet dictator which the Germans had consigned to him without too great exposure. Perhaps in that way there were avenues that could yet lead him to be less a phantom and more the tyrant of yore. In the interim, Buffarini Guidi took responsibility for some of the violent features of RSI life and for its deepening anti-Semitic practice. It was his choice on 30 November to tally and collect Italian Jews, 'even if exempted and irrespective of citizenship', and dispatch them to camps. He simultaneously ordered the confiscation of their property.[32] Buffarini Guidi's apparent racist dedication did not soften the parochialism and envy of Venetian Fascists, who, around this time, bewailed the fate of a country ruled by two Tuscans, one allegedly under the thumb of the Jews (Pavolini), the other of the Freemasons (Buffarini Guidi).[33] It was in Venice on 31 December 1943 and 17 August 1944 that the RSI authorities, without any specific orders from the Germans, rounded up the ancient local Jewish community, with deadly eventual effect.[34]

Meanwhile the fragile reality of RSI government was manifest in the difficulty that its ministries, scattered over northern Italian centres, had in communicating with each other. The Ministry of Foreign Affairs, for example, was based in Venice, just about as soft a posting as could be found in 1943–5. Although living at Gargnano and not Venice, Mussolini himself resumed the Ministry, with the respectable Serafino Mazzolini, once secretary of the ANI, doing the hack-work.[35] Work limped on. For many months, only one mutual telephone line functioned between the different parts of the administration and it was controlled by the Germans.[36]

Other personalities who reappeared at Salò were Graziani, now made Minister of National Defence and commander of a revived national army; Mezzasoma, the new head of Minculpop; and the intrepid or brutal half-blind war hero, Francesco Barracu, the Under-Secretary of the President of the Council and so the executor of much of Mussolini's domestic daily grind. Barracu was a Sard client of Pavolini, graphically defined by Farinacci as 'a sergeant-major lacking a baton in his knapsack'.[37] A German diplomat found his habit of appearing for everyday work with a machine gun slung over his shoulder theatrical and offensive and abhorred the way he threatened to shoot the next person he met.[38]

Carlo Alberto Biggini, born 1902 at Sarzana in Liguria, was a more respectable-seeming Fascist with Catholic contacts. He was another party chief who had won degrees in law and political science, being in 1941 nominated the youngest university rector in Italy. Now he remained as Minister of Education, a post to which he was first promoted in February 1943. In July 1943 Biggini had opposed the vote against the *Duce* on the prim grounds that any such move was unconstitutional. After September he busied himself vacuously in trying to draft a replacement constitution for the RSI, aiming to derail the extremism of Pavolini and his friends. In May 1944 he still had a wire open to Pope Pius XII and, during the final collapse in 1945, Biggini took sanctuary, perhaps appropriately, at the shrine of St Anthony of Padua.[39] Among more radical educationalists was Renato Ricci, the erstwhile Balilla chief, who in 1942 had been forced to deny further charges of corruption, now concerning a pig farm with mysteriously easy and cheap access to supplies.[40] Ricci returned as head of the party militia, the revived MVSN, from September to November 1943, when that body was merged into Graziani's national army. The institutional Darwinism which flourished mightily at Salò was soon evident, however, as almost immediately another paramilitary group, the Guardia Nazionale Repubblicana (National Republican Guard), came into existence. Under Ricci and financed by the Ministry of the Interior, the group initially boasted 150,000 cadres[41] and was ready to work collaboratively with the Germans, no matter how bloodily.

The most curious figure to acquire some prominence at Salò was the sometime Romagnole communist Nicola Bombacci. Personal financial troubles may have prompted Bombacci in 1931 and 1934 to approach Grandi for help and understanding. By the time of the Ethiopian war, Bombacci was ready to inform Mussolini of his admiration for the *Duce*'s 'unshakeable will in placing Italy and its People back on the road traced by Rome'. Minculpop subsidies in compensation for such agreeable views flowed. From 1936 to 1943 Bombacci edited a well-subsidized journal called *Verità* (Truth), meant to be the Fascist *Pravda*, expatiating on 'a proletarian Italy locked in struggle with capitalist imperialism'. In time *Verità* heralded the war as a battle for 'social justice among the nations'. Bombacci adhered to the RSI and became a familiar regime orator, touring factories with his gospel of a really existing social Fascism. As late as March 1945 he told a crowd at Genoa that 'Stalin will never make socialism; rather Mussolini will'.[42] Bombacci's other role was to be a special counsellor of the depressed *Duce*. As a rough and tumble familiar who evoked something of a lost youth of socialism and rebellion against convention, Bombacci could still bring a wan smile to his leader's face. A friend to the grave, Bombacci left Milan in April 1945 in Mussolini's own car, and was also to meet his death by Lago di Como.[43]

In the *Duce*'s mind Bombacci had become a substitute Farinacci, fulfilling what had once been his crucial informal role as the truth-teller of the regime, the genuine radical. The *ras* of Cremona had gone too far in toadying to the Germans after July 1943 and in urging himself forward as their man. Although he remained a person of some note in the RSI and, for a time, entertained himself by financing a defrocked priest who was bent on launching an 'Italic crusade', designed to promote schism with the Vatican (the Church, he wrote, was 'protean and Pharaonic'),[44] Farinacci found his sphere of influence mostly confined to his home town. For his part, Mussolini made plain his desire to avoid Farinacci's company.[45]

In the ostensibly more respectable and judicious world of high culture, the leading figures to rally to the RSI were Giovanni Gentile, stiffly proud of his intellect and austerity (and to be assassinated by partisans on 15 April 1944), F. T. Marinetti and Ardengo Soffici, each in the past insatiably importunate for fortune and fame, Giotto Dainelli, the geographer, Goffredo Coppola, the rector of Bologna university, and quite a few historians, among whom was the later Prime Minister, Giovanni Spadolini.[46] Coppola spoke in the spirit of his times in October 1943 when he demanded revenge on the 'cowards' of July and September. It behoved all good men, he urged, to efface the dishonour that had deeply stained the national escutcheon. With their 'infinite love for their land', he pronounced, Italians must make the RSI a 'State which punishes not only crime but also and above all deals with indifference and amorality of citizens ready to imitate Pilate in washing their hands' over contemporary developments.[47]

If his phrasing was less strident, Gentile did not demur from these literally murderous ideas. For him, too, a failure to take sides meant joining the 'party of the lazy, the egoists and the cowards'. After a betrayal, discipline was needed. It must 'inexorably strike' those most directly involved (Gentile was writing just before Ciano was shot). Fascists, the philosopher urged brutally, must bear down on 'the uncertain and irresolute'. Only then could the single flag of the united nation wave triumphant and 'order, justice and law' prevail.[48] Soffici, the intellectual who before 1939 had tirelessly urged his *Duce* to elevate his status and confirm his fortune,[49] now had the gall to claim that, although Fascism had not been a lie, it had contained a lie, one which was, he wrote in menacing metaphor, a 'plague pustule', demanding 'root and branch squeezing' from the body politic.[50] A few weeks later, Soffici varied his image a tad as he talked about 'suffocating and exterminating those canaille' who opposed Salò.[51] Dainelli concentrated on vaunting the superb racial unity of Italians, 'the most civilized of peoples', now, he thought, locked in a death struggle with 'brutal and primitive Bushmen and Australians' who, in his mind, staffed the Allied armies moving up the peninsula.[52] The journal in which these famous intellectuals, still revered in some circles today, wrote their pieces, contained examples of vicious anti-Semitism, with one journalist explaining clinically how the Jews were destined to disappear from the Europe of which they were the eternal and unforgiving enemy, just as old skin falls off new.[53]

While regime intellectuals went about their tawdry business, the character of the new state and of the society it governed was displayed at a congress at Verona in mid-November 1943. It was held under the auspices of the PFR and Pavolini. The reworked Fascist party, given a fresh tint with rhetoric about ideological purity and a special devotion to the productive proletariat, claimed to have signed on 250,000 paid-up members. A number, however, seem to have been coerced into joining and the bureaucratic processes of the PFR remained unreliable, despite its enthusiasts casting a slogan with some ring to it: 'all power to the Party'.[54] Mussolini himself, anxious as usual that there be no diminution of his charisma, but in practice an ever more woebegone figure, stayed away from the November meeting. On the 14th, the so-called 'Verona Manifesto' was approved. Its text was not so much a constitution as a sketch of where the RSI might go. The PFR and

Pavolini at once matched thought with squadrist action, breaking off from the convention on the 15th to raid Ferrara and wreak terrible revenge on those behind an anti-Fascist attack there. Eleven opponents of Fascism were killed and their bodies were exposed to public view with an unashamed brutality that would be imitated with sad frequency during the following months, reaching its bathetic end in the abuse and exhibition of the corpses of Mussolini, Pavolini, Bombacci, Starace and others at Piazzale Loreto in Milan on 29 April 1945.

Talk about a constitutive assembly continued over the following year but the legal basis of the RSI was never fully resolved. In December 1944 Mussolini moved successfully to have a final charter postponed until the war was over. None the less, the manifesto of November 1943 did stress that Italy had broken free from the 'traitorous and fugitive last King', that the nation should endorse its *Duce* in quinquennial referenda, that a corporate-style assembly must express the thoughts and interests of a range of economic and social groups, including soldiers and POWs, and that the party, hardened, purified and, by implication, reduced in number, should lead the people towards the achievement of the 'Revolutionary Idea'. 'The religion of the Republic shall be the apostolic Roman Catholic one. Every other cult that does not violate the law shall be respected,' the manifesto noted. Clause 7, in a slightly ambiguous choice of words but with the practical effect of having the RSI leadership underwrite the final solution, proclaimed that 'all those who belong to the Jewish race are foreigners. For the duration of the war they shall be regarded as being of enemy nationality.'

Further segments of the manifesto looked in more detail at aspects of foreign and social policy. The RSI was committed to retaining Italy's 'natural' Alpine and maritime borders (an empty warning here to the German rulers, settling in to govern Trento and Trieste). The new-style social fascists could be relied on to eliminate 'British intrigues' and press on with abolishing the entire 'capitalistic system', while simultaneously fomenting the overthrow of 'the world plutocracies'. These latest new men and women must subscribe to the development of Africa to the mutual benefit of metropolitan and 'native' peoples. Especially they must respect those extra-European peoples, 'who, like the Egyptian Muslims in particular, are already organized in social groupings'. At home, work stood as the basis of the republic but private property must be 'guaranteed by the State'. With an echo of the confusions of the 1930s it was now repeated that 'the State's sphere of action shall embrace everything that because of its dimensions or functions lies outside the private sector and falls within the collective interest'. An example might be the munitions industry. In factories, zealous efforts should be made to foster profit-sharing and worker participation; in agriculture, landowners, unable to render their land productive, could expect to be chastised by officialdom. Wages should be fair, prices should be stabilized, the black market rigorously suppressed. Seeking a final upbeat, the manifesto concluded with the plea: 'There is only one way to attain all of our social goals: "Fight! Work! Win!"'[55]

Both to impress the Germans and to convince themselves that they were constructing something new, the leaders of the Republic moved swiftly to punish the traitors of July, those members of the Grand Council who had voted against their *Duce*'s continuing control of the war effort and had precipitated Fascism's first fall. On 13 October a set of extraordinary provincial courts was established to this end. The assassination of the *federale* of Milan, Aldo Resega, on 18 December while he was boarding a tram taking him to work, magnified the fanaticism of Salò fascists and lifted their determination to create mayhem of their own.[56]

In January 1944 six eminent prisoners, including Galeazzo Ciano, were brought before judges sitting at Verona. Although the verdicts of their trials had long been prearranged, certain decencies were nevertheless observed. Throughout the proceedings Ciano was politely addressed as *Conte* and he did not forget to give the Roman salute when summoned to speak. The *genero* had also observed propriety by describing himself in a written memo to his prosecutors as 'of Aryan race, Catholic religion and a property owner'.[57] The six renegades from July were duly found guilty and, on the cold morning of 11 January, Ciano, De Bono, Marinelli and two others went before a firing squad. The only man to be saved from capital punishment was the Fascist unionist and, from April 1943, Minister of Corporations, Tullio Cianetti, who was jailed for thirty years. In his prison he wrote his memoirs, before escaping after the war to Mozambique and a second, perhaps still fascistoid, life as a *colon*.[58]

Ciano's execution carried a heavy implicit message. It signified the boasted liquidation of the bourgeois version of Fascism, with its weak acceptance that, in this wicked world, the family and *raccomandazioni*, corruption and high living, ideological equivocation and practical realism, are necessary parts of life. After Verona, it was suggested, the Fascism of Salò would surrender its capital F to symbolize the switch towards the purity, efficiency, dedication, fanaticism and blood lust of the Nazis. In this play without words, Ciano's shadow was thus the *Duce*, who from 1922 had accepted so many compromises about the meaning of Fascism and allowed so much delay in the implementation of social and cultural revolution. Mussolini had made evident his own comprehension of the matter when he told his secretary, Giovanni Dolfin, in October that Ciano was 'no better and no worse than the others. All the hatreds that focus on him are designed to strike against me.' The *Duce*, a coward of the most profound sort, willing to sacrifice his best-loved daughter's husband in order to conceal his own manifold failures and contradictions, with some nervousness and much after-the-event self-exculpation, knowingly let Ciano go to his doom in his stead.

After 1944, should the truth be known (and there were many whose present interest was to deny it), the *Duce* was an even hollower man than he had been before. He might on occasion bemoan that Pavolini erred when he sought to make the PFR 'a State within the State'.[59] He did not, however, move to check the secretary's fanaticism, preferring to let events run. His line was much the same in his dealings with the Germans. On occasion the *Duce* would politely beg that they behave more reasonably and display more solicitude towards Italians' needs and susceptibilities. But under pressure he always retreated. He might dream, as he let slip self-interestedly to friends, that his real hope was for an Italy free both of the Allies and of the Germans.[60] Yet, as Buffarini Guidi was already complaining in December 1943, his policy was 'perennially oscillating'; 'it seems impossible that a man of his intuition and flair is always for compromise', the Minister noted regretfully. 'He never loves sharp and defined situations.'[61]

While Mussolini fantasized with vanity and delusion about acting as a shield for the Italian people against German vengeance, some of his erstwhile friends took a shorter route to personal safety and contemplated the inadequacies in the story of Fascism, its *Duce* and themselves. The most prominent among the old leadership to find an exit from their past lives and commitments were Giuseppe Bottai, Dino Grandi and Giuseppe Volpi. Released from Regina Coeli on 8 September, the failed intellectual of the PNF managed successfully to conceal himself at the INPS office on the Via del Corso in central Rome before, in February 1944, transferring to become a guest at a Jesuit monastery. While still at INPS, Bottai philosophized happily about his innate ability to adapt to reduced living conditions and, for moral sustenance, read Shakespeare's *The Comedy of Errors* in Italian translation.[62] He also began a highly inadequate reckoning with his Fascist life, accepting that the regime had failed in any serious sense to implement what he was still inclined to regard as its attractive ideology. Current events at Salò, he wrote off; they embodied not 'the republic of the Italians but the republic of Mussolini',[63] a leader he now condemned as the person whose political 'dexterity' had been responsible for the wreck of the Fascist cause.[64] When Rome fell to the Allies, Bottai, able to summon his friends if not his courage to his assistance, again managed to flee. By 29 August 1944 he had reached Algiers where he enrolled in the French Foreign Legion, a suitably desperate refuge for one who had never plotted a convincing way to amalgamate his desire to be a philosopher and his need to be an activist. By 1947 an amnesty permitted Bottai to return to Italy where he survived until 1958. His son Bruno pursued a distinguished career in diplomacy, becoming Secretary-General of the Ministry of Foreign Affairs from 1987 to 1994 and also rejoiced in the office of Honorary President of the Federazione Italiana del Cricket.

Dino Grandi, the most exposed by the events of 25 July since the motion sacking the *Duce* had been presented in his name, rapidly abandoned his initial hopes that the King would summon him to form the next government and on 18 August escaped to Francoist Seville. Shortly thereafter, he moved to Salazar's Portugal, where he took up comfortable residence at Estoril. There, by his own account, he mixed easily with a wealthy and raffish set, which included Randolph Churchill and

Lord Beaverbrook, expanding in peacetime to embrace Winston Churchill. After 1947, rejecting a suggestion from Montanelli that he stay in Europe and collaborate in compiling a 'truthful' history of the dictatorship, Grandi departed to Brazil,[65] where he prospered commercially. He continued to avoid formal connection with Italian politics, resurfacing in the decade before his death in 1988 as a hero of Renzo De Felice's revisionist understanding of the Fascist regime. Under this historian's editorship or auspices, two volumes of memoirs, designed to display Grandi's virtue and understanding, were then published.[66] The RSI, Grandi repeated, mixing cliché and characteristic effrontery, amounted to a 'calvary' for the innocent Italian people, once they had missed the historical bus in July 1943 and had not rallied behind him in breaking with the appalling Nazis.[67]

Similarly blessed by fortune and good friends was Giuseppe Volpi. After 8 September the canny financier was arrested by the Germans and spent two uncomfortable months at Regina Coeli. Eventually, however, his lifetime strategy of keeping contacts open worked for him too. Graziani and Buffarini Guidi appealed on his behalf, as did the perhaps more influential Bernardino Nogara, master of Vatican finances. There may have been sympathy as well from Mussolini[68] and Volpi was transferred to comfortable house arrest at a villa on Lake Como. Thence he escaped to Switzerland in July 1944.[69]

Despite these and other defections, the RSI did undoubtedly find some base in Italian life. Why? Who were its supporters? What did they seek in this last throw at Fascist 'revolution'? Until the 1990s the standard response to these questions, conditioned by the flimsy nature of Salò government, was simple. The Germans had overwhelmed all and so bore responsibility for the destruction and murder from 1943 to 1945. Any *repubblichini* were their hirelings, a desperate crew of killers, whose motives scarcely deserved or needed further explanation. De Felicean revisionism, however, went near to turning this interpretation on its head. De Felice himself, in the posthumously published and unfinished last volume of his biography of Mussolini, announced that the PFR attracted members of both sexes and all classes out of their sense of 'moral and ideological coherence'. They may have been violent but so were their partisan enemies. Each side in the 'civil war' arose spontaneously and those who backed the RSI were not Nazis. Instead they embodied a 'wholly Italian tradition', although De Felice did concede that the Republic was riven by two 'souls', one 'extremist' and the other 'moderate'. Mussolini himself had initially returned reluctantly to politics to save his country from the 'fate of Poland' but was genuine in his talk about renewed socialization and a 'return to origins'. All in all, De Felice maintained, the RSI was a 'necessary republic'[70] and, seconding his research, quite a number of the regime's erstwhile servants now felt free to publish their self-justifications.

Vincenzo Costa defined himself as the 'last *federale*'; he assumed control of the PFR in Milan in April 1944. Only fourteen in 1914, Costa had falsified his age to fight strenuously in the First World War and in 1918–19 was based at Farinacci's Cremona, undertaking the welcome task of purging POWs corrupted with socialism. He joined the *fasci* in March 1919 and followed D'Annunzio to Fiume. Under the regime Costa did not rise far, however, and in 1940 returned to the army to fight in France. Costa greeted the events of 1943 with disdain as 'the betrayal of the *patria*'. On 25 July he deplored the sight of 'anti-Fascists creeping out of their secret holes, followed by the worst of the people, hungry for robbery and havoc'. The 8th of September he deemed still more infamous, involving as it did the 'cancellation of glorious pages of our history and [the surrender of] our independence'.

The real fighters for the RSI, he argued, those motivated by patriotism and the 'manly necessity to defend themselves and their families' from brutal and furtive partisan assault, were generally poor but honest folk, 'workers, middle-ranking members of the bourgeoisie, very seldom graduates'. They were impelled politically by a profound sense of honour that made them loyal to their ally to the war's end, even if, simultaneously, they hoped eventually to excise German control from Italy. A 'levantine' wheeler and dealer like Buffarini Guidi offended their innermost souls and Costa was delighted at his fall. Mussolini, by contrast, in his view really tried to act as a shield for the people and in April 1945 his return to Milan was motivated by his desire to be with them during the final crisis. If the years from 1943 to 1945 were a time of slaughter, that sad situation was not the special fault of the RSI but rather an effect of a deadly civil war, naturally 'scarred by ambush and betrayal'.[71]

If Costa justified himself as one seeking to keep honour bright in the party, Luigi Bolla argued a similar case for those public servants who, after September 1943, refused to follow the King and Badoglio south. Bolla, too, claimed to have reacted to 8 September with 'shame, bitterness and humiliation' and with an angry sense that the elites had 'behaved like complete cretins'. In the circumstances, Bolla believed that he must ensure that sound administration proceeded uninterrupted. He disliked the resuscitation at Salò of failed party fanatics but admired the way that the *Duce* accepted that he alone could rescue Italians from German fury. Bolla gagged at having to deal with such people as Vittorio Mussolini, the *Duce*'s son, 'one of the fattest louts on the face of the earth', superior only to his rag-tag following of 'athletes, boxers and denizens of the gym', with his language suggesting that Bolla was one Italian bureaucrat still to locate his manhood in the sporting life.[72] Yet, despite such problems, Bolla urged solemnly, service, national service, must dominate all.

The sentiments expressed by Costa, Bolla and many others who adhered to the RSI are all very well. Presumably a number were, by some definition, men and women of honour. It is true that the civil conflict that swept over parts of Italy in 1943 fractured Italians with something more than ideology. On each side, there were a number who fought for what they deemed to be the nation, just as there were crusaders for their perceived class. Revisionism goes too far, however, when historians or memoirists urge a moral equivalence between the competing sides. Some who worked for the party, the state and even the armies of Salò, may have seen themselves as fighting against the Germans by working with them. In this view, however, they were deluded and, had there been a Nazi victory, their backing of the RSI would have been a terrible error, both for Italians and any to be left under their direct rule.

One malign figure, who could rely on Nazi backing and was likely to acquire greater influence after a German victory, was the fanatical anti-Semite Preziosi. In March 1944 he was made Inspector-General of Race, a post from which he had to report only to the *Duce*. Two months earlier, he had spelled out his views in a lengthy memorandum demanding the 'total elimination' of Jews, 'half-breeds', any with a drop of Semitic blood in their veins and any who sympathized with them (in his manic understanding these last were certain to be 'polluted', too). Trimmers, he had written, amounted to a Trojan horse that must be destroyed.[73] Somewhat paradoxically, however, Preziosi, the Nazi client, remained prickly about too overt a German interference in Italian politics and his welcome for the German version of the final solution was not unalloyed.[74]

With or without his divagations, the practice of anti-Semitism remained complex at Salò. Buffarini Guidi twisted away from his actions in November 1943 and, for whatever amalgam of motives, a number of officials engaged in their old methods of procrastination or obfuscation when their German colleagues tried to press the Jewish question. It is instructive that Primo Levi, the most subtle and moving of reporters on what came to be called the Holocaust, preferred, when he was arrested by Salò militia in January 1944, to identify himself as an 'Italian citizen of Jewish race'. Nothing in his experience of what he recalled as four years of Fascist racial laws (actually six) counselled otherwise. Rather, Levi feared that openly calling himself an anti-Fascist 'would have meant torture and certain death'.[75] Yet, for all the lingering contradiction in Italian racism, it is hard to conceive of a post-war 'new order' Italy where Jews, blacks, Arabs and Slavs would not have suffered grossly for their alleged racial inferiority.

Such a conclusion does not entail any return to the interpretation that saw only sacrifice and heroism on the part of the anti-Fascists. One Italian who did not succumb to the appeal of the RSI, and who exposes some of the contradictions on his side of the front, was the patriotic young historian of empire, Corrado Zaghi. On 8 September Zaghi was lying low in a Rome hospital being treated for an allegedly 'major debilitating eye problem'. In fact, with his path smoothed by his class, his intellect and his contacts, he had spent eight and a half months trotting contentedly from one hospital to the next, always with the complicity of 'friendly or compliant doctors', given that he did not want to serve in a Fascist war. He, too, was scandalized by the flight of the King and the breakdown of the nation's most fundamental institutions but he read in these events the need to reforge social unity around anti-Fascism. *Repubblichini* he disdained as 'a frantic and unruly mob, violent by instinct and drunk with bombastic talk, who made violence and arbitrary acts their law in life, coming from the extremist parts of the Fascism that had been and from the most heterogeneous segments of society and of employment. Professional men without clients and a future, frustrated individuals lacking art or any real sense of belonging, soldiers of adventure who passed at a stroke from corporal to captain, . . . outcasts from every job and career.' Zaghi joined the Resistance out of a sense of repugnance for such unlovely people and, he recalled, out of a more general 'shame at past indolence' in his generation's tolerance of the dictatorship and 8 September.[76] Having developed close ties with the PCI, he was arrested at Ferrara in October 1944 but saved from execution when the local prefect intervened on his behalf, arguing somewhat speciously that Zaghi was still a public servant employed by the colonial exhibition in Naples, a job he could not resume given that city's 'liberation'. In prison in Padua, Zaghi cheered himself by reading the highly patriotic letters of Captain Vittorio Bottego, a pioneer of the national presence in Ethiopia.[77]

Nuto Revelli, an officer bitterly disillusioned by his experience of the Fascist failure to arm or protect its troops on the Eastern front,[78] took a different path. He was appalled by the chaos of 8 September which he endured at Cuneo. His fellows were utterly demoralized, looting anything they could lay their hands on, including 'trucks, food, blankets, office and hospital supplies'. On the market of those days, a truck, he remembered, could be swapped for a civilian suit. To escape this hell of selfishness, Revelli concluded that the only answer was to head for the hills and fight. In so doing, his aim was to restore the honour of the army (and the nation), always 'something greater and better than Fascism'. In their hearts, the peasantry around, he believed, agreed with him but cautiously, since there was not a family that did not anxiously await a boy lost somewhere at a front.[79] For the moment, Revelli despised all politics but his track headed leftwards and he eventually linked himself to the liberal socialist Partito d'Azione, heirs of the murdered Rossellis' Giustizia e Libertà movement.

Throughout 1943–5 the number of active partisans was not high, perhaps 4,000 in September 1943, 10,000 in January 1944, 60,000 in July, 100,000 in October and back to 60,000 in December 1944, surpassing 100,000 only in March 1945. About half were

communists. Factory workers were estimated to compose about 30
per cent, peasants 20 per cent (there could be rivalry and lack of comprehension between the two), artisans 11.7 per cent, students 11.2 per
cent, office workers 10 per cent and officers and other ranks 5.3 per
cent.[80] Out of a final official tally of 200,000, 35,000 were women[81]
but, whatever its legacy in the belated granting of female suffrage after
1945, the Resistance did not, in its liberated areas, allow women
to vote.[82]

According to one historian's tabulation, in the period from 1943 to
1945, 44,720 anti-Fascist fighters perished in battle of some kind and
9,980 in Fascist reprisals; another 21,000 were wounded.[83] The character of those who took up arms varied greatly, ranging from communists to conservative nationalists like Edgardo Sogno, who, after
the war, became a reactionary plotter against the Italian state.[84]
Within and between each political grouping and even within each partisan band there was little psychological or ethical unity. Fire-fights
between one formation and another were not unknown. Some bands
scrupulously endeavoured to pursue a policy of direct democracy, not
always an easy task under the imminent threat of death; others rallied
behind charismatic leaders of some alleged political persuasion.
Southerners adrift in the north, emigrants of a kind, were reported to
stick together against the imponderable northerners. News of raids by
the Anglo-American planes was unlikely to be welcome and some partisans were cheered by false rumours that an American city had been
severely bombed. Patriotic and even racist nostalgia for the lost Italian
empire could linger.[85]

Meanwhile, on the contested northeastern frontier, partisans split
over what might constitute an appropriate ethnic, strategic or ideological border between Italy and Yugoslavia. In this region, Italian
communists were likely to work with their Titoist Yugoslav comrades
and oppose national claims. At the Risiera di San Sabba in Trieste the
Germans, led by the mass murderer Odilo Globocnik, managed the
only extermination camp on Italian territory, liquidating up to 4,000
victims, most of them partisans, quite a number of whom were gassed
to death in vans. A territorial settlement in the region was not resolved
until 1954, with Italy hanging on to Trieste but losing Istria and the
ports further south. There were further border adjustments in the

west, where General De Gaulle snaffled some Alpine valleys for France but failed in his larger ambition to annex the Val d'Aosta.

Among the communist partisans, a hard-liner like Giovanni Pesce would never outgrow the brutal Stalinist recipe for conflict: 'a partisan was a fighter who never betrayed his companions . . . In every case, when a man became a potential danger to us, he automatically became an enemy' and could be eliminated at will.[86] Yet, after 1945, the PCI marketed itself as the humanist party of Antonio Gramsci and, for all the exaggeration and special pleading involved, there can be little doubt that the experience of surviving for a generation under a Fascist regime, committed by fair means and foul to root out communism, gave Italian communists a national and so Italian history which did separate them from the Russias that produced Stalinism. Certainly, among the 'Garibaldi brigades', as the communists with an eye to the past and the future called their forces, there were men and women open to humanist friendship and alliance with Catholics, socialists, democrats and other left-leaning anti-Fascists.

It was in part to answer the deepening communist domestic threat that RSI propaganda obsessively emphasized the regime's alleged commitment to socialization and so to a variety of fascist egalitarianism and an amplified fascist welfare state. Such rhetoric was destined to be treasured by post-war neo-fascists, anxious to be both radical and anti-communist. At the time, however, talk rarely produced much action or elicited much popular belief. In the regime's halcyon days, the ante-room to the Sala del Mappamondo in Palazzo Venezia had been a place where underlings, waiting for their moment with the *Duce*, plotted advantage over their fellows. Now a visit to Mussolini was a melancholy experience and a pall of pessimism about the present and future hung heavily over all, when, for example, in February 1944 the dim but enthusiastic Piero Parini commented to Dolfin that men and women of the people were reacting sceptically to the talk about socialization. 'Much interest or curiosity or diffidence among the workers,' he mused out loud. 'They do not believe in the decisive will of the government to make fully real the various decrees . . . Surprise, disorientation and hostility among the businessmen.'[87] As one historian has wisely concluded, the RSI was always destined to fail in its attempts to repoliticize a population Fascism had spent two generations depoliticizing and the Social Republic was always destined to collapse on the day German support was withdrawn.[88]

After all, neither the government nor the party was reliably in charge of pro-Fascist gunmen in the country at large. From their German imprisonment, between ten and sixteen thousand men were persuaded by the Nazis to enrol in each of the San Marco, Littorio, Monterosa and Italia brigades, which, after July 1944, resumed battle, either in Liguria against the partisans in mixed German and RSI groups or in the more dangerously stratified world on the northeastern frontier. Graziani's plans to construct a single national army were frustrated by this open German interference and, by January 1945, after the limited success of repeated efforts at conscription throughout the previous year, the Marshal accepted that the Germans would never treat Italian soldiers as their equals in combat.[89] He began moving towards retirement and that last sad refuge of a politician's vanity, his memoirs, where he explained that all his deeds had been inspired by self-sacrifice.[90] Much earlier, hopes of a prime role for the army in the Salò order had been challenged from within by the numerous semi-autonomous armed bands, operating under the aegis either of the party or of individuals brazen enough to act on their own behalf.

The most drastic step in this regard came in the summer of 1944, with the conversion of the PFR into the so-called 'Black Brigades' (*Brigate Nere* (BN)). Exactly what Pavolini, Farinacci and Mussolini envisaged can be disputed, with the *Duce* most anxious that any amendment in *repubblichino* practice or name should not derogate from his own power. As ever unashamed, Farinacci looked to his own political revival, was loud in his request that the new paramilitary version of the party punish any traitors they could find and was importunate in demanding that the BN display a prowess which might impress the Germans. When Paolo Zerbino succeeded as Minister of the Interior in February 1945, he endeavoured to fuse the varying RSI armed groups but without success.[91] The result was that the BN usually operated with a local purpose rather than a centralized one – there were cases here, too, of one gang firing on another. Throughout 1944–5 a slew of more or less 'Fascist' paramilitary forces stalked the land.

Pitiless in its tyranny was the so-called 'Ettore Muti Autonomous

Legion', named after the dead PNF secretary and established in Milan in March 1944.[92] Its leader, Francesco Colombo, once an aide of Giampaoli, the ruffianly *ras* of 1920s Milan, had then sought gain through running a protection racket over local shop-keepers but found sadly that his Fascist career did not prosper. In September 1943 Colombo had swiftly announced the revival of the squadrism of the happy early days of Fascism. Thereafter he and his not always fully disciplined men pursued an often vicious and bloody course of their own through the Salò Republic, backed financially by Farinacci and his business friends, formally rewarded by the Ministry of the Interior, mostly independent from Pavolini's BN and mocking Graziani's hopes of reconstructing a national army. The motivation of the Muti band's active core of some 1,500 men varied, with anti-Semitism, for example, not being a major factor.

The conflicting and potentially transitory philosophy of each of the armed groups was similarly expressed by Junio Valerio Borghese, the head of X-Mas, who, by 1944, was asserting ambitiously that his paramilitary force itself constituted 'the Italian state. Mussolini and the men of *Lago di Garda* are just folklore. We must free ourselves from them.'[93] From September 1943 Borghese had endeavoured with fluctuating success to open an independent wire to the German authorities and sought ruthlessly to use such contacts to justify the practical autonomy of himself and his gunmen. German intervention got him out of jail where Mussolini briefly put him in January 1944. In January 1945 Mezzasoma gave Borghese permission to publish a journal optimistically entitled *L'Orizzonte* (The Horizon). Its pages combined patriotic demands for the restoration of an Italian presence in the Adriatic with diatribes against the Vatican, Jews and Freemasons (Preziosi wrote for it).[94] The journal's sentiments were so unconfined that it was suppressed a month later, but during the last days of Fascism Mussolini remained neurotically fearful that Borghese was plotting a coup against him, while Graziani sought belated means to impose a national discipline over X-Mas, as over the other paramilitary forces.

The tale need not continue. When the Nazi-fascist rhetoric is set aside, what Borghese, the Muti band and the rest stood for was Behemoth,[95] the brutal chaos of Darwinian warlordism, familiar enough before and after 1945 in Third World societies where central government has collapsed. Contrary to some revisionist views of recent years, the men and women who served such forces were less likely to be bewitched adepts of a new political religion[96] than thugs anxious to kill and to profit, if doubtless often individuals for whom the choice of their brigade or political brand retained an accidental side. Although Salò propaganda labelled partisans 'terrorists', and perhaps some resisters did to some degree deserve the label, the more drastic practitioners of terror, only partially inspired by their ideological commitment rather than a lust to kill, were the members of these semi-independent Fascist gangs.

The brutality and unpredictability of these gunmen did not encourage fond receptions by any outside their immediate circle; indeed, their fighting spirit largely sprang from the fate of being hated and embattled by their surrounding society. Rather, when politics emerged from below between 1943 and 1945, it hinted at the survival of attitudes and practices that Fascism claimed to have destroyed. In March 1944 a series of strikes, engaging somewhere between 500,000 and 1,000,000 workers,[97] further convinced the German overlords, never fans of the radical strain in the new social-fascist economic line, that a firm hand was the best policy to be deployed with undisciplined Italians. The Nazis became steadily less hesitant in plundering what they could of the Italian economy and transporting its leavings across the Alps, where hundreds of thousands of Italian guest workers and POWs were still harnessed to the German war machine. For ordinary Italians, the breakdown of government and society was everywhere apparent. In 1945 the lira retained only 3.5 per cent of its pre-war buying power. In Bologna, already in the summer of 1944, the authorities were forced to admit to their dismay that 50 per cent of goods were sold at prices approved by the state and 50 per cent at the much higher ones, available on the black market.[98] By then, Mussolini had been warned by his police that 'the party out in the provinces is met with general unpopularity', even if, it was alleged, some respect for the Republic's government lingered.[99]

At around that time, Edoardo Moroni, the Minister of Agriculture, conceded resignedly that the central government could do little: 'each province works for itself'.[100] As on other occasions in Italian history, anyone seeking to understand what life was like for those away from the political spotlight is driven to local studies. In the province of Pavia, for example, the historian Giulio Guderzo has deftly portrayed the many ways in which different Italians endured this last stage of the war.

Those who lived in the city and those who resided in the country-side, whether on the Po plain or in the steep Apennines, had rejoiced in July 1943, not so much at the fall of Fascism – however weak the meaning of that ideology had been in practice – as at the outbreak of peace. After 8 September, with the state an 'escapee', the lineaments of a regional society can be traced. In November 1943 the Germans estimated that 2 per cent of the population had willingly associated themselves with the RSI and in February 1944 they wrote off support for that regime as trifling. Efforts in the summer of 1944 to conscript young men encouraged most to head for the hills, there to seek sanc-tuary or to join the Resistance. Despite pressure from Milan and Salò, in September 1944 only 3,000 fascists could be counted in Pavia, 500 of them being female. There were plenty of reasons to be apolitical. Rations supplied 150 grams of bread per day, 150 of meat and 1,200 of pasta per month, well below subsistence levels. The absence of salt supplies made it impossible any more to locate such staple products as cheese and salami.[101] Doubts deepened about each individual's and each family's ability to survive from this day to the next.

In this tumult, people from Pavia sought to make do amid a jarring anarchy with menace all about from *repubblichini* and from the Nazis and their mercenary troops. In autumn 1944 Waffen SS from Turkestan were deployed to suppress dissidence in some hill villages, where the locals believed that such troops, always described as *mon-goli* (Mongols), were brutally ready to rob and to rape 'women, girls and even tiny tots'. It was the Nazis, however, who in one hilly area, burned the harvest, committing an act regarded by local peasants as portending the apocalypse.[102] Felice Fiorentini, a seemingly respectable bourgeois ex-air force officer and director of a back rail-way, became the ferocious chief of pro-Nazi gunmen, the local war-lord. His ties with the Nazis, he maintained, elevated him above the discipline of Salò. Fiorentini spread murder about him; even a priest found his charity exhausted by someone who was so 'unbalanced' and so violent and unpredictable in his responses. Betrayed in the final days by his German friends, Fiorentini, whether to protect him from lynching or to exhibit his wolfish cruelty, was sent in a cage to Milan. He was executed on 3 May.[103]

In Pavia province, some villages, although exposed to German-led hostile raids, won for themselves an anti-Fascist autonomy. Their political tint could be communist – at the *paese* of Varzi there was time for the worthy establishment of a *circolo popolare di cultura politica* (popular club for political debate) – and could herald a new era of free expression.[104] Marxist internationalism of some type co-existed with an intense localism, while priests again proved key figures in trying to lead their parishioners through the valley of the shadow of death. For the most part, also in Pavia town, there was little zest for bloodshed, with people of all social ranks wishing the war away from their families and hoping against hope that it would soon end. Occasionally, however, the inhabitants of one *paese* would wreak revenge on another, claiming to be working in an ideological cause. Other more fortunate places survived their clear and present danger without the war ever visiting their streets.

In this tale encompassing the particular and the local, some general conclusions emerge. It may be that it was only in March–April 1945 that the citizens of city and countryside could imagine post-Fascist life in a polity somehow run by the anti-Fascist forces, united in the Comitato di Liberazione Nazionale (CLN, National Liberation Council). Yet, from September 1943, the theories and practices of restored Nazi-fascism had little purchase in Pavia. Socialization meant nothing and even Mussolini's charisma had long been dispersed. It was *Annales* historian Marc Ferro who argued that the October revolution in Russia was 'a fact before it happened', given that society in all the Russias had dissolved well in advance of the Bolsheviks' storming of the Winter Palace. The death of Fascism was similarly a story long foretold by the attitudes and actions of ordinary Italians. The recent tendency to re-examine the Salò Republic with charitable eyes should not conceal the fact that it failed in any serious sense to rule its Italy, whether in the first domestic duty of a state to provide food and justice or in the second great task of saving its people from the depredations of foreigners.

As the new year of 1945 commenced, the RSI was whimpering towards its end. In December 1944 Mussolini, ill, depressed, lethargic but intelligent enough to know that his war was definitively lost, came back to Milan to deliver one last public speech. The event has been romanticized among Fascist sympathizers as a moment of considerable weight. A recent sympathetic biographer believes that the *Duce*, understanding that he had been thwarted and overthrown by conservative and traditionalist Italy, genuinely preached the virtues of socialization and was greeted by 'spontaneous and deafening applause'. In this newly pious account, the Milanese treated their leader to 'a hero's welcome' when, subsequently, he toured war-damaged streets.[105] In reality, however, Mussolini had prated without conviction or depth about the way Italians could now assert their equality with their German and Japanese war partners and ritually condemned socialist internationalism and Judeo-Masonic cosmopolitanism.[106] Not far beneath the failing *Duce*'s phrases and beneath his reception, whatever may have been its appearance, lay desperation and emptiness.

In February 1945 the *Duce* tried one last Cabinet reshuffle, dropping Buffarini Guidi and replacing him with the socially and morally similar figure of ex-prefect Paolo Zerbino. But hardly had Zerbino been installed in office, with an agenda to reassert the authority of the state over the party, than rumours of corruption began to circle around him.[107] By now the main talk, apart from Mussolinian forays into writing a favourable history of himself or into arming 'social mines', which might disrupt good order after his departure, was about a heroic last stand, a death with some glory. Trieste, sentinel of *italianità* against barbarian marauders, was reluctantly dismissed as a possible site, since it was under de facto German rule. It was decided instead that the last withdrawal should be to the Valtellina, on the Swiss border. A medley of surviving radical fascists from Pavolini and Bruno Spampanato to Graziani and the clerical Biggini were ostensibly willing to contemplate a final glorious immolation.[108] No military resistance was ever organized, however. Mussolini and the other surviving Fascist bosses were captured by partisans well short of any final redoubt and, should the truth be admitted, were utterly unclear where they were going. The *Duce* was taken by Resistance fighters, near a village called Musso, while he was endeavouring to slink away from the nation and his past, concealed in a German greatcoat and on a German truck. He was shot the next day, 28 April 1945. There was no *Götterdämmerung* in this *Duce*'s end, just the banal last moments that failed tyrants have endured and have deserved to endure down the ages. Mussolini had long outlived even an aspiration to greatness and a friable Fascism, exhausted of credible meaning or social purpose, had long since crumbled into nothingness.

18

The Fascist heritage

During the late 1990s many erstwhile members of the Movimento Sociale Italiano (Italian Social Movement or MSI), Italy's most enduring post-war neo-fascist party, freshly labelled by their leader Gianfranco Fini as 'post-Fascists', evinced a stubborn desire to cling to their familiar history. Even if only 3 per cent of the party were willing to claim that Fascist dictatorship 'is still the best regime', more than 60 per cent believed that, 'apart from some questionable decisions, it was a good regime' and a meagre 0.2 per cent accepted that 'it was a brutal dictatorship'. In wider society, the responses to such questions were very different and yet fewer than 40 per cent of Italians agreed that 'brutality and tyranny' best summarized the Mussolini years, and between 1996 and 2001 the number of such critics only marginally declined (from 38.9 to 38.1 per cent).[1] In any case, throughout its public discourse, Berlusconi's Italy has sought to persuade its public that the sins of Fascism should now be forgotten. Fini, a youthfully ardent Fascist, now deputy Prime Minister and a pledged democrat of some kind, visited Israel, expressed heartfelt contrition about national responsibility for the Holocaust on a tour of the Yad Vashem memorial and in 2003 was hailed by the Jewish Defence League as its Man of the Year.

At around the same time Prime Minister Berlusconi told the press expansively that Mussolini had never killed anyone, joking crassly that those anti-Fascists pent up in *confino* on Ponza, Lipari or the Tremiti islands had actually endured a variety of 'holiday camp'.[2] Popular histories and biographies, their prose warmed with a romantic glow about the Fascist years, multiplied; even Starace's career was deemed worthy of revision. He was, a new biographer maintained, 'a loyal and fundamentally honest party official, generous in the extreme in his service of the idea in which he believed'.[3] According to another commentator, Ettore Muti, Starace's successor as PNF secretary, was a heroic soldier, bold sportsman and a Fascist who never seriously blotted his escutcheon as a man of honour.[4] Yet another popular historian, Marcello Staglieno, painted a friendly diptych of the happy collaboration between the Mussolini brothers,[5] although it was the English journalist Nicholas Farrell who wove the hope of resurrection into the title of his self-consciously revisionist biography of the *Duce*, entitled *Mussolini: a new life*.[6] At a much more austerely academic level, the internationally renowned historian Roberto Vivarelli was only one who found the late 1990s the ideal moment to 'come out' concerning his youthful past as a Fascist true believer to the last moment of the war. For his generation, Vivarelli attested: 'Fascism was a myth which had filled our life and to which we had fervently adhered.' When looking back on the history of his lawyer-squadrist and volunteer father as a Fascist in Siena, Vivarelli did not find much to regret, except the cruelty of his death. Instead there was admiration for an alleged paternal 'indomitable will' and sacrifice. Even though converted to democracy after the war, Vivarelli pronounced that he was glad to bear the imprint of his parents' teaching about patriotism and ethics. The German alliance (and Auschwitz), he explained away. As a youth, he now asserted, he had pigeon-holed the Nazis as allies positioned offstage; their anti-Semitism and its final solution had played no part in his Fascist understanding of past, present or future.[7]

No doubt the drift of this literature in large part reflects the contemporary cultural, economic and political strength of neo-conservatism and has parallels in many present-day societies. Similarly influential in powering such revisionism is a curtailment of historical interest in the general crisis of the Second World War. When its moral legacy to the present is confined to the planned global liquidation of the Jews by the 'mad' Hitler and all other aspects of the tyrannies of the 'locust decades' of the inter-war are obscured, then it is easy enough to forgive Mussolini and Fascism. In those circles where the 'black book' of communism rules unchallenged[8] or where the communist, socialist and liberal democratic beliefs of anti-Fascism are viewed as malign in their post-war effect and false in their reckoning with history, then the Fascist dictatorship might as well become another site for infotainment, a zany time enlivened by the movement and colour in its story.

A potential allure for advertisers and sentimental chronicle is one thing; positive ideological identification another. The fact that Mussolini and the Italian version of fascism have attracted political devotees into the third post-war generation must provoke some head-shaking. After all, in 1945 Italy – even if its Second World War had scarcely compared in devastation with the conflict on the Eastern front, in Yugoslavia and the rest of the Balkans or in China – was indeed battered by the two decades of dictatorship. 'Liberated' Naples was inscribed by both foreign and Italian journalists as the abyss of contemporary degeneration (while the people of the city were reported to yearn for the time when Naples had been a real capital and to blame Rome and so 'Italy' for their fate).[9] In Naples, it was said, people possessed 'no pride anymore, or dignity'; there could be found only the 'animal struggle for existence'. Scrabbling for food was what mattered and subsistence was won 'at the cost of any debasement or depravity'.[10] The ex-Fascist and now communist writer Curzio Malaparte, still seeking some kind of national revenge for the city's fate, penned an overheated narrative of a place of reconstituted virgins, where 'Latin civilization' used cunning as its last resort against the racial *mélange* of the American army and its ludicrous hope of implanting its naive and Puritan morality on Mediterranean shores. All, Malaparte contended, was summed up in a scene where liveried waiters, once spruce servants of the exquisite local aristocracy, had to appear deferential while feeding US officers with carrot soup, 'seasoned with vitamin D and disinfected with two per cent solution of chlorine' and spam, lying inert 'in purple slices on a thick carpet of boiled maize'. Never, claimed Malaparte, had he observed more profound contempt: 'it was the contempt – inscrutable, historic, deferential, serene – of the Neapolitan servant for the uncouth foreign master in his every shape and form'.[11]

From a different background but in not dissimilar vein, Benedetto Croce hoped that his prostrate country could rise again through its unique 'patrimony of spiritual riches', casting aside Fascism while simultaneously neutralizing the 'impurity' which afflicted contemporary culture.[12] Those who aspired to intellectual leadership were likely to summon up such ideas since, although Italy's casualty lists in the war had been relatively small, of the greater powers only France had to pull itself from the mire of an equivalent moral failure and in that country General De Gaulle had constructed himself as a shield behind which, for a generation, most French citizens hid the trauma of their memory of the conflict and disguised the national failure involved.[13] The nature of the Italian war effort, which combined diplomatic greed and military and social incompetence, had exposed to general view the contradictions and inadequacies, deeply etched into the nation-state. It was now that jokes circulated in every foreign mess about how the Italians only stayed on the same side in war from beginning to end when they changed sides twice. An Australian journalist expostulated that, 'by their sheer incapacity in war, the Italians have earned a reputation unique in the world. They are more dangerous to their allies than to their enemies.'[14] Anthony Eden, still nourishing his Italophobia, endorsed the views of his Foreign Office officials who contemptuously dismissed Italy's declaration of war against Japan in July 1945 as another 'stab in the back'.[15]

The Americans may have tried harder to be sympathetic but their experts were similarly vulnerable to painting the contemporary scene in hues coloured by past stereotypes. The American consul in Florence, W. W. Orebaugh, who was himself no stylist, complained about the way too many locals were 'contaminated with the corrupt methodology of nationalistic reasoning'. With their 'innate emotional instability' and 'passion for rhetoric and dialectics', the Italians, he concluded sadly, entirely lacked 'the American concept of cooperation and leadership'. Rather, he warned, enfeebled by the Fascist practice of welfare, they still dreamed of 'a state which provides everything to carry on a normal existence'.[16] In the post-war atmosphere, the new regime's sagacious changing of the pompous name of the road leading out of Rome towards the sea from the Via Imperiale (Imperial Street) to the Via Cristoforo Colombo (Christopher Columbus Street) was not enough to appease American suspicion that the Italians were a lightweight people.

Even to more literate commentators, Mussolini, rather than proving to the bitter end a 'Great Dictator', had perished in humiliation and dishonour, running he knew not where, impotent even at the task of discarding his annoying last mistress. During the Salò Republic, this feeble *Duce* had bathetically acted as a puppet dictator of the Germans and, well before July 1943, ill-health and the glaring contradictions and inadequacies of his regime had deepened his own patent spiral to despair. Any charisma once inscribed on to the *Duce*'s body and mind had leeched away, most observers concluded. So, at home, from 8 September 1943 and even more so from May 1945, Italians of whatever political persuasion turned to the urgent task of building a new state and girding it with new myths. In the aftermath of Fascism they must pave a road to a new society or, at a minimum, provide a wholly fresh gloss to national reality. For the majority of initial political leaders of this Republic, their new system must be anti-Fascist or nothing.

Yet contradictions soon surfaced. With the Cold War rapidly setting in, the fate of Italy's place in the world did not long preoccupy the peacemakers but they did remember to strip away the Italian empire, be it Fascist or Liberal. Democratic Italian negotiators complained bitterly about the loss to the nation and somewhat carelessly tagged the peace treaty a *Diktat*, a word that had played a pernicious role in inter-war European history.[17] In July 1946 Christian Democrat Prime Minister Alcide De Gasperi (he held the office in eight different administrations from December 1945 to August 1953) evoked another dangerously redolent metaphor when he bewailed the 'painful territorial mutilation' Italy was suffering.[18] He seemed therefore to agree with Bottai, who jotted into his diary sour words about the Allies being engaged in cutting 'living flesh' from the nation.[19] However, somewhere beneath their phrases, those who had taken over from the Fascists did not mind too much that the administration of Libya, Somalia and Eritrea was henceforth someone else's problem. It may or may not be true, as more recent patriotic historians have proclaimed, that 'no one' in Italy viewed the peace signed in February 1947 as 'just',[20] yet few in the new leadership repined at a destiny which had at last fully relegated Italy from the list of the great powers. Resuscitating a vocabulary familiar before 1914, De Gasperi and his friends were soon encouraging the resumption of emigration from Italian shores as a social necessity and safety-valve. Liberal economist Mario Einaudi depicted a manpower surplus as an inevitable national characteristic; this 'peasant country' was in reality a 'small nation' which could be relied on never again to disturb the international system.[21] Those of good sense should accept this fact and make the best of it.

In this and many other public ways, Italian history resumed a course which was indeed not alien to that pursued in the Liberal era before 1922. Croce's (self-interested) claims that Fascism amounted to no more than a parenthesis in the *longue durée* of national history had some basis in fact. It was true that on 2 June 1946 the monarchy was voted out and the Republic in, if in a fairly close fought and notably regionally skewed poll – the north preferred change, the south remained sympathetic to the King. But the Savoy dynasty had never fully convinced the Italian public of its appeal and purpose and few mourned when, a year later, Victor Emmanuel III died in exile in Egypt. Similarly, although the constitution resoundingly approved by Parliament in 1947 by 453 to 62 was marked by some radical-sounding clauses about the primacy of work and the need for social equality, the elections of 1948, won sweepingly by the Christian Democrats, enriched by Washington's favour, made sure that Italy cleaved to the American-inspired 'West'. The Marshal Plan had been sold on the enticing slogan: 'You [Italians] can be like us [Americans]', while Gary Cooper, Bing Crosby and Dinah Shore all seconded the anti-communist cause during the electoral campaign.[22] De Gasperi and his Christian Democrats simultaneously worked on a more traditional estimate of national preoccupations when they warned the electorate that, at the polling stations, 'God sees you, but Stalin does not'.[23] Such preaching might stem the reported tendency of some peasants to bracket in their minds San Giuseppe, Giuseppe Garibaldi and Giuseppe Stalin.[24] The staunchly anti-communist Church of Pius XII could rely not just on American largesse but also on help from the pious throughout the world. In Eire, for example, more than £50,000 was now collected and transferred to the coffers of the Democrazia Cristiana (DC).[25] The confirmation of the Catholic party's rule, which occurred in 1948 and which was to last two generations, ensured that any post-Fascist move towards economic and cultural equality would proceed haltingly, if at all.

Whether the government was in the hands of radicals or conservatives, eliminating the Fascist past was to prove not so simple a matter as it might initially have seemed. It was true that the second fall of Fascism in 1945 had prompted a wave of killings, notably in the so-called 'triangle of death' in the Emilia-Romagna. Whereas the collapse in July 1943 had been greeted with popular joy but few cases of vendetta, now a disputed number of Fascists were hunted to their graves, perhaps 8,000,[26] perhaps 12,000 of them (hardline Fascists came up with the absurdly gargantuan tally of 300,000). Although in August 1945 the crafty Communist party secretary, Palmiro Togliatti, had deemed it in the PCI's interest publicly to condemn continuing social violence, some of the killings had been at party behest. However, most acts were spontaneous, prompted by an array of motives which ran from a stubbornly nourished memory of squadrist murder and brutality in 1920–25 to a more immediate lust for financial and political gain, mingling histories sprung from both Italy and the Italies. The most controversial prey of the communist killers was the dissident Fascist Leandro Arpinati, who was eliminated at his family estate of Malacappa on 22 April 1945, just before his sometime *Duce*. Exactly what sort of payback was involved is contested, all the more because Arpinati, after his slide from political grace, had forsworn his Fascist past and, during Salò, opened contacts with the Resistance.[27]

A massacre at the northern textile town of Schio, when fifty-five Fascists died,[28] and in February 1945 the 'Porzus affair', when patriotic partisans fell victim to assault by a combined force of Italian and Yugoslav communists, were other brutal slayings, never altogether forgotten or forgiven thereafter. With the fate of Trieste and the northeastern border remaining unresolved until 1954 and with up to 300,000 nationals having been expelled from Istria and the other territories that passed into Yugoslav hands, many Italians have continued to regard events on the frontier as proof of the barbarism of their neighbours. They have reworked what had once been a visceral Fascist and nationalist belief in the moral inferiority of 'Slavs', by seeing the *foibe*, crevasses on the Carso above Trieste, as the tombs of countless patriots, cut down, whether Fascist or anti-Fascist, by the malevolence of the ancient enemy.[29] Border nationalism, sometimes drifting towards border fascism, survived and survives in the Republic.

In recent times, revisionist commentators have taken special pains to deplore the turmoil of the first months of peace, just as they have easily moralized about the execution of Mussolini and the subsequent outrages perpetrated against his corpse in Milan's Piazzale Loreto[30] or the liquidation of some fifty-two Fascist priests, thirty-three before Liberation and nineteen after it.[31] Murder is never to be condoned or written off as collateral damage. Yet a historian must take into account the violent context of an Italy which had lived through dictatorship and then a kind of civil war, made harsher by invasion, as well as enduring runaway inflation and the seemingly unstoppable spread of the black market. In July 1944, for example, 3.4 per cent of food in Rome was estimated to be gleaned by a suffering people through the official ration, 22.6 per cent from the free market and 74 per cent using extra-legal means. In this costly sanctuary charges were more than three times those set by the government.[32] Another relativity surfaces in the knowledge that, by 1946–7, Sicily, Campania and Calabria had resumed their traditional sad regional supremacy in the nation's tally of murders.[33] In the south, this killing from 'the Italies' at large was deemed 'social'. When it did possess a political side, it was likely that the victims possessed some identification with the left and were eliminated at the orders of landowners – in 1946, unaffected by purported Fascist egalitarianism, 1 per cent of them were estimated to own half of Sicily's land[34] – and Mafia-style bosses, who had a short and bloody answer to any flirtation by their fellow citizens with social democracy.

If the violence in Italy between 1943 and 1945 was a civil battle separating brother from brother and father from son, it is not surprising that the social dislocation then aroused took a while to settle. In the USSR, conflicts with some reflex from the Russian civil war had not been fully pacified a decade after communist 'totalitarianism' proved victorious. In any case, in that Italy, where history during the twentieth century moved with lighter tread than it did in the Russias, some Fascists soon found ways to survive the victory of anti-Fascism and to rally. Even while the world conflict continued, a political force came into existence in the liberated south, armed with an ideology drawing to some degree on Fascism and tapping into an electorate of those reluctant altogether to break from the recent past. On 27 December 1944 a new weekly hit the streets of Rome. It was entitled *L'Uomo Qualunque* (The Common Man) and bore on its masthead the slogan: 'Abbasso tutti!' ('Down with everybody!'). Its editor, the leader of the movement which took the paper's name, was Guglielmo Giannini, a writer and sometime radio comedian. The run of 25,000 copies of the first edition of *L'Uomo Qualunque* and an additional 55,000 copies, quickly reprinted, sold out. Giannini had exposed a vein of national opinion or at least one that beat hard in those parts of the country so far liberated by the Allies.

The UQ's chief had been born in Pozzuoli, west of Naples, in 1891, to an English mother and a Neapolitan journalist father of Apulian origin. Giannini quickly made a name for himself in southern journalism, mixing comic writing with depictions of high society. Long years of military service in Libya and the first World War followed, but in the post-war Giannini resumed his press career as the founding editor of the cinematic review *Cines*, film being a congenial arena for one of Giannini's ebullient and yet socially deferential nature. With the pseudonym 'Zorro' he also prospered as a song writer. Under the dictatorship he found no particular reason to quarrel with Fascism but did not actually take out a party ticket until 1941, although a little earlier, in a letter to Alessandro Pavolini, he had fawningly paralleled the *Duce* with Lorenzo Il Magnifico, each a master of all the arts. During the Fascist years, Giannini best embodied those southern fellow travellers who had an unFascist taste for quiet politically but knew that a minimal obeisance towards Fascist habits and preoccupations could allow their lives to remain unruffled in most circumstances.

In 1943 Giannini was not stirred to fight for the Fascism of Salò but became and, by most accounts, remained a convinced anti-Fascist. None the less, the Uomo Qualunque movement, with its mix of populism and a profoundly political condemnation of ideological politics, attitudes that can still earn electoral advantage, soon threatened to become a major force. Although Giannini had often been acerbic about the fatuities of nationalism, he now took to hailing Italy as 'Our Great Mother' and other once-Fascist phrases began to stud his speeches. Liberal and Marxist anti-Fascists he wrote off as deluded camp-followers of foreign ideas. Sales of *L'Uomo Qualunque* spiralled to 200,000 in February 1945 and to 800,000 six months later, with readers won over by the cheerful vulgarity and the aggression of what Giannini, with unrepentant language, called his 'verbal squadrism'. His targets were a promiscuous bunch including Togliatti, socialist Pietro Nenni and the dead dictator, mocked as the 'buffoon from Predappio'.

It was only now that UQ developed a political form, with Giannini taking the title of *fondatore* (founder) of a 'Front of the Common Man', while 'Zorro' came out of retirement to compose the movement's anthem.[35] UQ cells sprang into being more or less spontaneously in many parts of Italy but especially in the south. The spread of this 'anti-party' provoked alarm among Italy's mainstream politicians and Giannini was soon claiming that he was personally responsible for the fall in December 1945 of the radical democrat government of the anti-Fascist Ferruccio Parri.[36] As the months passed, UQ's base solidified on the right and in May 1946 *L'Uomo Qualunque* published a letter urging all those proud of the past to swing behind Giannini. In the November 1946 local elections, UQ did well, topping the poll at Palermo, Foggia and Lecce, entering coalition administrations at Bari, Catania, Messina and Salerno, while heading the opposition in Rome. The founder, however, lacked the staying power of a true politician, while his fondness for diatribes sometimes harmed his cause, for example when he excoriated the Big Business league, Confindustria, for cowardice and failing to display a real sense of class.

The political comet of Giannini had reached its zenith. De Gasperi and others in 1947 persuaded the Church that the DC was their party and managed to douse the dalliance between Giannini and the clerical interest. Meanwhile, Togliatti, as skilled as anyone at hard politics, trapped Giannini into calling him 'a gentleman, with a real heart and intellect' and then stepped back from their talks, with the greater political damage being borne by the UQ, shown up as no longer a limpid anti-communist force. Such Christian Democrats as the young Giulio Andreotti in Rome, already challenging Togliatti in flexibility and toughness, ruthlessly adapted the political language of the recent past to condemn a covert 'Giannini–Togliatti Axis'.[37] A few months earlier, Andreotti had joined Giannini in attacking the idea of too radical a purge of the once Fascist administration. In his canny plea for mercy the coming Christian Democrat chief was thought to express the views of Pope Pius XII himself.[38]

Fascists, too, now looked beyond Giannini in their attempts to map a future. In autumn 1946 Giorgio Almirante, born 1914 at Salsomaggiore and by the late 1930s a member of the editorial team of such ferociously racist and radical Fascist journals as *La Difesa della Razza* and *Il Tevere* and more recently *chef de cabinet* of Minculpop at Salò, sought ways to resuscitate Fascism. Almirante's first preoccupation was to merge the gamut of Fasci di Azione rivoluzionaria, which had revived in various parts of Italy, and marshal into a single cause the ideology being revoiced in a medley of small journals. Among those active in this Fascist revival were Giuseppe Caradonna, once the *ras* of Bari; Giorgio Pini, a journalist happiest when making a splash in Fascist high society who had been a belated Under-Secretary of the Interior after October 1944; E. M. Gray, the sometime paranoid Nationalist, who, during the 1930s, had been one of the more loud-mouthed and fanatical of radio 'megaphones' for the regime; and Arturo Michelini, a more moderate figure who best embodied a nostalgia for the alleged law and order and respect for 'social betters' of the Fascist years. Michelini had for a time been vice-secretary of the PNF in Rome but he was a career accountant and did his best to retail a careful image of himself. In December 1946 a union of these forces constituted the Movimento Sociale Italiano. Those in the know were said to understand that the real import of the letters MSI was that they stood for *Mussolini sempre immortale* (always immortal Mussolini) but the key word in the title was 'Sociale'. The MSI was meant to be the rallying point for those who had backed Salò.

Positive talk about the inheritance of the Repubblica Sociale Italiana and so of 'Fascist revolution' and the allegedly heroic and sacrificial Fascist part in civil war soon blotted out the jolly and now frivolous-seeming sounds orchestrated by Giannini. Faced with overwhelming assault on all fronts, the UQ crumbled. Members drifted away in dismay at the crudity or eccentricity of the *fondatore*'s style. Financial woes beset the movement and Giannini had to be rescued from imminent bankruptcy with funds from elements in the Vatican who still approved of him.[39] By the time of the 1948 elections, UQ could obtain only 3.8 per cent of the vote and five seats in the Chamber of Deputies. Its moment as a protest party was over.

The emergence of the MSI to challenge the UQ was proof that the commitment to an *epurazione* or purge of the residue of Fascism from Italian power structures, political, economic, cultural and legal, had rapidly faded in the evolving post-war context. Italy's lowly status as the lesser of the fascist dictatorships, not even the equal in remembered evil to imperial Japan, had been demonstrated in the ease with which the Allies relinquished any suggestion that Mussolini's major henchmen should be faced with a Nuremberg- or Tokyo-style trial. An analyst of this non-event has noted that the auspices of far-reaching change were poor from the moment that the liberating forces disembarked in the Mezzogiorno. This region, unreformed in its 'traditionalist, patron–client heritage, maintained an atmosphere where Fascist and conservative demarcations blurred and where attempts to pinpoint groups for punishment' were easily diverted, and was not an ideal 'testing ground for defascistization'. An invasion proceeding from south to north meant that, from the very beginning, those demanding retribution or drastic amendment were destined to be frustrated. Of the Allies, both the Americans, with Italian immigrant and Catholic votes to appease – no priest was ever jailed for his Fascism, although some were murdered in revenge killings – and the Soviets (and Togliatti's PCI), programmed by their combination of ideology and weakness to seek contacts and advantage wherever they might be found, failed to cauterize any Fascism which might remain in the body politic. The British, in 1940 affronted by what they viewed as Mussolini's jackal act in entering the war when they were down and stirred by their own traditional sense of racial superiority over feckless Italians, were readier to pursue a hard line. But, for them, Italy was a secondary arena and the punishment of Italians was not top of their agenda either.[40]

As a result, the process of examining those Fascists surviving in the Italian bureaucracy or in political or economic authority pursued a zig-zag course. In Naples, an Allied general was reported to have admitted, when asked why he was reliant for day-to-day administration on a notorious ex-Fascist, that the man was a scoundrel. But, he added, 'he's my scoundrel and he's going to stay'. When, after the liberation of Rome, the Italians took over the purge for themselves, its rhythm did not accelerate. On 27 July 1944, Prime Minister Ivanoe Bonomi, an aged social democrat possessed of a not altogether shiny record with regard to Fascism during its rise, instituted an Alto Commissariato per le sanzioni contro il fascismo (High Commission for sanctions against Fascism). The second clause of its mission statement promised the severest penalties, life imprisonment and death, for those guilty of having 'compromised and betrayed the nation' under the dictatorship. Heading the Commission was Carlo Sforza, another elderly politician reappearing from Liberal days, assisted by Mario Berlinguer, a Sardinian follower of Parri, and Mauro Scoccimarro from the PCI.

During an initial burst of activity, quite a few government employees were asked to account for themselves. Yet the knell sounded for few careers. In Naples, twenty-three ex-Fascists lost their jobs out of a total of 128,837 bureaucrats; in Palermo, five out of 26,636. All in all, among 277,701 state employees in the provinces liberated by the end of 1944, 143,781 had their cases reviewed, 13,737 were sent to judgment, 1,476 were sacked. There were moments of high publicity, for example during the trial of Pietro Caruso, the *questore* who had worked directly with the Germans in carrying through the Ardeatine caves massacre. Judicial proceedings were at once stained by the lynching of the subordinate figure of Donato Carretta, the ex-head of the Regina Coeli prison and a witness in the case, by a band led by Maria Ricottini, a Roman woman of the people bent on avenging a son executed by the Germans.[41] Carretta received his *coup de grâce* as he tried to flee across the Tiber. His corpse was removed from the river, carried by a shouting crowd of some 10,000 across Rome to his prison, hung and beaten there. The event was photographed.

The case was also complicated by the fact that the chief judge, Lorenzo Maroni, was an official who had served Fascism until 1943. In September 1944 Caruso was sentenced to be shot and died bravely, with even anti-Fascist observers reporting that his last cries to his executioners had been 'Viva l'Italia!' and 'Fire straight!'[42] Worse, public opinion as expressed in the press was doubtful about the capital penalty, at least for future cases. In part a 'wind from the south' had blown and brought with it that cynicism which said that no one ever really believed in political ideologies. To this depressed realism was added a sense of Catholic mercy and an acceptance that, through two decades, everyone who mattered had been some sort of Fascist. By January 1945 any purging of the country from Rome southward virtually ceased.

Nor were matters so different after April 1945 in the north, despite the more tender memories and more profoundly rooted political allegiances evident there and the viciousness of the civil contest between the partisans and the followers of Salò. To a great degree, the real purging was done through the largely spontaneous killings in the weeks just before and after the war's end. These murders were haphazard and brutal and alarmed the Allies, who took care to save some of their more distinguished prisoners. Marshal Rodolfo Graziani, head of Salò's armies, for example, was carried off from Milan's San Vittore prison to Algeria. That was just as well for Graziani, since San Vittore remained in chaos until 1946 and between 600 and 3,000 shootings were perpetrated there, many victims being Fascists.[43] The soldier and his rescuer, it was said, once in the North African sanctuary, enjoyed a 'bottle of very fine old cognac' together. Only in February 1946 was Graziani returned to the Italian authorities.

Some leading Fascists did go to trial, among them Attilio Teruzzi, with an appalling record in the empire but with a low profile under Salò. Teruzzi was sentenced to thirty years and died in prison in 1950. Guido Buffarini Guidi, one of the most prominent party chiefs under the Salò Republic, received the death penalty and was executed in a scene close to riot when he was dragged out of San Vittore and bashed before being shot.[44] As in the case of Caruso, the unseemly brutality of his fate prompted doubts over the whole purge. Trials did continue in 1945–6 (including eventually that of Graziani) but the capital penalty was applied sparsely, escapes were not unknown, commutations and amnesties increasingly common. Republican politicians of a humanist cast were anxious again to abolish the death sentence, while those who deemed themselves more realistic were appalled at the idea of a thoroughgoing critical legal examination of the relationship between Italian banking, business and law and their political masters under the dictatorship. By 1948 it was clear that many personnel in the national armed forces, police, bureaucracy, legal system, academic, intellectual and commercial worlds who had once been Fascists were to be permitted and were ready to serve the Republic. The structures of Italian civil society were not at a stroke made anti-Fascist.

Despite the new constitution, the law and more informal practice in many areas of life carried a powerful legacy from the Fascist past. The police code approved in 1931 remained in operation for decades after 1945. Plenty of ex-Fascist judges held on to office and seemed happy to visit the rigour of the law on any ex-partisans who came before them. It was typical that magistrates and diplomats collaborated in avoiding too rigorous a pursuit of German war criminals, who, between 1943 and 1945, polluted a number of Italian towns with blood as Nazi armies retreated north. By 1950 only five German soldiers were held in Italian prisons compared with 1,300 in France, 1,700 in Yugoslavia, 300 in Holland and 150 in Norway. The bureaucratic love for stasis, once thought to have leavened the Italian role in the Holocaust, now flourished in regard to the war-time massacres, with inactivity enhanced by the desire to work in European harness with Christian Democrat-governed West Germany. Messy discussion of the role of Salò fascists in acting as friends and allies of the Nazis was avoided as was any review of the partisans' own toleration of the sacrifice of civilian populations to their resistance. In January 1960 Enrico Santacroce, the Procuratore generale militare, thought he had buried the files of 695 Nazi-fascist crimes by locking them in a ministry cupboard in a process of *archiviazione provvisoria*, the allegedly temporary but actually permanent removal of material from public view. The archive only came to light in 1994 by accident during the trial of ex-SS lieutenant Erich Priebke for his role in the Ardeatine caves massacre.[45] There were to be many reasons why Italy's translation out of Fascism was a longer process than might have seemed likely in the heady first days of a democratic republic. Rapid change was not to be an obvious feature of the new regime, as is demonstrated in the statistic which reveals that, in the mid-1970s, almost three quarters of a million claims for war damage to housing stocks were still being processed.[46]

Thereafter the operation of the law in the Republic altered slowly. The permitting of divorce, confirmed in a referendum in 1974, and abortion, approved in 1981, was tardy and troubled, although the delays were due as much to Catholicism as to Fascism and also reflected, especially in the case of marital separation, the extreme caution in social reform of the Liberal regime before 1914. Perhaps the most lasting legacies of the dictatorship lay less formally in the way law was regarded in Italy. The state usually inched its way towards action while demanding a maximum of attention to legalistic detail and a studied deference to officialdom during the endless process. The crime of *oltraggio* (insulting a public servant) could always be invoked to defend worthy bureaucrats against impetuosity and impatience. In many senses, Italy inherited from Fascism the theory of a strong state and the reality of a weak one and the resultant intermeshing blocked change with a wall of words. As if in reflection, the Italian Parliament became a gold medallist in passing *leggine* (little laws). By the 1990s it was estimated that some 90,000 laws existed on national statute books as against 7,325 in France and 5,587 in Germany.[47] Respect for any of them remained problematic.

While covert currents were coursing through Italian society, the MSI was being confirmed as the post-war expression of what was called 'neo-fascism'. In the 1948 elections the MSI still failed to match UQ's tally, garnering only 2.2 per cent across the nation. This support converted to six seats, because the party amassed almost 70 per cent of its votes south of Rome. By the next national elections, the MSI vote rose to 5.8 per cent, an appreciable total in a multi-party system. For the following forty years the MSI became entrenched as the fourth party in Italian politics, behind the Christian Democrats, the Communists and the Socialists, with the peak of its attraction, until its reconstruction or rebranding in the 1990s, being reached in 1972 at 8.7 per cent. According to political scientist Piero Ignazi, the author of the most scholarly history of the party,[48] during these decades the MSI, emboldened by its relative success, acted as the guide of the European extreme right as a whole.[49] Although itself not fully legitimated as a player in the national political game, the MSI boasted resources and a status which could not be equalled by the other European neo-fascist groups, always a prey to schism, both ideological and personal, and occupying a world where, as the graphic saying goes, 'everyone wants to be *Führer*'.

Successful in its way, the MSI nevertheless was beset by its own divisions and dilemmas, most of which originated in the contradictions once present in the Fascist regime, now worsened by attempts to manipulate its history into an unarguable positive. One issue was regional. Throughout its existence the MSI remained essentially a southern party, so long as that term can be understood to embrace Rome. Catania, Reggio Calabria, Latina (the renamed Fascist model city of Littorio) and quite a few other southern towns were the MSI's fortresses and it never lost a following in Rome, where the bureaucrats of the suburbs clung to fond memories of their status under dictatorship.[50] By contrast, the MSI seldom earned much profile in the great industrial and commercial cities of the north. When, during the 1950s, it won majority support among students in Italy's still far from democratized universities, its most numerous fans were in Catania and Rome. For a time the MSI also dominated the University of Perugia, which still reflected its history as the creation of Mussolini's regime and a jewel of Fascist tertiary education.[51]

This identification with the centre–south and its society carried many ambiguities. Historic Fascism had been a northern movement and, with few exceptions, the cities and regions of the south only rallied to Mussolini after the March on Rome. Southern Fascists frequently seemed to possess a particularly opportunist reading of party ideology, delighting in patron–client networks and a more familial definition of the world than that favoured in the philosophy and oratory of Fascist modernization. Similarly the south was powerfully influenced by the Church and, to a lesser degree, by the monarchy, those two rival sources of charisma and historical meaning to that of the *Duce*, while Benedetto Croce's liberalism had also been rooted in Naples, nourished by powerful currents from the past of the elite southern intellectual enlightenment. Fascist racism was especially absurd in the south – German Nazis and Anglo-Saxon liberators agreed, as one of the latter put it, that the north was where you found the 'best type of Italians, very different from the southern stock' – although quite a few southerners were anxious to distinguish themselves from populations across the Mediterranean in ways that might include the 'racial'.[52]

More recent history also separated a neo-fascism in the southern regions from any to be found in the north. Sicily, Calabria and most of Apulia had, after all, been liberated before 8 September 1943. The civil war, with its brutal battles between 'left' and 'right', was fought out in great part north of Rome. The Salò Republic's propaganda campaigns about socialization and a renewed revolution had been targeted at a northern audience. Similarly, the PCI for many reasons had its own citadels in the north and so anti-communism, in the Cold War to be the most saleable of the ideas marketed by the MSI, made more direct sense in the north of the country than in the south.

Given these and other contradictions it was predictable that the first years of the MSI were characterized by infighting, manifest in a regular turnover of party secretaries. Giorgio Almirante held the post from 1946 to January 1950 and was seen to be taking the party in a leftist direction, although he preferred the word 'social', conceiving himself as a soldier of a Fascist revolution which had nothing in common with Marxism but rather surpassed it. Even after the 1948 elections Almirante was still inveighing against the *Diktat* imposed by the Allies and at first he refused to cheer Italian membership of NATO, eagerly approved by De Gasperi in April 1949.[53] Almirante pronounced the party fundamentally anti-capitalist, for a time rejecting any deals with monarchists or liberals. His faction's strident slogan was that 'there are three solutions – Russia, the United States or [the] MSI'.

The Cold War, however, was making anti-communism the first plank of any political force with ambitions on the right (or centre) in Italy as elsewhere and Almirante was forced to step down from his secretaryship to be replaced by the more pliable Augusto De Marsanich. Born in 1891 in Rome, De Marsanich had been an important if second-rank figure throughout the dictatorship, near to Bottai. He had published in *Critica Fascista*, was promoted to be Under-Secretary of Communications from 1935 to 1943, while remaining long-time head of the PNF's legal office. De Marsanich, unlike Bottai, had adhered to Salò, working there only indirectly in politics, being charged instead with the management of Alfa Romeo and the Banco di Roma. In 1950, with his connections to bureaucracy, business and Church, the new secretary speedily steered the MSI back towards the more orthodox right, while not forgetting to speak up both for those who had fought for Salò and for ex-legionaries of the MVSN. De Marsanich's parliamentary bargaining skills and the new anti-anti-Fascist mentality swiftly ensured that these two groups were granted government pensions.

De Marsanich also curried favour with Pius XII's Church, zealously anxious to engage in an anti-communist crusade, and in April 1952 the MSI won considerable Vatican backing for the prospect that, in the local Rome elections, it should campaign in full alliance with the DC and the monarchists. The leadership's contacts with the Church also helped to ensure that the 'Scelba Law', passed in June 1952 and banning a reconstituted Fascist party, was never applied to the MSI. Eleven months later, Andreotti, by now a major figure among Christian Democrats in Rome and still very near to De Gasperi, publicly embraced Rodolfo Graziani at his home in the Sabine hills near the capital. The retired Fascist general and war criminal, amnestied in 1950 from a nineteen-year term of imprisonment, had been elevated to the Honorary Presidency of the MSI. Similarly favouring a clerical path was ex-*quadrumvir* and man of 25 July, Cesare De Vecchi, who returned from a decade's exile in South America briefly to assume a role in the MSI. Despite the party's electoral successes and its gaining of a place in a host of local coalition administrations, factional conflict bubbled and in October 1954, Arturo Michelini, described as 'a skilful organizer and a clever mediator in the roaring jungle of the MSI',[54] replaced De Marsanich and reinforced the party's moderate and southernist line. Michelini remained in office until his death in June 1969. Under his guidance the party acquired its own trade union organization (CISNAL, the Confederazione Italiana Sindacati Nazionali Liberi), its own daily paper (*Il Secolo*) and its own youth and university associations (Giovane Italia and the Fronte Universitario di Azione Nazionale).

The nature of Michelini's MSI was best displayed in the politics of 1950s Naples and its ship-building magnate mayor, Achille Lauro, technically a monarchist and a chief of the Partito Nazionale Monarchico (PNM) but also reliant on MSI backing in 1952 to win office (it was Michelini who urged him forward). Thereafter Lauro delighted to work in harness with the neo-fascists. Born in 1887 into an already wealthy family, Lauro had multiplied his fortune under Fascism and then cynically denied the dictatorship in 1943 (although he did serve twenty-two months in a British prison as a possible war criminal).[55] Rebuffed both by the PCI and the DC when he tried to join their ranks, he found the UQ more accommodating and for a while helped finance Giannini's group. When the UQ began to stagger, Lauro switched to one of the monarchist factions, knowing that his city in 1946 had rejected the Republic (only 20.1 per cent of Naples' vote went to it).[56] According to a sociologist who investigated Neapolitan politics, the PNM's backers saw the world in simple terms, ones that encapsulated a southern yen for the idea of government by a 'strong man'. As one voter put it in words which he might once have fixed on Mussolini rather than Victor Emmanuel III: 'I am for the King who thinks only of himself and so does good for the citizens. The state nowadays is made up of too many people who want to eat out of the plate where only one ate before. I think that under the King everything was all right; nobody was too greedy and stealing was not too obvious . . . I and my father were always poor but under the King you knew whom you were supposed to obey. Now they're all talking and you don't know whom to vote for.'[57] Michelini's MSI, in other words, gave greater weight to populism and anti-communism than to the more drastic social revolutionary or racist-expansionist ideas of the Fascist past. The fuzziness of its stance was meant eventually to result in its legitimation as a respectable part of the national right, worthy to participate not just in local and regional administrations in the south but potentially a member of a national coalition.

The zenith of this trajectory occurred in the summer of 1960 when the Christian Democrat Prime Minister Fernando Tambroni was on the point of granting the MSI a place in his new government, until frustrated by a massive hostility expressed in northern Italy about the idea and by widespread and violent demonstrations which spread from Genoa, where the MSI planned to hold a congress. The so-called 'Tambroni affair' ensured that, for another twenty years, the MSI would be the 'excluded pole' of national politics, whatever its influence in local matters or, more covertly, in the secret service, police and important sectors of the bureaucracy, law and business. In 1961 Clare

Boothe Luce, during the 1950s the ambassador of the Republican US administration, found a somewhat surprising historical exception to her country's usual view that the business of business was business: 'There can be no question that Mussolini's "corporate state" made some welcome and much-needed reforms and, in its initial days, revived a sense of individual hope and public purpose in the new nation,' she pronounced.[58] Boothe Luce as ambassador had acted as the patron of rightists who dominated the various branches of the Italian secret service. Their control had been confirmed shortly after the 1948 elections when ex-partisans were purged, while sometime Fascists, with service in Italian East Africa, territories in the Balkans occupied during the war or more straightforward domestic careers under the dictatorship, returned to employment.[59]

Yet, for all the condoning of the new right from across the Atlantic and for all Michelini's calmness and negotiating skill, the MSI did not settle down to become another reformist conservative party. In many of its branches and in its more loosely associated extra-parliamentary groups, fascist fervour lingered. The most public face of this continuing radicalism was Almirante. As a young racist, Almirante had been sure that journalism must be removed from its Jewish control, affirming that right-thinking Americans agreed with his view of the world, having both in their past and in their ideal future battled for white civilization against its 'black' and 'yellow' enemies.[60] Now Almirante continued to emphasize that neo-fascism must pride itself on being an 'alternative to the system'.[61] When, in 1969, he returned as party secretary, a post which he was not to relinquish until 1987 (he died in May 1988), Almirante promised a more ideological course than that plotted by Michelini, praising the extremists of Ordine Nuovo (New Order), for example, as the 'military wing of the silent majority'.[62] Office quickly tempered such verbal radicalism, however. Almirante's MSI mostly accepted the rules of the parliamentary game in a way not dissimilar from the party's behaviour under Michelini, while its electorate continued to be southern and petit bourgeois in regional and class character.

Beyond Almirante but very likely in continuing contact with him and his two-faced policy of 'the cudgel and the double-breasted suit',[63] lay a loose constellation of more fanatical bands, many of whom were committed to the terrorist overthrow of Italy's democratic institutions. Most prominent among their leaders were Julius Evola and Pino Rauti, each in his own view an intellectual. Evola, insistent that he and fascists like him composed a new aristocracy, pledged to put an effete bourgeoisie in its place.[64] Evola, only a teenager when Mussolini took office, had become a highly fertile philosopher of race during the Fascist years, writing frequently for such organs as *La Difesa della Razza* and *La Vita Italiana*. His own cloudy mind was easily drawn to conspiracy theory. In 1932 he had found sense in the manic world-view of the German general Erich von Ludendorff, even though Evola deplored the Protestant Teutonic claim that Catholic Rome was a natural ally of the communists of Moscow, the Free-masons of Paris and the Jews. Actually, he contended stoutly, Fascist Italy was the firmest enemy of such malignly occult forces.[65] The Nazis, he counselled, should set aside that materialism, which tended to distort their racism, prompting them to silly beliefs about Aryans, and reach a more religious comprehension of racial being.[66] They must allow Fascism to overcome some of the over-simplifications and narrowness of Nazism.[67]

The onset of the Ethiopian war and the sanctions campaign convinced Evola that the purblind materialists were really the British, whose empire was based on force and was thus destined to lose out to a Fascism which could rally in its cause the 'spiritual, the ethical, the hierarchical and the supernational', those qualities which had once girded imperial Rome.[68] By the end of the decade, Evola was sure that Freud[69] and psychoanalysis and Einstein and his theories of relativity were part of a Jewish plot to undermine the respectable and respectful social order.[70] Even though, in the hope that there was something deep in his ideas, the Nazis translated Evola,[71] he continued to nourish doubts about Hitlerian racism, separating himself from its pseudo-science and insisting that race was a spiritual matter and that humankind was most moved by myth.[72]

His differences with the Nazis could vanish easily enough. When racial legislation was being drafted in Italy, Evola evinced sympathy for the frequent patriotic traditions of Italian Jewry and yet, he stated, all Jewish roads really ran to Jerusalem and 'the Jew must cease to be Jewish. This is the real dilemma.' Jewish immorality, he warned, lay at the root of all crime.[73] None the less, Evola, despite rejoicing in the prospect that Nazism and Fascism were marching together against their overt and covert foes,[74] kept to an idiosyncratic course. Surviving the war, Salò and the ineffectual post-1945 purge, Evola lived on to 1974. He cheerfully reshouldered the task of being the most pertinacious advocate of a fascist racism, owing more to the vaporous world-view of Corneliu Zelea Codreanu, 'martyred' Romanian leader of the 'Legion of the Archangel Michael' and other East European theorists (at least in their own minds) of a racism of the soul. In the post-war period, Evola liked to avow that '<u>between the real Right and the economic Right, there is no identity of views, but rather a totally clear-cut antithesis</u>' [sic], while admitting that, when reviewing the story of Mussolini's regime, a thoroughly spiritual fascist must acknowledge a record speckled by 'lights and shadows'.[75] Mussolini, Evola conceded, was actually a crude thinker and his regime, he charged, had regrettably lost its revolutionary élan under the weight of its bureaucratization.[76]

Pino Rauti, a generation younger than Evola, was born 1926 at Catanzaro. He preferred history to philosophy[77] but was similarly insistent that 'Fascism entailed revolution: in political institutions, in economic and social structures and in its conception of life.' Convinced that 'great men' embodied their national stocks (*stirpi*), Rauti was sure that Mussolini was neither opportunist nor buffoon but rather a prophet whose words must eventually register. Mussolini's ideas were potentially momentous ones but, always fighting on two fronts against capitalism and communism, the *Duce* and the Europe that identified with him had been led to a terrible defeat, which dogged his successors. During the prelude to the world conflict, Mussolini had been forced to occupy himself with foreign policy and so delay the revolution he, his ideology and his true followers wanted above all. 'Fascism lost the war – and with Fascism, Italy lost it and with Italy so did Europe – not because the regime was imperialist, expansionist and aggressive but because it was so little imperialist, so meagrely expansionist, so timidly aggressive.' 'The only really serious weakness of the Fascist regime was that it was insufficiently Fascist,' Rauti explained. Contrary to legend, he pronounced, Italy had 'fought well' for its forty months of war to September 1943 and, with its Nazi ally, had stoutly projected 'a change of the guard at the helm of the white race: here was the ultimate meaning of the Second World War'.

The best historical moment for Fascism and the source of its richest legacy to the present, Rauti naturally maintained, was the Social Republic. Then, in heroic battle with the monarchy and the old order, Mussolini had experienced 'a time of absolute and elevated serenity'. For its crusaders, the RSI incarnated 'a <u>choice</u>: an ethical, political and intellectual, choice'. In its fiery crucible, 'real <u>new men</u>' had been forged from the masses in the way Fascism had always planned.[78]

In 1956 Rauti, after the defeat of a faction with which he had collaborated for a while with Almirante,[79] withdrew from the MSI, preferring to work with such paramilitary bodies as Ordine Nuovo (New Order) and Avanguardia Nazionale (National Vanguard), avoiding party discipline and keeping himself uncorrupted by the compromises of the MSI, led by Michelini. In 1969, with Almirante's return to the secretaryship, Rauti brought himself in from the cold and he remained the most radical voice of the party until his own brief and unsuccessful tenure as secretary in 1990–91. He survived thereafter as the leader of the rump Movimento Sociale-Fiamma Tricolore, still purist in its defence of Nazi-fascism.

The tribulations confronting Rauti as he moved through his political life multiplied among the more nebulous and revolutionary Fascist groups outside the formal control of the MSI. Here a modicum of unity was provided by the existence of a sort of fascist International, with some ironical inheritance from the lacklustre organization briefly patronized by Mussolini in 1933–4 but, in most ways, in uneasy parallel with the other, more established and more useful world-ranging institutions of the contemporary world. Dictators in South America, Spain, Portugal and Greece and the apartheid regime in South Africa usually looked favourably on such forces, as did segments of the American far right, ready to bless terrorists so long as they were reliably anti-communist. The occasional rightist academic proffered a gloss of scholarly acceptance, with one argument being that Fascism had not been killed in the Second World War but rather was the unacknowledged guide to developing societies.[80] Some neofascists disliked such globalization and saw their task as to rally Europe – in the 1950s there was talk of a 'European Social

Movement'[81] – in a common crusade against the USA, the USSR and the uppity Third World.

Typical of those who inhabited this semi-legal political space was Stefano delle Chiaie, the self-consciously charismatic leader of Avanguardia Nazionale and a man who spent a lot of time outside Italy as one of the Latin American contacts of Klaus Barbie, the SS 'Butcher of Lyon' and chief of a network of Nazi-fascist refugees.[82] For such new generation fascists, their ideology had three key characteristics. They were racists of a generic kind but with anti-Semitism always providing the first base of their prejudice – in 1957 one of Mussolini's nephews was arraigned for boasting about how his sort had once 'burned Jews in the furnaces'.[83] Such men were violent, often for violence's sake, unashamed to be 'terrorists of the right'. They were also 'revolutionaries', committed to destroying the current system. In this amalgam, the inheritance from Mussolini and the Fascist dictatorship was tenuous. In their not-so-secret hearts, this variety of neo-fascist found their historical inspiration not in the *Duce* but rather in Adolf Hitler. They lusted to match his purism, purpose and what seemed to them the technological beauty of his death, so much more dramatic and meaningful in their understanding than was Mussolini's sordidly traditional demise. If other models were sought from the inter-war period, then Codreanu and José Antonio Primo De Rivera, the 'poetic fascist' killed at the beginning of the Spanish Civil War, were their heroes and the slogan 'Long live death' their own. The only way Mussolini could become their inspiration was if his trimming and contradiction could be obscured and he could be read as a lifetime fanatic and revolutionary. There was quite a bit of irony in the continued use of the label 'Fascist' to define such people, when Nazi or Nazi-fascist (implying a broader social and cultural radicalism than that approved by the incorrigibly petit-bourgeois Hitler) was the more accurate term. Perhaps the durability of the Italian word was the result of their Marxist enemies' adoption of it. 'Fascism' rather than Nazism had been depicted as the foe in the USSR's 'Great Patriotic War', the Stalin regime's version of a Second World War.

In so far as the national history of Italy was concerned, a significant memory could best be fixed on the days of squadrism from 1919 to 1925 or on the Salò Republic. Even if the *Duce* was by 1943 ill, depressed, tardy in action and a prey to choices he preferred not to make, the word '*sociale*' could migrate from its ambiguous deployment then into an apparently numinous present and future. Fascists were the slaves of neither capital nor labour, precisely because they hoped for a 'social alternative', that is policies that would follow a fascist third way. In 2004, after she found herself unable to cope further with Fini's criticism of the *Duce*, Mussolini's granddaughter Alessandra bathetically fought the European and administrative elections as the *ducessa* of a tiny group calling itself Alternativa Sociale.

Questing too hard for philosophical consistency and seriousness among the extra-parliamentary neo-fascists is a fruitless task. For many such people, their political pleasure and any meaning contained in it began and ended with violence. The punch-up on this campus or that or in some area of a city proclaimed a 'no-go' area, the fire-bombing of the meeting places of 'reds', gays or 'racial inferiors', the caressing of a pistol or bomb, gave definition to the lives of quite a few neo-fascist youths.[84] So, too, did a masculine congress with a football crowd on the terraces. In this setting, a lexicon of fascism, often couched in explicit racism, became and remained[85] part of the ritual for many fans, although it was rare for their behaviour to carry serious political meaning beyond a dumb sense of alienation. The MSI more directly courted the fantasy movement among the young, perhaps sensing in it a savagery and a racism that could be reconciled with fascism. Certainly in the late 1970s the party youth organizations began holding what they called 'Hobbit camps', social occasions, they boasted, where 'anything' could be discussed.[86]

More bloodily, when Italy entered its terrorist decade in the 1970s and endured the so-called 'crisis of the Italian crisis', rightist terrorists led the way. Between 1969 and 1975 sixty-three out of ninety-two assassinations were perpetrated by the right, with one analyst reckoning that neo-fascists were responsible for 83 per cent of political violence during those years. In the second half of the 1970s, most notably with the kidnapping and murder of the Christian Democrat leader Aldo Moro, the far right was outdistanced in murder by the far left, although the bombing of the railway station at Bologna, long a PCI redoubt, on 2 August 1980, when eighty-five died, was a fascist crime.

Some scanned further horizons. In 1964 General Giovanni De Lorenzo[87] and in 1970 Prince Junio Valerio Borghese – since 1968 head of the so-called Fronte nazionale rivoluzionario, aspiring to rally extra-parliamentary neo-fascism under his leadership – plotted coups against the Republic. Their plans for the overthrow of democracy were nourished by ongoing contacts between the far right and elements in the Italian secret service, and opposed any final legitimation of the PCI.

Yet the PCI never did head a national government and so speculating about what might in the circumstances have turned into a new civil war is a pointless exercise. In the actual history of Italy, the Moro murder and its aftermath signalled a swing away from the left and entailed a new scepticism about such forces' own key historical myth, that of anti-Fascism.[88] With the collapse of the Soviet Union and its accompanying 'end of history', the Italian Republic began what, more than a decade later, is a still incomplete task of reworking its institutions, myths and history. All the political parties that had conditioned so much of national life since 1945 now dissolved and took new names.

Among the neo-fascists the apparent winner in this rebranding process was Gianfranco Fini, who, by the new millennium, was installed as the most impressive figure on the national political right. Although his family nourished the memory of a cousin, hunted down and murdered by partisans in 1945, Fini, born 3 January 1952 (the 27th anniversary of Mussolini's assumption of the dictatorship), was educated in the post-war world. His father was a prosperous Bolognese manager of the local office of Gulf Oil. Fini claims that his own political choice was made in 1968, when he rejected calls from his classmates at the Galvani *liceo* to strike; soon, they have recalled, he was a sort of leader of the opposition, given to browsing ostentatiously during school breaks through the pages of *Mein Kampf* and Mussolini's *Opera omnia*. Quickly thereafter, Fini, having moved with his family to Rome in 1971 to attend university, where he took a degree in education, was rising through the MSI's youth organization. In 1977 he became its chief, beating off the challenge from Mario Tarchi, a follower of Rauti, even though his foes within the party continued to use the free discussions of Hobbit camps to deride him.[89] Fini's victory in the party youth bureaucracy, occurring at a troubled period in the Almirante secretaryship, ensured that the MSI leader viewed Fini as his dauphin. At thirty-one Fini won a seat in Parliament and in 1987 replaced his protector as MSI secretary. By that time, the auspices for the MSI's coming in from the political cold were good, with Italian journalists coining the perhaps inappropriate term of *sghettizzazione* (de-ghettoizing) to describe meetings between Almirante and the socialist Prime Minister Bettino Craxi in 1983–4.[90] Fini's conflict with the more ideological side of neo-fascism was resolved in 1990–91, with the disastrous Rauti secretaryship and Fini's own reclaiming of the MSI leadership. The way was now open for Fini to design a new mission for his electorate in the post-communist world and become a 'post-fascist'.

Fini's step beyond fascism was not immediate. Well into the 1990s he did not demur when party members hailed him as the *Duce* or burst into renditions of 'Giovinezza' or 'All'armi, siam fascisti'. On public occasions the young party secretary took pains to hymn Mussolini for saving Italy from communism in 1922 and to laud his foreign policy. In March 1994 he still argued that Mussolini had been 'the only Italian statesman of the century'. Two years earlier, he had contended that, when history writing reached an appropriate serenity, it would want 'squares and monuments' throughout the country to take the *Duce*'s name as presently they did those of Cavour, Garibaldi and Mazzini. He was still sure that he and other members of the MSI could never deny 'our roots'.

Yet what Fini was engaged on was indeed a reworking of history, which, by the time he was serving as Berlusconi's deputy, a post he shared in an unlikely manner with Umberto Bossi, charismatic leader of the regionalist Lega Nord, had been polished into a fine recipe for further political success. Fini's promotion in November 2004 to be Minister of Foreign Affairs made it likely that this interpretation would become the established one for official Italy. Some line countering Fini's may eventually emerge but it is hard not to believe that the new minister, like many of his predecessors, will appoint clients and friends to the ministry and ensure that his world-view will last beyond the term of his appointment.

What, then, was this new history? For Fini, as for Berlusconi, historic Fascism, that linked with the name and image of Mussolini, was now confined to a past with which contemporary Italy had few obvious bonds. Debate about it could be left to historians or, better, to the entertainment industry which could focus on the bright lights of the inter-war period and avoid too much moralizing. The only real problem with the Mussolini dictatorship, it now appeared, was its alliance with Hitler, the 'criminal' and 'madman',[91] and thereby its indirect part in the tragic murder of the Jews. Fascism's use of weapons of mass destruction, its suppression of parliament, unions, the press and women, its corruption of the law, its racist killing of Arabs, blacks and Slavs as well as Jews, its hypocrisy and failure, its pre-emptive wars, with their major collateral damage, none mattered, none was worthy of continuing historical review. For Fini and those of his supporters who had really sloughed off their Fascist pasts, only the brave new world of the future was significant.

There were some problems with this adaptation. What did Fini and his post-fascists really make of Silvio Berlusconi, with his populist but ageing anti-communism, his crudely trite patriotism and his curious background as a businessman who had flourished mightily in legally dubious association with a still interventionist state? Some commentators have portrayed the Prime Minister as a revived Mussolini, another authoritarian patrimonialist,[92] but, for a Fascist purist, it was not a convincing picture. What, too, did Fini's followers make of their ally Bossi, with his plans for regional autonomy and a weakening of centralized power? What did they make of globalization, a process likely to harm the economic position of the relatively uneducated and frequently southern backers of the new Alleanza Nazionale (AN)? Was it not globalization, for example, which had converted Italy from a country of emigration to one of immigration, a place where post-fascists were aghast at the infringement of the national 'colour' and 'stock'? There are no obvious answers to these questions. Perhaps that absence is an appropriate place to end a history of the practice of Italian Fascism. Fini's opportunism and cynicism in his studied egress from his Fascist inheritance may make him a worthy heir of Benito Mussolini and many other bosses in inter-war Italy, who, when their lives are subject to historical analysis, demonstrate that, to understand the era of Fascist politics and society, a reader must go beyond Fascism. Neo-fascism, like Fascism itself, turned out to be a matter not well explained merely by leafing through the works of the movement's intellectuals. Its practice bore, and bears, a fractured relationship with its theory. Its future will not have a simple and single past.

Conclusion

This book began with Adolf Hitler but he has seldom overtly troubled its pages since. Yet the picture that has been drawn of the patchiness of Fascism's intrusion into the everyday lives of all manner of people under Mussolini's regime has demonstrated that clichés about Nazi rule ill accord with the reality of how Italians lived their dictatorship. Following what can be called the vulgar model of Nazism, it might be expected that any account of a totalitarian regime would need to focus on a fanatical or 'mad' leader who intruded his fundamentalism into every nook and cranny of his subjects' minds. According to this simplistic version of the past, the Italian people, utterly alienated from their class and other social identities, wiped clean of their roots and histories, should have surrendered their individual and collective characters to the dogmas of their leader. Programmed to 'believe, obey and fight', Fascist Italians, to a man and a woman, should have become Mussolini's willing executioners, automatic adepts of a new 'civil religion' and, therefore, crusaders in every bloody task their leader's insanity and the malignity of his ideology, his party and state might suggest. First and foremost, they should have looked to impose a final solution on the 'Jewish problem'.

In fact, however, this book has demonstrated that being Italian between 1922 and 1945 was not like that. Even Fascism's deplorable racism was, for the most part, as focused on Arabs, blacks, 'Slavs' and fellow Italians as it was on Jews. As Salvatore Lupo, the author of a recent penetrating analysis of politicking during Mussolini's ascendancy, has argued, this dictatorship was not a place where ideas and rhetoric meshed neatly or inexorably with practice. Rather, Lupo maintains: 'the tales of anonymous letters, of secret dossiers, of

complex plots and scheming, organized by competing factions and
different and competing authorities, prove that a sense of loyalty to a
group, faction or set of clients survived [under the regime] and managed to find for itself a role in the new politics which was not different from that which it had held in the old'. The essence of Fascist party
history, he concludes, is to be sought in the contrast between what it
was and what it ought to have been.[1]

Nor does this perspective vary greatly when, as has often occurred
in this book, attention switches further down the social scale, either
to examine the careers of rough and tumble local Fascists or to review
the behaviour of workers and peasants, those men, women and children, who, whether consciously or not, tried to keep modern ideology
confined to one sector of their minds. Whether they were Roberto
Farinacci, the *ras*, or Lorenzo Boccaccio, the builders' labourer,
Giuseppe Bottai, the party intellectual, or Angelo Rossi, the itinerant
musician and provider of a village news service, Margherita Sarfatti,
the *Duce*'s Jewish mistress and woman about town, or Rosalba
Valente, the deluded prophetess of the Gargano, most Italians in this
story had their activities indelibly coloured by the regime to which
they were subject. From 1922 to 1945 (and beyond) Fascism was in
some sense an inescapable part of being Italian. Even peasants, still in
many cases automatically suspicious of all modern ideologies and
indeed all modernization, could not reliably repel its intrusions. Yet,
throughout the generation of their experience of this dictatorship they
and other Italians continued to draw their identities from, and craft
their behaviour around, other strands of their lives, woven from their
multilayered comprehension of culture, class, family, gender, region,
age, religion and a host of other factors, whether stable or shifting.

At its most strident, Fascism declared that it would amend the language Italians spoke, control the way in which its devotees held and
used their bodies (be it for leisure or reproduction), and temper the
very content of their souls. So much was ambition or theory. But
pigeon-fanciers, bee-keepers, philosophers of play and the toy, intellectuals in many fields, priests, the royal family, Arturo Bocchini and
his secret police, *carabinieri* in the provinces, each of these individuals or groups sought to wrench the official ideology into a course
familiar to their existing preoccupations and understandings.

Confronted by insistent intrusions, where even Maranzana in the province of Alessandria boasted a Via del Littorio (Lictor's Street) and very many citizens yielded to the temptation to act as police informers, the great majority nevertheless remained unrepentant lobbyists, determined to defend and enhance their own interests and social position. On every occasion when the Fascist 'revolution' sought to manipulate and control Italians, Italians were hard at work manipulating and adapting Fascism. Like all modern and most ancient ideologies, Fascism talked as though it wanted to impose only one version of history on its people. In reality, however, Italians at the interstices where ideology and practice met clung stubbornly to many pasts and presents and vested their hopes in many futures.

Some historians of ideas may be dismayed by this conclusion. In reaching it, they may charge, I am 'taking the mind out of history', as Lewis Namier was once blamed for doing to the English eighteenth century, with his focus on everyday interests, everyday arrived at. Potentially contradicting my stance, there is a vast literature concentrating on what Fascists said about themselves, their principles, regime and society. The more committed advocates of this line contend that, in recent times, a 'new consensus' has been achieved in the definition of that small 'f' fascism of which Italian capital 'F' Fascism was the most obvious progenitor and, on occasion, a generous continuing patron, if one that, after 1933, could seldom compete with the terrifying allure of the German Nazis. Despite its inability to match what became its German ally, Fascism, according to some of its historians, carried through a genuine 'cultural revolution'. For all its occasional contradiction and manifest inadequacies, Fascism preached a new party gospel and genuinely converted very many Italians to its cause. Historians who are convinced that these matters lie at the heart of the only viable model of fascism may view revelations about corruption and contradiction, mutability and manipulation, as *lèse-majesté* to the superior world of ideas, banal in their emphasis on banality, trifling in their unveiling of lasting nuance in human motivation and achievement, narrow in its emphasis on the breadth of life.

In response, it might be argued that the quest for a definition of fascism has become absurdly laboured. Why opt for a long list of factors or a paragraph of rococo ornateness when Mussolini, on a number of occasions, informed people he regarded as convertible to his cause that Fascism was a simple matter? All that was needed was a single party, a single youth organization, a single institution binding employers and their workforce, a *dopolavoro*, and, he did not have to add, a *Duce* (with a Bocchini to repress dissent) and a will to exclude the foe (somehow defined).[2] To be still more succinct, as Mussolini told Franco in October 1936, what the Spaniard should aim at was a regime that was simultaneously 'authoritarian', 'social' and 'popular'.[3] That amalgam, the *Duce* advised, was the basis of universal fascism.

Perhaps any caution against too florid an accounting of Fascism is unnecessary; the battlelines of historical debate may not be as starkly drawn as I have been intimating. In 2004 two major new works have amplified the field of fascism studies and proffered analyses that fit some of the evidence collected in this book. The sociologist Michael Mann stresses the high importance that must be accorded to Fascist ideas. 'Fascist ideology', he states, 'must be taken seriously, in its own terms', lest a fascist 'return' somehow happen. Moreover, Mann is sure that fascism 'was made in Italy'. A 'movement of the lesser intelligentsia', while sometimes more simply resembling a 'violent, male, teenage gang', Fascism drew its determined inspiration and fearsome thrust from organic nationalism, radical statism and paramilitarism. In Mann's definition, almost as brief as that of Mussolini, fascism is 'the pursuit of a transcendent and cleansing nation-statism through paramilitarism'. When ideas turned into action, the movement was violent and aggressive, 'always uniformed, marching, armed, dangerous and radically destabilizing of the existing order'. It flourished in those parts of Europe characterized by 'the crisis of the dual state, the semi-authoritarian, semi-liberal state found across half of Europe'.[4] It menaced civilization.

All but the last of these conclusions would not have seemed amiss to such *militi* as Mario Piazzesi or Edgardo Sulis (at least in his writings). Yet something troubles Mann when he ponders the detail of the Italian case. Is he still doubtful in his generalizations, he asks, implausibly given the massive scholarly research done during the last two decades, because the available evidence about Italy is 'fairly flimsy'? Or does the meaning of Italian Fascism blur because Mussolini, as often as not, was an 'opportunist', a less than militant figure, fond of 'zig-zags'? Italian Fascism, Mann underlines again, cannot be understood only in material terms. 'Transcendence' was its 'central plank'; Fascism's 'main attraction' was 'the intensity of its message'. Yet its practice, he concedes, was always 'problematic'. Perhaps, Mann suggests, because it seized power early and with relative ease, the Italian variant of fascism was 'rather conservative and bourgeois in outcome'. Mussolini's movement, Mann, with what a historian might think is a sociologist's rashness, pronounces in a cascade of final strictures, 'killed democracy, and a few thousand Italians . . . Ignoring Africa and the last year of the war . . . Italian fascism was the most benign fascist movement. That is why self-proclaimed "neo-fascists" re-emerged in Italy in recent years.'[5]

Approving some of Mann's generalizations and providing evidence to contest others, the historian Robert Paxton has followed the rules of his discipline to study the nature of what he says was 'the main political innovation of the twentieth century and the source of much of its pain'. Like Mann, Paxton is anxious to take the movement and its ideas seriously, all the more because he is convinced that fascism is not dead and buried but rather has left seeds 'within all democratic countries – not excluding the United States'. Yet Paxton cannot but be suspicious of narrowly intellectual investigations of the movement. 'Mood', he is sure, outweighed 'culture': 'Fascism was an affair of the gut more than of the brain, and a study of the roots of fascism that treats only the thinkers and the writers misses the most powerful impulses of all.'

Fascist rule, Paxton continues in words which have been frequently endorsed in this book, was 'more nakedly dependent on <u>charisma</u> than any other kind' and was, as a result, perpetually 'brittle'. 'Fascist regimes could not settle down into a comfortable enjoyment of power' since they 'had to produce an impression of driving momentum – "permanent revolution" – in order to fulfil their promises. They could not survive without that headlong, inebriating rush forward.' Although he duly admits the contradictions and backslidings common in Italian practice during Mussolini's dictatorship, Paxton boldly adds his own final definition to the existing store. For him, fascism was and is 'a form of political behaviour marked by obsessive preoccupation with community decline, humiliation, or victimhood and by compensatory cults of unity, energy, and purity, in which a mass-based party of committed nationalist militants, working in uneasy but effective collaboration with traditional elites, abandons democratic liberties and pursues with redemptive violence and without ethical or legal restraints goals of internal cleansing and external expansion'.[6]

When measured against the evidence assembled in this book, both Mann and Paxton have points worth making. Yet their generalizations continue to exhibit troubling features if they are meant to summarize fully the Italian population's experience of Fascism and accurately to delineate the reality of Fascist rule as distinct from its mythology. To pick just one of Paxton's phrases, that referring to a lack of legal restraint: was not one of the more frightening and salutary aspects of Mussolini's dictatorship that it mostly acted with legal cover and could regularly rely on its repressive policies and pre-emptive acts being approved by a lingering parliament and by a court system inherited from Liberal times and never ruthlessly purged? Were not many Fascist chiefs themselves lawyers by training or profession? Equally, is Fascism's fraught but often accommodating relationship with the Catholic hierarchy well described as utterly lacking in ethical base? Definitions may be contested but I doubt that these things were so.

In any case, although my questions in this book have often been framed by concepts drawn from accounts of generic fascism, for the most part I have preferred to pursue the social historian's trade of recounting the particular and recording the detail. Some summary in that regard may be useful. In my reckoning, the rise of Fascism did not destroy a democracy since Liberal Italy was very doubtfully democratized politically and, despite regional variation, even less so socially. Giolittian Italy may have been making economic progress before 1914 but the country was, and remained, poor. Even in 1930, *Baedeker* still advised visitors against drinking the water available in the small towns of central Italy (red wine, they helpfully counselled, was the best substitute) and warned tourists who ventured outside the walls of Rome to be back in their rooms by sunset lest they fall victim to the mosquito. The guide also cautioned the traveller to 'refrain from airing his political views, from taking photographs of beggars, etc'.[7] This last comment is a reminder that, despite Fascist fanfare, *la miseria* (poverty), until well after the Second World War, was the first reality in the life and culture of a majority of Italians.

Along with the scarcity of goods and arguably its natural accompaniment was the quick and common recourse to violence, be it manifest in the poor on poor killings of the south that so dismayed the northern criminologist Cesare Lombroso, or in punitive acts of a more organized kind. The Mafia in Sicily, landowners in Puglia, the rich of Bologna, Nationalists over the then border in Trieste – none drew back from the bludgeon and the gun when needed to impose their will. Traces of what might be deemed a proto-fascism can be detected in these and other places under Liberal rule. Yet to repeat Omer Bartov's memorable dictum, only with its participation in the First World War did Italy really become a society with 'murder in its midst'.[8] It was then that sporadic social blood-letting became channelled into 'paramilitarism', to use Mann's term. Readers of this book have been able to trace the way in which the future Fascist bosses, Roberto Farinacci, Italo Balbo, Dino Grandi and their friends and associates, were 'made' politically by Italy's war. As a result, they became Fascist militants before the meeting at the Piazza San Sepolcro, let alone the foundation of the PNF. After 1922, despite it being peacetime, Italian politics and society retained the mentality established when fighting. 'Total war' (Italian style) begat totalitarianism.

Modern (or modern-ish) war meant 'organization', an intrusive state favouring industry and the machine and a nation embodying national 'truth'. One of the most significant comments to appear from the writings of those linked to the ANI was the idea of an 'Italian truth' which was not identical to the French, German, British or any 'foreign' truths but should be accepted by every good citizen. Limitless war or permanent Darwinian struggle entailed the proselytizing among the people of a single history, the one that justified the nation's ambitions and, after 1919, the one that defended the nature and purpose of the great conflict. The Fascist mustering of peacetime life as war by other means entailed a profound belief in the virtue of the simple and single answer, the final (and national) solution, life (to use the *Duce*'s own catchphrase) as defined with 'mathematical certainty'.

Fascism rose swiftly to power in the aftermath of the Italian victory over the Austrians at Vittorio Veneto (and Mann is right to suggest that some 'liteness' resulted in the practice of this dictatorship as a result of this rapid triumph). In the course of their victory, Fascists were motivated to beat and to kill in order to impose a positive history of the war on non-Italians, now uneasily housed within the nation's new frontiers. Border fascism was one of the earliest and most durably influential strands of the movement; the evil metaphors of ethnic cleansing were always a key strain in the Fascist medley. But, in most of the country, the enemy was defined socially and was constituted by socialists and their unionized workers and peasants or by their Catholic equivalents. Fascism may on occasion have excoriated liberalism and, during the last stages of the Second World War, a desperate and despairing Mussolini may have dreamed fitfully of converting that conflict into a crusade against plutocratic capitalism as expressed among the Anglo-Saxons, while Fascist socialization united the people at home. But the *Duce*'s efforts to deflect Hitler from his visceral determination to liquidate Judeo-Bolshevism and to transmute him into a social radical were most unlikely to succeed and should not be read as somehow explaining Fascism (or fascism) as a whole.

Rather, during the 1920s at least, Mussolini can often be found endorsing aspects of liberalism, even if always with the proviso that its gentler, kinder side had lost its purpose with and in the war. Acerbo, Ricci, Costanzo Ciano and many other leading figures in the PNF were still flirting with liberalism in 1919 until some event or opportunity hardened them into being Fascists. Then and thereafter, many Liberal fathers spawned Fascist sons. However twisted their nature, lingering Fascist ideas about great individuals, private property and the (Darwinian) freedom to achieve always drew on liberal antecedents. Fascism was as surely the bastard, post-First World War child of liberalism as communism was of social democracy.

Virulent nationalists and implacable anti-Marxists, Fascists were also the crusaders, the storm-troopers of peacetime for whom savagery was a positive, a pleasure, the chief spur of their masculinity and their gut response to the world. The followers of Mussolini may have in the main drawn back from fully endorsing the mystical slogan 'long live death' but they did enjoy the punch-up and the forcing of their captured foes to drink castor oil, the raid on an enemy redoubt, its sacking and burning. And on occasion they indulged in murder, without reservation or doubt. Mussolini himself was certain that he was a savage, a frightening feline ready to claw and to kill (if also from time to time a purringly clever negotiator, adept at getting his own way). Savagery and Fascism went together. In 'civilized' Italy a tyranny was required to stiffen the national will, to oust the 'slipper-wearers', to escape the tourists and their condescension, to conquer an empire (however belatedly by European standards) and to allow the nation to stand tall 'again'. Paxton is right to underline the essential role of restlessness in the Fascist mix. Here was a revolution that would contradict itself if it were to settle down; it was 'permanent' or it was nothing.

Yet, after 1922 and especially after 1925, the regime had to prove that it did rule and did so with legislation, order, discipline and formality, all the more since Mussolini was rarely happy for long at the thought of crass vulgarity, as expressed by Farinacci, Giampaoli or Arpinati and their louche crews, establishing itself at the summit of party or national power. This institutionalizing of Fascism soon showed itself a lengthy and flawed process. What part should the old bureaucracy play in the new system? What was the corporate state? What was Fascist society? How repressive should the regime be and who were the police policing? What exactly did totalitarianism mean when, for example, a deal needed to be worked out with the Church and business or an accommodation maintained with the monarchy or the army officer corps? Fascist intellectuals, with Bottai in the vanguard, were only too happy to answer these questions with floods of words. Yet somehow the questions were unanswerable. Certainly the verbiage, whatever its power in 1932, no longer reads as credible or accurate. Through its perpetual longing for pre-emption, Fascism by definition contradicted itself. It is impossible to live by action alone.

It is thus unsurprising to find that, somehow, the 'real' start of the full-scale revolution was always only to be glimpsed around the corner. Endless postponement in turn entailed persistent uneasiness and inveterate contradiction. If, despite the clamour of the Decennale and its Mostra della Rivoluzione, the labour of a decade had not eliminated Pope and King, landowner and peasant, and had failed even to refashion bourgeois women, still sadly slim and fond of Paris gowns, then 'go to the people' and encourage a cretin like Starace to voice the catch-cries of populism to refurbish Fascism for a second decade in power. If that solution began to seem threadbare and Italians again were not fused into a mystical union, tightly bound by the party's rope and axes, erect in a single cause, then invade Ethiopia, join the Spanish Civil War, draw near to Nazi Germany in the Axis, take over Albania and talk big about war preparations of an unparalleled degree (but do not in any hard sense prepare either the armed forces or domestic society for global conflict). Maybe even favour an Italian form of legislative racism and put anti-Semitism, at least for a while, at its centre. One or the other or all these choices might somehow at last spark a genuine revolution (and paradoxically sustain the ageing and tiring Mussolini through further years of office, given that Fascism at no stage faced up to what might eventuate should the *Duce* retire or die).

With these factors propelling Fascism either into being ever more a propaganda state or to the viciousness on show under the Salò Republic, for most of the time plenty of other histories, behaviour patterns and ideas were able to survive among the diverse classes and regions of Italy and also between men and women. Fascism's modernity was meant to offer welfare. ONMI, INPS and other institutions did purvey advice and benefit of some kind. Yet the Fascist social state was uneven in its functioning; a political test could always bring advantage or failure. As the Vivarelli case displayed, the worthy wife of a squadrist from Siena could win from the *Duce* a special payment of fifty times the amount of an ordinary widow's pension. The drunken singing of a politically incorrect song could earn a poor peasant called Boccaccio a long stretch in the Basilicata.

But the road to Fascist fortune or well-being was not rendered bumpy by politics alone. Rather, out in the towns and countryside, ideology was perpetually conditioned by Italians' recourse to familial and other forms of loyalty and patronage whose cast was as frequently local as it was Italian, let alone Fascist. The Siena lawyer-squadrist's wife had the prefect and the president of the local bank speaking for her; many prisoners cheered when their terms were suddenly shortened after this or that notable or some member of their family pleaded their cause. Fascists swore that their revolution would purge the *raccomandazione* and the 'special case' from Italian lives. But, in practice, the chance to be a *furbo* (smart one) survived and flourished, as the surgeons who sought jobs and the historians who arranged favourable reviews for their books through contact with Farinacci well knew. In this dictatorship (and, very likely, in all others), the law and every other matter that impinged on the human condition could not automatically be relied on to say what it meant. Meaning remained negotiable. Throughout its history, but in an accelerated manner as the 1930s came to a cruel end, Fascism both was and was not.

In the *longue durée*, the absences, the cynicism, the corruption and the incompetence outweighed the rest in building a legacy for those Italians who survived into the new Republic after 1946. Despite the boasted revolution, the fact was that every one of the great slogans of Fascism had turned out to be false. Mussolini, anything but the greatest statesman of the twentieth century, had not proved himself to be always right. His people had not marched straight ahead. The plough had not been the guarantor of the nation's economic future or the sword the weapon of modern choice, and in any event battle mostly brought death and dishonour, not gain. The world was not destined to belong to the Fascists. Life was scarcely sustained merely by book and rifle. Given the enduring power of the structures of life, it was absurd and impossible to contemplate living one day as a lion. Italians, both under the dictatorship and after, were more suspicious than believing. They were by no means automatically obedient to the rules either of their social betters or their party chiefs. If doubtless able to kill, they were never fighters and merely that. Plainly, the best formula for happy times was not 'win, win, win'. Every message had to be decoded, rearranged and denied. The propaganda jingles thus came to resemble that long list of film titles, given new resonance by those in the know in 1942, where the dictator himself was hidden under the title *Un'ora sola che vorrei* (An hour is enough with you). For all their blatant ferocity, Fascist words were regularly open to negotiation and amendment in their meaning. Moreover, words apart, Fascism did not proffer a sunlit third way to its people but instead visited upon them the Second World War, humiliation in Greece, the casual loss of the Liberal and Fascist overseas empires, mass murder in Slovenia and other Balkan territories, the withering away of the nation on 8 September 1943 and the death toll of the RSI, German and Allied occupation and a kind of civil war which was prolonged for some months after Mussolini's death. It was an appalling record but one that was as meretricious as it was vile. When all the huffing and puffing had been done, Italians had not become the fervent adepts and peerless warriors of a new political faith. Instead, in the best parts of their minds, they had found solace in the understanding that, under a dictatorship such as Benito Mussolini's, to endure was all.

Notes

Preface

1. P. Ginsborg, *Silvio Berlusconi: television, power and patrimony* (London, 2004), p. 131.

Introduction

1. S. Drakulic, *The Balkan express: fragments from the other side of the war* (New York, 1994), p. 3.
2. For an able restatement of the model of fascism, see R. O. Paxton, *The anatomy of fascism* (London, 2004).
3. Carte Roberto Farinacci, 32, 18 November 1939, Farinacci to Pedrazza.
4. P. Corner, 'Italian Fascism: whatever happened to dictatorship?', *Journal of Modern History*, 74, 2002, p. 344.

1 One Italy or another before 1914

1. B. Mussolini, *Opera omnia* (ed. E. and D. Susmel) (Florence, 1952–) (hereafter BMOO), vol. XXIX, pp. 403–5.
2. R. and E. Packard, *Balcony Empire: Fascist Italy at war* (New York, 1942).
3. B. Tobia, 'Riti e simboli di due capitali (1846–1921)', in V. Vidotto (ed.), *Roma capitale* (Bari, 2002), p. 374.
4. For scathing comments in the US Catholic press, see P. R. D'Agostino, *Rome in America: transnational Catholic ideology from the Risorgimento to Fascism* (Chapel Hill, 2004).
5. M. Casciato, 'Lo sviluppo urbano e il disegno della città' in V. Vidotto (ed.), *Roma capitale* (Bari, 2002), p. 153.
6. Tobia, 'Riti e simboli di due capitali (1846–1921)', p. 374.

7. Casciato, 'Lo sviluppo urbano e il disegno della città', p. 153.

8. Quoted in S. J. Woolf (ed.), *Nationalism in Europe, 1815 to the present: a reader* (London, 1996), p. 50.

9. A. Riccardi, 'La vita religiosa' in V. Vidotto (ed.), *Roma capitale* (Bari, 2002), p. 279.

10. Anon., 'Le commemorazioni patriottiche del 1911', *Civiltà Cattolica*, 62, 1911, pp. 145–7.

11. W. H. McNeill, *Arnold J. Toynbee: a life* (Oxford, 1989), p. 42.

12. BMOO III, p. 190.

13. Woolf (ed.), *Nationalism in Europe*, p. 53.

14. N. Brancaccio, *In Francia durante la guerra* (Milan, 1916), p. 171.

15. V. Castronovo, *Economia e società in Piemonte dall'Unità al 1914* (Milan, 1969), pp. 165–76, 183, 196, 320.

16. V. Castronovo, *Giovanni Agnelli: la Fiat dal 1899 al 1945* (Turin, 1977), pp. 51, 58–9.

17. E. Lussu, *Il cinghiale del diavolo e altri scritti sulla Sardegna* (Turin, 1976), p. 49.

18. There is a massive literature about the life and ideas of Gramsci, and his own writings have been extensively translated into English. For a telling account of the historiographical disputes over the meaning of his career, see G. Liguori, *Gramsci conteso: storia di un dibattito 1922–1996* (Rome, 1996).

19. L. Passerini, *Fascism in popular memory: the cultural experience of the Turin working class* (Cambridge, 1984), p. 45.

20. For a further account of Venice in these years, see R. J. B. Bosworth, 'Venice between Fascism and international tourism, 1911–45', *Modern Italy*, 4, 1999, pp. 5–23.

21. See the cover of P. V. Cannistraro and B. R. Sullivan, *Il Duce's other woman* (New York, 1993).

22. Cited by M. Gibson, *Prostitution and the state in Italy, 1860–1915* (New Brunswick, 1986), pp. 140–41.

23. M. De Giorgio, *Le italiane dall'Unità a oggi: modelli culturali e comportamenti sociali* (Bari, 1992), pp. 39, 422, 431. In 1881, female life expectancy was only thirty-four years.

24. Ibid., pp. 159–60, 226.

25. L. Freddi, *Bandiere nere: contributo alla storia del Fascismo* (Rome, nd), pp. 193–9.

26. Cannistraro and Sullivan, *Il Duce's other woman*, p. 116.

27. G. D'Annunzio, *The Flame* (London, 1991), pp. 9, 55. The novel was first published in Italian in 1900.

28. There is no proper scholarly study of Volpi. But see the family-approved

S. Romano, *Giuseppe Volpi. Industria e finanza tra Giolitti e Mussolini* (Milan, 1979).

29. E. M. Gray, *The bloodless war* (New York, 1916), p. 168.

30. G. Boatti, *La terra trema: Messina 28 dicembre 1908. I trenta secondi che cambiarono l'Italia, non gli italiani* (Milan, 2004), p. 156.

31. O. Browning (ed.), *Macmillan's guide to Italy and Sicily* (London, 1911), pp. xxxii–xxxiii.

32. See, for example, J. Carrère, *La terre tremblante: Calabre et Messine 1907–1908–1909* (Paris, 1909), p. 13. For a more general introduction to gays in the Mediterranean, see R. Aldrich, *The seduction of the Mediterranean: writing, art and homosexual fantasy* (London, 1993).

33. T. D'A. Smith, *Love in earnest: some notes on the lives and writings of the 'Uranian' poets from 1889 to 1930* (London, 1970), p. 63.

34. E. Palermi and B. Cimino, *Nelle città della morte!! . . .* (Milan, 1909), p. 48.

35. *La Tribuna*, 2 January 1909.

36. Boatti, *La terra trema*, p. 180.

37. *Il Mattino*, 4 January 1909.

38. *Il Corriere della Sera*, 17 January 1909.

39. M. L. Salvadori, *Gaetano Salvemini* (Turin, 1963), p. 22.

40. *Avanti!*, 8 January 1909.

41. See, notably, G. Salvemini, *Under the axe of Fascism* (London, 1936), a work circulated by the Left Book Club.

42. Salvadori, *Gaetano Salvemini*, p. 23.

43. F. F. Rizi, *Benedetto Croce and Italian Fascism* (Toronto, 2003), p. 13.

44. I. Silone, *Emergency Exit* (London, 1969), pp. 59–60. For an account of Silone's alleged dealings with Fascism, see D. Biocca and M. Canali, *L'informatore: Silone, i comunisti e la Polizia* (Milan, 2000).

45. S. Giuliani, *Le 19 provincie create dal duce, la ricostruzione di Reggio e Messina* (Milan, 1928), p. 340.

46. SPDCO 172249, 15 December 1937, Mussolini to Ministry of Public Works.

47. N. Malatino (ed.), *1908–1958: cinquant' anni dal terremoto* (Messina, 1958), p. 129.

48. A. Barreca, *Episodio memorando di un superstite nel terremoto di Messina 28 dicembre 1908* (Siracusa, 1931), p. 15.

49. Ibid., p. 20.

50. M. Malatesta, 'Introduction: the Italian professions from a comparative perspective' in M. Malatesta (ed.), *Society and the professions in Italy, 1860–1914* (Cambridge, 1995), p. 16.

51. *Il Corriere della Sera*, 3, 4, 11 January 1911; *La Tribuna*, 7 January 1909.

52. Ministero Interno, Serie Diverse, Comitato Soccorso Terremoto Calabria e Sicilia, 2/1.D, 11 January 1909, minutes.

53. *La Tribuna*, 1, 4, 5 January 1909.

54. *Critica Sociale*, 16 January 1909.

55. *Avanti!*, 9 January 1909.

56. R. Trevelyan, *Princes under the volcano* (New York, 1973), p. 349.

57. For the statistics, see G. Rosoli, *Un secolo di emigrazione italiana: 1876–1976* (Rome, 1978), pp. 350–64.

58. Cited by L. Avagliano (ed.), *L'emigrazione italiana: testi e documenti* (Naples, 1976), pp. 112–13.

59. L. Luzzatti, *Memorie*, vol. III, 1901–1927 (Milan, 1966), p. 14.

60. O. Malagodi, *Imperialismo: la civiltà industriale e le sue conquiste: studii inglesi* (Milan, 1901), pp. 228–9.

61. E. Corradini, *Il nazionalismo italiano* (Milan, 1914), pp. 53–4, 58–9, 68.

62. G. B. Scalabrini, *Trent'anni di Apostalato: memorie e documenti* (ed. A. Scalabrini) (Rome, 1909), pp. 3, 363.

63. R. Murri, 'Impressioni d'America', *Nuova Antologia*, f. 985, 1 January 1913, pp. 78–89.

64. R. Murri, 'Gl'Italiani nell'America latina', *Nuova Antologia*, f. 991, 1 April 1913, p. 437.

65. Rosoli, *Un secolo di emigrazione italiana*, pp. 365–74.

66. A. Dumini, *Diciassette colpi* (Milan, 1958), p. 17.

67. J. J. Tighino, *Edmondo Rossoni from revolutionary syndicalism to Fascism* (New York, 1991), pp. 50, 59.

68. See, for example, *Il Corriere della Sera*, 19 December 1915, as quoted by D. Mack Smith, *Storia di cento anni di vita italiana visti attraverso il Corriere della Sera* (Milan, 1978), p. 199.

69. D. De Castro, *Memorie di un novantenne: Trieste e l'Istria* (Trieste, 1999), pp. 7–20.

70. For a sympathetic account of Battisti's career, see V. Calì, *Patrioti senza patria: i democratici trentini fra Otto e Novecento* (Trento, 2003).

71. C. E. Gadda, *Giornale di guerra e di prigionia* (Turin, 1965), p. 191.

72. *Avanti!*, 4 November 1921.

2 Liberal and dynastic war

1. J. Dunnage, *Twentieth-century Italy: a social history* (London, 2002), p. 24.

2. V. Zamagni, *The economic history of Italy 1860–1990* (Oxford, 1993), p. 189.

3. E. D. Whitaker, *Measuring mamma's milk: Fascism and the medicalization of maternity in Italy* (Ann Arbor, 2000), p. 89.

4. See the table in A. J. P. Taylor, *The struggle for mastery in Europe 1848–1914* (London, 1954), p. xxix.

5. C. E. Gadda, *Giornale di guerra e di prigionia* (Turin, 1980), p. 191.

6. Zamagni, *The economic history of Italy*, p. 40.

7. See R. A. Webster, *Industrial imperialism in Italy 1908–1915* (Berkeley, 1975), who largely endorses this view.

8. Zamagni, *The economic history of Italy*, p. 195.

9. P. Kennedy, *The rise and fall of the Great Powers: economic and military conflict from 1500 to 2000* (New York, 1987), p. 210.

10. Dunnage, *Twentieth-century Italy*, p. 24.

11. See S. Patriarca, *Numbers and nationhood: writing statistics in nineteenth-century Italy* (Cambridge, 1996).

12. S. Satta, *The day of judgment* (London, 1988), p. 29.

13. A. L. Maraspini, *The study of an Italian village* (Paris, 1968), pp. 25, 57–8.

14. See E. Magrì, *Musolino: il brigante dell'Aspromonte* (Milan, 1989).

15. R. Bachi, *L'alimentazione e la politica annonaria in Italia* (Bari, 1926), pp. 22, 127.

16. Zamagni, *The economic history of Italy*, p. 188.

17. P. Bevilacqua, 'Emigrazione transoceanica e mutamenti dell'alimentazione contadina calabrese fra otto e novecento' in P. Borzomati (ed.), *L'emigrazione calabrese dall'unità ad oggi* (Rome, 1982), pp. 65–78.

18. Bachi, *L'alimentazione e la politica annonaria in Italia*, p. 24.

19. C. S. Calogero, *Ferramonti: la vita e gli uomini del più grande campo d'internamento fascista (1940–1945)* (Florence, 1987), p. 178.

20. A. Nasalli Rocca, *Memorie di un prefetto* (Rome, 1946), pp. 124–5.

21. F. M. Snowden, '"Fields of death": malaria in Italy, 1861–1962', *Modern Italy*, 4, 1999, pp. 41–4.

22. Cited by F. M. Snowden, 'Cholera in Barletta 1910', *Past and Present*, 132, 1991, p. 95.

23. F. Mercadante (ed.), *Il terremoto di Messina* (Rome, 1962), p. 18.

24. P. Del Negro, *Esercito, stato, società* (Bologna, 1979), p. 227.

25. Taylor, *The struggle for mastery in Europe*, p. 283.

26. *Il Corriere della Sera*, 2 January 1909; E. Palermi and B. Cimino, *Nelle città della morte!! . . .* (Milan, 1909), p. 53.

27. For literary evocation, see M. Serao, *The conquest of Rome* (ed.

A. Caesar) (New York, 1992). Her novel was first published in 1884 and attempts both to evoke the mystique of parliament and urge a Man to 'conquer' the city and its past.

28. P. Farneti, *Sistema politica e società civile: saggi di teoria e di ricerca* (Turin, 1971), pp. 182, 240–54, 328–9.

29. P. Melograni, *Storia politica della grande guerra 1915–1918* (rev. ed.) (Milan, 1998), p. 8.

30. F. M. Snowden, *Violence and great estates in the south of Italy: Apulia, 1900–1922* (Cambridge, 1986), pp. 3, 143.

31. For more detail on this Mussolini, see R. J. B. Bosworth, *Mussolini* (London, 2002), pp. 87–9, 109.

32. M. G. Rossi, *Le origini del partito cattolico: movimento cattolico e lotta di classe nell'Italia liberale* (Rome, 1977), pp. 20–24, 210.

33. A. Del Boca, *Gli Italiani in Africa: Tripoli bel suol d'amore 1860–1922* (Bari, 1986), pp. 145, 153.

34. For the case of Tuscan gentleman, landowner, man of culture, imperial administrator and, in 1914, Minister of Colonies, Ferdinando Martini, see A. Del Boca, *Gli Italiani in Africa orientale dall'unità alla marcia su Roma* (Bari, 1976), pp. 751–9.

35. For further detail, see R. J. B. Bosworth, *Italy, the least of the Great Powers: Italian foreign policy before the First World War* (Cambridge, 1979), pp. 95–126.

36. 'G. De Frenzi', *Per l'italianità del "Gardasee"* (Naples, 1909), p. 6.

37. 'G. De Frenzi', *L'Italia nell'Egeo* (Rome, 1913), p. vi.

38. L. Federzoni, *La Dalmazia che aspetta* (Bologna, 1915), pp. 29, 49.

39. M. Alberti, *L'irredentismo senza romanticismi* (Como, 1936), p. 83.

40. *Il Mare Nostro: Stirpe Italica*, January 1934.

41. M. Barbagli, *Educating for unemployment: politics, labor markets and the school system – Italy 1859–1973* (New York, 1982), p. 37.

42. R. C. Fried, *The Italian Prefects: a study in administrative politics* (New Haven, 1963), p. 120.

43. Nasalli Rocca, *Memorie di un prefetto*, pp. 46, 150.

44. C. Moffa, 'I deportati libici della guerra 1911–12', *Rivista di storia contemporanea*, 19, 1990, pp. 32–56.

45. R. Canosa, *Storia della criminalità 1845–1945* (Turin, 1991), pp. 180–88, 256.

46. See, for example, M. G. Sarfatti, 'Clericalismo vecchio e nuovo', *Utopia*, II, 30 January 1914, pp. 44–9. She argued sagely that there was nothing wrong with Christianity as distinct from Catholicism, a position of potential compromise which once would have been eschewed by her *Duce*.

47. R. De Felice, *Mussolini il rivoluzionario 1883–1920* (Turin, 1965), p. 108.

48. See further Bosworth, *Mussolini*, p. 81.

49. C. Seton-Watson, *Italy from Liberalism to Fascism 1870–1925* (London, 1967), p. 394.

50. J. Dunnage, *The Italian police and the rise of Fascism: a case study of the province of Bologna, 1897–1925* (Westport, Conn., 1997), p. 66.

51. BMOO VI, p. 214.

52. For further background, see Bosworth, *Mussolini*, pp. 100–111.

53. For a eulogistic biography, see R. Colapietra, *Leonida Bissolati* (Milan, 1958). Bissolati switched to supporting war entry by 2 October, a fortnight before Mussolini's public conversion (p. 215).

54. S. Lupo, *Il Fascismo: la politica in un regime totalitario* (Rome, 2000), p. 77.

55. H. Fornari, *Mussolini's gadfly: Roberto Farinacci* (Nashville, 1971), p. 15.

56. For a study of his early years, see P. Nello, *Dino Grandi: la formazione di un leader fascista* (Bologna, 1987).

57. C. G. Segrè, *Italo Balbo: a Fascist life* (Berkeley, 1987), pp. 6, 19.

58. B. Vigezzi, 'Le "radiose giornate" del maggio 1915 nei rapporti dei prefetti', *Nuova Rivista Storica*, XLIII, 1960, p. 329.

59. A. Bravo, 'Donne contadine e prima guerra mondiale', *Società e Storia*, III, 1980, p. 850.

60. Gadda, *Giornale di guerra e di prigonia*, p. 43.

61. For further detail, see R. J. B. Bosworth, *Italy and the approach of the First World War* (London, 1983), pp. 121–41.

62. R. J. B. Bosworth, 'The *Touring Club Italiano* and the nationalization of the Italian bourgeoisie', *European History Quarterly*, 27, 1997, pp. 383, 388.

63. A. Monticone, 'Salandra e Sonnino verso la decisione dell'intervento', *Rivista di studi politici internazionali*, XXIV, 1957, p. 69.

64. J. R. Rodd, *Social and diplomatic memories 1902–1919* (London, 1925), vol. III, p. 253.

65. T. N. Page, *Italy and the world war* (London, 1921), p. 43.

66. F. Martini, *Diario 1914–1918* (ed. G. De Rosa) (Milan, 1966), p. 415.

67. *Il Corriere della Sera*, 4 June 1915.

68. *Il Corriere della Sera*, 19 December 1915.

69. M. De Marco, *Il Gazzettino: storia di un quotidiano* (Venice, 1976), p. 38.

70 R. Romeo, *L'Italia unita e la prima guerra mondiale* (Bari, 1978), p. 157.

This view was again implicitly endorsed in 2000 by Italian President Carlo Azeglio Ciampi. See his preface to M. R. Stern (ed.), *1915–1918: La guerra sugli altipiani: testimonianze di soldati al fronte* (Vicenza, 2000), p. viii.

71. F. Grassi, *Il tramonto dell'età giolittiana nel Salento* (Bari, 1973), p. 288.

72. P. Melograni, *Storia politica della grande guerra* (Milan, 1998), pp. 6–7, 10–11.

73. L. Gasparotto, *Diario di un fante* (Milan, 1919) as cited in Stern (ed.), *1915–1918: La guerra sugli altipiani*, p. 73.

74. E. De Bono, *Nell'esercito nostro prima della guerra* (Milan, 1931), pp. 188, 205.

75. Melograni, *Storia politica della grande guerra*, p. 21.

76. Vigezzi, 'Le "radiose giornate" del maggio 1915 nei rapporti dei prefetti', p. 110.

77. Melograni, *Storia politica della grande guerra*, p. 112.

78. P. Pieri, *L'Italia nella prima guerra mondiale* (Turin, 1965), pp. 69, 77.

79. J. Gooch, 'Preface' to M. A. Morselli, *Caporetto 1917: victory or defeat?* (London, 2001), p. viii.

80. L. Tosi, *La propaganda italiana all'estero nella prima guerra mondiale: rivendicazioni territoriali e politica delle nazionalità* (Pordenone, 1977), pp. 55–7, 87.

81. G. Petracchi, *Diplomazia di guerra e rivoluzione: Italia e Russia dall'ottobre 1916 al maggio 1917* (Bologna, 1974), pp. 58–9, 99.

82. Gooch, 'Preface' to M. A. Morselli, *Caporetto 1917*, p. ix.

83. In one incident Arditi abused an English general and his chauffeur for interfering where they did not belong. See L. Bissolati, *Diario di guerra: appunti presi sulle linee, nei comandi, nei consigli interalleati* (Turin, 1935), p. 95.

84. G. Fortunato, *Carteggio 1912–1922* (ed. E. Gentile) (Bari, 1979), pp. 276–7, 282–3, 285. Letters successively to Croce, Salandra and Giolitti. He was still lamenting the event ten weeks after it happened.

85. R. Farinacci, *Storia della rivoluzione fascista, vol. I, Il 1919* (Cremona, 1937), p. 14.

3 Popular and national war

1. G. Procacci, 'The disaster of Caporetto', in J. Dickie, J. Foot and F. M. Snowden, *Disastro: Disasters in Italy since 1860: culture, politics and society* (London, 2002), p. 151.

2. *Il Soldato*, 18 November 1917.

3. BMOO X, pp. 8–10, 36–8, 55–7, 67–8 (articles in *Il Popolo d'Italia*, 31 October, 10, 16, 20 November 1917).

4. P. Melograni, *Storia politica della grande guerra, 1915–1918* (Bari, 1969), pp. 165–6.

5. M. Abrate, *La lotta sindacale nella industrializzazione in Italia 1906–1926* (Turin, 1967), pp. 160–63.

6. L. Tomassini, 'Industrial mobilisation and the labour market in Italy during the First World War', *Social History*, 16, 1991, p. 63.

7. V. Zamagni, *The economic history of Italy 1860–1990* (Oxford, 1993), pp. 211, 219–21.

8. R. Paci, 'Le trasformazioni ed innovazioni nella struttura economica italiana' in A. Caracciolo (ed.), *Il trauma dell'intervento: 1914–19* (Florence, 1968), pp. 37–42.

9. Zamagni, *The economic history of Italy*, p. 221.

10. M. Clark, *Antonio Gramsci and the revolution that failed* (New Haven, 1977), pp. 14, 22.

11. Melograni, *Storia politica della grande guerra*, p. 119.

12. Zamagni, *The economic history of Italy*, p. 224.

13. G. Rochat and G. Massobrio, *Breve storia dell'esercito italiano dal 1861 al 1943* (Turin, 1978), p. 184.

14. A. Camarda and S. Peli, *L'altro esercito: la classe operaia durante la prima guerra mondiale* (Milan, 1980), p. 31.

15. Paci, 'Le trasformazioni ed innovazioni nella struttura economica italiana', p. 34.

16. D. Mack Smith, *Italy: a modern history* (Ann Arbor, 1969), p. 313.

17. N. Ferguson, *The pity of war* (Harmondsworth, 1999), p. 323.

18. Melograni, *Storia politica della grande guerra*, pp. 46, 92–3, 113, 310, 318.

19. G. Procacci, *Soldati e prigionieri italiani nella Grande Guerra: con una raccolta di lettere inedite* (Rome, 1993), p. 25. The real total was probably nearer 1,200.

20. G. Rochat, *L'esercito italiano da Vittorio Veneto a Mussolini (1919–1925)* (Bari, 1967), pp. 121–2.

21. E. Forcella and A. Monticone, *Plotone di esecuzione: i processi della prima guerra mondiale* (Bari, 1968), pp. 3–6; for further commentary, cf. Forcella's introduction 'Apologia della paura', pp. ix–lxii. It was not until the rise of critical history in the 1960s that any acknowledgement came of this tyranny.

22. Ibid., pp. 24–30.

23. M. A. Morselli, *Caporetto 1917: victory or defeat?* (London, 2001), p. 100.

24. Forcella and Monticone, *Plotone di esecuzione*, pp. 66–7, 99–100, 128–9.

25. Melograni, *Storia politica della grande guerra*, p. 105.

26. C. E. Gadda, *Giornale di guerra e di prigionia* (Turin, 1980), pp. 101, 236. For more about the role of grappa in the army, see E. Lussu, *Sardinian brigade* (London, 2000).

27. Procacci, *Soldati e prigionieri italiani nella Grande Guerra*, p. 90.

28. A. Frescura, *Diario di un imboscato* (Milan, 1981), pp. 163, 170. Frescura's book was first published in 1919.

29. Melograni, *Storia politica della grande guerra*, pp. 89, 92.

30. Frescura, *Diario di un imboscato*, p. 84.

31. Melograni, *Storia politica della grande guerra*, p. 295.

32. Procacci, *Soldati e prigionieri italiani nella Grande Guerra*, pp. 150, 160–65, 299, 333–7.

33. U. Levra, *Il colpo di stato della borghesia: la crisi politica di fine secolo in Italia 1896–1900* (Milan, 1975), p. 192.

34. Forcella and Monticone, *Plotone di esecuzione*, p. lviii.

35. R. J. B. Bosworth, *Italy the least of the Great Powers: Italian foreign policy before the First World War* (Cambridge, 1979), pp. 120–24.

36. L. Tosi, *La propaganda italiana all'estero nella prima guerra mondiale: rivendicazioni territoriali e politica delle nazionalità* (Pordenone, 1977), p. 25.

37. Frescura, *Diario di un imboscato*, pp. 287–8.

38. Unione degli insegnanti italiani per la guerra nazionale, 'Le mire dei nostri nemici', 1918.

39. L. Tosi, 'Romeo A. Gallenga Stuart e la propaganda di guerra all'estero (1917–1918)', *Storia contemporanea*, II, 1971, pp. 519–43.

40. Frescura, *Diario di un imboscato*, pp. 113, 123, 212.

41. J. Bourke, *An intimate history of killing: face-to-face killing in twentieth-century warfare* (London, 1999), p. 14.

42. L. Spitzer, *Lettere di prigionieri di guerra italiani 1915–1918* (Turin, 1976), p. 24.

43. Frescura, *Diario di un imboscato*, p. 192.

44. Spitzer, *Lettere di prigionieri di guerra italiani*, pp. 52, 55–8.

45. Frescura, *Diario di un imboscato*, pp. 37, 46–7, 192, 208–9, 288.

46. M. Puccini, *Cola o il ritratto di un italiano* (1927) as cited in M. R. Stern (ed.), *1915–1918: La guerra sugli altipiani: testimonianze di soldati al fronte* (Vicenza, 2000), p. 126. According to Lussu, forgetting their women was another one of the reasons why officers devoted themselves to hard liquor. See Lussu, *Sardinian brigade*, p. 158.

47. Gadda, *Giornale di guerra e di prigionia*, pp. 304–5.

48. Frescura, *Diario di un imboscato*, p. 17.

49. Bourke, *An intimate history of killing*, pp. 1, 31, 142.

50. See, for example, G. Stuparich, *Guerra del '15* (Turin, 1961), p. 40.

51. P. Jahier, *L'Antico 'Giornale delle Trincee'*, as anthologized in M. R. Stern (ed.), *1915–1918: La guerra sugli altipiani*, pp. 498–9.

52. L. Bissolati, *Diario di guerra: appunti presi sulle linee, nei comandi, nei consigli interalleati* (Turin, 1935), p. 34.

53. For the list, see *L'Alpino*, 15 November 1926.

54. R. J. B. Bosworth, *Mussolini* (London, 2002), p. 170.

55. See B. Mussolini, *Il mio diario di guerra (1915–1917)* (Milan, 1923); for an analysis of its myth, see L. Passerini, *Mussolini immaginario: storia di una biografia 1915–1939* (Milan, 1991), pp. 15–32.

56. See Mussolini preface to A. Turati, *Ragioni ideali di vita fascista* (Rome, 1926), p. 8.

57. Bourke, *An intimate history of killing*, pp. 103–38, 345–68.

58. V. Solaro del Borgo, *Giornate di guerra del re soldato* (Milan, 1931), p. 22.

59. Frescura, *Diario di un imboscato*, pp. 224, 321.

60. Rochat and Massobrio, *Breve storia dell'esercito italiano*, p. 185.

61. Melograni, *Storia politica della grande guerra*, pp. 221–3.

62. R. Festorazzi, *Starace: il mastino della rivoluzione fascista* (Milan, 2002), p. 22.

63. Forcella and Monticone, *Plotone di esecuzione*, p. 31.

64. P. Corner, *Fascism in Ferrara 1915–1925* (Oxford, 1975), p. 37.

65. Forcella and Monticone, *Plotone di esecuzione*, pp. 243, 346–7.

66. A. Malatesta, *I socialisti italiani durante la guerra* (Milan, 1926), pp. 71–2, 229–31.

67. G. Procacci, *La lotta di classe in Italia agli inizi del secolo XX* (Rome, 1970), p. 100.

68. G. Amendola, *Fascismo e movimento operaio* (Rome, 1975), p. 27, notes that, in Ferrara, the Socialists won 55 per cent of the vote in 1911, 75 per cent in 1919 and 24 per cent in 1921.

69. G. Arfè, *Storia del socialismo italiano (1892–1926)* (Turin, 1965), pp. 16, 19.

70. M. Degl'Innocenti, *Il socialismo italiano e la guerra di Libia* (Rome, 1976), p. 297.

71. E. Ragionieri, *Un comune socialista: Sesto Fiorentino* (Rome, 1976), p. 186.

72. Melograni, *Storia politica della grande guerra*, p. 301.

73. Zamagni, *The economic history of Italy*, p. 213.

74. Camarda and Peli, *L'altro esercito*, p. 32.

75. For a detailed description, see P. Spriano, *Torino operaio nella grande guerra* (Turin, 1960), pp. 235–51.

76. C. Cartiglia, *Rinaldo Rigola e il sindacalismo riformista in Italia* (Milan, 1976), p. 80.

77. Clark, *Antonio Gramsci and the revolution that failed*, pp. 24–7.

78. P. Pieri, *L'Italia nella prima guerra mondiale (1915–1918)* (Turin, 1965), p. 175.

79. Malatesta, *I socialisti italiani durante la guerra*, pp. 160–62, 167–73.

80. E. Vercesi, *Il Vaticano, l'Italia e la guerra* (Milan, 1925), pp. 31, 213, 266–7, 299.

81. H. Fornari, *Mussolini's gadfly: Roberto Farinacci* (Nashville, 1971), pp. 18–19.

82. F. Meda, *I Cattolici italiani nella prima guerra mondiale* (Milan, 1965), p. ix (the book was first published in 1928).

83. Ibid., p. 5. In his account of the war, he spent some time justifying the Italian seizure of the Palazzo Venezia, until August 1916 owned by the Habsburgs and housing their embassy to the Vatican.

84. F. E. Manuel, 'The Palestine question in Italian diplomacy, 1917–1920', *Journal of Modern History*, 27, 1955, p. 272. The Dominicans were believed to be less enthusiastic about the nation.

85. A. Ventrone, *La seduzione totalitaria: guerra, modernità, violenza politica (1914–1918)* (Rome, 2003), p. 38.

86. Melograni, *Storia politica della grande guerra*, pp. 131–4.

87. R. Giuliani, *Gli arditi: breve storia dei reparti d'assalto della Terza Armata* (Milan, 1926), pp. 14–15, 34, 61, 204.

88. P. L. Meloni, 'I cattolici e la grande guerra nella pubblicistica perugina' in M. C. Giuntella, G. Pellegrini and L. Tosi (eds), *Cattolici e società in Umbria tra Ottocento e Novecento* (Rome, 1984), pp. 373, 408–11.

89. G. Corni, 'L'occupazione austro-germanica del Veneto nel 1917–18: sindaci, preti, austriacanti e patrioti', *Rivista di storia contemporanea*, 18, 1989, pp. 388, 401–6.

90. See, for example, N. Brancaccio, *In Francia durante la guerra* (Milan, 1926), pp. 161–3.

91. For the detail, see R. L. Hess, 'Italy and Africa: colonial ambitions in the First World War', *Journal of African History*, 4, 1963, pp. 105–26.

92. G. Giordano, *Carlo Sforza: la diplomazia 1896–1921* (Milan, 1987), p. 77.

93. L. Federzoni, *Paradossi di ieri* (Milan, 1926), p. 12.

94. F. Gaeta (ed.), *La stampa nazionalista* (Rocca San Casciano, 1965), p. 7.

95. Quoted by A. J. De Grand, 'The Italian Nationalist Association in the period of Italian neutrality, August 1914–May 1915', *Journal of Modern History*, 43, 1971, p. 407.

96. On 24 October 1918, before hostilities ended, in *Il Corriere della Sera* D'Annunzio had already urged care lest 'our victory be maimed'. E. Di Nolfo, *Mussolini la politica estera italiana, 1919–1933* (Padua, 1960), p. 5.

4 1919

1. A. R. Fusilli, *Giampaoli (con prefazione di Mario Carli)* (Rome, 1928), pp. 12, 138–9.

2. See files in ACS, SPDCR 46 and especially 30 September 1927, police report.

3. R. J. Evans, *The coming of the Third Reich* (London, 2003), p. 72.

4. P. Bolzon, *'Le verghe e le scure': Il dado gittato: commento spirituale di una crociera rivoluzionaria* (Florence, 1923), p. 31.

5. L. Salvatorelli and G. Mira, *Storia d'Italia nel periodo fascista* (Milan, 1969), vol. 1, p. 11.

6. R. Albrecht-Carrié, *Italy at the Paris Peace Conference* (Hamden, Conn., 1966), p. 43.

7. L. Aldrovandi Marescotti, *Guerra diplomatica* (Milan, 1937), p. 199.

8. L. A. Cretella, 'A lost opportunity: Italian banks and Anatolian railroads in 1920', *Risorgimento*, 1, 1980, p. 343.

9. BMOO XII, pp. 110–12.

10. BMOO XII, p. 108.

11. BMOO XIII, p. 83.

12. G. Giuriati, *La parabola di Mussolini nei ricordi di una gerarca* (ed. E. Gentile) (Bari, 1981), pp. 9–10.

13. R. Farinacci, *Storia della rivoluzione fascista, vol. I, Il 1919* (Cremona, 1937), p. 72.

14. S. Crespi, *Alla difesa d'Italia in guerra e a Versailles* (Milan, 1937), pp. 702–4.

15. BMOO XIII, p. 72.

16. BMOO XIII, p. 89.

17. BMOO XIII, p. 205.

18. BMOO XIII, p. 218.

19. For the best recent study of these matters, see D. J. Forsyth, *The crisis of Liberal Italy: monetary and financial policy, 1914–1922* (Cambridge, 1993).

Forsyth provides a detailed statistical appendix of Italy's fiscal position (pp. 295–330).

20. Ibid., pp. 197, 230.

21. G. Giuriati, *Con D'Annunzio e Millo in difesa dell'Adriatico* (Florence, 1954), p. 2.

22. A. Tasca, *The rise of Italian Fascism 1918–1922* (New York, 1966), p. 59.

23. For figures, see V. Zamagni, *The economic history of Italy 1860–1990* (Oxford, 1993), p. 239. Railway workers were also doing badly.

24. R. Vivarelli, *Storia delle origini del fascismo: L'Italia dalla grande guerra alla marcia su Roma* (Bologna, 1991), pp. 299–300.

25. R. De Felice, *Mussolini il rivoluzionario 1883–1920* (Turin, 1965), p. 426.

26. G. Procacci, 'Appunti in tema di crisi dello Stato liberale e di origini del fascismo' in G. Sabbatucci (ed.), *La crisi italiana del primo dopoguerra: la storia e la critica* (Bari, 1976), p. 65.

27. Vivarelli, *Storia delle origini del fascismo*, p. 211.

28. G. Rochat, *L'esercito italiano in pace e guerra(:) studi di storia militare* (Padua, 1991), p. 160.

29. A. Gramsci, *Selections from political writings (1910–1920)* (ed. Q. Hoare) (London, 1977), pp. 89, 128, 136, 190.

30. G. Vettori (ed.), *Canzoni italiane di protesta*, pp. 126–7, 369. The song was then popular 'all over Italy'.

31. Vivarelli, *Storia delle origini del fascismo*, pp. 317–18.

32. For an introduction in English, see M. Clark, *Antonio Gramsci and the revolution that failed* (New Haven, 1977), p. 88.

33. F. M. Snowden, *The Fascist revolution in Tuscany 1919–1922* (Cambridge, 1989), pp. 51–3.

34. Cited by A. L. Cardoza, *Agrarian elites and Italian Fascism: the province of Bologna 1901–1926* (Princeton, 1982), p. 285.

35. A. L. Carlotti, *Storia del partito fascista sanmarinese* (Milan, 1973), p. 7.

36. *Il Gazzettino*, 9 September 1919.

37. *Il Gazzettino*, 12 January 1920.

38. A. Roveri, *Le origini del fascismo a Ferrara 1918–1921* (Milan, 1974), p. 37.

39. S. Colarizi, 'Le leghe contadine in Puglia nel primo dopoguerra', *Storia contemporanea*, 1, 1970, p. 904.

40. F. M. Snowden, *Violence and great estates in the south of Italy: Apulia, 1900–1922* (Cambridge, 1986), p. 31.

41. S. Colarizi, *Dopoguerra e fascismo in Puglia (1919–1926)* (Bari, 1971), p. 13.

42. Snowden, *Violence and great estates*, p. 163.

43. G. Miccichè, *Dopoguerra e fascismo in Sicilia 1919–1927* (Rome, 1976), p. 18.

44. A. A. Kelikian, *Town and country under Fascism: the transformation of Brescia 1915–26* (Oxford, 1986), p. 94.

45. G. Sabbatucci, *I combattenti nel primo dopoguerra* (Bari, 1974), pp. 29, 43, 55, 98, 117–19, 197–8.

46. For a full account, see S. Sechi, *Dopoguerra e fascismo in Sardegna: il movimento autonomistico nella crisi dello stato liberale (1918–1926)* (Turin, 1969).

47. E. Lussu, *Enter Mussolini* (London, 1936), pp. 9–10.

48. Giuriati, *Con D'Annunzio e Millo*, p. 100.

49. M. Franzinelli, *Squadristi: protagonisti e techniche della violenza fascista 1919–1922* (Milan, 2003), p. 169.

50. F. Vecchi, *Arditismo civile* (Milan, 1920), p. 36.

51. D. L. Rusinow, *Italy's Austrian heritage, 1919–1946* (Oxford, 1969), p. 46.

52. A. J. Rhodes, *The poet as superman: a life of Gabriele D'Annunzio* (London, 1959), p. 130.

53. Ibid., pp. 20–21; T. Antongini, *D'Annunzio* (London, 1938), pp. 1–3.

54. Antongini, *D'Annunzio*, pp. 3–4, 235.

55. M. A. Ledeen, *The first Duce: D'Annunzio at Fiume* (Baltimore, 1977), p. 17.

56. Antongini, *D'Annunzio*, pp. 278, 530.

57. Giuriati, *Con D'Annunzio e Millo*, p. 55.

58. Rhodes, *The poet as superman*, p. 147.

59. Ledeen, *The first Duce*, p. 47.

60. For the case of Comm. Prof. Harukichi Shimoi, see SPDCO 128083.

61. Ledeen, *The first Duce*, p. 173.

62. R. De Felice, *D'Annunzio politico 1918–1938* (Bari, 1978), pp. 61–2.

63. Ledeen, *The first Duce*, pp. 164–76.

64. Giuriati, *Con D'Annunzio e Millo*, pp. 56–8.

65. Ledeen, *The first Duce*, p. vii.

66. BMOO X, pp. 140–42.

67. De Felice, *Mussolini il rivoluzionario 1883–1920*, pp. 412–18.

68. BMOO XI, pp. 8–9.

69. BMOO XI, pp. 241–3.

70. BMOO XII, p. 28.

71. BMOO XII, pp. 52–5.

72. BMOO XII, p. 309.

73. P. Bolzon, *'Le verghe e le scure': Roveto ardente: commento spirituale di una crociera rivoluzionaria* (Florence, 1923), p. xi.

74. De Felice, *Mussolini il rivoluzionario*, pp. 476–7.

75. D. Detragiache, 'Le fascisme féminin de San Sepolcro à l'affaire Matteotti', *Revue d'histoire moderne et contemporaine*, 30, 1983, pp. 366–400.

76. Sechi, *Dopoguerra e fascismo in Sardegna*, p. 45.

77. De Felice, *Mussolini il rivoluzionario*, pp. 510–11.

78. G. Ricci, *Squadrismo forlivese* (Forlì, 1942), p. 139.

79. BMOO XI, pp. 270–72.

80. See, for example, BMOO XI, p. 384, where, ironically given later developments, he contrasted the 'young' United States with 'old' Europe.

81. For the programme, see De Felice, *Mussolini il rivoluzionario*, pp. 742–3.

82. BMOO XIII, pp. 61–3.

83. R. Cantagalli, *Storia del fascismo fiorentino 1919–1925* (Florence, 1972), p. 79.

84. E. Mariano, 'Significati e strutture letterarie del carteggio' in R. De Felice and E. Mariano (eds), *Carteggio D'Annunzio–Mussolini (1919–1938)* (Milan, 1971), pp. lxix–lxx.

85. De Felice, *Mussolini il rivoluzionario*, p. 533.

86. See A. Longoni, *Fascismo ed aviazione: gli aviatori nella rivoluzione fascista* (Milan, 1931) for an account of these 'aerial Fascists', including, for example, the Duchessa Fiammetta Carafa d'Andria. Attilio's brother, Edgardo, another journalist and 'Fascist of the first hour', was a more wide-ranging pioneer of modern sports.

87. BMOO XIV, pp. 43–5, 133.

5 Becoming a Fascist

1. F. Cammarano, 'The professions in parliament', in M. Malatesta (ed.), *Society and the professions in Italy, 1860–1914* (Cambridge, 1995), p. 311.

2. BMOO X, p. 188.

3. L. Salvatorelli and G. Mira, *Storia d'Italia nel periodo fascista* (Milan, 1969), vol. 1, p. 12.

4. E. Scarfoglio, *La guerra della sterlina contro il marco vista dall'Italia* (Rome, 1915), p. 17.

5. Unione Generale degli Insegnanti Italiani per la Guerra Nazionale, 'Un nuovo alleato'. This pamphlet bore no date but was printed in 1918.

6. M. Canali, *Cesare Rossi: da rivoluzionario a eminenza grigia del fascismo* (Bologna, 1991), p. 128.

7. N. S. Onofri, *La strage di palazzo d'Accursio: origine e nascita del fascismo bolognese* (Milan, 1980), p. 10.

8. M. Vaini, *Le origini del fascismo a Mantova (1914–1922)* (Rome, 1961), p. 73.

9. *Giovinissima: rivista mensile di educazione fascista*, 5, February 1935.

10. D. R. Forsyth, *The crisis of Liberal Italy: monetary and financial policy, 1914–1922* (Cambridge, 1993), pp. 230–35.

11. P. Spriano, *The occupation of the factories: Italy 1920* (London, 1975), pp. 42–3.

12. Forsyth, *The crisis of Liberal Italy*, pp. 236–60.

13. See table in ibid., p. 325.

14. See table, V. Zamagni, *The economic history of Italy 1860–1990* (Oxford, 1993), p. 213.

15. Ibid., pp. 238–9. Working from a 1913 index of 100, Zamagni places the real wages of agricultural workers at 107 in 1918, 130 in 1919, 118 in both 1920 and 1921 and 123 in 1922; factory workers were at 79 in 1918, 109 in 1919, 137 in 1920, 138 in 1921 and 134 in 1922.

16. Spriano, *The occupation of the factories*, pp. 41, 65.

17. A. Gramsci, *Selections from the political writings (1910–1920)* (ed. Q. Hoare) (London, 1977), p. 326.

18. V. Castronovo, *Giovanni Agnelli: la Fiat dal 1899 al 1945* (Turin, 1977), pp. 177–82.

19. R. De Felice, *Mussolini il rivoluzionario 1883–1920* (Turin, 1965), pp. 629–34.

20. Spriano, *The occupation of the factories*, pp. 75, 92, 97.

21. His biography can be followed through these years in H. Fornari, *Mussolini's gadfly: Roberto Farinacci* (Nashville, 1971), pp. 17–50.

22. G. Cremonesi, *Voci e moniti della vecchia Italia: dalla democrazia di Ettore Sacchi alla signoria di Roberto Farinacci* (Cremona, 1946), pp. 212–13.

23. R. Farinacci, *Squadrismo* (Rome, 1933), p. 17.

24. S. Lupo, *Il Fascismo: la politica in un regime totalitario* (Rome, 2000), p. 77.

25. See, for example, *Il Regime Fascista*, 28 May 1935, and the republication then of Bissolati's 'war diary'. L. Bissolati, *Diario di guerra: appunti presi sulle linee, nei comandi, nei consigli interalleati* (Turin, 1935).

26. SPDCR 40, with the identical works, though each has a different title, by Farinacci and by Stefano Marenghi.

27. M. Franzinelli, *Squadristi: protagonisti e techniche della violenza fascista 1919–1922* (Milan, 2003), p. 103.

28. Fornari, *Mussolini's gadfly*, p. 38.

29. De Felice, *Mussolini il rivoluzionario*, p. 594.

30. For a classic description of one of these raids, see Farinacci, *Squadrismo*, pp. 75–6.

31. De Felice, *Mussolini il rivoluzionario*, p. 635.

32. E. Gentile, *Storia del Partito Fascista 1919–1922: movimento e milizia* (Bari, 1989), pp. vii, 518.

33. Balbo's biography can be followed in C. G. Segrè, *Italo Balbo: a Fascist life* (Berkeley, 1987) and G. B. Guerri, *Italo Balbo* (Milan, 1984).

34. I. Balbo, *Diario 1922* (Milan, 1932), p. 6.

35. A. Roveri, *Le origini del fascismo a Ferrara 1918–1921* (Milan, 1974), p. 20.

36. Ibid., pp. 60, 68, 86.

37. P. Corner, *Fascism in Ferrara 1915–1925* (Oxford, 1975), pp. 55–6, 114–15, 121.

38. Segrè, *Italo Balbo*, p. 41.

39. Roveri, *Le origini del fascismo a Ferrara*, pp. 168–73.

40. R. Camurri, 'L'Ottocento e il Novecento', *Istituto della Enciclopedia Italiana* (Rome, 2002), p. 1383.

41. D. Grandi, 'Il diario della marcia su Roma', *Epoca*, 15 October 1972, p. 80.

42. P. Nello, *Dino Grandi: la formazione di un leader fascista* (Bologna, 1987), p. 44.

43. D. Grandi, *Giovani* (Bologna, 1941), pp. 85, 96, 105, 133.

44. Ibid., pp. 160–61, 189–90.

45. A. L. Cardoza, *Agrarian elites and Italian Fascism: the province of Bologna 1901–1926* (Princeton, 1982), p. 278.

46. T. Nanni, *Leandro Arpinati e il fascismo bolognese* (Bologna, 1927), p. 104.

47. G. Bergamo, *Il Fascismo visto da un repubblicano* (Bologna, 1921), pp. 9, 13–14.

48. Nello, *Dino Grandi*, pp. 67–73. He was still expressing this view in March 1921.

49. Cardoza, *Agrarian elites and Italian Fascism*, p. 377.

50. BMOO XVI, pp. 25–6.

51. BMOO XVI, p. 25.

52. R. De Felice, *Mussolini il fascista 1. La conquista del potere 1921–1925* (Turin, 1966), pp. 92, 136, 158.

53. Cardoza, *Agrarian elites and Italian Fascism*, p. 329.

54. Gentile, *Storia del Partito Fascista*, pp. 37–8.

55. De Felice, *Mussolini il rivoluzionario*, pp. 596, 636.

56. De Felice, *Mussolini il fascista 1. La conquista del potere*, pp. 74–5.

57. For examples, see A. Lyttelton, *The seizure of power: Fascism in Italy 1919–1929* (London, 1973), pp. 52–3.

58. De Felice, *Mussolini il fascista 1. La conquista del potere*, pp. 183–4.

59. Gentile, *Storia del Partito Fascista*, p. 365.

60. Corner, *Fascism in Ferrara*, p. 72.

61. D. M. Tuninetti, *La vita di Michele Bianchi* (Rome, 1935), p. 81.

62. Cited by Lyttelton, *The seizure of power: Fascism*, p. 45.

63. SPDCR 100, 17 August 1929, police report on the allegedly corrupt activities of Marchesa Maria De Seta.

64. For a classic example, see R. J. B. Bosworth, *Mussolini* (London, 2002), p. 230.

65. For a summary of his career, see Canali, *Cesare Rossi: da rivoluzionario a eminenza grigia del fascismo*.

66. See R. De Felice, 'Prefazione' to M. Piazzesi, *Diario di uno squadrista toscano 1919–1922* (ed. M. Toscano)(Rome, 1981), pp. 7–10.

67. M. Toscano, 'Introduzione' to M. Piazzesi, *Diario di uno squadrista toscano*, p. 23.

68. See B. F. Smith, *Heinrich Himmler: a Nazi in the making, 1900–1926* (Stanford, 1971), pp. 48–66, for his bitter disappointment in not quite making it to the front and his rapid joining of the local Free Corps in partial compensation.

69. For his own eventual memoirs, see M. Terzaghi, *Fascismo e Massoneria* (Milan, 1950).

70. M. Piazzesi, *Diario di uno squadrista toscano*, pp. 48–54.

71. Ibid., pp. 56, 193, 199.

72. Ibid., pp. 64–5, 164, 223.

73. B. Frullini, *Squadrismo fiorentino* (Florence, 1933), pp. 13–14, 51.

74. For a description by an anti-Fascist historian, see R. Cantagalli, *Storia del fascismo fiorentino 1919–1925* (Florence, 1972), pp. 177–95.

75. De Felice, *Mussolini il fascista 1. La conquista del potere*, p. 31.

76. See G. Gregori, *La strage di Empoli* (Rome, 1932), pp. 71–2, 82–3, written for the Fascist Decennale of that year.

77. M. Piazzesi, *Diario di uno squadrista toscano*, pp. 119–22. For a rival communist memoir, see J. Busoni, *Nel tempo del fascismo* (Rome, 1975), pp. 61–80.

78. M. Piazzesi, *Diario di uno squadrista toscano*, pp. 163–4.

79. L. Freddi, *Bandiere nere: contributo alla storia del Fascismo* (Rome, nd), p. 14.

80. Cited by Gentile, *Storia del Partito Fascista*, p. 499.

81. T. Cianetti, *Memorie dal carcere di Verona* (ed. R. De Felice) (Milan, 1983), pp. 67–70.

82. Gentile, *Storia del Partito Fascista*, p. 533.

83. G. Mayda, *Il pugnale di Mussolini: storia di Amerigo Dumini, sicario di Matteotti* (Bologna, 2004), p. 84.

84. See CP 1001, file on Michele Terzaghi. He was sentenced to five years but amnestied after six months.

85. Terzaghi, *Fascismo e Massoneria*, p. 131.

86. Mayda, *Il pugnale di Mussolini*, p. 87.

87. Cantagalli, *Storia del fascismo fiorentino*, pp. 110, 119, 197–202.

88. F. M. Snowden, *The Fascist revolution in Tuscany 1919–1922* (Cambridge, 1989), p. 113.

89. See, for example, the grovelling account by C. Mansueti, 'Il monumento a Giovanni Buitoni a Sansepolcro e le Opere insigne del nipote', *Il Mare Nostro-Stirpe Italica*, December 1936.

90. SPDCR 97, 19 June 1934, D. Ghetti to Sebastiani.

91. M. Franzinelli, *I tentacoli dell'Ovra: agenti, collaboratori e vittime della polizia politica fascista* (Turin, 1999), pp. 8–9.

92. For a summary of her early career, see V. De Grazia, *How Fascism ruled women: Italy 1922–1945* (Berkeley, 1992), pp. 32–3 and cf. the potted biography, E. Romano, 'Elisa Majer Rizzioli', *Il Mare Nostro-Stirpe Italica*, June 1934.

93. *La Vetta d'Italia*, 14 May 1922.

94. BMOO XIV, pp. 372–3, 379–80, 396–8. Cf. also XVI, pp. 101–3 when, in January 1921, almost a purist liberal, he again stated that Fascism stood for the gradual 'demobilization of the state'.

95. BMOO XIV, pp. 469–71.

96. BMOO XV, pp. 55–7.

97. BMOO XV, pp. 269–70.

98. BMOO XVI, pp. 5–8.

99. BMOO XV, pp. 152–4.

100. BMOO XV, p. 299.

101. BMOO XV, p. 287.

102. Corner, *Fascism in Ferrara*, p. 146.

103. BMOO XVI, pp. 170–73.

104. BMOO XVI, pp. 186–8.

105. BMOO XVI, pp. 211–13.

106. BMOO XVI, pp. 270–71.

107. F. Perfetti, *Fascismo monarchico: i paladini della monarchia assoluta fra integralismo e dissidio* (Rome, 1988), pp. 13–16.

108. De Felice, *Mussolini il fascista 1. La conquista del potere*, p. 92.

6 Learning to rule in the provinces

1. P. Togliatti, *Lectures on Fascism* (London, 1976), p. 1.

2. R. De Felice, *Mussolini il fascista 1. La conquista del potere 1921–1925* (Turin, 1966), p. 7.

3. E. R. Tannenbaum, 'The goals of Italian Fascism', *American Historical Review*, 74, 1969, p. 1188.

4. De Felice, *Mussolini il fascista 1. La conquista del potere*, pp. 6–11. For Bocchini, see R. J. B. Bosworth, *Mussolini* (London, 2002), pp. 220–22.

5. G. De Falco, *Il Fascismo milizia di classe: commenti alla cronaca* (Bologna, 1921), p. 15. Cf. the similar views of the sometime radical Fascist G. Bergamo, *Il Fascismo visto da un repubblicano* (Bologna, 1921), p. 32.

6. E. Apih, *Italia fascismo e antifascismo nella Venezia Giulia (1918–1943)* (Bari, 1966), p. 12.

7. G. Piemontese, *Il movimento operaio a Trieste: dalle origini all'avvento del fascismo* (Rome, 1974), pp. 135, 210.

8. Apih, *Italia fascismo e antifascismo nella Venezia Giulia*, pp. 20, 92.

9. See D. L. Rusinow, *Italy's Austrian heritage, 1919–1946* (Oxford, 1969).

10. In 1923, the city was thought to be second in the world in its suicide rate (behind San Francisco). See Apih, *Italia fascismo e antifascismo nella Venezia Giulia*, p. 208.

11. Ibid., pp. 93–5.

12. S. Lupo, *Il Fascismo: la politica in un regime totalitario* (Rome, 2000), p. 55.

13. P. Bolzon, *'Le verghe e le scure': Roveto ardente: commento spirituale di una crociera spirituale* (Florence, 1923), pp. 175–6.

14. P. Bolzon, *'Le verghe e le scure': Il Dado gittato: commento spirituale di una crociera rivoluzionaria* (Florence, 1923), pp. 131–2.

15. F. Giunta, *Essenza dello squadrismo* (Rome, 1931), pp. 50, 70–72, 183.

16. F. Giunta, *Un po' di Fascismo* (Milan, 1935), pp. 50–53.

17. Apih, *Italia fascismo e antifascismo nella Venezia Giulia*, p. 131.

18. BMOO XV, pp. 38–9.

19. Giunta, *Un po' di Fascismo*, pp. 12–13.

20. D. A. Binchy, *Church and state in Fascist Italy* (Oxford, 1941), pp. 556–7.

21. Apih, *Italia fascismo e antifascismo nella Venezia Giulia*, pp. 181–5.

22. See *Le Vie d'Italia*, XXV, May 1919, pp. 97–100.

23. A. M. Preziosi, *Borghesia e fascismo in Friuli negli anni 1920–1922* (Rome, 1980), p. 11.

24. See A. Lyttelton, *The seizure of power: Fascism in Italy 1919–1929* (London, 1973), p. 276.

25. De Felice, *Mussolini il fascista 1. La conquista del potere*, pp. 10–11.

26. Preziosi, *Borghesia e fascismo in Friuli*, pp. 35–6.

27. Lyttelton, *The seizure of power*, pp. 165–6.

28. Preziosi, *Borghesia e fascismo in Friuli*, p. 105.

29. S. Romano, *Giuseppe Volpi: industria e finanza tra Giolitti e Mussolini* (Milan, 1979), pp. 85–93.

30. F. Piva, *Lotte contadine e origini del fascismo Padova-Venezia; 1919–1922* (Venice, 1977), p. 79.

31. Romano, *Giuseppe Volpi*, p. 74.

32. R. De Felice, *Mussolini il rivoluzionario 1883–1920* (Turin, 1965), p. 647.

33. Piva, *Lotte contadine e origini del fascismo*, pp. 84, 141–4.

34. *Il Gazzettino*, 19 August 1921.

35. *Il Gazzettino*, 24 January 1922.

36. M. Franzinelli, *Squadristi: protagonisti e tecniche della violenza fascista 1919–1922* (Milan, 2003), pp. 221–2.

37. A. L. Savona and M. L. Straniero, *Canti dell'Italia fascista (1919–1945)* (Milan, 1979), pp. 72–3.

38. Franzinelli, *Squadristi*, p. 156.

39. Ibid., pp. 134–8. Riccardi published his own account of these times. See R. Riccardi, *Pagine squadristiche* (Rome, 1939).

40. For a recent eulogy, see G. Picardo, *Aurelio Padovani: il fascista intransigente* (Naples, 2003).

41. De Felice, *Mussolini il fascista 1. La conquista del potere*, p. 189.

42. P. Varvaro, *Una città fascista: potere e società a Napoli* (Palermo, 1990), p. 18.

43. S. Sechi, *Dopoguerra e fascismo in Sardegna: il movimento autonomisitico nella crisi dello Stato liberale (1918–1926)* (Turin, 1969), pp. 26–7, 150, 153, 243.

44. De Felice, *Mussolini il fascista 1. La conquista del potere*, pp. 10–11.

45. CP 584, file on Emilio Lussu, 8 August 1929, report.

46. Sechi, *Dopoguerra e fascismo in Sardegna*, pp. 326, 352.

47. G. Miccicchè, *Dopoguerra e fascismo in Sicilia 1919–1927* (Rome, 1976), pp. 119, 146.

48. MI DGPS G-1, b. 94, 26 May 1921, Prefect (Porro) to Minister.

49. MI DGPS G-1, b. 119, 22 August 1922, Prefect (Porro) to Minister.

50. MI DGPS G-1, b. 119, 27 September 1922, Prefect to DGPS.

51. P. Arlacchi, *Mafia, peasants and great estates: society in traditional Calabria* (Cambridge, 1983), pp. 5, 44, 124, 172, 179.

52. G. Cingari, *Reggio Calabria* (Bari, 1988), pp. 257, 273.

53. A. Lyttelton, *Italian Fascism from Pareto to Gentile* (London, 1973), p. 193.

54. SPDCR 87, 2 July 1934, Lanzillo to Mussolini.

55. F. M. Snowden, *Violence and great estates in the south of Italy: Apulia, 1900–1922* (Cambridge, 1986), pp. 1, 174–6, 196.

56. A. Lanzillo, *Le rivoluzioni del dopoguerra* (Città di Castello, 1922) as quoted by De Felice, *Mussolini il fascista 1. La conquista del potere*, p. 12.

57. BMOO XVII, pp. 10–14.

58. BMOO XVII, pp. 17–18.

59. De Felice, *Mussolini il fascista 1. La conquista del potere*, pp. 144, 149.

60. P. Nello, *Dino Grandi: la formazione di un leader fascista* (Bologna, 1987), p. 126.

61. De Felice, *Mussolini il fascista 1. La conquista del potere*, p. 139.

62. BMOO XVII, p. 67.

63. BMOO XVII, pp. 103–5.

64. De Felice, *Mussolini il fascista 1. La conquista del potere*, p. 151.

65. See the accounts in the *Bollettino* of the Unione Spirituale Dannunziana, 1 August 1923.

66. De Felice, *Mussolini il fascista 1. La conquista del potere*, p. 153.

67. BMOO XVII, pp. 196–7.

68. BMOO XVII, p. 220.

69. BMOO XVII, p. 360.

70. BMOO XVIII, p. 44.

71. *La Vetta d'Italia*, 20 August 1922.

72. BMOO XVII, p. 348.

73. *La Vetta d'Italia*, 14 May 1922. Roma Gilardini was the author.

74. BMOO XVIII, pp. 16–18, 36.

75. BMOO XVIII, p. 119.

76. BMOO XVIII, p. 418.

77. BMOO XVIII, p. 138; cf. also pp. 347–50.

78. BMOO XVIII, pp. 189–91, 282.

79. I. Balbo, *Diario 1922* (Milan, 1932), pp. 95–110.

80. De Felice, *Mussolini il fascista 1. La conquista del potere*, p. 275.

81. Balbo, *Diario 1922*, pp. 115–37.

82. De Felice, *Mussolini il fascista 1. La conquista del potere*, p. 300.

83. E. Ferraris, *La Marcia su Roma veduta dal Viminale* (Rome, 1946), pp. 48–9.

84. L. Salvatorelli and G. Mira, *Storia d'Italia nel periodo fascista* (Turin, 1969), vol. 1, pp. 230–31. Salandra was speaking at Troia near Bari and so was implicitly endorsing the vicious Fascism of his region.

85. Lyttelton, *The seizure of power*, p. 102.

86. G. Acerbo, *Fra due plotoni di esecuzione: avvenimenti e problemi dell'epoca fascista* (Rocca San Casciano, 1968), pp. 176–7.

87. De Felice, *Mussolini il fascista 1. La conquista del potere*, p. 376.

88. Lyttelton, *The seizure of power*, p. 109.

89. De Felice, *Mussolini il fascista 1. La conquista del potere*, pp. 392–4, 401.

90. Balbo, *Diario 1922*, pp. 163–7.

91. De Felice, *Mussolini il fascista 1. La conquista del potere*, p. 345, for the plan.

92. H. Woller, *Roma, 28 ottobre 1922. L'Europa e la sfida dei fascismi* (Bologna, 2001), p. 15.

93. Giunta, *Un po' di Fascismo*, p. 95.

94. M. Rocca, *Come il fascismo divenne una dittatura* (Milan, 1952), p. 113.

95. *L'Alpino*, 20 November–5 December 1922.

96. BMOO XVIII, pp. 462–3.

97. BMOO XVIII, pp. 468–9.

98. A. De Ambris, 'Mussolini: la leggenda e l'uomo' (1930) in R. De Felice (ed.), *Benito Mussolini; quattro testimonianze* (Florence, 1976), pp. 35, 42, 72.

7 Learning to rule from Rome

1. Carte Bianchi, b. 4, f. 80, 4 May 1923, report.

2. Carte Bianchi, b. 1, f. 10, 18 September 1923, report.

3. G. Fortunato, *Carteggio 1912–1922* (ed. E. Gentile) (Bari, 1979), pp. 416–19.

4. A. Lessona, *Un ministro di Mussolini racconta* (Milan, 1973), pp. 22–8.

5. For a contemporary account, see D. Manetti, *Gente di Romagna: Aldo Oviglio* (Bologna, 1924), pp. 402–3.

6. G. Salvemini, *Carteggio 1921–1926* (ed. E. Tagliacozzo) (Bari, 1985), p. 147.

7. F. Marcoaldi, *Vent'anni di economia e politica: La carte De' Stefani (1922–1941)* (Milan, 1986), p. 18.

8. B. Mussolini, *Corrispondenza inedita* (ed. D. Susmel) (Milan, 1972), p. 47.

9. N. D'Aroma, *Vent'anni insieme: Vittorio Emanuele e Mussolini* (Rocca San Casciano, 1957), p. 141.

10. C. Casalengo, *La Regina Margherita* (Turin, 1956), pp. 224–5.

11. BMOO XIX, pp. 74–6.

12. P. Scoppola, *La Chiesa e il Fascismo: documenti e interpretazioni* (Bari, 1971), pp. 63–7.

13. M. Rocca, *Come il fascismo divenne una dittatura* (Milan, 1952), p. 115.

14. For the documentation, see A. Aquarone, *L'organizzazione dello stato totalitario* (Turin, 1965), pp. 15–21, 332–5.

15. A. Teruzzi, *La milizia delle camicie nere e le sue specialità* (Milan, 1933), pp. 19–43.

16. S. Lupo, *Il Fascismo: la politica in un regime totalitario* (Rome, 2000), p. 166.

17. MI DGPS G-1, b. 119, 29 November 1922, Prefect to Ministry of the Interior.

18. MI DGPS G-1, b. 119, 30 November 1922, N. L. Tassone (mayor of Pallapolio), phone message to Mussolini.

19. MI DGPS G-1, b. 85, 26 December 1922, Prefect to Ministry of the Interior.

20. MI DGPS G-1, b. 119, 17 December 1922, Prefect to Ministry of the Interior.

21. MI DGPS G-1, b. 85, report of acts of violence in December 1922, sent to Ministry of the Interior.

22. BMOO XIX, pp. 4–5.

23. Carte Bianchi, b. 1, f. 12, 18 November 1922, Balbo to Bianchi.

24. Aquarone, *L'organizzazione dello stato totalitario*, pp. 338–9.

25. For a detailed account, see R. De Felice, *Fascismo, Antifascismo, Nazione: note e ricerche* (Rome, 1996), pp. 63–104.

26. See, for example, P. Gorgolini, *The Fascist movement in Italian life* (with a preface by B. Mussolini) (London, 1923). This book was strenuously nationalist in tone but argued for the present that Italy needed 'absolute quiet' and remembered to hail Mussolini as 'young in the most absolute sense of the word' (pp. 32, 101).

27. SPDCR 4, 26 June 1923, Prefect (Palmieri) to Mussolini.

28. SPDCR 4, 18 December 1922, Mussolini to De Vecchi.

29. Cited by Aquarone, *L'organizzazione dello stato totalitario*, pp. 336–7.

30. MRF 52/122, [nd but 1928], Turati to Provincial PNF *federali*.

31. R. De Felice, *Mussolini il fascista 1. La conquista del potere 1921–1925* (Turin, 1966), p. 407.

32. SPDCR 87, 31 January 1938, De Bono to Starace. The claim was that the joining only occurred in 1924 but was moved back to 28 October 1922.

33. S. Romano, *Giuseppe Volpi: industria e finanza tra Giolitti e Mussolini* (Milan, 1979), p. 197.

34. De Felice, *Mussolini il fascista 1. La conquista del potere 1921–1925*, pp. 410–11.

35. Carte Bianchi, b. 4, f. 8, 30 January 1924, G. Fiorlunga to Bianchi.

36. G. Cingari, *Reggio Calabria* (Bari, 1988), pp. 292–3.

37. SPDCR 87, 7 January 1925, Lanzillo to Mussolini.

38. A. M. and E. Nasalli Rocca, *Realismo nazionale: per una coscienza politica dei cattolici italiani* (Rome, 1926), p. 191.

39. De Felice, *Mussolini il fascista 1. La conquista del potere 1921–1925*, pp. 585–6.

40. BMOO XX, pp. 13–14.

41. Carte Bianchi, b. 1, f. 13.

42. Aquarone, *L'organizzazione dello stato totalitario*, pp. 340–41.

43. J. Dunnage, *The Italian police and the rise of Fascism: a case study of the province of Bologna, 1897–1925* (Westport, Ct., 1997), p. 158.

44. C. G. Segrè, *Italo Balbo: a Fascist life* (Berkeley, 1987), pp. 130–31.

45. Aquarone, *L'organizzazione dello stato totalitario*, pp. 344–6.

46. BMOO XV, p. 284.

47. BMOO XV, p. 299.

48. BMOO XVI, p. 45.

49. BMOO XVII, pp. 414–15.

50. BMOO XVIII, pp. 160–61.

51. G. Salvemini, *Carteggio 1921–1926*, p. 238.

52. S. Colarizi, *I democratici all'opposizione: Giovanni Amendola e l'Unione nazionale (1922–1926)* (Bologna, 1973), p. 67.

53. BMOO XVI, p. 118.

54. See the advertisements in O. Del Buono, *Eia, Eia, Eia, Alalà! La stampa italiana sotto il fascismo 1919–1943* (Milan, 1971), p. 45.

55. A. L. Savona and M. L. Straniero, *Canti dell'Italia fascista (1919–1945)* (Milan, 1979), pp. 53–63; for a Fascist account of the song's development, see L. Freddi, *Bandiera nera: contributo alla storia del Fascismo* (Rome, nd), pp. 39–48.

56. BMOO XIV, pp. 126–7.

57. G. Cresciani, 'Political songs of modern Italy', *Teaching History*, 12, 1978, pp. 37–8.

58. H. Taubman, *The Maestro: the life of Arturo Toscanini* (New York, 1951), pp. 156–7.

59. SPDCR 102, 24 June 1926, Mascagni to Mussolini.

60. *Il Gazzettino*, 25, 26 February 1928.

61. SPDCR 91, undated report of talk between Mussolini and Starace at a dinner at the palatial Excelsior Hotel.

62. *Gioventù Fascista*, 10 April XI [1932].

63. In this last regard, see E. De Bono, *Anno XIIII: the conquest of an empire* (London, 1937).

64. *L'Alpino*, 31 October 1927.

65. E. Gentile, *Storia del Partito Fascista 1919–1922: movimento e milizia* (Bari, 1989), pp. 525–33.

66. MRF 52/122/3, 9 December 1929, A. Turati circular to secretaries of provincial Fascist federations.

67. G. Bottai, *Diario 1944–1948* (ed. G. B. Guerri) (Milan, 1988), p. 316.

68. For an example of his self-interested cringing to Mussolini, see SPDCR 48, 28 November 1925, Panunzio to Mussolini.

69. *Critica Fascista*, 1, 15 June 1923.

70. *Critica Fascista*, 1, 1 July 1923.

71. *Critica Fascista*, 1, 15 July 1923.

72. *Critica Fascista*, 1, 1 December 1923.

73. The story of the thug who actually beat him (and another Fascist) can be traced in CP 142, file on Enrico Boselli, 26 March 1929, Carabinieri (Milan) to Carabinieri (Rome); 9 May 1929, Prefect (Milan) to Ministry of the Interior; August 1929, Boselli appeal.

74. CP 853, file on Giovanni Redaelli, 31 July 1929, Prefect (Milan) to Ministry of the Interior.

75. CP 646, files on Leopoldo and Umberto Maurelli, 6 April 1929, Carabinieri (Milan) to Carabinieri (Rome); 3 May 1929, Prefect (Milan) to Ministry of the Interior; 8 July 1929, Carabinieri (Milan) to Carabinieri (Rome); 29 July 1929, Prefect (Milan) to Ministry of the Interior.

76. CP 646, 22 May 1929, L. Maurelli to Mussolini.

77. CP 646, 6 April 1929, Carabinieri (Milan) to Carabinieri (Rome).

78. CP 113, file on Ettore Biddau, 19 June 1929, Prefect (Milan) to Ministry of the Interior; 21 August 1929, Ministry of the Interior report.

79. CP 113, 4 March 1929, Biddau appeal. Cf. Carte Roberto Farinacci 5, 5 June 1930, in which Biddau tried to offer himself as a client to Farinacci.

80. CP 113, 19 June 1929, Prefect (Milan) to Ministry of the Interior.

81. C. Duggan, *Fascism and the Mafia* (New Haven, 1989), pp. 121–4.

82. C. Mori, *Con la Mafia ai ferri corti* (Milan, 1932), pp. 230, 249–50.

83. Duggan, *Fascism and the Mafia*, pp. 179, 257–8, 261.

84. M. Canali, *Il delitto Matteotti: affarismo e politica nel primo governo Mussolini* (Bologna, 1997), p. 218.

85. See also G. Rossini (ed.), *Il delitto Matteotti tra il Viminale e l'Aventino: dagli atti del processo De Bono davanti all'Alta Corte di Giustizia* (Bologna, 1966), p. 609.

86. De Felice, *Mussolini il fascista 1. La conquista del potere 1921–1925*, p. 632.

87. *Daily Telegraph*, 15 September 1924, editorial.

88. *Daily Telegraph*, 22 November 1924, editorial.

89. For a description of his behaviour in these months, see R. J. B. Bosworth, *Mussolini* (London, 2002), pp. 194–203.

90. Carte Bianchi b. 1, f. 2, 16 June 1924, Bianchi to Mussolini.

91. SPDCR 4, 23 July 1924, Bottai to Mussolini.

92. Two years later, he was to be expelled from the party. He eventually ascribed Mussolini's victory after the Matteotti murder to his peasant canniness. See M. Terzaghi, *Fascismo e Massoneria* (Milan, 1950), p. 102.

93. See, especially, the brilliant C. Malaparte, *Kaputt* (London, 1948).

94. De Felice, *Mussolini il fascista 1. La conquista del potere 1921–1925*, pp. 664, 712, 715.

95. BMOO XXI, pp. 235–41.

8 Building a totalitarian dictatorship

1. BMOO XXI, p. 425.

2. See, for example, T. Napolitano, 'Il "fascismo" di Stalin', *Critica Fascista*, 15, 15 July 1937.

3. A. Aquarone, *L'organizzazione dello stato totalitario* (Turin, 1965), pp. 347–8, 395–6, 412–13.

4. See, for example, S. Fabbri, 'Il diritto della donna all'elettorato', *Gerarchia*, V, May 1925, pp. 293–5.

5. L. Salvatorelli and G. Mira, *Storia dell'Italia nel periodo fascista* (Turin, 1969), vol. I, p. 412.

6. Aquarone, *L'organizzazione dello stato totalitario*, p. 349.

7. BMOO XXI, pp. 248–50.

8. E. Decleva, 'Il Giornale d'Italia', in B. Vigezzi (ed.), *1919: dopoguerra e*

fascismo: politica e stampa in Italia (Bari, 1965), pp. 54–5.

9. P. V. Cannistraro, *La fabbrica del consenso: fascismo e mass media* (Bari, 1975), p. 76.

10. For Ferretti's eventual troubles (he was replaced at the Press Office in 1931) and the revocation of his temporary expulsion from the PNF, accompanied by fawning to Mussolini, see SPDCR 84.

11. Cannistraro, *La fabbrica del consenso*, p. 88.

12. M. Cesari, *La censura nel periodo fascista* (Naples, 1978), p. 32.

13. For a droll compendium of photos of the *Duce* deemed unsuitable for public consumption, see M. Franzinelli and E. V. Marino, *Il Duce proibito: le fotografie di Mussolini che gli italiani non hanno mai visti* (Milan, 2003).

14. Cesari, *La censura nel periodo fascista*, pp. 28–30.

15. For a narration of the paper's vicissitudes during these years, see D. Mack Smith, *Storia di cento anni di vita italiana visti attraverso il Corriere della Sera* (Milan, 1978), pp. 296–9.

16. Aquarone, *L'organizzazione dello stato totalitario*, p. 91.

17. M. De Marco, *Il Gazzettino: storia di un quotidiano* (Venice, 1936), p. 102.

18. P. Gobetti, *On liberal revolution* (ed. N. Urbanati) (New Haven, 2000), p. 58.

19. L. Freddi, *Bandiere nere: contributo alla storia del fascismo* (Rome, nd), pp. 10–12.

20. E. Amicucci, *La stampa della rivoluzione e del regime* (Milan, 1938), pp. 56–7.

21. For somewhat unlikely hagiography, see R. Farinacci, *Costanzo Ciano* (Bologna, 1940).

22. For his accounts, see G. Ansaldo, *L'antifascista riluttante: memorie del carcere e del confino 1926–1927* (ed. M. Staglieno) (Bologna, 1992); *Il giornalista di Ciano: diari 1932–1943* (Bologna, 2000).

23. Cannistraro, *La fabbrica del consenso*, pp. 227, 229–31.

24. T. H. Koon, *Believe, obey, fight: political socialization of youth in Fascist Italy 1922–1943* (Chapel Hill, 1985), p. 156.

25. P. Ortoleva, 'Telefono', in V. De Grazia and S. Luzzatto (eds), *Dizionario del fascismo* (Turin, 2003), vol. II, pp. 721–2.

26. P. Leprohon, *The Italian cinema* (London, 1972), p. 51.

27. G. P. Brunetta, *Storia del cinema italiano 1895–1945* (Rome, 1979), pp. 242–3, 323–9.

28. CP 385, file on Mario Fabbri, 25 April 1939, Questura (Florence) to Prefect (Florence) contains a long list of seized works which ran from *Fanny*

Hill and Italian translations of French novels to works about physiology and ones expressing neo-Malthusian ideas.

29. SPEP 19, 29 March 1929, Guglielmotti to Melchiori.

30. See, for example, issues of the journal *Sii preparata*, 1924–6.

31. G. Zanzanaini, *Renato Ricci: fascista integrale* (Milan, 2004), pp. 11–12, 82.

32. S. Setta, *Renato Ricci: dallo squadrismo alla Repubblica Sociale Italiana* (Bologna, 1986), p. 61.

33. SPDCR 48.

34. A. Grandi, *I giovani di Mussolini: Fascisti convinti, fascisti pentiti, antifascisti* (Milan, 2001), p. 141.

35. CP 273, file on Giovanni Maria Concina, 8 December 1926, Prefect (Udine) to Ministry of the Interior, 8 August 1927, Concina appeal.

36. D. D. Roberts, *The syndicalist tradition and Italian Fascism* (Manchester, 1979), pp. 252–6, 279.

37. T. Cianetti, *Memorie dal carcere di Verona* (Milan, 1983), p. 97.

38. P. Melograni, *Gli industriali e Mussolini: rapporti tra Confindustria e Fascismo dal 1919 al 1929* (Milan, 1972), pp. 68–9, 109.

39. *Il Secolo*, 10 August 1924, cited in ibid., p. 79.

40. Melograni, *Gli industriali e Mussolini*, p. 45.

41. F. Guarneri, *Battaglie economiche fra le due guerre* (ed. L. Zani) (Bologna, 1988), p. 152.

42. R. De Felice, *Mussolini il fascista 1. La conquista del potere 1921–1925* (Turin, 1966), pp. 594–5.

43. J. Morris, 'Retailers, Fascism and the origins of the social protection of shopkeepers in Italy', *Contemporary European History*, 5, 1996, pp. 285–318.

44. J. Morris, 'The Fascist "disciplining" of the Italian retail sector, 1922–1940', *Business History*, 40, 1998, p. 158.

45. V. De Grazia, *How Fascism ruled women: Italy 1922–1945* (Berkeley, 1992), p. 101.

46. See Aquarone, *L'organizzazione dello stato totalitario*, p. 439.

47. R. De Felice, *Mussolini il fascista 2. L'organizzazione dello stato fascista 1925–1929* (Turin, 1968), pp. 265–6.

48. A. Rocco, *La trasformazione dello Stato: dallo Stato Liberale allo Stato Fascista* (Rome, 1927), pp. 14, 16–17, 25.

49. Aquarone, *L'organizzazione dello stato totalitario*, pp. 442–51.

50. See, for example, G. Bottai, 'Significato della "Carta del Lavoro"', *Gerarchia*, VII, May 1927, pp. 322–4.

51. A. O. Olivetti, *Dal sindacalismo rivoluzionario al corporativismo* (Rome, 1984), pp. 288–9, 477–81.

52. SPDCR 91, reports of 11 March, 29 March and 24 November 1928.

53. J. Dunnage, *Twentieth century Italy: a social history* (London, 2002), p. 76.

54. V. De Grazia, *The culture of consent: mass organisation of leisure in fascist Italy* (Cambridge, 1981), pp. 24–34.

55. *Lo Sport Fascista*, I, June 1928.

56. *Lo Sport Fascista*, I, July 1928.

57. *L'Artigiano*, 29 August 1933.

58. *Lo Sport Fascista*, I, August 1928.

59. P. Dogliani, *L'Italia fascista 1922–1940* (Milan, 1999), p. 176.

60. *Lo Sport Fascista*, II, January 1929.

61. See, for example, *Gerarchia*, VII, January 1927, editorial.

62. G. Volpi di Misurata, *Finanza fascista* (Rome, 1929), p. 209.

63. R. Sarti, 'Mussolini and the Italian industrial leadership in the battle of the lira 1925–1927', *Past and Present*, 47, 1990, p. 97.

64. G. Rochat, *L'esercito italiano da Vittorio Veneto a Mussolini (1919–1925)* (Bari, 1967).

65. De Felice, *Mussolini il fascista 2. L'organizzazione dello stato fascista 1925–1929*, pp. 76–9.

66. Rochat, *L'esercito italiano*, p. 565.

67. Carte Farinacci 2, 27 August 1925, Baldini to Farinacci.

68. C. M. Fiorentino, 'Spie di Mussolini all'ombra di San Pietro: l'attività informativa fascista in Vaticano', *Nuova Storia Contemporanea*, 2, 1998, p. 73. Mons. Pucci was listed on Bocchini's payroll for these services.

69. D. Alvarez, 'Vatican communications security, 1914–18', *Intelligence and National Security*, 7, 1992, p. 445.

70. P. Scoppola, *La Chiesa e il Fascismo: documenti e interpretazioni* (Bari, 1971), p. 54.

71. N. D'Aroma, *Vent'anni insieme: Vittorio Emanuele e Mussolini* (Rocca San Casciano, 1957), p. 192.

72. For his own account, see F. Pacelli, *Diario della Conciliazione con verbali e appendice di documenti* (ed. M. Maccarrone) (Rome, 1959).

73. For the narrative of this event, see R. J. B. Bosworth, *Mussolini* (London, 2002), pp. 236–40.

74. See A. Riccardi (ed.), *Le chiese di Pio XII* (Bari, 1986).

75. P. R. D'Agostino, *Rome in America: transnational Catholic ideology from the Risorgimento to Fascism* (Chapel Hill, 2004), p. 202.

76. H. Fornari, *Mussolini's gadfly: Roberto Farinacci* (Nashville, 1978), p. 93.

77. R. Farinacci, *In difesa dell'assassino Dumini* (Rome, 1945), p. 44.

78. R. Farinacci, *Un periodo aureo del Partito Nazionale Fascista: raccolta di discorsi e dichiarazioni* (ed. R. Bacchetta) (Foligno, 1927), pp. 17, 59, 225–9, 263.

79. G. Bottai, 'Mussolini, dittatore del partito', *Critica Fascista*, 4, September 1926, pp. 342–4.

80. G. Bottai, 'Ritorno ai problemi del Partito', *Critica Fascista*, 5, 1 June 1927, pp. 201–3.

81. SPDCR 41, 6 September 1924, Mussolini to Farinacci.

82. SPDCR 43, 19 April 1925, note.

83. SPDCR 41, 13 June 1933, telephone tap of E. Settimelli.

84. SPDCR 43, October 1932, note.

85. SPDCR 41, 4 July 1925, Mussolini to Prefect at Messina.

86. SPDCR 41, 18 July 1925, Mussolini to Prefect at Messina.

87. SPDCR 43, 14 May 1925. 'Prof.' Mussolini used the Latin *Principi e Triari*.

88. SPDCR 43, 13 October 1925, Mussolini to Prefect at Cremona; 16 November 1925, Mussolini to Farinacci.

89. De Felice, *Mussolini il fascista 2. L'organizzazione dello stato fascista 1925–1929*, pp. 186–8.

90. SPDCR 40, 6 January 1926, Farinacci to party *federali*.

91. SPDCR 44, 17 May 1934, Farinacci telephone tap.

92. SPEP 6, 19 July 1933.

93. Carte Farinacci 12, 2 September 1936.

94. *Gioventù Fascista*, 30 November XI [1932].

95. Carte Farinacci 12, 18 April 1935, Farinacci to Ciano.

96. MRF 52/122/4, 14 June 1929, Turati to Fascist Members of Parliament.

97. *Annuario diplomatico e delle carriere direttive* (Rome, 1980), p. 593.

98. For the details of his death, see the bathetic account by his English-language biographer, H. Fornari, *Mussolini's gadfly: Roberto Farinacci*, pp. 214–15.

99. See the typical letter, Carte Farinacci 12, 12 August 1927, Farinacci to C. Ciano.

100. Carte Farinacci 2, 4 July 1932, Farinacci to Arpinati.

101. See, for example, Carte Farinacci 2, undated *raccomandazione* for a surgeon, Arpinati to Farinacci; 15, 27 March 1930, Crollalanza to Farinacci, for a skin doctor.

102. See, for example, Carte Farinacci, 29 July 1926, Stringher to Farinacci, in which the director of the Banca d'Italia apologized for not being able to appoint a Farinaccian to a bank job at Mantua but left the hope that the client would get the next available position. Cf. 22, 7 December 1935,

A. Frigessi to Farinacci, in which the president of the insurance group, the *Riunione Adriatica di Sicurtà*, spelled out their tax exemption requirements for opening a branch office at Cremona.

103. Carte Farinacci 25, 16 December 1931, P. Grillo to Farinacci, complaining that his enemies had organized an unwanted transfer for him within the army from Piacenza to distant and uncivilized Udine. Cf. a similar case: Carte Farinacci 10, 4 September 1939, O. Carletti to Farinacci. On this occasion, the petitioner was Cremona's Senator, acting on behalf of his own brother.

104. Carte Farinacci 30, 21 February 1934, C. Migliavacca to Farinacci. Migliavacca believed that he was being held back by the army bosses because of his reputation as an erstwhile squadrist. On 24 February, Farinacci did write to intervene on his behalf.

105. Carte Farinacci 37, 15 February 1938, Zoppi to Farinacci. For Zoppi's role earlier in assisting the military career of Farinacci's brother, see Bosworth, *Mussolini*, p. 259.

106. Carte Farinacci 21, 7 April 1939, C. Franchetti to Farinacci (and later letters).

107. Carte Farinacci 8, 9 July 1937, Farinacci to Buffarini Guidi.

108. Carte Farinacci 10, 30 January 1928, G. Carnevale to Farinacci.

109. Carte Farinacci 20, 21 September 1931, E. Ferrante to Farinacci.

110. Carte Farinacci 36, 8 March 1939, F. Vecchi to Farinacci. The non-payer was Léon Degrelle, charismatic leader of the Belgian Rexists.

111. Carte Farinacci 37, 1 July 1940, G. Volpe to Farinacci.

112. See, for example, a set of undated correspondence from Luigi Freddi in 1925 (Freddi was endeavouring to secure the moral and financial backing of Farinacci, who then was PNF Secretary, for Freddi's version of a Fascist paper). Carte Farinacci 22.

113. See, for example, Carte Farinacci 12, 12 August 1927, Farinacci to C. Ciano, complaining about the persecution of his followers among those employed by the Italian state railways.

114. Carte Farinacci 30, 21 January 1936, Medici del Vascello to Farinacci.

115. SPDCR 41, 13 April 1934, telephone tap.

116. Carte Farinacci 30, 30 April 1928, Farinacci to Masi. Farinacci feared that Turati had malignly arranged the appointment.

117. See further CP 59, 293, files on Danilo Barabaschi and Leonardo Cottarelli. The latter was a *sansepolcrista* who had soon fallen out with Farinacci.

118. CP 638, file on Giorgio Masi, 27 October 1937, Farinacci to Mussolini. Masi himself penned a gushing ten-page letter of apology to the *Duce*,

suggesting in a way that must appeal to an Australian reader that he be sent to the colonies to redeem himself. Farinacci had earlier petitioned the police chief, Arturo Bocchini, on Masi's behalf. See Carte Farinacci 30, 27 August 1927, Farinacci to Masi, again claiming that the only problem really was Masi's *cretineria filosofica*.

119. Carte Farinacci 32, 18 November 1939, Farinacci to Pedrazza.

120. *L'Alveare*, May 1930.

121. *L'Alveare*, December 1928.

122. *L'Alveare*, February 1929.

123. A. Turati, *Il partito e i suoi compiti* (Rome, 1928), pp. 55–6. The opportunity to play, he announced, must be extended to all Italians.

124. A. Turati, *Un popolo, un'idea, un uomo* (Milan, 1927), pp. 7–9.

125. Turati, *Il partito e i suoi compiti*, p. 11.

126. S. Lupo, *Il Fascismo: la politica in un regime totalitario* (Rome, 2000), p. 367.

127. BMOO XXI, p. 349.

128. De Felice, *Mussolini il fascista 2. L'organizzazione dello stato fascista 1925–1929*, p. 208.

129. Aquarone, *L'organizzazione dello stato totalitario*, pp. 427–9.

130. De Felice, *Mussolini il fascista 2. L'organizzazione dello stato fascista 1925–1929*, pp. 469–70.

131. M. R. Catti De Gasperi, *De Gasperi: uomo solo* (Milan, 1964), pp. 114–22, 143.

132. Aquarone, *L'organizzazione dello stato totalitario*, pp. 103–4.

133. G. Leto, *Ovra: fascismo-antifascismo* (Rocca San Casciano, 1952), p. 33.

134. For the embarrassing circumstances, see Bosworth, *Mussolini*, pp. 220–22.

135. M. Franzinelli, *I tentacoli dell'Ovra: agenti, collaboratori e vittime della polizia politica fascista* (Turin, 1999), pp. 377, 388.

136. A. Turati, *Fuori dell'ombra della mia vita: dieci anni nel solco del fascismo* (ed. A. Frappini)(Brescia, 1973), p. 99.

137. For the story and some examples, see U. Guspini, *L'orecchio del regime: le intercettazioni al tempo del fascismo* (Milan, 1973).

138. CP 487, file on Eugenio Giovanardi. For further background, see M. Franzinelli, *Delatori: spie e confidenti anonimi: l'arma segreta del regime fascista* (Milan, 2001), pp. 120–24.

139. Franzinelli, *Delatori: spie e confidenti anonimi*, pp. 16, 49.

140. C. Ipsen, *Dictating demography: the problem of population in Fascist Italy* (Cambridge, 1996), p. 147.

141. E. D. Whitaker, *Measuring mamma's milk: Fascism and the medicalization of maternity in Italy* (Ann Arbor, 2000), p. 179.

142. V. De Grazia, *How Fascism ruled women*, pp. 60–68.

143. BMOO XXII, pp. 360–90.

144. Turati, *Un popolo, un'idea, un uomo*, pp. 7–8.

145. Turati, *Il partito e i suoi compiti*, pp. 190–91.

146. De Felice, *Mussolini il fascista 2. L'organizzazione dello stato fascista 1925–1929*, pp. 437–8.

147. G. Bottai, unsigned editorial, *Critica Fascista*, 15 March 1929.

148. B. Dalla Casa, *Attentato al duce: le molte storie del caso Zamboni* (Bologna, 2000), pp. 44–9, 89, 201, 222.

149. See C. Ginzburg, *The cheese and the worms: the cosmos of a sixteenth century miller* (London, 1980).

9 Forging Fascist society

1. SPDCR 47, 22 February 1931, Giuriati to Mussolini.

2. G. Giuriati, *La parabola di Mussolini nei ricordi di un gerarca* (ed. E. Gentile) (Bari, 1981), pp. 39, 100, 105–6.

3. CP 254, file on Roberto Ciniselli, 2 October 1929, Carabinieri (Milan) to Carabinieri (Rome); 14 October 1929, Prefect (Milan) to Ministry of the Interior.

4. CP 417, file on Giovanni Fiumi, 24 April 1929, appeal. See also the police report on him, 29 January 1929, Questore (Milan) to Prefect (Milan).

5. CP 40, file on Leandro Arpinati, 23 October 1934, Rina Arpinati to Leandro.

6. CP 40, 1 October 1934, Arpinati to Rina.

7. CP 40, 25 October 1934, Arpinati to Giancarlo Arpinati.

8. CP 425, file on Gaetano Fornaciari, 6 September 1934, Carabinieri (Bologna) to Carabinieri (Rome); 23 July, 18 September 1934, letters, Fornaciari to Ceci.

9. CP 425, 9 August 1934, Fornaciari appeal to Ministry of the Interior.

10. CP 69, file on Ettore Bartolazzi, 30 August 1934, Prefect (Bologna) to Ministry of the Interior; 4 September 1934, Carabinieri (Bologna) to Carabinieri (Rome).

11. CP 854, file on Marcello Reggiani, 3 August 1934, Carabinieri (Bologna) to Questura (Bologna); 4 August 1934, Questura (Bologna) to Provincial Commissioner; 12 March 1935, Rita Reggiani to Mussolini.

12. Among his friends and associates were members of the Guidi and Boattini

families, with direct ties to the Mussolinis. See also CP 122, file on Giovanni Boattini.

13. CP 40, file on Settimio Arpinati, 10 August 1934, Carabinieri (Forlì) to Questore (Forlì).

14. CP 40, 31 March 1934, S. Arpinati statement.

15. For further on his case, see SPDCR 42, 23 February, 29 May 1930, both Farinacci to Arpinati.

16. CP 84, file on Ernesto Belloni, 1 February 1932, police to Bocchini.

17. G. Casini, 'Compiti delle città italiane', *Critica Fascista*, 15 December 1929.

18. CP 711, file on Giuseppe Nicastri, 10 May 1939, Prefect (Palermo) to Ministry of the Interior; 10 June 1939, Carabinieri (Palermo) to Carabinieri (Rome).

19. For the best period example, see G. C. Chapman, *Milocca: a Sicilian village* (London, 1973).

20. CP 489, file on Francesco Giua, 28 July 1940, Questore (Sassari) to Prefect (Sassari).

21. D. A. Binchy, *Church and State in Fascist Italy* (rev. ed.) (Oxford, 1970), p. 105.

22. *Observer*, 10 February 1929.

23. M. R. Catti De Gasperi, *De Gasperi: uomo solo* (Milan, 1964), pp. 135–6.

24. C. M. De Vecchi, *Tra Papa, Duce e Re: il conflitto tra Chiesa cattolica e Stato fascista nel diario 1930–1931 del primo ambasciatore del Regno d'Italia presso la Santa Sede* (ed. S. Setta) (Rome, 1998), p. 148.

25. DDI 7s, XV, 270, 21 May 1934, Mussolini–De Vecchi talk; 1 June 1934, Pacelli–De Vecchi talk.

26. De Vecchi, *Tra Papa, Duce e Re*, p. 89.

27. A. and B. Mussolini, *Vita di Sandro e Arnaldo Mussolini* (Milan, 1934), p. 45.

28. De Vecchi, *Tra Papa, Duce e Re*, p. 278.

29. G. Guidi, *Pio XI* (Milan, 1938), p. 7.

30. *Lo Sport Fascista*, II, March 1929.

31. *L'Alpino*, 15 February 1929.

32. S. Setta, 'Introduzione' to De Vecchi, *Tra Papa, Duce e Re*, p. 24.

33. DDI 8s, 461, 7 April 1938, Pignatti to Ciano.

34. DDI 8s, IX, 53, 5 May 1938, Pignatti to Ciano.

35. DDI 8s, VIII, 397, 25 March 1938, Pignatti to Ciano; 401, 26 March 1938, Ciano to Pignatti.

36. DDI 8s, IX, 336, 26 July 1938, Pignatti to Ciano.

37. I. Schuster, 'My last meeting with Mussolini' in B. Mussolini, *Memoirs 1942–1943 with documents relating to the period* (London, 1949), p. 258.

38. A. J. Rhodes, *The Vatican in the age of the dictators, 1922–1945* (London, 1973), p. 355.

39. P. C. Kent, *The Pope and the Duce: the international impact of the Lateran agreements* (London, 1981), pp. 63, 113.

40. See Mussolini's record of the meeting in DDI 7s, XI, 205, 11 February 1932, Mussolini to Victor Emmanuel III and cf. R. De Felice, *Mussolini il duce: 1. Gli anni del consenso 1929–1936* (Turin, 1974) pp. 272–3.

41. *Regni il Cuore Sacerdotale di Gesù*, 16–19 September 1936.

42. *Regni il Cuore Sacerdotale di Gesù*, 19–22 May 1937; 15–18 December 1937.

43. CP 25, file on Salvatore Anastasio, 23 January 1942, Questore (Naples) note.

44. CP 714, file on Vincenzo Nisticò, 8 August 1939, Carabinieri (Catanzaro) to Questura (Catanzaro); 29 August 1939, Questura (Catanzaro) to Prefect (Catanzaro). Nisticò and his two brothers got five years' *confino* in the Basilicata but were amnestied after three.

45. Anonymous article on 'La Santa Messa e l'Ora dell'Agricoltura', in *La Radio rurale*, VI, 29 March 1939.

46. See G. Poggi, *Catholic Action in Italy: the sociology of a sponsored organization* (Stanford, 1967), pp. 15–19.

47. J. F. Pollard, *The Vatican and Italian Fascism 1929–1932: a study in conflict* (Cambridge, 1985), pp. 24–5, 39, 120.

48. Anonymous editorial, *Critica Fascista*, 9, 15 July 1931.

49. Pollard, *The Vatican and Italian Fascism*, pp. 158–9.

50. For a review, see R. J. Ciruzzi, 'The *Federazione universitaria cattolica italiana*: Catholic students in Fascist Italy', *Risorgimento* 3, 1982, pp. 61–78.

51. De Felice, *Mussolini il duce: 1. Gli anni del consenso*, pp. 267–8.

52. Anonymous editorial, *Critica Fascista*, 9, 1 June 1931.

53. SPEP 19, anonymous report, 26 October 1933.

54. R. J. B. Bosworth, *Italy, the Least of the Great Powers: Italian foreign policy before the First World War* (Cambridge, 1979), pp. 342–3.

55. See J. F. Pollard, 'The Vatican and the Wall Street Crash: Bernardino Nogara and papal finances in the early 1930s', *Historical Journal*, 42, 1999, pp. 1077–91.

56. Pollard, *The Vatican and Italian Fascism*, p. 73.

57. V. De Grazia, *How Fascism ruled women: Italy 1922–1945* (Berkeley, 1992), p. 197.

58. The number of those admitted to secondary schools actually declined

from 337,000 in 1922–3 to 237,000 in 1926–7, though numbers rose thereafter. M. Barbagli, *Educating for unemployment: politics, labor markets, and the school system: Italy 1859–1973* (New York, 1982), p. 133.

59. SPEP 26, 21 June 1935, report.

60. M. De Giorgio, *Le italiane dall'Unità a oggi: modelli culturali e comportamenti sociali* (Bari, 1982), p. 464.

61. T. Tomasi, *L'educazione infantile tra Chiesa e Stato* (Florence, 1978), pp. 129–30.

62. M. Clark, *Modern Italy 1871–1982* (London, 1984), p. 256.

63. MRF 52/122/1, 28 January 1930, Turati to the provincial delegates of the Fasci femminili.

64. MRF 53/122/7, February 1930, debate of report of party situation in Ravenna.

65. M. Guasco, 'Il modello del prete fra tradizione e innovazione' in A. Riccardi (ed.), *Le chiese di Pio XII* (Bari, 1986), pp. 87–8.

66. *Regni il Cuore Sacerdotale di Gesù*, 17–20 February 1937.

67. *Regni il Cuore Sacerdotale di Gesù*, 31 May to 2 June 1939.

68. L. Caldwell, 'Reproducers of the nation: women and the family in Fascist policy' in D. Forgacs (ed.), *Rethinking Italian Fascism: capitalism, populism and culture* (London, 1986), p. 121.

69. De Giorgio, *Le italiane dall'Unità a oggi*, p. 163.

70. *Stirpe Italica*, June 1934.

71. P. R. Willson, 'Flowers for the doctor: pro-natalism and abortion in Fascist Milan', *Modern Italy*, 1, 1996, pp. 44–62.

72. L. Passerini, *Fascism in popular memory: the cultural experience of the Turin working class* (Cambridge, 1987), pp. 161–2.

73. F. Marconcini, *Culle vuote: il declino delle nascite in Europa: sviluppo – cause – rimedi* (Como, 1935), pp. 5, 77–92.

74. Ibid., pp. 214, 247, 255.

75. Ibid., pp. 432–7.

76. Ibid., pp. 160, 443–8.

77. A. Spektorowski and E. Mizrachi, 'Eugenics and the welfare state in Sweden: the politics of social margins and the idea of a productive society', *Journal of Contemporary History*, 39, 2004, p. 333.

78. For some figures, see E. R. Tannenbaum, *Fascism in Italy: society and culture 1922–1945* (London, 1973), p. 158; cf. the fuller tables in C. Ipsen, *Dictating demography*, pp. 19–20.

79. Cited by L. Villari, *Il capitalismo italiano del novecento* (Bari, 1992), p. 77.

80. BMOO XL, 27 May 1927, Mussolini to Prefects.

81. I. Insolera, *Roma moderna: un secolo di storia urbanistica 1870–1970* (Turin, 1976), p. 144.

82. A. Treves, *Le migrazioni interne nell'Italia fascista* (Turin, 1976), p. 33.

83. P. R. Willson, *Peasant women and politics in Fascist Italy: the Massaie Rurali* (London, 2002), pp. 15, 59, 171.

84. P. R. Willson, 'Cooking the patriotic omelette': women and the Italian Fascist ruralization campaign', *European History Review*, 27, 1997, p. 534.

85. Willson, *Peasant women and politics in Fascist Italy*, p. 129.

86. Willson, 'Cooking the patriotic omelette', p. 541.

87. See a demonstration on the island of Limina in 1935. CP 68, file on Placido Barra, 29 December 1935, Questore (Messina) to Prefect (Messina).

88. SPEP 27, 8 February 1933, report.

89. SPEP 19, 13 March 1934, Starace report.

90. See, for example, issues of *La Fiera del Levante*, II, May 1932; III, October, November 1933.

91. S. Petrucci, *In Puglia con Mussolini* (Rome, 1935), pp. 18, 25, 45.

92. *Riassunto Bollettini di Statistica: Comune di Bari*, 1933–4.

93. O. Bianchi, 'Ascesa e declino di una economia urbana tra regione e Mediterraneo' in F. Tateo (ed.), *Storia di Bari: il Novecento* (Bari, 1997), pp. 244, 253.

94. P. Corner, 'Fascist agrarian policy and the Italian economy in the inter-war years' in J. A. Davis (ed.), *Gramsci and Italy's passive revolution* (London, 1979), p. 248.

95. N. Revelli, *Il mondo dei vinti: testimonianze di vita contadina* (Turin, 1977), vol. II, p. 98.

96. G. Cingari, *Reggio Calabria* (Bari, 1988), p. 326.

97. See, for example, G. Dobbert (ed.), *L'economia fascista: problemi e fatti* (Florence, 1935) and the more critical but still intrigued W. G. Welk, *Fascist economic policy: an analysis of Italy's economic experiment* (rev. ed.) (New York, 1968).

98. C. Di Marzio, 'Aspetti di questo nuovo mondo', *Critica Fascista*, 8, 15 July 1930.

99. G. Bottai, 'Per noi fascisti da dieci anni', *Critica Fascista*, 10, 1 February 1932.

100. See, for example, P. Chimienti, 'Il regime degli Stati Uniti ed il regime fascista', *Gerarchia*, 13, February 1933; B. De Ritis, 'L'America scopre se stessa: lettera dall'America del Nord', *Critica Fascista*, 11, 1 June 1933; E. Brunetta, 'Esperimento di Roosevelt', *Critica Fascista*, 11, 1 September 1933; P. Sacerdoti, 'L'America verso il fascismo', *Gerarchia*, 13, September 1933.

101. L. Barzini, 'L'Italia ha ragione', *Gerarchia*, 13, August 1933.

102. *Gioventù Fascista*, 20 January XI [1933].

103. F. Guarneri, *Battaglie economiche fra le due guerre* (ed. L. Zani) (Bologna, 1988), pp. 834–5. Guarneri was another who came to his moderate version of Fascism through interventionism, while his elder brother was a bishop. His landowning family in Cremona province was a social cut above Farinacci.

104. S. La Francesca, *La politica economica del fascismo* (Bari, 1972), pp. 48, 77.

105. C. S. Maier, 'The economics of Fascism and Nazism' in his *In search of stability: explorations in historical political economy* (Cambridge, 1987), p. 91.

106. V. Zamagni, *The economic history of Italy 1860–1990* (Oxford, 1993), pp. 245–6, 290.

107. For the differences in wording to the constitution of 1929, see A. Aquarone, *L'organizzazione dello stato totalitario* (Turin, 1965), pp. 506–13, 518–29.

108. *Il Comune di Bologna: rivista mensile municipale*, XIX, July 1932.

109. J. T. Schnapp, 'Epic demonstrations: Fascist modernity and the 1932 exhibition of the Fascist revolution' in R. J. Golsan (ed.), *Fascism, aesthetics and culture* (Hanover, NH, 1992), p. 5.

110. M. Stone, 'Staging Fascism: the Exhibition of the Fascist Revolution', *Journal of Contemporary History*, 28, 1993, pp. 234–5. For further decoding of the event, see M. S. Stone, *The patron state: culture and politics in Fascist Italy* (Princeton, 1998), pp. 128–76.

111. A. Melchiori (ed.), 'Martirologia Fascista' in Associazione Nazionale Volontari di Guerra, *Il Decennale* (Florence, 1929), pp. 239–41.

112. Stone, *The patron state*, p. 59.

113. It is available in English as B. Mussolini, 'The political and social doctrine of Fascism', *Political Quarterly*, 4, 1933, pp. 341–56.

114. G. Volpe, 'L'"Enciclopedia italiana" è compiuta', *Nuova Antologia*, f. 1575, 1 November 1937, pp. 5–18.

115. Stone, *The patron state*, p. 27.

116. R. Ben-Ghiat, *Fascist modernities: Italy, 1922–1945* (Berkeley, 2001), p. 20.

117. M. Salvati, *Il regime e gli impiegati: la nazionalizzazione piccolo-borghese nel ventennio fascista* (Bari, 1992), pp. 134, 145, 201, 214–15.

10 Placing Italy in Europe

1. CP 82, file on Eugenio Bellemo, 5 August 1932, Carabinieri (Venice) to Carabinieri (Rome).

2. CP 82, 27 May 1932, Prefect (Venice) to Ministry of the Interior.

3. CP 142, file on Marcello Teodoro Boscolo, 14 June 1932, Carabinieri (Venice) report; 2 June 1932, Prefect (Venice) to Ministry of the Interior. Boscolo got two years' *confino* at Termoli (Campobasso) but was amnestied after four months.

4. CP 82, 27 May 1932, Prefect (Venice) to Ministry of the Interior; 31 August 1932, Prefect (Venice) to the Ministry of the Interior.

5. R. De Felice, *Mussolini il fascista 1. La conquista del potere, 1921–1925* (Turin, 1966), p. 758.

6. G. Rumi, *Alle origini della politica estera fascista (1918–1923)* (Bari, 1968), pp. 128, 146–7.

7. See, for example, E. Corradini, 'Costruire lo Stato', *La Vita italiana*, f. 104, 15 August 1921.

8. L. Ferraris, 'A proposito dell'insurrezione egiziana', *La Vita italiana*, f. 85, 15 January 1920.

9. O. Sinigaglia, 'Italia e Caucaso (a proposito della Missione italiana nel Caucaso)', *La Vita italiana*, f. 86, 15 February 1920.

10. O. Sinigaglia, 'Lega italiana per la tutela degli interessi nazionali', *La Vita italiana*, f. 91, 15 July 1920. For further on his idiosyncratic career, cf. L. Villari, *Le avventure di un capitano d'industria* (Turin, 1991).

11. See, for example, O. Sinigaglia, 'L'oscuro futuro economico dell'Italia', *La Vita italiana*, f. 88, 15 April 1920.

12. V. Scialoja, *I problemi dello stato italiano dopo la guerra* (Bologna, 1918), p. 178.

13. F. S. Nitti, *Peaceless Europe* (London, 1922), p. 76.

14. For an example, see R. Mallett, *Mussolini and the origins of the Second World War, 1933–1940* (London, 2003), p. 16.

15. E. Di Nolfo, *Mussolini e la politica estera italiana (1919–1933)* (Padua, 1960), pp. 1, 309.

16. BMOO XV, pp. 175–7.

17. BMOO XVI, p. 159.

18. BMOO XVIII, p. 466.

19. DDI 7s, I, 7, 31 October 1922, Mussolini to Poincaré and Bonar Law.

20. BMOO XXI, pp. 377–8.

21. N. D'Aroma, *Vent'anni insieme: Vittorio Emanuele e Mussolini* (Rocca San Casciano, 1957), p. 161.

22. G. Volpe, 'A crisi superata: constatazione e previsioni', *Gerarchia*, 2, October 1923, p. 1257.

23. See, for example, M. Rocca, 'Fascismo e paese' and U. D'Andrea, 'Il "cocente realismo" inglese e la sua maschera ideologica', each in *Critica Fascista*, I, 15 September 1923.

24. A. Signoretti, 'Contro la retorica universalistica sul fenomeno fascista', *Critica Fascista*, 1, 15 November 1923. Cf. the very similar line in A. Tamaro, 'Il fascismo in Germania e nell'Europa centrale', *Critica Fascista*, 3, 1 March 1925.

25. A. Pavolini, 'Le cose di Francia e l'universalità del fascismo', *Critica Fascista*, 4, 15 January 1926.

26. A. Palmieri, 'Il fascismo giapponese', *Critica Fascista*, 3, 1 April 1925.

27. *Critica Fascista*, 2, 16 February 1924.

28. See, for example, E. Corradini, 'L'emigrazione e la Società delle nazioni', *Critica Fascista*, 2, 15 May 1924.

29. E. Corradini, 'La forza dominante', *Gerarchia*, 6, March 1926, p. 142.

30. A. Dudan, 'La Dalmazia e la più grande turlupineria del secolo', *Gerarchia*, 7, September 1927, pp. 833–43.

31. DDI 7s, IV, 448, 2 October 1926, Mussolini to Badoglio.

32. M. Knox, *Common destiny: dictatorship, foreign policy, and war in Fascist Italy and Nazi Germany* (Cambridge, 2000), pp. 122–3.

33. Di Nolfo, *Mussolini e la politica estera italiana*, pp. 223–4.

34. J. J. Sadkovich, *Italian support for Croatian separatism 1927–1937* (New York, 1987), pp. 3–4.

35. R. De Felice, *Mussolini il duce: 1. Gli anni del consenso 1929–1936* (Turin, 1974), pp. 515–16.

36. Sadkovich, *Italian support for Croatian separatism*, pp. 33, 45–6.

37. De Felice, *Mussolini il duce: 1. Gli anni del consenso*, p. 516.

38. Mallett, *Mussolini and the origins of the Second World War*, p. 18; cf. p. 20 for his commentary on another spat and another burst of 'planning' in 1931.

39. DDI 7s, II, 616, 3 February 1924, Mussolini to Caetani.

40. G. G. Migone, *Gli Stati Uniti e il fascismo: alle origini dell'egemonia americana in Italia* (Milan, 1980), pp. 103, 125–6, 219.

41. I. Kershaw, *Making friends with Hitler: Lord Londonderry and Britain's road to war* (London, 2004), p. 39.

42. DDI 7s, I, 217, 9 December 1922, Mussolini memorandum on reparations and inter-allied debt.

43. DDI 7s, V, 213, 19 May 1927, Mussolini to Chiaramente Bordonaro.

44. DDI 7s, X, 151, 21 March 1931, Grandi to Attolico.

45. Rumi, *Alle origini della politica estera fascista*, p. 237.

46. DDI 7s, I, 705, 12 April 1923, Mussolini to Diaz.

47. DDI 7s, X, 224, 26 April 1931, De Bono to Grandi.

48. See, for example, DDI 7s, III, 797, 11 April 1925, Mussolini to Farinacci.

49. DDI 7s, VIII, 489, 13 April 1930, Grandi to Mussolini.

50. DDI 7s, IX, 122, 29 June 1930, Grandi to Mussolini.

51. See, for example, DDI 7s, III, 204, 18 December 1925, De Martino to Contarini.

52. See, for example, DDI 7s, V, 256, 8 June 1927, Grandi to Turati.

53. DDI 7s, IV, 414, 10 September 1926, Scalea to Mussolini.

54. DDI 7s, V, 154, 21 April 1927, Paternò to Mussolini.

55. For his own account, see R. Guariglia, *Ricordi 1922–1946* (Naples, 1949).

56. DDI 7s, XII, 223, 27 August 1932, Guariglia to Mussolini.

57. G. Bevione, 'Il patto Kellogg', *Gerarchia*, 8, August 1928.

58. E. R. Tannenbaum, *Fascism in Italy: society and culture 1922–1945* (London, 1973), p. 138.

59. CP 59, file on Italo Barattini.

60. SPDCR 48, 10 July 1926, Mussolini to Ricci.

61. S. Setta, *Renato Ricci. Dallo squadrismo alla Repubblica Sociale Italiana* (Bologna, 1986), p. 132.

62. F. Mezzasoma, *Essenza del G.U.F.* (Genoa, 1937), p. ii.

63. T. H. Koon, *Believe, obey, fight: political socialization of youth in Fascist Italy* (Chapel Hill, 1985), p. 103.

64. A. Scotto di Luzio, *L'appropriazione imperfetta: editori, biblioteche e libri per ragazzi durante il fascismo* (Bologna, 1996), p. 172.

65. *L'Artigiano*, 24 November 1935.

66. *L'Artigiano*, 6 December 1936.

67. *L'Artigiano*, 31 January 1937.

68. *L'Artigiano*, 24 December 1939.

69. *L'Artigiano*, 12 March 1939.

70. P. Dogliani, *L'Italia fascista 1922–1940* (Milan, 1999), p. 301.

71. *L'Artigiano*, 29 May 1938.

72. *L'Artigiano*, 18 July 1937.

73. *Rivista dell'ONB di Bolzano*, 1, March–April 1931.

74. *Rivista dell'ONB di Bolzano*, 1, March–April 1931.

75. M. Ostenc, 'Una tappa della fascistizzazione: la scuola e la politica dal 1925 al 1928', *Storia contemporanea*, 4, 1973, p. 482.

76. Tannenbaum, *Fascism in Italy: society and culture*, p. 184.

77. *Rivista dell'ONB di Bolzano*, 1, May–June 1931.

78. G. Buitoni, *Storia di un imprenditore* (Milan, 1972), pp. 22–3.

79. I. Balbo, *My air armada* (London, 1934), p. 192.

80. *L'Alpino*, 1 January 1931.

81. Balbo, *My air armada*, p. 202.

82. R. J. B. Bosworth, *Italy, the Least of the Great Powers: Italian foreign policy before the First World War* (Cambridge, 1979), p. 324.

83. D. Mack Smith, *Cavour* (London, 1985), p. 153.

84. For further commentary in this regard, see D. Mack Smith, *Cavour and Garibaldi 1860: a study in political conflict*, rev. ed. (Cambridge, 1985), p. 91.

85. For extensive background, see C. Duggan, *Francesco Crispi 1818–1901: from nation to nationalism* (Oxford, 2002).

86. A. Del Boca, 'I crimini del colonialismo fascista' in A. Del Boca (ed.), *Le guerre coloniali del fascismo* (Bari, 1991), pp. 237–8.

87. A. Del Boca (ed.), *I gas di Mussolini: il fascismo e la guerra d'Etiopia* (Rome, 1996), p. 20.

88. *L'Alpino*, 1 April 1936.

89. G. W. Baer, *Test case: Italy, Ethiopia and the League of Nations* (Stanford, 1976), pp. 238–9.

90. A. Lustig, 'Ricordi storici della guerra con i gas', *Esercito e Nazione*, II, June 1927.

91. 'Z', 'L'aviazione in Cirenaica', *Rivista Aeronautica*, VI, December 1930.

92. G. Rochat, 'L'impiego di gas nella guerra d'Etiopia 1935–6', *Rivista di storia contemporanea*, 17, 1988, p. 79.

93. See, for example, G. Douhet, 'Probabili aspetti della guerra futura', *Rivista Aeronautica*, IV, April 1928.

94. G. Douhet, 'Per l'arte della guerra aerea', *Rivista Aeronautica*, IV, May 1928.

95. *Corriere Emiliano*, 19 May 1935.

96. *Stirpe Italica*, December 1935.

97. See, for example, G. Montelucci, 'Cenni sulla guerra aero-chimica', *Rivista Aeronautica*, IX, December 1933.

98. C. Rossi, 'Guerra e chimica', *L'Ala d'Italia: La Gazzetta dell'aviazione*, 28 October 1932, pp. 37–8.

99. R. Graziani, *Ho difeso la patria* (Cernusco sul Naviglio, 1947), p. 109.

100. For English-language introduction, see C. G. Segrè, 'Douhet in Italy: prophet without honor', *Aerospace Historian*, 26, 1979, pp. 69–80.

101. V. Ferretti, 'La guerra batteriologica', *Rivista Aeronautica*, VII, February 1931.

102. For the fullest expression of this line, see A. Hitler, *Hitler's Secret Book* (ed. T. Taylor), (New York, 1961).

103. A. Kuzibek, *Young Hitler: the story of our friendship* (London, 1954), pp. 140–43.

104. H. Trevor-Roper (ed.), *Hitler's table talk 1941–1944* (London, 1953), pp. 10, 267, 704.

105. DDI 8s, IX, 310, 15 July 1938, Pariani to Mussolini.

106. DDI 8s, X, 14, 13 September 1938, Attolico to Ciano.

107. E. Reut-Nicolussi, *Tyrol under the axe of Italian Fascism* (London, 1930), pp. 8, 228–9, 264.

108. D. Irving, *The war path: Hitler's Germany 1933–1939* (London, 1983), p. 47.

109. DDI 7s, V, 692, 21 December 1927, Grandi to his ambassadors.

110. DDI 7s, X, 287, 23–24 May 1931, Grandi to Mussolini.

111. *La Vita italiana*, f. 266, 15 May 1935.

112. DDI 8s, IX, 11, 25 April 1938, Magistrati to Ciano.

113. BMOO XXIII, p. 122.

114. P. Buchignani, *Un fascismo impossibile: l'eresia di Berto Ricci nella cultura del ventennio* (Bologna, 1994), p. 300.

115. B. Ricci, *Avvisi* (Florence, 1943), p. 164.

116. Ibid., pp. 10, 61–2. For an English translation of this last, see F. T. Marinetti, *The Futurist cookbook* (ed. L. Chamberlain), (London, 1989).

117. R. Farinacci, 'Rilievi mensili', *La Vita italiana*, f. 223, 15 October 1931.

118. R. Farinacci, 'Rilievi mensili', *La Vita italiana*, f. 234, 15 September 1932.

119. R. Farinacci, 'Rilievi mensili', *La Vita italiana*, f. 239, 15 February 1933.

120. P. C. Kent, *The Pope and the Duce: the international impact of the Lateran agreements* (London, 1981), pp. 149–52.

121. R. Farinacci, 'Rilievi mensili', *La Vita italiana*, f. 241, 15 April 1933.

122. R. Farinacci, 'Rilievi mensili', *La Vita italiana*, f. 245, 15 August 1933.

123. Mallett, *Mussolini and the origins of the Second World War*, p. 21.

124. R. Quartararo, *Roma tra Londra e Berlino: la politica estera fascista dal 1931 al 1940* (Rome, 1980), p. 38.

125. H. S. Hughes, *The United States and Italy* (rev. ed., New York, 1968), p. 107.

126. For background, see G. Petracchi, *Da San Pietroburgo a Mosca: la diplomazia italiana in Russia 1861–1941* (Rome, 1993), pp. 341–2.

127. See, for example, DGPS, DPP, 46/8 c11/58/9, file on the matter in Naples.

128. For the personal ramifications of these matters, see R. J. B. Bosworth, *Mussolini* (London, 2002), pp. 280–84.

129. *Stirpe Italica*, September 1934.

130. *Mare Nostro: Stirpe Italica*, March 1935.

131. Governatorato di Roma, *Giardino zoologico di Roma: relazione sull'esercizio, 1933* (Rome, 1934), p. 9.

132. *Corriere Emiliano*, 19 May 1935.

11 Going to the people

1. See his editorial in *Civiltà Fascista*, 1, January 1934.

2. See, for example, G. De Michelis, *La corporazione nel mondo* (Milan, 1934). In this second edition of his book, he argued that the Four Power Pact provided the ideal global setting for cosmopolitan corporatism.

3. G. Bottai, 'Una rivoluzione nella Rivoluzione: la nuova legge Corporativa', *Critica Fascista*, 11, 15 December 1933.

4. G. Bottai, 'Insistiamo: corporativizzare l'azienda', *Critica Fascista*, 13, 15 May 1935.

5. G. Bottai, 'Abissinia: impresa rivoluzionaria', *Critica Fascista*, 13, 15 July 1935.

6. G. Salvemini, *Under the axe of Fascism* (London, 1936), pp. 127–35, 147, 164.

7. English-language readers can trace most of the text of this bill in C. F. Delzell (ed.), *Mediterranean Fascism 1919–1945* (New York, 1970), pp. 126–8.

8. V. Zamagni, *The economic history of Italy 1860–1990* (Oxford, 1993), pp. 299–302.

9. SPDCR 4, telephone tap, 6 February 1933.

10. See D. Musiedlak, *Lo stato fascista e la sua classe politica 1922–1943* (Bologna, 2003), pp. 139–40.

11. F. Mancini Lapenna, *In Campidoglio con Alberto Mancini* (Florence, 1958), p. 156.

12. *La Proprietà Edilizia*, January–March 1931.

13. *La Proprietà Edilizia*, March 1931.

14. *La Proprietà Edilizia*, January 1932. The author was Mario Ricca-Barberis.

15. *La Proprietà Edilizia*, May 1932.

16. *La Proprietà Edilizia*, January 1932.

17. L. Gaetani, 'Civiltà rurale del Fascismo', *La Radio rurale*, VI, 28 February 1938.

18. *La Proprietà Edilizia*, January–February 1933.

19. *La Proprietà Edilizia*, September 1933.

20. *La Proprietà Edilizia*, September–October 1934.

21. E. Conti, 'Difendiamo il lavoro italiano!', *Gerarchia*, XII, April 1932.

22. *La Proprietà Edilizia*, June–July 1934.

23. *La Proprietà Edilizia*, January–March 1937.

24. *La Proprietà Edilizia*, March–April 1935. The author was Virgilio Testa.

25. *La Proprietà Edilizia*, July–September 1937.

26. For further background, see R. J. B. Bosworth, *Mussolini* (London, 2002), pp. 98, 164, 210–11 and cf. L. Passerini, *Mussolini immaginario: storia di una biografia 1915–1939* (Bari, 1991).

27. B. Bianchini, *Dizionario mussoliniano: mille affermazioni e definizioni del Duce* (Milan, 1939), p. viii.

28. O. Dinale, *La rivoluzione che vince (1914–1934)* (Rome, 1934), pp. 95, 143, 153–4.

29. L. Masciangioli, *Mussolini da lontano* (Sulmona, 1937), pp. 39, 50.

30. G. Bottai, 'Il libro e la cultura del popolo', *Critica Fascista*, 15, 1 July 1937.

31. SPDCO 540382, 4 August 1942, President of the Monte dei Paschi di Siena; 17 June 1943, Prefect (Siena) each to Segreteria particolare del Duce; 4 June 1943, Margherita Vivarelli to Segreteria particolare del Duce.

32. SPDCO 204784, 22 April 1940, appeal to Mussolini and attached note.

33. SPDCO 519255, 27 August 1941, Petronio to Segreteria particolare del Duce.

34. SPDCO 165496, 31 December 1927, Bonasoro to Segreteria particolare del Duce.

35. SPDCO 157286, 26 June 1933, Campbell to Mussolini; 29 August 1933, Campbell to Mussolini.

36. SPDCO 155248, 19 October 1934, Mussolini to Chiang.

37. S. Fitzpatrick, *Everyday Stalinism: ordinary life in extraordinary times: Soviet Russia in the 1930s* (Oxford, 1999); 'The world of Ostap Bender: Soviet confidence men in the Stalin period', *Slavic Review*, 61, 2002, pp. 535–57.

38. See, for example, I. A. Ilf and E. Petrov, *The twelve chairs* (London, 1961); *The golden calf* (London, 1971).

39. See, for example, CP 714, file on Cesare Nirobba, 18 April 1939, Questore (Rome) to Prefect (Rome).

40. See, for example, CP 627, file on Carlo Marmini, a young man who tried to justify what the police called his 'feckless life' with claims that he was Bocchini's nephew. Ministry of the Interior note, 19 March 1938.

41. CP 550, file on Alcide Landini, 20 August 1937, Carabinieri (Savona) to Questura (Savona).

42. CP 245, file on Salvatore Chimenti, 10 October 1936, Questore (Modena) to Prefect (Modena).

43. CP 384, file on Anita Fabbri. In the police account, Rachele is too formidable a person to be named openly but is instead referred to as an 'Alta Personalità'. See 23 January 1936, A. Fabbri confession.

44. CP 985, file on Giuseppe Sturano, 25 May 1937, Carabinieri (Milan) to Carabinieri (Rome).

45. CP 276, file on Giovanni Gastone Conti, 26 May 1939, Carabinieri (Bologna) to Carabinieri (Rome).

46. CP 276, 6 May 1939, Prefect (Bologna) to Ministry of the Interior.

47. CP 275, file on Vittorio Contarini, 3 February 1943, Carabinieri (Milan) to Carabinieri (Rome).

48. R. Bracalini, *Il re 'vittorioso': la vita, il regno e l'esilio di Vittorio Emanuele III* (Milan, 1980), p. 202.

49. For a notable example, see the treatment of the King in the most widespread of party texts, R. Forges Davanzati, *Il balilla Vittorio: racconto. Il libro della V classe elementare* (Rome, 1938). The model Fascist boy, starstruck by his *Duce*, none the less bore the name of his King.

50. *La Rivista di Bergamo: mensile illustrato*, IV, 47, November 1925. The piece was written by Giulio Pavoni.

51. *Il Balilla del Trentino*, 20 November 1930 and following issues.

52. *Il Legionario*, 13 July 1935.

53. *L'Artigiano*, 14 April 1935.

54. *Il Legionario*, 24 August 1935.

55. M. Mureddu, *Il Quirinale del Re* (Milan, 1977), pp. 16–17.

56. *Il Balilla del Trentino*, 16 January and 10 March 1931.

57. See the editorial in *Oltremare*, 2, May 1928.

58. MRF 52/122/3, 30 November 1929, Turati to Federali.

59. *Lo Sport Fascista*, II, December 1929.

60. M. De Giorgio, *Le italiane dall'Unità a oggi: modelli culturali e comportamenti sociali* (Bari, 1982), pp. 189–90.

61. M. De Giorgio, *Le italiane dall'Unità a oggi*, p. 360.

62. M. C. Giusti, 'È nata una principessa', *Giovanissima*, V, November 1934.

63. *Il Mare Nostro-Stirpe Italica*, February 1937. The piece was written by Angela Pulcini who promiscuously visited similar prose on other royals and on Mussolini. Cf., for example, her description of Queen Elena as a 'Heavenly apparition' in *Il Mare Nostro-Stirpe Italica*, October 1936.

64. *Il Legionario*, 24 February 1937.

65. *Il Legionario*, 1 December 1937.

66. See, for example, O. F. Tencajoli, 'Vittorio Amedeo II Re di Sicilia, alto

sovrano di Malta', *Oltremare*, 4, February 1930, pp. 78–81; R. Micaletti, 'Il viaggio africano della Duchessa d'Aosta Madre', *Oltremare*, 7, April 1933, pp. 153–4.

67. *Il Legionario*, 17 March 1937.

68. A. Degasperi, *Trento '43* (Trento, 1991), p. 48.

69. *L'Alpino*, 1 May 1934.

70. *Giovanissima*, May 1935.

71. For a description, see D. Lasansky, 'Tableau and memory; the Fascist revival of the Medieval/Renaissance festival in Italy', *The European Legacy*, 4, 1999, pp. 26–53.

72. *Il Balilla del Trentino*, 27 April 1930.

73. CP 537, file on Nicola Ippolito, a returned soldier from AOI and fond of a drink, who was charged with responsibility for the affray.

74. CP 382, file on Antonio Errichiello, 30 January 1937, Questura (Avellino) to Prefect (Avellino).

75. CP 875, file on Carolina Rogger, 14 July 1939, Questura (Bolzano) to Provincial Commissioner; 20 July 1939, Prefect (Bolzano) note.

76. Clara Cirillo, 'Il mese Mariano', *La Rivista della Venezia Tridentina*, XVII, May–June 1935.

77. F. F. Nitti, *Escape: the personal narrative of a political prisoner who was rescued from Lipari: the Fascist 'Devil's Island'* (New York, 1930), p. v. For a further useful English-language account, see S. G. Pugliese, *Carlo Rosselli: socialist heretic and Antifascist exile* (Cambridge, Mass., 1999).

78. For a detailed account of his background, see N. Tranfaglia, *Carlo Rosselli dall'interventismo a 'Giustizia e Libertà'* (Bari, 1968).

79. J. Lussu, *Freedom has no frontiers* (London, 1969), p. 145.

80. R. De Felice, *Mussolini il duce: 1. Gli anni del consenso 1929–1936* (Turin, 1974), pp. 116–17.

81. A. Grandi, *I giovani di Mussolini: Fascisti convinti, fascisti pentiti, antifascisti* (Milan, 2001), p. 59.

82. R. Caccavale, *Comunisti italiani in Unione Sovietica: proscritti da Mussolini, soppressi da Stalin* (Milan, 1995), p. 25.

83. A. Davidson, *The theory and practice of Italian communism* (London, 1982), vol. 1, p. 188.

84. T. J. Jackson Lears, 'The concept of cultural hegemony: problems and possibilities', *American Historical Review*, 90, 1985, p. 567.

85. G. Amendola, *Un'isola* (Milan, 1980), pp. 131, 142.

86. A. Misuri, *'Ad bestias!' (Memorie di un pregiudicato)* (Rome, 1944), p. 215.

87. G. Cerreti, *Con Togliatti e Thorez: quarant'anni di lotte politiche* (Milan,

1973), p. 11. Togliatti was allegedly the master of eleven languages and was fascinated by philology.

88. See, for example, P. Treves, *What Mussolini did to us* (London, 1940), p. 202.

89. C. Ravera, *Diario di trent'anni 1913–1943* (Rome, 1973), p. 538.

90. See further details on her period in *confino* in CP 416, file on Cesira Fiori.

91. C. Fiori, *La confinata* (Milan, 1979), pp. 7–8, 10.

92. For a polemical account of this tendency, see P. Neglie, *Fratelli in camicia nera: comunisti e fascisti dal corporativismo alla CGIL (1928–1948)* (Bologna, 1996).

93. P. Nenni, *La battaglia socialista contro il fascismo 1922–1944* (ed. D. Zucàro) (Milan, 1977), pp. 411, 447.

94. CP 84, file on Mario Bellucci, 12 July 1930, Prefect (Florence) note.

95. CP 1, file on Luigi Abbiati, 26 January 1942, Coviello to Ministry of the Interior.

96. C. Ghini and A. Dal Pont, *Gli antifascisti al confino 1926–1943* (Rome, 1971), p. 35.

97. For a full list, including those in occupied territories, see C. S. Capogreco, *I campi del duce: l'internamento civile nell'Italia fascista* (Turin, 2004), pp. 177–282.

98. For a rebuttal of Berlusconi's views on the matter, see S. Corvisieri, *La villeggiatura di Mussolini: il confino da Bocchini a Berlusconi* (Milan, 2004).

99. Ghini and Dal Pont, *Gli antifascisti al confino*, p. 114.

100. Capogreco, *I campi del duce*, p. 66.

101. C. S. Capogreco, *Ferramonti: la vita e gli uomini del più grande campo d'internamento fascista (1940–1945)* (Florence, 1987), pp. 47, 117, 178.

102. E. Rossi, *Elogio della galera: lettere 1930–1943* (Bari, 1968), p. 62.

103. F. Gambetti, *Gli anni che scottano* (Milan, 1967), p. 144.

104. *Il Commercio Vinicolo*, 11 November 1933.

105. CP 86, file on Giovanni Benazzo, 12 April 1933, Questore (Alessandria) to Provincial Commissioner for *confino*; 22 September 1933, Ministry of the Interior note.

106. CP 122, file on Lorenzo Boccaccio, 12 April 1933, Questore (Alessandria) to Prefect.

107. CP 86, 17 September 1933, Prefect (Alessandria) to Ministry of the Interior.

108. CP 122, 22 September 1933, Prefect (Alessandria) to Ministry of the Interior.

109. CP 122, 27 July 1933, Luigi Boccaccio to Mussolini.

110. CP 122, 21 May 1933, Carabinieri (Alessandria) to Carabinieri (Rome).

111. See the editorial in *Critica Fascista*, 15, 1 November 1937.

12 Dictating full-time

1. SPEP 19, 22 August 1932, PNF report.
2. J. Harris, 'Was Stalin a weak dictator?', *Journal of Modern History*, 75, 2003, pp. 375–86.
3. Further commentary on all these matters can be tracked in R. J. B. Bosworth, *Mussolini* (London, 2002).
4. C. Silvestri, *Matteotti, Mussolini e il dramma italiana* (Milan, 1981), p. 30.
5. M. Canali, *Il delitto Matteotti* (Bologna, 2004), pp. 298–301.
6. SPDCR 40, 4 July 1934, police report noting that Farinacci had bought her a rifle costing 17,000 lire.
7. SPDCR 40, 20 September 1933, police report; cf. also 20 July 1935 and SPDCR 44, 7 August 1936, both occasions when the pair showed up at the Venice Biennale and stayed at the Hotel Excelsior.
8. SPDCR 44, 24 July 1936, police report.
9. See, for example, the telephone tap read by Mussolini in which Pederzini declared roundly that the only thing which she and Farinacci really had in common was bed. SPDCR 43 (Farinacci), 14 February 1935, telephone tap.
10. SPDCR 43, 11 October 1934, Avvocato Salvatore Pantano to Farinacci.
11. SPEP 19, 16 September 1932, PNF report.
12. SPDCR 104, 15 February 1925, medical report.
13. L. Federzoni, *1927: diario di un ministro fascista* (ed. A. Macchi) (Florence, 1993), p. 27.
14. See further Bosworth, *Mussolini*, pp. 364–5, 385–9, 404–6.
15. F. Bandini, *Claretta: profilo di Clara Petacci e dei suoi tempi* (Milan, 1960), p. 55.
16. BMOO XXXVIII, p. 40.
17. For the story, see P. V. Cannistraro and B. R. Sullivan, *Il Duce's other woman* (New York, 1993).
18. For a description of this psychologically revealing tie, see Bosworth, *Mussolini*, pp. 91–5.
19. For racy detail, see A. Spinosa, *I figli del Duce* (Milan, 1983), pp. 24–5, 98–102.
20. SPDCR 113, 1 November 1925, Mussolini to school head.
21. SPDCR 113, 15 October 1928, Mussolini to Edda.
22. For pious evocation, see P. Mastri, *La Rocca delle Caminate (Il castello del Duce)* (Bologna, 1927).

23. C. Petacci, *Il mio diario* (n.p., 1946), pp. 63–4.

24. For an anthropological study of the region of the Marsica where their estates were notorious, see C. White, *Patrons and partisans: a study of politics in two southern Italian Comuni* (Cambridge, 1980). Cf. the great anti-Fascist novels by I. Silone, *Fontamara* (London, 1934) and *Bread and Wine* (London, 1962). Silone came from the Marsica where the Torlonias were large landowners.

25. See, for example, SPDCR 108, 17 April 1936, Mussolini to Vittorio and Bruno.

26. V. Mussolini, *Voli sulle Ambe* (Florence, 1937).

27. It can be found in separate edition or in BMOO XXXIV, pp. 193–269.

28. SPDCR 112, 5 November 1942, school report; E. Amicucci, *I 600 giorni di Mussolini: dal Gran Sasso a Dongo* (Rome, 1948), p. 81. For Romano's own coffee-table account of family life, see R. Mussolini, *Benito Mussolini: apologia del mio padre* (Bologna, 1969).

29. A. Spinosa, *I figli del Duce*, pp. 115–17.

30. A. Lessona, *Un ministro di Mussolini racconta* (Milan, 1973), p. 174.

31. SPDCR 43, 10 July 1936, Farinacci to Mussolini.

32. The best edition is G. Ciano, *Diario 1937–1943* (ed. R. De Felice) (Milan, 1980).

33. For further on the Fascist attitude towards golf, see R. J. B. Bosworth, 'Golf and Italian Fascism', in M. R. Farrally and A. J. Cochran (eds), *Science and Golf III: proceedings of the 1998 World Scientific Congress of Golf*, (London, 1999).

34. P. Pedrazza, *Giornalismo di Mussolini* (Milan, 1937), p. 113; V. Emiliani, *Il paese dei Mussolini* (Turin, 1984), p. 34.

35. For an apologetic study of the brothers' relationship, see M. Staglieno, *Arnaldo e Benito: due fratelli* (Milan, 2003).

36. Canali, *Il delitto Matteotti*, p. 80.

37. Ibid., p. 171.

38. D. Susmel (ed.), *Carteggio Arnaldo–Benito Mussolini* (Florence, 1954), p. 30.

39. Ibid., p. 18.

40. *Le Vie d'Italia*, XXXIV, February 1928.

41. Canali, *Il delitto Matteotti*, pp. 78–9.

42. M. Canali, *Le spie del regime* (Bologna, 2004), p. 200.

43. A. Mussolini, *Scritti e discorsi* (Milan, 1934), vol. II, pp. 18–20.

44. *Carteggio Arnaldo–Benito Mussolini*, p. 184.

45. For the circumstances, see Bosworth, *Mussolini*, p. 26.

46. A. and B. Mussolini, *Vita di Sandro e Arnaldo* (Milan, 1934).

47. For a typically overblown example, see G. S. Spinetti, *Mistica fascista nel pensiero di Arnaldo Mussolini* (Milan, 1936).

48. For examples, see Bosworth, *Mussolini*, p. 323.

49. BMOO XXVIII, pp. 136–9; XLIV, p. 199.

50. V. Panunzio, *Il 'secondo fascismo' 1936–1943: la reazione della nuova generazione alla crisi del movimento e del regime* (Milan, 1988), p. 63; Q. Navarra, *Memorie del cameriere di Mussolini* (Milan, 1946), pp. 60–61.

51. See, for example, D. Mack Smith, *Mussolini* (London, 1981).

52. N. D'Aroma, *Mussolini segreto* (Rocca San Casciano, 1958), p. 278.

53. Ibid., p. 120.

54. BMOO XXIX, p. 53.

55. G. Ciano, *Diario 1937–1943*, p. 284.

56. C. M. De Vecchi, *Tra Papa, Duce e Re: il conflitto tra Chiesa cattolica e Stato fascista nel diario 1930–1931 del primo ambasciatore del Regno d'Italia presso la Santa Sede* (ed. S. Setta) (Rome, 1998), p. 210.

57. F. Bojano, *In the wake of the goose-step* (London, 1944), p. 41.

58. D'Aroma, *Mussolini segreto*, p. 121.

59. Ibid., p. 33.

60. G. Ciano, *Diario 1937–1943*, p. 570.

61. Y. De Begnac, *Palazzo Venezia: storia di un regime* (Rome, 1950), p. 567.

62. BMOO XLIV, pp. 67–70.

63. A. Pozzi, *Come li ho visti io: dal diario di un medico* (Milan, 1947), pp. 118–19.

64. F. Anfuso, *Roma Berlino Salò (1936–1945)* (Milan, 1950), pp. 85–6.

65. C. Delcroix, *Un uomo e un popolo* (Florence, 1928), p. 3.

66. Y. De Begnac, *Taccuini mussoliniani* (Bologna, 1990), p. 5.

67. F. Anfuso, *Da Palazzo Venezia al Lago di Garda (1936–1945)* (Rome, 1996), p. 71.

68. De Begnac, *Palazzo Venezia*, p. 651.

69. Anfuso, *Da Palazzo Venezia al Lago di Garda*, p. 71.

70. For many examples, see Bosworth, *Mussolini*.

71. DDI 7s, IV, 387, 8 August 1926, Mussolini to Volpi.

72. The detail of the war in Ethiopia can be further tracked in Bosworth, *Mussolini*, pp. 287–309.

73. For a careful account, see J. F. Coverdale, *Italian intervention in the Spanish Civil War* (Princeton, 1975).

74. R. De Felice, *Mussolini il fascista 2. L'organizzazione dello stato fascista 1925–1929* (Turin, 1968), p. 313.

75. D. Musiedlak, *Lo stato fascista e la sua classe politica 1922–1943* (Bologna, 2003), pp. 146–9.

76. Ibid., p. 563.

77. M. Salvati, *Il regime e gli impiegati: la nazionalizzazione piccolo-borghese nel ventennio fascista* (Bari, 1992).

78. R. C. Fried, *The Italian Prefects: a study in administrative politics* (New Haven, 1963), p. 174.

79. See, for example, the case of Federzoni, Musiedlak, *Lo stato fascista e la sua classe politica*, pp. 173–5.

80. Canali, *Le spie del regime*, p. 63.

81. Ibid., pp. 133–5, 152, 265.

82. For introduction, see H. Krausnick et al., *Anatomy of the SS State* (London, 1968) and for positioning of debates about it in the historiography, cf. I. Kershaw, *The Nazi dictatorship: problems and perspectives of interpretation*, 4th ed. (London, 2000), pp. 55–65.

83. For an example, see G. Bonsaver, 'Fascist censorship on literature and the case of Elio Vittorini', *Modern Italy*, 8, 2003, pp. 165–86.

84. Canali, *Le spie del regime*, p. 122.

85. G. Bottai, *Diario 1935–1944* (ed. G. B. Guerri) (Milan, 1989), p. 337.

86. F. Bandini, *Claretta: profilo di Clara Petacci e i suoi tempi* (Milan, 1960), pp. 13–15.

87. C. Alvaro, *Quasi una vita: giornale di uno scrittore* (Milan, 1950), p. 121.

88. Cannistraro and Sullivan, *Il Duce's other woman*, pp. 518, 528.

89. E. Sturani, *Otto milioni di cartoline per il Duce* (Turin, 1995), p. 39.

90. Petacci, *Il mio diario*, p. 48.

91. See U. Guspini, *L'orecchio del regime: le intercettazioni telefoniche al tempo del fascismo* (Milan, 1973) and for further background, Bosworth, *Mussolini*, pp. 276–8.

92. E. Cerruti, *Ambassador's wife* (London, 1952), p. 224.

93. SPDCR 104, article in *Il Messaggero*, 16 November 1937.

94. Bandini, *Claretta*, pp. 103–11.

95. For her empty memoirs, punning tastelessly on the Fascist slogan 'Chi si ferma è perduto', see M. Petacci, *Chi ama è perduta: mia sorella Claretta* (Gardolo di Trento, 1988).

96. SPDCR 103, 10 May 1938, Petacci to Sebastiani.

97. Ibid., undated, Sebastiani to Professor Perez.

98. *Evening Standard*, 22 May 1933.

99. N. Sigillino, *Mussolini visto da me* (Rome, 1935), p. 24.

13 Becoming imperialists

1. A. Del Boca, *L'Africa nella coscienza degli italiani: miti, memorie, errori, sconfitte* (Bari, 1992), p. 35.

2. BMOO XXVII, p. 268.

3. BMOO XXVII, p. 266.

4. A. V. Savona and M. L. Straniero, *Canti dell'Italia fascista (1919–1945)* (Milan, 1979), p. 271.

5. G. De Vecchi, *Dubàt: gli arditi neri* (Milan, 1936), p. 129.

6. B. Sorgoni, *Parole e corpi: antropologia, discorso giuridico e politiche sessuali interrazziali nella colonia Eritrea* (Naples, 1998), p. 153.

7. A. Castaldi, 'La cucina abissina', *Rivista delle colonie*, 5, March 1931, pp. 208–10.

8. C. Savoia, 'Appunti del buon gusto', *Meridiani*, 2, April–May 1936.

9. R. De Felice, *Mussolini il duce: 1. Gli anni del consenso 1929–1936* (Turin, 1974), p. 642.

10. N. Labanca, *Oltremare: storia dell'espansione coloniale italiana* (Bologna, 2002), p. 56.

11. The actual death toll at Dogali was 430. See G. Finaldi, 'Italy's scramble for Africa from Dogali to Adowa' in J. Dickie, J. Foot and F. M. Snowden (eds), *Disastro! Disasters in Italy since 1860: culture, politics, society* (London, 2002), pp. 82–6.

12. It is available in English translation: L. Barzini, *Peking to Paris: a journey across two continents in 1907* (London, 1972). For typical enthusiasm, see the accounts in the *Rivista mensile del Touring* in 1907 and 1908. Borghese was inevitably a member and, after his victory in the race, was given a special reception and a gold medal by the gratified club.

13. G. Piazza, *La fiamma bilingue: momenti del dissidio ideale 1913–1923* (Milan, 1924), p. 52.

14. L. Federzoni, *Presagi alla nazione: discorsi politici* (Milan, 1924), p. 129.

15. Labanca, *Oltremare*, p. 169.

16. A. Bertarelli, 'Il Guidone del Touring nell'Eritrea', *Rivista mensile del Touring*, XIV, February 1908, pp. 59–66.

17. See, for example, Luigi Bertarelli editorial, *Rivista mensile del Touring*, XXI, January 1915, p. 1.

18. V. Cacciami, 'Slavi, Germani e Franchi', *Rivista mensile del Touring*, XX, September 1914, pp. 581–90.

19. L. Medici del Vascello, *Per l'Italia!* (Bari, 1916), pp. 183–5.

20. Cited in F. Gaeta, *La stampa nazionalista* (Rocca San Casciano, 1965), p. 21.

21. R. Cantalupo, *L'Italia musulmana* (Rome, 1928), p. 155.

22. S. A. Stehlin, *Weimar and the Vatican 1919–1933: German–Vatican diplomatic relations in the interwar years* (Princeton, 1983), p. 159.

23. P. Lanza di Scalea, 'La politica coloniale' in T. Sillani (ed.), *L'Italia di Vittorio Emanuele III 1900–1925* (Rome, 1926), p. 173.

24. See C. Duggan, *Francesco Crispi 1818–1901: from nation to nationalism* (Oxford, 2002), pp. 682–715.

25. Labanca, *Oltremare*, pp. 168–9.

26. M. Tendrini and M. Shandrick, *The Duke of the Abruzzi: an explorer's life* (Seattle, 1997), pp. 12, 94, 101.

27. G. Speroni, *Il Duca degli Abruzzi* (Milan, 1991), pp. 6–7.

28. See, for example, Labanca, *Oltremare*, p. 129, who talks about the new regime being 'possessed' by an 'anxiety' for empire, or A. Del Boca, *Gli italiani in Libia dal fascismo a Gheddafi* (Bari, 1988), pp. 6–7.

29. C. De Vecchi di Val Cismon, *Orizzonti d'Impero: cinque anni in Somalia* (Milan, 1935), pp. 3–4, 16, 285.

30. 'Marga', *Piccolo Mondo Fascista* (Florence, 1932), pp. 93–101.

31. De Vecchi, *Dubàt: gli arditi neri*, p. 15.

32. A. Bullotta, *La Somalia sotto due bandiere* (Cernusco del Naviglio, 1949), p. xiii.

33. Jama Mohamed, '"The evils of locust bait": popular nationalism during the 1945 anti-locust control rebellion in colonial Somaliland', *Past and Present*, 174, 2002, pp. 184–216.

34. Bullotta, *La Somalia sotto due bandiere*, pp. xxi, 4–5, 39–40, 117–18.

35. Del Boca, *L'Africa nella coscienza degli italiani*, pp. 41–3.

36. For a fine narration of his story, see ibid., pp. 45–57.

37. C. Bertacchi, 'L'impero dell'Africa Orientale Italiana', *La vita italiana*, f. 302, 15 May 1938.

38. See, for example, R. Sertoli Salis, *Le isole italiane dell'Egeo dall'occupazione alla sovranità* (Rome, 1939).

39. C. Marongiu Buonaiuti, *La politica religiosa del Fascismo nel Dodecanneso* (Naples, 1979), pp. 99–106.

40. N. Doumanis, *Myth and memory in the Mediterranean: remembering Fascism's empire* (London, 1997), p. 49.

41. Del Boca, *L'Africa nella coscienza degli italiani*, p. 32.

42. S. Romano, *Giuseppe Volpi: industria e finanza tra Giolitti e Mussolini* (Milan, 1979), p. 107.

43. R. Graziani, *Ho difeso la patria* (Cernusco sul Naviglio, 1948), p. 10.

44. A. Del Boca, *Gli italiani in Libia dal fascismo a Gheddafi* (Bari, 1988), p. 13.

45. For a detailed history of this group, see R. De Felice, *Ebrei in un paese arabo* (Bologna, 1978).

46. Del Boca, *Gli italiani in Libia dal fascismo a Gheddafi*, pp. 25–52.

47. See, for example, R. Graziani, *Pace romana in Libia* (Milan, 1937).

48. Del Boca, *Gli italiani in Libia dal fascismo a Gheddafi*, pp. 121, 124, 183.

49. Ibid., pp. 196–7; A. Del Boca, 'I crimini del colonialismo fascista' in A. Del Boca (ed.), *Le guerre coloniali del fascismo* (Bari, 1991), pp. 237–8.

50. B. Pace, 'L'occupazione di Cufra e la politica con la Senussia', *Riviste delle Colonie*, 5, May 1931, pp. 327–41.

51. G. Giambalino De Gregorio, 'Un problema coloniale d'attualità: lo spopolamento libico', *Il Mare Nostro-Stirpe Italica*, November 1936.

52. By one account, he told Badoglio, who had sent him conventional congratulations, that the soldier's sorrow at leaving was not matched by Balbo's at arriving. G. De Luna, *Badoglio: un militare al potere* (Milan, 1974), p. 129.

53. SPDCR 84, 28 September 1934, De Bono to Bocchini; [1939], undated financial report.

54. M. Moore, *Fourth shore: Italy's mass colonization of Libya* (London, 1940), pp. 18–20, 96.

55. Del Boca, *Gli italiani in Libia dal fascismo a Gheddafi*, p. 267.

56. C. G. Segrè, *Fourth shore: the Italian colonization of Libya* (Chicago, 1974), pp. 123, 164, 167.

57. For the statistics, see G. Rosoli (ed.), *Un secolo di emigrazione italiana 1876–1976* (Rome, 1978), p. 347.

58. A. Sbacchi, *Ethiopia under Mussolini: Fascism and the colonial experience* (London, 1985), pp. 108–11.

59. For an example involving Rachele Mussolini and for Farinacci's exposure of the dilemmas of Fascist rule in East Africa, see R. J. B. Bosworth, *Mussolini* (London, 2002), p. 321.

60. See the lavish and officially sponsored English version of his account of the war, P. Badoglio, *The war in Abyssinia* (London, 1937).

61. Sbacchi, *Ethiopia under Mussolini*, p. 47.

62. SPDCR 67, 22 January 1937, Farinacci to Mussolini.

63. The rumours in this regard came from the circle around De Bono. SPDCR 67, 28 July 1937, report.

64. SPDCR 67, 5 April 1937, Lessona to Prince Colonna, the Governor of Rome. The city was to pay two million, the Ministries of Colonies and War half a million each.

65. Sbacchi, *Ethiopia under Mussolini*, p. 99.

66. A. Del Boca, *Il Negus: vita e morte dell'ultimo re dei re* (Bari, 1995), pp. 205–6. It is suggested that 275,000 soldiers and civilians died in 1935–6, 75,000 or more in 1936–41 from direct Fascist actions, while a further 300,000 perished in villages stricken by the political turmoil of the years of imperial occupation.

67. See, for example, P. M. Masotti, *Ricordi d'Etiopia di un funzionario coloniale* (Milan, 1981), p. 53.

68. For the case of Alberto Pollera, see L. Goglia, 'Una diversa politica razziale coloniale in un documento inedito di Alberto Pollera del 1937', *Storia contemporanea*, XVI, 1985, pp. 1071–91.

69. R. Pickering-Iazzi, 'Mass-mediated fantasies of feminine conquest, 1930–1940', in P. Palumbo (ed.), *A place in the sun: Africa in Italian colonial culture from post-unification to the present* (Berkeley, 2003), p. 207.

70. Sorgoni, *Parole e corpi*, p. 186.

71. CP 1088, file of Abele Zanichelli, 3 February 1936, Carabinieri (Bologna) to Carabinieri (Rome).

72. CP 23, file on Aurelio Amici, 15 October 1935, Questura (Forlì) to Prefect (Forlì).

73. CP 1043, file on Italo Valesani, 30 September 1935, Questura (Belluno) to Prefect (Belluno).

74. CP 273, files on Leandro and Francesco Concetti, 14 September 1935, Carabinieri (Ascoli Piceno) to Questura (Ascoli Piceno).

75. *Il Regime Fascista*, 28 May 1935.

76. CP 82, file on Ferdinando Belli, 29 November 1935, Questura (Cremona) to Prefect (Cremona).

77. CP 1050, file on Stefano Vassallo, 16 August 1936, Questura (Imperia) to Prefect (Imperia). Vassallo was sentenced to five years but let off in February 1937.

78. Luciani's use of the ancient and general term '*i mori*' to describe the Ethiopians is splendid evidence of how far off from his Italy was their country, at least in his imagination.

79. CP 581, file on Luigi Luciani, 18 July 1936, Carabinieri (Padova) to Questura (Padova).

80. L. Polezzi, 'Imperial reproductions: the circulation of colonial images across popular genres and media in the 1920s and 1930s', *Modern Italy*, 8, 2003, pp. 31–47, provides some background to the ambiguities of Italians' constructions of gender identities in their empire.

81. CP 1015, file on Filippo Torquati, 28 October 1937, Questura (Ascoli Piceno) to Prefect (Ascoli Piceno). Torquati's amnesty came through by December 1937.

82. For more context, see R. J. B. Bosworth, *Italy and the wider world* (London, 1996), p. 94.

83. Labanca, *Oltremare*, pp. 260–61.

84. K. von Henneberg, 'Monuments, public space and the memory of empire in modern Italy', *History and Memory*, 16, 2004, p. 53.

85. Rosoli (ed.), *Un secolo di emigrazione italiana*, p. 346.

86. R. Michels, 'La politica demografica' in G. Dobbert, *L'economia fascista* (Florence, 1935), p. 85.

87. R. Santinon, *I fasci italiani all'estero* (Rome, 1991), p. 16.

88. BMOO XX, p. 345, in a letter of 15 February to the durable migration expert, Giuseppe De Michelis.

89. BMOO XXI, p. 212.

90. P. V. Cannistraro and G. Rosoli, 'Fascist emigration policy in the 1920s: an interpretative framework', *International Migration Review*, XIII, 1979, p. 687.

91. Rosoli (ed.), *Un secolo di emigrazione italiana*, p. 346.

92. Z. Ciuffoletti and M. Degl'Innocenti, *L'emigrazione nella storia d'Italia 1868–1975* (Florence, 1978), vol. ii, p. 156.

93. *I Fasci italiani all'estero*, 3 January 1925, editorial.

94. Ciuffoletti and Degl'Innocenti, *L'emigrazione nella storia d'Italia*, vol. ii, p. 128.

95. G. Cresciani, *Fascism, Anti-Fascism and Italians in Australia 1922–1945* (Canberra, 1980), pp. 30–31.

96. See, for example, the decidedly 'unpolitical' collection, L. DiStasi (ed.), *Una storia segreta: the secret history of Italian-American evacuation and internment during World War II* (Berkeley, 2001).

97. C. Baldoli, *Exporting Fascism: Italian Fascists and Britain's Italians in the 1930s* (Oxford, 2003), p. 74.

98. E. Ciccotosto and M. Bosworth, *Emma: a translated life* (Fremantle, 1990), p. 34.

99. For a wildly exaggerated account of its achievement, see A. Grande, *La Legione Parini (da Sabaudia a Diredawa)* (Florence, 1937).

100. SPDCO 519235, 29 July 1935, Parini to Mussolini.

101. Father Parini was briefly jailed for his part in the kidnapping of the corpse and then for a while sent to a sort of religious *confino* in South America, where he was *persona grata* among Fascists fled there. For his own account of the event, see A. Parini, 'La nostra vicenda' in P. Scarpa (ed.), *Cronistoria di una salma famosa e Diario di 42 giorni di carcere* (Milan, 1947).

102. BMOO XXXI, p. 130.

103. CP 752, file on Alberto Parini, 4 December 1942, Prefect (Mantova) to Ministry of the Interior; 12 December 1942, Questura (Mantova) to Prefect (Mantova). Parini remained a Franciscan friar until his death in February 1971. For a eulogistic obituary, see *Acta Provinciae Medioterrensis S. Caroli Borromei*, 62, 1969–1976, pp. 56–7.

104. CP 752, 29 December 1942, Farinacci to Senise.

105. CP 275, file on Galliano Conte, 25 May 1938, Carabinieri (Treviso) to Questura (Treviso).

106. CP 984, file on Virgilio Stucchi, 4 September 1941, Carabinieri (Naples) to Ministry of the Interior.

107. See, for example, CP 385, file on Giuseppina Fabbri, a worker from Conselice, 5 August 1942, Questura (Bologna) to Prefect (Bologna).

14 Embracing Nazi Germany

1. A. Bollati, *La campagna italo-etiopica nella stampa militare estera (previsioni, critiche, riconoscimenti e deduzioni)* (Rome, 1938), pp. 8–12.

2. See, for example, the editorial in *The Times*, London, 21 February 1936.

3. *The Times*, 31 March 1936.

4. *The Times*, 8 April 1936.

5. *The Month*, September 1935.

6. G. Salvemini, *Under the axe of Fascism* (London, 1936); G. Seldes, *Sawdust Caesar: the untold history of Mussolini and Fascism* (London, 1936).

7. G. L. Steer, *Caesar in Abyssinia* (London, 1936), p. 233.

8. G. Giglio, *The triumph of Barabbas* (Sydney, 1937); cf. A. Borghi, *Mussolini: red and black* (London, 1935).

9. S. K. B. Asante, *Pan-African protest: West Africa and the Italo-Ethiopian crisis, 1934–1941* (London, 1977), pp. 40–42.

10. J. T. Sammons, *Beyond the ring: the role of boxing in American society* (Urbana, Ill, 1988), pp. 101–2.

11. G. Mondaini, 'Il significato storico dell'impresa etiopica nella evoluzione coloniale contemporanea', *Rivista delle colonie*, 10, June 1936, pp. 609–20.

12. G. Gentile, 'Dopo la fondazione dell'Impero', *Civiltà Fascista*, 3, May 1936, pp. 321–34.

13. I. Montanelli, 'Dentro la guerra', *Civiltà Fascista*, 3, January 1936, pp. 38–9.

14. I. Montanelli, 'Dopo la guerra', *Civiltà Fascista*, 3, May 1936, pp. 290–91.

15. G. Pistillo, 'Il problema ebraico in Italia', *La Vita italiana*, f. 281, 15 August 1936.

16. BMOO XXVII, pp. 76–80, speech of 25 May 1935.

17. R. De Felice, *Mussolini il duce: 1. Gli anni del consenso 1929–1936* (Turin, 1974), p. 667.

18. F. Suvich, *Memorie 1932–1936* (ed. G. Bianchi) (Milan, 1984), pp. 278–80.

19. The fullest narrative can be found in J. F. Coverdale, *Italian intervention in the Spanish Civil War* (Princeton, 1978).

20. D. M. Tuninetti, *La mia missione segreta in Austria 1937–1938* (Milan, 1946), p. 87.

21. G. B. Guerri, *Italo Balbo* (Milan, 1984), p. 315. SPDCR 38, 11 February 1937, police report.

22. See, for example, DDI 8s, VII, 191, 9 August 1937, Mussolini to Viola.

23. R. De Felice, *Mussolini il duce: 2 Lo stato totalitario 1936–1940* (Turin, 1981), p. 465.

24. CP 23, file on Pasquale Ameri, 23 September 1937, Carabinieri (Genoa) to Prefect (Genoa).

25. See, for example, CP 30, file on Ciro Angrisano, 15 January 1938, Prefect (Naples) to Ministry of the Interior.

26. For further detail, see R. J. B. Bosworth, *Mussolini* (London, 2002), pp. 315–19.

27. BMOO XXVIII, pp. 67–72.

28. Tuninetti, *La mia missione segreta*, pp. 16, 49.

29. R. Quartararo, *Roma tra Londra e Berlino: la politica estera fascista dal 1931 al 1940* (Rome, 1980), p. 400.

30. DDI 8s, X, 203, 1 October 1938, Grandi to Ciano.

31. DDI 8s, X, 344, 28 October 1938, memoir of Mussolini, Ciano, Ribbentrop talk.

32. G. Landra, 'Scienza: per una carta della razza italiana in Francia', *La Difesa della Razza*, II, 20 January 1939.

33. C. Gencarelli, 'L'Albania e il suo popolo', *La Difesa della Razza*, II, 5 August 1939.

34. DDI 8s, IX, 42, 2 May 1938, Ciano to Mussolini.

35. B. J. Fischer, *Albania at war 1939–1945* (London, 1999), pp. 33–4, 40, 48.

36. Istituto per gli studi di politica internazionale, *Albania* (Milan, 1940), pp. 10, 91; cf. F. Jacomoni di San Savino, *La politica dell'Italia in Albania* (Rocca San Casciano, 1965), p. 7, who was still maintaining this claim after the war.

37. Fischer, *Albania at war*, pp. 22, 56.

38. Jacomoni di San Savino, *La politica dell'Italia in Albania*, pp. 158–64.

39. DDI 8s, XII, 59, 30 May 1939, Mussolini to Hitler.

40. De Felice, *Mussolini il duce: 1. Gli anni del consenso*, p. 784.

41. A. De Grand, 'Mussolini's follies: Fascism in its imperial and racist phase, 1935–1940', *Contemporary European History*, 13, 2004, p. 133.

42. V. Zamagni, *The economic history of Italy 1860–1990* (Oxford, 1993), p. 267.

43. De Felice, *Mussolini il duce: 2. Lo stato totalitario 1936–1940*, p. 181.

44. B. Mantelli, *'Camerati del lavoro': i lavoratori italiani emigrati nel Terzo Reich nel periodo dell'Asse 1938–1943* (Florence, 1992), p. 33.

45. Ibid., p. 43.

46. DDI 9s, VIII, 429, 4 April 1942, Scorza to De Cesare.

47. DDI 8s, IX, 338, 26 July 1938, Pignatti to Ciano.

48. Mantelli, *'Camerati del lavoro'*, p. 54.

49. M. Magistrati, *L'Italia a Berlino (1937–1939)* (Milan, 1956), pp. 16–17, 87.

50. *L'Artigiano*, 4 February 1934.

51. *L'Artigiano*, 20 May 1934.

52. Anon., 'Echi del primo scambio di trasmissioni scolastiche tra Italia e Germania', *La Radio rurale*, VI, 29 October 1938.

53. 'Voci dalla Germania: transmissione radiofonica del giorno 8 marzo 1939', *La Radio rurale*, VI, 29 March 1939.

54. DDI 8s, V, 101, 23 September 1936, Mussolini–Frank talk.

55. D. Mack Smith, *Mussolini* (London, 1981), p. 215.

56. R. Bianchi Bandinelli, *Dal diario di un borghese* (ed. M. Barbanera) (Rome, 1996), pp. 120–23.

57. DDI 8s, IX, 85, 13 May 1938, Grandi to Ciano.

58. O. Vergani, *Ciano: una lunga confessione* (Milan, 1974), p. 59.

59. G. P. Brunetta, *Storia del cinema italiano 1895–1945* (Rome, 1979), p. 285.

60. *Il Primato*, I, 1 October 1940.

61. *Gioventù Fascista*, 10 December XI [1933].

62. G. C. Viganò, 'Funzione e mete dello sport', *Gerarchia*, XVII, May 1937.

63. CP 646, file on Wais Mattiolini, 19 November 1939, Questura (Florence) to Prefect (Florence).

64. *Stirpe Italica*, November 1934.

65. CP 84, file on Italo Belluzzi, 12 August 1939, Prefect (Bologna) to Ministry of the Interior.

66. F. Gambetti, *Gli anni che scottano* (Milan, 1967), p. 255.

67. O. Vergani, *Ciano: una lunga confessione* (Milan, 1974), p. 80.

68. See, for example, *Bollettino quindicinale: Federazione Provinciale Fascista dei Commercianti* (Trento), 1 February 1929.

69. See, for example, G. Devoto, 'Lingue speciali: le cronache del calcio', *Lingua Nostra*, I, February 1939, pp. 17–21.

70. E. De Felice, 'La terminologia del pugilato', *Lingua Nostra*, III, May 1941, pp. 56–9.

71. V. Martelli, 'Ancora sulla nomenclatura scientifica', *Lingua Nostra*, III, May 1941, pp. 83–5.

72. *L'Alpino*, 1 December 1935.

73. S. Malfatti, 'Il nome italiano del bridge', *Lingua Nostra*, II, July 1941.

74. B. Migliorini, 'La sostituzione dei forestierismi: improvvisa o graduale', *Lingua Nostra*, III, November 1941, pp. 138–40.

75. A. Menarini, 'Appunti sull'autarchia della lingua', *Lingua Nostra*, V, January 1943, pp. 18–22.

76. B. Mussolini, *Memoirs 1942–1943 with documents relating to the period* (London, 1949), p. 146.

77. G. Bottai, *Diario 1935–1944* (ed. G. B. Guerri) (Milan, 1989), pp. 112–13.

78. E. Ghersi, 'Di alcune questioni di politica indigena', *Rivista delle Colonie*, 10, July 1936, pp. 770–81.

79. R. Sertoli Salis, 'Sulla sudditanza dell'AOI', *Rivista delle Colonie*, 10, October 1936.

80. A. Del Boca, 'I crimini del colonialismo fascista' in A. Del Boca (ed.), *Le guerre coloniali del fascismo* (Bari, 1991), p. 247.

81. H. S. Hughes, *Prisoners of hope: the silver age of Italian Jews 1924–1974* (Cambridge, Mass., 1983), p. 20.

82. R. De Felice, *Storia degli ebrei italiani sotto il fascismo* (Turin, 1961), p. 85.

83. A. Stille, *Benevolence and betrayal: five Italian Jewish families under Fascism* (New York, 1993), pp. 21–2.

84. A. Momigliano, *Storia tragica e grottesca del razzismo fascista* (Milan, 1946), p. 47.

85. E. Ovazza, *Sionismo bifronte* (Rome, 1935), p. 93.

86. L. Villari, *Le avventure di un capitano d'industria* (Turin, 1991), pp. 192–3.

87. I. Pavan, '"Ebrei" in affari tra realtà e pregiudizi. Paradigmi storiografici di ricerca dall'Unità alle leggi razziali', *Quaderni storici*, 38, 2003, p. 787.

88. D. V. Segre, *Memoirs of a fortunate Jew: an Italian story* (London, 1987), p. 47.

89. De Felice, *Storia degli ebrei italiani*, p. 29.

90. Stille, *Benevolence and betrayal*, p. 11.

91 G. Mosse, *Confronting history: a memoir* (Madison, 2000), pp. 108–9.

92. E. M. Robertson, 'Race as a factor in Mussolini's policy in Africa and Europe', *Journal of Contemporary History*, 23, 1988, p. 39.

93. See M. Lolli, *Ebrei, Chiesa e Fascismo* (Tivoli, 1938).

94. A. Soffici, 'Mie relazioni con Mussolini' (ed. G. Parlato), *Storia contemporanea*, 30, 1994, p. 825.

95. As republished in G. Preziosi, *Giudaismo-bolscevismo plutocrazia massoneria* (Milan, 1941). This collection of past articles was published by the prestigious Arnaldo Mondadori.

96. See, for example, V. Mantegazza, *Note e ricordi* (Milan, 1910), pp. 133–4.

97. G. Buffarini Guidi, *La vera verità* (Milan, 1970), p. 20; cf. De Felice, *Storia degli ebrei italiani*, p. 282.

98. R. De Felice, *Ebrei in un paese arabo* (Bologna, 1978), pp. 261–2, 267.

99. DDI 8s, IX, 508, 10 September 1938, Grandi to Ciano.

100. DDI 8s, XII, 185, 11 June 1939, Grandi to Ciano.

101. G. Sacerdoti, *Ricordi di un ebreo bolognese: illusioni e delusioni 1919–1945* (Rome, 1983), p. 66.

102. G. Ciano, *Diary 1937–1938* (London, 1952), p. 74.

103. DDI 8s, IX, 335, 26 July 1938, Ciano to all representatives.

104. *Critica Fascista*, 16, 1 August 1938, leading article.

105. *Critica Fascista*, 16, 15 August, 1 September 1938, leading articles.

106. *Critica Fascista*, 16, 15 October 1938.

107. A. Ventura, 'La persecuzione fascista contro gli ebrei nell'università italiana', *Rivista Storica Italiana*, 109, 1997, p. 175.

108. A. Gillette, *Racial theories in Fascist Italy* (London, 2002), pp. 55–71.

109. See, for example, P. Orano (ed.), *Inchiesta sulla razza* (Rome, 1939), pp. 38–9; cf. his *Gli ebrei in Italia* (Rome, 1937), one of the first signals of the new line.

110. De Felice, *Storia degli ebrei italiani*, p. 83.

111. MRF 53/122/7, February 1930, debate on report of party in Forlì province.

112. S. Zuccotti, *The Italians and the holocaust: persecution, rescue and survival* (New York, 1987), p. 22.

113. SPEP 7, 25 November 1938.

114. G. Almirante, 'Roma antica e i giudei', *La Difesa della Razza*, I, 5 September 1938.

115. G. Almirante, 'Nè con 98 nè con 998', *La Difesa della Razza*, I, 20 October 1938.

116. Gillette, *Racial theories in Fascist Italy*, p. 79.

117. E. Sulis, *Imitazione di Mussolini* (Milan, 1934), p. 111.

118. E. Sulis, 'Accuso le costituzioni', *Gerarchia*, XVII, September 1937. Cf. also De Felice, *Mussolini il duce: 2. Lo stato totalitario 1936–1940*, p. 42.

119. E. Sulis, *Rivoluzione ideale* (Florence, 1939), pp. 7, 29, 33, 175–9, 245–52.

120. E. Sulis, introduction to his *Processo alla borghesia* (Rome, 1939). Cf., too, his earlier disquisition, *Accuso la civiltà meccanica* (Rome, 1934).

121. Sulis, introduction to his *Processo alla borghesia*, p. 7.

122. Sulis, 'La borghesia', in ibid., p. 9. He added (pp. 15–16) that the bourgeoisie was also painfully devoted to bureaucratic form and detail.

123. This case was argued by B. Ricci, 'Categoria spirituale e categoria sociale', in Sulis (ed.), *Processo alla borghesia*, pp. 25–41.

124. E. Sulis, 'Introduzione' to E. Sulis (ed.), *Mussolini e il Fascismo* (Rome, 1941), pp. ix, xix, xxii–xxiii, xxxii.

125. CP 762, file on Rosario Patanè, sentenced to three years in 1930, rather appropriately for the Sulis story, for being a credit shark in his home town of Acireale.

126. SPDCO 590534, undated letter, E. Sulis to Mussolini's secretariat. His son indeed claimed both that he had been an army officer and that he had established the *fascio* at Villanovatulo.

127. CP 986, file on E. Sulis, 13 December 1932, Prefect (Nuoro) to Ministry of the Interior.

128. CP 986, 2 April 1933, Prefect (Nuoro) to Ministry of the Interior.

129. CP 986, 2 April 1933, Prefect (Nuoro) to Ministry of the Interior.

130. SPDCO 590534, 25 May 1932, E. Sulis letter.

131. SPDCO 590534, undated letter, A. Sulis to Prefect (Nuoro).

132. Certainly Antonio Sulis is not mentioned in a contemporary study of the local Fascist movement, emphatic about its commitment to radical revolution. See S. Ruinas, *Figure del fascismo sardo* (Rome, [1928]).

133. CP 986, 29 November 1932, Carabinieri report.

134. CP 986, 10 October 1932, Carabinieri report.

135. SPDCO 590534, 13 August 1934, Prefect (Nuoro) to Mussolini's Secretariat.

136. CP 986, 11 March 1933, A. Sulis to Ministry of the Interior. Assunta was behaving in a way highly typical of Italian mothers in the circumstances.

137. SPDCO 590534, 23 June 1932, Prefect (Nuoro) to Mussolini's Secretariat.

138. SPDCO 590534, undated letter, E. Sulis to Mussolini's secretariat.

139. CP 986, 4 November 1932, E. Sulis appeal. He wrote patriotically on Vittorio Veneto day.

140. CP 986, 20 October 1933, note; 5 December 1933, Prefect (Nuoro) to Ministry of the Interior.

141. SPDCO 590534, 23 April 1939, Prefect (Nuoro) to Mussolini's Secretariat.

142. SPDCO 590534, 10 December 1939, Prefect (Rome) report.

143. For a contemporary account of the meeting, see SPDCO 514829/1–2.

144. National Archives, Washington, Personal papers of Benito Mussolini, 26/012640. Apart from what he earned from his work with Ricci, Sulis received extraordinary payments of 1,000 lire in 1937, 5,000 in 1938, 2,000 in 1939 and 1,000 in 1940. See SPDCO 590534, reports.

145. SPDCO 590534, 17 June 1938, Sulis to Mussolini.

146. SPDCO 590534, 18 June 1938, Sulis to Mussolini.

147. SPDCO 590534, 2 March 1939, Alfieri to Sebastiani.

148. SPDCO 590534, 18 June 1938, Sulis to Mussolini.

149. SPDCO 590534, 1 December 1939, Sulis to Mussolini.

150. SPDCO 590534, 22 March 1939, Sulis to Mussolini.

151. SPDCO 590534, 28 March 1940, Sulis to Mussolini.

152. SPDCO 590534, 1 July 1940, Sulis to Mussolini.

153. SPDCO 590534, 1 July 1940, Sulis to Mussolini.

154. SPDCO 590534, 21 December 1941, De Cesare note about another rejection.

155. SPDCO 590534, November 1942, note by Mussolini's Secretariat.

156. I owe this information to correspondence with the Archivio di Stato of Cagliari.

15 Lurching into war

1. R. Zangrandi, 'Un giovane per i giovani: il problema della disoccupazione giovanile', *Gerarchia*, 17, October 1937.

2. R. P. Domenico, *Remaking Italy in the twentieth century* (Lanham, Maryland, 2002), p. 124.

3. M. Barbagli, *Educating for unemployment: politics, labor markets, and the school system – Italy, 1859–1973* (New York, 1982), pp. 168, 183–4.

4. H. S. Hughes, *The United States and Italy* (rev. ed.) (Cambridge, Mass., 1965), p. 91.

5. M. Barbagli, *Educating for unemployment*, pp. 200–201.

6. R. Zangrandi, *Il lungo viaggio attraverso il fascismo: contributo alla storia di una generazione* (Milan, 1964), pp. 22–44.

7. *Il Comune di Bologna: rivista mensile municipale*, 19, July 1932.

8. Zangrandi, *Il lungo viaggio attraverso il fascismo*, pp. 104–5.

9. *Gioventù Fascista*, 10 May X [1932].

10. N. Tripodi, *Italia Fascista in piedi! Memorie di un Littore* (Rome, 1960), pp. 57–60. Tripodi, a Fascist also after 1945, won the prize in the segment on the 'doctrine of Fascism' in the games at Palermo in 1938.

11. *Il Primato*, I, 1 April, 1 May, 1940.

12. E. R. Tannenbaum, *Fascism in Italy: society and culture 1922–1945* (New York, 1972), p. 185.

13. G. Bottai, *La carta della scuola* (Milan, 1939), pp. 83–4.

14. *Critica Fascista*, 17, 1 June 1939.

15. Bottai, *La carta della scuola*, pp. 6–8, 209–10.

16. J. Dunnage, *Twentieth century Italy: a social history* (London, 2002), p. 83.

17. T. M. Mazzatosta, *Il regime fascista tra educazione e propaganda (1935–1943)* (Bologna, 1978), pp. 135, 189.

18. A. Grandi, *I giovani di Mussolini: Fascisti convinti, fascisti pentiti, antifascisti* (Milan, 2001), pp. 39, 46, 83, 95, 141, 272.

19. F. Gambetti, *Gli anni che scottano* (Milan, 1967), p. 118.

20. For some introduction, see R. Aldrich, *The seduction of the Mediterranean: writing, art and homosexual fantasy* (London, 1993), pp. 143–52.

21. CP 509, file on Vittorio Grillo, 4 September 1938, Molina to Prefect (Catania).

22. See, for example, CP 417, file on Lorenzo Fisichella, 20 January 1939, Molina to Prefect (Catania); 2 February 1939, Molina report.

23. CP 391, file on Salvatore Fallica, 28 May 1940, Ministry of the Interior report.

24. G. J. Giles, '"The most unkindest cut of all": castration, homosexuality and Nazi justice', *Journal of Contemporary History*, 27, 1992, pp. 41–61.

25. C. M. De Vecchi di Val Cismon, *Bonifica fascista della cultura* (Milan, 1937), pp. 21–3, 46.

26. See, for example, the brilliant description in E. Sereni, *Il capitalismo nelle campagne (1860–1900)* (rev. ed.) (Turin, 1968), pp. 167–72.

27. C. Langobardi, *Land-reclamation in Italy: rural revival in the building of a nation* (London, 1936), pp. iv, 132–47.

28. O. Gaspari, *L'emigrazione veneta nell'Agro Pontino durante il periodo fascista* (Brescia, 1985), pp. 21, 86, 105, 108–17, 152–4.

29. F. M. Snowden, '"Fields of death": malaria in Italy 1861–1962', *Modern Italy*, 4, 1999, p. 46.

30. P. Orano, 'Premessa' to 'Felsineus', *L'azione fascista nelle ferrovie* (Rome, 1936), pp. 11–13.

31. L. Bortolotti, *Storia della politica edilizia in Italia: proprietà, imprese edili e lavori pubblici dal primo dopoguerra ad oggi (1919–1970)* (Rome, 1978), pp. 118, 122, 152–4.

32. For a highly critical account, see A. Cederna, *Mussolini urbanista: lo sventramento di Roma negli anni del consenso* (Bari, 1979).

33. P. Baxa, 'Piacentini's window: the modernism of the Fascist master plan of Rome', *Contemporary European History*, 13, 2004, p. 18. Piacentini, the leading architect of the regime, survived allegations of plagiarism, corrupt dealing and sexual misconduct. See SPDCR 103.

34. F. Sapori, *L'Arte e il Duce* (Milan, 1932), pp. 126–7.

35. D. Ghirardo, '*Città fascista*: surveillance and spectacle', *Journal of Contemporary History*, 31, 1996, pp. 347–72.

36. For a period account, see Anon., *Studio per il risanamento igienico-edilizio del 'Sass' di Trento*, Trento, nd.

37. M. Quine, *Italy's social revolution: charity and welfare from liberalism to Fascism* (Basingstoke, 2002), pp. 115–18, 145.

38. P. Pieri and G. Rochat, *Pietro Badoglio* (Turin, 1974), p. 19.

39. Ibid., p. 734.

40. G. Rochat and G. Massobrio, *Breve storia dell'esercito italiano dal 1861 al 1943* (Turin, 1978), p. 225.

41. M. Knox, *Mussolini unleashed 1939–1941: politics and strategy in Fascist Italy's last war* (Cambridge, 1982), p. 26.

42. Rochat and Massobrio, *Breve storia dell'esercito italiano*, p. 283.

43. G. Zanzanaini, *Renato Ricci: fascista integrale* (Milan, 2004), p. 115.

44. D. Ferrari, 'La mobilitazione dell'esercito nella seconda guerra mondiale', *Storia contemporanea*, 23, 1992, p. 1013.

45. Knox, *Mussolini unleashed*, p. 26.

46. N. Revelli, *La Guerra dei poveri* (Turin, 1962), pp. 4–5, 10.

47. G. Vannutelli, *Il Mediterraneo e la civiltà mondiale dalle origini all'impero fascista della Nuova Italia* (Bologna, 1936), pp. 65, 223, 228.

48. R. Mallett, *The Italian navy and Fascist expansionism 1935–1940* (London, 1998), p. 54.

49. Knox, *Mussolini unleashed*, p. 20.

50. Mallett, *The Italian navy and Fascist expansionism*, pp. 70, 172.

51. J. Rohwer and M. Monakov, 'The Soviet Union's ocean-going fleet, 1935–1956', *International History Review*, 18, 1996, pp. 846–7.

52. Vannutelli, *Il Mediterraneo e la civiltà mondiale*, p. 228.

53. A. Gatt, 'Futurism, proto-Fascist Italian culture and the sources of Douhetism', *War and Society*, 15, 1997, p. 51.

54. *L'Ala d'Italia: La Gazzetta dell'aviazione*, 22 May 1932.

55. *L'Ala d'Italia*, February 1933 (the journal had now become a monthly).

56. *L'Ala d'Italia*, 5 June 1932.

57. Knox, *Mussolini unleashed*, pp. 23, 31.

58. M. Knox, *Hitler's Italian Allies: Royal Armed Forces, Fascist regime, and the war of 1940–1943* (London, 2000), pp. 43–4.

59. G. Rochat, *Italo Balbo: aviatore e ministro dell'aeronautica 1926–1933* (Ferrara, 1979), p. 156.

60. P. Kennedy, *The rise and fall of the Great Powers* (Glasgow, 1989), p. 354.

61. G. Ciano, *Diario 1937–1943* (ed. R. De Felice) (Milan, 1980), pp. 290, 305.

62. Mallett, *The Italian navy and Fascist expansionism*, pp. 95, 111.

63. *Il Popolo d'Italia*, 5 June 1939.

64. M. S. Finkelstein, 'Curzio Malaparte' in P. V. Cannistraro (ed.), *Historical dictionary of Fascist Italy* (Westport, Conn., 1982), p. 520.

65. This is certainly the view of revisionist Italian historians. See R. Quartararo, *Roma tra Londra e Berlino: la politica estera fascista dal 1931 al 1940* (Rome, 1980), p. 461.

66. U. von Hassell, *The Von Hassell diaries 1938–1944* (London, 1948), p. 44.

67. *Il Popolo d'Italia*, 3 and 4 June 1939.

68. *Il Popolo d'Italia*, 10 July 1939.

69. CP 30, file on Francesco Anrather, 11 May 1939, Questura (Trento) to Prefect (Trento).

70. G. Aly, *'Final Solution': Nazi population policy and the murder of the European Jews* (London, 1999), pp. 24–6.

71. CP 509, files on Bruno and Elisabetta Grillo, 17 March 1940, Questura (Bolzano) to Provincial Commissioner; 5 April 1940, B. Grillo to Provincial Commissioner.

72. G. B. Guerri, *Galeazzo Ciano: una vita 1903–1944* (Milan, 1979), p. 34.

73. D. Susmel, *Vita sbagliata di Galeazzo Ciano* (Milan, 1962), p. 56.

74. O. Vergani, *Ciano: una lunga confessione* (Milan, 1974), pp. 54–5.

75. Guerri, *Galeazzo Ciano*, p. 92.

76. B. Bottai, *Fascismo famigliare* (Casale Monferrato, 1997), p. 44.

77. Guerri, *Galeazzo Ciano*, p. 70.

78. M. Pellegrinotti, *Sono stato il carceriere di Ciano* (Milan, 1975), p. 64.

79. G. Gafencu, *The last days of Europe: a diplomatic journey in 1939* (London, 1947), p. 128.

80. For his official accounts, see DDI 8s, XIII, 1, 4 and 21, 12 and 13 August 1939, Ciano reports.

81. G. Ciano, *Diario 1937–1943*, p. 327.

82. G. Ansaldo, *Il giornalista di Ciano: diari 1932–1943* (Bologna, 2000), pp. 178–9.

83. G. Ciano, *Diario 1937–1943*, pp. 330–32.

84. DDI 8s, XIII, 136, 21 August, 250, 25 August, 293, 26 August, 304, 26 August 1939, all Mussolini to Hitler.

85. G. Ciano, *Diario 1937–1943*, p. 341.

86. C. Senise, *Quando ero capo di polizia 1940–1943* (Rome, 1946), p. 35.

87. P. Melograni, *Rapporti segreti della polizia fascista* (Bari, 1979), p. 24.

88. CP 417, file on Silvestro Fiorioli della Lena, 6 April 1939, report.

89. CP 260, file on Umberto Cleva, 17 May 1939, Questura (Trieste) to Prefect (Trieste).

90. CP 254, file on Vincenzo Cinalli, 13 June 1939, Carabinieri (Ancona) to Questura (Chieti).

91. CP 850, file on Giovanni Re, 5 November 1939, Questura (Milan) to Prefect (Milan).

92. CP 714, file on Ambrogio Nini, 11 January 1940, Questura (Milan) to Prefect (Milan).

93. CP 479, file on Enrico Gianrossi, 1 May 1940, Carabinieri (Genoa) to Carabinieri (Rome).

94. G. Ciano, *Diario 1937–1943*, pp. 343, 355.

95. L. Simoni, *Berlino ambasciata d'Italia 1939–1943* (Rome, 1946), p. 25.

96. D. Varè, *The two imposters* (London, 1949), p. 203.

97. See his collected writings, R. Riccardi, *La collaborazione economica europea* (Rome, 1943).

98. For a laudatory biography, see A. Petacco, *Ammazzate quel fascista! Vita intrepida di Ettore Muti* (Milan, 2002). For rumours of corruption, see SPDCR 47, 31 October 1940, memo.

99. G. Ciano, *Diario 1937–1943*, p. 172.

100. P. Dogliani, *L'Italia fascista, 1922–1940* (Milan, 1999), p. 86.

101. R. De Felice, *Mussolini il duce: 2. Lo stato totalitario 1936–1940* (Turin, 1981), pp. 703–5.

102. F. Mezzasoma, 'Il centro di preparazione politica per i giovani', *Gerarchia*, XX, January 1940.

103. Anon., 'La posizione dell'Italia', *Critica Fascista*, 18, 15 September 1939.

104. Anon., 'Il Partito', *Critica Fascista*, 18, 15 November 1939.

105. See, for example, E. Canevari, 'La guerra totale e la qualità degli eserciti: politica e tecnica della guerra', *Critica Fascista*, 18, 15 March 1940. The author was a pronounced anti-Semite and one of the team at *La Vita italiana*.

106. *La Vita italiana*, f. 322, 15 January 1940.

107. A. Milward, *War, economy and society 1939–1945* (Berkeley, 1977), p. 97.

108. Knox, *Mussolini unleashed*, pp. 61–2.

109. G. Ciano, *Diario 1937–1943*, p. 400.

110. P. Badoglio, *Italy in the Second World War* (London, 1948), p. 11.

111. G. Ciano, *Diario 1937–1943*, pp. 416, 457.

112. T. Cianetti, *Memorie dal carcere di Verona* (ed. R. De Felice) (Milan, 1983), p. 317.

113. SPEP 6, 28 May 1940, report.

114. SPEP 19, 20 May 1940, report.

115. SPEP 19, 10 May 1940, report.

116. SPEP 19, 16 May 1940, report.

117. For a further development of this thesis, see Bosworth, *Mussolini*, pp. 357–71.

118. For some heralding of this racially diverse force, see *L'Alpino*, 1 September 1940.

119. DDI 9s, V, 516, 29 August 1940, Ciano to Mussolini.

120. R. Moore, 'Turning liabilities into assets: British government policy toward German and Italian Prisoners of War during the Second World War', *Journal of Contemporary History*, 32, 1997, p. 123.

121. C. G. Segrè, *Italo Balbo: a Fascist life* (Berkeley, 1987), pp. 398–400.

122. R. De Felice, *Mussolini l'alleato 1940–1945: 1. L'Italia in guerra 1940–1943*, vol. II, *Crisi e agonia del regime* (Turin, 1990), pp. 725–6.

123. SPEP 6, 12 June 1940, report.

124. CP 627, file on Alfredo Marletta, 10 July 1940, Questura (Catania) to Prefect (Catania).

125. CP 580, file on Angelo Lucantoni, 27 July 1940, Questura (Rome) to Prefect (Rome).

126. CP 554, file on Cosimo Vito Lassandro, 27 August 1940, Questura (Bari) to Prefect (Bari).

127. CP 275, file on Gaetano Conte, 16 December 1940, Carabinieri (Milan) to Carabinieri (Rome).

128. CP 884, file on Adele Rossi, 26 November 1941, Questura (Cuneo) to Prefect (Cuneo).

129. CP 112, file on Giuseppe Biasini, 8 October 1940, Questura (Brescia) to Prefect (Brescia).

130. CP 884, file on Umberto Rossetti, 30 September 1940, Prefect (Reggio nell'Emilia) to Ministry of the Interior; 6 November 1940, Carabinieri (Reggio nell'Emilia) to Carabinieri (Rome).

131. C. Fiori, *La confinata* (Milan, 1979), pp. 53–4.

132. See, for example, DDI 8s, IV, 805, 28 August 1936, Mussolini to Boscarelli.

133. DDI 9s, I, 166, 12 September 1939, Mussolini to Grazzi.

134. G. Ciano, *Diario 1937–1943*, p. 472.

135. Q. Armellini, *Diario di guerra: nove mesi al Comando Supremo* (Cernusco sul Naviglio, 1946), p. 127.

136. P. Cavallo, *Italiani in guerra: sentimenti e immagini dal 1940 al 1943* (Bologna, 1997), p. 59.

16 The wages of Fascist war

1. A. V. Savona and M. L. Straniero, *Canti dell'Italia fascista (1919–1945)* (Milan, 1979), pp. 332–3.

2. S. Visconti Prasca, *Io ho aggredito la Grecia* (Milan, 1946), pp. 63–4.

3. M. Knox, *Hitler's Italian allies: royal armed forces, Fascist regime, and the war of 1940–1943* (Cambridge, 2000), p. 80.

4. F. Pricolo, *Ignavia contro eroismo: l'avventura italo-greca: ottobre 1940–aprile 1941* (Rome, 1946), pp. 7–8.

5. Knox, *Hitler's Italian allies*, p. 41.

6. M. Cervi, *The hollow legions: Mussolini's blunder in Greece, 1940–41* (New York, 1971), p. xxi.

7. SPDCR 44, 9 November 1940, Farinacci to Mussolini.

8. See, for example, MI, DGPS, SCP 1, 4 February 1941, Questura (Milan) to Senise.

9. CP 30, file on Terzilio Anzaghi, 16 September 1941, Questura (Perugia) to Prefect (Perugia).

10. CP 489, file on Carlo Giretti, 13 February 1941, Questura (Turin) to Prefect (Turin).

11. U. Cavallero, *Comando supremo: diario 1940–43 del Capo di S.M.G.* (Bologna, 1948), pp. 8, 30.

12. G. Ciano, *Diario 1937–1943* (ed. R. De Felice) (Milan, 1980), pp. 334–5.

13. Knox, *Hitler's Italian allies*, p. 102.

14. M. Roatta, *Otto milioni di baionette: l'esercito italiano in guerra dal 1940 al 1944* (Milan, 1946), p. 85.

15. P. Cavallo, *Italiani in guerra: sentimenti e immagini dal 1940 al 1943* (Bologna, 1997), p. 80.

16. Knox, *Hitler's Italian allies*, p. 27.

17. K. Schmider, 'The Mediterranean in 1940–1941: crossroads of lost opportunities?', *War and Society*, 15, 1997, p. 22.

18. J. Goebbels, *The Goebbels diaries 1939–1941* (ed. F. Taylor) (London, 1982), pp. 201, 208–9, 214. In the next year, Pavolini warned Ciano of surviving German ambitions on these lands. See DDI 9s, VII, 509, 25 August 1941, Pavolini to Ciano.

19. Knox, *Hitler's Italian allies*, p. 101.

20. Cavallo, *Italiani in guerra: sentimenti e immagini dal 1940 al 1943*, p. 232.

21. DDI 9s, V, 114, 26 June 1940, Ciano to Pietromarchi.

22. E. G. H. Pedaliu, 'Britain and the "hand-over" of Italian war criminals to Yugoslavia, 1945–48', *Journal of Contemporary History*, 39, 2004, p. 509.

23. DDI 9s, V, 200, 7 July 1940, Ciano to Mussolini; 242, 13 July 1940, Hitler to Mussolini.

24. See, for example, DDI 9s, V, 492, 25 August 1940, Mussolini to Franco; VI, 501, 25 January 1941, Lequio to Ciano.

25. DDI 9s, VI, 568, 12 February 1941, memo of Mussolini–Franco–Serrano Suñer talks.

26. DDI 9s, VI, 942, 19 April 1941, Suppiej to Mussolini.

27. DDI 9s, VI, 936, 18 April 1941, Conti to Anfuso.

28. See, for example, DDI 9s, VI, 956, 21 April 1941; 967, 22 April 1941, both Ciano to Mussolini, reporting on unsuccessful talks with Ribbentrop; VII, 131, 17 May 1941, Menichella (the manager of IRI) to Mussolini.

29. DDI 9s, VII, 260, 15 June 1941, memo of Ciano–Ribbentrop talks; 268, 17 June 1941, Alfieri to Ciano.

30. DDI 9s, VII, 299, 23 June 1941, Mussolini to Hitler.

31. See, for example, DDI 9s, VII, 410, 20 July 1941, Hitler to Mussolini.

32. DDI 9s, VII, 426, 25 July 1941, Alfieri to Ciano.

33. DDI 9s, VII, 602, 29 September 1941, Alfieri to Ciano; 647, 13 October 1941, Ciano to Alfieri.

34. DDI 9s, VII, 808, 3 December 1941, memo of Mussolini talk with Horikari.

35. SCP 6, 17 December 1941, Questore (Bologna) to Senise.

36. SCP 6, 23 December 1941, Questore (Bologna) to Senise.

37. DDI 9s, VII, 786, 24–27 November 1941, Ciano to Mussolini.

38. DDI 9s VIII, 26, 15 December 1941, memo on Ciano–Pavelic talk.

39. DDI 9s, VIII, 536, 12 May 1942, Giustiniani (Zagreb) to Ciano.

40. See J. Steinberg, *All or nothing: the Axis and the Holocaust 1941–1943* (London, 1990).

41. For further on the matter, see R. J. B. Bosworth, *Mussolini* (London, 2002), pp. 392–3.

42. M. Michaelis, *Mussolini and the Jews: German–Italian relations and the*

Jewish question in Italy 1922–1945 (Oxford, 1978), p. 342.

43. See S. Zuccotti, *Under his very windows: the Vatican and the Holocaust in Italy* (New Haven, 2002).

44. For his case, see SPDCO 540404.

45. See, for example, the debate R. Farinacci, G. Acerbo and G. Preziosi, 'Per la serietà degli studi italiani sulla razza', *La Vita italiana*, f. 329, 15 August 1940.

46. See, for example, A. Stefanelli, *Biologia delle razze umane (con cenni sulla razza italiana)* (Bari, 1942).

47. For divagations in this regard in which blacks were deemed the most alien of people to Italians, see G. Maggiore, *Razza e fascismo* (Palermo, 1939), p. 20.

48. D. Rodogno, *Il nuovo ordine mediterraneo: le politiche dell'Italia fascista in Europa (1940–1943)* (Turin, 2003), p. 27.

49. T. Ferenc (ed.), *La provincia 'italiana' di Lubiana: documenti 1941–1942* (Udine, 1994), p. 5.

50. G. Ciano, *Diario 1937–1943*, pp. 572.

51. Ferenc (ed.), *La provincia 'italiana' di Lubiana*, pp. 23, 73–4, 484.

52. DDI 9s, VIII, 79, 29 December 1941, Mussolini to Hitler.

53. Rodogno, *Il nuovo ordine mediterraneo*, pp. 190, 352–3.

54. M. Mazower, *Inside Hitler's Greece: the experience of occupation, 1941–44* (New Haven, 2001), pp. 25–9, 92.

55. Rodogno, *Il nuovo ordine mediterraneo*, pp. 145–6, 210, 278.

56. DDI 9s, VIII, 638, 20 June 1942, Mussolini to Hitler.

57. DDI 9s, VIII, 645, 4 July 1942, Hitler to Mussolini.

58. DDI 9s, IX, 23, 5 August 1942, Alfieri to Ciano.

59. DDI 9s, IX, 379, 5 December 1942, Grazioli to Mussolini.

60. DDI 9s, IX, 535, 21 January 1943, Alfieri to Ciano.

61. See, for example, DDI 9s, X, 198, 6 April 1943, Bastianini to Mussolini.

62. See, for example, DDI 9s, X, 312, 12 May 1943, Ciano to Maglione.

63. For a splendid example, see DDI 9s, X, 406, 9 June 1943, Vitetti–Acquarone talk.

64. R. De Felice, *Mussolini l'alleato 1940–1945, 1. L'Italia in guerra 1940–1943, vol. I, Dalla guerra 'breve' alla guerra lunga* (Turin, 1990), p. 98.

65. R. De Felice, *Mussolini l'alleato 1940–1945, 1. L'Italia in guerra 1940–1943, vol. II, Crisi e agonia del regime* (Turin, 1990), p. 969.

66. Carte Farinacci 35, 24 August 1941, Farinacci to Serena.

67. S. Lupo, *Il Fascismo: la politica in un regime totalitario* (Rome, 2000), p. 424.

68. De Felice, *Mussolini l'alleato 1940–1945, 1. L'Italia in guerra 1940–1943, vol. II, Crisi e agonia del regime*, p. 899.

69. SCP 7, 20 September 1942, Questore (Bologna) to Senise.

70. SPDCR 44, 19 November 1942, Farinacci to Mussolini.

71. De Felice, *Mussolini l'alleato 1940–1945, 1. L'Italia in guerra 1940–1943, vol. II, Crisi e agonia del regime*, pp. 907–8.

72. Cavallero, *Comando supremo*, p. 146.

73. F. Rossi, *Mussolini e lo stato maggiore: avvenimenti del 1940* (Rome, 1951), p. 10.

74. G. Rochat, *L'esercito italiano in pace e in guerra: studi di storia militare* (Milan, 1991), p. 270.

75. G. Bottai, *Diario 1937–1943* (ed. G. B. Guerri) (Milan, 1989), p. 305.

76. CP 762, file on Leonardo Patanè, 24 February 1942, Questura (Milan) to Prefect (Milan).

77. CP 875, file on Sergio Rodomonte, 8 August 1942, Carabinieri (Udine) to Ministry of the Interior.

78. M. Franzinelli, *Delatori: spie e confidenti anonimi: l'arma segreta del regime fascista* (Milan, 2001), pp. 99–103.

79. CP 762, file on Leonardo Patanè.

80. CP 962, file on Pietro Sommavilla, 16 February 1941, Questura (Cuneo) to Prefect (Cuneo).

81. CP 72, file on Domenico Bassi, 1 February 1941, Questura (Trieste) to President of the Provincial Commission (Trieste). Bassi declared himself a nationalist and Germanophobe and, according to the police, was notorious for being 'presumptuous and a malicious gossiper'. In other words, he had probably long made public his doubts about the current war.

82. CP 1022, file on Rachele Traverso, 19 September 1941, Carabinieri (Genoa) to Carabinieri (Rome). She also declared her preference for Britain over Germany.

83. See further Bosworth, *Mussolini*, p. 386.

84. CP 479, file on Ivo Gianrossi, 17 January 1942, Carabinieri (La Spezia) to Carabinieri (Rome). Gianrossi denied the story, claiming that it was prompted by a vendetta against him by a number of local women he had loved and left.

85. CP 532, file on Antonio Immovili, 5 April 1941, report. Immovili was informed on by local nuns to whom he had stated this view. He had once been an emigrant in Chile and later in Brazil.

86. CP 670, file on Cesare Milani, 5 April 1942, Questura (Rome) to Prefect (Rome). Milani was another now charged with long expressing negative thoughts about the regime and its policies.

87. CP 260, file on Achille Attilio Clerici, 11 February 1941, police report.

88. CP 471, file on Renato Ghidoni, 14 September 1941, Questura (Turin) to Provincial Commissioner.

89. CP 305, file on Basilio D'Abbraccio, 30 December 1941, Carabinieri (Raviscanina) to Commandant, Piedimonte d'Alife; 19 February 1942, Questura (Benevento) to Prefect (Benevento).

90. CP 254, file on Maria Ciocca, 27 June 1941, Carabinieri (Turin) to Questura (Turin).

91. SPDCR 50, 28 September 1942, Vidussoni memo to Mussolini.

92. CP 884, file on Angelo Benedetto Rossi, 4 February 1943, Questura (Rome) to Prefect (Rome).

93. B. Spampanato, *Contromemoriale vol. 1 Da Monaco all'armistizio* (Rome, nd), p. 277.

94. D. Susmel, *Vita sbagliata di Galeazzo Ciano* (Milan, 1962), p. 260.

95. SPDCR 53, 9 January 1942, report.

96. See, for example, SCP 5, 17 September 1941, Inspector-General (Rome) to Senise.

97. SPDCR 38, 19 February 1941, telephone tap; SPDCO 545962, file on B. Gigli, 23 November 1941, report on his dealings with the Agnellis.

98. SPDCR 67, 10 January 1942, report.

99. DDI 9s, VIII, 211, 28 January 1942, memo on Mussolini–Göring talk.

100. R. Riccardi, *La collaborazione economica europea* (Rome, 1943), pp. 96–100.

101. G. Ciano, *Diario 1937–1943*, p. 628.

102. SPDCR 44, 24 April 1941, memo; 8 June 1941, Farinacci to Mussolini.

103. D. Grandi, *Bonifica umana: decennale delle leggi penali e della riforma penitenziaria*, 2 vols (Rome, 1941).

104. A. Milward, *War, economy and society 1939–1945* (Harmondsworth, 1987), p. 108; Knox, *Hitler's Italian allies*, p. 39.

105. CP 245, file on F. Chilanti, 8 June 1942, Questura (Rome) to Prefect (Rome).

106. CP 495, file on Giuseppe Golia, 3 November 1941, Questura (Treviso) to Prefect (Treviso).

107. SPDCR 98, 3 August 1942, Carabinieri report.

108. *Il Gazzettino*, 9 August 1941.

109. M. Legnani, 'Guerra e governo delle risorse: strategie economiche e soggetti sociali nell'Italia 1940–1943', *Italia contemporanea*, 179, 1990, p. 256.

110. De Felice, *Mussolini l'alleato 1940–1945, 1. L'Italia in guerra 1940–1943, vol. I, Dalla guerra 'breve' alla guerra lunga*, p. 551.

111. De Felice, *Mussolini l'alleato 1940–1945*, 1. *L'Italia in guerra 1940–1943*, *vol. II, Crisi e agonia del regime*, p. 716.

112. A. Soffici and G. Prezzolini, *Diari 1939–1945* (Milan, 1962), p. 108.

113. O. Bonacina, *Obiettivo Italia: i bombardamenti aerei delle città italiane dal 1940 al 1945* (Milan, 1970), p. 265.

114. E. Ortona, *Diplomazia di guerra: diari 1937–1943* (Bologna, 1993), p. 229.

115. Cavallo, *Italiani in guerra: sentimenti e immagini dal 1940 al 1943*, pp. 264, 340–44.

116. G. Zingoli, *L'invasione della Sicilia (1943): avvenimenti militari e responsabilità politiche* (Catania, 1962), pp. 8, 27–8, 51.

117. A. Cassels, *Fascist Italy* (London, 1969), p. 99.

118. Zingoli, *L'invasione della Sicilia*, pp. 33–8, 53, 68–9.

119. Savona and Straniero, *Canti dell'Italia fascista*, p. 356.

120. L. Meneghello, 'Razza e costume nella formazione della coscienza fascista', *Gerarchia*, 19, June 1940.

121. N. Pende, 'Femminilità e cultura femminile', *Gerarchia*, 20, May 1941.

122. E. Sulis, 'Il lavoro e la nuova civiltà', *Gerarchia*, 22, January 1943.

123. E. Sulis, 'Democrazia nemico n. 1: Mussolini contro il mito di Demos', *Critica Fascista*, 20, 1 November 1942.

124. See, for example, G. Bottai, *Diario 1937–1943*, pp. 275, 307.

125. Anon. editorial, 'Guerra di principi', *Critica Fascista*, 18, 1 June 1940.

126. G. Paresca, 'Peccato di superbia: lettera inglese da Roma', *Critica Fascista*, 18, 15 July 1940.

127. Anon. editorial, 'Popolo, guerra e rivoluzione', *Critica Fascista*, 19, 1 January 1941.

128. Anon. editorial, 'Irredentismo dell'Impero', *Critica Fascista*, 20, 15 May 1942.

129. See, for example, the editorial in *Il Primato*, I, 15 June 1940.

130. G. Bottai, 'Latinità e germanesimo', *Il Primato*, II, 1 January 1941.

131. E. M. Rosini, 'I popoli e la guerra', *Il Campano*, XV, May 1941.

132. *Il Primato*, II, 15 May 1941.

133. Anon. editorial, 'Fine del cosidetto enigma sovietico', *Critica Fascista*, 19, 1 July 1941.

134. G. Bottai, 'Sangue contro oro', *Critica Fascista*, 19, 15 July 1941.

135. Editorial, *Il Primato*, II, 1 July 1941.

136. S. Panunzio, 'Terza ondata: direttrici politiche del Regime', *Critica Fascista*, 20, 1 November 1941.

137. Editorial, *Il Primato*, III, 1 January 1942.

138. Anon. editorial, 'Vittoria di un popolo', *Critica Fascista*, 20, 1 July

1942; G. Bottai, 'La giovinezza come ordine nuovo', *Critica Fascista*, 20, 15 July 1942. Bottai enjoyed his prose so much that he simultaneously published the piece in *Il Primato*, III, 15 July 1942.

139. See, for example, G. Bottai, 'Bilancio morale dei tre anni', *Critica Fascista*, 20, 15 September 1942; Anon. editorial, 'Ragioni d'un intransigenza', *Critica Fascista*, 21, 1 December 1942; Anon. editorial, 'Il popolo sul "fronte interno"', *Critica Fascista*, 21, 1 January 1943.

140. Editorial, *Il Primato*, III, 1 November 1942.

141. G. Bottai, 'Funzione rivoluzionaria della critica: nostri vent'anni', *Critica Fascista*, 21, 15 May 1943.

142. Editorial, *Il Primato*, IV, 15 July 1943.

143. M. Appelius, *Parole dure e chiare* (Milan, 1942), p. 75.

144. *Il Gazzettino*, 15 May 1941.

145. *Il Gazzettino*, 11 August 1942.

146. G. Ortolani, *Le responsabilità di F. Delano Roosevelt (1936–1942)* (Milan, 1943), p. 251.

147. C. Bermani, *Al lavoro nella Germania di Hitler: racconti e memorie dell'emigrazione italiana 1937–1945* (Turin, 1998), pp. 58–62.

148. See, for example, the report DDI 9s, VII, 318, 26 June 1941, Attolico to Ciano.

149. M. Franzinelli, *Il riarmo dello spirito: i cappellani militari nella seconda guerra mondiale* (Padova, 1991), p. 64.

150. *Il Gazzettino*, 8 May 1943.

151. See De Felice, *Mussolini l'alleato 1940–1945, 1. L'Italia in guerra 1940–1943, vol. II, Crisi e agonia del regime*, p. 756.

152. Franzinelli, *Il riarmo dello spirito*, pp. 71–7, 84, 154.

153. CP 320, file on Angelina De Benedictis, one of the backers, 15 June 1942, Questura (Foggia) to Prefect (Foggia).

154. J. Cornwell, *Hitler's Pope: the secret history of Pius XII* (Harmondsworth, 1999).

155. SPDCR 4, 25 January 1941, Farinacci to Mussolini.

156. For Italian reports on the matter, see DDI 9s, IX, 124, 14 September and 129, 17 September, 145, 22 September 1942, all Guariglia to Ciano; 191, 6 October 1942, Ciano to Alfieri.

157. SCP 1, 24 December 1940, Questore (Bologna) to Senise.

158. SCP 3, 4 June 1941, Questore (Bologna) to Senise.

159. SCP 3, 3 June 1941, Ispettore Generale (Puglia and Matera) to Senise.

160. SCP 1, 19 February 1941, Questore (Rome) to Senise.

161. SCP 2, 4 March 1941, Questore (Venice) to Senise.

162. SCP 2, 8 April 1941, Questore (Milan) to Senise.

163. SCP 3, 6 May 1941, Questore (Bologna) to Senise.

164. See T. Mason, 'The Turin strikes of March 1943', in his *Nazism, Fascism and the working class* (ed. J. Caplan) (Cambridge, 1995), pp. 274–94.

165. For a case study, see C. Dellavalle, *Operai, industriali e partito comunista nel Biellese 1940–1945* (Milan, 1978), pp. 1–56.

166. A. Pirelli, *Taccuini 1922–1943* (ed. D. Barbone) (Bologna, 1984), pp. 428–60.

167. C. Scorza, *Il segreto di Mussolini* (Lanciano, 1933), p. 369.

168. *Credere-obbedire-combattere: notiziario del Fascio di Combattimento di Trento*, 30 April 1943.

169. SPDCR 49, 7 June 1943 memorandum. It is printed in full as an appendix to De Felice, *Mussolini l'alleato 1940–1945, 1. L'Italia in guerra 1940–1943, vol. II, Crisi e agonia del regime*, pp. 1528–35.

170. For a more detailed account, see Bosworth, *Mussolini*, pp. 400–402.

171. *Il Gazzettino*, 4 August 1943.

172. See, for example, E. Aga Rossi, *L'Italia nella sconfitta: politica interna e situazione internazionale durante la seconda guerra mondiale* (Naples, 1985), p. 110.

17 Losing all the wars

1. R. Katz, *Death in Rome* (London, 1967), pp. 7–8.
2. A. Portelli, *The order has been carried out: history, memory, and meaning of a Nazi massacre in Rome* (London, 2003), p. 240.
3. For the detail, see G. Contini, *La memoria divisa* (Milan, 1997).
4. P. Pezzino, *Anatomia di un massacro: controversia sopra una strage tedesca* (Bologna, 1997). Cf. also the more general study, M. Battini and P. Pezzino, *Guerra ai civili: occupazione tedesca e politica del massacro. Toscana 1944* (Venice, 1997), which includes many documents and examines, for example, the still equivocal case of the killing in July of more than 500 assembled in the *duomo* of San Miniato, a story that was turned into film in the Taviani brothers' *La notte di San Lorenzo*. The historians do not know whether the bomb was German or American, although probability favours the latter.
5. Pezzino, *Anatomia di un massacro*, pp. 145–7.
6. Portelli, *The order has been carried out*, pp. 13, 136.
7. Ibid., p. 77. Portelli's figures of 'perhaps' 3,000 dead and 10,000 injured ill accord with the claims in the main monograph on the subject that 717 civilians perished in the raid and 1,599 were wounded. One hundred and fifty

thousand Romans, however, were said to have fled the city. O. Bonacina, *Obiettivo Italia: i bombardamenti aerei delle città italiane dal 1940 al 1945* (Milan, 1970), p. 211.

8. Portelli, *The order has been carried out*, p. 9.

9. For my further critique, see R. J. B. Bosworth, 'Film memories of Fascism' in R. J. B. Bosworth and P. Dogliani (eds), *Italian Fascism: history, memory and representation* (London, 1999), pp. 106–10.

10. For the context, see R. J. B. Bosworth, *Explaining Auschwitz and Hiroshima: history writing and the Second World War 1945–1990* (London, 1993), p. 11.

11. L. Klinkhammer, *L'occupazione tedesca in Italia 1943–1945* (Turin, 1993), p. 32.

12. R. Rahn, *Ambasciatore di Hitler a Vichy e a Salò* (Milan, 1950), pp. 266, 271, 323.

13. I. Kershaw, *Hitler 1936–45: nemesis* (London, 2000), p. 834.

14. J. Goebbels, *Diaries* (ed. L. P. Lochner) (London, 1948), p. 349.

15. E. Aga Rossi, *Una nazione allo sbando: l'armistizio italiano del settembre 1943* (Bologna, 1993), p. 129.

16. G. Cadoni (ed.), 'La cattura e l'internamento dei militari italiani nei Balcani da parte dei tedeschi dopo l'8 settembre nel diario del maggiore Proto Cadini', *Storia contemporanea*, 20, 1989, p. 856.

17. R. De Felice, *Mussolini l'alleato 1940–1945, 2. La guerra civile 1943–1945* (Turin, 1997), p. 1585.

18. See, for example, the account of the Italian military chaplain, R. Formato, *L'eccidio di Cefalonia* (Milan, 1975), pp. 97–139.

19. Or so De Felice argued. See R. De Felice, 'La Resistenza e il Regno del Sud', *Nuova Storia Contemporanea*, 3, 1999, p. 9.

20. O. Skorzeny, *Skorzeny's special missions* (London, 1957), pp. 45–6.

21. BMOO XXXII, pp. 1–5.

22. B. Frullini, *Squadrismo fiorentino* (Florence, 1933), p. 51.

23. F. Anfuso, *Roma Berlino Salò (1936–1945)* (Milan, 1950), p. 446.

24. A. Petacco, *Il superfascista: vita e morte di Alessandro Pavolini* (Milan, 1998), p. 31.

25. J. T. Schnapp, *Staging Fascism: 18BL and the theater of masses for masses* (Stanford, 1996), p. 9.

26. See the boasts in A. Pavolini, *Disperata* (Florence, 1937).

27. SPDCR 48, notes, 30 January, 25 March and 26 May 1942.

28. E. Amicucci, *I 600 giorni di Mussolini (dal Gran Sasso a Dongo)* (Rome, 1948), p. 26. The claim had also been recorded in Mussolini's secretariat in 1942, when an anonymous denunciation blamed the relationship for the

many failings of the national theatre. See SPDCR 102.

29. M. Canali, *Il dissentismo fascista: Pisa e il caso Santini 1923–1925* (Rome, 1983), p. 40.

30. E. F. Moellhausen, *La carta perdente: memorie diplomatiche 25 luglio 1943–2 maggio 1945* (Rome, 1948), pp. 203–6.

31. G. Buffarini Guidi, *La vera verità* (Milan, 1970), pp. 138, 143.

32. M. Michaelis, *Mussolini and the Jews: German–Italian relations and the Jewish question in Italy 1922–1945* (London, 1978), p. 351.

33. Carte Bruno Spampanato, diary entry, 5 November 1943.

34. M. Toscano, 'Gli ebrei in Italia e la politica antisemita del Fascismo', in N. Caracciolo, *Gli ebrei italiani e l'Italia durante la guerra 1940–45* (Rome, 1986), p. 29.

35. L. Bolla, *Perché a Salò: diario della Repubblica Sociale Italiana* (ed. G. B. Guerri) (Milan, 1982), pp. 45, 59.

36. Amicucci, *I 600 giorni di Mussolini*, p. 45.

37. De Felice, *Mussolini l'alleato 1940–1945*, 2. *La guerra civile 1943–1945*, p. 362.

38. Moellhausen, *La carta perdente*, pp. 74, 202.

39. L. Garibaldi (ed.), *Mussolini e il professore: vita e diari di Carlo Alberto Biggini* (Milan, 1983), pp. 13–15, 248.

40. SPDCR 48, 30 July 1942, police report.

41. L. Ganapini, *La repubblica delle camicie nere* (Milan, 1999), p. 12.

42. G. Salotti, *Nicola Bombacci da Mosca a Salò* (Rome, 1986), pp. 107, 202.

43. P. Pisenti, *Una repubblica necessaria (RSI)* (Rome, 1977), p. 169.

44. C. Pavone, *Una guerra civile: saggio storico sulla moralità nella Resistenza* (Turin, 1991), p. 294.

45. H. Fornari, *Mussolini's gadfly: Roberto Farinacci* (Nashville, 1971), pp. 206–15.

46. See, for example, G. Spadolini, 'Responsabilità', *Italia e Civiltà*, 15 January 1944.

47. G. Coppola, 'A viso aperto', *L'Assalto*, 15 October 1943.

48. G. Gentile, 'Questione morale', *Italia e Civiltà*, 8 January 1944.

49. For examples, see SPDCR 14.

50. A. Soffici, 'La verità', *Italia e Civiltà*, 8 January 1944.

51. A. Soffici, 'Collaborazione degli intellettuali', *Italia e Civiltà*, 24 January 1944.

52. G. Dainelli, 'Materie prime e guerra', *Italia e Civiltà*, 15 January 1944. Cf. also his similar piece 'Caso di coscienza', *Italia e Civiltà*, 12 February 1944.

53. B. Occhini, 'Degli ebrei', *Italia e Civiltà*, 13 May 1944.

54. M. Ludovici, 'La Romagna nel regime fascista' in M. Ludovici (ed.), *Fascismi in Emilia Romagna* (Cesena, 1998), p. 100. The propagandist was Pino Romualdi, a distant relative of the *Duce*, who remained a Fascist after 1945.

55. The English translation is from C. F. Delzell (ed.), *Mediterranean fascism 1919–1945* (New York, 1970), taken from A. Tamaro, *Due anni di storia, 1943–1945* (Rome, 1949), pp. 249–52.

56. Amicucci, *I 600 giorni di Mussolini*, p. 62.

57. V. Cerosimo, *Dall'istruttoria alla fucilazione: storia del processo di Verona* (Milan, 1961), pp. 61, 67, 204.

58. T. Cianetti, *Memoire dal carcere di Verona* (ed. R. De Felice) (Milan, 1983).

59. G. Dolfin, *Con Mussolini nella tragedia: diario del capo della segreteria particolare del Duce 1943–1944* (Cernusco sul Naviglio, 1949), pp. 29, 138.

60. B. Spampanato, *Contromemoriale vol. 1 Da Monaco all'Armistizio* (Rome, nd), p. 218.

61. Dolfin, *Con Mussolini nella tragedia*, p. 142.

62. G. Bottai, *Diario 1935–1944* (ed. G. B. Guerri) (Milan, 1982), pp. 438–9.

63. G. Bottai, *Diario 1944–1948* (ed. G. B. Guerri) (Milan, 1988), p. 51.

64. G. Bottai, *Diario 1935–1944*, p. 475.

65. D. Grandi, *Il mio paese: ricordi autobiografici* (ed. G. B. Guerri) (Bologna, 1985), pp. 657–8, 669–70.

66. Apart from the above, see also D. Grandi, *La politica estera dell'Italia dal 1929 al 1932* (ed. P. Nello) (Rome, 1985).

67. D. Grandi, *Il mio paese*, pp. 661–4.

68. Amicucci, *I 600 giorni di Mussolini*, p. 93.

69. S. Romano, *Giuseppe Volpi: industria e finanza tra Giolitti e Mussolini* (Milan, 1979), p. 236.

70. De Felice, *Mussolini l'alleato 1940–1945, 2. La guerra civile 1943–1945*, pp. 66–7, 125, 136, 359. De Felice here echoed the title of the memoirs of the RSI Minister of Justice, P. Pisenti, *Una repubblica necessaria*.

71. V. Costa, *L'ultima federale: memorie della guerra civile 1943–1945* (Bologna, 1997), pp. 6, 10, 36, 81, 83, 181, 194, 219–21.

72. Bolla, *Perché a Salò*, pp. 96, 100–105, 158.

73. See, for example, G. Preziosi, 'Per la soluzione del problema ebraico', *La Vita italiana*, f. 354, 15 September 1942.

74. Michaelis, *Mussolini and the Jews*, p. 350.

75. P. Levi, *If this is a man* and *The truce* (Harmondsworth, 1979), pp. 19–20.

76. C. Zaghi, *Terrore a Ferrara durante i 18 mesi della repubblica di Salò*

(Bologna, 1992), pp. 14–16, 75, 98.

77. Ibid., pp. 180, 273–7, 316.

78. For his textured account, see N. Revelli, *L'ultimo fronte: lettere di soldati caduti o dispersi nella seconda guerra mondiale* (Turin, nd).

79. N. Revelli, *La guerra dei poveri* (Turin, 1962), pp. 118, 127–8.

80. R. Absalom, 'The armed resistance in Italy (1943–45): the politics of history and the recovery of "national legitimation"' in E. Cahm and V. C. Fisera (eds), *Socialism and nationalism in contemporary Europe (1848–1945)*, (Nottingham, 1980), p. 89.

81. J. Slaughter, *Women and the Italian Resistance 1943–1945* (Denver, 1997), p. 33.

82. A. Bravo and A. M. Bruzzone, *In guerra senza armi: storie di donne 1940–1945* (Bari, 1995), p. 21.

83. Pavone, *Una guerra civile*, p. 413.

84. For his account, see E. Sogno, *La Franchi: storia di un'organizzazione partigiana* (Bologna, 1996).

85. Pavone, *Una guerra civile*, pp. 124–33, 140, 200–203.

86. G. Pesce, *And no quarter: an Italian partisan in World War II* (Athens, Ohio, 1972), p. 243.

87. Dolfin, *Con Mussolini nella tragedia*, p. 257.

88. Pavone, *Una guerra civile*, pp. 231, 243.

89. Ganapini, *La repubblica delle camicie nere*, pp. 12, 70–71.

90. R. Graziani, *Ho difeso la patria* (Cernusco sul Naviglio, 1947), p. 382.

91. D. Gagliani, *Brigate nere: Mussolini e la militarizzazione del Partito Fascista Repubblicano* (Turin, 1999), pp. 199–200, 219.

92. M. Griner, *La 'pupilla' del Duce: la legione autonoma mobile Ettore Muti* (Turin, 2004), p. 3.

93. G. Bocca, *La repubblica di Mussolini* (Bari, 1977), p. 281.

94. R. Lazzero, *La Decima Mas* (Milan, 1984), pp. 72–3, 173–5.

95. Pavone, *Una guerra civile*, p. 235.

96. For an extreme example, see C. Mazzantini, *I balilla andarono a Salò: l'armata degli adolescenti che pagò il conto della storia* (Venice, 1995).

97. Absalom, 'The armed resistance in Italy (1943–45): the politics of history and the recovery of "national legitimation"', p. 89.

98. Klinkhammer, *L'occupazione tedesca in Italia 1943–1945*, pp. 129, 237.

99. De Felice, *Mussolini l'alleato 1940–1945, 2. La guerra civile 1943–1945*, p. 147.

100. Klinkhammer, *L'occupazione tedesca in Italia 1943–1945*, p. 248.

101. G. Guderzo, *L'altra guerra: neofascisti, tedeschi, partigiani, popolo in una provincia padana: Pavia 1943–1945* (Bologna, 2002), pp. 122, 352.

102. Ibid., pp. 320, 464–73.
103. Ibid., pp. 223–4, 543, 793–4.
104. Ibid., p. 418.
105. N. Farrell, *Mussolini: a new life* (London, 2003), pp. 453–4.
106. BMOO XXXII, pp. 126–39.
107. Ganapini, *La repubblica delle camicie nere*, p. 295.
108. Garibaldi (ed.), *Mussolini e il professore*, p. 320.

18 The Fascist heritage

1. P. Ignazi, *Extreme Right Parties in Western Europe* (Oxford, 2003), pp. 46, 51.
2. For a jaundiced response, see S. Corvisieri, *La villeggiatura di Mussolini: il confino da Bocchini a Berlusconi* (Milan, 2004).
3. R. Festorazzi, *Starace: il mastino della rivoluzione fascista* (Milan, 2002), p. 10.
4. A. Petacco, *Ammazzate quel Fascista! Vita intrepida di Ettore Muti* (Milan, 2002).
5. M. Staglieno, *Arnaldo e Benito: due fratelli* (Milan, 2003).
6. N. Farrell, *Mussolini: a new life* (London, 2003).
7. R. Vivarelli, *La fine di una stagione: memoria 1943–1945* (Bologna, 2000), pp. 15, 18, 24, 104.
8. See S. Courtois, *Le livre noir du communisme: crimes, terreurs et repression* (Paris, 1997).
9. G. Blake Palmer, *Italian journey* (Auckland, 1945), p. 10.
10. Alan Moorehead in his work *Eclipse* (London, 1945), as quoted by D. Ellwood, *Italy 1943–1945* (Leicester, 1985), p. 49.
11. C. Malaparte, *The Skin* (London, 1952), pp. 205–6.
12. A. Giovannini, *Travaglio per la libertà 1943–1947* (Rocca San Casciano, 1962), p. 173.
13. For an account, see H. Rousso, *The Vichy syndrome: history and memory in France since 1944* (Cambridge, Mass., 1991).
14. F. Clune, *All roads lead to Rome* (Sydney, 1950), p. 27.
15. Ellwood, *Italy 1943–1945*, p. 10.
16. R. Absalom (ed.), *Gli alleati e la ricostruzione in Toscana (1944–1945): documenti anglo-americani* (Florence, 1988), pp. 317–21.
17. For Croce on the matter, see P. Cacace, *Venti anni di politica estera italiana (1943–1963)* (Rome, 1986), p. 265.
18. Ibid., p. 200.

19. G. Bottai, *Diario 1944–1948* (ed. G. B. Guerri) (Milan, 1988), p. 350.
20. R. Quartararo, *Italia e Stati Uniti: gli anni difficili (1945–1952)*, p. 27.
21. M. Einaudi, 'The economic reconstruction of Italy', *Foreign Affairs*, 22, 1944, pp. 298–308.
22. J. E. Miller, 'Roughhouse diplomacy: the United States confronts Italian communism 1945–1958', *Storia delle relazioni internazionali*, 5, 1989, p. 293.
23. E. Di Nolfo, *Le paure e le speranze degli italiani (1943–1953)* (Milan, 1986), p. 264.
24. At least according to novelist Leonardo Sciascia, *Sicilian Uncles* (Manchester, 1986), p. 69.
25. D. Keogh, 'Ireland, the Vatican and the Cold War: the case of Italy, 1948', *Historical Journal*, 34, 1991, p. 947.
26. N. S. Onofri, *Il triangolo rosso (1943–1947): la verità sul dopoguerra in Emilia-Romagna attraverso i documenti d'archivio* (Rome, 1994), p. 8.
27. G. Arpinati, *Malacappa: diario di una ragazza* (ed. B. Dalla Casa) (Bologna, 2004).
28. For an account of the event, see S. Morgan, *Rappresaglie dopo la Resistenza. L'eccidio di Schio tra guerra civile e guerra fredda* (Milan, 2002) or, in briefer English version, her 'The Schio killings: a case study of partisan violence in post-war Italy', *Modern Italy*, 5, 2000, pp. 147–60.
29. For an English-language account of the controversy, see G. Sluga, 'Italian national memory, national identity and Fascism' in R. J. B. Bosworth and P. Dogliani (eds), *Italian Fascism: history, memory and representation* (London, 1999), pp. 178–94.
30. For further on the background, see R. J. B. Bosworth, *Mussolini* (London, 2002), pp. 410–13.
31. For the tally, see Onofri, *Il triangolo rosso*, p. 103. Di Nolfo offers another perplexing background to the new democracy by pointing out that, during their occupation to 1946, the Allies managed to kill 3,584 Italians on the roads while injuring 20,192. Di Nolfo, *Le paure e le speranze degli italiani*, p. 82.
32. Ellwood, *Italy 1943–1945*, p. 130.
33. Onofri, *Il triangolo rosso*, p. 65.
34. R. Aya, *The missed revolution: the fate of rural rebels in Sicily and Southern Spain 1840–1950* (Amsterdam, 1975), p. 19.
35. S. Setta, *L'Uomo Qualunque 1944–1948* (Bari, 1945), pp. 3, 36–8, 57, 60–61, 72–4, 123, 137.
36. Parri had an unusual record in that he had been amnestied from *confino*

through Mussolini's direct intervention and allegedly because of his 'merits in the [First World] war'. See CP 755, file on Ferruccio Parri.

37. Setta, *L'Uomo Qualunque*, pp. 126, 188, 196–211, 225.

38. R. Orfei, *Andreotti* (Milan, 1975), p. 49.

39. Setta, *L'Uomo Qualunque*, p. 265.

40. For a sensible account, see E. G. H. Pedaliu, 'Britain and the "hand-over" of Italian war criminals to Yugoslavia, 1945–48', *Journal of Contemporary History*, 39, 2004, pp. 503–29.

41. R. P. Domenico, *Italian fascists on trial, 1943–1948* (Chapel Hill, 1991), pp. 12, 31, 62, 76, 89, 97.

42. Z. Algardi, *Il processo Caruso: resoconto stenografico* (Rome, 1945), pp. 108–11, 289–301.

43. J. Foot, 'The tale of San Vittore: prisons, politics, crime and Fascism in Milan, 1943–1946', *Modern Italy*, 3, 1998, p. 29.

44. Domenico, *Italian fascists on trial*, pp. 154, 175.

45. M. Franzinelli, *Le strage nascoste: l'armadio della vergogna: impunità e rimozione dei crimini di guerra nazifascisti 1943–2001* (Milan, 2002), pp. 10, 123.

46. M. Clark, *Modern Italy 1871–1982* (London, 1984), p. 339.

47. P. Ginsborg, *Italy and its discontents: family, civil society, state 1980–2001* (London, 2001), p. 217.

48. P. Ignazi, *Il polo escluso: profilo del Movimento Sociale Italiano* (Bologna, 1989).

49. Ignazi, *Extreme Right Parties in Western Europe*, p. 21.

50. P. Ginsborg, *A history of contemporary Italy: society and politics 1943–1988* (Harmondsworth, 1990), p. 144.

51. Ignazi, *Il polo escluso*, p. 72.

52. Absalom (ed.), *Gli alleati e la ricostruzione in Toscana*, p. 120.

53. Ignazi, *Il polo escluso*, pp. 55–8.

54. A. Del Boca and M. Giovana, *Fascism today: a world survey* (London, 1970), pp. 62–5, 82, 141, 149.

55. P. A. Allum, *Politics and society in post-war Naples* (Cambridge, 1973), pp. 275–6, 284.

56. G. Amendola, *Gli anni della Repubblica* (Rome, 1976), p. 55.

57. Allum, *Politics and society in post-war Naples*, p. 95.

58. C. Boothe Luce, 'Italy after one hundred years', *Foreign Affairs*, 39, 1961, p. 223.

59. G. De Lutiis, *Storia dei servizi segreti in Italia* (Rome, 1984), pp. 44–50, 61.

60. See, for example, G. Almirante, 'Una razza alla conquista di un conti-

nente', *La Difesa della Razza*, 2, 5 November 1938; 'Giornalismo', 5 July 1939.

61. M. Tarchi, *Dal MSI ad AN: organizzazione e strategie* (Bologna, 1997), p. 42.

62. M. Battaglini, 'Il movimento politico Ordine nuovo. Il processo di Roma del 1973' in V. Borraccetti (ed.), *Eversione di destra, terrorismi, stragi: i fatti e l'intervento giudiziario* (Milan, 1986), p. 29.

63. M. Caciagli, 'The Movimento Sociale Italiano-Destra Nazionale and neo-fascism in Italy', *West European Politics*, 11, 1989, p. 24.

64. See, for example, J. Evola, 'Significato dell'aristocrazia per il fronte anti-borghese', *La Vita italiana*, f. 327, 15 June 1940.

65. J. Evola, 'L'internazionale ebraica e la profezia della nuova guerra mondiale secondo Ludendorff', *La Vita italiana*, f. 236, 15 November 1932.

66. See, for example, J. Evola, 'Osservazioni critiche sul "razzismo" nazionalsocialista', *La Vita italiana*, f. 248, 15 November 1933.

67. J. Evola, 'Noi tedeschi e il fascismo di Mussolini: sondaggi europei', *La Vita italiana*, f. 283, 15 October 1936.

68. J. Evola, 'Imperium Britannicum ovvero: Due Diritti', *La Vita italiana*, f. 272, 15 November 1935.

69. See, for example, J. Evola, 'I tre gradi del problema della razza', *La Difesa della Razza*, 2, 5 January 1939.

70. J. Evola, 'Gli ebrei e la matematica', *La Difesa della Razza*, 3, 20 February 1940. For a fuller account emphasizing the problem that Mussolini, with his usual intellectual ambition, had earlier labelled Fascism a 'super relativist movement' and invoked Einstein to do so, see G. Israel and P. Nastasi, *Scienza e razza nell'Italia fascista* (Bologna, 1998), p. 310.

71. Israel and Nastasi, *Scienza e razza nell'Italia fascista*, p. 312.

72. See, for example, J. Evola, 'Le razze e il mito delle origini di Roma', *La Difesa della Razza*, 3, 20 April 1940; 'La mistica razziale in Roma antica', 20 May 1940.

73. 'Arthos' (a pseudonym of Evola), 'Gli ebrei in Italia e il vero problema ebraico: fra color che sono sospesi', *La Vita italiana*, f. 291, 15 June 1937; 'Moralità ebraiche', *La Vita italiana*, f. 303, 15 June 1938.

74. See, for example, J. Evola, 'Nord e Sud: superamento di una opposizione', *La Difesa della Razza*, 2, 5 June 1939.

75. J. Evola, *Il fascismo: saggio di una analisi critica dal punto di vista della Destra* (Rome, 1964), pp. 8, 15.

76. F. Ferraresi, 'La destra eversiva' in D. Della Porta (ed.), *Terrorismi in Italia* (Bologna, 1984), p. 253.

77. See, at great length, the five volumes of G. Rauti and R. Sermonti, *Storia*

del fascismo (Rome, 1976–7) and cf. Rauti's *Le idee che mossero il mondo* (Rome, 1965).

78. G. Rauti, *L'immane conflitto. Mussolini, Roosevelt, Stalin, Churchill, Hitler* (Rome, 1966), pp. 14–15, 163, 171, 178, 186, 190–91.

79. Tarchi, *Dal MSI ad AN*, p. 36.

80. See, for example, the works of A. J. Gregor, and cf. A. J. Joes, *Fascism in the contemporary world: ideology, evolution, resurgence* (Boulder, Colorado, 1978).

81. D. Eisenberg, *The re-emergence of fascism* (London, 1967), p. 23.

82. M. Linklater, I. Hilton and N. Ascherson, *The Fourth Reich: Klaus Barbie and the neo-Fascist connection* (London, 1985), pp. 204–5, 289. Among them were the Belgian Rexist Léon Degrelle and some Croatian Ustasha.

83. Del Boca and Giovana, *Fascism today*, p. 156.

84. For a telling autobiography, see G. Salierno, *Autobiografia di un picchiatore fascista* (Turin, 1976).

85. For an evocative account, see T. Parks, *A season with Verona: travels around Italy in search of illusion, national character and . . . goals!* (New York, 2002).

86. Ignazi, *Extreme Right Parties in Western Europe*, p. 40.

87. For more on his background, see De Lutiis, *Storia dei servizi segreti*, pp. 61–74.

88. For my own account of such matters, see R. J. B. Bosworth, *Explaining Auschwitz and Hiroshima: history writing and the Second World War 1945–1990* (London, 1993), pp. 118–41.

89. G. Locatelli and D. Martini, *Duce addio: la biografia di Gianfranco Fini* (Milan, 1994), pp. 11, 29, 60–61.

90. See, for example, *L'Espresso*, 25 November 1984.

91. Locatelli and Martini, *Duce addio*, pp. 117, 216–17.

92. See, notably, P. Ginsborg, *Silvio Berlusconi: television, power and patrimony* (London, 2004), pp. 128–31.

Conclusion

1. S. Lupo, *Il Fascismo: la politica in un regime totalitario* (Rome, 2000), p. 24.

2. DDI 8s IV, 805, 28 August 1936, Mussolini to Boscarelli.

3. DDI 8s V, 154, 4 October 1936, Mussolini to De Rossi.

4. M. Mann, *Fascists* (Cambridge, 2004), pp. ix, 2–4, 13, 16, 77–9, 93, 102.

5. Ibid. pp. 15, 22, 134–7, 360, 364.

6. R. O. Paxton, *The anatomy of fascism* (London, 2004), pp. 3, 41–2, 126, 148, 218–19.

7. K. Baedeker, *Rome and Central Italy: handbook for travellers* (Leipzig, 1930), pp. xxix–xxxii.

8. See O. Bartov, *Murder in our midst: industrial killing and representation* (New York, 1996).

Index

abortion, 21, 242, 265–7, 365, 546
Abruzzi, 40, 189, 194
Acerbo, Giacomo, 179–181, 185,
   191, 193–4, 357, 471, 568
Agnelli, Giovanni, 17–19, 95, 125,
   190, 224, 310, 481
   see also Fiat
al Mukhtàr, Omar, 381
Albania, 2, 59, 96, 278–9, 283,
   358, 388, 394, 404–5,
   449–50, 451, 462, 464–5,
   473, 504, 570
   annexation of, 388, 404–5
   occupation of, 405, 464–6, 504
Albertini, Luigi, 111, 121, 180, 218
Alessandria, 162, 333, 338, 563
Alfieri, Dino, 274–5
Alighieri, Dante, 35, 63, 75, 122,
   149, 156–7, 173, 197–8, 203,
   249–50, 300, 370, 440
Almirante, Giorgio, 421, 541, 548,
   551, 554, 558
Alpini, the, 55, 70, 78, 129, 132,
   139, 208, 324
Aly, Götz, 448
Amendola, Giorgio, 329
Amendola, Giovanni, 180, 196,
   218, 329, 379
Amici, Aurelio, 385
Amicucci, Ermanno, 219

AN (Alleanza Nazionale, National
   Alliance), 559
ANC (Associazione Nazionale dei
   Combattenti, the National
   Returned Soldiers' League),
   106–8, 117, 129, 132, 156,
   166–7
Ancona, 52, 178
Andreotti, Giulio, 262, 540–41, 549
Anrather, Francesco, 448
Ansaldo, 69, 115, 124
Ansaldo, Giovanni, 219
anti-clericalism, 15, 31, 54, 87–8,
   116, 126, 128, 139, 147, 156,
   159, 160, 176, 187, 231, 257,
   415
anti-colonialism, 373–4, 386–8,
   398
anti-Comintern pact, 403, 445
anti-communism, 26, 141, 259,
   285–6, 489, 505, 523, 536,
   540, 548–50, 554, 559
   see also anti-socialism
anti-Fascism, 26, 162, 167, 177,
   189, 191, 241, 241–2, 257,
   308, 327–31, 333, 338,
   380–81, 391, 402, 411,
   416–18, 444, 452, 485,
   498–502, 505, 507, 513, 520,
   521–2, 523, 528, 531–2, 535,

anti-Fascism – *cont.*
537, 538, 539–40, 543, 545, 557
anti-Semitism *see* racism
anti-socialism, 48, 56, 84, 106, 129, 130, 132, 138–41, 143–4, 152, 156–9, 161–2, 163–4, 168–9, 170, 172–3, 175–6, 185, 189, 197, 212, 216, 223, 259, 285–6, 304, 331, 454–5, 472
    see also anti-communism
Anzaghi, Terzilio, 465
AOI (Africa Orientale Italiana, Italian East Africa), 319, 368, 370, 373, 377, 378, 383, 385, 394, 459, 468
    see also Eritrea; Ethiopia; Somalia
Aosta, Duke of, 29, 107, 181, 187, 228, 375, 378, 385, 394
Appelius, Mario, 391, 488
architecture, fascist, 326, 376, 380, 440–42, 640
Ardeatine caves massacre, 498–501, 543, 545
Arditi, the, 79, 111–12, 117, 131, 139, 144–5, 157, 197, 376
Arezzo, 144
Arlacchi, Pino, 169
Arpinati, Leandro, 133–5, 185, 238, 240, 251–4, 273, 440, 537, 569
Arpinati, Settimio, 253
Asinari di San Marzano, Enrico, 187
Associazione Colombofila Nazionale (National Pigeon Fanciers' Association), 228
Associazione Nazionalista Italiana, 31, 53
Associazione Provinciale degli Agricoltori (Provincial Landowners' Association), 133
Austria, 215, 284, 300–301, 305, 337, 388–9, 400–401, 403–4, 503
Austria-Hungary, 34–5, 37–8, 43–4, 49, 60, 62–4, 71, 73, 75–76, 81–3, 88–91, 96, 106, 110, 121, 129, 154–5, 158–9, 404, 442–3, 502, 504, 567
Avanti!, 22, 36, 43, 47, 52–3, 83, 119, 218–19, 342
Aventine secession, 212–13, 218
aviation, 18, 55, 69, 284, 289, 294–5, 445–6
Azione Cattolica (Catholic Action), 249, 261–5

Badoglio, Pietro, 17, 230, 283–4, 288, 298–9, 380, 384, 397–8, 443–4, 464–5, 471, 481, 495–7, 502, 504, 519
Bachi, Riccardo, 69
Balabanoff, Angelica, 354
Balbo, Italo, 7, 55–6, 79, 82, 95, 129–136, 143, 168, 173–4, 177–81, 189, 194–5, 204, 211, 240, 294–5, 298, 381–3, 402, 417–19, 445, 459, 567
Banca Commerciale Italiana, 23, 160
Banca Italiana di Sconto, 124
Banco di Roma, 39, 88, 186, 373, 548
Bari, 41, 153, 270–71, 540
Barletta, 43
Barracu, Francesco, 509–10
Barreca, Antonio, 27–9
Bartolazzi, Ettore, 252
Bartolomasi, Angelo, 89, 155, 157, 489

Bartov, Omer, 567
Barzini, Luigi, 74, 272
Barzini, Luigi (Snr), 371
Basilicata, 192, 194, 241, 252–3, 330–31, 338
Bassi, Domenico, 478
Bastianini, Giuseppe, 474, 492
Battisti, Cesare, 34–5, 71, 322, 326–7, 442
bee-keeping, 239, 562
Bellemo, Eugenio, 277–9, 296
Belli, Ferdinando, 386, 394
Belloni, Ernesto, 228, 254–5
Benazzo, Giovanni, 334–8
Benedict XV, Pope (1914–22) 21–2, 57, 80, 87, 95, 119, 157, 257, 261, 373
Beneduce, Alberto, 309
Bergamini, Alberto, 217
Bergamo, Guido and Mario, 133
Berlinguer, Mario, 543
Berlusconi, Silvio, 10, 215, 354, 498, 500, 531, 558–9
Bertarelli, Luigi Vittorio, 57–8
Bianchi, Michele, 55–6, 121, 136–8, 170–71, 179, 181, 184, 188–9, 191, 194, 196, 212
Biasini, Giuseppe, 460
Biddau, Ettore, 208–9, 599
Biggini, Carlo Alberto, 510, 529
birth rate, 21, 77, 244, 265–6, 268–9
  see also pro-natalism
Bismarck, Otto von, 43–4, 193–4
Bissolati, Leonida, 47, 54, 63, 78, 121, 126–7
'Black brigades' (BN, Brigate Nere), 524
Blasetti, Alessandro, 220
Boattini, Ferdinando, 482, 607–8
Boccaccio, Lorenzo, 333–8, 562, 570

Boccaccio, Luigi, 336
Bocchini, Arturo, 5, 29, 50, 153, 195, 242, 327–8, 333, 340–41, 361–2, 436, 449, 456, 562, 564, 603, 606, 608, 619, 622
Bolla, Luigi, 519
Bollettino dell'Emigrazione, 31, 595
Bologna, 52, 84, 101, 104–5, 117, 132–4, 149, 153, 188, 195, 217, 222, 240, 249, 251–3, 269, 273, 319, 390, 412, 418, 432, 440, 470, 476, 491, 499, 505, 511, 526, 556, 567
Bolzano, 326–7
Bolzon, Piero, 94, 116–17, 156, 168
Bombacci, Nicola, 86, 510–11, 513
Bonasoro, Giuseppe, 316–17
Bonghi, Ruggero, 370–1
Bonomelli, Geremia, 48
Bonomi, Ivanoe, 47, 63, 172–3, 185, 543
Boothe Luce, Clare, 550–51
Bordiga, Amedeo, 101–2
Borelli, Aldo, 218
Borghese, Junio Valerio, 525, 557, 627
Borghese, Scipione, 371
Boscolo, Marcello Teodoro, 278–9, 613
Boselli, Paolo, 63, 88
Bossi, Umberto, 558–9
Bottai, Giuseppe, 7, 79, 116, 194, 204–6, 208, 210, 212, 221, 227, 233, 246, 261, 272, 275, 298, 302, 306, 307–8, 313–14, 337, 363, 410, 412–13, 419, 421, 431, 433–4, 455–6, 471, 477, 481, 485–7, 491, 493, 516, 535, 548–9, 562, 650
Bourke, Joanna, 76, 78, 80
Brescia, 75, 106, 239–40, 460

Briand, Aristide, 284, 288–9
Britain, 2, 281–2, 258–9, 281–2,
    285, 297, 299, 304–6, 357,
    366, 385, 392, 397–8, 401,
    406, 452, 458, 460, 479, 480,
    487–8, 618
Bruno, Giordano, 15, 126
Buffarini Guidi, Guido, 361, 508–9,
    515, 517–18, 520, 529, 544
Bullotta, Antonia, 377
Buozzi, Bruno, 125–6
bureaucracy, 15, 27–9, 40, 50, 81,
    194, 203, 260, 276, 359–60,
    432
    peasant perceptions of, 40
    and implementation of *Duce*'s
        decisions, 360
    residues of fascism in post-war,
        542–3
Buronzo, Vincenzo, 408
Bush, George W., 498–501
business, 18, 23, 57–9, 67–9, 77,
    95, 99, 106, 116, 123, 151,
    158, 161, 176, 180, 211–12,
    219, 222–30, 280, 308–10,
    312–14, 360, 413, 490–91,
    523, 540, 544–5, 548–50

Cabrini, Angiolo, 47
Cadorna, Luigi, 17, 61–3, 71, 74,
    89, 190, 329
Cagliari, 116, 167, 170
Calabria, 24–30, 40–42, 168–70,
    184, 192, 241, 271, 386, 484,
    504, 538, 547–8
Camorra, 41
Campbell, Eric, 317
Canali, Mauro, 211, 348, 361–2
Cantalupo, Roberto, 373
Capasso Torre di Pastene, Giovanni,
    217

capitalism, 3, 10, 97–8, 195–6, 211,
    224, 272, 295, 302, 348, 406,
    409, 428, 553, 568
    see also business
Caporetto, battle of, 64–7, 71–2,
    74–5, 77–9, 80–82, 84, 86–7,
    89, 91, 117, 129, 154, 156,
    159, 204, 230, 301, 335,
    462
Capponi, Countess, 139
Caradonna, Giuseppe, 541
Carli, Mario, 117
Carnazza, Gabriele, 168, 194
Carocci, Cesira, 342
Carrère, Jean, 30
Carretta, Donato, 543
Carta del Carnaro, 113
Carta del Lavoro (Labour Charter),
    227
Caruso, Pietro, 543–4
Casalini, Armando, 213
Castelletti, Giuseppe, 159
Catanzaro, 189, 436
Catholic Church
    and colonialism, 373–4, 405
    and education, 263–4, 433
    and emigration, 31, 88
    and fascism, 3, 15, 54, 80, 187,
        197, 203, 231–2, 256–63,
        324, 326, 333, 423, 443, 488,
        490, 496, 547; *see also*
        Lateran Pacts
    and film, 221
    finance, 39, 263; *see also* Banco
        di Roma
    and First World War, 57,
        87–90
    and homosexuality, 435
    and Liberal state, 45, 88–90
    and Matteotti murder, 211
    and Nazism, 490

popular devotion to, 147, 324–6, 496
and PPI, 106, 187–8, 193
and priesthood, 265, 277–9
and racism, 258–9, 415, 417, 420
and scouts, 222–3
and Second World War, 488–90
and socialism, 47, 259, 489
and unionism *see* Confederazione Italiana del Lavoro (CIL)
and welfare, 443
and women, 264–70
youth organizations, 261–2
see also Azione Cattolica (Catholic Action); Christian Democrats; festivals and ritual; PPI; anti-clericalism; Gentiloni Pact
carabinieri, 19, 85, 103, 134, 187, 264, 277, 325–6, 330, 453, 562
Cassino, 116
Catholic Social Studies Association (Unione cattolica per gli studi sociali), 47
Cavallero, Ugo, 464–5, 481
Cavazzoni, Stefano, 186
Cavour, Camillo Benso di, 17, 61, 297, 332, 558
Cephalonia, 504
CGdL (Confederazione Generale del Lavoro, General Confederation of Labour), 46–7, 87, 101, 104, 127, 136, 172, 225
chemical and biological weapons, 10, 297–300, 381, 396, 397
Chiang Kai-shek, 317
Chilanti, Felice, 482
children, 70, 72, 77, 84, 110, 146,

227, 244, 245, 247, 263–4, 267–8, 289, 290, 291–4, 305, 316, 322, 324–6, 371, 376–7, 379, 381, 385, 408, 442
Chioggia, 277–9, 296
Christian Democrats (DC, Democrazia Cristiana), 106, 262, 308, 430, 433, 535–6, 540–41, 545–6, 549, 550, 556
Churchill, Winston, 11, 58, 467, 477, 517
Cianetti, Tullio, 141–3, 223, 457, 514
Ciano, Constanzo, 219, 449, 482, 568
Ciano, Edda *see* Mussolini, Edda
Ciano, Galeazzo, 219, 235–6, 257, 274–5, 319–20, 322, 346–7, 350, 358, 363, 388, 401, 403–5, 409, 413–14, 416–19, 446–7, 449–51, 454–7, 461–2, 466, 468, 469–70, 474–8, 481–2, 491–3, 506–8, 512, 514–15
Cinalli, Vincenzo, 452–3
Ciniselli, Roberto, 250–51
Ciocca, Maria, 479–80
Civitavecchia, 179
class, 34, 55, 70–74, 76, 81, 83, 98, 101–2, 108–9, 115, 125–6, 130, 135, 140–41, 143, 150–51, 160, 328–9, 383, 390, 392, 412, 415, 422, 427, 431, 442, 449, 480, 499, 507, 519, 561, 562
Clemenceau, Georges, 67, 98
Clerici, Achille, 479
Clerici, Ugo, 132, 207
Cleva, Umberto, 452
clientelism, 4, 29, 32, 45, 54–5, 82, 127–8, 137, 166, 168, 170,

clientelism – *cont.*
192, 194, 207, 237–9,
250–51, 254–6, 279, 319,
337, 405, 420, 428, 542, 547,
558, 562, 570–71
see also corruption; *raccomandazione*
clothing, 21–2, 162, 197, 200, 202,
221, 267, 294
Cold War, 505, 535, 548
Collacchioni, Countess, 139
Colmayer, Giovanni, 319–20
Colombo, Francesco, 525
Comitato di azione contro il lusso
(Association against
Exaggerated Luxury among
Women), 146
Communist party, 17, 101, 189,
328–30, 537
PCd'I (Partito Comunista
d'Italia) 19, 102, 149–50,
329–30
PCI (Partito Comunista Italiano),
521, 523, 537, 542, 548, 550,
557
see also socialism
Compagnia Italiana Grandi
Alberghi (CIGA), 161
Concetti family, 385–6
Concina, Giovanni Maria, 222–3
Confederazione Italiana del Lavoro
(CIL), 47–8
Confindustria, 67, 99, 162, 226,
540
see also business
confino see punishment
Contarini, Vittorio, 320
Conte, Gaetano, 460
Conte, Galliano, 395
Conti, Ettore, 312
Conti, Giovanni Gastone, 319–20

Coppola, Goffredo, 511
Corner, Paul, 5
corporatism, 2, 91, 95, 113, 118,
156, 122, 226–7, 240, 272,
276, 307–13, 388, 398, 406,
423, 455, 483–4, 486, 551,
618
see also economy
Corradini, Enrico, 31, 54–5, 95, 99,
280, 283, 311
Corridoni, Filippo, 121
corruption, 4, 5, 27, 32, 54, 127,
137, 165, 192, 194–5, 207–8,
235–6, 242, 250, 289, 307–8,
315, 318, 332–3, 340, 347–9,
360, 387, 405, 420, 480, 482,
492, 494, 515, 563, 571
see also clientelism; *raccomandazione*
Costa, Vincenzo, 518–19
Craxi, Bettino, 558
Cremona, 117, 126–9, 131, 153,
156, 177, 188, 233, 235,
238–9, 386, 460, 518
Cremona Nuova, 232
crime
banditry, 41, 42
criminology, 51
murder rates, 51, 109, 538
organized, 41, 167, 209–10, 538,
567
as a way to adapt to fascism,
317–18
see also punishment; police; law
Crispi, Francesco, 15, 31, 73, 77,
194, 297, 370, 374
Crispo Moncada, Francesco, 242
Critica Fascista, 204–6, 220, 239,
255, 261–2, 272, 275, 282–3,
419, 456, 485–7
Croatia, 4, 259, 284, 470–71

Croce, Benedetto, 26, 184, 328, 505, 533, 536, 545, 547
Croci, Piero, 218
Crotone, 169–70
Cucco, Alfredo, 210
Cufra, 3, 381

D'Abbraccio, Basilio, 479
Dainelli, Giotto, 375, 511–12
Dallolio, Alfredo, 68–9, 86
Dalmatia, 49, 59, 96, 113–14, 129, 147, 155, 283, 472
Dalser, Ida Irena, 343
D'Annunzio, Gabriele, 22, 67, 80–1, 95, 110–15, 119, 130, 133, 136, 146, 161, 174–5, 180, 182, 195, 201, 213, 221, 243 267, 274, 303, 375, 446, 507, 518, 585
D'Aragona, Ludovico, 104
dating system, fascist, 201
DC see Christian Democrats
De Ambris, Alceste, 113, 121, 136, 177, 182–3, 223
De Bono, Emilio, 61, 79, 181, 188, 190, 194, 286, 380, 493–4, 514
De Castro, Diego, 34
De Cesarò, Giovanni Colonna, 179
De Felice, Renzo, 135, 180, 234, 369–70, 418–19, 517–18
De Gasperi, Alcide, 106, 180, 241, 257, 535–6, 540, 548, 549
De Lorenzo, Giovanni, 557
De Nava, Giuseppe, 170
De Nicola, Enrico, 172
De' Stefani, Alberto, 186, 224, 229
De Vecchi, Cesare Maria, 79, 117, 172, 180–81, 188, 190, 375–6, 378, 433–4, 436–7, 490, 549
De Vecchi, Giorgio, 376

Decennale, 130, 274–5, 298, 306, 314, 441, 569
Del Boca, Angelo, 377
Delcroix, Carlo, 194, 353
Delle Chiaie, Stefano, 555
Depretis, Agostino, 194
Di San Giuliano, Antonino, 296
Diaz, Armando, 95, 186, 286
Dinale, Ottavio, 314
diseases
  cholera, 20, 43, 51
  malaria, 20, 42, 43, 385, 437–9, 497, 484, 505
  typhus, 51
Dodecanese islands, 49, 96–7, 296, 378–9
  see also Greece
Dolfin, Giovanni, 515, 523
Douhet, Giulio, 298–9, 446
Drakulic, Slavenka, 1
Duce see Mussolini, Benito
Dumini, Amerigo, 33, 143–5, 211, 232, 340, 349, 382
Duranti, Doris, 508

earthquakes, 24–30, 38, 43–4
Ebert, Friedrich, 104
economy, 2, 38–9, 69–70, 100–101, 109, 123–4, 150, 155, 158, 161, 175–6, 186, 224, 266, 272–3, 276, 307–13, 360, 406–7, 447, 455, 466–7, 482, 506, 526
  autarchy, 2, 70, 229–30, 291, 312–13, 406, 412, 447
  national budgets, 39, 124, 184, 186, 224, 308, 360–61
  currency valuation, 229–30, 356, 405–6
  and world depression, 272–3, 311
  see also corporatism

Eden, Anthony, 397, 534
education, 43, 118, 122, 158,
    186–7, 263–4, 273–4, 294,
    410, 419, 431–4, 434, 436–7,
    471, 510, 547
  and Catholic Church, 263–4, 433
  and gender, 290, 432, 434
  and Jews, 434, 471
  Littoriali (youth) games, 432–4,
    507
  schools, fascist, 118, 122, 263–4,
    291, 294, 324, 371, 408, 420,
    431, 432–3, 609–10
  teachers, 40, 75, 89, 263–4,
    269, 294, 416, 420–21, 423,
    431, 434
  universities, 419, 433–4, 436–7
EIAR (Ente Italiano Audizioni
    Radiotelefoniche, Italian
    Radio Company), 220, 369
Einaudi, Luigi, 180
Einaudi, Mario, 536
elections, 48, 50, 101, 104, 108–9,
    134, 149, 172, 191, 193–5,
    246, 402, 536, 540
Elena, Queen, 23, 322, 332, 620
emigration, 6, 24, 30–34, 42, 70,
    88, 95, 272, 279–81, 335–8,
    363, 383, 389–90, 391, 393,
    407, 535–6, 559
  extent of fascisization among
    emigrants, 391–3
  and Marxism, 389–90
  and policing, 391
  rates of, 389
  regime hostility to, 393, 407
  see also Fasci all'estero
Emilia-Romagna, 22, 40, 51,72, 146,
    177, 194, 264, 344, 390, 537
Emmanuel II, King Victor
    (1861–78), 12, 17

Emmanuel III, King Victor,
    (1900–1946) 15, 18, 26, 44,
    47, 57, 79–80, 95–6, 142,
    180–82, 187, 199, 201, 211,
    231, 265, 269, 282, 317,
    321–7, 332, 352, 374, 376,
    409, 413, 417, 444, 491–2,
    495–6, 497, 502–4, 508–9,
    513, 516, 520, 536, 569, 620
employment, 17, 40, 77, 100, 107,
    113, 155, 227, 243, 271–5,
    316, 406, 431–2, 438
Empoli, 140–41, 331
Eritrea, 57, 367–8, 370, 372, 374,
    377, 535
  see also AOI
Ethiopia, 2, 3, 9, 24, 43, 48, 57,
    140, 270, 288, 296–8, 304–5,
    308, 325, 327, 330, 333,
    356–8, 367–70, 383–5, 391,
    396–8, 401, 406–7, 414–15,
    452, 459, 625
  see also AOI; imperialism;
    facism; genocide
ethnic cleansing, 10, 49–50, 154–8,
    171, 179, 326, 381, 389, 448,
    473, 568
  see also fascism, border
'everyday Mussolinism', 11, 169,
    249–52, 254, 273, 561, 563
Evola, Julius, 552–3

Fabbri, Anita, 318–19, 620
Fabbri, Giuseppina, 632
'Faccetta nera', 368–9, 463
Facta, Luigi, 177, 179, 181, 185
Fagiuoli, Ettore, 326
family, 76–8, 108, 139, 203, 245,
    262, 265, 268–9, 335–7, 350,
    383, 388, 422, 430, 503, 515,
    546, 562, 570

Farinacci, Franco, 235–7
Farinacci, Roberto, 4, 54, 64–5, 79,
    87–8, 95, 98, 126–9, 135,
    143, 153, 160, 173, 175, 178,
    185–6, 188–9, 191, 204–5,
    210, 212–13, 230–39, 250,
    254, 259, 287, 302–4, 341,
    346, 349–50, 384, 386, 394,
    400, 402, 419–20, 439, 450,
    464, 471, 475–6, 482,
    490–91, 493, 495, 506, 509,
    511, 518, 524–5, 562, 567,
    569, 571
Farrell, Nicholas, 532
fasces, 5, 13–14, 122, 202, 217,
    226, 232, 430
Fasci all'estero (Fascists abroad),
    318, 321, 391
Fasci di combattimento, 33, 93,
    116–17, 120, 123, 280
Fascio d'azione interventista, 33
Fascio d'azione rivoluzionaria (the
    union for revolutionary
    action), 56, 121, 541
Fascism
    and anti-Anglo-Saxon sentiment,
        470, 474, 486, 568
    border, 157–8, 245, 537–8, 568
    class analysis of, 150–51, 160
    collapse of, 496–7, 505, 530,
        537
    and Catholic Church, 3, 15, 54,
        80, 187, 197, 203, 231–2,
        256–63, 324, 326, 333, 423,
        443, 488, 490, 496, 547; see
        also Lateran Pacts
    as 'civic religion', 3, 67, 80,
        140–41, 158, 197–8, 202,
        263, 265, 273–4, 296, 347,
        421, 496
    and corporatism see corporatism

economy policy see corporatism
    and emigration, 390–95
    and 'fascist martyrs', 134,
        140–41, 202, 274, 326–7,
        350, 415, 427
    foreign policy see foreign policy
    government see government,
        fascist
    historiography of, 532–4, 564–6
    ideology, 116, 120, 122, 129,
        137–8, 142–3, 151–3, 160,
        186, 189, 196, 205–6, 210,
        259–60, 275–6, 282–3,
        302–3, 351, 364, 421–4,
        485–7, 511–12, 516, 560,
        562, 564, 568–9
    and labour practices, 223–7
    and local power, 143, 154,
        173–4, 192, 207–10, 239,
        250, 254, 424–7, 563
    meeting at Piazza San Sepolcro,
        116–17, 127, 131, 145, 415
    multiple meanings of, 434–5,
        515
    and 'Mussolinism', 165, 167,
        172, 175, 205–6, 233, 315,
        339, 355, 422, 434, 486; see
        also Mussolini, personality
        cult of
    and the 'spirit of the trenches',
        79–80
    and non-Catholic religious, 260
    as 'permanent revolution', 5,
        569–70
    popular representations of,
        531–4
    popular support for, 307–38,
        369–70
    'post-fascism', 558–9
    post-war political devotion to,
        500, 505, 523, 533, 541–2,

Fascism – *cont.*
    551–4; *see also* Republic,
      Italian; MSI; UQ; MSN; inter-
      national neo-fascist move-
      ments
    pre-1922 programme, 109,
      115–18, 147–9
    profile of the word 'fascism',
      121–2
    propaganda *see* propaganda
    repression of dissidence, 195,
      216, 240–43, 246, 327–8,
      331–8
    as social and cultural revolution,
      142, 182–5, 188, 201–3,
      215–16, 232, 246, 254, 257,
      276, 281, 287, 296–7, 307–8,
      313, 340, 342–3, 347, 387,
      392, 432, 436–7, 458, 485,
      563
    southern, 255–7, 547
    and *trincerocrazia*, 115–16
    and fascist unions, 141, 148,
      176, 223–6, 491
    and violence, 123, 127–8, 133,
      134, 136, 138, 140, 144,
      145–6, 149, 162, 164, 168–9,
      173–4, 177–9, 189–90,
      207–8, 211–12, 250–51,
      568–9
    women's *fasci*, 145–6, 176,
      269–70
    and youth, 118, 152, 168, 180,
      199, 221–3, 289–94, 432–3,
      476
Fascist Party (PNF, Partito
    Nazionale Fascista)
    control of social institutions,
      221, 232, 249, 268, 273, 279,
      330, 363, 475–6
    creation of, 33, 175

electoral performance, 120, 149,
    193
fasci congress, 107, 120, 175,
    180
and fascist ideology, 245, 249,
    267–8, 279, 282, 249–50,
    475, 513
leadership, 165–6, 168, 184,
    232, 234, 239–40, 249, 262,
    263, 273, 341–2, 455, 475–6,
    492, 507, 518, 532, 541
membership, 6, 117, 151–4,
    158–9, 167, 170, 191–2, 233,
    415, 455, 475, 512, 517;
    backdating, 6, 192, 274, 449,
    465; class composition,
    151–2, 160, 234; regional
    breakdown, 153–4
merger of PNF with Nationalist
    Association, 186
renaming to PFR (Partito
    Fascista Repubblicano), 507
see also government, fascist
Favagrossa, Carlo, 456–7
Favia, Nicola, 107
Federazione Nazionale Fascista della
    Proprietà Edilizia (Real Estate
    Agents Association), 310–11
Federazione Nazionale Fascista delle
    Massaie Rurali (Rural House-
    wives Association), 269–70
see also fascism, and women;
    women
Federterra, 46, 126–7, 162, 225
Federzoni, Luigi, 49–50, 63, 91, 95,
    155, 186, 209, 211, 213,
    216–17, 232, 298, 342, 372,
    381, 490, 508
feminism, 21, 117, 146, 176, 267,
    269, 485
Ferrara, 33, 55, 105, 130, 131–3,

148, 153, 177, 188–9, 195,
240, 390, 417, 513, 521
Ferraris, Dante, 99
Ferraris, Luigi, 280
Ferretti, Lando, 217–18
Ferro, Marc, 528
festivals and rituals
Church, 201–3, 325, 326
fascist, 112, 201, 273, 391, 335
Befana Fascista, 202, 291–2,
322, 391
sabato fascista, 413
local, 202, 325, 507
see also music; salutes; flags
Fiat, 17–18, 69, 104, 125, 144, 229,
251, 331, 354, 446, 507
Fiera del Levante, 270–71
Figaia, Cirillo, 222
Filippelli, Filippo, 211, 232
film, 220–21, 265, 295, 345, 391,
409–10, 413, 431, 435,
477–8, 501, 508, 539, 571
see also Instituto Luce
finance, 16, 39, 48, 186, 229–30,
309, 348, 272, 415
see also economy; business
Fini, Gianfranco, 531, 556–9
Finzi, Aldo, 188, 194, 211, 415,
446
Finzi, Gino, 211
FIOM (Federazione Italiana degli
operai metallurgici, the metalworkers' union), 124–5
Fiorentini, Felice, 527–8
Fiori, Cesira, 330, 461
Fiorioli della Lena, Silvestro, 452
First World War,
battles, 62–4, 94–5, 154, 158–9
and business, 67–9
casualties, 37, 62, 64, 73, 458
and Catholic Church, 87

conditions, 71–2
cost of, 60
division between combatants and
non-combatants, 76–8
end of, 94–7
entry into, 44, 51, 59
and Fascism, 79–80, 163
internal unrest during, 64–5
killing, 78–9
military strength, 60, 63
and neutralism, 36, 53–8, 61, 81,
90, 114
and pursuit of 'leadership',
80–81, 95
as 'total war', 67
war aims, 90, 95, 154
see also military interventionism;
prisoners of war
Fiume, 96, 98, 108, 110–14, 119,
130, 133, 136, 146–7, 155,
160–61, 183, 195, 221, 375,
411, 503, 518
Fiumi, Giovanni, 251
flags, 132, 134, 141, 170, 198,
202–3, 376, 478
Florence, 15, 109, 116, 120, 127,
129, 139, 140–42, 144, 153,
180, 213, 234, 246, 269, 325,
343, 409, 411, 416, 439, 446,
483, 505, 507, 534
food, 41–2, 142, 184, 251, 266, 270,
272, 282, 303, 334–6, 369,
438, 456, 479–84, 495, 538
during First World War, 60, 72,
75
during Second World War, 479,
482–4, 490–91, 527
foreign policy, 2, 48, 176, 281, 286,
337, 373, 389, 403
and Albania, 277–9, 283, 358,
462

foreign policy – *cont.*
    and Austria, 284, 305, 400, 403
    belligerency of fascist, 283–4,
       286, 289, 297, 299, 304–5
    and Britain, 281–2, 285, 304–6,
       366, 618
    and Croatia, 284
    domestic promotion of Italian
       world primacy, 289–94,
       296–7, 299, 303–4, 337, 400;
       see also youth; organizations;
       aeroplanes
    extent of *Duce*'s influence over,
       281–2, 287–8, 304, 357–9
    and the Fascist 'International',
       303, 554
    and France, 281–2, 286, 305,
       366, 618
    and Greece, 461–2; Corfu crisis,
       282; and Dodecanese islands,
       378
    and Germany, 282, 301–6, 358,
       366, 403, 407, 618; *see also*
       Germany
    and Hungary, 284
    and Japan 282–3, 303, 405, 470
    and liberal internationalism, 283,
       288–9, 302
    Ministry of, 48, 185, 287–8, 307,
       347, 401, 449, 474, 509, 516
    and Spain, 284, 358, 401–4; *see*
       also Spanish Civil War
    and Turkey, 286
    and United States, 285, 295
    and USSR, 285, 305
    and Yemen, 288
    and Yugoslavia, 283–5
    see also imperialism; irredentism
Forges Davanzati, Roberto, 284
Forlì, 38, 117, 164, 253, 333,
    342–4, 385, 482

Fornaciari, Gaetano, 252
Fortunato, Giustino, 64–5, 184–5
Four Power Pact, 304, 306, 366,
    618
    see also foreign policy
France, 2, 9, 25, 58, 67, 73, 93,
    98–9, 113–14, 161, 206, 218,
    223, 267, 281, 284, 286, 279,
    304–6, 335, 337–8, 370, 379,
    381, 401, 404, 406, 418, 420,
    445, 452–3, 456–8, 460–61,
    468, 470, 497, 518, 523, 534
    see also foreign policy, and
    France
Franco, Francisco, 141, 215, 242,
    259–60, 286, 342, 401–2,
    461, 468, 564
Frank, Hans, 408
Frassati, Alfredo, 218
Freddi, Luigi, 141, 218, 605
Freemasonry, 45, 54, 126, 139, 212,
    247, 525, 552
Frescura, Attilio, 72–3, 76–8, 80–81
Friuli, 158–60, 222
Frullini, Bruno, 139–40
Futurism, 22, 95, 116–19, 131, 168,
    204, 303, 408, 483

Gabeto, Antonio, 333–8
Gadda, Carlo Emilio, 38, 72, 77
Gaggioli, Olao, 116, 131
Galbiati, Enzo, 493
Gallarotti, Carlo, 162
Gallenga Stuart, Romeo, 75
Gargano, 489–90, 562
Garibaldi, Giuseppe, 110, 127, 136,
    183, 327, 523, 536, 558
Gasparri, Pietro, 187
Gayda, Virginio, 74–5
Gazzetta Ferrarese, 56
Gazzetta Ufficiale, 484

Gemelli, Agostino, 106, 243
Genco, Bernardo Attilio, 310–12
gender, 21, 35, 76–7, 122, 143, 257, 267–8, 318, 333, 335–7, 392, 422, 432, 434, 436, 438, 562, 630
  see also feminism
Genoa, 37, 101, 117, 124, 373, 444, 459, 502, 511, 550
Gentile, Emilio, 129, 202, 249
Gentile, Giovanni, 186–7, 275, 294, 307, 398–9, 431, 433, 511–12
'Gentiloni Pact', 48, 88
  see also Catholic Church
Gerarchia (Hierarchy), 176, 202, 282–3, 289, 410, 421, 431, 455, 485
Germany
  border with Italy, 98
  economic relationship with Italy, 24, 39
  Imperial, alliance with Italy, 44, 358
  population transfers, 448
  war against, 62, 73
  Weimar, 109, 178, 225
  see also foreign policy, and Germany; Germany, Nazi
Germany, Nazi
  alliance with Italy, 2, 4, 9, 200, 358, 403–5, 408, 423, 429, 448, 453–4, 459–61, 466–7, 469, 479, 485, 490, 501–2, 570; and Italy's 'parallel war', 401, 461, 466–7; popular reactions to, 465, 491–3; soldiers' reactions to, 466; Nazi reactions to, 467, 503; see also anti-Comintern pact
  Anschluss, 403

  bellicosity, 451
  and Catholic Church, 490
  collaboration with in Spanish Civil War, 402–3
  cultural exchange, 408
  invasion of Czechoslovakia, 404
  occupation of the north see Salo Republic
  racism see racism, Nazi
  relations with, 400–401
  response to partisan attacks, 498–500
  response to fall of Mussolini, 502–3
  rise of, 300
  war criminals, 545
  worker exchange, 406–8
Ghidoni, Renato, 479
Giampaoli, Mario, 93–5, 206–9, 254, 349, 440, 569
Giannini, Guglielmo, 539–41, 550
Gianrossi, Enrico, 454
Gianrossi, Ivo, 478, 647
Gibson, Violet, 374
Ginsborg, Paul, xxiv
Ginzburg, Carlo, 247
Gioda, Mario, 190
Giolitti, Giovanni, 12, 17–18, 23, 28–9, 45, 48, 50, 56–7, 59, 90, 95, 114, 123–4, 126, 130, 132, 148–9, 155, 160, 166, 171–2, 180, 191, 194–5, 224, 263, 273, 357, 371, 373, 566
Giordani, Giulio, 134
Gioventù Universitaria Fascista (GUF, Fascist University Youth) 200–201, 272, 289–290, 410, 433, 435
  see also youth, organizations; education

Giretti, Carlo, 465
Giua, Francesco, 256–7
Giuliani, Reginaldo, 89
Giunta, Francesco, 107, 129, 155–8, 181, 188–9, 273, 279
Giuriati, Giovanni, 7, 97, 100, 113, 161, 172, 185, 249–50, 262, 280
Giustizia e Libertà, 327–8, 521
Globocnik, Odilo, 522
Gobbi, Goffredo, 186
Gobetti, Piero, 218
Goebbels, Josef, 467, 504
Gorgolini, Pietro, 190
Göring, Hermann, 409, 446, 448, 470, 481
Gorizia, 76, 154, 503
government, fascist, 185–8, 190–91, 194, 210–11, 212, 216, 240, 567
    Chamber of Fasces and Corporations, 308, 359
    Grand Council (Gran Consiglio), 141, 188, 347, 359, 493–5, 514
    local administrations (*podestà*) 216
    Ministries: Air, 227; Colonies, 54, 59, 186, 369; Communications, 219; Corporations, 227, 307, 514; Education, 186, 419, 431, 433–4, 436, 510; Exchange Controls, 272; Finance, 186, 229, 415, 455; Foreign Affairs, 48, 55, 62, 185, 227, 235, 287–8, 307, 401, 449, 474, 509, 516, 558; Foreign Trade, 224; the Interior, 179–80, 185, 211–13, 217, 227, 232, 481, 508–10, 524–5; Justice, 91, 185, 226, 455, 482; National Defence, 509; the Navy, 227; Occupied Territories, 185; Popular Culture (Minculpop), 236, 413, 427, 507–9, 541; Posts and Telegraphs, 28; Public Works, 27, 168; War, 227
Gramsci, Antonio, 17–19, 102, 109, 125, 150, 190, 241, 329, 425, 523, 574
Grandi, Dino, 54–5, 95, 173–5, 185, 188, 204, 279–80, 285, 287–8, 301, 307, 390, 392, 404, 409, 413, 418–19, 449, 455, 482, 491, 493–5, 510, 516–17, 567
Grassini, Margherita, 22
Gray, Ezio Maria, 23, 162–3, 541
Graziani, Rodolfo, 299, 377–81, 384, 398, 459, 480, 509–10, 517, 524–5, 529, 544, 549
Greco, Paolo, 166
Greece, 215, 230, 337, 379, 461–6, 468–9, 473, 478, 490, 504, 554, 571
    attacks on, 2, 463–4, 466
    occupation of Dodecanese islands, 96
    wartime occupation of, 468, 473–4, 504
Grillo, Bruno, 448–9
Grillo, Vittorio, 436
Guariglia, Raffaele, 288
Guarneri, Felice, 224, 272, 447, 455, 680
Guderzo, Giulio, 527
Guidi, Augusta, 320
Guidi, Rachele, *see* Mussolini, Rachele

Habsburg Empire *see* Austria-Hungary
Haile Selassie, Emperor, 367–8, 384, 386, 398
health and medicine, 37, 41, 42, 43, 266, 274, 365, 432, 484
see also disease; life expectancy
Himmler, Heinrich, 139, 235, 346, 361–2, 493, 502
Hitler, Adolf, 1, 2, 235, 258, 300–301, 340–41, 346, 361, 371, 405–6, 408–9, 451, 454, 458, 467–70, 473–5, 506, 532, 561, 568
perceptions of in Italy, 256, 282, 304–5, 307, 454, 477
historiography of, 490, 532
and neo-fascism, 552, 555, 559
Holocaust, 1, 3, 10, 112, 288, 331, 362, 389, 394, 415, 470, 501, 513, 520, 531–2, 545, 561
see also ethnic cleansing
homosexuality, 25, 242, 435–6, 501
housing, 20, 27, 166, 253, 271, 311–13, 385, 442, 502, 545
Hungary, 94, 113, 147, 284

I Lupi della Valsesia (the Valsesia wolves), 162
Ignazi, Piero, 546
Il 1919, 93–4
Il combattente mantovano, 122
Il Corriere della Maestra, 264
Il Corriere della Sera, 59, 111, 180, 218
Il Corriere di Napoli, 489
Il Corriere italiano, 211
Il Fascio, 175
Il Fuoco, 23
Il Gazzettino, 59, 218, 496

Il Giornale d'Italia, 49, 119, 187, 217
Il Grido del Popolo, 19
Il Legionario, 321–3
Il Mondo, 218
Il Popolo, 35
Il Popolo d'Italia, 53–4, 97, 115, 120, 146, 170, 173, 187, 208, 257, 347–8, 391, 427–8, 447
Il Popolo di Trieste, 156–7
Il Primato, 410, 486–7
Il Regime Fascista, 236, 287
Il Resto del Carlino, 49, 55, 278
Il Soldato, 66
Il Telegrafo, 219
illiteracy, 21, 40, 253, 329, 405
immigration to Italy, 559
Immovili, Antonio, 478–9, 647
imperialism, 88, 91, 97–9, 279–80, 367–95
asserts relationship with classical Rome, 371–3
compared with Nazi colonial policy, 389
concentration camps, 377, 381,
domestic support for, 280, 367, 388–9, 393, 398–9
European, 286, 375
and genocide, 286, 380–81, 389
international perceptions of, 396–7
Liberal, 369–75, 388–9
and monarchy, 374
Mostra delle terre d'Oltremare (Exhibition of overseas territories), 387–8
post-war perceptions of, 535
resistance to, 385–8
wartime ambitions, 468
see also Libya; Ethiopia; Somalia;

imperialism – *cont.*
AOI; Dodecanese islands;
Greece; Albania
industry, 15, 45, 68–9, 176, 224,
226, 333, 348, 567
agricultural, 42, 124
automobile, 17, 18, 69, 124
aeronautic, 69
building and real estate, 310,
313
cinema *see* film
electricity, 23
fishing, 277–9
heavy, 15,17, 124, 161
insurance, 48
leather, 444
minerals, 38, 39, 211
munitions, 60, 69, 444, 514
regional variation, 40
'Sovietization' of, 104
tourist, *see* tourism
wine, 333
see also IRI; Confindustria;
business
Ingrao, Pietro, 433
INPS (Istituto Nazionale di
Previdenza Sociale, National
Insurance Institute), 442, 516,
570
insurance, *see* INPS
intellectuals, 20–21, 23, 26, 31, 40,
43, 53, 101, 107, 117, 133,
170, 176, 194, 196, 204–6,
212–13, 275–6, 278, 310,
485–7, 507, 511–12, 552,
560, 569
Interlandi, Telesio, 417
international neo-fascist movements, 554–7
interventionism, 33, 53–6, 61, 79,
83, 88, 90, 92–3, 112–13,
116, 121–3, 132–3, 135, 137,
141, 161, 165, 167
irredentism, 34–5, 96–7, 154, 249,
283
IRI (Istituto per la Ricostruzione
Industriale, Institute for the
Reconstruction of Industry),
309–10
Isonzo, 62, 63
Istria, 34, 59, 114, 197, 210, 522,
537

Jacomoni, Francesco, 405
Jews, 3, 131–2, 154, 332, 379–80,
400, 403, 410, 415–20, 447,
454, 456, 468–72, 486, 488,
498–9, 501, 508–9, 512–13,
519–20, 531–2, 552, 555,
559, 561–2
see also racism; anti-Semitism;
Zionism
John XXIII, Pope (1958–63), 489
journalism, 15, 41, 45, 74–5, 77,
217, 219, 267, 298, 299, 305,
321, 355, 362, 390, 427, 429,
449, 456, 533, 551, 558
Jung, Guido, 309, 415–6

Kellogg–Briand pact, 288–9
Kesselring, Field Marshal Albert, 503
Knox, Macgregor, 284, 446, 464,
467

L'Artigiano, 228–9, 408
L'Assalto, 134–5
L'Azione, 55
La Conquista dello Stato, 213
La Difesa della Razza, 421, 471,
541, 552
L'Echo de Paris, 217
La Fontaine, Pietro, 161

La Gazzetta dello Sport, 217, 364
L'Idea Nazionale, 48–9, 92
La Nave, 22
L'Ordine Nuovo, 102, 190
L'Osservatore Romano, 257, 459
La Proprietà Edilizia, 310
La Rivista della Venezia Trentina,
    326
La rivoluzione liberale, 218
La Squilla, 54, 126
La Stampa, 17–18, 74, 218, 281
La Tribuna, 29
L'Unità, 218
L'Universale, 302, 427
L'Uomo Qualunque (The Common
    Man), 539–40
  see also UQ
La Vetta d'Italia, 146
La Vita italiana, 378, 400, 522
La Voce del Popolo Sovrano, 128
La Voce repubblicana, 218
Lago, Mario, 378–9
Landini, Alcide, 318
landowners, 38, 44–6, 50, 72, 90,
    104, 118, 127, 130–31, 133,
    148, 151, 166, 169–71,
    223–4, 238, 312, 401, 438,
    505, 514, 538, 567
Landra, Guido, 404
Langobardi, Cesare, 437
language and dialect, 17, 20, 32,
    34–5, 49, 75–6, 154, 158,
    179, 330, 369, 411–12, 472,
    534, 562
Lanzillo, Agostino, 170–171, 193
Lassandro, Cosimo, 460
Lateran Pacts, 15, 231, 239, 257,
    263, 324, 349, 358
Lauro, Achille, 549–50
Lavagnini, Spartaco, 140
Laval, Pierre, 306

law
  Acerbo law, 191, 193
  constitution, 203, 212, 321, 536
  corporatist, 309
  courts and tribunals, 167, 191,
    216, 241–2, 247, 514, 566
  and lawyers, 45, 149, 151, 191,
    220, 256, 359, 432, 566
  and power of the *Duce,* 332–3
  significance of to the dictator-
    ship, 191, 216, 566, 569
Lazio, 40, 194, 441
Le Bon, Gustave, 196
League of Nations, 87, 133, 283,
    297, 367, 396, 403, 406
Lega Nord, 558
Lega patriottica, 126–7
Legnano, 250
leisure, 3, 562, 410, 293, 562
  bridge, 412
  dopolavoro clubs, *see* OND
  Littoriali (youth) games, 432–5,
    507
  sports, 156, 161–2, 217–18,
    228–9, 264, 267, 290–91,
    346–7, 364, 410–11
  toys, 291–3
Leo XIII, Pope (1878–1903), 22
Lessona, Alessandro, 185, 192, 382,
    384
Levi, Carlo, 336
Levi, Primo, 520
Li Causi, Girolamo, 329
Liberal government, 27, 29–31, 43,
    50, 177, 566–7
  Chamber of Deputies, 45, 46, 48,
    51, 95, 108, 172,
  continuities with post-war
    government, 536
  parliament, 45, 47, 92, 176–7
  and Mussolini, 179–80

Liberal government – *cont.*
  in wartime, 63, 65, 67, 73, 75,
    90–92
Libya, 3, 286, 297–9, 337, 357,
    373–4, 379–83, 388, 407,
    417–18, 535
  in First World War, 57
  genocide in, 380–81
  governors of, 295, 380–82, 459
  internees from, 50
  invasion of, 18, 47, 48, 379,
    396
  Jewish community in, 417–18
  migration to, 382–3
  minerals in, 39, 447
  in Second World War, 459, 466
  and TCI, 58
Licata, Vincenzo, 255–6
life expectancy, 21, 37, 574
Liguria, 40, 63, 173, 510, 524
lira, 29, 100, 123, 229–30, 242,
    405–6, 441, 526
  see also economy, currency
    valuation
Lissa, 43, 49
Liuzzi, Alberto, 416
literature, 23, 111, 291–2, 363,
    371, 624
Livorno, 140, 219, 418
Lombardy, 40, 194, 405
Lombroso, Cesare, 21, 51, 243–4,
    567
Longhi, Silvio, 311
Longoni, Attilio, 120, 588
Low, David, 366
Lucantoni, Angelo, 459–60
Luciani, Luigi, 387
Lupo, Salvatore, 189, 561
Lussu, Emilio, 108, 167, 241, 328
Luzzatti, Luigi, 31, 123, 415

Machiavelli, Nicolo, 6, 474
Mafia *see* crime, organized
Maffi, Maffio, 218
Magistrati, Massimo, 302, 319–20,
    408
Malagodi, Olindo, 31
Malaparte, Curzio, 213, 533
Malta, 259, 461, 474
Majer Rizzioli, Elisa, 145–6
Mann, Michael, 564–7
Mantua, 122, 153, 172, 479, 604
Maranzana, 333–8
March on Athens, 462
March on Bolzano, 180
March on Rome, 130, 132,177,
    180–82, 184, 188–90, 196,
    201, 213, 215, 222, 224,
    253, 293, 300, 415, 419, 449,
    457
March on Ravenna, 173
March on Sarzana, 173
March on Treviso, 173
Marche, 47
Marconcini, Federico, 267
Marconi, Guglielmo, 219
Maremma, 42
Margherita, Queen, 187, 375
Maria José, Princess, 322–3
Maria Pia, Princess, 323
Marinetti, Filippo Tommaso, 22,
    95, 116–17, 119, 139, 145,
    303, 511
Marletta, Alfredo, 459
Maroni, Lorenzo, 543
marriage, 169, 268, 469
  see also family
Marsich, Pietro, 161–2, 173–5
Martini, Ferdinando, 54, 59
Marxism, Italian, 17, 20, 46,
    150–51, 390, 548,
  see also socialism;

Communist Party

Mascagni, Pietro, 199

masculinity, 3, 76, 139, 143, 178,
    185, 222, 237, 302, 411, 440,
    446, 518, 556

Masi, Corrado, 313

Masi, Giorgio, 238–9, 605–6

Matteotti, Giacomo 33, 137, 143,
    145, 211–14, 217, 232, 234,
    250, 256, 340, 348–9, 382,
    415, 424, 508

Matteotti, Velia, 340

Mattiolini, Wais, 411

Maurelli, Leopoldo and Umberto,
    207–8, 211

Mazza, Francesco, 29

Mazzini, Giuseppe, 6, 55, 127–9,
    165, 169, 328, 558

Mazzolini, Serafino, 509

Mazzucchetti, Enrico, 378

Meda, Filippo, 63, 88

Medici del Vascello, Luigi, 372

Meneghello, Luigi, 485

Messina, 24–30, 43–4, 163, 540

Metaxas, Ioannis, 215, 461, 464

Mezzasoma, Fernando, 290, 455,
    509, 525

Michelini, Arturo, 541, 549–51, 554

Michels, Robert, 6, 389

Miglioli, Guido, 54, 87–8, 106, 128

Milan, 15, 37, 45, 93, 116–17, 120,
    128, 132, 145–9, 153, 159,
    170–71, 181–2, 206–9,
    211–12, 218, 228, 235, 252,
    271, 342, 348–50, 420, 428,
    439, 440, 452–3, 457, 459–60,
    477–8, 483, 491, 502, 513,
    514, 518, 525, 529, 538

Milani, Cesare, 479

military
    air force, 445–7

Bersaglieri, 126, 140, 165

Brigata Sassari (Sassari Brigade),
    166

and catholicism, 88–9

comradeship 78–9

disintegration of, 504

equipment, 443–4, 464, 466,
    473–4

esprit, 61, 465

expenditure, 42, 60, 69–8, 456

fascist reform of, 230–31, 444

leadership, 61–3, 71–2, 443,
    464–5

and Matteotti murder, 212

navy, 43, 444–5

officer corps, 17, 60–63, 71–2,
    79, 443–4, 473–4

recruits, 40, 43, 444, 476,

training, 43

soldiers, 70–72, 473–4, 476–7

wages, 70

weaponry, 60, 69, 443–4, 456,
    466

see also Alpini, the; Arditi, the;
    chemical and biological
    weapons

Minniti, Giuseppe, 192

Minzoni, Giovanni, 106, 195

Misuri, Alfredo, 142

Mondaini, Gennaro, 398

Montanelli, Indro, 367, 399–400,
    414, 517

Montessori, Maria, 264

Montini, Giovanni Battista, 262

monuments, 12–14, 36, 59, 268,
    326, 388, 415, 440–41,
    500–501, 558

Morabito, Antonio, 107

Moravia, Alberto, 363

Morgagni, Manlio, 481

Morgari, Oddino, 30

Mori, Cesare, 209–10
Moro, Aldo, 262, 433, 556–7
Moroni, Edoardo, 526–7
Mosca, Gaetano, 133
Mosse, George, 417
Mostra della Rivoluzione Fascista
    (Exhibition of the Fascist
    Revolution), 263, 274, 569
    see also Decennale
mothers and motherhood, 21–2,
    141, 145–6, 244–5, 266–8,
    323, 325, 442, 485
    see also pro-natalism; ONMI
MSI (Movimento Sociale Italiano,
    Italian Social Movement,
    neo-fascists), 210, 531, 541–2,
    546–51, 554, 556, 558
    and the Catholic Church, 549
    and the European extreme right,
    546–7
    ideology, 449–554, 556, 558
    leadership, 548–9, 554, 557–8
    and 'post-fascism', 531, 558–9
    regional base, 547–8
    support for, 546–8
    'Tambroni affair', 550–51
Munich conference, 404–6
Murri, Romolo, 32–3, 88
music 23
    'All'armi', 163–4, 558
    'Bandiera rossa', 334–8
    'Battaglione M', 484–5
    'Canto del Lavoro', 199–200
    Carnevale, 199
    'Faccetta nera' ('Little black
        face'), 368–9, 463
    fascist, 163–4, 197–200,
        197–200
    'Giovinezza', 112, 141, 197–200,
        219, 558
    'Horst Wessel Song', 448

jazz, 346
Royal March, 199
    socialist, 103
    subversive, 169
    'Tirol ist Mein Heimat', 326
    UQ anthem, 540
    'Vincere', 463–4
Musiedlak, Didier, 359–360
Musolino, Giuseppe, 41
Mussolini, Alessandra, 556
Mussolini, Alessandro, 349
Mussolini, Anna Maria, 343, 346
Mussolini, Arnaldo, 209, 211, 220,
    231, 311, 318, 347–50
Mussolini, Benito
    administrative style, 351–7, 360,
        362, 473
    as adroit politician, 179–83, 189,
        315, 357, 419
    arrest of, 495
    assassination attempts, 240–41,
        246
    authority as Duce, 174–5, 189,
        217, 295, 357, 362, 473
    as aviator, 120
    and Catholicism, 119, 147, 187,
        231–2, 257
    and D'Annunzio, 114, 119,
        174
    daily activity, 355, 360, 366
    execution, 511, 529–30, 538
    and First World War, 79, 95
    and Hitler, Adolf 4, 352, 408–9,
        454, 461–2, 469, 473, 515
    and imperialism, 99, 147, 373,
        396
    as intellectual, 26, 40, 52, 53,
        147–8,
    international perceptions of,
        396–7
    as interventionist, 53–5

and Matteotti murder, 211–12, 214
and Mussolini family, 51, 342–51
and neo-fascism, 555
oratory, 9, 116, 352–3, 529
physical characteristics, 200–201, 217–18, 314, 341–2
personality, 136, 343, 350–5, 515
personality cult of, 3, 204, 218, 233, 273, 295, 313–15, 321–7, 351, 565
plots to dispose of, 475, 491, 493–4
post-war interpretations of, 532, 535, 540, 553–4
public support for, 491
and racism, 147, 419–20, 461–2
rescue of, 506
responsibility for entry into Second World War, 457–8
responsibility for use of poison gas, 299
role in the 'making' of fascists, 135, 137, 142–3, 567
and Salo Republic, 506, 509, 515
sexual relationships, 22, 52, 342–3, 363–5
as socialist, 16, 22, 47, 52, 53, 115, 118, 126, 147–8, 175–6
and violence, 173–4, 189–90, 216, 234, 340–41, 568
and Wilson, Woodrow, 97, 147
youth, 51–2, 476
and Zionism, 147
see also fascism, and 'Mussolinism'; 'everyday Mussolinism'; propaganda
Mussolini, Bruno, 343, 345–6, 478
Mussolini, Edda, 219, 236, 257, 322, 342–4, 346–7, 363, 409, 449

Mussolini, Rachele, 52, 318–20, 332, 343–4, 347, 482, 495, 508, 620, 629
Mussolini, Romano, 343, 346
Mussolini, Sandro, 258
Mussolini, Vittorio, 221, 343, 345, 431, 519
Muti, Ettore, 455, 475, 524–5, 532
MVSN (Milizia volontaria per la sicurezza nazionale, Voluntary Militia for National Security), 188, 190, 208, 230, 402, 416, 424, 491, 493, 510, 549

Namier, Lewis, 563
Naples, 15, 17, 37, 41, 117, 153, 165–6, 246, 260, 272, 387–8, 479–80, 488, 504–5 533, 542–3, 547, 549–50
Nardò, 105, 142
Nathan, Ernesto, 415
Nationalist Association (ANI, Associazione Nazionalista Italiana) 48, 49, 50, 52, 53, 61, 91, 99–101, 139, 147, 149, 168, 182, 186, 280, 288, 372, 389, 509, 567
nationalization,14, 16, 30, 32, 35, 38, 46, 57–8, 65, 67, 72, 75–6, 80–82, 88–90, 152, 154, 159, 221, 255, 279, 336, 371, 437–9
Nenni, Pietro, 330–31, 540
Nicastri, Giuseppe, 255–6
Nini, Ambrogio, 453–4
Nitti, Francesco, 66, 68, 95, 100, 110, 114, 123, 139, 155, 180, 281, 290, 309
Nogara, Bernardino, 263, 492, 517
Novara, 162, 177, 471, 479
Nuova Antologia, 32

Observer, 257
Ojetti, Ugo, 218
Olivetti, Gino, 67–8, 176
Omodeo, Adolfo, 72
OND (Opera Nazionale Dopolavoro, National After-work Group), 228, 330, 391, 453, 564
ONMI (Opera Nazionale per la Protezione della Maternità e dell'Infanzia, (National agency for mothers and children), 244–5, 265, 323, 442–3, 570
Opera Nazionale Balilla (Fascist boy scouts), 221–3, 289–93, 305, 321, 325, 391, 510
see also youth
Orano, Paolo, 66, 167, 439
Orlando, Emma, 392–3
Orlando, Vittorio Emanuele, 66, 75, 95–6, 98–9, 107, 132, 180, 191
Ovazza, Ettore, 416
Oviglio, Aldo, 185–6

Pacelli, Francesco, 231
Pact of Pacification, 136–7, 172–3, 175
Padovani, Aurelio, 165–6
Palazzo Venezia, 9, 11–14, 273, 311, 364, 493, 523, 584
Palazzo Vidoni pact, 226–7
Palermo, 37, 46, 116, 167, 210, 540, 543
Pantaleoni, Maffeo, 48
Panunzio, Sergio, 205, 486
parades, 95, 201–2, 216, 222, 264, 290–92, 326–7, 370, 412–13
see also salutes, Roman
Parenti, Rino, 452

Pareto, Vilfredo, 133, 196
Parini, Alberto, 393–4, 631–2
Parini, Piero, 321–3, 391–4, 523
Paris, 22, 38, 97, 111, 217, 410, 442, 569
Parisi, Enrico, 310–12
Parma, 149, 177–8
Parri, Ferruccio, 241, 540, 543, 657
Partito agrario, 167–8
Partito d'Azione, 521
Partito Comunista d'Italia, *see* Communist Party
Partito del Lavoro, 159
Partito di Rinnovamento (Renewal Party), 108
Partito economico, 106, 167–8
Partito Nazionale Fascista *see* Fascist Party
Partito Popolare Italiano *see* PPI
Pasella, Umberto, 135–8, 151–5, 172
Patanè, Leonardo, 477–8
Paul VI, Pope (1963–78), 262
Pavelić, Ante, 4, 284, 469
Pavolini, Alessandro, 283, 507–10, 512–13, 515, 524–5, 529, 539
Paxton, Robert, 565–9, 573
peasants, 6, 19, 24–5, 29, 30–31, 38, 40–43, 45–7, 50–51, 57, 61, 64, 70, 72, 76, 87, 90, 101, 104–6, 108, 124, 126–8, 142, 154–5, 158, 165–7, 169–71, 184–5, 266, 269–71, 383, 481–2, 487, 499, 562
Pederzini, Gianna, 341, 623
Pelloux, Luigi, 45
Pende, Nicola, 485
Perugia, 89, 145, 181, 234, 294, 371, 547
Pesce, Giovanni, 523
Petacci, Claretta, 345, 363–5, 448

Petacci, Francesco Saverio, 363, 365
Petacci, Marcello Cesare Augusto, 365–6
Petacci, Maria, 365
Petronio, Enrichetta, 316
photography, 25, 44, 290, 314, 375, 410, 413, 435
Piazzesi, Mario, 138–44, 151, 564
Piccinini, R., 177
Piedmont, 17–20, 40, 57, 59, 62–3, 162, 230, 246, 271, 322–3, 333, 444
Pini, Giorgio, 387, 541
Pirano, 34
Pirelli, Alberto, 312, 491–2
Pisenti, Piero, 159–60, 188
Pius XI, Pope (1922–39), 15, 176, 180, 231, 257–9, 261–3, 265, 352, 357, 363–4, 374, 407, 415, 435
Pius XII, Pope (1939–58), 39, 265, 363, 374, 490, 510, 536, 541, 549
PNF (Partito Nazionale Fascista, National Fascist Party) see Fascist party
PNM (Partito Nazionale Monarchico, National Monarchist Party), 549–50
Po valley, 33, 40, 42, 46, 64, 84, 153, 162, 209, 502, 505
police, 2, 106, 138, 186, 214, 220, 230–32, 235, 241–2, 260, 318, 333–6, 341, 362–3, 402, 411, 420, 448, 452, 457, 459, 465, 477, 481, 482, 491, 562
    budget for, 360–61
    carabinieri, 131
    chiefs (Questori), 50
    Mussolini's involvement in, 362–3

OVRA (secret police), 318
    and poverty, 270
    repressive practices, 50, 240–41
    response to fascist violence, 164, 173, 194, 208–9
poison gas, see chemical and biological weapons
Pontine marshes, 42, 437–8, 505
    see also reclamation (bonifica)
Ponzio, Giacomo, 187
pornography, 221, 369
Portelli, Alessandro, 500–501, 651
Poveromo, Amleto, 145
poverty, 20, 41, 101, 105, 166, 169–70, 210, 270, 335–6, 437–9, 484, 566–7
PPI (Partito Popolare Italiano, Italian Popular Party, Catholics), 47, 106–8, 131, 149, 188, 193, 262
Predappio, 33, 38, 51, 117, 233, 344, 482
prefects, 50
press
    fascist control of, 195, 217–18, 362
    Ufficio Stampa, 217
    and women, 267–8
    see also journalism
Preziosi, Anna Maria, 159
Preziosi, Giovanni, 302, 417, 456, 471, 508, 519–20, 525
Priebke, Erich, 500, 545
Primo de Rivera, José Antonio, 401, 555
Priolo, Giovanni, 170
prisoners of war
    Ethiopian, 377
    in First World War, 64, 73, 75–7
    in Second World War, 402, 459, 466, 513, 518, 526

pro-natalism, 244–5, 266–8, 290, 586
see also ONMI
propaganda
Fascist, 74, 80, 122, 220, 273, 315, 353, 356–7, 404, 413–14, 442, 455–6, 479, 484, 571; see also Ministries: Popular Culture under goverment, fascist
during First World War, 66–7, 74–5, 78, 80–81
during Second World War, 484, 507, 523, 526, 548, 570–71
Fascist Italy as 'propaganda state', 6, 414, 442, 570–71
public works, 436–42
railways, 439
roads, 439–40
urban planning, 440–42
see also reclamation (bonifica), of land; architecture, fascist
Puglia, 47, 105, 142, 171, 271, 567
Pugliese, Samuele, 131–2, 181
punishment
for abortion and contraception, 265–6
capital, 51, 241–2, 514
of children, 293–4
confino, 6, 50, 144, 206, 222, 238, 241, 251–6, 279, 319–20, 329, 331–2, 335–8, 362, 386, 393, 411, 426, 436, 449, 452, 460, 478, 495, 531, 609, 613, 622, 657
for homosexuality, 436
military, 70–72, 82
Mussolini's involvement in, 362, 477
of non-Catholic religious, 260
for political crimes, 185, 242–3, 247–8, 320–23, 335–8
prison, 167, 241, 247–8, 329–31, 482
of war crimes, 542
see also police

quadrumviri, 181–2, 190, 286, 375, 380, 549
Quirinal Palace, 44, 47, 187, 200, 327, 409

raccomandazione, 4, 184, 237–9, 276, 317–18, 332–3, 349, 361, 365–6, 394, 455, 515, 571, 604
racism, 10, 240–45, 372, 376, 400, 416, 420–21, 430, 454, 456, 471–2, 485–7, 512, 547, 561;
anti-Italian, 33, 392, 397;
anti-Semitic, 243, 250, 400, 415–20, 430, 454, 456, 470–72, 512, 561; legislation, 2, 379, 418–21, 471, 520
in Salò republic, 3, 512, 520
religious, 415, 417; wartime, 470–71
anti-Slav, 49, 91, 109, 154–8, 243, 372, 472, 472, 536–7, 561
anti-southern, 243–4, 300, 547
and Catholic Church, 258, 490
colonialist, 48, 49, 368–9, 378, 380, 384–6, 394–5, 399–400, 414–15, 418, 420, 561; race legislation in Ethiopia, 414–15; race legislation in Libya, 417–18
and idea of 'spiritual' Italian race, 244–5, 552–3

Nazi, 258, 268, 300–301, 416–17, 469, 504; Italian reactions to, 420, 469
and the Republic, 551–3
'scientific', 16, 110–11, 240, 243, 268, 300–301, 404, 414, 471–2; eugenics, 268, 472
see also pro-natalism; xenophobia
'Radiant May', 56, 59–60, 62, 80, 83–4, 86
radio, 219–20, 261, 312, 323, 325, 408, 429, 466
see also EIAR (Ente Italiano Audizioni Radiotelefoniche, Italian Radio Company)
Rafanelli, Mazzetto, 500
Rafanelli, Leda, 342, 363
Rahn, Rudolf, 503
railways, 24, 27, 41, 127, 238, 274, 437, 439, 440, 502, 586
ras, 28, 117, 152, 179, 191, 196, 232, 240–41, 269–70, 493
Rassegna Femminile Italiana, 146
Rauti, Pino, 552–4, 557–8
Ravenna, 153, 173, 177
Ravera, Camilla, 329
Re, Giovanni, 453
reclamation (*bonifica*)
of land, 383, 436–9, 505
human (*umana*), 414, 482
Redaelli, Giovanni, 206–8
Reggiani, Marcello, 253
Reggio, 193
regionalism, 5, 16–30, 34–5, 38, 40–43, 56, 73, 75, 108–9, 139, 150–84, 188, 192, 228, 270–71, 330–31, 371, 424, 427, 430, 438, 480, 483, 527, 540–41, 547–8, 559
Renaissance, 9, 11, 325, 371
Renan, Ernest, 14, 16

Republic, Italian, 536–60
constitution and laws, 536, 545–6
and 'de-fascistization', 542–5, 549, 551
and extra-parliamentary neo-fascists, 554–7
government, 536–7, 546
political parties, 536–7, 540–42, 546–50; *see also* Christian Democrats; UQ; MSI; PNM; AN; Lega Nord; PPI
public administration, 546
referendum for, 44, 536
Repubblica Sociale Italiana, *see* Salò Republic
Resistance, *see* anti-Fascism
Resegna, Aldo, 514
Revelli, Nuto, 271, 444, 521
Ribbentrop, Joachim 404, 451, 453, 469, 645
Riccardi, Raffaelo, 164–5, 455, 482
Ricci, Berto, 302–3, 349, 427, 434
Ricci, Renato, 221–2, 289–90, 293, 510
Ricottini, Maria, 543
Rigola, Rinaldo, 47, 85–6, 104
Rimini, 177, 344–5
Risorgimento 12, 15, 21, 34, 45, 55, 59, 61, 64, 81, 88, 108, 199, 231, 250, 257, 282, 296, 415, 458
Roatta, Mario, 443–4, 466, 472–3
Robotti, Mario, 472
Rocco, Alfredo, 91, 95, 226, 231
Rodomonte, Sergio, 477
Rombiolo, 169
Rome, 9, 11–17, 37, 41, 116–17, 139, 153, 175, 182, 184, 196, 199, 201, 211, 222, 229, 232, 246, 250, 258–9, 268–70,

Rome – *cont.*
274, 303–4, 314, 348, 363,
371–3, 390–91, 398–9, 415,
417, 440–41, 480–83,
500–502, 505, 508, 510, 533,
538, 543, 547, 552, 566
Romeo, Rosario, 60
Roosevelt, Franklin, 272, 325, 488,
490
Roselli, Aldo, 328, 416–17, 450, 521
Rosselli, Carlo, 241, 327–8,
416–17, 450, 521
Rosselli, Roberto, 501
Rossetti, Umberto, 460–61
Rossi, Adele, 460
Rossi, Angelo, 480, 562
Rossi, Cesare, 137–8, 145, 172,
175, 188, 200, 211, 217
Rossi, Ernesto, 332
Rossoni, Edmondo, 33, 136,199,
223–6, 228
RSI, *see* Salò Republic
Ruini, Meuccio, 30
Russian Revolution, 63, 101–2,
133, 247

Salandra, Antonio, 56, 58, 60–64,
68, 100,105, 121, 179, 191,
580, 596
Salento, 41
Salgari, Emilio, 371
Salò Republic, 3, 160, 499, 503–30,
570
anti-Semitism in, 509–13,
519–20, 525
and 'black brigades' and paramilitary forces, 524–6
borders, 503–5
economy, 526
extent of Italian support for,
517–19, 527; *see also* MSI

extermination camp, 522
failure of, 528–9
government of, 507–10, 529;
'Verona Manifesto', 512–14
historicization of, 500–501
violence in, 512–13, 525–6,
537
meaning of Fascism in, 515,
523–4
resistance to, 520–22, 526,
528–9; propaganda, 523;
strikes, 526
trial and execution of 'traitors of
July', 513–14
salutes
Heil Hitler, 408, 448
Roman, 202, 229, 236, 273,
294, 331, 354, 413, 514
Salvemini, Gaetano, 25–6, 74, 99,
107–8, 180, 186, 196, 308,
373, 396–7, 507
San Marino, 105
Sansanelli, Nicola, 165–7, 172, 188
Santacroce, Enrico, 545
Sardinia, 19, 40–41, 108, 117,
166–7, 193–4, 208, 256–7,
424–5, 428–9, 437, 582
Sarfatti, Margherita, 21–3, 52, 145,
176, 342, 363, 415, 418, 562,
578
Sarfatti, Cesare, 22
Sarti, Roland, 229–30
Sassaiolo fiorentino, 144
Savoia-Aosta, Amedeo, 323, 378
Scalabrini, Giovanni Battista, 31–2,
88
Scalea, Pietro Lanza di, 106, 167,
168, 288, 374
Schanzer, Carlo, 28
Schio, 537
Scialoja, Vittore, 75, 280–81

Scoccimarro, Mauro, 543
Scorza Carlo, 262, 407, 492–3, 495
scouts, *see* Opera Nazionale Balilla
Second World War
    Allied occupation of the south,
       493, 497, 502, 504–5
    ambiguity of Italian 'enemies' in,
       472–4
    armistice, 504
    attack on Greece, 463–4
    battles, 467, 474, 502
    bombing, 483, 502
    casualties, 458, 502
    and 'defeatists', 459–61, 477–91
    entry of Italy into, 457
    historiography of, 532–4
    Italian non-belligerency, 451–7
    war aims, 458, 468, 474, 479
    wartime society, 475, 477–91,
       496
    see also military; prisoners of
       war
Segre, Dan, 416
Seldes, George, 396–7
Senise, Carmine, 242–3, 362, 394,
    491
Serena, Adelchi, 475–6
Serrati, Giacinto Menotti, 102
Sestri Ponente, 177
Sezione studentesca dell'Alleanza di
    difesa cittadina (Student
    branch of the alliance for
    citizen's defence), 139, 144
Sforza, Carlo, 97, 114, 543
Shakespeare, William, vii, 516
shopping, 225–6, 413, 417
Sicily, 24–30, 41, 105, 167–8, 193,
    207, 209–11, 390, 437, 477,
    482–3, 538, 548, 567
Silone, Ignazio, 26
Sinigaglia, Oscar, 111, 280, 416

'skinheads', 200–201
Slovenia, 10, 49–50, 146, 154–5,
    157–8, 469, 472–3, 486
Snowden, Frank, 46–7
socialism, 17, 19, 20, 26, 33, 35,
    36, 43, 46, 47–8, 52–4, 82–3,
    101–6, 108, 113, 118, 124–6,
    128, 135, 138, 140, 149, 152,
    158, 162, 177–8, 193,
    328–31, 510–11
    see also Socialist Party, anti-
      socialism
Socialist party, Italian (PSI), 46–7,
    55, 101, 107
Società Giordano Bruno, 126–7
Soffici, Ardengo, 483, 511–12
Sogno, Edgardo, 522
Somalia, 190, 368, 374–7, 458, 535
    British raid on, 458–9
    and children's literature, 376
    concentration camp, 377
    fascist police force in, 376
    see also AOI; Italian East Africa
Sommavilla, Pietro, 478
Sonnino, Sidney, 46, 58, 61–3,
    74–5, 91, 95, 98–100, 415
Sorel, Georges, 196
Spadolini, Giovanni, 511
Spain, 2, 4, 14, 37, 215, 284, 304,
    313, 337, 358, 401–405, 416,
    420, 449, 468, 476, 484,
    554
Spanish Civil War, 2, 141, 242,
    259–60, 269, 330, 346, 358,
    401–404, 468, 555, 570
sport *see* leisure, sport
squadrism, 2, 47, 88, 119, 128,
    132, 134, 136, 138, 140–41,
    143–5, 149, 156–7, 160–62,
    164–5, 168–70, 174–5,
    177–9, 188–90, 202, 207–9,

squadrism – *cont.*
211–13, 216, 416, 513, 525, 537, 568–9
see also MVSN
Staglieno, Marcello, 532
Stalin, Joseph, 215, 327–9, 339–40, 353, 468, 474, 511, 523, 536
standard of living, 2, 20, 270–71
see also poverty
Starace, Achille, 7, 79, 81, 171, 174, 179, 200–201, 236–7, 251, 268–9, 272–3, 276, 291, 298, 315, 349, 354, 361, 363, 410–12, 418, 432–4, 443, 452, 455–6, 475, 491, 513, 531–2, 570
Steer, G. L., 397
stereotypes, 9–10, 16, 215, 420, 501, 534
Stille, Alexander, 417
Stirpe Italica, 266, 305
Streicher, Julius, 201
strikes, 47, 63, 68, 71, 86, 104–5, 124–6, 127–8, 130, 142, 161, 167, 176–7, 226, 491, 526
'occupation of the factories', 124–6
Stringher, Bonaldo, 187, 604
Stucchi, Virgilio, 395
Sturano, Giuseppe, 318–19
Sturzo, Luigi, 47, 106, 187–8
Suckert, Curzio, *see* Malaparte, Curzio
Sulis, Edgardo, 421–31, 485, 491, 564
Sursum corda, 154
Suvich, Fulvio, 158, 307, 401
syndicalism, 33, 46, 131, 133, 135–7, 152, 165, 167, 223, 226–7

Tacchi Venturi, Pietro, 262, 318
Taddei, Paolino, 179
Tambroni, Fernando, 550
Tangorra, Vincenzo, 186
Taylorism, 18, 19, 292
taxation, 69–70, 265, 482
TCI (Touring Club Italiano), 57, 58, 159, 203, 348, 372
telephones, 181, 220, 224, 234, 242, 509
television, 447
Terni, 179
Terruzzi, Regina, 117, 269–70
Teruzzi, Attilio, 380, 544
Terzaghi, Michele, 139, 144, 212, 592
Thaon di Revel, Paolo, 186, 286, 455
Tiburtina, 182
Toeplitz, Giuseppe, 23
Togliatti, Palmiro, 17, 150, 329, 330, 537, 540, 542
Torcellan, Emilia, 316
Tornato, Antonio, 334–8
Torquati, Filippo, 387
totalitarianism, 3, 39, 67, 143, 174, 194, 203, 215–16, 216, 226, 233, 242–3, 246–8, 254, 290, 295, 303, 308, 315, 359–64, 398–9, 422–3, 438, 452, 472, 475, 488, 496, 561, 567, 572
'catholic totalitarianism', 259, 262
and corporatism, 307–8
origins of word 'totalitarian', 215
see also punishment; propaganda; Mussolini, personality cult of
tourism, 16, 20, 24–5, 39, 49, 158–9, 161, 202, 217, 440–41

tourism of war, 158–9
and Italian, 411–12
Toynbee, Arnold, 16
trade unionism, 3, 17, 33, 46–7,
106, 124–5, 177, 223–6
transport, 40–41, 206, 483–4
Traverso, Rachele, 478
Treaty of Lausanne, 23
Treaty of London, 58–9, 87, 90,
100
Treaty of Rapallo, 114, 119,
160–61
Trentino, 34–5, 59, 171, 176, 239,
260, 321–2, 325–6, 411
Trento, 34–5, 96, 179, 239, 241,
249, 326–7, 343, 442, 448,
503, 513
Treves, Claudio, 47, 60, 86
Trieste, 24, 55, 59, 62, 96, 117,
146, 153–8, 179, 181, 249,
270, 279, 370, 453, 476, 513,
522, 529, 537, 567
Tripepi, Silvio, 170
Triple Alliance, 44, 95
Triple Entente, 44
Turati, Augusto, 191, 203, 220,
234, 237, 239, 241–2, 245,
249, 264, 349
Turati, Filippo, 43, 60, 79, 84, 86,
104, 160, 173
Turin, 15, 17,-20, 37, 104, 117 124,
153, 172, 190, 218, 234,
266–7, 375, 459, 502
Turkey, 62, 91, 96, 135, 160, 286,
378, 379
Toscanini, Arturo, 197
Toscano, Mario, 471
Touring Club Italiano, see TCI
Tuscany, 42, 51, 104, 138–40, 153,
162, 194, 300, 344, 491,
500

Umberto, Crown Prince, 322
Umberto I, King (1878–1900), 17,
44, 55, 374
Unione democratica, 219
Unione Italiana del Lavoro (UIL,
Italian Labour Union, syndicalists), 33, 136
Unione Spirituale Dannunziana (the
D'Annunzian spiritual league),
174, 595
UQ (Uomo Qualunque, Common
Man Party), 539–42, 546,
550
USA
business methods, 18, 348–9
cultural influence of, 409–10,
534
emigration to, 2, 30, 31, 32, 33
entry into First World War, 63,
90
popular perceptions of, 295, 470,
479, 488
post-war relationship with,
498–501, 536
trade with, 348–9
wars against, 2, 470
USSR, 2, 113, 178, 202, 215, 242,
246, 282, 285, 305, 317,
328–9, 374, 432, 445, 455,
465–6, 469–70, 474, 479,
486, 492, 538, 555
war against, 2, 469–70, 474
Ustasha, 4, 284, 469–70, 660

Valente, Rosalba, 489, 562
Valenti, Giuseppe, 164–5
Valesani, Italo, 385
Vassallo, Stefano, 387
Vecchi, Ferruccio, 95, 107, 118
Veneto, 23, 40, 47, 64, 96, 106,
162, 194, 390

Venice, 20–24, 105, 116–17, 160–62, 170, 178, 200, 218, 250, 278, 305, 344, 488–9, 496, 509, 574

Verona, 153, 319, 512, 514

Versailles Treaty, 99–100, 132, 147

Victor Emmanuel, Prince, 323

Vidussoni, Aldo, 10, 472, 476–7, 480, 482

Villelli, Gennaro, 168

Viterbo, 177

Vittoriale, 110, 506–7

Vittoriano, 12–14, 36
  see also architecture

Vittorio Veneto, victory of, 13, 79, 96, 156, 158, 184, 201, 281, 391, 452, 567

Vivarelli, Lavinio, 316

Vivarelli, Margherita, 316, 570

Vivarelli, Roberto, 532

Volpe, Gioacchino, 275, 282, 291

Volpi, Albino, 145–6, 211

Volpi, Giuseppe 23–4, 160–63, 183, 192, 218, 229, 356–7, 379, 380, 473, 516–17, 574

von Glöden, Wilhelm, 25, 435

von Hassell, Ulrich, 401

von Hötzendorff, Conrad, 25

welfare, 5, 27, 29, 175, 227, 243–4, 268, 442–3, 570
  see also INPS; ONMI

Wilson, Woodrow, 10, 63, 87, 90, 97–8, 283, 302, 488

women, 6, 21, 22, 32, 41–2, 45, 57, 69, 76–7, 117, 145–6, 176, 216–18, 225–7, 244–5, 264–70, 290–91, 438, 456, 475

xenophobia, 155, 282, 291, 305, 411, 461

X-Mas, 525

youth, 3, 66, 165, 180, 221–3, 289–94, 476–7, 482
  organizations, 289–94; Opera Nazionale Balilla (Fascist boy scouts), 221–3, 289–91, 293, 305, 325, 391, 510; Gioventù Universitaria Fascista (GUF, Fascist University Youth) 200–201, 272, 289–91, 410, 433, 435

Yugoslavia, 2, 44, 98, 114, 121, 468–70, 472, 504

Zaghi, Corrado, 520–21

Zamboni, Anteo, 222, 240, 246

Zamboni family, 246–9

Zangrandi, Ruggero, 431–2

Zanichelli, Abele, 385

Zara, 113, 114, 117

Zerbino, Paolo, 524, 529

Zingoli, Gaetano, 483–4

Zionism, 21, 147, 416–17

Zog, King, 279, 337, 388, 464

Zuccheretti, Piero, 500

Zupelli, 63